Minority Recruitment Data

This book identifies in specific detail where the nation's minorities (black, Hispanic, Asian, and Native American) receive their undergraduate degrees. Available by institution and stratified by minority group and disciplinary division, the data are further aggregated within a 60-mile radius of major airports so that an effective, cost-efficient recruitment strategy can be initiated. It can be used as a resource by both educators and personnel directors to address the issue of minority underrepresentation in graduate and professional education and in business and industry as well.

Minority Recruitment Data

An Analysis
of Baccalaureate Degree Production
in the United States

Donald R. Deskins, Jr.

ROWMAN & ALLANHELD
PUBLISHERS

 ROWMAN & ALLANHELD

Published in the United States of America in 1983
by Rowman & Allanheld
(A division of Littlefield, Adams & Company)
81 Adams Drive, Totowa, New Jersey 07512

Library of Congress Cataloging in Publication Data

Deskins, Donald Richard.
  Minority recruitment data.

  Bibliography: p.
  1. Minority college graduates—United States—
Recruiting—Statistics. 2. Minority college graduates
—United States—Statistics. I. Title.
HD6278.U5D48 1983   331.6'0973   83-19159
ISBN 0-86598-145-0

83 84 85/10 9 8 7 6 5 4 3 2 1

Printed in the United States of America

TABLE OF CONTENTS

LIST OF TABLES

DISCIPLINARY FIELD SPECIFIC DATA

LIST OF MAPS

PREFACE

This book is an attempt to identify institutions where significant numbers of minorities receive their baccalaureate degrees. In this way it is possible to establish a national pool of minority candidates which can be used by educators in graduate and professional schools, as well as personnel directors in industry, to improve recruiting efforts. It is hoped that the book will fulfill a need, since many business and educational institutions have yet to achieve their goal of increasing minority participation. The book's basic assumption is that in identifying a readily available pool of minority students, both leaders in education and business will be better able to reach their goals. The book also hopes to counter the mistaken notion that there is no available pool of minority students. In this sense, the pool data provided will help close this information gap by identifying schools with the greatest concentration of minority students. It is my belief that with adequate information, educators can achieve their goals of increasing minority participation, even during a time of gloomy economic predictions, declining enrollments, and shortages of funding sources. Moreover, I believe that increased minority participation can be achieved within the parameters of present programs, if the data on minority degree production contained in this volume are considered thoughtfully and sincere efforts are made to use it in meeting recruitment goals.

The data pool are presented in a format designed to enhance the efforts of both universities and business enterprises in developing recruitment strategies compatible with their size, needs and available resources. The information in this book is divided into sections detailing the number of baccalaureate degrees held by Blacks, Hispanics, Asians and Native Americans. This information is then stratified by institution, state, and the institutional proximity to nearest airport. In short, the book identifies the available pool of minority students, as well as its size, location, distribution and accessibility. The information is further stratified by field of study, which permits the recruiting institution to focus on specific disciplines in search of potential candidates.

A debt of gratitude is owed to many people and agencies for assistance received during various stages of this project. The study would not have been completed if it were not for the generous financial support of the Graduate and Professional Opportunity Program's Institutional Grant, U.S. Department of Education, the Vice President for Academic Affairs and Provost and the Vice President for Graduate Studies and Research both at The University of Michigan. Special appreciation is extended to Glenn Moultrie, Office of Civil Rights, U.S. Department of Education who provided me with the data tapes essential for completing this study and also for his advice and patience when I needed further clarification of the material. Special thanks to Michael Merlo who took care of the tedious task of processing and arranging much of the material. A debt of gratitude is also due my office staff for their patience, general assistance, and support throughout the duration of the project. Special acknowledgements go to Marina Seeman, Lynette Wanless, Joanne Gosling and Ethel Thoms who spent countless hours at the word processor typing the manuscript and its numerous tables.

Donald R. Deskins, Jr.

INTRODUCTION

Long before the United States faced the prospects of economic decline, experts recognized that for a nation to prosper, it had to utilize its human and economic resources wisely. The maladies of social discrimination in the workplace and in the academy were deemed injurious to the nation, and imprudent for the welfare of the individuals and groups who have yet to benefit from the economic prosperity enjoyed by most Americans.

The national outrage about under-utilization of our human resources coalesced with a series of legislative actions on both the national and state levels culminating in a national policy to address the issues of minority access and equal opportunity. Foremost among this legislation was Title VI of the Civil Rights Act of 1964, and the 1965 Executive Order 11246, providing minority access to employment and higher education. This legislation specifically prohibited discrimination on the basis of race in programs receiving federal funding. Any violation of this law would result in the termination of these funds.[1]

Much of the impetus for these legislative actions, initiated in the mid-1960's, was focused upon the plight of black Americans. However, history clearly indicates that there are strong parallels between the experience of blacks and other minority groups, particularly Chinese and Japanese Americans and Hispanic Americans. Of all minority groups, Native Americans have endured the most extreme hardships because of racial discrimination and have benefitted very little from the social legislation of the 1960's. Perhaps one of the greatest failures of American democracy is its failure to share its benefits with all minority groups. This is readily apparent in any census data, which clearly document the extent of minority underrepresentation in many of the nation's major insitutions.

Many argue that minority underrepresentation is primarily due to the lack of training or experience, rather than racial or ethnic discrimination. Verification of this argument should lead to an examination of both the formal and informal record of minority educational achievement in order to measure the extent of this lack of training. What such an examination does reveal is that opportunities for minorities to acquire the necessary training for meaningful participation in society are almost non-existent. To help provide solutions to this problem the record of minority educational achievement must be examined. The task is made relatively easy by the availability of records, detailing both minority enrollment in

educational institutions and number of degrees earned. Both indicate
that the level of minority achievement is well below that of the
national average. The data clearly show that minorities are generally
underrepresented on all levels of the educational hierarchy,
especially in graduate and professional schools where the nation's
leadership emerges.   It is at this crucial level where minority
representation is the lowest.[2]

The problem of minority participation must be addressed and
dealt with simultaneously on all levels of the educational hierarchy if
minority participation is to increase both within higher education as
well as in business and industry.[3]   The problem is further
compounded by the lack of proportional representation of minorities
in the various academic disciplines and programs.[4] Lack of minority
representation in academic areas such as the physical sciences,
engineering, or the humanities is generally attributed to lack of
adequate preparation by most minority students before entering the
university. Far from being accurate, this argument seems to be a
further attempt to excuse failures to seek out competent minority
students who can meet the requirements. An underlying assumption
is that the available pool of minority students does not exist or
remains too small to be of any consequence. To challenge such
assumptions, a serious effort to document the available pool of
potential minority graduate and professional students must be made.
Such efforts enhance the possibility of increasing minority access to
higher education as well as to employment, particularly in those
areas where participation is either low or does not exist and where
institutional initiatives, based upon the assumption that no pool
exists, are weak.

PURPOSE

The purpose of this effort is to address the issue of low minority
participation in graduate and professional schools as well as in
business and industry.   This involves, first, identifying and locating
the national minority student pool. The pool will then be categorized
by disciplinary group with the data presented in a format consisting
of a series of maps and tables. Data in this form can enhance and
expedite the development of recruitment strategies designed to
increase minority access by optimizing the accessibility to the
minority pool and minimizing the cost of this access.

RATIONALE

Some progress toward minorities access and equity in graduate
and professional education as well as in industrial and business
employment has been achieved since the enactment of Civil Rights
legislation in the mid-1960's.[5] However, full minority access was
never realized and there are ominous signs that the gains made are
now being lost.   The alarming decline in the level of black
participation in post-baccalaureate education is a clear indicator that

the initiatives which lead to increases in black enrollment in graduate and professional schools are eroding rapidly and should serve as a signal to other minoritity groups which have recently experienced similar increases.

Alarmed by the rapidly decreasing rate at which blacks are participating in graduate and professional education, the National Advisory Committee on Black Higher Education and Black Colleges and Universities, an advisory committee to the Secretary of Education, issued a report, A Losing Battle: The Decline in Black Participation in Graduate and Professional Education, less than three years ago in October 1980, specifically documenting this decline, as well as advancing plausible social, political and economic explanations for its occurrence. The report also made an attempt to assess the impact of this decline and outline actions to be taken to halt and reverse this downward trend. In the report, the committee noted that black enrollment in post–baccalaureate programs has not kept up with black undergraduate enrollment in recent years. According to the report, the percentage of black graduate students fell from 6.0 percent of the total graduate student enrollment in 1976, to 5.7 percent by 1980. Similar declines are observed in the number of blacks enrolled in medical schools, which fell 5.7 percent in 1978-79, to the lowest level since 1972-73.   While overall law school enrollment increased by 9.3 percent between 1976-77 and 1978-79, black enrollment fell to 4.5 percent, its lowest level during the same period.[6] Collectively, these data clearly document that the proportion of blacks participating in graduate and professional degree programs is rapidly diminishing.

Considering the decreasing trend in black participation in post-baccalaureate education, the committee took the position in one of its recommendations:

> That graduate and professional schools assume the
> initiative for increasing black participation since theirs
> is the responsibility for selection and that faculty and
> administrative staff of predominantly white institutions
> become active in recruiting black students into
> underrepresented fields.[7]

As recently as this year the Commission on the Higher Education of Minorities in its final report, concerned with efforts to improve the educational opportunities for several categorically disadvantaged minority groups, Chicanos, Puerto Ricans, Native Americans, and blacks, also recommends:

> That graduate and professional schools make special
> efforts to increase their pools of minority graduate
> students.[8]

Both of these commissions, in their recommendations, reached a consensus that the identification of a minority graduate and professional student pool would contribute to breaking one of the

barriers to minority access to post-baccalaureate educational
opportunities. They strongly suggested that adequate pool information is vital to efforts to increase minority participation in programs
in institutions at the pinnacle of the educational hierarchy.

DATA

Successful recruitment of minorities depends heavily upon having
accurate knowledge of the minority pool's size and location. To
identify and locate the pool adequately requires an analysis of the
minority record of participation in educational programs at four-year
institutions, which goes beyond the mere examination of enrollment
data. The record of minority recipients of baccalaureate degrees is
well suited to this task because it provides sound information on pool
size. Comprehensive data on minority bacccalaureate recipients
have been available for public scrutiny since 1973, through the
various Higher Education General Information Surveys (HEGIS), which
have been conducted since then.[9]

Comprehensiveness
Collectively, the institutional reports on the "1978-79 HEGIS
Earned Degree Tapes," the primary data base for this analysis, is the
most comprehensive single source of information on the status of
baccalaureate production available in the United States.[10] The 1,658
schools that responded to the survey provide nationwide coverage
since it accounts for 84.5 percent of the 1,962 four-year degree
granting institutions in the United States.[11] These data are available
in a format such that the total, as well as minority baccalaureate
production, can be determined for each institution stratified by
twenty-four disciplinary divisions. For the purposes of this analysis,
these data are valuable in at least three ways:

1. they represent the most comprehensive data
    available on baccalaureate degree production in the
    United States,

2. they can be used to delineate the size of the
    minority baccalaureate degree recipient pool, and

3. they can be used to identify and locate the
    institutions where significant numbers of
    baccalaureate degrees are being conferred on
    minority students.

Minority Groups Represented
Blacks, Hispanics, Asians and Native Americans are the four
minority groups represented in this data source and are the groups
considered throughout this study. It is obvious that these groups have
been selected because they are underrepresented in higher education
and they are the groups that have historically been categorically
disadvantaged in gaining access to higher education. A full definition

of the minority group designations which apply here are found in Appendix A.

Disciplinary Stratification

Besides being broken down by minority group, baccalaureate production is further stratified into the following twenty-four disciplinary divisions: (0100) Agriculture and Natural Resources; (0200) Architecture and Environmental Design; (0300) Area Studies; (0400) Biological Sciences; (0500) Business and Management; (0600) Communications; (0700) Computer and Information Sciences; (0800) Education; (0900) Engineering; (1000) Fine and Applied Arts; (1100) Foreign Languages; (1200) Health Professions; (1300) Home Economics; (1400) Law; (1500) Letters; (1600) Library Science; (1700) Mathematics; (1800) Military Sciences; (1900) Physical Sciences; (2000) Psychology; (2100) Public Affairs and Services; (2200) Social Sciences; (2300) Theology and (2400) Interdisciplinary Studies. Each of these disciplinary divisions are comprised of numerous disciplines and programs. The taxonomy used in this study is consistent with that used by HEGIS and the disciplines included under each division are listed in Appendix B.

Magnitude

These data show that a total of 916,247 baccalaureate degrees were conferred at U.S. Institutions of higher learning in 1978-79, 10.8 percent of which went to minority students—blacks, Hispanics, Asians and Native Americans. Of the 98,886 baccalaureate degrees conferred on minority students, 60.8 percent went to blacks, 20.3 percent to Hispanics, 15.5 percent to Asians and 3.4 percent to Native Americans, indicating the approximately one out of every ten baccalaureate degrees conferred in the United States was awarded to a minority (Table 1).

Temporal Stability

The total number of baccalaureate degrees conferred nationally has exceeded nine hundred thousand annually since 1973-74, although there is a slight decline since that time. In contrast, the number of minority degrees conferred during the same period has experienced absolute and relative increases for each minority group. The largest increases were experienced by Asians and Hispanics. Although the increase in black baccalaureate degrees has not been as striking, they still account for more than 60 percent of all minority baccalaureate production, while the number of Native Americans receiving baccalaureate degrees has remained quite small, never exceeding 3,500 in a single year.

Reliability

Earned baccalaureate degree data reported by the 1978-79 HEGIS survey are drawn from the entire universe of four-year institutions. When comparing the 1973-74 HEGIS data with the American Council on Education's Higher Education Panel (HEP) sample survey for the same year the national estimates derived by a

Data

weighing procedure were found to be within 3.6 percent of each other. [12] Based upon the correspondence between the counts of baccalaureate degrees generated by each of these independent surveys, the HEGIS data used in this study are presumed to be a reliable data source, representative of the U.S. minority baccalaureate degree production.

It can be concluded from these data that the size of the minority graduate and professional school recruitment pool in terms of baccalaureate degree production has been increasing since 1973-74 (Table 1). Although there are fluctuations in baccalaureate degree production among the minority groups considered, it can be assumed that the trends identified will continue in the near future, thus the 1978-79 data are useful in establishing the parameters for contemporary recruitment, as well as the development of future minority recruitment strategies.

TABLE 1

BACCALAUREATE DEGREES CONFERRED AT U.S.
INSTITUTIONS OF HIGHER EDUCATION BY
ETHNICITY AND RACE

Year	Blacks	Hispanics	Asians	Native Americans	Total Minority	Total
1978-79	60,127	20,025	15,336	3,398	98,886	916,247
1976-77	58,515	18,663	13,745	3,319	94,242	915,131
1975-76	59,122	17,964	11,193	3,494	91,777	918,329
1973-74	52,427	12,860	8,903	2,968	77,158	989,200

Data Reduction

The 1,658 institutions reporting data on minority baccalaureate production are an unwieldy number to use effectively in the development of a recruitment strategy. For these data to be useful requires that the number of institutions be minimized as much as possible, while at the same time maximizing the size of the pool represented by the number of minority baccalaureate degrees conferred. Only those institutions are considered where the number of minority baccalaureate degrees awarded for a single group was at least 49 in 1978-79. This criterion was applied to all the minority groups considered in the study with the exception of Native Americans where, due to their small numbers, the threshold was lowered to 15 degrees awarded annually to members of this group. Employing this criterion 362 institutions, of which a subset of 92 are predominantly minority, emerged with an aggregate production of 80,051 minority baccalaureate degrees. In this study 80,051 minority baccalaureate degrees are presumed to be the effective minority graduate and professional student pool.

Effective Pool
     This minimization-maximization procedure employed to derive the effective minority pool reveals that 80.2 percent of all minority baccalaureate production is concentrated at 21.8 percent of the institutions awarding degrees. Nearly 82 percent of the nation's black baccalaureate degrees and 80 percent of the respective Hispanic and Asian baccalaureate degrees are conferred at this set of 362 institutions, where nearly 74 percent of the Native American baccalaureate degree production is also concentrated (Table 2). From here on, the analysis is based upon the aggregate of 80,051 minority baccalaureate degrees conferred at the 362 institutions selected, which produce a total of 495,427 baccalaureate degrees.

TABLE 2

MINORITY BACCALAUREATE DEGREES
AWARDED IN THE U.S.
1978-79

Minority Group	Total Number Of Degrees	Degrees For Selected Institutions	
		Number	Percentage
Blacks	60,127	49,116	81.7
Hispanics	20,025	16,037	80.1
Asians	15,336	12,394	80.1
Native Americans	3,398	2,504	73.7
Total Minorities	98,886	80,051	80.2
Number of Institutions	1,658	362	21.8

DISTRIBUTION OF THE POOL

     A prerequisite for a sound recruitment strategy is a comprehensive knowledge of the pool. It is important to know the size of the pool, as well as to have knowledge of its location by state and institution. The rank order of minority baccalaureate production by institution is also important information to have available.

Location by State
     The 80,051 minority baccalaureate degrees conferred at the institutions selected for this study are found in all but nine states: Alaska, Iowa, Kansas, Maine, Nevada, South Dakota, Vermont and

Wyoming, where minority populations are very small. It would be a misinterpretation to believe that minorities do not receive baccalaureate degrees in these states. These states are excluded because the number of degrees conferred on minorities at each of the institutions in these states are not sufficient to meet the criterion specified for inclusion in the study.

California produces more minority undergraduate degrees than any other state with New York second, Texas third and Florida, fourth. Illinois is fifth, with slightly more than 3,800 minority baccalaureate degrees being conferred annually at institutions in the state (Table 3). For blacks, New York ranks first in baccalaureate production, followed by North Carolina, California and Illinois in descending order. The next six highest ranking states in the production of black baccalaureate degrees are all located in the south. Hispanic baccalaureate production is highest in Texas, followed closely by California, New York and Florida. Together these four states produce 71.5 percent of all the baccalaureate degrees conferred on Hispanics nationally. Two of every five undergraduate degrees received by Asians are conferred in California. Hawaii is the next ranking state followed by New York, which accounts for 9.3 percent of all baccalaureate degrees conferred upon Asians. California also leads the nation in the number of baccalaureate degrees conferred on Native Americans with Oklahoma and Texas ranking second and third, respectively, and New York in fourth position.

It is clear from Table 3 that the highest minority baccalaureate production generally occurs in the states with the largest populations. This generalization also holds when considering the baccalaureate production for each of the minority groups separately. These data also show the black production is concentrated in the south, as well as in our most populous states, while Hispanic production is concentrated in the west and southwest, for the most part, with other nodes in Florida and the more urbanized states.

Asian baccalaureate production is concentrated mainly in California and Hawaii and is generally a west coast phenomenon. The distribution of Native American production generally follows the Hispanic distribution pattern with the major exception being Oklahoma, the state with the second highest number of degrees awarded to this group, and North Carolina and New Mexico, which rank fifth and sixth respectively. Two other states where production is significant are also among the most highly urbanized. The spatial characteristics of the distributions of baccalaureate production for blacks, Hispanics, Asians and Native American are displayed on Maps 1-4, which locates and shows each institution's production as the square root of the actual number of degrees conferred.

The number of minority baccalaureate degrees conferred by state and institutions stratified by minority group are found on Table 4. These data are extremely useful since they provide the foundation upon which to develop a recruitment strategy because it is possible to concentrate recruitment efforts on the states and institutions where

the level of minority baccalaureate degree production is significant
enough to justify such activity.

TABLE 3

TEN LEADING STATES IN
MINORITY BACCALAUREATE PRODUCTION

Rank	Black State	%	Hispanic State	%	Asian State	%	Native American State	%	Total Minority State	%
1	NY	11.1	TX	25.6	CA	44.2	CA	23.7	CA	16.4
2	NC	7.3	CA	23.3	HI	17.3	OK	12.1	NY	11.1
3	CA	6.8	NY	13.2	NY	9.3	TX	9.1	TX	9.3
4	IL	5.7	FL	9.4	IL	4.0	NY	6.8	FL	5.0
5	LA	5.7	NM	6.0	TX	3.0	NC	4.8	IL	4.8
6	TX	5.5	NJ	3.6	WA	2.8	NM	4.2	NC	4.7
7	AL	5.0	IL	3.1	NJ	1.7	PA	3.9	LA	3.7
8	VA	4.6	AZ	2.9	FL	1.6	IL	3.3	AL	3.3
9	FL	4.6	CO	2.6	MI	1.5	MI	3.1	VA	2.9
10	MS	4.4	PA	1.0	MA	1.3	NJ	2.6	MI	2.9
		60.7%		90.7%		86.7%		73.6%		64.1%
	n=49,116		n=16,037		n=12,394		n=2,504		n=80,051	

Production by Institution

To further facilitate a recruitment strategy focused upon the
magnitude of minority baccalaureate degree production, the 362
institutions on Table 4 are rank ordered for each minority group.
From these data it is easy to determine which are the institutions
with the greatest production and highest recruitment potential. Such
information sharpens the process of selecting institutions where
recruitment activities may be directed.

For example, an examination of the rank ordered list of
institutions where blacks received their baccalaureate degrees
reveals that large numbers of blacks also received their degrees at
non-minority institutions. This fact, although it may be obvious to
some, is still important because the position of these non-minority
institutions in the ranking can greatly influence a recruitment
initiative. It is still common practice to recruit blacks from only
predominantly black institutions. This practice was sound at its

10

DISTRIBUTION OF BLACK BACCALAUREATE DEGREES   MAP 1

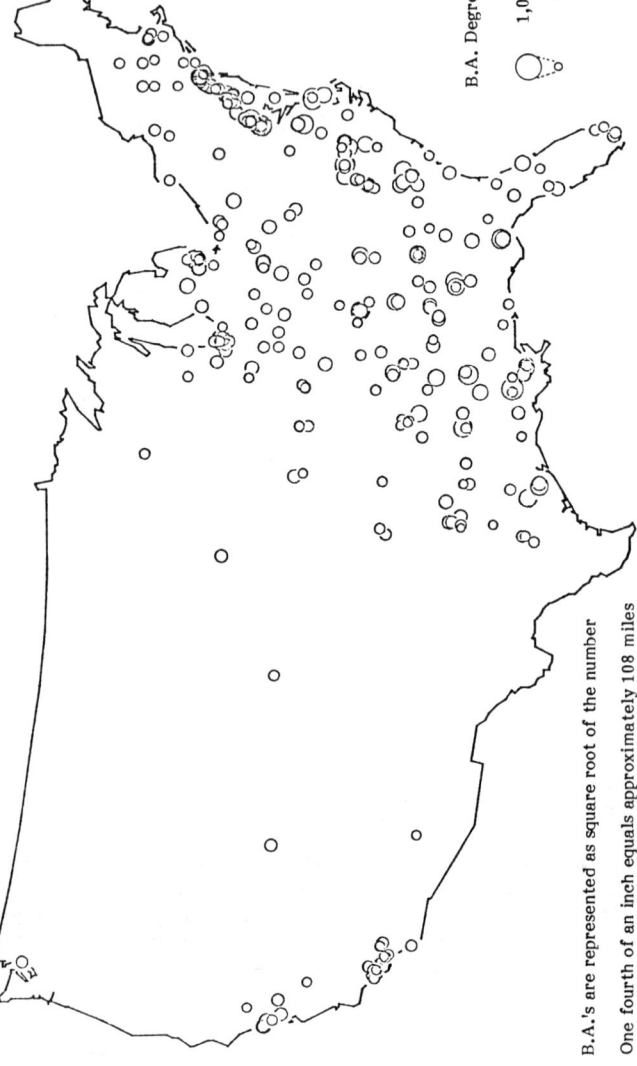

B.A. Degrees

1,000
15

B.A.'s are represented as square root of the number

One fourth of an inch equals approximately 108 miles

11

DISTRIBUTION OF HISPANIC BACCALAUREATE DEGREES   MAP 2

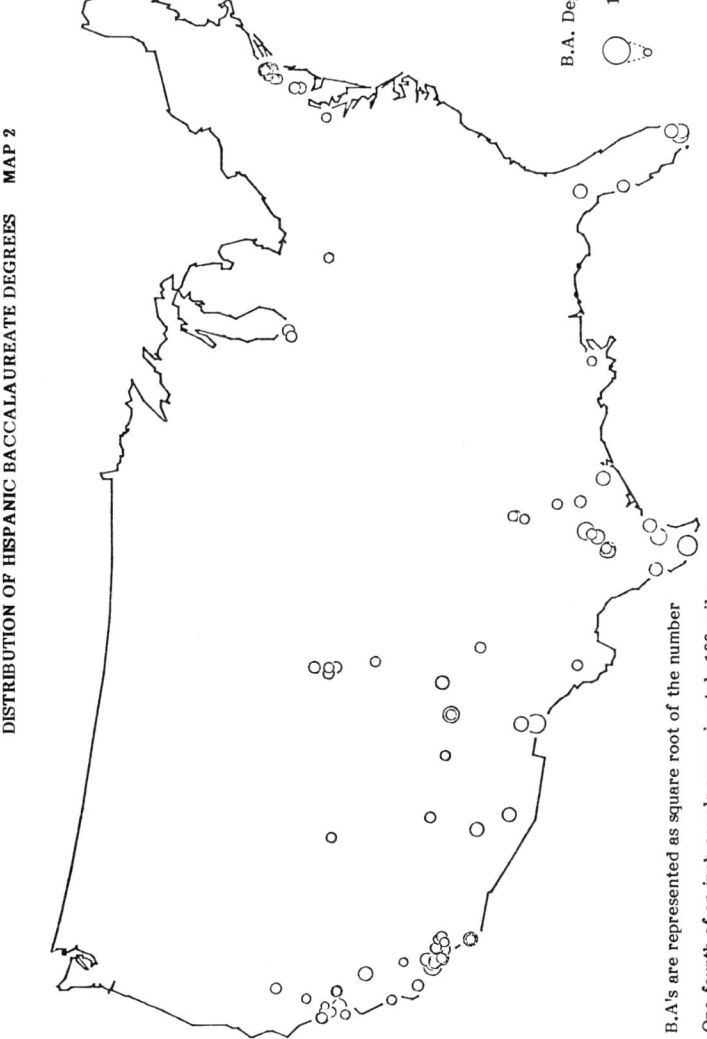

B.A. Degrees

○ 1,000

○ 15

B.A's are represented as square root of the number

One fourth of an inch equals approximately 108 miles

12

DISTRIBUTION OF ASIAN BACCALAUREATE DEGREES   MAP 3

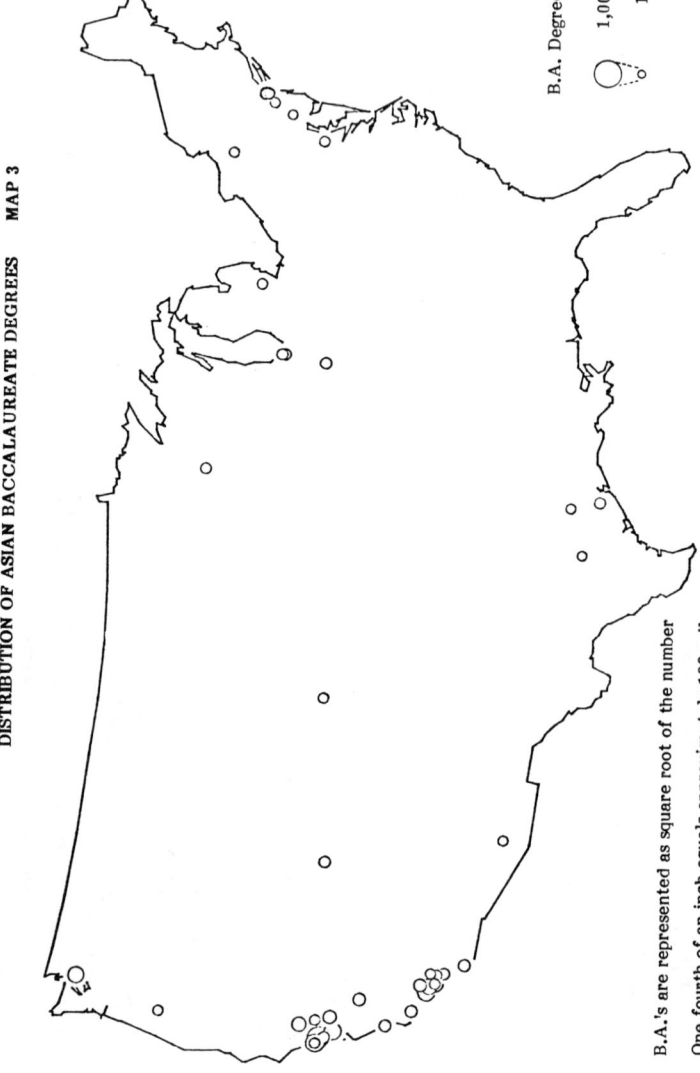

B.A. Degrees

1,000

15

B.A.'s are represented as square root of the number

One fourth of an inch equals approximately 108 miles

DISTRIBUTION OF NATIVE AMERICAN BACCALAUREATE DEGREES   MAP 4

B.A. Degrees

1,000

15

B.A.'s are represented as square root of the number

One fourth of an inch equals approximately 108 miles

TABLE 4

TOTAL (0100–2400)
MINORITY BACCALAUREATE DEGREES
BY STATE AND INSTITUTION

STATE/SCHOOL	MINORITY GROUP			
	Black	Hispanic	Asian	Native American
Alabama				
Alabama A&M University*	390			
Alabama State University*	400			
Jacksonville State University	87	7	11	
Miles College*	142			
Oakwood College*	187			
Stillman College*	131	2		
Talladega College*	109			
Troy State University - Main Campus	128	8	2	
Troy State University - Montgomery	62	2		
Tuskegee Institute*	430	1	1	
University of Alabama	175			
U of Alabama in Birmingham	160	1	7	
University of South Alabama	61	1	6	4
	2,462	**22**	**27**	**4**
Arizona				
Arizona State University	52	198	49	8
Northern Arizona University	15	79	10	54
University of Arizona	44	195	63	53
	111	**472**	**122**	**115**
Arkansas				
Arkansas Baptist College*	45			
Arkansas State U - Main Campus	70	1	1	3
Henderson State University	94			
Philander Smith College*	63			
University of Arkansas - Pine Bluff*	341			
University of Central Arkansas	49		1	
	662	**1**	**2**	**3**

(0100-2400)

STATE/SCHOOL	MINORITY GROUP			
	Black	Hispanic	Asian	Native American
California				
Cal Poly State U – San Luis Obispo	23	59	114	44
Cal State College – Bakersfield	16	41	10	31
Cal State College – San Bernadino	59	76	9	7
Cal State Poly U – Pomona	38	127	67	37
Cal State University – Chico	25	85	43	14
Cal State U – Dominguez Hills	369	69	80	13
Cal State University – Fresno	57	215	143	16
Cal State University – Fullerton	53	207	86	29
Cal State University – Hayward	128	61	94	9
Cal State University – Long Beach	174	226	338	31
Cal State University – Los Angeles	341	447	422	20
Cal State University – Northridge	110	161	148	68
Cal State University – Sacramento	129	108	159	33
Chapman College	78	33	26	12
Loyola Marymount University	54	91	32	2
Pacific Christian College	71	6	14	5
Pepperdine University	90	20	36	4
San Diego State University	98	218	126	22
San Francisco State University	221	138	526	29
San Jose State University	156	223	382	47
Stanford University	75	82	99	5
U of Cal – Berkeley	165	98	856	21
U of Cal – Davis	50	50	227	15
U of Cal – Irvine	45	33	104	8
U of Cal – Los Angeles	186	163	547	17
U of Cal – Riverside	47	51	28	2
U of Cal – San Diego		59	49	7
U of Cal – San Francisco	10	12	60	
U of Cal – Santa Barbara	34	100	117	7
U of Cal – Santa Cruz		57	17	
University of LaVerne	46	87	10	2

16

(0100-2400)

STATE/SCHOOL	MINORITY GROUP			
	Black	Hispanic	Asian	Native American
California (cont)				
University of Redlands	126	73	33	
University of San Francisco	107	80	94	14
University of Southern California	138	156	311	18
University of the Pacific	27	27	76	4
	3346	**3739**	**5483**	**593**
Colorado				
Colorado State University	14	107	24	7
Metropolitan State College	78	93	13	14
U of Colorado at Boulder	37	84	66	6
U of Northern Colorado	34	67	15	8
U of Southern Colorado	14	68	6	4
	177	**419**	**124**	**39**
Connecticut				
University of Connecticut	49	20	9	3
Yale University	59	47	46	2
	108	**67**	**55**	**5**
Delaware				
Delaware State College*	133	1		
University of Delaware	62	5	9	2
	195	**6**	**9**	**2**
District of Columbia				
American University	173	27	14	2
George Washington University	73	38	45	3
Howard University*	778		5	
University of DC*	441	31	10	8
	1465	**96**	**74**	**13**
Florida				
Bethune Cookman College*	287	1		
Biscayne College*	37	203		1
Edward Waters College*	76			
Florida Agr & Mech University*	615	3	9	

(0100-2400)

STATE/SCHOOL	MINORITY GROUP			
	Black	Hispanic	Asian	Native American
Florida (cont)				
Florida Atlantic University	84	43	3	1
Florida International University	176	529	45	3
Florida Memorial College*	69			
Florida State University	269	43	10	5
University of Central Florida	55	26	15	1
St. Leo College	75	24		1
University of Florida	138	209	48	2
University of Miami	102	276	34	4
University of South Florida	195	132	20	6
University of West Florida	71	17	12	3
	2249	**1506**	**196**	**27**
Georgia				
Albany State College*	229			
Clark College*	296			
Fort Valley State College*	146			
Georgia College	56		1	
GA Inst of Tech – Main Campus	52	23	15	1
Georgia State University	211	3	6	6
Morehouse College*	214			
Morris Brown College*	173			
Paine College*	88			
Savannah State College*	161			
Spelman College*	273		1	
University of Georgia	100	9	5	8
Valdosta State College	49			
	2,048	**35**	**28**	**15**
Hawaii				
Chaminade University of Honolulu	5	4	57	
University of Hawaii at Hilo*		6	102	
University of Hawaii at Manoa*	7	29	1,984	1
	12	**39**	**2143**	**1**

18

(0100–2400)

STATE/SCHOOL	MINORITY GROUP			
	Black	Hispanic	Asian	Native American
Illinois				
Bradley University	51	2	9	2
Chicago State University*	552	19	2	2
College of St. Francis	166	11	11	
Columbia College	90	12	10	8
Daniel Hale Williams University*	70			
DePaul University	107	39	16	2
Eastern Illinois University	73	1	6	
Governors State University	154	10	2	
Illinois State University	165	21	18	18
Loyola University of Chicago	82	44	20	
Northern Illinois University	149	18	25	2
Northeastern Illinois University	112	86	29	2
Northwestern University	133	19	33	2
Roosevelt University	287	28	91	
Southern Illinois U – Carbondale	198	28	26	26
Southern Illinois U – Edwardsville	110	1	9	1
U of Illinois – Chicago Circle	216	121	101	6
U of Illinois – Urbana Campus	91	34	91	12
	2,806	**494**	**499**	**83**
Indiana				
Ball State University	76	5	2	3
Ind-Purdue U – Indianapolis	74	4	6	5
Indiana State U – Main Campus	98	3	6	4
Indiana University – Bloomington	133	20	25	5
Indiana University – Northwest	50	12		
Purdue University – Main Campus	103	25	41	4
	534	**69**	**80**	**21**
Kentucky				
Eastern Kentucky University	81			
Kentucky State University*	110			

(0100–2400)

STATE/SCHOOL	MINORITY GROUP			
	Black	Hispanic	Asian	Native American
Kentucky (cont)				
University of Louisville	73	7	15	2
Western Kentucky University	53	2		1
	317	**9**	**15**	**3**
Louisiana				
Dillard University*	188			
Grambling State University*	526			
Louisiana State U & A&M College	62	15	5	3
Louisiana Tech University	69	2	3	
McNeese State University	54	3	5	1
Northeast Louisiana University	124	1	2	
Southeastern Louisiana U	54		1	
Sthrn U A&M College - Main Cam*	904			
Southern U in New Orleans*	295			
Tulane U of Louisiana	28	55	11	5
University of New Orleans	88	23	8	
U of Southwestern Louisiana	144	16	3	15
Xavier University of Louisiana*	257		11	
	2793	**115**	**49**	**24**
Maryland				
Bowie State College*	140			
Coppin State College*	142			1
Morgan State University*	438		4	
Towson State University	140	6	7	3
University of Baltimore	107	1	3	1
U of MD - Baltimore Co Campus	88		1	4
U of MD - Baltimore Prof School	60	6	19	
U of MD - College Park Campus	216	53	72	42
U of MD - Eastern Shore*	87	1		
U of MD - University College	103	14	14	6
	1521	**81**	**120**	**57**

20

STATE/SCHOOL	MINORITY GROUP			
	Black	Hispanic	Asian	Native American
Massachussetts				
Boston State College	71	17	7	3
Boston University	65	21	18	4
Harvard University	108	28	45	6
Radcliffe College	51	11	16	1
Tufts University	67	21	30	3
U of Mass – Amherst Campus	54	33	41	7
	416	**131**	**157**	**24**
Michigan				
Detroit Institute of Technology	52		6	
Eastern Michigan University	175	14	7	25
Mercy College of Detroit	70	2	1	
Michigan State University	271	42	38	13
Oakland University	76	5	7	5
Shaw College at Detroit*	68			
University of Detroit	163	9	13	
U of Michigan – Ann Arbor	233	41	79	10
Wayne State University	635	29	31	14
Western Michigan University	143	17	7	11
	1,886	**159**	**189**	**78**
Minnesota				
U of Minn – Minneapolis/St. Paul	72	32	86	16
	72	**32**	**86**	**16**
Mississippi				
Alcorn State University*	286		1	
Delta State University	71		2	
Jackson State University*	653			1
Mississippi Industrial College*	40			
Mississippi State University	175	3	2	2
Mississippi University for Women	50		1	
Mississippi Valley State Univ*	375	1		
Rust College*	117			

(0100-2400)

STATE/SCHOOL	MINORITY GROUP			
	Black	Hispanic	Asian	Native American
Mississippi (cont)				
Tougaloo College*	127			
U of Mississippi – Main Campus	90	2	8	2
U of Southern Mississippi	164	3	8	
	2,148	**9**	**22**	**5**
Missouri				
Columbia College	91	7	1	2
Harris Stowe College*	54			
Lincoln University	84			
Park College	165	42		2
St. Louis U – Main Campus	94	9	11	2
U of Missouri – Columbia	54	8	25	6
U of Missouri – Kansas City	49	8	9	6
U of Missouri – St. Louis	93	15	7	6
Washington University	59	16	25	
Webster College	50	1		
	793	**106**	**78**	**24**
Montana				
Montana State University	1	4	7	17
	1	**4**	**7**	**17**
Nebraska				
U of Nebraska at Omaha	49	21	3	1
	49	**21**	**3**	**1**
New Hampshire				
Dartmouth College	70	3	7	6
	70	**3**	**7**	**6**
New Jersey				
Glassboro State College	156	104	5	31
Jersey City State College	109	43	9	
Kean College of New Jersey	134	67	9	4
Montclair State College	53	64	13	18
New Jersey Inst Technology	69	35	29	

(0100–2400)

STATE/SCHOOL	MINORITY GROUP			
	Black	Hispanic	Asian	Native American
New Jersey (cont)				
Princeton University	63	33	36	5
Rutgers U – Camden Campus	72	6	2	1
Rutgers U – New Brunswick	272	82	65	1
Rutgers U – Newark Campus	181	49	18	
St. Peter's College	34	70	8	
Seton Hall University	66	8	6	1
Trenton State College	117	9	8	5
	1326	**570**	**208**	**66**
New Mexico				
Eastern NM U – Main Campus	24	84	4	15
New Mexico Highlands U*	4	171		5
NM State U – Main Campus	19	235	5	17
University of Albuquerque	5	77	1	6
U of NM – Main Campus	18	345	12	58
Western New Mexico University	4	58	1	4
	74	**970**	**23**	**105**
New York				
Adelphi University	169	43	1	1
College of New Rochelle	133	33	3	
Cornell U Endowed College	67	36	65	6
CUNY Bernard Baruch College	374	162	130	5
CUNY Brooklyn College	650	224	50	23
CUNY City College	597	285	166	22
CUNY College of Staten Island	70	42	15	2
CUNY Graduate School & U Center	60	27	12	2
CUNY Hunter College	308	182	68	15
CUNY John Jay College – Crim Jus	171	82	10	12
CUNY Lehman College	171	202	48	2
CUNY Medgar Evers College*	122	1		
CUNY Queen's College	307	84	90	7
CUNY York College	185	39	10	5

(0100–2400)

STATE/SCHOOL	MINORITY GROUP			
	Black	Hispanic	Asian	Native American
New York (cont)				
Fordham University	136	139	20	
Long Island U – Brooklyn Center	174	54	21	
Long Island U – C W Post Center	56	12	5	
Mercy College	154	81	12	2
New York University	204	57	79	12
Pace University New York	91	33	29	2
Polytechnic Institute New York	28	22	72	
Pratt Institute	105	39	25	
St. Francis College	197	13	41	
St. John's University	51	39	33	5
St. Joseph's College – Main Campus	271	11	13	
SUNY at Albany	65	38	16	13
SUNY at Buffalo – Main Campus	67	9	26	2
SUNY at Stony Bk – Main Campus	54	31	46	2
SUNY College at Buffalo	85	16	7	13
SUNY College at New Paltz	51	19	6	15
SUNY College – Old Westbury	80	20	1	
SUNY Empire State College	100	20	7	2
Syracuse University – Main Campus	99	26	22	
	5452	**2121**	**1149**	**170**
North Carolina				
Barber–Scotia College*	51			
Bennett College*	85			
Duke University	51	11	14	1
East Carolina University	92	2	1	1
Elizabeth City State U*	301		1	
Fayetteville State University*	294	5	4	2
Johnson C Smith University*	200			
Livingstone College*	129			
NC Agrl & Tech State University*	602			
NC Central University*	614	2		1

24

STATE/SCHOOL	MINORITY GROUP			
	Black	Hispanic	Asian	Native American
North Carolina (cont)				
NC State U - Raleigh	88	8	3	3
Pembroke State University	46		1	96
St. Augustine's College*	202		2	
Shaw University*	193			
U of NC at Chapel Hill	156	10	8	13
U of NC at Charlotte	64	7	4	1
U of NC at Greensboro	84	4	2	2
Winston-Salem State University*	309			
	3561	**49**	**40**	**120**
North Dakota				
U of North Dakota - Main Campus	7	3	4	29
	7	**3**	**4**	**29**
Ohio				
Antioch University	194	61	4	5
Bowling Green State U - Main Cam	142	15	7	2
Central State University*	224		1	
Franklin University	56	2	7	1
Kent State U - Main Campus	135	6	2	6
Oberlin College	53	6	26	2
Ohio State U - Main Campus	138	8	28	3
Ohio University - Main Campus	197	3	3	6
U of Akron - Main Campus	92	3	8	3
U of Cincinnati - Main Campus	224	11	10	2
University of Dayton	64	8	7	3
University of Toledo	58	8	17	6
Wilberforce University*	112			
Wright State U - Main Campus	55	1	1	1
	1,744	**132**	**121**	**40**
Oklahoma				
Cameron University	41	12	1	16
Central State University	98	12	7	18

(0100-2400)

STATE/SCHOOL	MINORITY GROUP			
	Black	Hispanic	Asian	Native American
Oklahoma (cont)				
East Central Oklahoma State U	12	2	1	24
Langston University*	77			
Northeast Oklahoma State U	61	1	4	118
Oklahoma State U – Main Campus	45	13	26	40
Southeast Oklahoma State U	23	1	3	21
Southwest Oklahoma State U	16	2	2	17
U of Oklahoma – Norman Campus	45	11	12	48
	418	**54**	**56**	**302**
Oregon				
Oregon State University	6	8	41	21
University of Oregon – Main Campus	23	20	69	11
	29	**28**	**110**	**32**
Pennsylvania				
Cheyney State College*	303			
Drexel University	61	2	15	
Lincoln University*	172			
Pennsylvania State U – Main Campus	96	20	25	7
St. Joseph's University	47	3	2	51
Temple University	446	102	41	23
University of Pennsylvania	113	28	50	3
U of Pittsburgh – Main Campus	251	8	4	14
West Chester State College	55	2	1	
	1544	**165**	**138**	**98**
Rhode Island				
Brown University	71	10	26	1
	71	**10**	**26**	**1**
South Carolina				
Allen University*	66			
Baptist College at Charleston	58			
Benedict College*	296			
Claflin College*	147			

26

(0100-2400)

STATE/SCHOOL	MINORITY GROUP			
	Black	Hispanic	Asian	Native American
South Carolina (cont)				
Morris College*	89			
South Carolina State College*	468		2	
U of South Carolina at Columbia	250	18	11	3
Voorhees College*	164			
Winthrop College	72	1		
	1,610	**19**	**13**	**3**
Tennessee				
Austin Peay State University	50	2	3	2
Fisk University*	217			
Knoxville College*	104			
Lane College*	109			
LeMoyne-Owen College*	114			
Memphis State University	271	5	28	1
Middle Tennessee State U	71	2	18	2
Tennessee State University*	500			
U of Tennessee - Knoxville	125	9	15	4
U of Tennessee - Martin	70	1	4	
	1,631	**19**	**68**	**9**
Texas				
Angelo State University	18	68		1
Bishop College*	155			
Corpus Christi State University	4	174	4	3
East Texas State University	200	42	13	7
Huston-Tillotson College*	67	1		
Incarnate Word College	18	86		
Jarvis Christian College*	45			
Lamar University	25	2	11	104
Laredo State University*		163		
North Texas State University	175	62	11	4
Our Lady of Lake University*	27	136	1	
Pan American University*	4	719	5	1

(0100-2400)

STATE/SCHOOL		MINORITY GROUP		
	Black	Hispanic	Asian	Native American
Texas (cont)				
Paul Quinn College*	44			
Prairie View A&M University*	461	6	21	
St. Edward's University	13	81		
St. Mary's U - San Antonio	12	153	19	
Sam Houston State University	89	2	59	9
Southwest Texas State University	78	229	4	1
Sul Ross State University	6	75		
Texas A&I University	22	335		
Texas A&M U - Main Campus	15	110	17	41
Texas College*	99			
Texas Southern University*	462	7		
Texas Women's University	125	70	12	6
Trinity University	10	72	3	
U of Houston - Central Campus	203	212	93	8
U of Texas at Arlington	84	55	17	5
U of Texas at Austin	103	453	53	12
U of Texas at El Paso	49	584	23	11
U of Texas at San Antonio	12	202	8	4
Wiley College*	93			
	2718	**4099**	**374**	**227**
Utah				
Brigham Young University - Main			25	37
University of Utah	21	35	31	16
	21	**35**	**56**	**53**
Virginia				
Hampton Institute*	444			
Norfolk State College*	603			
Old Dominion University	62	11	13	5
St. Paul's College*	102			
U of Virginia - Main Campus	68	3	7	

(0100–2400)

STATE/SCHOOL	MINORITY GROUP			
	Black	Hispanic	Asian	Native American
Virginia (cont)				
Virginia Commonwealth University	222	9	10	6
Virginia State College*	593		1	
Virginia Union University*	162			
	2,256	**23**	**31**	**11**
Washington				
Evergreen State College	19	7	5	17
University of Washington	121	40	343	29
	140	**47**	**348**	**46**
West Virginia				
West Virginia State College	97	1	6	
	97	**1**	**6**	
Wisconsin				
U of Wisconsin – Madison	65	32	34	10
U of Wisconsin – Milwaukee	111	25	13	6
	176	**57**	**47**	**16**
TOTALS	**49,116**	**16,037**	**12,394**	**2,504**

*Predominantly minority institutions are those where at least 50% of total BA Degrees awarded are to one of the minority groups considered.

inception and survives because predominantly black institutions are relatively easy to identify and, due to the nature of their enrollment, concentrations of black degree recipients are always available at these institutions. However, the content of Table 5 suggests that this strategy, although it still has some validity, is not as sound as it was several decades ago because of increases in the numbers of blacks receiving baccalaureate degrees at non-minority institutions.

The largest producer of black bachelor's degrees in the U.S. is Southern University in Baton Rouge, Louisiana with 904 annually conferred. Howard University is second with 778 degrees conferred and Jackson State University, in Mississippi, with 653 ranks third. These are all predominantly black schools. Number four is CUNY's Brooklyn College with 650 and number five is Wayne State University with 635. Moving down the list past the intervening predominantly black schools, City College of New York with 597 degrees appears in tenth place. Temple University is eighteenth, twenty-sixth is CUNY's Bernard Baruch, followed by California State University-Dominguez Hills and California State University-Los Angeles. The next non-minority institutions on the list are Hunter College and Queen's College of the CUNY system while Chicago's Roosevelt University is ranked thirty-ninth. It is obvious from this ranked list that significant black baccalaureate production takes place at non-minority institutions. It is not surprising that much of this production is at institutions located in heavily urbanized areas. However, it is surprising that among those institutions ranked between 43 and 69 are some of the nation's largest institutions: Rutgers University-New Brunswick (43), Michigan State University (44), the University of Pittsburgh-Main Campus (49), the University of Michigan (51), the University of Cincinnati-Main Campus (54), all located in the northeast and middle west. More interesting is the fact that large state institutions in the south are now appearing on this list: Memphis State University (46), Florida State University (47), University of South Carolina at Columbia (50) and the University of Maryland-College Park Campus (60).

Among the top sixty ranked schools in black baccalaureate production, twenty-three are non-minority institutions. These data suggests that efforts to recruit blacks need to extend beyond the 92 predominantly minority institutions identified in this study, 85 of which are predominantly black institutions. Sufficient attention needs to be given to the recruitment of blacks at the remaining 270 non-minority institutions if the full potential of the minority baccalaureate pool is to be realized.

There are very few predominantly Hispanic institutions in the U.S.; only five are identified among the 362 schools being examined, one each in Florida and New Mexico and three in Texas. Pan American University in Texas, one of the predominantly Hispanic institutions identified, heads the list in Hispanic baccalaureate production with 719 degrees conferred. Due to the fact that there are few predominantly Hispanic institutions, the ranked list of baccalaureate production by institution is especially useful since it lists the institutions where the large clusters of Hispanic bachelor's

TABLE 5

TOTAL (0100-2400)
BLACK BACCALAUREATE DEGREES RANKED BY INSTITUTION

Rank	Institution	B.A.'s	Rank	Institution	B.A.'s
1	Sthrn U A&M C-Main Cam*	904	29	U of Arkansas-Pine Bluff*	341
2	Howard University*	778	30	Winston-Salem State U*	309
3	Jackson State U*	653	31	CUNY Hunter C	308
4	CUNY Brooklyn College	650	32	CUNY Queen's C	307
5	Wayne State University	635	33	Cheyney State C*	303
6	Florida Agrl & Mech U*	615	34	Elizabeth City State U*	301
7	NC Central U*	614	35	Clark C*	296
8	Norfolk State C*	603	36	Benedict C*	296
9	NC Agrl & Tech State U*	602	37	Southern U in New Orleans*	295
10	CUNY City C	597	38	Fayetteville State U*	294
11	Virginia State C*	593	39	Roosevelt U	287
12	Chicago State U*	552	40	Bethune Cookman C*	287
13	Grambling State U*	526	41	Alcorn State U*	276
14	Tennessee State U*	500	42	Spelman C*	273
15	South Carolina State C*	468	43	Rutgers U-New Brunswick	272
16	Texas Southern U*	462	44	Michigan State U	271
17	Prairie View A&M U*	461	45	St. Joseph's C-Main Campus	271
18	Temple U	446	46	Memphis State U	271
19	Hampton Institute*	444	47	Florida State U	269
20	U of DC*	441	48	Xavier U of Louisiana*	257
21	Morgan State U*	438	49	U of Pittsburgh-Main Campus	251
22	Tuskegee Institute*	430	50	U of South Carolina at Columbia	250
23	Alabama State U*	400	51	U of Michigan-Ann Arbor	233
24	Alabama A&M U*	390	52	Albany State C*	229
25	Mississippi Valley State U*	375	53	U of Cincinnati-Main Campus	250
26	CUNY Bernard Baruch C	374	54	Central State U*	224
27	Cal State U-Dominguez Hills	369	55	Virginia Commonwealth U	222
28	Cal State U-Los Angeles	341	56	San Francisco State U	221

Black B.A.'s (0100-2400)

Rank	Institution	B.A.'s	Rank	Institution	B.A.'s
57	Fisk U*	217	90	Adelphi U	169
58	U of Illinois-Chicago Circle	216	91	C of St. Francis	166
59	U of MD-College Park Campus	216	92	Illinois State U	165
60	Morehouse C*	214	93	Park C	165
61	Georgia State U	211	94	U of Cal-Berkeley	165
62	New York U	204	95	U of Southern Mississippi	164
63	U of Houston-Central Campus	203	96	Voorhees C*	164
64	St. Augustine's C*	202	97	U of Detroit	163
65	Johnson C Smith U*	200	98	Virginia Union U*	162
66	East Texas State U	200	99	Savannah State C*	161
67	Southern Illinois U-Carbondale	198	100	U of Alabama in Birmingham	160
68	Ohio U-Main Campus	197	101	U of NC at Chapel Hill	156
69	St. Franics C	197	102	San Jose State U	156
70	U of South Florida	195	103	Glassboro State C	156
71	Antioch U	194	104	Bishop C*	155
72	Shaw U*	193	105	Governors State U	154
73	Dillard U*	188	106	Mercy C	154
74	Oakwood C*	187	107	Northern Illinois U	149
75	U of Cal-Los Angeles	186	108	Claflin C*	147
76	CUNY York C	185	109	Fort Valley State C*	146
77	Rutgers U-Newark Campus	181	110	U of Southeastern Louisiana	144
78	Florida International U	176	111	Western Michigan U	143
79	Eastern Michigan U	175	112	Coppin State C*	142
80	Mississippi State U	175	113	Bowling Green State U-Main Ca	142
81	U of Alabama	175	114	Miles C*	142
82	North Texas State U	175	115	Bowie State C*	140
83	Cal State U-Long Beach	174	116	Towson State U	140
84	Long Island U-Brooklyn Center	174	117	U of Florida	138
85	Morris Brown C*	173	118	Ohio State U-Main Campus	138
86	American U	173	119	U of Southern California	138
87	Lincoln U*	172	120	Fordham U	136
88	CUNY Lehman C	171	121	Kent State U-Main Campus	135
89	CUNY John Jay C-Crim Jus	171	122	Kean C of New Jersey	134

32

Black B.A.'s (0100-2400)

Rank	Institution	B.A.'s	Rank	Institution	B.A.'s
123	Indiana U-Bloomington	133	156	Pratt Institute	105
124	Delaware State C*	133	157	Knoxville C*	104
125	Northwestern U	133	158	Purdue U-Main Campus	103
126	C of New Rochelle	133	159	U of MD-University C	103
127	Stillman C*	131	160	U of Texas at Austin	103
128	Cal State U-Sacramento	129	161	U of Miami	102
129	Livingstone C*	129	162	St. Paul's C*	102
130	Cal State U-Hayward	128	163	SUNY Empire State C	100
131	Troy State U-Main Campus	128	164	U of Georgia	100
132	Tougaloo C*	127	165	Syracuse U-Main Campus	99
133	U of Redlands	126	166	Texas C*	99
134	U of Tennessee-Knoxville	125	167	Indiana State U-Main Campus	98
135	Texas Women's U	125	168	Central State U	98
136	Northeast Louisiana U	124	169	San Diego State U	98
137	CUNY Medgar Evers C*	122	170	West Virginia State C	97
138	U of Washington	121	171	Pennsylvania State U-Main Cam	96
139	Trenton State C	117	172	St. Louis U-Main Campus	94
140	Rust C*	117	173	Henderson State U	94
141	Le Moyne-Owen C*	114	174	U of Missouri-St. Louis	93
142	U of Pennsylvania	113	175	Wiley C*	93
143	Northeastern Illinois U	112	176	East Carolina U	92
144	Wilberforce U*	112	177	U of Akron-Main Campus	92
145	U of Wisconsin-Milwaukee	111	178	Columbia C	91
146	Kentucky State U*	110	179	U of Illinois-Urbana Campus	91
147	Southern Illinois U-Edwardsville	110	180	Pace U-New York	91
148	Cal State U-Northridge	110	181	Columbia C	90
149	Jersey City State C	109	182	Pepperdine U	90
150	Talladega C*	109	183	U of Mississippi-Main Campus	90
151	Lane C*	109	184	Sam Houston State U	89
152	Harvard U	108	185	Morris C*	89
153	DePaul U	107	186	U of MD-Baltimore Co Campus	88
154	U of Baltimore	107	187	U of New Orleans	88
155	U of San Francisco	107	188	Paine C*	88

Black B.A.'s (0100-2400)

Rank	Institution	B.A.'s	Rank	Institution	B.A.'s
189	NC State U-Raleigh	88	222	Brown U	71
190	U of MD-Eastern Shore*	87	223	Mercy C of Detroit	70
191	Jacksonville State U	87	224	CUNY C of Staten Island	70
192	SUNY C at Buffalo	85	225	Daniel Hale Williams U*	70
193	Bennett C*	85	226	Dartmouth C	70
194	U of NC at Greensboro	84	227	Arkansas State U-Main Campus	70
195	Florida Atlantic U	84	228	U of Tennessee-Martin	70
196	Lincoln U	84	229	Louisiana Tech U	69
197	U of Texas at Arlington	84	230	New Jersey Inst Technology	69
198	Loyola U of Chicago	82	231	Florida Memorial C*	69
199	Eastern Kentucky U	81	232	Shaw C at Detroit*	68
200	SUNY C-Old Westbury	80	233	U of Virginia-Main Campus	68
201	Chapman C	78	234	Cornell U Endowed C	67
202	Metropolitan State C	78	235	SUNY at Buffalo-Main Campus	67
203	Southwest Texas State U	78	236	Tufts U	67
204	Langston U*	77	237	Huston-Tillotson C*	67
205	Edward Waters C*	76	238	Seton Hall U	66
206	Ball State U	76	239	Allen U*	66
207	Oakland U	76	240	SUNY at Albany	65
208	St. Leo C	75	241	Boston U	65
209	Stanford U	75	242	U of Wisconsin-Madison	65
210	Ind-Purdue U-Indianapolis	74	243	U of Dayton	64
211	Eastern Illinois U	73	244	U of NC at Charlotte	64
212	George Washington U	73	245	Princeton U	63
213	U of Louisville	73	246	Philander Smith C*	63
214	U of Minn-Minneapolis/St. Paul	72	247	Louisiana State U & A&M C	62
215	Rutgers U-Camden Campus	72	248	U of Delaware	62
216	Winthrop C	72	249	Troy State U-Montgomery	62
217	U of West Florida	71	250	Old Dominion U	62
218	Boston State C	71	251	Northeast Oklahoma State U	61
219	Pacific Christian C	71	252	Drexel U	61
220	Middle Tennesee State U	71	253	U of South Albama	61
221	Delta State U	71	254	CUNY Graduate School & U Ctr	60

34

Black B.A.'s (0100-2400)

Rank	Institution	B.A.'s	Rank	Institution	B.A.'s
255	U of MD–Baltimore Prof School	60	288	Indiana U–Northwest	50
256	Washington U	59	289	Webster C	50
257	Yale U	59	290	U of Cal–Davis	50
258	Cal State C–San Bernadino	59	291	Mississippi U for Women	50
259	U of Toledo	58	292	Austin Peay State U	50
260	Baptist C at Charleston	58	293	Valdosta State C	49
261	Cal State U–Fresno	57	294	U of Missouri–Kansas City	49
262	Franklin U	56	295	U of Central Arkansas	49
263	Georgia C	56	296	U of Texas at El Paso	49
264	Long Island U–C W Post Center	56	297	U of Cal–Riverside	47
265	University of Central Florida	55	298	St. Joseph's U	47
266	Wright State U–Main Campus	55	299	Pembroke State U	46
267	West Chester State C	55	300	U of La Verne	46
268	Southeastern Louisiana U	54	301	U of Oklahoma State U–Main Ca	45
269	U of Mass–Amherst	54	302	Oklahoma State U–Main Campus	45
270	U of Missouri–Columbia	54	303	Arkansas Baptist C*	45
271	McNesse State U	54	304	U of Cal–Irvine	45
272	SUNY at Stony Bk–Main Campus	54	305	Jarvis Christian C*	45
273	Loyola Marymount U	54	306	U of Arizona	44
274	Harris Stowe C*	54	307	Paul Quinn C*	44
275	Western Kentucky U	53	308	Cameron U	41
276	Oberlin C	53	309	Mississippi Industrial C*	40
277	Cal State U–Fullerton	53	310	Cal State U–Pomona	38
278	Montlcair State C	53	311	U of Colorado at Boulder	37
279	Detroit Institute Technology	52	312	Biscayne C	37
280	GA Inst of Tech–Main Campus	52	313	U of Cal–Santa Barbara	34
281	Arizona State U	52	314	U of Northern Colorado	34
282	Duke U	51	315	St. Peter's C	34
283	SUNY C at New Paltz	51	316	Tulane U of Louisiana	28
284	Bradley U	51	317	Polytechnic Institute New York	28
285	Barber–Scotia C*	51	318	U of the Pacific	27
286	Radcliffe C	51	319	Our Lady of the Lake U	27
287	St. John's U	51	320	Cal State U–Chico	25
			321	Lamar University	25

*predominantly black institutions

Institutions not ranked have less than 25 degrees conferred on blacks.

degree recipients are found (Table 6).

Only two predominantly Asian institutions are found in the U.S., both of which are in Hawaii, making Table 7 extremely valuable in identifying those institutions where significant numbers of baccalaureate degrees are conferred on Asians. The University of Hawaii at Manoa, one of the two predominantly Asian institutions, heads the list with 1,984 degrees conferred. Next on this list is the University of California-Berkeley with 856. The list continues with high rankings for other institutions in California and west coast states. Although there are concentrations on the west coast, Asians receive degrees from nearly all the major universities, even though the number of degrees conferred at each of these institutions falls well below the number of baccalaureate degrees conferred on Asians at institutions in California and Hawaii.

Native Americans, the only indigenous Americans included in this study, are so scattered and small in number that there is not a single surviving accredited four year degree-granting predominantly Native American institution in the United States. Northeastern Oklahoma State, with 118 degrees conferred, ranks first in Native American baccalaureate production. Lamar University in Texas ranks next with 104, followed by North Carolina's Pembroke State University with 96 and California State University at Northridge conferring 68 degrees, ranking fourth (Table 8).

Disciplinary Concentration

The total minority student pool has been identified. Now the discussion can focus upon how the 80,051 minority degree recipients are distributed over the various disciplinary fields and how the minority disciplinary distributional patterns differ from that observed for all baccalaureate degree recipients at the schools included in this study. By comparing the precentage of each minority baccalaureate degree distribution by disciplinary fields with that for all degrees conferred, it is possible to discuss how the minority percentage for each disciplinary field differ from each other and how they compare with percentages for total degrees conferred.

Eighteen percent of the degrees that go to all baccalaureate recipients are concentrated in Business and Management, followed by Education in second place, which accounts for 12.8 percent of all degrees conferred and Social Sciences in third place with 11.8 percent. The number of degrees conferred in Law (pre-law), Military Sciences, Theology, and Library Science are so small that they will not be discussed individually but are presented under the heading "Other".

Recent black degree recipients are most concentrated in Education where 20.1 percent of all degrees conferred to this group are found. The proportion of black bachelor's degree production in this field is quite high compared to 12.8 percent found in this category for all other recipients. Although another 19.2 percent of black degrees are conferred in Business and Management, this portion is only slightly larger than the norm. Social Sciences, with 14.5 percent, is another area where the proportions of blacks receiving degrees exceed that of the total recipients. From the data on

TABLE 6

TOTAL (0100–2400)
HISPANIC BACCALAUREATE DEGREES RANKED BY INSTITUTION

Rank	Institution	B.A.'s	Rank	Institution	B.A.'s
1	Pan American U*	719	29	Laredo State U*	163
2	U of Texas at El Paso	584	30	CUNY Bernard Baruch C	162
3	Florida International U	529	31	Cal State U-Northridge	161
4	U of Texas at Austin	453	32	U of Southern California	156
5	Cal State U-Los Angeles	447	33	St. Mary's U-San Antonio	153
6	U of NM-Main Campus	345	34	Fordham U	139
7	Texas A&I U	335	35	San Francisco State U	138
8	CUNY City C	285	36	Our Lady of the Lake U*	136
9	U of Miami	276	37	U of South Florida	132
10	NM State U-Main Campus	235	38	Cal State Poly U-Pomona	127
11	Southwest Texas State U	229	39	U of Illinois-Chicago Circle	121
12	Cal State U-Long Beach	226	40	Texas A&M U-Main Campus	110
13	CUNY Brooklyn C	224	41	Cal State U-Sacramento	108
14	San Jose State U	223	42	Colorado State U	107
15	San Diego State U	218	43	Glassboro State C	104
16	Cal State U-Fresno	215	44	Temple U	102
17	U of Houston-Central Campus	212	45	U of Cal-Santa Barbara	100
18	U of Florida	209	46	U of Cal-Berkeley	98
19	Cal State U-Fullerton	207	47	Metropolitan State C	93
20	Biscayne C*	203	48	Loyola Marymount U	91
21	CUNY Lehman C	202	49	U of La Verne	87
22	U of Texas at San Antonio	202	50	Northeastern Illinois U	86
23	Arizona State U	198	51	Incarnate Word C	86
24	U of Arizona	195	52	Cal State U-Chico	85
25	CUNY Hunter C	182	53	Eastern NM U-Main Campus	84
26	Corpus Christi State U	174	54	CUNY Queen's C	84
27	New Mexico Highlands U*	171	55	U of Colorado at Boulder	84
28	U of Cal-Los Angeles	163	56	Rutgers U-New Brunswick	82

Hispanic B.A.'s (0100-2400)

Rank	Institution	B.A.'s	Rank	Institution	B.A.'s
57	CUNY John Jay C-Crim Jus	82	90	Rutgers U-Newark Campus	49
58	Stanford U	82	91	Yale U	47
59	Mercy C	81	92	Loyola U of Chicago	44
60	St. Edward's U	81	93	Adelphi U	43
61	U of San Francisco	80	94	Florida Atlantic U	43
62	Northern Arizona U	79	95	Jersey City State C	43
63	U of Albuquerque	77	96	Florida State U	43
64	Cal State C-San Bernardino	76	97	Michigan State U	42
65	Sul Ross State U	75	98	Park C	42
66	U of Redlands	73	99	CUNY C of Staten Island	42
67	Trinity U	72	100	East Texas State U	42
68	St. Peter's C	70	101	U of Michigan-Ann Arbor	41
69	Texas Women's U	70	102	Cal State C-Bakersfield	41
70	Cal State U-Dominguez Hills	69	103	U of Washington	40
71	U of Southern Colorado	68	104	St. John's U	39
72	Angelo State U	68	105	Pratt Institute	39
73	Kean C of New Jersey	67	106	CUNY York C	39
74	U of Northern Colorado	67	107	DePaul U	39
75	Montclair State C	64	108	SUNY at Albany	38
76	North Texas State U	62	109	George Washington U	38
77	Cal State U-Hayward	61	110	Cornell U Endowed C	36
78	Antioch U	61	111	New Jersey Inst Technology	35
79	U of Cal-San Diego	59	112	U of Utah	35
80	Cal Poly State-San Luis Obispo	59	113	U of Illinois-Urbana Campus	34
81	Western New Mexico U	58	114	C of New Rochelle	33
82	U of Cal-Santa Cruz	57	115	U of Cal-Irvine	33
83	New York U	57	116	Princeton U	33
84	Tulane U of Louisiana	55	117	Chapman C	33
85	U of Texas at Arlington	55	118	Pace U-New York	33
86	Long Island U-Brooklyn Center	54	119	U of Mass-Amherst Campus	33
87	U of MD-College Park Campus	53	120	U of Minn-Minneapolis/St. Paul	32
88	U of Cal-Riverside	51	121	SUNY U of Wisconsin-Madison	32
89	U of Cal-Davis	50	122	SUNY at Stony Bk-Main Campus	31

38

Hispanic B.A.'s (0100-2400)

Rank	Institution	B.A.'s	Rank	Institution	B.A.'s
123	U of DC	31	130	American U	27
124	Wayne State U	29	131	U of Pacific	27
125	U of Hawaii at Manoa	29	132	CUNY Graduate School & U Ctr	27
126	Southern Illinois U-Carbondale	28	133	U of Central Florida	26
127	Roosevelt U	28	134	Syracuse U-Main Campus	26
128	Harvard U	28	135	Purdue U-Main Campus	25
129	U of Pennsylvania	28	136	U of Wisconsin-Milwaukee	25

*predominantly Hispanic institutions

Institutions not ranked have less than 25 degrees conferred on Hispanics.

TABLE 7

TOTAL (0100-2400)
ASIAN BACCALAUREATE DEGREES RANKED BY INSTITUTION

Rank	Institution	B.A.'s	Rank	Institution	B.A.'s
1	U of Hawaii at Manoa*	1984	29	U of Minn-Minneapolis/St. Paul	86
2	U of Cal-Berkeley	856	30	Cal State U-Fullerton	86
3	U of Cal-Los Angeles	547	31	Cal State U-Dominquez Hills	80
4	San Francisco State U	526	32	New York U	79
5	Cal State U-Los Angeles	422	33	U of Michigan-Ann Arbor	79
6	San Jose State U	382	34	U of the Pacific	76
7	U of Washington	343	35	Polytechnic Institute New York	72
8	Cal State U-Long Beach	338	36	U of MD-College Park Campus	72
9	U of Southern California	311	37	U of Oregon-Main Campus	69
10	U of Cal-Davis	227	38	CUNY Hunter C	68
11	CUNY City C	166	39	Cal State Poly U-Pomona	67
12	Cal State U-Sacramento	159	40	U of Colorado at Boulder	66
13	Cal State U-Northridge	148	41	Cornell U Endowed C	65
14	Cal State U-Fresno	143	42	Rutgers U-New Brunswick	65
15	CUNY Bernard Baruch C	130	43	U of Arizona	63
16	San Diego State U	126	44	U of Cal-San Francisco	60
17	U of Cal-Santa Barbara	117	45	Sam Houston State U	59
18	Cal Poly State-San Luis Obispo	114	46	Chaminade U of Honolulu	57
19	U of Cal-Irvine	104	47	U of Texas at Austin	53
20	U of Hawaii at Hilo*	102	48	CUNY Brooklyn C	50
21	U of Illinois-Chicago Circle	101	49	U of Pennsylvania	50
22	Stanford U	99	50	U of Cal-San Diego	49
23	Cal State U-Hayward	94	51	Arizona State U	49
24	U of San Francisco	94	52	U of Florida	48
25	U of Houston-Central Campus	93	53	CUNY Lehman C	48
26	Roosevelt U	91	54	Yale U	46
27	U of Illinois-Urbana Campus	91	55	SUNY at Stony Bk-Main Campus	46
28	CUNY Queen's C	90	56	George Washington U	45

40

Asian B.A.'s (0100-2400)

Rank	Institution	B.A.'s	Rank	Institution	B.A.'s
57	Harvard U	45	77	Pace U-New York	29
58	Florida International U	45	78	New Jersey Inst Technology	29
59	Cal State U-Chico	43	79	Northeastern Illinois U	29
60	St. Francis C	41	80	Ohio State U-Main Campus	28
61	Purdue U-Main Campus	41	81	U of Cal-Riverside	28
62	Oregon State U	41	82	Memphis State U	28
63	U of Mass-Amherst Campus	41	83	Oklahoma State U-Main Campus	26
64	Temple U	41	84	SUNY at Buffalo-Main Campus	26
65	Michigan State U	38	85	Southern Illinois U-Carbondale	26
66	Pepperdine U	36	86	Oberlin C	26
67	Princeton U	36	87	Chapman C	26
68	U of Miami	34	88	Brown U	26
69	U of Wisconsin-Madison	34	89	U of Missouri-Columbia	25
70	U of Redlands	33	90	Northern Illinois U	25
71	Northwestern U	33	91	Pratt Institute	25
72	St. John's U	33	92	Indiana U-Bloomington	25
73	Loyola Marymount U	32	93	Brigham Young U-Main Campus	25
74	Wayne State U	31	94	Washington U	25
75	U of Utah	31	95	Pennsylvania State U-Main Cam	25
76	Tufts U	30			

*predominantly Asian institutions

Institutions not ranked have less than 25 degrees conferred on Asians.

TABLE 8

TOTAL (0100-2400)
NATIVE AMERICAN BACCALAUREATE DEGREES RANKED BY INSTITUTION

Rank	Institution	B.A.'s	Rank	Institution	B.A.'s
1	Northeast Oklahoma State U	118	29	Temple U	23
2	Lamar U	104	30	CUNY City C	22
3	Pembroke State U	96	31	San Diego State U	22
4	Cal State U-Northridge	68	32	Southeast Oklahoma State U	21
5	U of NM-Main Campus	58	33	U of Cal-Berkeley	21
6	Northern Arizona U	54	34	Oregon State U	21
7	U of Arizona	53	35	Cal State U-Los Angeles	20
8	St. Joseph's U	51	36	Montclair State C	18
9	U of Oklahoma-Norman Campus	48	37	U of Southern California	18
10	San Jose State U	47	38	Central State U	18
11	Cal Poly State-San Luis Obispo	44	39	Illinois State U	18
12	U of MD-College Park Campus	42	40	Montana State U	17
13	Texas A&M U-Main Campus	41	41	NM State U-Main Campus	17
14	Oklahoma State U-Main Campus	40	42	Southwest Oklahoma State U	17
15	Cal State Poly U-Pomona	37	43	U of Cal-Los Angeles	17
16	Brigham Young U-Main Campus	37	44	Evergreen State C	17
17	Cal State U-Sacramento	33	45	U of Minn-Minneapolis/St. Paul	16
18	Cal State U-Long Beach	31	46	Cameron U	16
19	Glassboro State C	31	47	Cal State U-Fresno	16
20	Cal State C-Bakersfield	31	48	U of Utah	16
21	San Francisco State U	29	49	CUNY Hunter C	15
22	Cal State U-Fullerton	29	50	U of Cal-Davis	15
23	U of North Dakota-Main Campus	29	51	Eastern NM U-Main Campus	15
24	U of Washington	29	52	U of Southwestern Louisiana	15
25	Southern Illinois U-Carbondale	26	53	SUNY C at New Paltz	15
26	Eastern Michigan U	25	54	Metropolitan State C	14
27	East Central Oklahoma State U	24	55	Wayne State U	14
28	CUNY Brooklyn C	23	56	U of San Francisco	14

42

Native American B.A.'s (0100-2400)

Rank	Institution	B.A.'s	Rank	Institution	B.A.'s
57	Cal State U-Chico	14	66	New York U	12
58	U of Pittsburgh-Main Campus	14	67	U of Illinois-Urbana Campus	12
59	SUNY at Albany	13	68	U of Texas at Austin	12
60	SUNY C at Buffalo	13	69	Western Michigan U	12
61	Michigan State U	13	70	Southwest Texas State U	11
62	U of NC at Chapel Hill	13	71	U of Oregon-Main Campus	11
63	Cal State U-Dominguez Hills	13	72	U of Texas at El Paso	11
64	CUNY John Jay C-Crim Jus	12	73	U of Michigan-Ann Arbor	10
65	Chapman C	12	74	U of Wisconsi-Madison	10

Institutions not ranked have less than 10 degrees conferred on Native Americans.

Table 9, it is possible to compare the proportion of black degree concentration in each field with that for all degree recipients and address the issue of over- and underrepresentation as the respective minority proportion deviates from the percentage found in the total column. These data reveal that black's are clearly overrepresented in Education, Psychology, Public Affairs and Services, Social Sciences and Interdisciplinary Studies and are clearly underrepresented in Agriculture and Natural Resources, Architecture and Environmental Design, Biological Sciences, Communications, Computer and Information Sciences, Engineering, Foreign Languages, Health Professions, Letters and Physical Sciences.

The pattern of black over- and underrepresentation among the disciplinary areas matches, for the most part, that of the Hispanics and Native Americans with some minor variations. Hispanics are overrepresented in Architecture and Environmental Design and Area Studies, where blacks and Native Americans both fall below the norm. Although Hispanics are overrepresented in Education, they are near the norm, while blacks and Native Americans are considerably over. Of the three groups, the proportion of Native American degree recipients in Fine Arts, Home Economics and Interdisciplinary Studies exceeds that for total baccalaureate degree recipients, as well as each group. Similarly, Hispanic proportions are highest in Foreign Languages. Other than these differences, the respective black, Hispanic and Native American patterns of over- and underrepresentation are very much alike.

Asians, on the other hand, have a rather unique pattern, which is inverse to the patterns of over- and underrepresentation observed for Blacks, Hispanics and Native Americans. Asians are significantly overrepresented in the sciences; Agriculture and Natural Resources, Architecture and Environmental Design, Area Studies, Biological Sciences, Business and Management, Engineering, Psychology, Computer and Information Sciences and Mathematics. Clearly, they are underrepresented in Social Sciences, Public Affairs and Services, Communications, Education and Letters. These data are useful if minority underrepresentation is a factor considered in recruitment. Table 10 shows what percentage of the total degrees conferred in each disciplinary field is represented by minority degree recipients. These data can be viewed as the rate of minority production in each disciplinary area. For example, of all the degrees conferred in Business and Management, 10.3 percent go to blacks. Another way to state this relationship is that one out of every ten degrees conferred in Business and Management goes to a black. Although this rate data may be useful, they are only rates for the 362 institutions included in the study and are not national rates. The national rates would be much lower, nearly half the rate of those recorded on Table 10 where the total baccalaureate production is 495,427 for the 362 institutions selected compared to 916,247 for the entire universe of 1,658 institutions.

44

TABLE 9

MINORITY PERCENTAGE BY DISCIPLINARY DIVISION

DIVISION	MINORITY GROUP					
	Black	Hispanic	Asian	Native American	Total Minority	Total
Agriculture & Natural Resources (0100)	.6	1.0	2.2	2.7	1.0	3.0
Architecture & Environmental Design (0200)	.5	1.3	1.6	.9	.8	1.2
Area Studies (0300)	.1	.4	.6	.1	.3	.3
Biological Sciences (0400)	4.2	5.3	9.5	4.4	5.2	5.4
Business & Management (0500)	19.2	15.9	21.0	14.4	18.6	18.5
Communications (0600)	3.5	2.2	2.0	2.2	2.9	3.7
Computer & Information Sciences (0700)	.9	.8	1.7	.4	.1	1.1
Education (0800)	20.1	15.8	4.8	20.5	16.9	12.8
Engineering (0900)	2.9	5.8	12.4	5.2	5.0	7.4
Fine & Applied Arts (1000)	2.8	3.4	4.3	4.7	3.2	4.3
Foreign Languages (1100)	.5	4.9	1.5	.7	1.6	1.3
Health Professions (1200)	5.4	4.9	6.3	5.3	5.4	6.4
Home Economics (1300)	2.1	.9	2.8	2.6	2.0	2.3
Letters (1500)	3.4	2.9	2.7	3.2	3.2	4.2
Mathematics (1700)	1.1	.9	1.9	1.2	1.2	1.1
Physical Sciences (1900)	1.1	1.5	2.2	1.8	1.4	2.3
Psychology (2000)	5.1	6.1	5.3	5.5	5.3	4.7
Public Affairs & Services (2100)	7.5	6.4	2.8	5.6	6.5	4.4
Social Sciences (2200)	14.5	14.9	10.4	13.5	14.0	11.8
Interdisciplinary Studies (2400)	4.1	4.5	3.9	4.7	4.1	3.7
Others	.3	.1	.1	.2	.2	.1
All Divisions	100.0	100.0	100.0	100.0	100.0	100.0
(n)	49,116	16,037	12,394	3,504	80,051	495,427

TABLE 10

MINORITY GROUP PERCENTAGE IN EACH DISCIPLINARY DIVISION

DIVISION				MINORITY GROUP			
	Black	Hispanic	Asian	Native American	Total Minority	Total	(n)
Agriculture & Natural Resources(0100)	2.1	1.1	1.9	.4	5.5	100.0	14,880
Architecture & Environmental Design (0200)	4.1	3.4	3.2	.3	11.0	100.0	6,164
Area Studies (0300)	4.4	4.8	4.9	.1	14.2	100.0	1,457
Biological Sciences (0400)	7.8	3.2	4.4	.4	15.8	100.0	26,536
Business & Management (0500)	10.3	2.8	2.8	.4	16.3	100.0	91,781
Communications (0600)	9.4	2.0	1.3	.3	13.0	100.0	18,097
Computer & Information Sciences (0700)	8.2	2.4	4.0	.2	14.8	100.0	5,378
Education (0800)	15.6	4.0	.9	.8	21.3	100.0	63,369
Engineering (0900)	3.8	2.5	4.2	.4	10.9	100.0	36,774
Fine & Applied Arts(1000)	6.4	2.6	2.5	.6	12.1	100.0	21,169
Foreign Languages (1100)	4.1	12.5	2.9	.2	19.7	100.0	6,304
Health Professions (1200)	8.4	2.5	2.5	.4	13.8	100.0	31,494
Home Economics (1300)	9.0	1.2	3.1	.6	13.9	100.0	11,502
Letters (1500)	8.1	2.2	1.6	.4	12.3	100.0	20,727
Mathematics (1700)	9.7	2.6	4.2	.5	17.0	100.0	5,673
Physical Sciences (1900)	4.9	2.1	2.4	.4	9.8	100.0	11,301
Psychology (2000)	10.8	4.3	2.8	.6	18.5	100.0	23,096
Public Affairs & Services (2100)	16.8	4.6	1.6	.7	23.7	100.0	22,023
Social Sciences (2200)	12.2	4.1	2.2	.6	19.1	100.0	58,566
Interdisciplinary Studies (2400)	10.8	3.9	2.6	.6	17.9	100.0	18,438
Other	19.8	3.0	1.1	.6	24.5	100.0	698
All Divisions	9.9	3.2	2.5	.5	16.1	100.0	495,427

CHARACTERISTICS OF A POOL

Although knowledge of the minority pool size and its location is fundamental for recruitment initiatives, additional information on the institutions where degrees are conferred is also useful and should be considered when formulating a recruitment strategy. Knowledge of (1) an institution's minority designation, (2) its control, (3) its environmental setting, (4) its comparative size, (5) its formal affiliation with other institutions, (6) its academic classification and (7) its census division location is also valuable in selecting recruitment sites. All higher education institutions are not the same; they differ along these dimensions, which have an impact on the nature of the programs offered and ultimately the degrees conferred.

Minority Designation

An institution's minority designation is an important factor to consider when the minority baccalaureate pool is being examined. Of the 362 institutions considered herein, 92 have minority degree production that exceeds fifty percent and are designated as minority institutions. In terms of the percentage of total minority baccalaureate production, 69.5 percent of all minority graduates receive their bachelor's degree at non-minority institutions (Table 11). Even in the case of black baccalaureate degree recipients who are heavily concentrated at the 85 predominantly black institutions included in the minority institution category, approximately 57 percent of the degrees awarded to blacks are conferred at non-minority institutions, whereas Hispanics and Native Americans, respectively, receive more than ninety percent of their bachelor's degrees at non-minority institutions, while over eighty percent of all baccalaureate degrees received by Asians are conferred at similar institutions.

TABLE 11

MINORITY BACCALUAREATE DEGREES CONFERRED
AT MINORITY AND NON-MINORITY INSTITUTIONS

MINORITY GROUP PERCENTAGE BY TYPE OF INSTITUTION

Type of Institution	Number of Institutions	Black	Hispanic	Asian	Native American	Total Minority	Total
Minority	25.4	42.6	8.2	17.5	0.7	30.5	6.1
Non-Minority	74.6	57.4	91.8	82.5	99.3	69.5	93.9
Total	100.0	100.0	100.0	100.0	100.0	100.0	100.0
(n)	362	49,116	16,037	12,394	2,504	80,051	495,427

TABLE 11 (Continued)

MINORITY GROUP PERCENTAGE IN EACH TYPE OF INSTITUTION

Type of Institution	Black	Hispanic	Asian	Native American	Total Minority	Total	(n)
Minority	68.8	4.3	7.1	0.1	80.3	100.0	30,428
Non-Minority	6.1	3.2	2.2	0.5	12.0	100.0	464,999
Total	9.9	3.2	2.5	0.5	16.2	100.0	495,427

Institutional Control

Private schools account for 24.3 percent of minority baccalaureate production nationally; therefore, minority baccalaureate production is primarily a public institution phenomenon. At least seventy percent of degrees awarded to minority groups are awarded at public institutions. The percentages range from a low of 71.4 percent for blacks to a high of 89.3 percent for Native Americans, with Hispanics and Asians each converging on 85 percent.

Nearly one out of four degrees received from private institutions go to minority students, a rate which exceeds that for public schools where minorities received 14.6 percent of all the baccalaureate degrees awarded (Table 12). Therefore, the rate of minority degree production is nearly twice as high at private institutions.

TABLE 12

MINORITY BACCALAUREATE DEGREES CONFERRED
PRIVATE AND PUBLIC INSTITUTIONS

MINORITY GROUP PERCENTAGE BY TYPE OF INSTITUTION

Type of Institution	Number of Institutions	Black	Hispanic	Asian	Native American	Total Minority	Total
Private	33.7	28.6	20.2	15.8	10.7	24.3	16.5
Public	66.3	71.4	79.8	84.2	89.3	75.7	83.5
Total	100.0	100.0	100.0	100.0	100.0	100.0	100.0
(n)	362	49,116	16,037	12,394	2,504	80,051	495,427

MINORITY GROUP PERCENTAGE IN EACH TYPE OF INSTITUTION

Type of Institution	Black	Hispanic	Asian	Native American	Total Minority	Total	(n)
Private	17.2	4.0	2.4	0.3	23.9	100.0	81,852
Public	8.5	3.1	2.5	0.5	14.6	100.0	413,575
Total	9.9	3.2	2.5	0.6	16.2	100.0	495,427

Size of Institution

Four categories, based upon the total institutional B.A. production, are used for size of institution comparisons. A small school annually produces from one to 499 individuals with baccalaureate degrees, a medium-sized school from 500 to 999 and a large institution from 1,000 to 1,999. A very large school graduates 2,000 or more students with bachelor's degrees each year. In terms of their contributions to the minority pool, small schools produce 22.2 percent of all minority degrees, medium-sized institutions 19.3 percent and large institutions 23.5 percent. The very large institutions produce 34.9 percent of all minority baccalaureate degrees (Table 13). For each minority group, the largest percentage of production is at the very large schools with the exception of blacks, where 32 percent of the degrees conferred are at the small schools and 22.5 and 22.6 percent respectively are awarded at the large and very large institutions.

The rate of minority degree production is highest at the smallest schools. For instance, only ten percent of baccalaureates conferred at very large institutions go to minority students, compared to approximately 54 percent at small schools. The smaller the school, the larger the proportion of minority degrees conferred. The large institutions produce greater absolute numbers of minority bachelor's degrees but do not have the highest rates of degree production.

TABLE 13

MINORITY BACCALAUREATE DEGREES CONFERRED
BY SIZE OF INSTITUTION

MINORITY GROUP PERCENTAGE BY SIZE OF INSTITUTION

Size of Institution	Number of Institutions	Black	Hispanic	Asian	Native American	Total Minority	Total
Small (1-499)	32.0	31.1	11.2	4.1	8.8	22.3	6.7
Medium (500-999)	18.5	23.8	16.6	5.7	14.6	19.3	9.6
Large (1000-1999)	27.1	22.5	30.1	18.1	29.0	23.5	28.6
Very Large (2000+)	22.4	22.6	42.1	72.1	47.6	34.9	55.1
Total	100.0	100.0	100.0	100.0	100.0	100.0	100.0
(n)	362	49,116	16,037	12,394	2,504	80,051	495,427

TABLE 13 (Continued)

MINORITY GROUP IN EACH SIZE OF INSTITUTION

Size of Institution	Black	Hispanic	Asian	Native American	Total Minority	Total	(n)
Small	46.1	5.4	1.5	0.7	53.7	100.0	33,128
Medium	24.6	5.6	1.5	0.8	32.5	100.0	47,390
Large	7.8	3.4	1.6	0.5	13.3	100.0	141,813
Very Large	4.1	2.5	3.3	0.4	10.3	100.0	273,096
Total	9.9	3.2	2.5	0.5	16.2	100.0	495,427

Environmental Setting

Nearly 50 percent of all minority students receive their degrees from institutions that are located in an urban environment, with another 24 percent in the suburbs and only 26 percent at institutions in rural areas. Therefore, minority education is not a rural phenomenon. In fact, a greater proportion of minority students receive their degrees from urban institutions than do non-minority students, with the exception of Native Americans where 40 percent of their degrees are conferred at institutions located in rural America.

At urban schools, one out of five degrees conferred goes to a minority student. The rate falls off when institutions in suburban surroundings are considered; only 13.9 percent of all baccalaureate degrees awarded go to minority students. At rural institutions, only twelve percent of all bachelor's degrees are awarded to minority students (Table 14). For definitions of environmental setting categories used (urban, suburban and rural), see Appendix C.

TABLE 14

MINORITY BACCALAUREATE DEGREES CONFERRED AT INSTITUTIONS BY ENVIRONMENTAL SETTING

MINORITY GROUP PERCENTAGE BY ENVIRONMENTAL SETTING

Institution's Environmental Setting	Number of Institutions	Black	Hispanic	Asian	Native American	Total Minority	Total
Urban	40.9	49.7	47.2	55.1	35.2	49.6	38.7
Suburban	21.6	19.1	28.5	34.0	25.8	23.5	27.4
Rural	37.5	31.2	24.3	10.9	39.0	26.9	33.9
Total	100.0	100.0	100.0	100.0	100.0	100.0	100.0
(n)	362	49,116	16,037	12,394	2,504	80,051	495,427

TABLE 14 (Continued)

MINORITY GROUP PERCENTAGE IN EACH ENVIRONMENTAL SETTING

Institution's Environmental Setting	Black	Hispanic	Asian	Native American	Total Minority	Total	(n)
Urban	12.7	3.9	3.6	0.5	20.7	100.0	191,802
Suburban	6.9	3.4	3.1	0.5	13.9	100.0	135,719
Rural	9.1	2.3	0.8	0.6	12.8	100.0	167,906
Total	9.9	3.2	2.5	0.5	16.1	100.0	495,427

Groups of Institutions

Many of the institutions considered in this study belong to a consortia and/or large university system. An examination of the differences in levels of minority participation in graduate education at these sets of institutions is worthwhile, if indeed differences exist, since these groups of schools are organized quite differently and cluster regionally. The Ivy League, the Committee on Institutional Cooperation (CIC), the California University System, the California State University and College System, the City University of New York System (CUNY) and the State University of New York System (SUNY) are the six groups of institutions being considered. Lists of the institutions comprising each of these groupings are found in Appendix D.

The separate contribution of each of these groupings or consortia to the national minority bachelor's degree pool is relatively small. The Ivy League contributes only 1.4 percent, the CIC 3.3 percent, the University of California 4.0 percent, the California State University System 9.6 percent, CUNY 6.3 percent and SUNY only 1.0 percent. However, together, these consortia and systems which include some of the most prestigious institutions in the United States, significantly contribute to the minority pool because collectively they account for 25.6 percent of all the baccalaureate degrees awarded nationally to minority students.

As these consortia and systems vary in the absolute number of degrees awarded to minority students, they also vary in terms of the rate of minority degree production. For example, one out of every ten bachelor's degrees conferred in the Ivy League goes to a minority graduate. In the University of California System, 16 percent of all degrees awarded go to minorities. For the California State University System, the rate is higher yet with 20.1 percent. The CUNY System in New York City at 38 percent has the highest rate nationally and SUNY has 7.5 percent of its bachelor's production in the minority category (Table 15).

TABLE 15

MINORITY BACCALAUREATE DEGREES CONFERRED
BY GROUPS OF INSTITUTIONS

MINORITY GROUP PERCENTAGE BY GROUP OF INSTITUTIONS

Group	Number of Institutions	Black	Hispanic	Asian	Native American	Total Minority	Total
Ivy League	2.2	1.2	1.2	2.3	1.2	1.4	2.2
CIC	3.0	3.2	2.5	4.6	3.5	3.3	10.1
UCS	2.5	1.1	3.9	16.2	3.1	4.0	4.1
CSUS	4.4	4.1	15.3	22.2	17.9	9.6	7.8
CUNY	3.0	6.1	8.3	4.8	3.8	6.3	3.8
SUNY	1.9	1.0	1.0	0.9	1.9	1.0	2.2
Other	83.0	83.3	67.8	49.0	68.6	74.4	69.8
Total	100.0	100.0	100.0	100.0	100.0	100.0	100.0
(n)	362	49,116	116,037	12,394	2,504	80,051	495,427

MINORTIY GROUP PERCENTAGE IN EACH GROUP OF INSTITUTIONS

Group	Black	Hispanic	Asian	Native American	Total Minority	Total	(n)
Ivy League	5.6	1.8	2.7	0.3	10.4	100.0	10,763
CIC	3.1	0.8	1.1	0.2	5.2	100.0	49,800
UCS	2.7	3.1	9.9	0.4	16.1	100.0	20,200
CSUS	5.2	6.5	7.2	1.2	20.1	100.0	38,133
CUNY	22.7	10.0	4.5	0.7	37.9	100.0	13,276
SUNY	4.6	1.4	1.0	0.4	7.4	100.0	10,850
Other	11.6	3.1	1.7	0.5	16.9	100.0	352,405
Total	9.9	3.2	2.5	0.5	16.1	100.0	495,427

Carnegie Categories

Educational institutions not only vary in size, they also differ in curricula offered, organizational structure, range and number of degrees offered and level of research activity carried out. Collectively, data along these dimensions allow institutions to be categorized. The Carnegie Classification of Institutions of Higher Education is quite useful for this purpose because it multi-dimensionally groups institutions in four major classes and nineteen categories of which fourteen categories are represented among the institutions considered here.[13] The major classes and categories are:

52   Characteristics

I. Research and Doctorate-Granting Institutions, which include (1.1) Research Universities I, (1.2) Research Universities II, (1.3) Doctorate-Granting Universities I and (1.4) Doctorate-Granting Universities II.

II. Comprehensive Universities and Colleges, including (2.1) Comprehensive Universities and Colleges I and (2.2) Comprehensive Universities and Colleges II.

III. Liberal Arts Colleges, including (3.1) Liberal Arts Colleges I and (3.2) Liberal Arts Colleges II.

IV. Specialized Institutions, which include (5.2) Medical Schools and Medical Centers, (5.4) Schools of Engineering and Technology, (5.5) Schools of Business and Management, (5.8) Teachers Colleges, (5.9) Other Specialized Institutions and (6.0) Institutions for Non-Traditional Study.

This classification scheme is primarily based upon the size of institution, breadth of program offerings, academic specialization and research capacity. For example, category (1.1) Research Universities I includes some of the nation's largest and most prestigious research institutions. This class is defined by the number of Ph.D.'s granted, research dollars received and the number of disciplinary areas covered. Research Universities II have some of the same attributes but the magnitudes of the activity are less. The same difference in the magnitude of activities distinguishes the difference in categories within the major groups, except for the Specialized Institutions, which are categorized by the uniqueness of their specialization. A detailed description of the Carnegie Classification System is provided for each of these classes in Appendix E.

Approximately 35.3 percent of all minority bachelor's degrees are awarded at the nation's Ph.D. granting institutions, nearly half of which, 16.6 percent, are awarded at the (1.1) Research Universities I Twenty-eight percent of all black degrees, 36.1 percent of Hispanic, 60.7 percent of all Asian and 41.9 percent of Native American bachelor's degrees are granted at Ph.D. granting institutions. However, the largest percentage of minority baccalaureate production is at the nation's comprehensive universities, a trend which respectively holds for all minority groups except Asians, where 60.7 percent of the degrees are awarded by the Ph.D. granting institutions.

In each of the four Ph.D. granting institution categories, minorities receive approximately nine percent of all baccalaureate degrees awarded. The rates of production are astonishingly higher in comprehensive universities, which include most of 92 predominantly minority institutions considered in this study (Table 16).

53

TABLE 16

MINORITY BACCALAUREATE DEGREES CONFERRED
BY INSTITUTIONS FOLLOWING THE CARNEGIE CLASSIFICATION

MINORITY GROUP PERCENTAGE BY INSTITUTIONAL CLASS

Institutional Class	Number of Institutions	Black	Hispanic	Asian	Native American	Total Minority	Total
Ph.D. Institution							
1.1	11.6	8.4	17.4	46.5	19.1	16.6	29.0
1.2	7.8	8.4	6.5	5.9	10.2	7.7	13.2
1.3	9.7	7.4	9.8	6.6	10.0	7.8	14.5
1.4	3.6	3.8	2.4	1.7	2.6	3.2	5.0
	32.7	28.0	36.1	60.7	41.9	35.3	61.7
Comprehensive University							
2.1	38.1	45.2	50.1	34.0	47.2	44.5	30.5
2.2	13.8	14.4	10.2	2.5	8.5	11.5	4.9
	51.9	59.6	60.3	36.5	55.7	55.6	35.4
Liberal Arts							
3.1	0.3	0.1	*	0.2	0.1	0.1	0.1
3.2	12.7	10.3	1.4	0.3	1.2	6.7	1.5
	13.0	10.4	1.4	0.5	1.3	6.8	1.6
Others							
5.2	0.5	0.1	0.1	0.6	0.0	0.2	0.2
5.4	0.5	0.3	0.2	0.3	0.0	0.2	0.2
5.5	0.3	0.8	1.0	1.0	0.2	0.8	0.3
5.8	0.3	0.1	0.0	0.0	0.0	0.1	*
5.9	0.3	0.3	0.5	0.1	0.5	0.3	0.1
6.0	0.5	0.5	0.2	0.2	0.3	0.3	0.4
	2.4	2.0	1.6	2.2	1.0	1.9	12.0
Total	100.0	100.0	100.0	100.0	100.0	100.0	100.0
(n)	362	49,116	16,037	12,394	2,504	8,051	495,427

* Less than .001 percent

TABLE 16 (Continued)

MINORITY GROUP PERCENTAGE IN EACH INSTITUTIONAL CLASS

Institutional Class	Black	Hispanic	Asian	Native American	Total Minority	Total	(n)
Ph.D. Institution							
1.1	2.9	1.9	4.0	0.3	9.1	100.0	143,641
1.2	6.3	1.6	1.1	0.4	9.4	100.0	65,400
1.3	5.0	2.2	1.1	0.4	8.7	100.0	71,652
1.4	7.5	1.6	0.8	0.3	10.2	100.0	24,831
Comprehensive University							
2.1	14.7	5.3	2.8	0.8	23.6	100.0	151,050
2.2	29.2	6.8	1.3	0.9	38.2	100.0	24,222
Liberal Arts							
3.1	7.8	0.9	3.9	0..3	12.9	100.0	667
3.2	65.9	3.0	0.6	0.4	69.9	100.0	7640
Others							
5.2	7.4	1.9	8.4	0.0	17.7	100.0	946
5.4	10.9	3.2	3.1	0.1	17.3	100.0	1,144
5.5	24.1	10.5	8.4	0.3	43.3	100.0	1,549
5.8	60.0	0.0	0.0	0.0	60.0	100.0	90
5.9	24.7	11.7	1.4	1.7	39.3	100.0	698
6.0	10.7	1.8	1.1	0.4	14.0	100.0	1,897
Total	9.9	3.2	2.5	0.5	16.1	100.0	495,427

Regional Concentration

Regionally, the South Atlantic produces 21.9 percent of all minority bachelor's degrees awarded. Undoubtedly, this high percentage of minority degree production is influenced by a high concentration of blacks and predominately black institutions in the region. The second highest regional production of minority degrees is 21.1 percent found on the west coast in the Pacific region. This high level of minority production is influenced by the large number of Asians and Hispanics receiving degrees at institutions located there. Third in the regional production of minority degrees is the Middle Atlantic region with 16.2 percent. The highest production in this region is not solely attributable to the concentration of a single group but rather to a high level of production resulting from significant representation of all the minority groups being considered. The regional comparisons in degree production are more meaningful when each minority group's pattern is examined independently.

The region of highest black degree production is the South Atlantic with 30.5 percent of the total black bachelor's degrees, reflecting the high concentration of black population, as well as being the area where the largest number of predominantly black institutions are located. The next area of significantly high black degree production is the populous Middle Atlantic region with 16.9 percent, followed by the East North Central region with 14.5 percent. These regions in the northeast and middle west contributed more to the minority pool than did the remaining two regions in the south – the East South Central and the West South Central, which each account for 13.4 percent of black baccalaureate production.

Hispanic baccalaureate production is the highest in both the West South Central and Pacific regions, which each account for 26.6 percent, followed by the Middle Atlantic region with 17.8 percent. These three regions together produce 71 percent of all Hispanic degrees conferred and this production follows the national distribution of Hispanic population, which is mainly a west coast, southwest and east coast phenomenon, with Mexican Americans concentrated in the west and southwest and Puerto Ricans in the Middle Atlantic area. The next highest region of Hispanic production is the South Atlantic region with 11.3 percent, much of which is associated with the Cuban population concentrated in Florida.

Sixty-six percent of all degres awarded to Asians are awarded on the west coast in the Pacific region, with the major concentration in California. The next highest concentration of Asian degree production, although it is significantly less, is found in the respective populous Middle Atlantic and East North Central regions.

The Pacific region also leads in the production of Native American degrees with 28.4 percent, as it does with Hispanics and Asians. The second highest Native American degree production is found in the West South Central region, which is also second in Hispanic production. The Middle Atlantic region is third with 13.3 percent of the Native American degrees awarded. Generally, the regionalization of Native American baccalaureate production follows the national Hispanic pattern.

Table 17 also shows that the regional rate of minority baccalaureate production varies widely. For example, in each of the three southern regions, one out of every five degrees awarded goes to a minority student, while the next highest rate of production is respectively found in the Pacific and Middle Atlantic regions. The highest regional rates of production for each minority group coincides closely with the regional concentration of each minority group's total population.

TABLE 17

MINORITY BACCALAUREATE DEGREES CONFERRED
AT INSTITUTIONS BY REGIONS

MINORITY GROUP PERCENTAGE BY MINORITY REGION

Region	Number of Institutions	Black	Hispanic	Asian	Native American	Total Minority	Total
New England	2.8	1.4	1.3	1.9	1.4	1.5	3.5
Middle Atlantic	14.9	16.9	17.8	12.1	13.3	16.2	15.8
East North-Central	13.8	14.5	5.7	7.6	9.5	11.5	20.1
West North-Central	3.6	1.9	1.0	1.4	2.8	1.7	3.7
South Atlantic	21.8	30.5	11.3	4.2	9.9	21.9	15.9
East South-Central	10.5	13.4	0.4	1.1	0.8	8.5	6.0
West South-Central	16.3	13.4	26.6	3.9	22.2	14.9	12.0
Mountain	3.3	0.4	9.2	1.7	11.6	2.7	4.5
Pacific	13.3	7.5	26.6	66.2	28.5	21.1	18.5
Total	100.0	100.0	100.0	100.0	100.0	100.0	100.0
(n)	362	49,116	16,037	12,394	2,504	80,051	495,427

MINORITY GROUP PERCENTAGE IN EACH REGION

Region	Black	Hispanic	Asian	Native American	Total Minority	Total	(n)
New England	3.8	1.2	1.4	0.2	6.6	100.0	17,436
Middle Atlantic	10.7	3.7	1.9	0.4	16.7	100.0	78,045
East North-Central	7.2	0.9	0.9	0.2	9.2	100.0	99,363
West North-Central	5.0	0.9	0.9	0.4	7.2	100.0	18,490
South Atlantic	18.9	2.3	0.7	0.3	22.2	100.0	79,230
East South-Central	22.0	0.2	0.4	0.1	22.7	100.0	29,752
West South-Central	11.1	7.2	0.8	0.9	20.0	100.0	59,315
Mountain	0.9	6.7	0.9	1.3	9.8	100.0	22,089
Pacific	4.0	4.7	9.0	0.8	18.5	100.0	91,706
Total	9.9	3.2	2.5	0.5	16.1	100.0	495,427

Examining minority baccalaureate production along these seven dimensions is a good preparation for formulating a recruitment strategy. From this examination, it is apparent that there is great diversity among the institutions where minorities earn their degrees. It is also apparent that the public institutions are dominant among the schools which grant minority baccalaureates and within this set of schools considerable numbers of minorities receive their degrees at large state-supported institutions. Although there is regional variance where minorities receive their degrees, within this variance a large portion of the degrees are generated at institutions located in highly urbanized areas. There are variations in the absolute numbers of degrees awarded among the institutions considered; there are also differences in the rate of production among these institutions. All of the dimensions used to characterize the institutions where minority bachelor's degrees are generated, with the exception of regional locations, are listed for each institution in Appendix F. These data are useful because they provide a profile for each institution along these dimensions and, since the total baccalaureate production is listed along with total minority B.A. production, it is possible to derive each institution's rate of minority production. It is also possible to establish the rates of production for each minority group by using the minority group specific data on total degree generation listed by institution on Table 4, in conjunction with the total production for each institution found in Appendix F.

ACCESSIBILITY TO POOL

Once the institutions where nearly eighty percent of the nation's minority baccalaureate production takes place have been identified, the issue of how to access this pool arises. This issue was partially considered when the decision was made to reduce the number of institutions which produce minority degrees from 1,658 to a manageable number of 362, fully realizing that it would be very difficult to access all the institutions where minorities earn bachelor's degrees. Now the task is to increase accessibility to the pool distributed among the 362 institutions identified.

It is obvious that these institutions can be communicated with by correspondence and telephone. It is also apparent that recruitment requires some face to face contact with students, which can be achieved by bringing all prospective candidates to the institution initiating the recruitment or by sending a representative from the institution to the school where large clusters of prospective candidates are. On a selective basis, it is reasonable to arrange for a prospective candidate to visit; however, such visitation programs are usually limited in size and costly. Thus access to the pool is restricted and expensive since each visitor's expenses are usually paid by the host institution. On the other hand, one institutional representative or recruiter can visit a campus where large numbers of minority degree recipients are at a cost which is nearly equivalent to that for one student visit to the host institution. Not only are the costs of sending a recruiter to the source areas of minority

baccalaureate production about the same as a single candidate's visit,
it also has the advantage of accessing a much larger segment of the
minority pool and on a per capita basis, the cost of access to each
student is very low.

Most recruitment strategies requires some travel; it cannot be
completely avoided. Also, most recruitment requires air travel since
this is the most convenient means of transportation, considering the
time constraints imposed by the short duration of the recruitment
season for graduate and professional schools, which generally runs
from the beginning of September to the end of November. Although
recruiters from business and industry are not faced with admission
deadlines and have a more leisurely recruitment schedule spread out
over the entire year, they, too, are forced to intensify their recruitment during this short recruitment season, if they are to compete
with the universities and professional schools for the best candidates.

Institutions by Nearest Airport
Since air travel is an important element in recruiting, it is
reasonable to know which of the institutions generating minority
degrees are in the vicinity of each airport. Each of the 362
institutions awarding baccalaureate degrees to minorities are listed
by nearest airport on Table 18. The availability of the information on
this table is valuable in planning travel itineraries.

Pool Within 60-Mile Radius of Airport
To further facilitate the planning of recruitment travel
itineraries that increase the potential for access to minority baccalaureate production, all institutions and the number of minority
bachelor's degrees they generate for each minority group are
aggregated by airport.[14] These data are first aggregated within a
sixty mile radius from each major airport in the United States. In
other words, each institution within the sixty mile radius of a major
airport is listed with the number of degrees awarded to Blacks,
Hispanics, Asians and Native Americans, as well as the total
production for each of these groups by airport. Data in this form are
used for developing recruitment itineraries because the size of the
pool in the vicinity of each airport is known and it allows a recruiter,
who has selected one or more institutions in the airport's region, to
focus his attention and also to realize what other opportunities are in
the vicinity of that airport. Thus, the recruiter increases the
opportunity for additional coverage of the existing minority pool
without excessive additional expenditures. The sixty mile radius was
decided upon because it approximates the one hour isochron, the
distance one can travel by car at approximately 55 miles per hour
within one hour's time.

Aggregate minority baccalaureate production within a sixty mile
radius from major airports in the United States is found on Table 19.
For example, if data for ATL=Atlanta, GA, a popular minority
recruitment site, is examined, the well-known predominantly black
institutions such as Clark College, Morehouse College, Morris Brown
College and Spelman College appear. Further examination indicates
that there is additional minority baccalaureate production at Georgia

TABLE 18

INSTITUTIONS AWARDING MINORITY BACCALAUREATE DEGREES
BY STATE AND NEAREST AIRPORT

STATE/SCHOOL	DISTANCE		
	Within 60 Miles	Between 61–80 Miles	Beyond 80 Miles
Alabama			
Alabama A&M University*	HSV**		
Alabama State University*	MGM		
Jacksonville State University		BHM,HVS,ATL	
Miles College*	BHM,TCL		
Oakwood College*	HSV		
Stillman College*	BHM,TCL		
Talladega College*	BHM	MGM	
Troy State University – Main Campus	MGM		
Troy State University – Montgomery	MGM		
Tuskegee Institute*	MGM		
University of Alabama	BHM,TCL		
U of Alabama in Birmingham	BHM,TCL		
University of South Alabama	MOB		
Arizona			
Arizona State University	PHX		
Northern Arizona University	FLG		
University of Arizona	TUS		
Arkansas			
Arkansas Baptist College*	LIT		
Arkansas State U – Main Campus		MEM	
Henderson State University		LIT	
Philander Smith College*	LIT		
University of Arkansas – Pine Bluff*	LIT		
University of Central Arkansas	LIT		

60

(Airports)

STATE/SCHOOL

DISTANCE

	Within 60 Miles	Between 61–80 Miles	Beyond 80 Miles
California			
Cal Poly State U – San Luis Obispo	SBP		
Cal State College – Bakersfield		LAX,SBA	
Cal State College – San Bernadino	LAX		
Cal State Poly U – Pomona	LAX		
Cal State University – Chico	CIC		
Cal State U – Dominguez Hills	LAX		
Cal State University – Fresno	FAT		
Cal State University – Fullerton	LAX		
Cal State University – Hayward	SFO		
Cal State University – Long Beach	LAX		
Cal State University – Los Angeles	LAX	SBA	
Cal State University – Northridge	LAX	SBA	
Cal State University – Sacramento		SFO	
Chapman College	LAX	SAN	
Loyola Marymount University	LAX	SBA	
Pacific Christian College	LAX		
Pepperdine University	LAX,SBA		
San Diego State University	SAN		
San Francisco State University	SFO		
San Jose State University	SFO		
Stanford University	SFO		
U of Cal – Berkeley	SFO		
U of Cal – Davis		SFO	
U of Cal – Irvine	LAX	SAN	
U of Cal – Los Angeles	LAX	SBA	
U of Cal – Riverside	LAX	SAN	
U of Cal – San Diego	SAN		
U of Cal – San Francisco	SFO		
U of Cal – Santa Barbara	SBA		
U of Cal – Santa Cruz		SFO	
University of LaVerne	LAX		

(Airports)

STATE/SCHOOL	DISTANCE		
	Within 60 Miles	Between 61–80 Miles	Beyond 80 Miles
California (cont)			
University of Redlands		LAX	
University of San Francisco	SFO		
University of Southern California	LAX		
University of the Pacific		SFO	
Colorado			
Colorado State University		DEN	
Metropolitan State College	DEN	COS	
U of Colorado at Boulder	DEN	COS	
U of Northern Colorado	DEN		
U of Southern Colorado	COS		
Connecticut			
University of Connectcut	BDL,PVD		
Yale University	BDL	JFK	
Delaware			
Delaware State College*	PHL	BAL,SBY	
University of Delaware	PHL,BAL		
District of Columbia			
American University	DCA,BAL		
George Washington University	DCA,BAL		
Howard University*	DCA,BAL		
University of DC*	DCA,BAL		
Florida			
Bethune Cookman College*	DAB		
Biscayne College*	MIA		
Edward Waters College*	JAX		
Florida Agr & Mech University*	TLH		

62

(Airports)

STATE/SCHOOL	DISTANCE		
	Within 60 Miles	Between 61-80 Miles	Beyond 80 Miles
Florida (cont)			
Florida Atlantic University	MIA		
Florida International University	MIA		
Florida Memorial College*	MIA		
Florida State University	TLH		
University of Central Florida	DAB	TPA	
St. Leo College	TPA		
University of Florida		JAX	
University of Miami	MIA		
University of South Florida	TPA		
University of West Florida	MOB		
Georgia			
Albany State College*		TLH	
Clark College*	ATL	MCN	
Fort Valley State College*	MCN		
Georgia College	MCN	ATL	
GA Inst of Tech - Main Campus	ATL	MCN	
Georgia State University	ATL	MCN	
Morehouse College*	ATL	MCN	
Morris Brown College*	ATL	MCN	
Paine College*		CAE	
Savannah State College*	SAV	CHS	
Spelman College*	ATL	MCN	
University of Georgia		ATL	
Valdosta State College		TLH	
Hawaii			
Chaminade University of Honolulu	NHL		
University of Hawaii at Hilo*	ITO		
University of Hawaii at Manoa*	HNL		

(Airports)

STATE/SCHOOL	DISTANCE		
	Within 60 Miles	Between 61–80 Miles	Beyond 80 Miles
Illinois			
Bradley University	PIA		
Chicago State University*	ORD		
College of St. Francis	ORD		
Columbia College	ORD		
Daniel Hale Williams University*	ORD		
DePaul University	ORD		
Eastern Illinois University	CMI		
Governors State University	ORD		
Illinois State University	CMI		
Loyola University of Chicago	ORD		
Northern Illinois University	ORD		
Northeastern Illinois University	ORD		
Northwestern University	ORD	MKE	
Roosevelt University	ORD		
Southern Illinois U – Carbondale	MDH		
Southern Illinois U – Edwardsville	STL		
U of Illinois – Chicago Circle	ORD		
U of Illinois – Urbana Campus	CMI		
Indiana			
Ball State University	IND		
Ind-Purdue U – Indianapolis	IND		
Indiana State U – Main Campus	CMI	IND	
Indiana University – Bloomington	IND		
Indiana University – Northwest	ORD		
Purdue University – Main Campus	IND	CMI	
Kentucky			
Eastern Kentucky University	LEX		
Kentucky State University*	LEX	CVG	

64

STATE/SCHOOL	DISTANCE		
	Within 60 Miles	Between 61–80 Miles	Beyond 80 Miles
Kentucky (cont)			
University of Louisville	LEX		
Western Kentucky University	BNA		
Louisiana			
Dillard University*	MSY	BTR	
Grambling State University*	SHV,MLU		
Louisiana State U & A&M College	BTR	MSY	
Louisiana Tech University	MLU	SHV	
McNeese State University	LCH		
Northeast Louisiana University	MLU		
Southeastern Louisiana U	BTR	MSY	
Sthrn U A&M College – Main Cam*	BTR		
Southern U in New Orleans*	MSY	BTR	
Tulane U of Louisiana	MSY	BTR	
University of New Orleans	MSY	BTR	
U of Southwestern Louisiana		BTR,LCH	
Xavier University of Louisiana*	MSY	BTR	
Maryland			
Bowie State College*	DCA,BAL		
Coppin State College*	DCA,BAL		
Morgan State University*	DCA,BAL		
Towson State University	DCA,BAL		
University of Baltimore	DCA,BAL		
U of MD – Baltimore Co Campus	DCA,BAL		
U of MD – Baltimore Prof School	DCA,BAL		
U of MD – College Park Campus	DCA,BAL		
U of MD – Eastern Shore*	SBY		
U of MD – University College	DCA,BAL		

(Airports)

STATE/SCHOOL	DISTANCE		
	Within 60 Miles	Between 61–80 Miles	Beyond 80 Miles
Massachussetts			
Boston State College	BOS,PVD	MHT	
Boston University	BOS,PVD	MHT	
Harvard University	BOS,MHT,PVD		
Radcliffe College	BOS,MHT,PVD		
Tufts University	BOS,MHT,PVD		
U of Mass – Amherst Campus	BDL	BOS,MHT,ALB, PVD	
Michigan			
Detroit Institute of Technology	DTW		
Eastern Michigan University	DTW		
Mercy College of Detroit	DTW		
Michigan State University		DTW,GRR	
Oakland University	DTW		
Shaw College at Detroit*	DTW		
University of Detroit	DTW		
U of Michigan – Ann Arbor	DTW		
Wayne State University	DTW		
Western Michigan University	GRR		
Minnesota			
U of Minn – Minneapolis/St. Paul	MSP		
Mississippi			
Alcorn State University*	JAN	MLU	
Delta State University	GLH		
Jackson State University*	JAN		
Mississippi Industrial College*	MEM	MKL	
Mississippi State University			TCL
Mississippi University for Women	TCL		
Mississippi Valley State Univ*	GLH		
Rust College*	MEM	MKL	

66

(Airports)

DISTANCE

	Within 60 Miles	Between 61-80 Miles	Beyond 80 Miles
Mississippi (cont)			
Tougaloo College*	JAN		
U of Mississippi - Main Campus		MEM	
U of Southern Mississippi		MOB,MSY	
Missouri			
Columbia College	COU		
Harris Stowe College*	STL		
Lincoln University	COU		
Park College	MCI		
St. Louis U - Main Campus	STL		
U of Missouri - Columbia	COU		
U of Missouri - Kansas City	MCI		
U of Missouri - St. Louis	STL		
Washington University	STL		
Webster College	STL		
Montana			
Montana State University		BTM	
Nebraska			
U of Nebraska at Omaha	OMA		
New Hampshire			
Dartmouth College	MHT		
New Jersey			
Glassboro State College	PHL		
Jersey City State College	JFK		
Kean College of New Jersey	JFK		
Montclair State College	JFK		
New Jersey Inst Technology	JFK		

(Airports)

STATE/SCHOOL	DISTANCE		
	Within 60 Miles	Between 61-80 Miles	Beyond 80 Miles
New Jersey (cont)			
Princeton University	JFK,PHL		
Rutgers U - Camden Campus	PHL		
Rutgers U - New Brunswick	JFK,PHL		
Rutgers U - Newark Campus	JFK		
St. Peter's College	JFK		
Seton Hall University	JFK		
Trenton State College	JFK,PHL		
New Mexico			
Eastern NM U - Main Campus			ROW
New Mexico Highlands U*			ABQ
NM State U - Main Campus		ALM	
University of Albuquerque	ABQ		
U of NM - Main Campus	ABQ		
Western New Mexico University	SVC		
New York			
Adelphi University	JFK		
College of New Rochelle	JFK	BDL	
Cornell U Endowed College	SYR		
CUNY Bernard Baruch College	JFK		
CUNY Brooklyn College	JKF		
CUNY City College	JFK		
CUNY College of Staten Island	JFK		
CUNY Graduate School & U Center	JFK		
CUNY Hunter College	JFK		
CUNY John Jay College - Crim Jus	JFK		
CUNY Lehman College	JFK		
CUNY Medgar Evers College*	JFK		
CUNY Queen's College	JFK		
CUNY York College	JFK		

(Airports)

STATE/SCHOOL	DISTANCE		
	Within 60 Miles	Between 61–80 Miles	Beyond 80 Miles
New York (cont)			
Fordham University	JFK		
Long Island U – Brooklyn Center	JFK		
Long Island U – C W Post Center	JFK		
Mercy College	JFK	BDL	
New York University	JFK		
Pace University New York	JFK		
Polytechnic Institute New York	JFK		
Pratt Institute	JFK		
St. Francis College	JFK		
St. John's University	JFK		
St. Joseph's College – Main Campus	JFK		
SUNY at Albany	ALB	BDL	
SUNY at Buffalo – Main Campus	BUF		
SUNY at Stony Bk – Main Campus	JFK		
SUNY College at Buffalo	BUF		
SUNY College at New Paltz		BDL,ALB,JFK	
SUNY College – Old Westbury	JFK		
SUNY Empire State College	ALB		
Syracuse University – Main Campus	SYR		
North Carolina			
Barber-Scotia College*	CLT	GSO	
Bennett College*	RDU,GSO		
Duke University	RDU,GSO	FAY	
East Carolina University		RDU	
Elizabeth City State U*	ORF		
Fayetteville State University*	RDU,FAY		
Johnson C Smith University*	CLT		
Livingstone College*	CLT,GSO		
NC Agrl & Tech State University*	RDU,GSO		
NC Central University*	RDU,GSO,FAY		

(Airports)

STATE/SCHOOL	DISTANCE		
	Within 60 Miles	Between 61-80 Miles	Beyond 80 Miles
North Carolina (cont)			
NC State U - Raleigh	RDU,FAY	GSO	
Pembroke State University	FAY		
St. Augustine's College*	RDU,FAY	GSO	
Shaw University*	RDU,FAY	GSO	
U of NC at Chapel Hill	RDU,GSO,FAY		
U of NC at Charlotte	CLT		
U of NC at Greensboro	RDU,GSO		
Winston-Salem State University*	GSO	CLT	
North Dakota			
U of North Dakota - Main Campus	GFK		
Ohio			
Antioch University	CVG	CMH	
Bowling Green State U - Main Cam		DTW	
Central State University*	CVG,CMH		
Franklin University	CVG		
Kent State U - Main Campus	BKL		
Oberlin College	BKL		
Ohio State U - Main Campus	CMH		
Ohio University - Main Campus		CMH	
U of Akron - Main Campus	BKL		
U of Cincinnati - Main Campus	CVG		
University of Dayton	CVG	CMH	
University of Toledo	DTW		
Wilberforce University*	CVG,CMH		
Wright State U - Main Campus	CVG	CMH	
Oklahoma			
Cameron University			PWA
Central State University	PWA		

70

(Airports)

DISTANCE

	Within 60 Miles	Between 61–80 Miles	Beyond 80 Miles
Oklahoma (cont)			
East Central Oklahoma State U		PWA	
Langston University*	PWA		
Northeast Oklahoma State U	TUL		
Oklahoma State U – Main Campus	PWA	TUL	
Southeast Oklahoma State U	SWI		
Southwest Oklahoma State U		PWA	
U of Oklahoma – Norman Campus	PWA		
Oregon			
Oregon State University	EUG		
University of Oregon – Main Campus	EUG		
Pennsylvania			
Cheyney State College*	PHL	BAL	
Drexel University	PHL		
Lincoln University*	PHL,BAL	DCA	
Pennsylvania State U – Main Campus	AOO		
St. Joseph's University	PHL		
Temple University	PHL		
University of Pennsylvania	PHL		
U of Pittsburg – Main Campus	PIT		
West Chester State College	PHL		
Rhode Island			
Brown University	BOS,PVD	BDL	
South Carolina			
Allen University*	CAE		
Baptist College at Charleston	CHS	SAV	
Benedict College*	CAE		
Claflin College*	CAE	CHS	

(Airports)

STATE/SCHOOL	DISTANCE		
	Within 60 Miles	Between 61–80 Miles	Beyond 80 Miles
South Carolina (cont)			
Morris College*	CAE		
South Carolina State College*	CAE	CHS	
U of South Carolina at Columbia	CAE		
Voorhees College*	CAE		
Winthrop College	CLT	CAE	
Tennessee			
Austin Peay State University	BNA		
Fisk University*	BNA		
Knoxville College*	TYS		
Lane College*	MKL	MEM	
LeMoyne–Owen College*	MEM		
Memphis State University	MEM	MKL	
Middle Tennessee State U	BNA	HSV	
Tennessee State University*	BNA		
U of Tennessee – Knoxville	TYS		
U of Tennessee – Martin	MKL		
Texas			
Angelo State University	SJT		
Bishop College*	DFW,SWI		
Corpus Christi State University	CRP		
East Texas State University	DFW,SWI	TYR	
Huston–Tillotson College*	AUS	SAT	
Incarnate Word College	SAT	AUS	
Jarvis Christian College*	TYR		
Lamar University		LCH	
Laredo State University*	LRD		
North Texas State University	DFW,SWI		
Our Lady of Lake University*	SAT	AUS	
Pan American University*	MFE		

72

(Airports)

STATE/SCHOOL	DISTANCE		
	Within 60 Miles	Between 61–80 Miles	Beyond 80 Miles
Texas (cont)			
Paul Quinn College*	ACT		
Prairie View A&M University*	IAH		
St. Edward's University	SAT	AUS	
St. Mary's U – San Antonio	SAT	AUS	
Sam Houston State University		IAH	
Southwest Texas State University	AUS,SAT		
Sul Ross State University			MAF,ELP
Texas A&I University	CRP		
Texas A&M U – Main Campus			AUS,IAH
Texas College*	TYR		
Texas Southern University*	IAH		
Texas Women's University	DFW,SWI		
Trinity University	SAT	AUS	
U of Houston – Central Campus	IAH		
U of Texas at Arlington	DFW	SWI	
U of Texas at Austin	AUS	SAT	
U of Texas at El Paso	ELP		
U of Texas at San Antonio	SAT	AUS	
Wiley College*	SHV,TYR		
Utah			
Brigham Young University – Main	SLC		
University of Utah	SLC		
Virginia			
Hampton Institute*	ORF	RIC	
Norfolk State College*	ORF	RIC	
Old Dominion University	ORF		
St. Paul's College*		RDU,RIC	
U of Virginia – Main Campus		RIC	

(Airports)

STATE/SCHOOL	DISTANCE		
	Within 60 Miles	Between 61–80 Miles	Beyond 80 Miles
Virginia (cont)			
Virginia Commonwealth University	RIC		
Virginia State College*	RIC	ORF	
Virginia Union University*	RIC		
Washington			
Evergreen State College	SEA		
University of Washington	SEA		
West Virginia			
West Virginia State College	CRW		
Wisconsin			
U of Wisconsin – Madison	MSN	MKE	
U of Wisconsin – Milwaukee	MKE	MSN	

*Predominately minority institutions are those where at least 50% of the total BA Degrees awarded are to one of the minority groups being considered.

**Airport codes follow those that appear in the Official Airline Guide, North American Edition.

74

TABLE 19

TOTAL (0100-2400)
MINORITY BACCALAUREATE DEGREES
WITHIN 60 MILE RADIUS OF AIRPORT

AIRPORT	MINORITY GROUP			
	Black	Hispanic	Asian	Native American
ABQ=Albuquerque, NM				
U of NM - Main Campus	18	345	12	58
University of Albuquerque	5	77	1	6
	23	**422**	**13**	**64**
ACT=Waco, TX				
Paul Quinn College*	44			
	44			
ALB=Albany, NY				
SUNY at Albany	65	38	16	13
SUNY Empire State College	100	20	7	2
	165	**58**	**23**	**15**
AOO=Altoona, PA				
Pennsylvania State U - Main Campus	96	20	25	7
	96	**20**	**25**	**7**
ATL=Atlanta, GA				
Clark College*	296			
GA Inst of Tech - Main Campus	52	23	15	1
Georgia State University	211	3	6	6
Morehouse College*	214			
Morris Brown College*	173			
Spelman College*	273		1	
	1219	**26**	**22**	**7**
AUS=Austin, TX				
Huston-Tillotson College*	67	1		
Southwest Texas State University	78	229	4	11
U of Texas at Austin	103	453	53	12
	248	**683**	**57**	**23**

Airport 60 (0100–2400)

AIRPORT	MINORITY GROUP			
	Black	Hispanic	Asian	Native American
BAL=Baltimore, MD				
University of Delaware	62	5	9	2
American University	173	27	14	2
George Washington Univesity	73	38	45	3
Howard University*	778		5	
University of DC*	441	31	10	8
Bowie State College*	140			
Coppin State College*	142			1
Morgan State University*	438		4	
Towson State University	140	6	7	3
U of MD – University College	103	14	14	6
U of MD – Baltimore Prof School	60	6	19	
U of MD – Baltimore Co Campus	88		1	4
U of MD – College Park Campus	216	53	72	42
University of Baltimore	107	1	3	1
Lincoln University*	172			
	3133	**181**	**203**	**72**
BDL=Hartford, CT/Springfield, MA				
Yale University	59	47	46	2
U of Mass – Amherst Campus	54	33	41	7
	113	**80**	**87**	**9**
BHM=Birmingham, AL				
Miles College*	142			
Stillman College*	131	2		
Talladega College*	109			
U of Alabama in Birmingham	160	1	7	
University of Alabama	175			
	717	**3**	**7**	
BKL=Cleveland-Lakefront, OH				
Kent State U – Main Campus	135	6	2	6
Oberlin College	53	6	26	2
U of Akron – Main Campus	92	3	8	3
	280	**15**	**36**	**11**

Airport 60 (0100-2400)

AIRPORT	MINORITY GROUP			
	Black	Hispanic	Asian	Native American
BNA=Nashville, TN				
Western Kentucky University	53	2		1
Austin Peay State University	50	2	3	2
Fisk University*	217			
Middle Tennessee State U	71	2	18	2
Tennessee State University*	500			
	891	**6**	**21**	**5**
BOS=Boston, MA				
Boston State College	71	17	7	3
Boston University	65	21	18	4
Harvard University	108	28	45	6
Radcliffe College	51	11	16	1
Tufts University	67	21	30	3
Brown University	71	10	26	1
	433	**108**	**142**	**18**
BTR=Baton Rouge, LA				
Louisiana State U & A&M College	62	15	5	3
Sthrn U A&M College - Main Cam*	904			
Southeastern Louisiana U	54		1	
	1020	**15**	**6**	**3**
BUF=Buffalo, NY				
SUNY at Buffalo - Main Campus	67	9	26	2
SUNY College at Buffalo	85	16	7	13
	152	**25**	**33**	**15**
CAE=Columbia, SC				
Allen University*	66			
Benedict College*	296			
Claflin College*	147			
Morris College*	89			
South Carolina State College*	468		2	
U of South Carolina at Columbia	250	18	11	3
Voorhees College*	164			
	1480	**18**	**13**	**3**

Airport 60 (0100-2400)

AIRPORT	MINORITY GROUP			
	Black	Hispanic	Asian	Native American
CHS=Charleston, SC				
Baptist College at Charleston	58			
	58			
CIC=Chico, CA				
Cal State University - Chico	25	85	43	14
	25	**85**	**43**	**14**
CLT=Charlotte, NC				
Barber-Scotia College*	51			
Johnson C Smith University*	200			
Livingstone College*	129			
U of NC at Charlotte	64	7	4	1
Winthrop College	72	1		
	516	**8**	**4**	**1**
CMH=Columbus, OH				
Central State University*	224		1	
Ohio State U - Main Campus	138	8	28	3
Wilberforce University*	112			
	474	**8**	**29**	**3**
CMI=Champaign, IL				
Eastern Illinois University	73	1	6	
Illinois State University	165	21	18	18
U of Illinois - Urbana Campus	91	34	91	12
Indiana State U - Main Campus	98	3	6	4
	427	**59**	**121**	**34**
COS=Colorado Springs, CO				
U of Southern Colorado	14	68	6	4
	14	**68**	**6**	**4**
COU=Columbia, MO				
Columbia College	91	7	1	2
Lincoln University	84			
U of Missouri - Columbia	54	8	25	6
	229	**15**	**26**	**8**

Airport 60 (0100–2400)

AIRPORT	MINORITY GROUP			
	Black	Hispanic	Asian	Native American
CRP=Corpus Christi, TX				
Corpus Christi State University	4	174	4	3
Texas A&I University	22	335		
	26	**509**	**4**	**3**
CRW=Charleston, WV				
West Virginia State College	97	1	6	
	97	**1**	**6**	
CVG=Cincinnati, OH				
Antioch University	194	61	4	5
Central State University*	224		1	
Franklin University	56	2	7	1
U of Cincinnati - Main Campus	224	11	10	2
University of Dayton	64	8	7	3
Wilberforce University*	112			
Wright State U - Main Campus	55	1	1	1
	929	**83**	**30**	**12**
DAB=Dayton Beach, FL				
Bethune Cookman College*	287	1		
University of Central Florida	55	26	15	1
	342	**27**	**15**	**1**
DCA=Washington–National, DC				
American University	173	27	14	2
George Washington University	73	38	45	3
Howard University*	778		5	
University of DC*	441	31	10	8
Bowie State College*	140			
Coppin State College*	142			1
Morgan State University*	438		4	
Towson State University	140	6	7	3

79

Airport 60 (0100-2400)

AIRPORT	MINORITY GROUP			
	Black	Hispanic	Asian	Native American
DCA (cont)				
U of MD - University College	103	14	14	6
U of MD - Baltimore Prof School	60	6	19	
U of MD - Baltimore Co Campus	88		1	4
U of MD - College Park Campus	216	53	72	42
University of Baltimore	107	1	3	1
	2899	**176**	**194**	**70**
DEN=Denver, CO				
Metropolitan State College	78	93	13	14
U of Colorado at Boulder	37	84	66	6
U of Northern Colorado	34	67	15	8
	149	**244**	**94**	**28**
DFW=Dallas/Fort Worth, TX				
Bishop College*	155			
East Texas State University	200	42	13	7
North Texas State University	175	62	11	4
Texas Woman's University	125	70	12	6
U of Texas at Arlington	84	55	17	5
	739	**229**	**53**	**22**
DTW=Detroit-Metropolitan, MI				
Detroit Institute of Technology	52		6	
Eastern Michigan University	175	14	7	25
Mercy College of Detroit	70	2	1	
Oakland University	76	5	7	5
Shaw College at Detroit*	68			
U of Michigan - Ann Arbor	233	41	79	10
University of Detroit	163	9	13	
Wayne State University	635	29	31	14
University of Toledo	58	8	17	6
	1530	**108**	**161**	**60**
ELP=El Paso, TX				
U of Texas at El Paso	49	584	23	1
	49	**584**	**23**	**11**

Airport 60 (0100-2400)

AIRPORT	MINORITY GROUP			
	Black	Hispanic	Asian	Native American
EUG=Eugene, OR				
Oregon State University	6	8	41	21
University of Oregon - Main Campus	23	20	69	11
	29	**28**	**110**	**32**
FAT=Fresno, CA				
Cal State University - Fresno	57	215	143	16
	57	**215**	**143**	**16**
FAY=Fayetteville, NC				
Fayetteville State University*	294	5	4	2
NC Central University*	614	2		1
NC State U - Raleigh	88	8	3	3
Pembroke State University	46		1	96
St. Augustine's College*	202		2	
Shaw University*	193			
U of NC at Chapel Hill	156	10	8	13
	1593	**25**	**18**	**115**
FLG=Flagstaff, AZ				
Northern Arizona University	15	79	10	54
	15	**79**	**10**	**54**
GLH=Greenville, MS				
Delta State University	71		2	
Mississippi Valley State U*	375	1		
	446	**1**	**2**	
GRR=Grand Rapids, MI				
Western Michigan University	143	17	7	11
	143	**17**	**7**	**11**
GSO=Greensboro/High Point, NC				
Bennett College*	85			
Duke University	51	11	14	1
Livingstone College*	129			
NC Agrl & Tech State University*	602			
NC Central University*	614	2		1

Airport 60 (0100–2400)

AIRPORT	MINORITY GROUP			
	Black	Hispanic	Asian	Native American
GSO (cont)				
U of NC at Chapel Hill	156	10	8	13
U of NC at Greensboro	84	4	2	2
Winston-Salem State University*	309			
	2030	**27**	**24**	**17**
HNL=Honolulu/Oahu, HI				
Chaminade University of Honolulu	7	29	1984	1
University of Hawaii at Manoa*	5	4	57	
	12	**33**	**2041**	**1**
HSV=Huntsville, AL/Decatur, GA				
Alabama A&M University*	390			
Oakwood College*	187			
	577			
IAH=Houston–Intercontinental,TX				
Prairie View A&M University*	461	6	21	
Texas Southern University*	462	7		
U of Houston – Central Campus	203	212	93	8
	1126	**225**	**114**	**8**
IND=Indianapolis, IN				
Ball State University	76	5	2	3
Ind-Purdue U – Indianapolis	74	4	6	5
Indiana University – Bloomington	133	20	25	5
Purdue University – Main Campus	103	25	41	4
	386	**54**	**74**	**17**
ITO=Hilo, HI				
University of Hawaii at Hilo*		6	102	
		6	**102**	
JAN=Jackson/Vicksburg, MS				
Alcorn State University*	286		1	
Jackson State University*	653			1
Tougaloo College*	127			
	1066		**1**	**1**

82

AIRPORT	MINORITY GROUP			
	Black	Hispanic	Asian	Native American
JAX=Jacksonville, FL				
Edward Waters College*	76			
	76			
JFK=New York, Kennedy Int'l, NY				
Jersey City State College	109	43	9	
Kean College of New Jersey	134	67	9	4
Montclair State College	53	64	13	18
New Jersey Inst of Technology	69	35	29	
Princeton University	63	33	36	5
Rutgers U – New Brunswick	272	82	65	1
Rutgers U – Newark Campus	181	49	18	
St. Peter's College	34	70	8	
Seton Hall University	66	8	6	1
Trenton State College	117	9	8	5
Adelphi University	169	43	1	1
College of New Rochelle	133	33	3	
CUNY Bernard Baruch College	374	162	130	5
CUNY Brooklyn College	650	224	50	23
CUNY College of Staten Island	70	42	15	2
CUNY City College	597	285	166	22
CUNY Graduate School & U Center	60	27	12	2
CUNY Hunter College	308	182	68	15
CUNY John Jay College – Crim Jus	171	82	10	12
CUNY Lehman College	171	202	48	2
CUNY Medgar Evers College*	122	1		
CUNY Queen's College	307	84	90	7
CUNY York College	185	39	10	5
Fordham University	136	139	20	
Long Island U – Brooklyn Center	174	54	21	
Long Island U – C W Post Center	56	12	5	
Mercy College	154	81	12	2

Airport 60 (0100–2400)

| AIRPORT | MINORITY GROUP | | | Native |
	Black	Hispanic	Asian	American
JFK (cont)				
New York University	204	57	79	12
Pace University New York	91	33	29	2
Polytechnic Institute New York	28	22	72	
Pratt Institute	105	39	25	
St. Francis College	197	13	41	
St. John's University	51	39	33	5
St. Joseph's College - Main Campus	271	11	13	
SUNY at Stony Bk - Main Campus	54	31	46	2
SUNY College - Old Westbury	80	20	1	
	6016	**2417**	**1201**	**153**
LAX=Los Angeles, CA				
Cal State College - San Bernardino	59	76	9	7
Cal State Poly U - Pomona	38	127	67	37
Cal State U - Dominguez Hills	369	69	80	13
Cal State University - Fullerton	53	207	86	29
Cal State University - Long Beach	174	226	338	31
Cal State University - Los Angeles	341	447	422	20
Cal State University - Northridge	110	161	148	68
Chapman College	78	33	26	12
Loyola Marymount University	54	91	32	2
Pacific Christian College	71	6	14	5
Pepperdine University	90	20	36	4
U of Cal - Irvine	45	33	104	8
U of Cal - Los Angeles	186	163	547	17
U of Cal - Riverside	47	51	28	2
University of Southern California	138	156	311	18
University of LaVerne	46	87	10	2
	1899	**1953**	**2258**	**275**
LCH=Lake Charles, LA				
McNeese State University	54	3	5	1
	54	**3**	**5**	**1**

84

Airport 60 (0100-2400)

AIRPORT	MINORITY GROUP			
	Black	Hispanic	Asian	Native American
LEX=Lexington/Frankfort, KY				
Eastern Kentucky University	81			
Kentucky State University*	110			
University of Louisville	73	7	15	2
	264	**7**	**15**	**2**
LIT=Little Rock, AR				
Arkansas Baptist College*	45			
Philander Smith College*	63			
University of Arkansas - Pine Bluff*	341			
University of Central Arkansas	49		1	
	498		**1**	
LRD=Laredo, TX				
Laredo State University*		163		
		163		
MCI=Kansas City-International, MO				
Park College	165	42		2
U of Missouri - Kansas City	49	8	9	6
	214	**50**	**9**	**8**
MCN=Macon, GA				
Fort Valley State College*	146			
Georgia College	56		1	
	202		**1**	
MDH=Carbondale, IL				
Southern Illinois U - Carbondale	198	28	26	26
	198	**28**	**26**	**26**
MEM=Memphis, TN				
Mississippi Industrial College*	40			
Rust College*	117			
Le Moyne-Owen College*	114			
Memphis State University	271	5	28	1
	542	**5**	**28**	**1**

Airport 60 (0100–2400)

AIRPORT	MINORITY GROUP			
	Black	Hispanic	Asian	Native American
MFE=McAllen, TX				
Pan American University*	4	719	5	1
	4	**719**	**5**	**1**
MGM=Montgomery, GA				
Alabama State University*	400			
Troy State University – Main Campus	128	8	2	
Troy State University – Montgomery	62	2		
Tuskegee Institute*	430	1	1	
	1020	**11**	**3**	
MHT=Manchester, NH				
Harvard University	108	28	45	6
Radcliffe College	51	11	16	1
Tufts University	67	21	30	3
Dartmouth College	70	3	7	6
	296	**63**	**98**	**16**
MIA=Miami, FL				
Biscayne College*	37	203		1
Florida Atlantic University	84	43	3	1
Florida International University	176	529	45	3
Florida Memorial College*	69			
University of Miami	102	276	34	4
	468	**1051**	**82**	**9**
MKE=Milwaukee, WS				
U of Wisconsin – Milwaukee	111	25	13	6
	111	**25**	**13**	**6**
MKL=Jackson, TN				
Lane College*	109			
U of Tennessee – Martin	70	1	4	
	179	**1**	**4**	
MLU=Monroe, LA				
Grambling State University*	526			
Louisiana Tech University	69	2	3	
Northeast Louisiana University	124	1	2	
	719	**3**	**5**	

86

Airport 60 (0100-2400)

AIRPORT	MINORITY GROUP			
	Black	Hispanic	Asian	Native American
MOB=Mobile, AL/Pasagoula, MS				
University of South Alabama	61	1	6	4
University of West Florida	71	17	12	3
	132	**18**	**18**	**7**
MSN=Madison, WS				
U of Wisconsin - Madison	65	32	34	10
	65	**32**	**34**	**10**
MSP=Minneapolis/St. Paul, MN				
U of Minn - Minneapolis/St. Paul	72	32	86	16
	72	**32**	**86**	**16**
MSY=New Orleans, LA				
Dillard University*	188			
Southeastern Louisiana U	54		1	
Southern U in New Orleans*	295			
Tulane U of Louisiana	28	55	11	5
University of New Orleans	88	23	8	
Xavier University of Louisiana*	257		11	
	910	**78**	**31**	**5**
ORD=Chicago-O'Hare Airport, IL				
Chicago State University*	552	19	2	2
College of St. Francis	166	11	11	
Columbia College	90	12	10	8
Daniel Hale Williams University*	70			
DePaul University	107	39	16	2
Governors State University	154	10	2	
Loyola University of Chicago	82	44	20	
Northern Illinois University	149	18	25	2
Northwestern University	133	19	33	2
Northeastern Illinois University	112	86	29	2
Roosevelt University	287	28	91	
U of Illinois - Chicago Circle	216	121	101	6
Indiana University - Northwest	50	12		
	2168	**419**	**340**	**24**

Airport 60 (0100-2400)

AIRPORT	MINORITY GROUP			
	Black	Hispanic	Asian	Native American
ORF=Norfolk/Virginia Beach, VA				
Elizabeth City State U*	301		1	
Hampton Institute*	444			
Norfolk State College*	603			
Old Dominion University	62	11	13	5
	1410	**11**	**14**	**5**
PHL=Philadelphia, PA/Wilmington, DE				
Delaware State College*	133	1		
University of Delaware	62	5	9	2
Glassboro State College	156	104	5	31
Princeton University	63	33	36	5
Rutgers U - Camden Campus	72	6	2	1
Rutgers U - New Brunswick	272	82	65	1
Trenton State College	117	9	8	5
Cheyney State College*	303			
Drexel University	61	2	15	
Lincoln University*	172			
St. Joseph's University	47	3	2	51
Temple University	446	102	41	23
University of Pennsylvania	113	28	50	3
West Chester State College	55	2	1	
	2072	**377**	**234**	**122**
PHX=Phoenix, AZ				
Arizona State University	52	198	49	8
	52	**198**	**49**	**8**
PIA=Peoria, IL				
Bradley University	51	2	9	2
	51	**2**	**9**	**2**
PIT=Pittsburgh, PA				
U of Pittsburgh - Main Campus	251	8	4	14
	251	**8**	**4**	**14**

88

Airport 60 (0100-2400)

AIRPORT	MINORITY GROUP			
	Black	Hispanic	Asian	Native American
PVD=Providence, RI				
Boston State College	71	17	7	3
Boston University	65	21	18	4
Harvard University	108	28	45	6
Radcliffe College	51	11	16	1
Tufts University	67	21	30	3
Brown University	71	10	26	1
	433	**108**	**142**	**18**
PWA=Oklahoma City-Wiley Post, OK				
Central State University	98	12	7	18
Langston University*	77			
Oklahoma State U - Main Campus	45	13	26	40
U of Oklahoma - Norman Campus	45	11	12	48
	265	**36**	**45**	**106**
RDU=Raleigh/Durham, NC				
Bennet College*	85			
Duke University	51	11	14	1
Fayetteville State University*	294	5	4	2
NC Agrl & Tech State University*	602			
NC Central University*	614	2		1
NC State U - Raleigh	88	8	3	3
St. Augustine's College*	202		2	
Shaw University*	193			
U of NC at Chapel Hill	156	10	8	13
U of NC at Greensboro	84	4	2	2
	2369	**40**	**33**	**22**
RIC=Richmond, VA				
Virginia Commonwealth University	222	9	10	6
Virginia State College*	593		1	
Virginia Union University*	162			
	977	**9**	**11**	**6**

Airport 60 (0100-2400)

AIRPORT		MINORITY GROUP		
	Black	Hispanic	Asian	Native American
SAN=San Diego, CA				
San Diego State University	98	218	126	22
U of Cal - San Diego		59	49	7
	98	**277**	**175**	**29**
SAT=San Antonio, TX				
Incarnate Word College	18	86		
Our Lady of Lake University*	27	136	1	
St. Edward's University	13	81		
St. Mary's U - San Antonio	12	153	19	
Southwest Texas State University	78	229	4	11
Trinity University	10	72	3	
U of Texas at San Antonio	12	202	8	4
	170	**959**	**35**	**15**
SAV=Savannah, GA				
Savannah State College*	161			
	161			
SBA=Santa Barbara, CA				
Pepperdine University	90	20	36	4
U of Cal - Santa Barbara	34	100	117	7
	124	**120**	**153**	**11**
SBP=San Luis Obispo, CA				
Cal Poly State U - San Luis Obispo	23	59	114	44
	23	**59**	**114**	**44**
SBY=Salisbury, MD				
U of MD - Eastern Shore*	87	1		
	87	**1**		
SEA=Seattle/Tacoma, WA				
Evergreen State College	19	7	5	17
University of Washington	121	40	343	29
	140	**47**	**348**	**46**

Airport 60 (0100–2400)

AIRPORT	MINORITY GROUP			
	Black	Hispanic	Asian	Native American
SFO=San Francisco/Oakland, CA				
Cal State University - Hayward	128	61	94	9
San Francisco State University	221	138	526	29
San Jose State University	156	223	382	47
Stanford University	75	82	99	5
U of Cal - Berkeley	165	98	856	21
U of Cal - San Francisco	10	12	60	
University of San Francisco	107	80	94	14
	862	**694**	**2111**	**125**
SHV=Shreveport, LA				
Grambling State University*	526			
Wiley College*	93			
	619			
SJT=San Angelo, TX				
Angelo State University	18	68		1
	18	**68**		**1**
SLC=Salt Lake City, UT				
Brigham Young University - Main			25	37
University of Utah	21	35	31	16
	21	**35**	**56**	**53**
STL=St. Louis, MO				
Southern Illinois U - Edwardsville	110	1	9	1
Harris Stowe College*	54			
St. Louis U - Main Campus	94	9	11	2
U of Missouri - St. Louis	93	15	7	6
Washington University	59	16	25	
Webster College	50	1		
	460	**42**	**52**	**9**
SVC=Silver City, NM				
Western New Mexico University	4	58	1	4
	4	**58**	**1**	**4**

Airport 60 (0100–2400)

AIRPORT	MINORITY GROUP			
	Black	Hispanic	Asian	Native American
SWI=Sherman, TX				
Southeast Oklahoma State U	16	1	3	21
Bishop College*	155			
East Texas State University	200	42	13	7
North Texas State University	175	62	11	4
Texas Woman's University	125	70	12	6
	671	**175**	**39**	**38**
SYR=Syracuse, NY				
Cornel U Endowed College	67	36	65	6
Syracuse U - Main Campus	99	26	22	
	166	**62**	**87**	**6**
TCL=Tuscaloosa, AL				
Miles College*	142			
Stillman College*	131	2		
U of Alabama in Birmingham	160	1	7	
University of Alabama	175			
Mississippi University for Women	50		1	
	658	**3**	**8**	
TLH=Tallahassee, FL				
Florida Agr & Mech University*	615	3	9	
Florida State University	269	43	10	5
	884	**46**	**19**	**5**
TPA=Tampa, FL				
St. Leo College	75	24		1
University of South Florida	195	132	20	6
	270	**156**	**20**	**7**
TUL=Tulsa, OK				
Northeast Oklahoma State U	61	1	4	118
	61	**1**	**4**	**118**
TUS=Tucson, AZ				
University of Arizona	44	195	63	53
	44	**195**	**63**	**53**

92

Airport 60 (0100–2400)

AIRPORT	MINORITY GROUP			
	Black	Hispanic	Asian	Native American
TYR=Tyler, TX				
Jarvis Christian College*	45			
Texas College*	99			
Wiley College*	93			
	237			
TYS=Knoxville, TN				
Knoxville College*	104			
U of Tennessee – Knoxville	125	9	15	4
	229	**9**	**15**	**4**

TABLE 20

TOTAL (0100-2400)
MINORITY BACCALAUREATE DEGREES
WITHIN 61-80 MILE ANNULUS OF AIRPORT

AIRPORT	MINORITY GROUP			
	Black	Hispanic	Asian	Native American
ALB=Albany, NY				
U of Mass - Amherst Campus	54	33	41	7
SUNY College at New Paltz	51	19	6	15
	105	**52**	**47**	**22**
ALM=Alamogordo, NM				
NM State U - Main Campus	19	235	5	17
	19	**235**	**5**	**17**
ATL=Atlanta, GA				
Jacksonville State University	87	7	11	
Georgia College	56		1	
University of Georgia	100	9	5	8
	243	**16**	**17**	**8**
AUS=Austin, TX				
Incarnate Word College	18	86		
Our Lady of Lake University*	27	136	1	
St. Edward's University	13	81		
St. Mary's U - San Antonio	12	153	19	
Trinity University	10	72	3	
U of Texas at San Antonio	12	202	8	4
	92	**730**	**31**	**4**
BAL=Baltimore, MD				
Delaware State College*	133	1		
Cheyney State College*	303			
	436	**1**		
BDL=Hartford, CT/Springfield, MA				
College of New Rochelle	133	33	3	
Mercy College	154	81	12	2

94

Airport 61-80 (0100-2400)

AIRPORT	MINORITY GROUP			
	Black	Hispanic	Asian	Native American
BDL (cont)				
SUNY at Albany	65	38	16	13
SUNY College at New Paltz	51	19	6	15
Brown University	71	10	26	1
	474	181	63	31
BHM=Birmingham, AL				
Jacksonville State University	87	7	11	
	87	7	11	
BOS=Boston, MA				
U of Mass - Amherst Campus	54	33	41	7
	54	33	41	7
BTM=Butte, MT				
Montana State University	1	4	7	17
	1	4	7	17
BTR=Baton Rouge, LA				
Dillard University*	188			
Southern U in New Orleans*	295			
Tulane U of Louisiana	28	55	11	5
U of Southwestern Louisiana	144	16	3	15
University of New Orleans	88	23	8	
Xavier University of Louisiana*	257		11	
	1000	94	33	20
CAE=Columbia, SC				
Paine College*	88			
Winthrop College	72	1		
	160	1		
CHS=Charleston, SC				
Savannah State College*	161			
Claflin College*	147			
South Carolina State College*	468		2	
	776		2	

Airport 61-80 (0100-2400)

AIRPORT	Black	Hispanic	Asian	Native American
CLT=Charlotte, NC				
Wintson-Salem State University*	309			
	309			
CMH=Columbus, OH				
Antioch University	194	61	4	5
Ohio University - Main Campus	197	3	3	6
University of Dayton	64	8	7	3
Wright State U - Main Campus	55	1	1	1
	510	**73**	**15**	**15**
CMI=Champaign, IL				
Purdue University - Main Campus	103	25	41	4
	103	**25**	**41**	**4**
COS=Colorado Springs, CO				
Metropolitan State College	78	93	13	14
U of Colorado at Boulder	37	84	66	6
	115	**177**	**79**	**20**
CRW=Charleston, WV				
Ohio University - Main Campus	197	3	3	6
	197	**3**	**3**	**6**
CVG=Cincinnati, OH				
Kentucky State University*	110			
	110			
DCA=Washington-National, DC				
Lincoln University*	172			
	172			
DEN=Denver, CO				
Colorado State University	14	107	24	7
	14	**107**	**24**	**7**
DTW=Detroit-Metropolitan, MI				
Michigan State University	271	42	38	13
Bowling Green State U - Main Cam	142	15	7	2
	413	**57**	**45**	**15**

Airport 61-80 (0100-2400)

AIRPORT	MINORITY GROUP			
	Black	Hispanic	Asian	Native American
FAY=Fayetteville, NC				
Duke University	51	11	14	1
	51	**11**	**14**	**1**
GRR=Grand Rapids, MI				
Michigan State University	271	42	38	13
	271	**42**	**38**	**13**
GSO=Greensboro/High Point, NC				
Barber-Scotia College*	51			
St. Augustine's College*	88	8	3	3
Shaw University*	202		2	
	193			
	534	**8**	**5**	**3**
HSV=Huntsville, AL/Decatur, GA				
Jacksonville State University	87	7	11	
Middle Tennessee State U	71	2	18	2
	158	**9**	**29**	**2**
IAH=Houston-Intercontinental,TX				
Sam Houston State University	89	2	59	9
	89	**2**	**59**	**9**
IND=Indianapolis, IN				
Indiana State U - Main Campus	98	3	6	4
	98	**3**	**6**	**4**
JAX=Jacksonville, FL				
University of Florida	138	209	48	2
	138	**209**	**48**	**2**
JFK=New York, Kennedy Int'l, NY				
Yale University	59	47	46	2
SUNY College at New Paltz	51	19	6	15
	110	**66**	**52**	**17**
LAX=Los Angeles, CA				
Cal State College - Bakersfield	16	41	10	31
University of Redlands	126	73	33	
	142	**114**	**43**	**31**

Airport 61–80 (0100–2400)

AIRPORT	MINORITY GROUP			
	Black	Hispanic	Asian	Native American
LCH=Lake Charles, LA				
U of Southwestern Louisiana	144	16	3	15
Lamar University	25	2	11	104
	169	**18**	**14**	**119**
LIT=Little Rock, AR				
Henderson State University	94			
	94			
MCN=Macon, GA				
Clark College*	296			
GA Inst of Tech – Main Campus	52	23	15	1
Georgia State University	211	3	6	6
Morehouse College*	214			
Morris Brown College*	173			
Spelman College*	273		1	
	1219	**26**	**22**	**7**
MEM=Memphis, TN				
Arkansas State U – Main Campus	70	1	1	3
U of Mississippi – Main Campus	90	2	8	2
Lane College*	109			
	269	**3**	**9**	**5**
MGM=Montgomery, GA				
Talladega College*	109			
	109			
MHT=Manchester, NH				
Boston State College	71	17	7	3
Boston University	65	21	18	4
U of Mass – Amherst Campus	54	33	41	7
	190	**71**	**66**	**14**
MKE=Milwaukee, WS				
Northwestern University	133	19	33	2
U of Wisconsin – Madison	65	32	34	10
	198	**51**	**67**	**12**

Airport 61-80 (0100-2400)

AIRPORT	MINORITY GROUP			
	Black	Hispanic	Asian	Native American
MKL=Jackson, TN				
Mississippi Industrial College*	40			
Rust College*	117			
Memphis State University	271	5	28	1
	428	**5**	**28**	**1**
MLU=Monroe, LA				
Alcorn State University*	286		1	
	286		**1**	
MOB=Mobile, AL/Pasagoula, MS				
U of Southern Mississippi	164	3	8	
	164	**3**	**8**	
MSN=Madison, WS				
U of Wisconsin - Milwaukee	111	25	13	6
	111	**25**	**13**	**6**
MSY=New Orleans, LA				
Louisiana State U & A&M College	62	15	5	3
Sthrn U A&M C - Main Cam*	904			
	966	**15**	**5**	**3**
ORF=Norfolk/Virginia Beach, VA				
Virginia State College*	593		1	
	593		**1**	
PVD=Providence, RI				
U of Mass - Amherst Campus	54	33	41	7
	54	**33**	**41**	**7**
PWA=Oklahoma City-Wiley Post, OK				
East Central Oklahoma State U	12	2	1	24
Southwest Oklahoma State U	23	2	2	17
	35	**4**	**3**	**41**
RDU=Raleigh/Durham, NC				
East Carolina University	92	2	1	1
St. Paul's College*	102			
	194	**2**	**1**	**1**

Airport 61-80 (0100-2400)

AIRPORT	MINORITY GROUP			
	Black	Hispanic	Asian	Native American
RIC=Richmond, VA				
Hampton Institute*	444			
Norfolk State College*	603			
St. Paul's College*	102			
U of Virginia - Main Campus	68	3	7	
	1217	**3**	**7**	
SAN=San Diego, CA				
Chapman College	78	33	26	12
U of Cal - Irvine	45	33	104	8
U of Cal - Riverside	47	51	28	2
	170	**117**	**158**	**22**
SAT=San Antonio, TX				
Huston-Tillotson College*	67	1		
U of Texas at Austin	103	453	53	12
	170	**454**	**53**	**12**
SAV=Savannah, GA				
Baptist College at Charleston	58			
	58			
SBA=Santa Barbara, CA				
Cal State College - Bakersfield	16	41	10	31
Cal State University - Los Angeles	341	447	422	20
Cal State University - Northridge	110	161	148	68
Loyola Marymount University	54	91	32	2
U of Cal - Los Angeles	186	163	547	17
	707	**903**	**1159**	**138**
SBY=Salisbury, MD				
Delaware State College*	133	1		
	133	**1**		
SFO=San Francisco/Oakland, CA				
Cal State University - Sacramento	129	108	159	33
U of Cal - Davis	50	50	227	15

100

Airport 61-80 (0100-2400)

AIRPORT	MINORITY GROUP			
	Black	Hispanic	Asian	Native American
SFO (cont)				
U of Cal - Santa Cruz		57	17	
University of the Pacific	27	27	76	4
	206	**242**	**479**	**52**
SHV=Shreveport, LA				
Louisiana Tech University	69	2	3	
	69	**2**	**3**	
SWI=Sherman, TX				
U of Texas at Arlington	84	55	17	5
	84	**55**	**17**	**5**
TLH=Tallahassee, FL				
Albany State College*	229		1	
Valdosta State College	49			
	278		**1**	
TPA=Tampa, FL				
University of Central Florida	55	26	15	1
	55	**26**	**15**	**1**
TUL=Tulsa, OK				
Oklahoma State U - Main Campus	45	13	26	40
	45	**13**	**26**	**40**
TYR=Tyler, TX				
East Texas State University	200	42	13	7
	200	**42**	**13**	**7**

TABLE 21

TOTAL (0100-2400)
MINORITY BACCALAUREATE DEGREES
MORE THAN 80 MILES FROM NEAREST AIRPORT

AIRPORT	MINORITY GROUP			
	Black	Hispanic	Asian	Native American
ABQ=Albuquerque, NM				
New Mexico Highlands U*	4	171		5
	4	171		5
AUS=Austin, TX				
Texas A&M U - Main Campus	15	110	17	41
	15	110	17	41
ELP=El Paso, TX				
Sul Ross State University	6	75		
	6	75		
IAH=Houston-Intercontinental, TX				
Texas A&M U - Main Campus	15	110	17	41
	15	110	17	41
MAF=Midland/Odessa, TX				
Sul Ross State University	6	75		
	6	75		
MSY=New Orleans, LA				
U of Southern Mississippi	164	3	8	
	164	3	8	
PWA=Oklahoma City-Wiley Post, OK				
Cameron University	40	12	1	16
	40	12	1	16
ROW=Roswell, NM				
Eastern NM U - Main Campus	24	84	4	15
	24	84	4	15
TCL=Tuscaloosa, AL				
Mississippi State University	175	3	2	2
	175	3	2	2

Institute of Technology, also in Atlanta, and at Georgia State University, which produces baccalaureate degrees at nearly the same numerical levels as the well-known predominantly black institutions. These institutions could be easily overlooked because they are not widely known for producing black baccalaureate degree recipients.

Pool Within 61-80 Mile Annulus of Airport
It should be apparent from Table 18 that not all of the 362 institutions being considered fall within a sixty mile radius of an airport. To account for those institutions that are located beyond sixty miles, minority baccalaureate production is aggregated for those institutions located in the 61-80 mile annulus of each airport (Table 20). These data have similar utility for planning travel itineraries.

Pool With Nearest Airport Beyond Eighty Miles
Even though minority baccalaureate production has been aggregated by sixty mile radii from airports and by the 61-80 mile annuulus around a major airport, there are still nine institutions which are more than eighty miles from the nearest major airport. Data for these institutions are found in Table 21. The information in Tables 18-21 adequately documents bachelor's degree production for each minority group at each institution in proximity to an airport and can be used to effectively plan recruitment trips.

UTILIZATION OF DATA

Now attention is directed to effectively utilizing the pool data available in this volume for recruiting minorities in a more integrated manner. The minority pool data, which has been presented thus far, are in formats that, if properly, conscientiously and creatively used, have the potential to enhance an institution's minority recruitment efforts. To demonstrate the utility of this pool data, a few minority recruitment strategies are outlined for a hypothetical institution, which could be an educational institution or a business or industrial firm.

Prerequisites for Recruitment
Before an institution undertakes a minority recruitment initiative, several preconditions have to exist if the program is to have any reasonable chance for success. First, the institution has to have a written policy relative to minority underrepresentation. This policy has to be clearly articulated, widely publicized, and fully understood throughout the organization, especially by those individuals in the organizational hierarchy who make decisions about who enters the institution. Second, the institution must make more than a verbal commitment to this policy; it must support this program by making the proper level of resource allocation, both in terms of adequate personnel and finances sufficient to support the program logistically.

The commitment must be articulated by the top eschelon of the institution's leadership; namely the president and chief executive and operating officers. These invidivudals are responsible for evaluating how effectively the institutional policy is being carried out. They possess the authority to call those responsible for minority recruitment activities and entry to account for their actions relative to achieving the institution's program goals. It is also obvious that those responsible for operationalizing a recruitment strategy must report directly to the institution's top leadership on a scheduled basis. In other words, recruitment must be centrally initiated, nurtured and monitored. Without such reporting arrangements and high-level commitment to minority recruitment, there is little chance for such a program to achieve and sustain success.

Finally, the institution must have a genuine commitment to its minority recruitment program; not one that is solely motivated and mandated by legislation but one which is based upon the premise that minority participation is considered positive and adds value to the institution. Such participation should enhance the institution's potential to achieve its overall mission, whether it is to seek truth and generate knowledge or to increase productivity. Minorities must be mainstreamed when brought into the institution, and there must also be adequate support given and efforts made to fully assimilate them into the organization's primary activities.

Establishing Program Parameters

Once the institution's commitment to minority recruitment is clearly established, adequately manned and with proper financial support, it is necessary to locate the minority pool within the context of the institution's policy, its capacity to accept minority participation and its need to add diversity to its demographic profile and, more specifically, to bring needed skills and different viewpoints to areas where minority representation is absent.

Table 4 "Total Minority Baccalaureate Degrees by State and Institution" documents 80.2 percent of the nation's minority baccalaureate production by number of degrees conferred by state and institution. By using these data, which are further stratified by minority group, preliminary planning for recruitment can commence. The data are such that the recruiting institution can decide upon the size of the recruitment program it wishes to undertake and whether the strategy should be one that is national, regional or local in coverage.

Refining Parameters

To fine-tune the parameters of the institution's recruitment program and to focus its efforts on a particular minority group, as well as on those institutions where large numbers of that minority group receive their degrees, the data on minority production is rank-ordered by size of each institution's production for each of the minority groups included in the study. From Tables 5 through 8, the institutions are ordered from largest to smallest number of baccalaureate degrees produced for each respective minority group.

If, for example, a recruiting institution chooses to focus its attention on a single minority group at the ten institutions that conferred the largest number of degrees on members of this group, these schools can easily be identified by using the rank-ordered information available on Tables 5 through 8. To illustrate this Single Minority Group Ten School Recruitment Strategy, Hispanic B.A. production is utilized. The top ten institutions in Hispanic baccalaureate production are (1) Pan American University, (2) University of Texas at El Paso, (3) Florida International University, (4) University of Texas at Austin, (5) California State University -Los Angeles, (6) University of New Mexico -Main Campus, (7) Texas A & I University, (8) CUNY City College, (9) University of Miami, Florida and (10) New Mexico State University - Main Campus (Table 6). Together, these ten institutions granted 4,208 Hispanic bachelor's degrees, which is 26.2 percent of the total Hispanic baccalaureate degrees conferred. Therefore, the data on the rank-ordered tables can be used in similar ways for the other minority groups represented. The focus and direction of a recruitment effort can be determined and the parameters of such efforts can be adjusted to specific institutional needs and policies by employing this rank ordered data.

Using Accessibility Data

A regional or national minority recruitment effort will require air travel. Each of the institutions included in this study are listed by distance to the nearest airport, first for institutions within a sixty-mile radius (Table 19), second for those institutions located within the sixty-one to eighy-mile annulus (Table 20) and, third, for those institutions where the distance to the nearest airport is beyond eighty miles (Table 21).

If an institution embarks upon a recruitment plan that directs its attention to those institutions which are the five largest producers of baccalaureate degrees for each minority group (blacks, Hispanics, Asians and Native Americans), Tables 5 through 7 can be used for this determination. As a result of a Five Largest School Recruitment Strategy, nineteen institutions emerge. The institutions selected for this hypothetical recruitment strategy are listed on Table 22.

By locating these institutions on Table 18, which lists each institution with the name of the nearest airport(s), it is possible to determine the appropriate airport for each institution selected thus providing direct access to the minority baccalaureate production at these targeted schools. Since the airport nearest to each institution is known, then Table 19, which reports the total minority baccalaureate degrees within a sixty-mile radius of the airport, can

TABLE 22

INSTITUTIONS SELECTED FOR THE
FIVE LARGEST SCHOOL RECRUITMENT STRATEGY

MINORITY GROUP

Rank	Black	Hispanic	Asian	Native American
1	Southern U*	Pan American U*	U of Hawaii-Manoa*	NE Oklahoma State U
2	Howard U*	U of Texas-El Paso	U of Cal-Berkeley	Lamar U
3	Jackson State U*	Florida Int'l U	U of Cal-LA	Pembroke U
4	Brooklyn C	U of Texas-Austin	SanFrancisco State U	Cal State U-Northridge
5	Wayne State U	Cal State U-LA	Cal State U-LA	U of New Mexico

*predominantly minority institution

Source: Tables 5 through 7

be consulted. This table provides aggregate baccalaureate production by institution and minority group for each airport. It is useful because it provides the recruiting institutions with comprehensive information on the minority pool within the vicinity of the targeted institution, which can be included in recruitment efforts with little additional expenditure of time or money.

If the recruitment carried out under the Five Largest School Recruitment Strategy was restricted only to the nineteen schools meeting the selection criterion, and included all of the baccalaureate degrees conferred to all four minority groups at these schools, then this option has only the potential for contacting 5,302 black, 3,952 Hispanic, 4,723 Asian and 587 Native American bachelor's degree recipients. By including all the schools within the sixty-mile radius of the airports where the targeted schools are located, the number of institutions that the recruiting institution will be exposed to is increased by ninety-five; and the total number of baccalaureate degrees exposed, including those for the target institution, would be 17,919 blacks, 8,899 Hispanics, 8,189 Asians and 1,148 Native Americans, which, when the total for all groups are considered, amounts to a 148 percent increase in potential contacts (Table 23).

With information on the aggregate baccalaureate production within a sixty-mile radius of an airport, it is easy to gain access to a larger pool, many of which receive their degrees at non minority institutions. Specific information on the magnitude of the minority pool is revealed when the tables on airport accessibility are examined in more detail. By using these data a recruiting institution can greatly increase its contacts at marginal costs.

TABLE 23

ADDITIONAL POOL ADDED BY INCLUDING ALL SCHOOLS WITHIN
THE SIXTY-MILE RADIUS OF AN AIRPORT
WHERE TARGETED INSTITUTION IS LOCATED

		MINORITY GROUP			
Institutions	Black	Hispanic	Asian	Native American	Total Minority
Targeted 19	5,302	3,952	4,723	587	14,564
Additional 95	12,617	4,947	3,466	561	21,591
Total 114	17,919	8,899	8,189	1,148	36,155

Source: Table 20

Again, it must be emphasized that each recruitment strategy is individually tailored to the recruiting institution, its size, range of programs available and its needs. It should also be recognized that all institutions where minority baccalaureate degrees are generated will not universally appear on all recruiting institutions' lists. Appendix F, which lists the characteristics of the degree-generating institutions, is particularly valuable in making the final selection of institutions as recruitment sites. By using this appendix, it is possible to stratify institutions by their minority status, type of control, size of institution, environmental setting and class of institution. It is possible, therefore, to restrict recruitment to any subset of institutions desired by the recruiting institutions by using the Carnegie Classification reported for each institution.

The utility of each of the major data tables on the minority pool have been briefly discussed, although the examples used as illustration were based only on the tables which report total minority baccalaureate production. By no means are the examples of how to use these tables exhaustive; they are just single illustrations. There are numerous creative ways to use these data for recruitment which can be adjusted to a specific recruitment strategy.

DISCIPLINARY FIELD SPECIFIC DATA

Many minority recruitment efforts are disciplinary specific. Firms are seeking individuals with engineering or business management degrees as are engineering colleges and graduate schools of business administration. To accomodate these specific needs, data on minority baccalaureate production are available for twenty-four disciplinary areas. All disciplinary divisions are included, except for Law, Library Science, Military Sciences and Theology. The number of degrees generated in these four areas is so small that it would not be reasonable to attempt to discuss them any further. The twenty remaining areas are available in table form, which include (1) minority baccalaureate degrees by state and institution; (2) baccalaureate degrees ranked by institution for each minority group; (3) minority baccalaureate degrees within a sixty-mile radius of an airport; within a 61- to 81-mile annulus from an airport and the nearest airport beyond eighty miles. Since these data are subsets of the total data on minority baccalaureate production and follow the same format already used in this study, it would be redundant to illustrate how to use each of these data sets, because strategies similar to those already illustrated would apply.

Therefore, the major data tables for each of the twenty disciplinary divisions included follows. From each of these data sets, disciplinary specific minority recruitment strategies can be developed. Appendix B lists disciplines in each division.

108

AGRICULTURE & NATURAL RESOURCES (0100)

AGRICULTURE AND NATURAL RESOURCES (0100)
MINORITY BACCALAUREATE DEGREES
BY STATE AND INSTITUTION

STATE/SCHOOL	MINORITY GROUP			
	Black	Hispanic	Asian	Native American
Alabama				
Alabama A&M University*	25			
Tuskegee Institute*	35			
	60			
Arizona				
Arizona State University	2	1	3	1
Northern Arizona University		1		
University of Arizona		4	2	2
	2	**6**	**5**	**3**
Arkansas				
Arkansas State U – Main Campus	1			
University of Arkansas – Pine Bluff*	13			
	14			
California				
Cal Poly State U – San Luis Obispo	5	13	26	13
Cal State Poly U – Pomona	1	9	12	7
Cal State University – Chico		3		1
Cal State University – Fresno	3	13	13	1
U of Cal – Berkeley	7	1	43	2
U of Cal – Davis		6	29	2
U of Cal – Riverside	1			
	17	**45**	**123**	**26**
Colorado				
Colorado State University	1	4	3	1
	1	**4**	**3**	**1**
Connecticut				
University of Connecticut	2	1	1	
	2	**1**	**1**	

110

(0100)

STATE/SCHOOL	MINORITY GROUP			
	Black	Hispanic	Asian	Native American
Delaware				
Delaware State College*	3			
University of Delaware	2	1		
	5	1		
District of Columbia				
University of DC*	7	1		
	7	1		
Florida				
Florida Agr & Mech University*	13		1	
University of Florida	2	8	3	
	15	8	4	
Georgia				
Fort Valley State College*	3			
University of Georgia	4	1		1
	7	1		1
Hawaii				
University of Hawaii at Hilo*		1	20	
University of Hawaii at Manoa*		1	69	
		2	89	
Illinois				
Southern Illinois U – Carbondale		2	1	1
U of Illinois – Urbana Campus	2	1	3	
	2	3	4	1
Indiana				
Purdue University – Main Campus	1	1		1
	1	1		1
Louisiana				
Louisiana State U & A&M College	1	1	1	
Louisiana Tech University	1			
McNeese State University	1			
Northeast Louisiana University	1			

(0100)

STATE/SCHOOL	MINORITY GROUP			
	Black	Hispanic	Asian	Native American
Delaware				
Delaware State College*	3			
University of Delaware	2	1		
	5	**1**		
D.C.				
University of D.C.*	7	1		
	7	**1**		
Florida				
Florida Agr & Mech University*	13		1	
University of Florida	2	8	3	
	15	**8**	**4**	
Georgia				
Fort Valley State College*	3			
University of Georgia	4	1		1
	7	**1**		**1**
Hawaii				
University of Hawaii at Hilo*		1	20	
University of Hawaii at Manoa*		1	69	
		2	**89**	
Illinois				
Southern Illinois U - Carbondale		2	1	1
U of Illinois - Urbana Campus	2	1	3	
	2	**3**	**4**	**1**
Indiana				
Purdue University - Main Campus	1	1		1
	1	**1**		**1**
Louisiana				
Louisiana State U & A&M College	1	1	1	
Louisiana Tech University	1			
McNeese State University	1			
Northeast Louisiana University	1			

(0100)

STATE/SCHOOL	MINORITY GROUP Black	Hispanic	Asian	Native American
Louisiana (cont)				
Sthrn U A&M College - Main Cam*	40			
U of Southwestern Louisiana	3	2		1
	47	**3**	**1**	**1**
Maryland				
U of MD - College Park Campus	1	5	3	3
U of MD - Eastern Shore*	1			
	2	**5**	**3**	**3**
Massachussetts				
U of Mass - Amherst Campus	1	1	6	2
	1	**1**	**6**	**2**
Michigan				
Michigan State University	13	2	4	2
U of Michigan - Ann Arbor	3	3	2	
Western Michigan University		1		
	16	**6**	**6**	**2**
Minnesota				
U of Minn - Minneapolis/St. Paul	2	1	6	2
	2	**1**	**6**	**2**
Mississippi				
Alcorn State University*	13			
Mississippi State University	5		1	
	18		**1**	
Missouri				
Lincoln University	2			
U of Missouri - Columbia	4	1		
	6	**1**		
Montana				
Montana State University	1		1	1
	1		**1**	**1**
New Jersey				
Rutgers U - New Brunswick	3	3		
	3	**3**		

(0100)

STATE/SCHOOL		MINORITY GROUP		
	Black	Hispanic	Asian	Native American
New Mexico				
Eastern NM U - Main Campus		1		
NM State U - Main Campus	2	24	1	3
	2	25	1	3
North Carolina				
NC Agrl & Tech State University*	18			
NC State U - Raleigh	3	2		
	21	2		
Ohio				
Ohio State U - Main Campus			3	1
Ohio University - Main Campus	1			
	1		3	1
Oklahoma				
Cameron University	1			1
Langston University*	4			
Oklahoma State U - Main Campus		1	3	
	5	1	3	1
Oregon				
Oregon State University		1	1	6
		1	1	6
Pennsylvania				
Pennsylvania State U - Main Campus	3	1	1	
	3	1	1	
Tennessee				
Middle Tennessee State U	2		2	
Tennessee State University*	18			
U of Tennessee - Knoxville	3		1	
U of Tennessee - Martin	2	1		
	25	1	3	
Texas				
East Texas State University	1		1	
Lamar University				1

114

STATE/SCHOOL	MINORITY GROUP			
	Black	Hispanic	Asian	Native American
Texas (cont)				
Prairie View A&M University*	5		3	
Sam Houston State University	3			2
Southwest Texas State University		1		
Sul Ross State University	1	3		
Texas A&I University		12		
Texas A&M U – Main Campus	2	19	2	8
	12	35	6	11
Utah				
Brigham Young University – Main				1
				1
Virginia				
Virginia State College*	11			
	11			
Washington				
University of Washington	1	3	6	1
	1	3	6	1
Wisconsin				
U of Wisconsin – Madison	2	3		
	2	3		
TOTALS	312	165	277	68

*Predominately minority institutions are those where at least 50% of the total BA Degrees awarded are to one of the minority groups being considered.

AGRICULTURE AND NATURAL RESOURCES (0100)
BLACK BACCALAUREATE DEGREES RANKED BY INSTITUTION

Rank	Institution	B.A.'s	Rank	Institution	B.A.'s
1	Sthrn U A&M C-Main Campus*	40	6	Alcorn State U*	13
2	Tuskegee Institute*	35	7	Florida Agrl & Mech U*	13
3	Alabama A&M U*	25	8	Michigan State U	13
4	NC Agrl & Tech State U*	18	9	U of Arkansas-Pine Bluff*	13
5	Tennessee State U*	18	10	Virginia State C*	11

*predominantly black institutions

Institutions not ranked have less than ten degrees conferred on blacks.

AGRICULTURE & NATURAL RESOURCES (0100)
HISPANIC BACCALAUREATE DEGREES RANKED BY INSTITUTION

Rank	Institution	B.A.'s	Rank	Institution	B.A.'s
1	NM State U-Main Campus	24	4	Cal State U-Fresno	13
2	Texas A&M U-Main Campus	19	5	Texas A&I U	12
3	Cal Poly State-San Luis Obispo	13			

Institutions not ranked have less than ten degrees conferred on Hispanics.

AGRICULTURE & NATURAL RESOURCES (0100)
ASIAN BACCALAUREATE DEGREES RANKED BY INSTITUTION

Rank	Institution	B.A.'s	Rank	Institution	B.A.'s
1	U of Hawaii at Manoa*	69	5	U of Hawaii at Hilo*	20
2	U of Cal-Berkeley	43	6	Cal State U-Fresno	12
3	U of Cal-Davis	29	7	Cal State Poly U-Pomona	12
4	Cal Poly State-San Luis Obispo	26			

*predominantly Asian institutions

Institutions not ranked have less than ten degrees conferred on Asians.

AGRICULTURE & NATURAL RESOURCES (0100)
NATIVE AMERICAN BACCALAUREATE DEGREES RANKED BY INSTITUTION

Rank	Institution	B.A.'s	Rank	Institution	B.A.'s
1	Cal Poly State-San Luis Obispo	13	3	Cal State Poly U-Pomona	7
2	Texas A&M U-Main Campus	8	4	Oregon State U	6

Institutions not ranked have less than five degrees conferred on Native Americans.

AGRICULTURE AND NATURAL RESOURCES (0100)
MINORITY BACCALAUREATE DEGREES
WITHIN 60 MILE RADIUS OF AIRPORT

AIRPORT	MINORITY GROUP			
	Black	Hispanic	Asian	Native American
AOO=Altoona, PA				
Pennsylvania State U – Main Campus	3	1	1	
	3	**1**	**1**	
AUS=Austin, TX				
Southwest Texas State University		1		
		1		
BAL=Baltimore, MD				
University of Delaware	2	1		
University of DC*	7	1		
U of MD – College Park Campus	1	5	3	3
	10	**7**	**3**	**3**
BDL=Hartford, CT/Springfield, MA				
U of Mass – Amherst Campus	1	1	6	2
	1	**1**	**6**	**2**
BNA=Nashville, TN				
Middle Tennessee State U	2		2	
Tennessee State University*	18			
	20		**2**	
BTR=Baton Rouge, LA				
Louisiana State U & A&M College	1	1	1	
Sthrn U A&M College – Main Cam*	40			
	41	**1**	**1**	
CIC=Chico, CA				
Cal State University – Chico		3		1
		3		**1**

118

Airport 60 (0100)

AIRPORT	MINORITY GROUP			
	Black	Hispanic	Asian	Native American
CMH=Columbus, OH				
Ohio State U - Main Campus	1		3	1
	1		3	1
CMI=Champaign, IL				
U of Illinois - Urbana Campus	2	1	3	
	2	1	3	
COU=Columbia, MO				
Lincoln University	2			
U of Missouri - Columbia	4	1		
	6	1		
CRP=Corpus Christi, TX				
Texas A&I University		12		
		12		
DCA=Washington-National, DC				
University of DC*	7	1		
U of MD - College Park Campus	1	5	3	3
	8	6	3	3
DFW=Dallas/Fort Worth, TX				
East Texas State University	1		1	
	1		1	
DTW=Detroit-Metropolitan, MI				
U of Michigan - Ann Arbor	3	3	2	
	3	3	2	
EUG=Eugene, OR				
Oregon State University		1	1	6
		1	1	6
FAT=Fresno, CA				
Cal State University - Fresno	3	13	13	1
	3	13	13	1

Airport 60 (0100)

AIRPORT	MINORITY GROUP			
	Black	Hispanic	Asian	Native American
FAY=Fayetteville, NC				
NC State U - Raleigh	3	2		
	3	2		
FLG=Flagstaff, AZ				
Northern Arizona University		1		
		1		
GRR=Grand Rapids, MI				
Western Michigan University		1		
		1		
GSO=Greensboro/High Point, NC				
NC Agrl & Tech State University*	18			
	18			
HNL=Honolulu, Oahu, HI				
University of Hawaii at Manoa*		1	69	
		1	69	
HSV=Huntsville, AL/Decatur, GA				
Alabama A&M University*	25			
	25			
IAH=Houston–Intercontinental, TX				
Prairie View A&M University*	5		3	
	5		3	
IND=Indianapolis, IN				
Purdue University - Main Campus	1	1		1
	1	1		1
ITO=Hilo, HI				
University of Hawaii at Hilo*		1	20	
		1	20	
JAN=Jackson/Vicksburg, MS				
Alcorn State University*	13			
	13			
JFK=New York, Kennedy Int'l, NY				
Rutgers U - New Brunswick	3	3		
	3	3		

Airport 60 (0100)

AIRPORT	MINORITY GROUP			
	Black	Hispanic	Asian	Native American
LAX=Los Angeles, CA				
Cal State Poly U - Pomona	1	9	12	7
U of Cal - Riverside	1			
	2	9	12	7
LCH=Lake Charles, LA				
McNeese State University	1			
	1			
LIT=Little Rock, AR				
University of Arkansas - Pine Bluff*	13			
	13			
MCN=Macon, GA				
Fort Valley State College*	3			
	3			
MDH=Carbondale, IL				
Southern Illinois U - Carbondale		2	1	1
		2	1	1
MGM=Montgomery, GA				
Tuskegee Institute*	35			
	35			
MKL=Jackson, TN				
U of Tennessee at Martin	2	1		
	2	1		
MLU=Monroe, LA				
Louisiana Tech University	1			
Northeast Louisiana University	1			
	2			
MSN=Madison, WS				
U of Wisconsin - Madison	2	3		
	2	3		
MSP=Minneapolis/St. Paul, MN				
U of Minn - Minneapolis/St. Paul	2	1	6	2
	2	1	6	2

Airport 60 (0100)

AIRPORT	MINORITY GROUP			
	Black	Hispanic	Asian	Native American
PHL=Philadelphia, PA/Wilmington, DE				
Delaware State College*	3			
University of Delaware	2	1		
Rutgers U - New Brunswick	3	3		
	8	**4**		
PHX=Phoenix, AZ				
Arizona State University	2	1	3	1
	2	**1**	**3**	**1**
PWA=Oklahoma City-Wiley Post, OK				
Langston University*	4			
Oklahoma State U - Main Campus		1	3	
	4	**1**	**3**	
RDU=Raleigh/Durham, NC				
NC Agrl & Tech State University*	18			
NC State U - Raleigh	3	2		
	21	**2**		
RIC=Richmond, VA				
Virginia State College*	11			
	11			
SAT=San Antonio, TX				
Southwest Texas State University		1		
		1		
SBP=San Luis Obispo, CA				
Cal Poly State U - San Luis Obispo	5	13	26	13
	5	**13**	**26**	**13**
SBY=Salisbury, MD				
U of MD - Eastern Shore*	1			
	1			
SEA=Seattle/Tacoma, WA				
University of Washington	1	3	6	1
	1	**3**	**6**	**1**

Airport 60 (0100)

AIRPORT	MINORITY GROUP			
	Black	Hispanic	Asian	Native American
SFO=San Francisco/Oakland, CA				
U of Cal – Berkeley	7	1	43	2
	7	1	43	2
SLC=Salt Lake City, UT				
Brigham Young University – Main				1
				1
SWI=Sherman, TX				
East Texas State University	1		1	
	1		1	
TLH=Tallahassee, FL				
Florida Agr & Mech University*	13		1	
	13		1	
TUS=Tucson, AZ				
University of Arizona		4	2	2
		4	2	2
TYS=Knoxville, TN				
U of Tennessee – Knoxville	3		1	
	3		1	

AGRICULTURE AND NATURAL RESOURCES (0100)
MINORITY BACCALAUREATE DEGREES
WITHIN 61-80 MILE ANNULUS OF AIRPORT

AIRPORT	MINORITY GROUP			
	Black	Hispanic	Asian	Native American
ALB=Albany, NY				
U of Mass - Amherst Campus	1	1	6	2
	1	**1**	**6**	**2**
ALM=Alamogordo, NM				
NM State U - Main Campus	2	24	1	3
	2	**24**	**1**	**3**
ATL=Atlanta, GA				
University of Georgia	4	1		1
	4	**1**		**1**
BAL=Baltimore, MD				
Delaware State College*	3			
	3			
BOS=Boston, MA				
U of Mass - Amherst Campus	1	1	6	2
	1	**1**	**6**	**2**
BTM=Butte, MT				
Montana State University	1		1	1
	1		**1**	**1**
BTR=Baton Rouge, LA				
U of Southwestern Louisiana	3	2		1
	3	**2**		**1**
CMI=Champaign, IL				
Purdue University - Main Campus	1	1		1
	1	**1**		**1**
DEN=Denver, CO				
Colorado State University	1	4	3	1
	1	**4**	**3**	**1**

124

Airport 61-80 (0100)

AIRPORT	MINORITY GROUP			
	Black	Hispanic	Asian	Native American
DTW=Detroit-Metropolitan, MI				
Michigan State University	13	2	4	2
	13	2	4	2
GRR=Grand Rapids, MI				
Michigan State University	13	2	4	2
	13	2	4	2
GSO=Greensboro/High Point, NC				
NC State U - Raleigh	3	2		
	3	2		
HSV=Huntsville, AL/Decatur, GA				
Middle Tennessee State U	2		2	
	2		2	
IAH=Houston-Intercontinental,TX				
Sam Houston State University	3			2
	3			2
JAX=Jacksonville, FL				
University of Florida	2	8	3	
	2	8	3	
LCH=Lake Charles, LA				
U of Southwestern Louisiana	3	2		1
	3	2		1
MEM=Memphis, TN				
Arkansas State U - Main Campus	1			
	1			
MHT=Manchester, NH				
U of Mass - Amherst Campus	1	1	6	2
	1	1	6	2
MKE=Milwaukee, WS				
U of Wisconsin - Madison	2	3		
	2	3		

Airport 61-80 (0100)

AIRPORT	MINORITY GROUP			
	Black	Hispanic	Asian	Native American
MLU=Monroe, LA				
Alcorn State University*	13			
	13			
MSY=New Orleans, LA				
Louisiana State U & A&M College	1	1	1	
Sthrn U A&M C – Main Cam*	40			
	41	1	1	
ORF=Norfolk/Virginia Beach, VA				
Virginia State College*	11			
	11			
PVD=Providence, RI				
U of Mass – Amherst Campus	1	1	6	2
	1	1	6	2
SAN=San Diego, CA				
U of Cal – Riverside	1			
	1			
SBY=Salisbury, MD				
Delaware State College*	3			
	3			
SFO=San Francisco/Oakland, CA				
U of Cal – Davis		6	29	2
		6	29	2
SHV=Shreveport, LA				
Louisiana Tech University	1			
	1			
TUL=Tulsa, OK				
Oklahoma State U – Main Campus		1	3	
		1	3	
TYR=Tyler, TX				
East Texas State University	1		1	
	1		1	

126

AGRICULTURE AND NATURAL RESOURCES (0100)
MINORITY BACCALAUREATE DEGREES
MORE THAN 80 MILES FROM NEAREST AIRPORT

AIRPORT	MINORITY GROUP			
	Black	Hispanic	Asian	Native American
AUS=Austin, TX				
Texas A&M U - Main Campus	2	19	2	8
	2	19	2	8
ELP=El Paso, TX				
Sul Ross State University	1	3		
	1	3		
IAH=Houston–Intercontinental, TX				
Texas A&M U - Main Campus	2	19	2	8
	2	19	2	8
MAF=Midland/Odessa, TX				
Sul Ross State University	1	3		
	1	3		
PWA=Oklahoma City–Wiley Post, OK				
Cameron University	1			1
	1			1
ROW=Roswell, NM				
Eastern NM U - Main Campus		1		
		1		
TCL=Tuscaloosa, AL				
Mississippi State University	5		1	
	5		1	

ARCHITECTURE & ENVIRONMENTAL DESIGN (0200)

ARCHITECTURE AND ENVIRONMENTAL DESIGN (0200)
MINORITY BACCALAUREATE DEGREES
BY STATE AND INSTITUTION

STATE/SCHOOL	MINORITY GROUP			
	Black	Hispanic	Asian	Native American
Alabama				
Tuskegee Institute*	10			
	10			
Arizona				
Arizona State University		1		
University of Arizona	3	9		
	3	10		
California				
Cal Poly State U – San Luis Obispo	4	4	15	2
Cal State Poly U – Pomona	3	8	17	3
San Jose State University			4	
U of Cal – Berkeley	9	6	31	
U of Cal – Davis	1		3	2
University of Southern California		6	4	1
	17	24	74	8
Colorado				
Metropolitan State College		1		
U of Colorado at Boulder	2		2	
	2	1	2	
Connecticut				
Yale University	2	1	3	
	2	1	3	
District of Columbia				
Howard University*	24			
University of DC*	4			
	28			

(0200)

STATE/SCHOOL	MINORITY GROUP			
	Black	Hispanic	Asian	Native American
Florida				
Florida Agr & Mech University*	3	1	1	
Florida International University	3	17	6	
Florida State University		1	1	
University of Florida	4	18	3	
University of Miami	2	24	4	
	12	**61**	**15**	
Georgia				
GA Inst of Tech - Main Campus	3	4	1	
	3	**4**	**1**	
Hawaii				
University of Hawaii at Manoa*			16	
			16	
Illinois				
Columbia College		2		
Northeastern Illinois University		3		
Roosevelt University	2			
Southern Illinois U - Carbondale	2			
U of Illinois - Chicago Circle	2	1	1	3
U of Illinois - Urbana Campus	3	2	3	
	9	**8**	**4**	**3**
Indiana				
Ball State University	1			
	1			
Kentucky				
Eastern Kentucky University	1			
Western Kentucky University	2			
	3			
Louisiana				
Louisiana State U & A&M College	1	1		
Louisiana Tech University	2			
Sthrn U A&M College - Main Campus*	15			

130

(0200)

STATE/SCHOOL

	MINORITY GROUP			
	Black	Hispanic	Asian	Native American
Louisiana (cont)				
Tulane U of Louisiana		2		
U of Southwestern Louisiana	1	3		
	19	**6**		
Maryland				
U of MD – College Park Campus		1		
		1		
Michigan				
Michigan State University	1		1	
University of Detroit	1	1	1	
U of Michigan – Ann Arbor	5		3	
	7	**1**	**5**	
Minnesota				
U of Minn – Minneapolis/St. Paul	1		5	1
	1		**5**	**1**
Mississippi				
Mississippi State University		1		
U of Southern Mississippi	1			
	1	**1**		
Missouri				
Washington University	1	1	2	
	1	**1**	**2**	
Nebraska				
U of Nebraska at Omaha	1			
	1			
New Jersey				
New Jersey Inst Technology	6	2		
Princeton University	1	1	2	1
Rutgers U – New Brunswick	1	1	1	
	8	**4**	**3**	**1**
New Mexico				
U of NM – Main Campus		7		
		7		

(0200)

STATE/SCHOOL	MINORITY GROUP			
	Black	Hispanic	Asian	Native American
New York				
Cornell U Endowed College	3	1	5	1
CUNY City College	45	22	15	1
Pratt Institute	9	8	6	
SUNY at Buffalo - Main Campus	1		1	
SUNY at Stony Bk - Main Campus			1	
SUNY College at Buffalo				2
Syracuse University - Main Campus	3		4	
	61	**31**	**32**	**4**
North Carolina				
East Carolina University	2			
NC State U - Raleigh		1		
Shaw University*	2			
U of NC at Charlotte		1		
	4	**2**		
Ohio				
Antioch University		1	1	1
Kent State U - Main Campus	3	1		
Ohio State U - Main Campus	2		1	
U of Cincinnati - Main Campus	4		2	
	9	**2**	**4**	**1**
Oklahoma				
Oklahoma State U - Main Campus			1	
U of Oklahoma - Norman Campus		1	2	1
		1	**3**	**1**
Oregon				
University of Oregon - Main Campus	1	3	2	
	1	**3**	**2**	
Pennsylvania				
Pennsylvania State U - Main Campus	3			
University of Pennsylvania	4		3	
	7		**3**	

132

(0200)

STATE/SCHOOL	MINORITY GROUP			
	Black	Hispanic	Asian	Native American
South Carolina				
Winthrop College	1			
	1			
Tennessee				
Middle Tennessee State U	2			
U of Tennessee – Knoxville		1	3	
	2	1	3	
Texas				
Incarnate Word College		2		
Prairie View A&M University*	17			
Texas A&M U – Main Campus		10		3
Trinity University		4		
U of Houston – Central Campus	5	3	3	
U of Texas at Arlington	1	4		
U of Texas at Austin	1	13	1	
	24	36	4	3
Utah				
Brigham Young University – Main			1	1
			1	1
Virginia				
Hampton Institute*	7			
U of Virginia – Main Campus			2	
	7		2	
Washington				
University of Washington	3	1	12	
	3	1	12	
Wisconsin				
U of Wisconsin – Madison	1			
	1			
TOTALS	**250**	**207**	**196**	**23**

Predominately minority institutions are those where at least 50% of total BA Degrees awarded are to one of the minority groups being considered.

ARCHITECTURE AND ENVIRONMENTAL DESIGN (0200)
BLACK BACCALAUREATE DEGREES RANKED BY INSTITUTION

Rank	Institution	B.A.'s	Rank	Institution	B.A.'s
1	CUNY City C	45	4	Sthrn U A&M C-Main Campus*	15
2	Howard U*	24	5	Tuskegee Institute*	10
3	Prairie View A&M U*	17			

*predominantly black institutions

Institutions not ranked have less than ten degrees conferred on blacks.

ARCHITECTURE & ENVIRONMENTAL DESIGN (0200)
HISPANIC BACCALAUREATE DEGREES RANKED BY INSTITUTION

Rank	Institution	B.A.'s	Rank	Institution	B.A.'s
1	U of Miami	24	4	Florida International U	17
2	CUNY City C	22	5	U of Texas at Austin	13
3	U of Florida	18	6	Texas A&M U-Main Campus	10

Institutions not ranked have less than ten degreees conferred on Hispanics.

ARCHITECTURE & ENVIRONMENTAL DESIGN (0200)
ASIAN BACCALAUREATE DEGREES RANKED BY INSTITUTION

Rank	Institution	B.A.'s	Rank	Institution	B.A.'s
1	U of Cal-Berkeley	31	4	CUNY City C	15
2	Cal State Poly U-Pomona	17	5	Cal Poly State-San Luis Obispo	15
3	U of Hawaii at Manoa*	16	6	U of Washington	12

*predominantly Asian institutions

Institutions not ranked have less than ten degrees conferred on Asians.

ARCHITECTURE AND ENVIRONMENTAL DESIGN (0200)
MINORITY BACCALAUREATE DEGREES
WITHIN 60 MILE RADIUS OF AIRPORT

AIRPORT	MINORITY GROUP			
	Black	Hispanic	Asian	Native American
ABQ=Albuquerque, NM				
U of NM - Main Campus		7		
		7		
AOO=Altoona, PA				
Pennsylvania State U - Main Campus	3			
	3			
ATL=Atlanta, GA				
GA Inst of Tech - Main Campus	3	4	1	
	3	**4**	**1**	
AUS=Austin, TX				
U of Texas at Austin	1	13	1	
	1	**13**	**1**	
BAL=Baltimore, MD				
Howard University*	24			
University of DC*	4			
U of MD - College Park Campus		1		
	28	**1**		
BDL=Hartford, CT/Springfield, MA				
Yale University	2	1	3	
	2	**1**	**3**	
BKL=Cleveland-Lakefront, OH				
Kent State U - Main Campus	3	1		
	3	**1**		
BNA=Nashville, TN				
Western Kentucky University	2			
Middle Tennessee State U	2			
	4			

Airport 60 (0200)

AIRPORT	MINORITY GROUP			
	Black	Hispanic	Asian	Native American
BTR=Baton Rouge, LA				
Louisiana State U & A&M College	1	1		
Sthrn U A&M College - Main Cam*	15			
	16	**1**		
BUF=Buffalo, NY				
SUNY at Buffalo - Main Campus	1		1	
	1		**1**	
CLT=Charlotte, NC				
U of NC at Charlotte		1		
Winthrop College	1			
	1	**1**		
CMH=Columbus, OH				
Ohio State U - Main Campus	2		1	
	2		**1**	
CMI=Champaign, IL				
U of Illinois - Urbana Campus	3	2	3	
	3	**2**	**3**	
CVG=Cincinnati, OH				
Antioch University		1	1	1
U of Cincinnati - Main Campus	4		2	
	4	**1**	**3**	**1**
DCA=Washington-National, DC				
Howard University*	24			
University of DC*	4			
U of MD - College Park Campus		1		
	28	**1**		
DEN=Denver, CO				
Metropolitan State College		1		
U of Colorado at Boulder	2		2	
	2	**1**	**2**	

Airport 60 (0200)

AIRPORT	MINORITY GROUP			
	Black	Hispanic	Asian	Native American
DFW=Dallas/Fort Worth, TX				
U of Texas at Arlington	1	4		1
	1	**4**		**1**
DTW=Detroit-Metropolitan, MI				
U of Michigan - Ann Arbor	5		3	
University of Detroit	1	1	1	
	6	**1**	**4**	
EUG=Eugene, OR				
University of Oregon - Main Campus	1	3	2	
	1	**3**	**2**	
FAY=Fayetteville, NC				
NC State U - Raleigh		1		
Shaw University*	2			
	2	**1**		
HNL=Honolulu/Oahu, HI				
U of Hawaii at Manoa*			16	
			16	
IAH=Houston-Intercontinental,TX				
Prairie View A&M University*	17			
U of Houston - Central Campus	5	3	3	
	22	**3**	**3**	
IND=Indianapolis, IN				
Ball State University	1			
	1			
JFK=New York, Kennedy Int'l, NY				
New Jersey Inst of Technology	6	2		
Princeton University	1	1	2	1
Rutgers U - New Brunswick	1	1	1	
CUNY City College	45	22	15	1
Pratt Institute	9	8	6	
SUNY at Stony Bk - Main Campus			1	
	62	**34**	**25**	**2**

Airport 60 (0200)

AIRPORT	MINORITY GROUP			
	Black	Hispanic	Asian	Native American
LAX=Los Angeles, CA				
Cal State Poly U – Pomona	3	8	17	3
University of Southern California	2	6	4	1
	5	**14**	**21**	**4**
LEX=Lexington/Frankfort, KY				
Eastern Kentucky University	1			
	1			
MDH=Carbondale, IL				
Southern Illinois U – Carbondale	2			
	2			
MGM=Montgomery, GA				
Tuskegee Institute*	10			
	10			
MIA=Miami, FL				
Florida International University	3	17	6	
University of Miami	2	24	4	
	5	**41**	**10**	
MKE=Milwaukee, WS				
U of Wisconsin – Milwaukee		1		
		1		
MLU=Monroe, LA				
Louisiana Tech University	2			
	2			
MSN=Madison, WS				
U of Wisconsin – Madison	1			
	1			
MSP=Minneapolis/St. Paul, MN				
U of Minn – Minneapolis/St. Paul	1		5	1
	1		**5**	**1**
MSY=New Orleans, LA				
Tulane U of Louisiana		2		
		2		

138

Airport 60 (0200)

AIRPORT	MINORITY GROUP			
	Black	Hispanic	Asian	Native American
ORD=Chicago-O'Hare Airport, IL				
Columbia College		2		
Northeastern Illinois University		3		
Roosevelt University	2			
U of Illinois - Chicago Circle	2	1	1	3
	4	**6**	**1**	**3**
ORF=Norfolk/Virginia Beach, VA				
Hampton Institute*	7			
	7			
PHL=Philadelphia, PA/Wilmington, DE				
Princeton University	1	1	2	1
Rutgers U - New Brunswick	1	1	1	
University of Pennsylvania	4		3	
	6	**2**	**6**	**1**
PHX=Phoenix, AZ				
Arizona State University		1		
		1		
PWA=Oklahoma City-Wiley Post, OK				
Oklahoma State U - Main Campus			1	
U of Oklahoma - Norman Campus		1	2	1
		1	**3**	**1**
RDU=Raleigh/Durham, NC				
NC State U - Raleigh		1		
Shaw University*	2			
	2	**1**		
SAT=San Antonio, TX				
Incarnate Word College		2		
Trinity University		4		
		6		
SBP=San Luis Obispo, CA				
Cal Poly State U - San Luis Obispo	4	4	15	2
	4	**4**	**15**	**2**

Airport 60 (0200)

AIRPORT	MINORITY GROUP			
	Black	Hispanic	Asian	Native American
SEA=Seattle/Tacoma, WA				
University of Washington	3	1	12	
	3	1	12	
SFO=San Francisco/Oakland, CA				
San Jose State University			4	
U of Cal - Berkeley	9	6	31	
	9	6	35	
SLC=Salt Lake City, UT				
Brigham Young University - Main			1	1
			1	1
STL=St. Louis, MO				
Washington University	1	1	2	
	1	1	2	
SYR=Syracuse, NY				
Cornel U Endowed College	3	1	5	1
Syracuse U - Main Campus	3		4	
	6	1	9	1
TLH=Tallahassee, FL				
Florida Agr & Mech University*	3	1	1	
Florida State University		1	1	
	3	2	2	
TUS=Tucson, AZ				
University of Arizona	3	9		
	3	9		
TYS=Knoxville, TN				
U of Tennessee - Knoxville		1	3	
		1	3	

ARCHITECTURE AND ENVIRONMENTAL DESIGN (0200)
MINORITY BACCALAUREATE DEGREES
WITHIN 61-80 MILE ANNULUS OF AIRPORT

AIRPORT	MINORITY GROUP			
	Black	Hispanic	Asian	Native American
AUS=Austin, TX				
Incarnate Word College		2		
Trinity University		4		
		6		
BTR=Baton Rouge, LA				
Tulane U of Louisiana		2		
U of Southwestern Louisiana	1	3		
	1	**5**		
CAE=Columbia, SC				
Winthrop College	1			
	1			
CMH=Columbus, OH				
Antioch University		1	1	1
		1	**1**	**1**
COS=Colorado Springs, CO				
Metropolitan State College		1		
U of Colorado at Boulder	2		2	
	2	**1**	**2**	
DTW=Detroit-Metropolitan, MI				
Michigan State University	1		1	
	1		**1**	
GRR=Grand Rapids, MI				
Michigan State University	1		1	
	1		**1**	
GSO=Greensboro/High Point, NC				
NC State U - Raleigh		1		
Shaw University*	2			
	2	**1**		

Airport 61-80 (0200)

AIRPORT	MINORITY GROUP			
	Black	Hispanic	Asian	Native American
HSV=Huntsville, AL/Decatur, GA				
Middle Tennessee State U	2			
	2			
JAX=Jacksonville, FL				
University of Florida	4	18	3	
	4	18	3	
JFK=New York, Kennedy Int'l, NY				
Yale University	2	1	3	
	2	1	3	
LCH=Lake Charles, LA				
U of Southwestern Louisiana	1	3		
	1	3		
MCN=Macon, GA				
GA Inst of Tech - Main Campus	3	4	1	
	3	4	1	
MKE=Milwaukee, WS				
U of Wisconsin - Madison	1			
	1			
MOB=Mobile, AL/Pasagoula, MS				
U of Southern Mississippi	1			
	1			
MSN=Madison, WS				
U of Wisconsin - Milwaukee		1		
		1		
MSY=New Orleans, LA				
Louisiana State U & A&M College	1	1		
Sthrn U A&M C - Main Cam*	15			
	16	1		
RDU=Raleigh/Durham, NC				
East Carolina University	2			
	2			

142

Airport 61-80 (0200)

AIRPORT	MINORITY GROUP			
	Black	Hispanic	Asian	Native American
RIC=Richmond, VA				
Hampton Institute*	7			
U of Virginia - Main Campus			2	
	7		2	
SAT=San Antonio, TX				
U of Texas at Austin	1	13	1	
	1	13	1	
SFO=San Francisco/Oakland, CA				
U of Cal - Davis	1		3	2
	1		3	2
SHV=Shreveport, LA				
Louisiana Tech University	2			
	2			
SWI=Sherman, TX				
U of Texas at Arlington	1	4		1
	1	4		1
TUL=Tulsa, OK				
Oklahoma State U - Main Campus			1	
			1	

ARCHITECTURE AND ENVIRONMENTAL DESIGN (0200)
MINORITY BACCALAUREATE DEGREES
MORE THAN 80 MILES FROM NEAREST AIRPORT

AIRPORT	Black	Hispanic	Asian	Native American
AUS=Austin, TX				
Texas A&M U - Main Campus		10		3
		10		**3**
IAH=Houston-Intercontinental, TX				
Texas A&M U - Main Campus		10		3
		10		**3**
MSY=New Orleans, LA				
U of Southern Mississippi	1			
	1			
TCL=Tuscaloosa, AL				
Mississippi State University		1		
		1		

(MINORITY GROUP)

144

AREA STUDIES (0300)

AREA STUDIES (0300)
MINORITY BACCALAUREATE DEGREES
BY STATE AND INSTITUTION

STATE/SCHOOL	MINORITY GROUP			
	Black	Hispanic	Asian	Native American
Alabama				
University of Alabama	2			
	2			
Arizona				
University of Arizona		2		
		2		
California				
Cal State University – Fullerton		4		1
Cal State University – Los Angeles	5	7	1	
San Diego State University	1	2		
San Francisco State University			1	
Stanford University		1	1	
U of Cal – Berkeley			4	
U of Cal – Davis			1	
U of Cal – Los Angeles	1	1	2	
U of Cal – Santa Barbara			1	
U of Cal – Santa Cruz		2		
University of the Pacific		2	4	
	7	19	15	1
Colorado				
U of Colorado at Boulder		2	1	
		2	1	
Connecticut				
Yale University	3	1	3	
	3	1	3	

146

(0300)

STATE/SCHOOL	MINORITY GROUP			
	Black	Hispanic	Asian	Native American
District of Columbia				
American University	2	1		
George Washington University	3			
Howard University*	1			
	6	1		
Florida				
Florida State University			1	
University of Florida	1			
University of Miami		2		
University of South Florida		1		
	1	3	1	
Hawaii				
University of Hawaii at Manoa*			24	
			24	
Illinois				
Roosevelt University	2			
U of Illinois - Chicago Circle	1	1		
U of Illinois - Urbana Campus			1	
	3	1	1	
Louisiana				
Tulane U of Louisiana		4		
		4		
Maryland				
U of MD - Baltimore Co Campus	1			
	1			
Massachussetts				
Harvard University	1	1	4	
Radcliffe College	1	1	2	
	2	2	6	
Michigan				
U of Michigan - Ann Arbor	2			
	2			

(0300)

STATE/SCHOOL	MINORITY GROUP			
	Black	Hispanic	Asian	Native American
Minnesota				
U of Minn – Minneapolis/St. Paul	1		1	1
	1		**1**	**1**
New Hampshire				
Dartmouth College	1			
	1			
New Jersey				
Princeton University	1			
Seton Hall University			2	
	1		**2**	
New York				
Adelphi University		1		
Cornell U Endowed College		1		
CUNY Brooklyn College	5	2		
CUNY City College	7	4	3	
CUNY College of Staten Island	1			
CUNY Hunter College	1	1		
CUNY Lehman College	4	6	1	
CUNY Queen's College	2			
Fordham University		1		
New York University			1	
St. John's University			1	
SUNY at Albany		1		
SUNY at Buffalo – Main Campus	1	2	1	
SUNY College – Old Westbury	4	3		
Syracuse University – Main Campus	1			
	26	**22**	**7**	
Ohio				
Antioch University			1	
Oberlin College			3	
			4	

148

(0300)

STATE/SCHOOL	MINORITY GROUP			
	Black	Hispanic	Asian	Native American
Pennsylvania				
Pennsylvania State U – Main Campus	1			
Temple University	2			
University of Pennsylvania	2		1	
	5		1	
Rhode Island				
Brown University	1			
	1			
Tennessee				
U of Tennessee – Knoxville	1			
	1			
Texas				
Pan American University*		2		
St. Edward's University		1		
St. Mary's U – San Antonio		1		
U of Texas at Austin	1	7		
U of Texas at El Paso		1		
	1	12		
Utah				
University of Utah		1		
		1		
Washington				
University of Washington			6	
			6	
TOTALS	**64**	**70**	**72**	**2**

*Predominately minority institutions are those where at least 50% of the total BA
Degrees awarded are to one of the minority groups being considered.

AREA STUDIES (0300)
ASIAN BACCALAUREATE DEGREES RANKED BY INSTITUTION

Rank	Institution	B.A.'s
1	U of Hawaii at Manoa*	24

*predominantly Asian institutions

Institutions not ranked have less than ten degrees conferred on Asians.

150

AREA STUDIES (0300)
MINORITY BACCALAUREATE DEGREES
WITHIN 60 MILE RADIUS OF AIRPORT

AIRPORT	MINORITY GROUP			
	Black	Hispanic	Asian	Native American
ALB=Albany, NY				
SUNY at Albany		1		1
		1		1
AOO=Altoona, PA				
Pennsylvania State U – Main Campus	1			
	1			
AUS=Austin, TX				
U of Texas at Austin	1	7		
	1	7		
BAL=Baltimore, MD				
American University	2	1		
George Washington Univesity	3			
Howard University*	1			
U of MD – Baltimore Co Campus	1			
	7	1		
BDL=Hartford, CT/Springfield, MA				
Yale University	3	1	3	
	3	1	3	
BHM=Birmingham, AL				
University of Alabama	2			
	2			
BKL=Cleveland-Lakefront, OH				
Oberlin College			3	
			3	
BOS=Boston, MA				
Harvard University	1	1	4	
Radcliffe College	1	1	2	
Brown University	1			
	3	2	6	

Airport 60 (0300)

AIRPORT	MINORITY GROUP			
	Black	Hispanic	Asian	Native American
BUF=Buffalo, NY				
SUNY at Buffalo - Main Campus	1	2	1	2
	1	2	1	2
CMI=Champaign, IL				
U of Illinois - Urbana Campus			1	
			1	
CVG=Cincinnati, OH				
Antioch University			1	
			1	
DCA=Washington-National, DC				
American University	2	1		
George Washington University	3			
Howard University*	1			
U of MD - Baltimore Co Campus	1			
	7	1		
DEN=Denver, CO				
U of Colorado at Boulder		2	1	
		2	1	
DTW=Detroit-Metropolitan, MI				
U of Michigan - Ann Arbor	2			
	2			
ELP=El Paso, TX				
U of Texas at El Paso		1		
		1		
HNL=Honolulu/Oahu, HI				
University of Hawaii at Manoa*			24	
			24	
JFK=New York, Kennedy Int'l, NY				
Princeton University	1			
Seton Hall University			2	
Adelphi University		1		
CUNY Brooklyn College	5	2		

152

Airport 60 (0300)

AIRPORT	MINORITY GROUP			
	Black	Hispanic	Asian	Native American
JFK (cont)				
CUNY College of Staten Island	1			
CUNY City College	7	4	3	
CUNY Hunter College	1	1		
CUNY Lehman College	4	6	1	
CUNY Queen's College	2			
Fordham University		1		
New York University			1	
St. John's University			1	
SUNY College - Old Westbury	4	3		
	25	18	8	
LAX=Los Angeles, CA				
Cal State University - Fullerton		4		1
Cal State U - Los Angeles	5	7	1	
U of Cal - Los Angeles	1	1	2	
	6	12	3	1
MFE=McAllen, TX				
Pan American University*		2		
		2		
MHT=Manchester, NH				
Harvard University	1	1	4	
Radcliffe College	1	1	2	
Dartmouth College	1			
	3	2	6	
MIA=Miami, FL				
University of Miami		2		
		2		
MSP=Minneapolis/St. Paul, MN				
U of Minn - Minneapolis/St. Paul	1		1	1
	1		1	1

Airport 60 (0300)

AIRPORT		MINORITY GROUP		
	Black	Hispanic	Asian	Native American
MSY=New Orleans, LA				
Tulane U of Louisiana		4		1
		4		**1**
ORD=Chicago–O'Hare Airport, IL				
Roosevelt University	2			
U of Illinois - Chicago Circle	1	1		
	3	**1**		
PHL=Philadelphia, PA/Wilmington, DE				
Princeton University	1			
Temple University	2			
University of Pennsylvania	2		1	
	5		**1**	
PVD=Providence, RI				
Harvard University	1	1	4	
Radcliffe College	1	1	2	
Brown University	1			
	3	**2**	**6**	
SAN=San Diego, CA				
San Diego State University	1	2		
	1	**2**		
SAT=San Antonio, TX				
St. Edward's University		1		
St. Mary's U - San Antonio		1		
		2		
SBA=Santa Barbara, CA				
U of Cal - Santa Barbara			1	
			1	
SEA=Seattle/Tacoma, WA				
University of Washington			6	
			6	

Airport 60 (0300)

AIRPORT	MINORITY GROUP			
	Black	Hispanic	Asian	Native American
SFO=San Francisco/Oakland, CA				
San Francisco State University			1	
Stanford University		1	1	
U of Cal – Berkeley			4	
		1	6	
SLC=Salt Lake City, UT				
University of Utah		1		
		1		
SYR=Syracuse, NY				
Cornel U Endowed College		1		
Syracuse U – Main Campus	1			
	1	1		
TCL=Tuscaloosa, AL				
University of Alabama	2			
	2			
TLH=Tallahassee, FL				
Florida State University			1	
			1	
TPA=Tampa, FL				
University of South Florida		1		
		1		
TUS=Tucson, AZ				
University of Arizona		2		
		2		
TYS=Knoxville, TN				
U of Tennessee – Knoxville	1			
	1			

155

AREA STUDIES (0300)
MINORITY BACCALAUREATE DEGREES
WITHIN 61-80 MILE ANNULUS OF AIRPORT

AIRPORT	MINORITY GROUP			
	Black	Hispanic	Asian	Native American
AUS=Austin, TX				
St. Edward's University		1		
St. Mary's U – San Antonio		1		
		2		
BDL=Hartford, CT/Springfield, MA				
SUNY at Albany		1		1
Brown University	1			
	1	**1**		**1**
BTR=Baton Rouge, LA				
Tulane U of Louisiana		4		1
		4		**1**
CMH=Columbus, OH				
Antioch University			1	
			1	
COS=Colorado Springs, CO				
U of Colorado at Boulder		2	1	
		2	**1**	
JAX=Jacksonville, FL				
University of Florida	1			
	1			
JFK=New York, Kennedy Int'l, NY				
Yale University	3	1	3	
	3	**1**	**3**	
SAT=San Antonio, TX				
U of Texas at Austin	1	7		
	1	**7**		

Airport 61-80 (0300)

AIRPORT	MINORITY GROUP			
	Black	Hispanic	Asian	Native American
SBA=Santa Barbara, CA				
Cal State University - Los Angeles	5	7	1	
U of Cal - Los Angeles	1	1	2	
	6	8	3	
SFO=San Francisco/Oakland, CA				
U of Cal - Davis			1	
U of Cal - Santa Cruz		2		
University of the Pacific		2	4	
		4	5	

BIOLOGICAL SCIENCES (0400)

BIOLOGICAL SCIENCES (0400)
MINORITY BACCALAUREATE DEGREES
BY STATE AND INSTITUTION

STATE/SCHOOL	MINORITY GROUP			
	Black	Hispanic	Asian	Native American
Alabama				
Alabama A&M University*	9			
Alabama State University*	25			
Jacksonville State University	5	1	1	
Oakwood College*	25			
Stillman College*	10			
Talladega College*	9			
Troy State University - Main Campus	1			
Tuskegee Institute*	45			
University of Alabama	8			
U of Alabama in Birmingham	7		2	
University of South Alabama	1		1	
	145	**1**	**4**	
Arizona				
Arizona State University		4	1	
Northern Arizona University		1	1	3
University of Arizona		13	7	
		18	**9**	**3**
Arkansas				
Arkansas State U - Main Campus	1			
Henderson State University	4			
Philander Smith College*	3			
University of Arkansas - Pine Bluff*	5			
University of Central Arkansas	1			
	14			
California				
Cal Poly State U - San Luis Obispo	1	3	4	2
Cal State College - Bakersfield		2		2

(0400)

STATE/SCHOOL	MINORITY GROUP			
	Black	Hispanic	Asian	Native American
California (cont)				
Cal State College - San Bernadino	2	2		
Cal State Poly U - Pomona	2	3	6	
Cal State University - Chico		2	2	
Cal State U - Dominguez Hills	7		8	2
Cal State University - Fresno		8	10	1
Cal State University - Fullerton	1	8	7	
Cal State University - Hayward	3	2	11	
Cal State University - Long Beach	3	10	33	1
Cal State University - Los Angeles	5	10	13	1
Cal State University - Northridge	3	4	8	1
Cal State University - Sacramento	1	3	9	2
Chapman College		1		2
Loyola Marymount University	5	15	5	1
Pepperdine University		1		
San Diego State University	2	3	6	2
San Francisco State University	8	5	31	
San Jose State University	5	10	26	1
Stanford University	14	21	29	
U of Cal - Berkeley	7	4	147	2
U of Cal - Davis	11	8	77	1
U of Cal - Irvine			31	
U of Cal - Los Angeles	6	12	86	1
U of Cal - Riverside	2	6	13	
U of Cal - San Diego		10	15	
U of Cal - Santa Barbara		4	10	
U of Cal - Santa Cruz		9	5	
University of Redlands	1			
University of San Francisco		4	11	
University of Southern California	8	14	48	3
University of the Pacific	2		14	
	100	**184**	**665**	**25**

160

(0400)

STATE/SCHOOL	MINORITY GROUP			
	Black	Hispanic	Asian	Native American
Colorado				
Colorado State University		2	1	1
Metropolitan State College	5	3		
U of Colorado at Boulder	1	4	14	
U of Northern Colorado		3		
U of Southern Colorado	2	5		
	8	**17**	**15**	**1**
Connecticut				
University of Connecticut	2	2	4	1
Yale University	9	11	7	
	11	**13**	**11**	**1**
Delaware				
Delaware State College*	3			
University of Delaware	2			
	5			
District of Columbia				
American University	3		1	
George Washington University	9	3	6	
Howard University*	76			
University of DC*	21	2		
	109	**5**	**7**	
Florida				
Bethune Cookman College*	7			
Biscayne College*		2		
Edward Waters College*	2			
Florida Agr & Mech University*	8			
Florida Atlantic University		2		
Florida International University		14		
Florida Memorial College*	1			
Florida State University	3	2	2	1
University of Central Florida	1	2		
University of Florida	2	11	1	

(0400)

STATE/SCHOOL	MINORITY GROUP			
	Black	Hispanic	Asian	Native American
Colorado				
Colorado State University		2	1	1
Metropolitan State College	5	3		
U of Colorado at Boulder	1	4	14	
U of Northern Colorado		3		
U of Southern Colorado	2	5		
	8	**17**	**15**	**1**
Connecticut				
University of Connecticut	2	2	4	1
Yale University	9	11	7	
	11	**13**	**11**	**1**
Delaware				
Delaware State College*	3			
University of Delaware	2			
	5			
D.C.				
American University	3		1	
George Washington University	9	3	6	
Howard University*	76			
University of D.C.*	21	2		
	109	**5**	**7**	
Florida				
Bethune Cookman College*	7			
Biscayne College*		2		
Edward Waters College*	2			
Florida Agr & Mech University*	8			
Florida Atlantic University		2		
Florida International University		14		
Florida Memorial College*	1			
Florida State University	3	2	2	1
University of Central Florida	1	2		
University of Florida	2	11	1	

162

(0400)

STATE/SCHOOL	MINORITY GROUP			
	Black	Hispanic	Asian	Native American
Florida (cont)				
University of Miami	1	17	5	1
University of South Florida	2	6	2	1
University of West Florida	2			
	29	56	10	3
Georgia				
Albany State College*	3			
Clark College*	14			
Fort Valley State College*	5			
Georgia College	2			
Georgia State University	5		1	
Morehouse College*	40			
Morris Brown College*	6			
Paine College*	8			
Savannah State College*	7			
Spelman College*	25			
University of Georgia	8		1	
Valdosta State College	2			
	125		2	
Hawaii				
Chaminade University of Honolulu			3	
University of Hawaii at Hilo*			13	
University of Hawaii at Manoa*	1	2	75	
	1	2	91	
Illinois				
Bradley University	1			
Chicago State University*	25	5		
College of St. Francis	1		1	
DePaul University	1	1	1	
Eastern Illinois University	1		2	
Governors State University			1	
Illinois State University	2			
Loyola University of Chicago	7	7	5	

(0400)

STATE/SCHOOL	MINORITY GROUP			
	Black	Hispanic	Asian	Native American
Illinois (cont)				
Northern Illinois University	4			
Northeastern Illinois University	1	3	1	
Northwestern University	7	3	7	
Roosevelt University	7			
Southern Illinois U – Carbondale	10	1	3	
Southern Illinois U – Edwardsville	4			
U of Illinois – Chicago Circle	12	9	21	
U of Illinois – Urbana Campus	4	8	15	
	87	**37**	**57**	
Indiana				
Ball State University	2			
Indiana State U – Main Campus	2		1	
Indiana University – Bloomington	5	2	3	
Indiana University – Northwest	5			
Purdue University – Main Campus	7	1	5	
	21	**3**	**9**	
Kentucky				
Kentucky State University*	4			
University of Louisville	1		2	
Western Kentucky University	1			
	6		**2**	
Louisiana				
Dillard University*	20			
Grambling State University*	19			
Louisiana State U & A&M College	5			
Louisiana Tech University	2			
McNeese State University	1			
Southeastern Louisiana U	2			
Sthrn U A&M College – Main Cam*	17			
Southern U in New Orleans*	9			
Tulane U of Louisiana	2	14	4	1

(0400)

STATE/SCHOOL	MINORITY GROUP			
	Black	Hispanic	Asian	Native American
Louisiana (cont)				
University of New Orleans	1	1		
U of Southwestern Louisiana	3			
Xavier University of Louisiana*	5			
	86	**15**	**4**	**1**
Maryland				
Bowie State College*	8			
Coppin State College*	4			
Morgan State University*	30			
Towson State University	3			
U of MD - Baltimore Co Campus	6			1
U of MD - College Park Campus	7	8	12	2
U of MD - Eastern Shore*	3			
U of MD - University College				
	61	**8**	**12**	**3**
Massachussetts				
Boston State College	3	1	1	
Boston University	4	2		1
Harvard University	27	6	18	1
Radcliffe College	12	3	6	
Tufts University	6	3	4	
U of Mass - Amherst Campus	2	1	3	
	54	**16**	**32**	**2**
Michigan				
Detroit Institute of Technology	6		1	
Eastern Michigan University	3	1	2	1
Mercy College of Detroit	1			
Michigan State University	5	5	5	1
Oakland University	4		1	
University of Detroit	1		1	
U of Michigan - Ann Arbor	12	2	12	1

(0400)

STATE/SCHOOL	MINORITY GROUP			
	Black	Hispanic	Asian	Native American
Michigan (cont)				
Wayne State University	16	1	2	1
Western Michigan University	3	1		3
	51	**10**	**24**	**7**
Minnesota				
U of Minn - Minneapolis/St. Paul	2		8	1
	2		**8**	**1**
Mississippi				
Alcorn State University*	26			
Jackson State University*	36			
Mississippi Industrial College*	5			
Mississippi State University	2	1		1
Mississippi University for Women	2			
Mississippi Valley State Univ*	16			
Rust College*	17			
Tougaloo College*	29			
U of Mississippi - Main Campus	2			
U of Southern Mississippi	3			
	138	**1**		**1**
Missouri				
Lincoln University	4			
Park College	1			
St. Louis U - Main Campus		3	1	
U of Missouri - Columbia	1		1	
U of Missouri - Kansas City	7	1	1	
U of Missouri - St. Louis	2	1		
Washington University	8	1	4	
Webster College	1			
	24	**6**	**7**	
Montana				
Montana State University		1	1	
		1	**1**	

166

(0400)

STATE/SCHOOL	MINORITY GROUP			
	Black	Hispanic	Asian	Native American
Nebraska				
U of Nebraska at Omaha	2	3		
	2	3		
New Hampshire				
Dartmouth College	3		1	2
	3		1	2
New Jersey				
Glassboro State College	1			2
Jersey City State College	1	1		
Kean College of New Jersey	8	1	1	
Montclair State College	3	1	1	
Princeton University	3	1	4	1
Rutgers U – Camden Campus	2			
Rutgers U – New Brunswick	22	6	9	
Rutgers U – Newark Campus	16	2	2	
St. Peter's College		4	1	
Seton Hall University		1	1	
Trenton State College	2			
	58	17	19	3
New Mexico				
New Mexico Highlands U*		12		
NM State U – Main Campus		8	1	2
University of Albuquerque		2		
U of NM – Main Campus	1	16		1
	1	38	1	3
New York				
Adelphi University		1		
College of New Rochelle	2	2		
Cornell U Endowed College	5	6	6	1
CUNY Brooklyn College	19	7	2	1
CUNY City College	53	25	15	2
CUNY College of Staten Island	3	2		
CUNY Hunter College	6	4	2	

(0400)

STATE/SCHOOL	Black	Hispanic	Asian	Native American
MINORITY GROUP				

STATE/SCHOOL	Black	Hispanic	Asian	Native American
New York (cont)				
CUNY Lehman College	6	6	2	
CUNY Medgar Evers College*	7			
CUNY Queen's College	7	2	2	
CUNY York College	13	2		
Fordham University	3	12	2	
Long Island U – Brooklyn Center	10	3	1	
Long Island U – C W Post Center	4			
Mercy College	2	1	6	
New York University	13	9	12	1
Pace University New York	6	1	1	
St. Francis College	2	1		
St. John's University	6	6	4	3
St. Joseph's College – Main Campus		1		
SUNY at Albany	3	2	3	1
SUNY at Buffalo – Main Campus	1		1	
SUNY at Stony Bk – Main Campus	12	8	3	
SUNY College at Buffalo	2			
SUNY College at New Paltz	3			
SUNY College – Old Westbury	11			
SUNY Empire State College		1		
Syracuse University – Main Campus	8	2		
	207	**104**	**62**	**9**
North Carolina				
Barber–Scotia College*	5			
Bennett College*	2			
Duke University	3		1	
East Carolina University	1		1	
Elizabeth City State U*	11		1	
Fayetteville State University*	7			
Johnson C Smith University*	8			
Livingstone College*	4			

(0400)

STATE/SCHOOL		MINORITY GROUP		
	Black	Hispanic	Asian	Native American
North Carolina (cont)				
NC Agrl & Tech State University*	11			
NC Central University*	32			
NC State U – Raleigh	6			1
Pembroke State University	1		1	9
St. Augustine's College*	4		1	
Shaw University*	3			
U of NC at Chapel Hill	11	1	2	2
U of NC at Charlotte	2			
U of NC at Greensboro	5	1		
Winston-Salem State University*	26			
	142	**2**	**7**	**12**
Ohio				
Antioch University				
Bowling Green State U – Main Cam	4	2	1	
Central State University*	5			
Kent State U – Main Campus	1			
Oberlin College	8		3	
Ohio State U – Main Campus	4	1	1	
Ohio University – Main Campus	14			
U of Akron – Main Campus			1	
U of Cincinnati – Main Campus	2	1	2	
University of Dayton	1	1		
University of Toledo	4		3	
Wilberforce University*	8			
Wright State U – Main Campus	1			
	52	**5**	**11**	
Oklahoma				
Cameron University				1
Central State University	2		1	
East Central Oklahoma State	1		1	
Langston University*	6			

(0400)

STATE/SCHOOL	MINORITY GROUP			
	Black	Hispanic	Asian	Native American
Oklahoma (cont)				
Northeast Oklahoma State U	2			1
Oklahoma State U - Main Campus	1		1	1
Southwest Oklahoma State U	1			1
U of Oklahoma - Norman Campus			1	1
	13		**4**	**5**
Oregon				
Oregon State University	1		5	
University of Oregon - Main Campus			2	1
	1		**7**	**1**
Pennsylvania				
Cheyney State College*	9			
Drexel University	1			
Lincoln University*	21			
Pennsylvania State U - Main Campus	3	2	3	
St. Joseph's University	4			3
Temple University	6			
University of Pennsylvania	7	5	6	
U of Pittsburgh - Main Campus	8	1		1
	59	**8**	**9**	**4**
Rhode Island				
Brown University	17	3	8	
	17	**3**	**8**	
South Carolina				
Allen University*	4			
Baptist College at Charleston	2			
Benedict College*	20			
Claflin College*	12			
Morris College*	1			
South Carolina State College*	16			
U of South Carolina at Columbia	14	1	1	
Winthrop College	2			
	71	**1**	**1**	

170

(0400)

STATE/SCHOOL	MINORITY GROUP			
	Black	Hispanic	Asian	Native American
Tennessee				
Austin Peay State University	4			
Fisk University*	33			
Knoxville College*	12			
Lane College*	6			
LeMoyne-Owen College*	11			
Memphis State University	9	1	4	
Middle Tennessee State U	5		2	
Tennessee State University*	34			
U of Tennessee – Knoxville	5		1	
U of Tennessee – Martin	7		1	
	126	**1**	**8**	
Texas				
Angelo State University		3		
Bishop College*	7			
Corpus Christi State University		3		
East Texas State University	6			1
Huston-Tillotson College*	2			
Incarnate Word College		6		
Jarvis Christian College*	2			
Lamar University	1			4
North Texas State University	6	2		
Our Lady of Lake University*	1	13		
Pan American University*		50		
Paul Quinn College*	2			
Prairie View A&M University*	21	1	5	
St. Edward's University		1		
St. Mary's U – San Antonio		37	2	
Sam Houston State University	1			2
Southwest Texas State University	1	4		
Sul Ross State University	1	2		
Texas A&I University		10		

(0400)

STATE/SCHOOL	MINORITY GROUP			
	Black	Hispanic	Asian	Native American
Texas (cont)				
Texas A&M U – Main Campus	1	6	3	5
Texas College*	15			
Texas Southern University*	10			
Texas Women's University	6			
Trinity University	2	9	1	
U of Houston – Central Campus	13	18	8	1
U of Texas at Arlington	4	3	1	
U of Texas at Austin	5	38	5	2
U of Texas at El Paso	2	44	1	1
U of Texas at San Antonio	1	18	3	1
Wiley College*	13			
	123	**268**	**29**	**17**
Utah				
Brigham Young University – Main			2	1
University of Utah			2	3
			4	**4**
Virginia				
Hampton Institute*	26			
Norfolk State College*	8			
Old Dominion University	4	2	1	1
St. Paul's College*	3			
U of Virginia – Main Campus	5		2	
Virginia Commonwealth University	12	1	2	
Virginia State College*	17			
Virginia Union University*	24			
	99	**3**	**5**	**1**
Washington				
University of Washington	6	1	21	1
	6	**1**	**21**	**1**

172

(0400)

STATE/SCHOOL	MINORITY GROUP			
	Black	Hispanic	Asian	Native American
West Virginia				
West Virginia State College	3		1	
	3		1	
Wisconsin				
U of Wisconsin – Madison	1	4	4	
U of Wisconsin – Milwaukee	4	1		
	5	5	4	
TOTALS	**2,065**	**852**	**1,172**	**110**

*Predominately minority institutions are those where at least 50% of the total BA Degrees awarded are to one of the minority groups being considered.

BIOLOGICAL SCIENCES (0400)
BLACK BACCALAUREATE DEGREES RANKED BY INSTITUTION

Rank	Institution	B.A.'s	Rank	Institution	B.A.'s
1	Howard U*	76	29	Brown U	17
2	CUNY City C	53	30	Sthrn U A&M C-Main Campus*	17
3	Tuskegee Institute*	45	31	Virginia State C*	17
4	Morehouse C*	40	32	Wayne State U	16
5	Jackson State U*	36	33	Rutgers U-Newark Campus	16
6	Tennessee State U*	34	34	South Carolina C*	16
7	Fisk U*	33	35	Mississippi Valley State U*	16
8	NC Central U*	32	36	Texas C*	15
9	Morgan State U*	30	37	Stanford U	14
10	Tougaloo C*	29	38	Ohio U-Main Campus	14
11	Harvard U	27	39	Clark C*	14
12	Alcorn State U*	26	40	U of South Carolin at Columbia	14
13	Winston-Salem U*	26	41	New York U	13
14	Hampton Institute*	26	42	U of Houston-Central Campus	13
15	Spelman C*	25	43	CUNY York C	13
16	Oakwood C	25	44	Wiley C*	13
17	Chicago State U*	25	45	SUNY at Stony Brook-Main Cam	12
18	Albama State U*	25	46	U of Illinois-Chicago Circle	12
19	Virginia Union U*	24	47	Knoxville C*	12
20	Rutgers U-New Brunswick	22	48	U of Michigan-Ann Arbor	12
21	Lincoln U*	21	49	Claflin C*	12
22	U of DC*	21	50	Radcliffe C	12
23	Prairie View A&M U*	21	51	Virginia Commonwealth U	12
24	Dillard U*	20	52	Elizabeth City State U*	11
25	Benedict C	20	53	SUNY C-Old Westbury	11
26	CUNY Brooklyn C	19	54	NC Agrl & Tech State U*	11
27	Grambling State U*	19	55	U of Cal-Davis	11
28	Rust C*	17	56	U of NC at Chapel Hill	11

174

Black B.A.'s (0400)

Rank	Institution	B.A.'s	Rank	Institution	B.A.'s
58	Southern Illinois U–Carbondale	10	60	Stillman C*	10
59	Long Island U–Brooklyn Center	10	61	Texas Southern U*	10

*predominantly black institutions

Institutions not ranked have less than ten degrees conferred on blacks.

BIOLOGICAL SCIENCES (0400)
HISPANIC BACCALAUREATE DEGREES RANKED BY INSTITUTION

Rank	Institution	B.A.'s	Rank	Institution	B.A.'s
1	Pan American U*	50	14	Tulane U of Louisiana	14
2	U of Texas at El Paso	44	15	U of Arizona	13
3	U of Texas at Austin	38	16	Our Lady of the Lake U*	13
4	St. Mary's U–San Antonio	37	17	New Mexico Highlands U*	12
5	CUNY City C	25	18	U of Cal–Los Angeles	12
6	Stanford U	21	19	Fordham U	12
7	U of Houston–Central Campus	18	20	U of Florida	11
8	U of Texas at San Antonio	18	21	Yale U	11
9	U of Miami	17	22	Cal State U–Long Beach	10
10	U of NM–Main Campus	16	23	Cal State U–Los Angeles	10
11	Loyola Marymount U	15	24	U of Cal–San Diego	10
12	U of Southern California	14	25	San Jose State U	10
13	Florida International U	14	26	Texas A&I U	10

*predominanty Hispanic institutions

Institutions not ranked have less than ten degrees conferred on Hispanics.

BIOLOGICAL SCIENCES (0400)
ASIAN BACCALAUREATE DEGREES RANKED BY INSTITUTION

Rank	Institution	B.A.'s	Rank	Institution	B.A.'s
1	U of Cal-Berkeley	147	15	U of Illinois-Urbana Campus	15
2	U of Cal-Los Angeles	86	16	CUNY City C	15
3	U of Cal-Davis	77	17	U of the Pacific	14
4	U of Hawaii at Manoa*	75	18	U of Colorado at Boulder	14
5	U of Southern California	48	19	Cal State U-Los Angeles	13
6	Cal State U-Long Beach	33	20	U of Cal-Riverside	13
7	San Francisco State U	31	21	U of Hawaii at Hilo*	13
8	U of Cal-Irvine	31	22	U of Michigan-Ann Arbor	12
9	Stanford U	29	23	U of MD-College Park Campus	12
10	San Jose State U	26	24	New York U	12
11	U of Illinois-Chicago Circle	21	25	Cal State U-Hayward	11
12	U of Washington	21	26	U of San Francisco	11
13	Harvard U	18	27	Cal State U-Fresno	10
14	U of Cal-San Diego	15	28	U of Cal-Santa Barbara	10

*predominantly Asian institutions

Institutions not ranked have less than ten degrees conferred on Asians.

BIOLOGICAL SCIENCES (0400)
NATIVE AMERICAN BACCALAUREATE DEGREES RANKED BY INSTITUTION

Rank	Institution	B.A.'s
1	Pembroke State U	9
2	Texas A&M U-Main Campus	5

Institutions not ranked have less than five degrees conferred on Native Americans.

BIOLOGICAL SCIENCES (0400)
MINORITY BACCALAUREATE DEGREES
WITHIN 60 MILE RADIUS OF AIRPORT

AIRPORT	MINORITY GROUP			
	Black	Hispanic	Asian	Native American
ABQ=Albuquerque, NM				
U of NM - Main Campus	1	16		1
University of Albuquerque		2		
	1	18		1
ACT=Waco, TX				
Paul Quinn College*	2			
	2			
ALB=Albany, NY				
SUNY at Albany	3	2	3	1
SUNY Empire State College		1		
	3	3	3	1
AOO=Altoona, PA				
Pennsylvania State U - Main Campus	3	2	3	
	3	2	3	
ATL=Atlanta, GA				
Clark College*	14			
Georgia State University	5		1	
Morehouse College*	40			
Morris Brown College*	6			
Spelman College*	25			
	90		1	
AUS=Austin, TX				
Huston-Tillotson College*	2			
Southwest Texas State University	1	4		
U of Texas at Austin	5	38	5	2
	8	42	5	2

Airport 60 (0400)

AIRPORT	MINORITY GROUP			
	Black	Hispanic	Asian	Native American
BAL=Baltimore, MD				
University of Delaware	2			
American University	3		1	
George Washington Univesity	9	3	6	
Howard University*	76			
University of DC*	21	2		
Bowie State College*	8			
Coppin State College*	4			
Morgan State University*	30			
Towson State University	3			
U of MD – Baltimore Co Campus	6			1
U of MD – College Park Campus	7	8	12	2
Lincoln University*	21			
	190	**13**	**19**	**3**
BDL=Hartford, CT/Springfield, MA				
Yale University	9	11	7	
U of Mass – Amherst Campus	2	1	3	
	11	**12**	**10**	
BHM=Birmingham, AL				
Stillman College*	10			
Talladega College*	9			
U of Alabama in Birmingham	7		2	
University of Alabama	8			
	34		**2**	
BKL=Cleveland-Lakefront, OH				
Kent State U – Main Campus	1			
Oberlin College	8		3	
U of Akron – Main Campus			1	
	9		**4**	

178

Airport 60 (0400)

AIRPORT	MINORITY GROUP			
	Black	Hispanic	Asian	Native American
BNA=Nashville, TN				
Western Kentucky University	1			
Austin Peay State University	4			
Fisk University*	33			
Middle Tennessee State U	5		2	
Tennessee State University*	34			
	77		2	
BOS=Boston, MA				
Boston State College	3	1	1	
Boston University	4	2		1
Harvard University	27	6	18	1
Radcliffe College	12	3	6	
Tufts University	6	3	4	
Brown University	17	3	8	
	69	18	37	2
BTR=Baton Rouge, LA				
Louisiana State U & A&M College	5			
Sthrn U A&M College - Main Cam*	17			
Southeastern Louisiana U	2			
	24			
BUF=Buffalo, NY				
SUNY at Buffalo - Main Campus	1		1	
SUNY College at Buffalo	2			
	3		1	
CAE=Columbia, SC				
Allen University*	4			
Benedict College*	20			
Claflin College*	12			
Morris College*	1			
South Carolina State College*	16			
U of South Carolina at Columbia	14	1	1	
	67	1	1	

Airport 60 (0400)

AIRPORT		MINORITY GROUP		
	Black	Hispanic	Asian	Native American
CHS=Charleston, SC				
Baptist College at Charleston	2			
	2			
CIC=Chico, CA				
Cal State University - Chico		2	2	
		2	2	
CLT=Charlotte, NC				
Barber-Scotia College*	5			
Johnson C Smith University*	8			
Livingstone College*	4			
U of NC at Charlotte	2			
Winthrop College	2			
	21			
CMH=Columbus, OH				
Central State University*	5			
Ohio State U - Main Campus	4	1	1	
Wilberforce University*	8			
	17	1	1	
CMI=Champaign, IL				
Eastern Illinois University	1		2	
Illinois State University	2			
U of Illinois - Urbana Campus	4	8	15	
Indiana State U - Main Campus	2		1	
	9	8	18	
COS=Colorado Springs, CO				
U of Southern Colorado	2	5		
	2	5		
COU=Columbia, MO				
Lincoln University	4			
U of Missouri - Columbia	1		1	
	5		1	

Airport 60 (0400)

AIRPORT	MINORITY GROUP			
	Black	Hispanic	Asian	Native American
CRP=Corpus Christi, TX				
Corpus Christi State University		3		
Texas A&I University		10		
		13		
CRW=Charleston, WV				
West Virginia State College	3		1	
	3		1	
CVG=Cincinnati, OH				
Central State University*	5			
U of Cincinnati - Main Campus	2	1	2	
University of Dayton	1	1		
Wilberforce University*	8			
Wright State U - Main Campus	1			
	17	2	2	
DAB=Dayton Beach, FL				
Bethune Cookman College*	7			
University of Central Florida	1	2		
	8	2		
DCA=Washington-National, DC				
American University	3		1	
George Washington University	9	3	6	
Howard University*	76			
University of DC*	21	2		
Bowie State College*	8			
Coppin State College*	4			
Morgan State University*	30			
Towson State University	3			
U of MD - Baltimore Co Campus	6			1
U of MD - College Park Campus	7	8	12	2
	167	13	19	3

Airport 60 (0400)

AIRPORT	MINORITY GROUP			
	Black	Hispanic	Asian	Native American
DEN=Denver, CO				
Metropolitan State College	5	3		
U of Colorado at Boulder	1	4	14	
U of Northern Colorado		3		
	6	10	14	
DFW=Dallas/Fort Worth, TX				
Bishop College*	7			
East Texas State University	6			1
North Texas State University	6	2		
Texas Woman's University	6			
U of Texas at Arlington	4	3	1	
	29	5	1	1
DTW=Detroit-Metropolitan, MI				
Detroit Institute of Technology	6		1	
Eastern Michigan University	3	1	2	1
Mercy College of Detroit	1			
Oakland University	4		1	
U of Michigan - Ann Arbor	12	2	12	1
University of Detroit	1		1	
Wayne State University	16	1	2	1
University of Toledo	4		3	
	47	4	22	3
ELP=El Paso, TX				
U of Texas at El Paso	2	44	1	1
	2	44	1	1
EUG=Eugene, OR				
Oregon State University	1		5	
University of Oregon - Main Campus			2	1
	1		7	1
FAT=Fresno, CA				
Cal State University - Fresno		8	10	1
		8	10	1

Airport 60 (0400)

AIRPORT	MINORITY GROUP			
	Black	Hispanic	Asian	Native American
FAY=Fayetteville, NC				
Fayetteville State University*	7			
NC Central University*	32			
NC State U - Raleigh	6			1
Pembroke State University	1		1	9
St. Augustine's College*	4		1	
Shaw University*	3			
U of NC at Chapel Hill	11	1	2	2
	64	**1**	**4**	**12**
FLG=Flagstaff, AZ				
Northern Arizona University		1	1	3
		1	**1**	**3**
GLH=Greenville, MS				
Mississippi Valley State U*	16			
	16			
GRR=Grand Rapids, MI				
Western Michigan University	3	1		3
	3	**1**		**3**
GSO=Greensboro/High Point, NC				
Bennett College*	2			
Duke University	3		1	
Livingstone College*	4			
NC Agrl & Tech State University*	11			
NC Central University*	32			
U of NC at Chapel Hill	11	1	2	2
U of NC at Greensboro	5	1		
Winston-Salem State University*	26			
	94	**2**	**3**	**2**
HNL=Honolulu/Oahu, HI				
Chaminade University of Honolulu			3	
University of Hawaii at Manoa*	1	2	75	
	1	**2**	**78**	

Airport 60 (0400)

AIRPORT	MINORITY GROUP			
	Black	Hispanic	Asian	Native American
HSV=Huntsville, AL/Decatur, GA				
Alabama A&M University*	9			
Oakwood College*	25			
	34			
IAH=Houston-Intercontinental,TX				
Prairie View A&M University*	21	1	5	
Texas Southern University*	10			
U of Houston - Central Campus	13	18	8	1
	44	**19**	**13**	**1**
IND=Indianapolis, IN				
Ball State University	2			
Indiana University - Bloomington	5	2	3	
Purdue University - Main Campus	7	1	5	
	14	**3**	**8**	
ITO=Hilo, HI				
University of Hawaii at Hilo*			13	
			13	
JAN=Jackson/Vicksburg, MS				
Alcorn State University*	26			
Jackson State University*	36			
Tougaloo College*	29			
	91			
JAX=Jacksonville, FL				
Edward Waters College*	2			
	2			
JFK=New York, Kennedy Int'l, NY				
Jersey City State College	1	1		
Kean College of New Jersey	8	1	1	
Montclair State College	3	1	1	
Princeton University	3	1	4	1
Rutgers U - New Brunswick	22	6	9	

184

Airport 60 (0400)

AIRPORT	MINORITY GROUP			
	Black	Hispanic	Asian	Native American
JFK (cont)				
Rutgers U – Newark Campus	16	2	2	
St. Peter's College		4	1	
Seton Hall University		1	1	
Trenton State College	2			
Adelphi University		1		
College of New Rochelle	2	2		
CUNY Brooklyn College	19	7	2	1
CUNY College of Staten Island	3	2		
CUNY City College	53	25	15	2
CUNY Hunter College	6	4	2	
CUNY Lehman College	6	6	2	
CUNY Medgar Evers College*	7			
CUNY Queen's College	7	2	2	
CUNY York College	13	2		
Fordham University	3	12	2	
Long Island U – Brooklyn Center	10	3	1	
Long Island U – C W Post Center	4			
Mercy College	2	1	6	
New York University	13	9	12	1
Pace University New York	6	1	1	
St. Francis College	2	1		
St. John's University	6	6	4	3
St. Joseph's College – Main Campus		1		
SUNY at Stony Bk – Main Campus	12	8	3	
SUNY College – Old Westbury	11			
	240	**110**	**71**	**8**
LAX=Los Angeles, CA				
Cal State College – San Bernardino	2	2		
Cal State Poly U – Pomona	2	3	6	
Cal State U – Dominguez Hills	7		8	2
Cal State University – Fullerton	1	8	7	

Airport 60 (0400)

AIRPORT	MINORITY GROUP			
	Black	Hispanic	Asian	Native American
LAX (cont)				
Cal State University - Long Beach	3	10	33	1
Cal State University - Los Angeles	5	10	13	1
Cal State University - Northridge	3	4	8	1
Chapman College		1		2
Loyola Marymount University	5	15	5	1
Pepperdine University		1		
U of Cal - Irvine			31	
U of Cal - Los Angeles	6	12	86	1
U of Cal - Riverside	2	6	13	
University of Southern California	8	14	48	3
	44	**86**	**258**	**12**
LCH=Lake Charles, LA				
McNeese State University	1			
	1			
LEX=Lexington/Frankfort, KY				
Kentucky State University*	4			
University of Louisville	1		2	
	5		**2**	
LIT=Little Rock, AR				
Philander Smith College*	3			
University of Arkansas - Pine Bluff*	5			
University of Central Arkansas	1			
	9			
MCI=Kansas City-International, MO				
Park College	1			
U of Missouri - Kansas City	7	1	1	
	8	**1**	**1**	
MCN=Macon, GA				
Fort Valley State College*	5			
Georgia College	2			
	7			

186

Airport 60 (0400)

AIRPORT	MINORITY GROUP			
	Black	Hispanic	Asian	Native American
MDH=Carbondale, IL				
Southern Illinois U – Carbondale	10	1	3	
	10	1	3	
MEM=Memphis, TN				
Mississippi Industrial College*	5			
Rust College*	17			
Le Moyne-Owen College*	11			
Memphis State University	9	1	4	
	42	1	4	
MFE=McAllen, TX				
Pan American University*		50		
		50		
MGM=Montgomery, GA				
Alabama State University*	25			
Troy State University - Main Campus	1			
Tuskegee Institute*	45			
	71			
MHT=Manchester, NH				
Harvard University	27	6	18	1
Radcliffe College	12	3	6	
Tufts University	6	3	4	
Dartmouth College	3		1	2
	48	12	29	3
MIA=Miami, FL				
Biscayne College*		2		
Florida Atlantic University		2		
Florida International University		14		
Florida Memorial College*	1			
University of Miami	1	17	5	1
	2	35	5	1
MKE=Milwaukee, WS				
U of Wisconsin - Milwaukee	4	1		
	4	1		

187

Airport 60 (0400)

AIRPORT	MINORITY GROUP			
	Black	Hispanic	Asian	Native American
MKL=Jackson, TN				
Lane College*	6			
U of Tennessee - Martin	7		1	
	13		1	
MLU=Monroe, LA				
Grambling State University*	19			
Louisiana Tech University	2			
	21			
MOB=Mobile, AL/Pasagoula, MS				
University of South Alabama	1		1	
University of West Florida	2			
	3		1	
MSN=Madison, WS				
U of Wisconsin - Madison	1	4	4	
	1	4	4	
MSP=Minneapolis/St. Paul, MN				
U of Minn - Minneapolis/St. Paul	2		8	1
	2		8	1
MSY=New Orleans, LA				
Dillard University*	20			
Southeastern Louisiana U	2			
Southern U in New Orleans*	9			
Tulane U of Louisiana	2	14	4	
University of New Orleans	1	1		
Xavier University of Louisiana*	5			
	39	15	4	
ORD=Chicago–O'Hare Airport, IL				
Chicago State University*	25	5		
College of St. Francis	1		1	
DePaul University	1	1	1	
Governors State University			1	
Loyola University of Chicago	7	7	5	

Airport 60 (0400)

AIRPORT		MINORITY GROUP		
	Black	Hispanic	Asian	Native American
ORD (cont)				
Northern Illinois University	4			
Northwestern University	7	3	7	
Northeastern Illinois University	1	3	1	
Roosevelt University	7			
U of Illinois – Chicago Circle	12	9	21	
Indiana University – Northwest	5			
	70	**28**	**37**	
ORF=Norfolk/Virginia Beach, VA				
Elizabeth City State U*	11		1	
Hampton Institute*	26			
Norfolk State College*	8			
Old Dominion University	4	2	1	1
	49	**2**	**2**	**1**
PHL=Philadelphia, PA/Wilmington, DE				
Delaware State College*	3			
University of Delaware	2			
Glassboro State College	1			2
Princeton University	3	1	4	1
Rutgers U – Camden Campus	2			
Rutgers U – New Brunswick	22	6	9	
Trenton State College	2			
Cheyney State College*	9			
Drexel University	1			
Lincoln University*	21			
St. Joseph's University	4			3
Temple University	6			
University of Pennsylvania	7	5	6	
	83	**12**	**19**	**6**
PHX=Phoenix, AZ				
Arizona State University		4	1	
		4	**1**	

Airport 60 (0400)

AIRPORT		MINORITY GROUP		
	Black	Hispanic	Asian	Native American
PIA=Peoria, IL				
Bradley University	1			
	1			
PIT=Pittsburgh, PA				
U of Pittsburgh - Main Campus	8	1		1
	8	**1**		**1**
PVD=Providence, RI				
Boston State College	3	1	1	
Boston University	4	2		1
Harvard University	27	6	18	1
Radcliffe College	12	3	6	
Tufts University	6	3	4	
Brown University	17	3	8	
	69	**18**	**37**	**2**
PWA=Oklahoma City-Wiley Post, OK				
Central State University	2		1	
Langston University*	6			
Oklahoma State U - Main Campus	1		1	1
U of Oklahoma - Norman Campus			1	1
	9		**3**	**2**
RDU=Raleigh/Durham, NC				
Bennet College*	2			
Duke University	3		1	
Fayetteville State University*	7			
NC Agrl & Tech State University*	11			
NC Central University*	32			
NC State U - Raleigh	6			1
St. Augustine's College*	4		1	
Shaw University*	3			
U of NC at Chapel Hill	11	1	2	2
U of NC at Greensboro	5	1		
	84	**2**	**4**	**3**

190

Airport 60 (0400)

| AIRPORT | MINORITY GROUP | | | |
	Black	Hispanic	Asian	Native American
RIC=Richmond, VA				
Virginia Commonwealth University	12	1	2	
Virginia State College*	17			
Virginia Union University*	24			
	53	**1**	**2**	
SAN=San Diego, CA				
San Diego State University	2	3	6	2
U of Cal – San Diego		10	15	
	2	**13**	**21**	**2**
SAT=San Antonio, TX				
Incarnate Word College		6		
Our Lady of Lake University*	1	13		
St. Edward's University		1		
St. Mary's U – San Antonio		37	2	
Southwest Texas State University	1	4		
Trinity University	2	9	1	
U of Texas at San Antonio	1	18	3	1
	5	**88**	**6**	**1**
SAV=Savannah, GA				
Savannah State College*	7			
	7			
SBA=Santa Barbara, CA				
Pepperdine University		1		
U of Cal – Santa Barbara		4	10	
		5	**10**	
SBP=San Luis Obispo, CA				
Cal Poly State U – San Luis Obispo	1	3	4	2
	1	**3**	**4**	**2**
SBY=Salisbury, MD				
U of MD – Eastern Shore*	3			
	3			

Airport 60 (0400)

AIRPORT	MINORITY GROUP			
	Black	Hispanic	Asian	Native American
SEA=Seattle/Tacoma, WA				
University of Washington	6	1	21	1
	6	**1**	**21**	**1**
SFO=San Francisco/Oakland, CA				
Cal State University - Hayward	3	2	11	
San Francisco State University	8	5	31	
San Jose State University	5	10	26	1
Stanford University	14	21	29	
U of Cal - Berkeley	7	4	147	2
University of San Francisco	1	4	11	
	38	**46**	**255**	**3**
SHV=Shreveport, LA				
Grambling State University*	19			
Wiley College*	13			
	32			
SJT=San Angelo, TX				
Angelo State University		3		
		3		
SLC=Salt Lake City, UT				
Brigham Young University - Main			2	1
University of Utah			2	3
			4	**4**
STL=St. Louis, MO				
Southern Illinois U - Edwardsville	4			
St. Louis U - Main Campus		3	1	
U of Missouri - St. Louis	2	1		
Washington University	8	1	4	
Webster College	1			
	15	**5**	**5**	

Airport 60 (0400)

AIRPORT	MINORITY GROUP			
	Black	Hispanic	Asian	Native American
SWI=Sherman, TX				
Bishop College*	7			
East Texas State University	6			1
North Texas State University	6	2		
Texas Woman's University	6			
	25	**2**		**1**
SYR=Syracuse, NY				
Cornel U Endowed College	5	6	6	1
Syracuse U - Main Campus	8	2		
	13	**8**	**6**	**1**
TCL=Tuscaloosa, AL				
Stillman College*	10			
U of Alabama in Birmingham	7		2	
University of Alabama	8			
Mississippi University for Women	2			
	27		**2**	
TLH=Tallahassee, FL				
Florida Agr & Mech University*	8			
Florida State University	3	2	2	1
	11	**2**	**2**	**1**
TPA=Tampa, FL				
University of South Florida	2	6	2	1
	2	**6**	**2**	**1**
TUL=Tulsa, OK				
Northeast Oklahoma State U	2			1
	2			**1**
TUS=Tucson, AZ				
University of Arizona		13	7	
		13	**7**	

Airport 60 (0400)

AIRPORT	MINORITY GROUP			
	Black	Hispanic	Asian	Native American
TYR=Tyler, TX				
Jarvis Christian College*	2			
Texas College*	15			
Wiley College*	13			
	30			
TYS=Knoxville, TN				
Knoxville College*	12			
U of Tennessee - Knoxville	5		1	
	17		1	

BIOLOGICAL SCIENCES (0400)
MINORITY BACCALAUREATE DEGREES
WITHIN 61-80 MILE ANNULUS OF AIRPORT

AIRPORT	MINORITY GROUP			
	Black	Hispanic	Asian	Native American
ALB=Albany, NY				
U of Mass - Amherst Campus	2	1	3	
SUNY College at New Paltz	3			
	5	1	3	
ALM=Alamogordo, NM				
NM State U - Main Campus		8	1	2
		8	1	2
ATL=Atlanta, GA				
Jacksonville State University	5	1	1	
Georgia College	2			
University of Georgia	8		1	
	15	1	2	
AUS=Austin, TX				
Incarnate Word College		6		
Our Lady of Lake University*	1	13		
St. Edward's University		1		
St. Mary's U - San Antonio		37	2	
Trinity University	2	9	1	
U of Texas at San Antonio	1	18	3	1
	4	84	6	1
BAL=Baltimore, MD				
Delaware State College*	3			
Cheyney State College*	9			
	12			
BDL=Hartford, CT/Springfield, MA				
College of New Rochelle	2	2		
Mercy College	2	1	6	

Airport 61-80 (0400)

AIRPORT	MINORITY GROUP			
	Black	Hispanic	Asian	Native American
BDL (cont)				
SUNY at Albany	3	2	3	1
SUNY College at New Paltz	3			
Brown University	17	3	8	
	27	8	17	1
BHM=Birmingham, AL				
Jacksonville State University	5	1	1	
	5	1	1	
BOS=Boston, MA				
U of Mass - Amherst Campus	2	1	3	
	2	1	3	
BTM=Butte, MT				
Montana State University		1	1	
		1	1	
BTR=Baton Rouge, LA				
Dillard University*	20			
Southern U in New Orleans*	9			
Tulane U of Louisiana	2	14	4	
U of Southwestern Louisiana	3			
University of New Orleans	1	1		
Xavier University of Louisiana*	5			
	40	15	4	
CAE=Columbia, SC				
Paine College*	8			
Winthrop College	2			
	10			
CHS=Charleston, SC				
Savannah State College*	7			
Claflin College*	12			
South Carolina State College*	16			
	35			

Airport 61-80 (0400)

AIRPORT	MINORITY GROUP			
	Black	Hispanic	Asian	Native American
CLT=Charlotte, NC				
Wintson-Salem State University*	26			
	26			
CMH=Columbus, OH				
Ohio University - Main Campus	14			
University of Dayton	1	1		
Wright State U - Main Campus	1			
	16	1		
CMI=Champaign, IL				
Purdue University - Main Campus	7	1	5	
	7	1	5	
COS=Colorado Springs, CO				
Metropolitan State College	5	3		
U of Colorado at Boulder	1	4	14	
	6	7	14	
CRW=Charleston, WV				
Ohio University - Main Campus	14			
	14			
CVG=Cincinnati, OH				
Kentucky State University*	4			
	4			
DCA=Washington-National, DC				
Lincoln University*	21			
	21			
DEN=Denver, CO				
Colorado State University		2	1	1
		2	1	1
DTW=Detroit-Metropolitan, MI				
Michigan State University	5	5	5	1
Bowling Green State U - Main Cam	4	2	1	
	9	7	6	1

Airport 61-80 (0400)

AIRPORT	MINORITY GROUP			
	Black	Hispanic	Asian	Native American
FAY=Fayetteville, NC				
Duke University	3		1	
	3		1	
GRR=Grand Rapids, MI				
Michigan State University	5	5	5	1
	5	5	5	1
GSO=Greensboro/High Point, NC				
Barber-Scotia College*	5			
NC State U - Raleigh	6			1
St. Augustine's College*	4		1	
Shaw University*	3			
	18		1	1
HSV=Huntsville, AL/Decatur, GA				
Jacksonville State University	5	1	1	
Middle Tennessee State U	5		2	
	10	1	3	
IAH=Houston-Intercontinental,TX				
Sam Houston State University	1			2
	1			2
IND=Indianapolis, IN				
Indiana State U - Main Campus	2		1	
	2		1	
JAX=Jacksonville, FL				
University of Florida	2	11	1	
	2	11	1	
JFK=New York, Kennedy Int'l, NY				
Yale University	9	11	7	
SUNY College at New Paltz	3			
	12	11	7	
LAX=Los Angeles, CA				
Cal State College - Bakersfield		2		2
University of Redlands	1			
	1	2		2

Airport 61-80 (0400)

AIRPORT	MINORITY GROUP			
	Black	Hispanic	Asian	Native American
LCH=Lake Charles, LA				
U of Southwestern Louisiana	3			
Lamar University	1			4
	4			4
LIT=Little Rock, AR				
Henderson State University	4			
	4			
MCN=Macon, GA				
Clark College*	14			
Georgia State University	5		1	
Morehouse College*	40			
Morris Brown College*	6			
Spelman College*	25			
	90		1	
MEM=Memphis, TN				
Arkansas State U - Main Campus	1			
U of Mississippi - Main Campus	2			
Lane College*	6			
	9			
MGM=Montgomery, GA				
Talladega College*	9			
	9			
MHT=Manchester, NH				
Boston State College	3	1	1	
Boston University	4	2		1
U of Mass - Amherst Campus	2	1	3	
	9	4	4	1
MKE=Milwaukee, WS				
Northwestern University	7	3	7	
U of Wisconsin - Madison	1	4	4	
	8	7	11	

Airport 61-80 (0400)

AIRPORT	MINORITY GROUP			
	Black	Hispanic	Asian	Native American
MKL=Jackson, TN				
Mississippi Industrial College*	5			
Rust College*	17			
Memphis State University	9	1	4	
	31	**1**	**4**	
MLU=Monroe, LA				
Alcorn State University*	26			
	26			
MOB=Mobile, AL/Pasagoula, MS				
U of Southern Mississippi	3			
	3			
MSN=Madison, WS				
U of Wisconsin - Milwaukee	4	1		
	4	**1**		
MSY=New Orleans, LA				
Louisiana State U & A&M College	5			
Sthrn U A&M C - Main Cam*	17			
	22			
ORF=Norfolk/Virginia Beach, VA				
Virginia State College*	17			
	17			
PVD=Providence, RI				
U of Mass - Amherst Campus	2	1	3	
	2	**1**	**3**	
PWA=Oklahoma City-Wiley Post, OK				
East Central Oklahoma State U	1		1	
Southwest Oklahoma State U	1			1
	2		**1**	**1**
RDU=Raleigh/Durham, NC				
East Carolina University	1		1	
St. Paul's College*	3			
	4		**1**	

Airport 61-80 (0400)

AIRPORT	MINORITY GROUP			
	Black	Hispanic	Asian	Native American
RIC=Richmond, VA				
Hampton Institute*	26			
Norfolk State College*	8			
St. Paul's College*	3			
U of Virginia - Main Campus	5		2	
	42		**2**	
SAN=San Diego, CA				
Chapman College		1		2
U of Cal - Irvine			31	
U of Cal - Riverside	2	6	13	
	2	**7**	**44**	**2**
SAT=San Antonio, TX				
Huston-Tillotson College*	2			
U of Texas at Austin	5	38	5	2
	7	**38**	**5**	**2**
SAV=Savannah, GA				
Baptist College at Charleston	2			
	2			
SBA=Santa Barbara, CA				
Cal State College - Bakersfield		2		2
Cal State University - Los Angeles	5	10	13	1
Cal State University - Northridge	3	4	8	1
Loyola Marymount University	5	15	5	1
U of Cal - Los Angeles	6	12	86	1
	19	**43**	**112**	**6**
SBY=Salisbury, MD				
Delaware State College*	3			
	3			
SFO=San Francisco/Oakland, CA				
Cal State University - Sacramento	1	3	9	2
U of Cal - Davis	11	8	77	1

Airport 61-80 (0400)

AIRPORT	MINORITY GROUP			
	Black	Hispanic	Asian	Native American
SFO (cont)				
U of Cal – Santa Cruz		9	5	
University of the Pacific	2		14	
	14	**20**	**105**	**3**
SHV=Shreveport, LA				
Louisiana Tech University	2			
	2			
SWI=Sherman, TX				
U of Texas at Arlington	4	3	1	
	4	**3**	**1**	
TLH=Tallahassee, FL				
Albany State College*	3			
Valdosta State College	2			
	5			
TPA=Tampa, FL				
University of Central Florida	1	2		
	1	**2**		
TUL=Tulsa, OK				
Oklahoma State U – Main Campus	1		1	1
	1		**1**	**1**
TYR=Tyler, TX				
East Texas State University	6			1
	6			**1**

202

BIOLOGICAL SCIENCES (0400)
MINORITY BACCALAUREATE DEGREES
MORE THAN 80 MILES FROM NEAREST AIRPORT

AIRPORT	Black	Hispanic	Asian	Native American
ABQ=Albuquerque, NM				
New Mexico Highlands U*		12		
		12		
AUS=Austin, TX				
Texas A&M U - Main Campus	1	6	3	5
	1	**6**	**3**	**5**
ELP=El Paso, TX				
Sul Ross State University	1	2		
	1	**2**		
IAH=Houston-Intercontinental, TX				
Texas A&M U - Main Campus	1	6	3	5
	1	**6**	**3**	**5**
MAF=Midland/Odessa, TX				
Sul Ross State University	1	2		
	1	**2**		
MSY=New Orleans, LA				
U of Southern Mississippi	3			
	3			
PWA=Oklahoma City-Wiley Post, OK				
Cameron University				1
				1
TCL=Tuscaloosa, AL				
Mississippi State University	2	1		1
	2	**1**		**1**

The column headers span: MINORITY GROUP

BUSINESS & MANAGEMENT (0500)

<table>
<tr><td align="center">Tables</td><td>Page</td></tr>
</table>

204

BUSINESS AND MANAGEMENT (0500)
MINORITY BACCALAUREATE DEGREES
BY STATE AND INSTITUTION

STATE/SCHOOL	MINORITY GROUP			
	Black	Hispanic	Asian	Native American
Alabama				
Alabama A&M University*	89			
Alabama State University*	65			
Jacksonville State University	29	2	5	
Miles College*	72			
Oakwood College*	11			
Stillman College*	46	1		
Troy State University – Main Campus	37	7	1	
Troy State University – Montgomery	24			
Tuskegee Institute*	60			
University of Alabama	42			
U of Alabama in Birmingham	20		2	
University of South Alabama	12		1	
	507	**10**	**9**	
Arizona				
Arizona State University	12	38	16	
Northern Arizona University	1	5	2	3
University of Arizona	7	24	14	3
	20	**67**	**32**	**6**
Arkansas				
Arkansas Baptist College*				
Arkansas State U – Main Campus	8			1
Henderson State University	13			
Philander Smith College*	20			
University of Arkansas – Pine Bluff*	58			
University of Central Arkansas	10			
	109			**1**

(0500)

STATE/SCHOOL		MINORITY GROUP		
	Black	Hispanic	Asian	Native American
California				
Cal Poly State U - San Luis Obispo	1	6	6	3
Cal State College - Bakersfield	3	9	1	5
Cal State College - San Bernadino	13	2	1	2
Cal State Poly U - Pomona	8	28	6	7
Cal State University - Chico		13	10	2
Cal State U - Dominguez Hills	88	9	32	5
Cal State University - Fresno	7	35	33	1
Cal State University - Fullerton	6	32	33	6
Cal State University - Hayward	28	13	49	1
Cal State University - Long Beach	29	27	118	5
Cal State University - Los Angeles	50	58	153	
Cal State University - Northridge	10	24	37	15
Cal State University - Sacramento	30	21	50	5
Chapman College	14	7	4	4
Loyola Marymount University	13	24	11	
Pacific Christian College	59	5	14	4
Pepperdine University	28	9	20	3
San Diego State University	14	33	33	1
San Francisco State University	16	20	171	2
San Jose State University	31	37	109	15
U of Cal - Berkeley	6	2	76	
U of Cal - Los Angeles			1	
U of Cal - Riverside	5	3	3	
U of Cal - Santa Barbara		10	20	
University of LaVerne	21	9	2	2
University of Redlands	101	57	24	
University of San Francisco	9	8	25	
University of Southern California	27	34	103	3
University of the Pacific		3	8	1
	617	**538**	**1153**	**92**

(0500)

STATE/SCHOOL	MINORITY GROUP			
	Black	Hispanic	Asian	Native American
Colorado				
Colorado State University		7	3	1
Metropolitan State College	15	16	2	2
U of Colorado at Boulder	5	15	9	1
U of Northern Colorado	7	10	2	1
U of Southern Colorado	1	10	1	1
	28	**58**	**17**	**6**
Connecticut				
University of Connecticut	14	3		
Yale University	2	2	3	
	16	**5**	**3**	
Delaware				
Delaware State College*	58			
University of Delaware	6		2	1
	64		**2**	**1**
District of Columbia				
American University	18	5	5	
George Washington University	18	3	15	
Howard University*	71			
University of DC*	87	6	4	1
	194	**14**	**24**	**1**
Florida				
Bethune Cookman College*	73			
Biscayne College*	5	51		
Edward Waters College*	19			
Florida Agr & Mech University*	137	1	1	
Florida Atlantic University	9	13	1	
Florida International University	25	137	18	
Florida Memorial College*	17			
Florida State University	37	10		
University of Central Florida	5	5	4	
St. Leo College	42	15		1

(0500)

STATE/SCHOOL	MINORITY GROUP			
	Black	Hispanic	Asian	Native American
Florida (cont)				
University of Florida	13	22	3	
University of Miami	17	64	6	
University of South Florida	28	30	3	
University of West Florida	10	5	2	1
	437	**353**	**38**	**2**
Georgia				
Albany State College*	57		1	
Clark College*	75			
Fort Valley State College*	22			
Georgia College	16			
GA Inst of Tech – Main Campus	13	3		
Georgia State University	64	3	2	
Morehouse College*	72			
Morris Brown College*	49			
Paine College*	28			
Savannah State College*	52			
University of Georgia	15	1		2
Valdosta State College	7			
	470	**7**	**3**	**2**
Hawaii				
Chaminade University of Honolulu	2	1	31	
University of Hawaii at Hilo*			24	
University of Hawaii at Manoa*		8	476	
	2	**9**	**531**	
Illinois				
Bradley University	12	1	2	
Chicago State University*	114	2	1	
Daniel Hale Williams University*	25			
DePaul University	35	9	8	
Eastern Illinois University	12		1	

208

(0500)

STATE/SCHOOL	MINORITY GROUP			
	Black	Hispanic	Asian	Native American
Illinois (cont)				
Governors State University	7		1	
Illinois State University	19	3	4	2
Loyola University of Chicago	12	5	5	
Northern Illinois University	26	6	8	
Northeastern Illinois University	6	4	4	
Northwestern University	2		1	
Roosevelt University	115	11	57	
Southern Illinois U - Carbondale	17	3	2	1
Southern Illinois U - Edwardsville	20		3	
U of Illinois - Chicago Circle	32	14	14	
U of Illinois - Urbana Campus	15	4	6	3
	469	**62**	**117**	**6**
Indiana				
Ball State University	11			
Ind-Purdue U - Indianapolis	18	2		
Indiana State U - Main Campus	11			
Indiana University - Bloomington	30	5	4	2
Indiana University - Northwest	19	5		
Purdue University - Main Campus	31	7	6	
	120	**19**	**10**	**2**
Kentucky				
Eastern Kentucky University	11			
Kentucky State University*	18			
University of Louisville	18	1	4	1
Western Kentucky University	7	1		
	54	**2**	**4**	**1**
Louisiana				
Dillard University*	48			
Grambling State University*	127			
Louisiana State U & A&M College	12	2		3

(0500)

STATE/SCHOOL		MINORITY GROUP		
	Black	Hispanic	Asian	Native American
Louisiana (cont)				
Louisiana Tech University	5			
McNeese State University	12	1		
Northeast Louisiana University	30			
Southeastern Louisiana U	13			
Sthrn U A&M College – Main Cam*	183			
Southern U in New Orleans*	120			
Tulane U of Louisiana	1	3		
University of New Orleans	27	7	2	
U of Southwestern Louisiana	41	1	1	4
Xavier University of Louisiana*	88			
	707	**14**	**3**	**7**
Maryland				
Bowie State College*	43			
Morgan State University*	129		2	
Towson State University	30	2	2	
University of Baltimore	49		3	1
U of MD – College Park Campus	33	6	14	7
U of MD – Eastern Shore*	18	1		
	302	**9**	**21**	**8**
Massachussetts				
Boston State College	19	2	2	1
Boston University	13	6	2	
U of Mass – Amherst Campus	9	3	11	2
	41	**11**	**15**	**3**
Michigan				
Detroit Institute of Technology	23		1	
Eastern Michigan University	38	2	2	4
Mercy College of Detroit	13		1	
Michigan State University	20	4	8	
Oakland University	9	1		2
Shaw College at Detroit*	28			

(0500)

STATE/SCHOOL	MINORITY GROUP			
	Black	Hispanic	Asian	Native American
Michigan (cont)				
University of Detroit	53		2	
U of Michigan – Ann Arbor	13	1	2	
Wayne State University	82	1	5	3
Western Michigan University	32	4		2
	311	**13**	**21**	**11**
Minnesota				
U of Minn – Minneapolis/St. Paul	7	2	11	1
	7	**2**	**11**	**1**
Mississippi				
Alcorn State University*	77			
Delta State University	24			
Jackson State University*	189			
Mississippi Industrial College*	12			
Mississippi State University	43			
Mississippi University for Women	14			
Mississippi Valley State Univ*	37			
Rust College*	24			
U of Mississippi – Main Campus	21		1	2
U of Southern Mississippi	28	1		
	469	**1**	**1**	**2**
Missouri				
Columbia College	33	5	1	
Lincoln University	20			
Park College	65	16		1
St. Louis U – Main Campus	17		3	
U of Missouri – Columbia	5		3	
U of Missouri – Kansas City		1	1	4
U of Missouri – St. Louis	31	4	2	
Washington University	9			
Webster College	10			
	190	**26**	**10**	**5**

(0500)

STATE/SCHOOL	MINORITY GROUP			
	Black	Hispanic	Asian	Native American
Montana				
Montana State University			2	1
			2	**1**
Nebraska				
University of Nebraska at Omaha	7	9		
	7	**9**		
New Jersey				
Glassboro State College	11	5	2	6
Jersey City State College	1			
Kean College of New Jersey	9	6	3	
Montclair State College	9	14	5	1
New Jersey Inst Technology	16	2		
Rutgers U - Camden Campus	11		1	
Rutgers U - New Brunswick	16	2	5	
Rutgers U - Newark Campus	58	9	1	
St. Peter's College	17	24	6	
Seton Hall University	11	3	2	1
Trenton State College	6			
	165	**65**	**25**	**8**
New Mexico				
Eastern NM U - Main Campus	3	21	2	5
New Mexico Highlands U*		28		
NM State U - Main Campus	3	40	2	2
University of Albuquerque	5	42	1	3
U of NM - Main Campus	1	32		1
Western New Mexico University	1	18		1
	13	**181**	**5**	**12**
New York				
Adelphi University	15	5	1	
College of New Rochelle	2			
Cornell U Endowed College	4	4	4	
CUNY Bernard Baruch College	288	130	103	5
CUNY Brooklyn College	86	35	9	2

212

(0500)

STATE/SCHOOL	MINORITY GROUP			
	Black	Hispanic	Asian	Native American
New York (cont)				
CUNY Hunter College	10	6	2	
CUNY Lehman College	23	19	6	1
CUNY Medgar Evers College*	36			
CUNY Queen's College	39	13	12	1
CUNY York College	3			
Fordham University	16	22	10	
Long Island U – Brooklyn Center	37	10	5	
Long Island U – C W Post Center	7	4	4	
Mercy College	55	20	2	1
New York University	14	3	22	
Pace University New York	61	22	27	
Pratt Institute	16	1	1	
St. Francis College	18	1	8	
St. John's University	11	4	8	
SUNY at Albany	15	5	1	2
SUNY at Buffalo – Main Campus	7	1	2	
SUNY College – Old Westbury	18	4		
SUNY Empire State College	37	8	2	
Syracuse University – Main Campus	15	5	4	
	833	**322**	**233**	**12**
North Carolina				
Barber–Scotia College*	17			
Bennett College*	6			
Duke University	9	1	2	
East Carolina University	12	2		
Elizabeth City State U*	69			
Fayetteville State University*	61			1
Johnson C Smith University*	42			
Livingstone College*	28			
NC Agrl & Tech State University*	116			
NC Central University*	170	1		

(0500)

STATE/SCHOOL	MINORITY GROUP			
	Black	Hispanic	Asian	Native American
North Carolina (cont)				
NC State U - Raleigh	15		1	
Pembroke State University	1			11
St. Augustine's College*	54			
Shaw University*	48			
U of NC at Chapel Hill	20	1	1	2
U of NC at Charlotte	12	1		
U of NC at Greensboro	12		1	1
Winston-Salem State University	71			
	763	**6**	**5**	**15**
North Dakota				
U of North Dakota - Main Campus	1		1	1
	1		**1**	**1**
Ohio				
Antioch University	4	1		
Bowling Green State U - Main Cam	23	2	1	
Central State University*	66		1	
Franklin University	53	2	7	1
Kent State U - Main Campus	16	1		
Ohio State U - Main Campus	16	2	6	
Ohio University - Main Campus	23		1	
U of Akron - Main Campus	10		2	
U of Cincinnati - Main Campus	44	1	1	1
University of Dayton	13	5	4	1
University of Toledo	12	3	1	2
Wilberforce University*	34			
Wright State U - Main Campus	12			
	326	**17**	**24**	**5**
Oklahoma				
Cameron University	15	1		3
Central State University	31	2	2	3
East Central Oklahoma State U		1		4

214

(0500)

STATE/SCHOOL	MINORITY GROUP			
	Black	Hispanic	Asian	Native American
Oklahoma (cont)				
Langston University*	15			
Northeast Oklahoma State U	12		2	21
Oklahoma State U – Main Campus	7	2	9	8
Southeast Oklahoma State U	1			2
Southwest Oklahoma State U	6	1		2
U of Oklahoma – Norman Campus	5	2	1	8
	92	**9**	**14**	**51**
Oregon				
Oregon State University	1	1	10	3
University of Oregon – Main Campus	1	2	17	2
	2	**3**	**27**	**5**
Pennsylvania				
Cheyney State College*	53			
Drexel University	26		5	
Lincoln University*	39			
Pennsylvania State U – Main Campus	10	3	2	
St. Joseph's University	21	2	2	25
Temple University	50	12	10	8
University of Pennsylvania	22	5	11	1
U of Pittsburgh – Main Campus	9		2	
West Chester State College	2			
	232	**22**	**32**	**34**
South Carolina				
Allen University*	10			
Baptist College at Charleston	16			
Benedict College*	78			
Morris College*	22			
South Carolina State College*	80			
U of South Carolina at Columbia	34	3	5	1
Voorhees College*	46			
Winthrop College	10			
	296	**3**	**5**	**1**

(0500)

STATE/SCHOOL	MINORITY GROUP			
	Black	Hispanic	Asian	Native American
Tennessee				
Austin Peay State University	8		1	
Fisk University*	41			
Knoxville College*	37			
Lane College*	35			
LeMoyne–Owen College*	28			
Memphis State University	88		9	1
Middle Tennessee State U	10		2	
Tennessee State University*	79			
U of Tennessee – Knoxville	23	1	3	
U of Tennessee – Martin	7		1	
	356	**1**	**16**	**1**
Texas				
Angelo State University	4	11		
Bishop College*	54			
Corpus Christi State University	2	28		
East Texas State University	31	5	6	1
Huston-Tillotson College*	26			
Incarnate Word College	4	3		
Jarvis Christian College*	15			
Lamar University	8	2		22
Laredo State University*		26		
North Texas State University	44	17	4	1
Our Lady of Lake University*	5	25		
Pan American University*		103	1	
Paul Quinn College*	18			
Prairie View A&M University*	68	1	4	
St. Edward's University	2	16		
St. Mary's U – San Antonio	4	21	9	
Sam Houston State University	16		11	3
Southwest Texas State University	7	7		
Sul Ross State University	1	16		

(0500)

STATE/SCHOOL	MINORITY GROUP			
	Black	Hispanic	Asian	Native American
Texas (cont)				
Texas A&I University	4	42		
Texas A&M U - Main Campus	3	13	2	8
Texas College*	39			
Texas Southern University*	96	2		
Texas Women's University	14	2		1
Trinity University	1	23	1	
U of Houston - Central Campus	69	44	31	2
U of Texas at Arlington	22	13	6	1
U of Texas at Austin	23	71	11	2
U of Texas at El Paso	14	125	4	3
U of Texas at San Antonio	3	61	3	2
Wiley College*	33			
	630	**677**	**93**	**46**
Utah				
Brigham Young University - Main			2	1
University of Utah		3	6	1
		3	**8**	**2**
Virginia				
Hampton Institute*	113			
Norfolk State College*	146			
Old Dominion University	9	2	1	1
St. Paul's College*	31			
U of Virginia - Main Campus	4	1		
Virginia Commonwealth University	38			1
Virginia State College*	168		1	
Virginia Union University*	21			
	530	**3**	**2**	**2**
Washington				
University of Washington	12	3	81	8
	12	**3**	**81**	**8**

(0500)

STATE/SCHOOL	MINORITY GROUP			
	Black	Hispanic	Asian	Native American
West Virginia				
West Virginia State College	13		1	
	13		**1**	
Wisconsin				
U of Wisconsin - Madison	2		2	
U of Wisconsin - Milwaukee	5	5	5	
	7	**5**	**7**	
TOTALS	**9,412**	**2,549**	**2,606**	**361**

*Predominately minority institutions are those where at least 50% of the total BA Degrees awarded are to one of the minority groups being considered.

BUSINESS AND MANAGEMENT (0500)
BLACK BACCALAUREATE DEGREES RANKED BY INSTITUTION

Rank	Institution	B.A.'s	Rank	Institution	B.A.'s
1	CUNY Bernard Baruch C	288	30	Morehouse C*	72
2	Jackson State U*	189	31	Miles C*	72
3	Sthrn U A&M C-Main Cam*	183	32	Winston-Salem State U*	71
4	NC Central U*	170	33	Howard U*	71
5	Virginia State C*	168	34	U of Houston-Central Campus	69
6	Norfolk State C*	146	35	Elizabeth City State U*	69
7	Florida Agrl & Mech U*	137	36	Prairie View A&M U*	68
8	Morgan State U*	129	37	Central State U*	66
9	Grambling State U*	127	38	Park C	65
10	Southern U in New Orleans*	120	39	Alabama State U*	65
11	NC Agrl & Tech State U*	116	40	Georgia State U	64
12	Roosevelt U	115	41	Pace U-New York	61
13	Chicago State U*	114	42	Fayetteville State U*	61
14	Hampton Institute*	113	43	Tuskegee Institute*	60
15	U of Redlands	101	44	Pacific Christian C	59
16	Texas Southern U*	96	45	Delaware State C	58
17	Alabama A&M U*	89	46	Rutgers U-Newark Campus	58
18	Xavier U of Louisiana*	88	47	U of Arkansas-Pine Bluff*	58
19	Cal State U-Dominguez Hills	88	48	Albany State C*	57
20	Memphis State U	88	49	Mercy C	55
21	U of DC*	87	50	St. Augustine's C*	54
22	CUNY Brooklyn C	86	51	Bishop C*	54
23	Wayne State U	82	52	Franklin U	53
24	South Carolina State C*	80	53	Cheyney State C*	53
25	Tennessee State U*	79	54	U of Detroit	53
26	Benedict C*	78	55	Savannah State C*	52
27	Alcorn State U*	77	56	Cal State U-Los Angeles	50
28	Clark C*	75	57	Temple U	50
29	Bethune Cookman C*	73	58	U of Baltimore	49

Black B.A.'s (0500)

Rank	Institution	B.A.'s	Rank	Institution	B.A.'s
59	Morris Brown C*	49	92	U of Illinois-Chicago Cirlce	32
60	Shaw U*	48	93	Western Michigan U	32
61	Dillard U*	48	94	Purdue U-Main Campus	31
62	Stillman C*	46	95	U of Missouri-St. Louis	31
63	Voorhees C*	46	96	San Jose State U	31
64	U of Cincinnati-Main Campus	44	97	East Texas State U	31
65	North Texas State U	44	98	Central State U*	31
66	Bowie State C*	43	99	St. Paul's C*	31
67	Mississippi State U	43	100	Northeast Louisiana U	30
68	St. Leo C	42	101	Towson State U	30
69	Johnson C Smith U*	42	102	Cal State U-Sacramento	30
70	U of Albama	42	103	Indiana U-Bloomington	30
71	Fisk U*	41	104	Cal State U-Long Beach	29
72	U of Southwest Lousiana	41	105	Jacksonville State U	29
73	Lincoln U*	39	106	Pepperdine U	28
74	CUNY Queen's C	39	107	Paine C*	28
75	Texas C*	39	108	Shaw C at Detroit*	28
76	Eastern Michigan U	38	109	Cal State U-Hayward	28
77	Virginia Commonwealth U	38	110	Livingstone C*	28
78	SUNY Empire State C	37	111	U of South Florida	28
79	Mississippi Valley State U*	37	112	U of Southern Mississippi	28
80	Long Island U-Brooklyn Center	37	113	Le Moyne-Owen C*	28
81	Florida State U	37	114	U of New Orleans	27
82	Troy State U-Main Campus	37	115	U of Southern California	27
83	Knoxville C*	37	116	Northern Illinois U	26
84	CUNY Medgar Evers C*	36	117	Drexel U	26
85	DePaul U	35	118	Huston-Tillotson C*	26
86	Lane C*	35	119	Daniel Hale Williams U*	25
87	Wilberforce U*	34	120	Florida International U	25
88	U of South Carolina at Columbia	34	121	Rust C*	24
89	U of MD-College Park Campus	33	122	Delta State U	24
90	Columbia C	33	123	Troy State U-Montgomery	24
91	Wiley C*	33	124	Bowling Green State U-Main Ca	23

Black B.A.'s (0500)

Rank	Institution	B.A.'s	Rank	Institution	B.A.'s
125	CUNY Lehman C	23	158	U of Miami	17
126	U of Tennessee-Knoxville	23	159	Barber-Scotia C*	17
127	Detroit Institute of Technology	23	160	Florida Memorial C*	17
128	U of Texas at Austin	23	161	St. Louis U-Main Campus	17
129	Ohio U-Main Campus	23	162	Southern Illinois U-Carbondale	17
130	U of Pennsylvania	22	163	Ohio State U-Main Campus	16
131	Morris C*	22	164	Rutgers U-New Brunswick	16
132	Fort Valley State C*	22	165	Pratt Institute	16
133	U of Texas at Arlington	22	166	Fordham U	16
134	U of Mississippi-Main Campus	21	167	Kent State U-Main Campus	16
135	St. Joseph's U	21	168	San Francisco State U	16
136	U of La Verne	21	169	New Jersey Institute Technology	16
137	Virginia Union U*	21	170	Sam Houston State U	16
138	Lincoln U*	20	171	Georgia C	16
139	U of NC at Chapel Hill	20	172	Baptist C at Chastleston	16
140	Southern Illinois U-Edwardsville	20	173	Syracuse U-Main Campus	15
141	Philander Smith C*	20	174	SUNY at Albany	15
142	Michigan State U	20	175	Cameron U	15
143	U of Alabama in Birmingham	20	176	U of Georgia	15
144	Indiana U-Northwest	19	177	NC State U-Raleigh	15
145	Illinois State U	19	178	Metropolitan State C	15
146	Boston State C	19	179	Langston U*	15
147	Edward Waters C*	19	180	U of Illinois-Urbana Campus	15
148	Kentucky State U*	18	181	Adelphi U	15
149	Ind-Purdue U-Indianapolis	18	182	Jarvis Christian C*	15
150	American U	18	183	San Diego State U	14
151	U of Louisville	18	184	New York U	14
152	St. Francis C	18	185	Chapman C	14
153	George Washington U	18	186	Texas Women's U	14
154	SUNY C-Old Westbury	18	187	Mississippi U for Women	14
155	U of MD-Eastern Shore*	18	188	U of Texas at El Paso	14
156	Paul Quinn C*	18	189	Mercy C of Detroit	13
157	St. Peter's C	17	190	U of Florida	13

Black B.A.'s (0500)

Rank	Institution	B.A.'s	Rank	Institution	B.A.'s
191	Southeastern Louisiana U	13	212	McNeese State U	12
192	Loyola Marymount U	13	213	Arizona State U	12
193	U of Dayton	13	214	U of Washington	12
194	Boston U	13	215	Rutgers U-Camden Campus	11
195	U of Michigan-Ann Arbor	13	216	Glassboro State C	11
196	Henderson State U	13	217	Eastern Kentucky U	11
197	GA Inst of Tech-Main Campus	13	218	Seton Hall U	11
198	Cal State C-San Bernardino	13	219	Indiana State U-Main Campus	11
199	West Virginia State C	13	220	St. John's U	11
200	Wright State U-Main Campus	12	221	Ball State U	11
201	U of NC at Charlotte	12	222	Oakwood C*	11
202	Northeastern Oklahoma State	12	223	Webster C	10
203	Eastern Illinois U	12	224	CUNY Hunter C	10
204	U of NC at Charlotte	12	225	Cal State U-Northridge	10
205	Loyola U of Chicago	12	226	Pennsylvania State U-Main Cam	10
206	East Carolina U	12	227	U of Akron-Main Campus	10
207	Louisiana State U & A&M C	12	228	Winthrop C	10
208	Mississippi Industrial C*	12	229	U of West Florida	10
209	Bradley U	12	230	Allen U*	10
210	U of Toledo	12	231	U of Central Arkansas	10
211	U of South Alabama	12	232	Middle Tennessee State U	10

*predominantly black institutions

Institutions not ranked have less than ten degrees conferred on blacks.

BUSINESS & MANAGEMENT (0500)
HISPANIC BACCALAUREATE DEGREES RANKED BY INSTITUTION

Rank	Institution	B.A.'s	Rank	Institution	B.A.'s
1	Florida International U	137	31	St. Peter's C	24
2	CUNY Bernard Baruch C	130	32	Loyola Marymount U	24
3	U of Texas at El Paso	125	33	U of Arizona	24
4	Pan American U*	103	34	Trinity U	23
5	U of Texas at Austin	71	35	Fordham U	22
6	U of Miami	64	36	Pace U-New York	22
7	U of Texas at San Antonio	61	37	U of Florida	22
8	Cal State U-Los Angeles	58	38	Eastern NM U-Main Campus	21
9	U of Redlands	57	39	Cal State U-Sacramento	21
10	Biscayne C*	51	40	St. Mary's U-San Antonio	21
11	U of Houston-Central Campus	44	41	Mercy C	20
12	U of Albuquerque	42	42	San Francisco State U	20
13	Texas A&I U	42	43	CUNY Lehman C	19
14	NM State U-Main Campus	40	44	Western New Mexico U	18
15	Arizona State U	38	45	North Texas State U	17
16	San Jose State U	37	46	Metropolitan State C	16
17	Cal State U-Fresno	35	47	Sul Ross State U	16
18	CUNY Brooklyn C	35	48	Park C	16
19	U of Soutern California	34	49	St. Edward's U	16
20	San Diego State U	33	50	St. Leo C	15
21	Cal State U-Fullerton	32	51	U of Colorado at Boulder	15
22	U of NM-Main Campus	32	52	U of Illinois-Chicago Circle	14
23	U of South Florida	30	53	Montclair State C	14
24	New Mexico Highlands U*	28	54	Florida Atlantic U	13
25	Cal State Poly U-Pomona	28	55	Cal State U-Hayward	13
26	Corpus Christi State U	28	56	Texas A&M U-Main Campus	13
27	Cal State U-Long Beach	27	57	CUNY Queen's C	13
28	Laredo State U*	26	58	U of Texas at Arlington	13
29	Our Lady of the Lake U*	25	59	Cal State U-Chico	13
30	Cal State U-Northridge	24	60	Temple U	12

Hispanic B.A.'s (0500)

Rank	Institution	B.A.'s	Rank	Institution	B.A.'s
61	Roosevelt U	11	65	U of Cal-Santa Barbara	10
62	Angelo State U	11	66	Florida State U	10
63	U of Southern Colorado	10	67	Long Island U-Brooklyn Center	10
64	U of Northern Colorado	10			

*predominantly Hispanic institutions

Institutions not ranked have less than ten degrees conferred on Hispanics.

224

BUSINESS & MANAGEMENT (0500)
ASIAN BACCALAUREATE DEGREES RANKED BY INSTITUTION

Rank	Institution	B.A.'s	Rank	Institution	B.A.'s
1	U of Hawaii at Manoa*	476	24	New York U	22
2	San Francisco State U	171	25	Pepperdine U	20
3	Cal State U-Los Angeles	153	26	U of Cal-Santa Barbara	20
4	Cal State U-Long Beach	118	27	Florida International U	18
5	San Jose State U	109	28	U of Oregon-Main Campus	17
6	U of Southern California	103	29	Arizona State U	16
7	CUNY Bernard Baruch C	103	30	George Washington U	15
8	U of Washington	81	31	U of MD-College Park Campus	14
9	U of Cal-Berkeley	76	32	Pacific Christian C	14
10	Roosevelt U	57	33	U of Illinois-Chicago Circle	14
11	Cal State U-Sacramento	50	34	U of Arizona	14
12	Cal State U-Hayward	49	35	CUNY Queen's C	12
13	Cal State U-Northridge	37	36	Loyola Marymount U	11
14	Cal State U-Fullerton	33	37	Sam Houston State U	11
15	San Diego State U	33	38	U of Minn-Minneapolis/St. Paul	11
16	Cal State U-Fresno	33	39	U of Pennsylvania	11
17	Cal State U-Dominguez Hills	32	40	U of Mass-Amherst Campus	11
18	Chaminade U of Honolulu	31	41	U of Texas at Austin	11
19	U of Houston-Central Campus	31	42	Oregon State U	10
20	Pace U-New York	27	43	Fordham U	10
21	U of San Francisco	25	44	Cal State U-Chico	10
22	U of Redlands	24	45	Temple U	10
23	U of Hawaii at Hilo*	24			

*predominantly Asian institutions

Institutions not ranked have less than ten degrees conferred on Asians.

BUSINESS & MANAGEMENT (0500)
NATIVE AMERICAN BACCALAUREATE DEGREES RANKED BY INSTITUTION

Rank	Institution	B.A.'s	Rank	Institution	B.A.'s
1	St. Joesph's U	25	12	U of MD-College Park Campus	7
2	Lamar U	22	13	Cal State Poly U-Pomona	7
3	Northeastern Oklahoma State	21	14	Cal State U-Fullerton	6
4	Cal State U-Northridge	15	15	Glassboro State C	6
5	San Jose State U	15	16	Cal State U-Sacramento	5
6	Pembroke State U	11	17	Eastern NM U-Main Campus	5
7	Texas A&M U-Main Campus	8	18	Cal State U-Long Beach	5
8	U of Oklahoma-Norman Campus	8	19	Cal State C-Bakersfield	5
9	Temple U	8	20	CUNY Bernard Baruch C	5
10	Oklahoma State U-Main Campus	8	21	Cal State U-DomingueZ Hills	5
11	U of Washington	8			

Institutions not ranked have less than five degrees conferred on Native Americans.

BUSINESS AND MANAGEMENT (0500)
MINORITY BACCALAUREATE DEGREES
WITHIN 60 MILE RADIUS OF AIRPORT

AIRPORT	MINORITY GROUP			
	Black	Hispanic	Asian	Native American
ABQ=Albuquerque, NM				
U of NM - Main Campus	1	32		1
University of Albuquerque	5	42	1	3
	6	**74**	**1**	**4**
ACT=Waco, TX				
Paul Quinn College*	18			
	18			
ALB=Albany, NY				
SUNY at Albany	15	5	1	2
SUNY Empire State College	37	8	2	
	52	**13**	**3**	**2**
AOO=Altoona, PA				
Pennsylvania State U - Main Campus	10	3	2	
	10	**3**	**2**	
ATL=Atlanta, GA				
Clark College*	75			
GA Inst of Tech - Main Campus	13	3		
Georgia State University	64	3	2	
Morehouse College*	72			
Morris Brown College*	49			
	273	**6**	**2**	
AUS=Austin, TX				
Huston-Tillotson College*	26			
Southwest Texas State University	7	7		
U of Texas at Austin	23	71	11	2
	56	**78**	**11**	**2**

Airport 60 (0500)

AIRPORT	MINORITY GROUP			
	Black	Hispanic	Asian	Native American
BAL=Baltimore, MD				
University of Delaware	6		2	1
American University	18	5	5	
George Washington Univesity	18	3	15	
Howard University*	71			
University of DC*	87	6	4	1
Bowie State College*	43			
Morgan State University*	129		2	
Towson State University	30	2	2	
U of MD - College Park Campus	33	6	14	7
University of Baltimore	49		3	1
Lincoln University*	39			
	523	**22**	**47**	**10**
BDL=Hartford, CT/Springfield, MA				
Yale University	2	2	3	
U of Mass-Amherst Campus	9	3	11	2
	11	**5**	**14**	**2**
BHM=Birmingham, AL				
Miles College*	72			
Stillman College*	46	1		
U of Alabama in Birmingham	20		2	
University of Alabama	42			
	180	**1**	**2**	
BKL=Cleveland-Lakefront, OH				
Kent State U-Main Campus	16	1		
U of Akron-Main Campus	10		2	
	26	**1**	**2**	
BNA=Nashville, TN				
Western Kentucky University	7	1		
Austin Peay State University	8		1	
Fisk University*	41			

228

Airport 60 (0500)

AIRPORT	MINORITY GROUP			
	Black	Hispanic	Asian	Native American
BNA (cont)				
Middle Tennessee State U	10		2	
Tennessee State University*	79			
	145	**1**	**3**	
BOS=Boston, MA				
Boston State College	19	2	2	1
Boston University	13	6	2	
	32	**8**	**4**	**1**
BTR=Baton Rouge, LA				
Louisiana State U & A&M College	12	2		3
Sthrn U A&M College - Main Cam*	183			
Southeastern Louisiana U	13			
	208	**2**		**3**
BUF=Buffalo, NY				
SUNY at Buffalo - Main Campus	7	1	2	
	7	**1**	**2**	
CAE=Columbia, SC				
Allen University*	10			
Benedict College*	78			
Morris College*	22			
South Carolina State College*	80			
U of South Carolina at Columbia	34	3	5	1
Voorhees College*	46			
	270	**3**	**5**	**1**
CHS=Charleston, SC				
Baptist College at Charleston	16			
	16			
CIC=Chico, CA				
Cal State University - Chico		13	10	2
		13	**10**	**2**

Airport 60 (0500)

AIRPORT	MINORITY GROUP			
	Black	Hispanic	Asian	Native American
CLT=Charlotte, NC				
Barber-Scotia College*	17			
Johnson C Smith University*	42			
Livingstone College*	28			
U of NC at Charlotte	12	1		
Winthrop College	10			
	109	**1**		
CMH=Columbus, OH				
Central State University*	66		1	
Ohio State U - Main Campus	16	2	6	
Wilberforce University*	34			
	116	**2**	**7**	
CMI=Champaign, IL				
Eastern Illinois University	12		1	
Illinois State University	19	3	4	2
U of Illinois - Urbana Campus	15	4	6	3
Indiana State U - Main Campus	11			
	57	**7**	**11**	**5**
COS=Colorado Springs, CO				
U of Southern Colorado	1	10	1	1
	1	**10**	**1**	**1**
COU=Columbia, MO				
Columbia College	33	5	1	
Lincoln University	20			
U of Missouri - Columbia	5		3	
	58	**5**	**4**	
CRP=Corpus Christi, TX				
Corpus Christi State University	2	28		
Texas A&I University	4	42		
	6	**70**		

Airport 60 (0500)

AIRPORT	MINORITY GROUP			
	Black	Hispanic	Asian	Native American
CRW=Charleston, WV				
West Virginia State College	13		1	
	13		**1**	
CVG=Cincinnati, OH				
Antioch University	4	1		
Central State University*	66		1	
Franklin University	53	2	7	1
U of Cincinnati - Main Campus	44	1	1	1
University of Dayton	13	5	4	1
Wilberforce University*	34			
Wright State U - Main Campus	12			
	226	**9**	**13**	**3**
DAB=Dayton Beach, FL				
Bethune Cookman College*	73			
University of Central Florida	5	5	4	
	78	**5**	**4**	
DCA=Washington-National, DC				
American University	18	5	5	
George Washington University	18	3	15	
Howard University*	71			
University of DC*	87	6	4	1
Bowie State College*	43			
Morgan State University*	129		2	
Towson State University	30	2	2	
U of MD - College Park Campus	33	6	14	7
University of Baltimore	49		3	1
	478	**22**	**45**	**9**
DEN=Denver, CO				
Metropolitan State College	15	16	2	2
U of Colorado at Boulder	5	15	9	1
U of Northern Colorado	7	10	2	1
	27	**41**	**13**	**4**

Airport 60 (0500)

AIRPORT	MINORITY GROUP			
	Black	Hispanic	Asian	Native American
DFW=Dallas/Fort Worth, TX				
Bishop College*	54			
East Texas State University	31	5	6	1
North Texas State University	44	17	4	1
Texas Woman's University	14	2		1
U of Texas at Arlington	22	13	6	1
	165	**37**	**16**	**4**
DTW=Detroit-Metropolitan, MI				
Detroit Institute of Technology	23		1	
Eastern Michigan University	38	2	2	4
Mercy College of Detroit	13		1	
Oakland University	9	1		2
Shaw College at Detroit*	28			
U of Michigan – Ann Arbor	13	1	2	
University of Detroit	53		2	
Wayne State University	82	1	5	3
University of Toledo	12	3	1	2
	271	**8**	**14**	**11**
ELP=El Paso, TX				
U of Texas at El Paso	14	125	4	3
	14	**125**	**4**	**3**
EUG=Eugene, OR				
Oregon State University	1	1	10	3
University of Oregon – Main Campus	1	2	17	2
	2	**3**	**27**	**5**
FAT=Fresno, CA				
Cal State University – Fresno	7	35	33	1
	7	**35**	**33**	**1**
FAY=Fayetteville, NC				
Fayetteville State University*	61			1
NC Central University*	170	1		
NC State U – Raleigh	15		1	

232

Airport 60 (0500)

AIRPORT	MINORITY GROUP			
	Black	Hispanic	Asian	Native American
FAY (cont)				
Pembroke State University	1			11
St. Augustine's College*	54			
Shaw University*	48			
U of NC at Chapel Hill	20	1	1	2
	369	**2**	**2**	**14**
FLG=Flagstaff, AZ				
Northern Arizona University	1	5	2	3
	1	**5**	**2**	**3**
GLH=Greenville, MS				
Delta State University	24			
Mississippi Valley State U*	37			
	61			
GRR=Grand Rapids, MI				
Western Michigan University	32	4		2
	32	**4**		**2**
GSO=Greensboro/High Point, NC				
Bennett College*	6			
Duke University	9	1	2	
Livingstone College*	28			
NC Agrl & Tech State University*	116			
NC Central University*	170	1		
U of NC at Chapel Hill	20	1	1	2
U of NC at Greensboro	12		1	1
Winston-Salem State University*	71			
	432	**3**	**4**	**3**
HNL=Honolulu/Oahu, HI				
Chaminade University of Honolulu	2	1	31	
University of Hawaii at Manoa*		8	476	
	2	**9**	**507**	

Airport 60 (0500)

AIRPORT		MINORITY GROUP		
	Black	Hispanic	Asian	Native American
HSV=Huntsville, AL/Decatur, GA				
Alabama A&M University*	89			
Oakwood College*	11			
	100			
IAH=Houston-Intercontinental,TX				
Prairie View A&M University*	68	1	4	
Texas Southern University*	96	2		
U of Houston - Central Campus	69	44	31	2
	233	**47**	**35**	**2**
IND=Indianapolis, IN				
Ball State University	11			
Ind-Purdue U - Indianapolis	18	2		
Indiana University - Bloomington	30	5	4	2
Purdue University - Main Campus	31	7	6	
	90	**14**	**10**	**2**
ITO=Hilo, HI				
University of Hawaii at Hilo*			24	
			24	
JAN=Jackson/Vicksburg, MS				
Alcorn State University*	77			
Jackson State University*	189			
	266			
JAX=Jacksonville, FL				
Edward Waters College*	19			
	19			
JFK=New York, Kennedy Int'l, NY				
Jersey City State College	1			
Kean College of New Jersey	9	6	3	
Montclair State College	9	14	5	1
New Jersey Inst of Technology	16	2		
Rutgers U - New Brunswick	16	2	5	
Rutgers U - Newark Campus	58	9	1	

234

Airport 60 (0500)

AIRPORT	MINORITY GROUP			
	Black	Hispanic	Asian	Native American
JFK (cont)				
St. Peter's College	17	24	6	
Seton Hall University	11	3	2	1
Trenton State College	6			
Adelphi University	15	5	1	
College of New Rochelle	2			
CUNY Bernard Baruch College	288	130	103	5
CUNY Brooklyn College	86	35	9	2
CUNY Hunter College	10	6	2	
CUNY Lehman College	23	19	6	1
CUNY Medgar Evers College*	36			
CUNY Queen's College	39	13	12	1
CUNY York College	3			
Fordham University	16	22	10	
Long Island U - Brooklyn Center	37	10	5	
Long Island U - C W Post Center	7	4	4	
Mercy College	55	20	2	1
New York University	14	3	22	
Pace University New York	61	22	27	
Pratt Institute	16	1	1	
St. Francis College	18	1	8	
St. John's University	11	4	8	
SUNY College - Old Westbury	18	4		
	898	**359**	**242**	**12**
LAX=Los Angeles, CA				
Cal State College - San Bernardino	13	2	1	2
Cal State Poly U - Pomona	8	28	6	7
Cal State U - Dominguez Hills	88	9	32	5
Cal State University - Fullerton	6	32	33	6
Cal State University - Long Beach	29	27	118	5

Airport 60 (0500)

AIRPORT	MINORITY GROUP			
	Black	Hispanic	Asian	Native American
LAX (cont)				
Cal State University - Los Angeles	50	58	153	
Cal State University - Northridge	10	24	37	15
Chapman College	14	7	4	4
Loyola Marymount University	13	24	11	
Pacific Christian College	59	5	14	4
Pepperdine University	28	9	20	3
U of Cal - Los Angeles			1	
U of Cal - Riverside	5	3	3	
University of Southern California	27	34	103	3
University of LaVerne	21	9	2	2
	371	**271**	**538**	**56**
LCH=Lake Charles, LA				
McNeese State University	12	1		
	12	**1**		
LEX=Lexington/Frankfort, KY				
Eastern Kentucky University	11			
Kentucky State University*	18			
University of Louisville	18	1	4	1
	47	**1**	**4**	**1**
LIT=Little Rock, AR				
Philander Smith College*	20			
University of Arkansas - Pine Bluff*	58			
University of Central Arkansas	10			
	88			
LRD=Laredo, TX				
Laredo State University*		26		
		26		
MCI=Kansas City-International, MO				
Park College	65	16		1
U of Missouri - Kansas City		1	1	4
	65	**17**	**1**	**5**

Airport 60 (0500)

AIRPORT		MINORITY GROUP		
	Black	Hispanic	Asian	Native American
MCN=Macon, GA				
Fort Valley State College*	22			
Georgia College	16			
	38			
MDH=Carbondale, IL				
Southern Illinois U – Carbondale	17	3	2	1
	17	**3**	**2**	**1**
MEM=Memphis, TN				
Mississippi Industrial College*	12			
Rust College*	24			
Le Moyne-Owen College*	28			
Memphis State University	88		9	1
	152		**9**	**1**
MFE=McAllen, TX				
Pan American University*		103	1	
		103	**1**	
MGM=Montgomery, GA				
Alabama State University*	65			
Troy State University – Main Campus	37	7	1	
Troy State University – Montgomery	24			
Tuskegee Institute*	60			
	186	**7**	**1**	
MIA=Miami, FL				
Biscayne College*	5	51		
Florida Atlantic University	9	13	1	
Florida International University	25	137	18	
Florida Memorial College*	17			
University of Miami	17	64	6	
	73	**265**	**25**	
MKE=Milwaukee, WS				
U of Wisconsin – Milwaukee	5	5	5	
	5	**5**	**5**	

Airport 60 (0500)

AIRPORT	MINORITY GROUP			
	Black	Hispanic	Asian	Native American
MKL=Jackson, TN				
Lane College*	35			
U of Tennessee - Martin	7		1	
	42		**1**	
MLU=Monroe, LA				
Grambling State University*	127			
Louisiana Tech University	5			
Northeast Louisiana University	30			
	162			
MOB=Mobile, AL/Pasagoula, MS				
University of South Alabama	12		1	
University of West Florida	10	5	2	1
	22	**5**	**3**	**1**
MSN=Madison, WS				
U of Wisconsin - Madison	2		2	
	2		**2**	
MSP=Minneapolis/St. Paul, MN				
U of Minn - Minneapolis/St. Paul	7	2	11	1
	7	**2**	**11**	**1**
MSY=New Orleans, LA				
Dillard University*	48			
Southeastern Louisiana U	13			
Southern U in New Orleans*	120			
Tulane U of Louisiana	1	3		
University of New Orleans	27	7	2	
Xavier University of Louisiana*	88			
	297	**10**	**2**	
ORD=Chicago–O'Hare Airport, IL				
Chicago State University*	114	2	1	
Daniel Hale Williams University*	25			
DePaul University	35	9	8	
Governors State University	7		1	

238

Airport 60 (0500)

AIRPORT	MINORITY GROUP			
	Black	Hispanic	Asian	Native American
ORD (cont)				
Loyola University of Chicago	12	5	5	
Northern Illinois University	26	6	8	
Northwestern University	2		1	
Northeastern Illinois University	6	4	4	
Roosevelt University	115	11	57	
U of Illinois - Chicago Circle	32	14	14	
Indiana University - Northwest	19	5		
	393	**56**	**99**	
ORF=Norfolk/Virginia Beach, VA				
Elizabeth City State U*	69			
Hampton Institute*	113			
Norfolk State College*	146			
Old Dominion University	9	2	1	1
	337	**2**	**1**	**1**
PHL=Philadelphia, PA/Wilmington, DE				
Delaware State College*	58			
University of Delaware	6		2	1
Glassboro State College	11	5	2	6
Rutgers U - Camden Campus	11		1	
Rutgers U - New Brunswick	16	2	5	
Trenton State College	6			
Cheyney State College*	53			
Drexel University	26		5	
Lincoln University*	39			
St. Joseph's University	21	2	2	25
Temple University	50	12	10	8
University of Pennsylvania	22	5	11	1
West Chester State College	2			
	321	**26**	**38**	**41**

Airport 60 (0500)

AIRPORT	MINORITY GROUP			
	Black	Hispanic	Asian	Native American
PHX=Phoenix, AZ				
Arizona State University	12	38	16	
	12	**38**	**16**	
PIA=Peoria, IL				
Bradley University	12	1	2	
	12	**1**	**2**	
PIT=Pittsburgh, PA				
U of Pittsburgh - Main Campus	9		2	
	9		**2**	
PVD=Providence, RI				
Boston State College	19	2	2	1
Boston University	13	6	2	
	32	**8**	**4**	**1**
PWA=Oklahoma City-Wiley Post, OK				
Central State University	31	2	2	3
Langston University*	15			
Oklahoma State U - Main Campus	7	2	9	8
U of Oklahoma - Norman Campus	5	2	1	8
	58	**6**	**12**	**19**
RDU=Raleigh/Durham, NC				
Bennet College*	6			
Duke University	9	1	2	
Fayetteville State University*	61			
NC Agrl & Tech State University*	116			
NC Central University*	170	1		
NC State U - Raleigh	15		1	
St. Augustine's College*	54			
Shaw University*	48			
U of NC at Chapel Hill	20	1	1	2
U of NC at Greensboro	12		1	1
	511	**3**	**5**	**4**

Airport 60 (0500)

AIRPORT	MINORITY GROUP			
	Black	Hispanic	Asian	Native American
RIC=Richmond, VA				
Virginia Commonwealth University	38			1
Virginia State College*	168		1	
Virginia Union University*	21			
	227		**1**	**1**
SAN=San Diego, CA				
San Diego State University	14	33	33	1
	14	**33**	**33**	**1**
SAT=San Antonio, TX				
Incarnate Word College	4	3		
Our Lady of Lake University*	5	25		
St. Edward's University	2	16		
St. Mary's U – San Antonio	4	21	9	
Southwest Texas State University	7	7		
Trinity University	1	23	1	
U of Texas at San Antonio	3	61	3	2
	26	**156**	**13**	**2**
SAV=Savannah, GA				
Savannah State College*	52			
	52			
SBA=Santa Barbara, CA				
Pepperdine University	28	9	20	3
U of Cal – Santa Barbara		10	20	
	28	**19**	**40**	**3**
SBP=San Luis Obispo, CA				
Cal Poly State U – San Luis Obispo	1	6	6	3
	1	**6**	**6**	**3**
SBY=Salisbury, MD				
U of MD – Eastern Shore*	18	1		
	18	**1**		

Airport 60 (0500)

AIRPORT	MINORITY GROUP			
	Black	Hispanic	Asian	Native American
SEA=Seattle/Tacoma, WA				
University of Washington	12	3	81	8
	12	**3**	**81**	**8**
SFO=San Francisco/Oakland, CA				
Cal State University - Hayward	28	13	49	1
San Francisco State University	16	20	171	2
San Jose State University	31	37	109	15
U of Cal - Berkeley	6	2	76	
University of San Francisco	9	8	25	
	90	**80**	**430**	**18**
SHV=Shreveport, LA				
Grambling State University*	127			
Wiley College*	33			
	160			
SJT=San Angelo, TX				
Angelo State University	4	11		
	4	**11**		
SLC=Salt Lake City, UT				
Brigham Young University - Main			2	1
University of Utah		3	6	1
		3	**8**	**2**
STL=St. Louis, MO				
Southern Illinois U - Edwardsville	20		3	
St. Louis U - Main Campus	17		3	
U of Missouri - St. Louis	31	4	2	
Washington University	9			
Webster College	10			
	87	**4**	**8**	
SVC=Silver City, NM				
Western New Mexico University	1	18		1
	1	**18**		**1**

242

Airport 60 (0500)

AIRPORT	MINORITY GROUP			
	Black	Hispanic	Asian	Native American
SWI=Sherman, TX				
Southeast Oklahoma State U	1		2	
Bishop College*	54			
East Texas State University	31	5	6	1
North Texas State University	44	17	4	1
Texas Woman's University	14	2		1
	144	24	10	5
SYR=Syracuse, NY				
Cornel U Endowed College	4	4	4	
Syracuse U – Main Campus	15	5	4	
	19	9	8	
TCL=Tuscaloosa, AL				
Miles College*	72			
Stillman College*	46	1		
U of Alabama in Birmingham	20		2	
University of Alabama	42			
Mississippi University for Women	14			
	194	1	2	
TLH=Tallahassee, FL				
Florida Agr & Mech University*	137	1	1	
Florida State University	37	10		
	174	11	1	
TPA=Tampa, FL				
St. Leo College	42	15		1
University of South Florida	28	30	3	
	70	45	3	1
TUL=Tulsa, OK				
Northeast Oklahoma State U	12		2	21
	12		2	21
TUS=Tucson, AZ				
University of Arizona	7	24	14	3
	7	24	14	3

Airport 60 (0500)

AIRPORT		MINORITY GROUP		
	Black	Hispanic	Asian	Native American
TYR=Tyler, TX				
Jarvis Christian College*	15			
Texas College*	39			
Wiley College*	33			
	87			
TYS=Knoxville, TN				
Knoxville College*	37			
U of Tennessee – Knoxville	23	1	3	
	60	1	3	

BUSINESS AND MANAGEMENT (0500)
MINORITY BACCALAUREATE DEGREES
WITHIN 61-80 MILE ANNULUS OF AIRPORT

AIRPORT	MINORITY GROUP			
	Black	Hispanic	Asian	Native American
ALB=Albany, NY				
U of Mass - Amherst Campus	9	3	11	2
	9	3	11	2
ALM=Alamogordo, NM				
NM State U - Main Campus	3	40	2	2
	3	40	2	2
ATL=Atlanta, GA				
Jacksonville State University	29	2	5	
Georgia College	16			
University of Georgia	15	1		2
	60	3	5	2
AUS=Austin, TX				
Incarnate Word College	4	3		
Our Lady of Lake University*	5	25		
St. Edward's University	2	16		
St. Mary's U - San Antonio	4	21	9	
Trinity University	1	23	1	
U of Texas at San Antonio	3	61	3	2
	19	149	13	2
BAL=Baltimore, MD				
Delaware State College*	58			
Cheyney State College*	53			
	111			
BDL=Hartford, CT/Springfield, MA				
College of New Rochelle	2			
Mercy College	55	20	2	1
SUNY at Albany	15	5	1	2
	72	25	3	3

Airport 61-80 (0500)

AIRPORT	MINORITY GROUP			
	Black	Hispanic	Asian	Native American
BHM=Birmingham, AL				
Jacksonville State University	29	2	5	
	29	2	5	
BOS=Boston, MA				
U of Mass – Amherst Campus	9	3	11	2
	9	3	11	2
BTM=Butte, MT				
Montana State University			2	1
			2	1
BTR=Baton Rouge, LA				
Dillard University*	48			
Southern U in New Orleans*	120			
Tulane U of Louisiana	1	3		
U of Southwestern Louisiana	41	1	1	4
University of New Orleans	27	7	2	
Xavier University of Louisiana*	88			
	325	11	3	4
CAE=Columbia, SC				
Paine College*	28			
Winthrop College	10			
	38			
CHS=Charleston, SC				
Savannah State College*	52			
South Carolina State College*	80			
	132			
CLT=Charlotte, NC				
Wintson-Salem State University*	71			
	71			
CMH=Columbus, OH				
Antioch University	4	1		
Ohio University – Main Campus	23		1	

Airport 61-80 (0500)

AIRPORT	MINORITY GROUP			
	Black	Hispanic	Asian	Native American
CMH (cont)				
University of Dayton	13	5	4	1
Wright State U - Main Campus	12			
	52	6	5	1
CMI=Champaign, IL				
Purdue University - Main Campus	31	7	6	
	31	7	6	
COS=Colorado Springs, CO				
Metropolitan State College	15	16	2	2
U of Colorado at Boulder	5	15	9	1
	20	31	11	3
CRW=Charleston, WV				
Ohio University - Main Campus	23		1	
	23		1	
CVG=Cincinnati, OH				
Kentucky State University*	18			
	18			
DCA=Washington-National, DC				
Lincoln University*	39			
	39			
DEN=Denver, CO				
Colorado State University		7	3	1
		7	3	1
DTW=Detroit-Metropolitan, MI				
Michigan State University	20	4	8	
Bowling Green State U - Main Cam	23	2	1	
	43	6	9	
FAY=Fayetteville, NC				
Duke University	9	1	2	
	9	1	2	
GRR=Grand Rapids, MI				
Michigan State University	20	4	8	
	20	4	8	

Airport 61-80 (0500)

AIRPORT	MINORITY GROUP			
	Black	Hispanic	Asian	Native American
GSO=Greensboro/High Point, NC				
Barber-Scotia College*	17			
NC State U - Raleigh	15		1	
St. Augustine's College*	54			
Shaw University*	48			
	134		**1**	
HSV=Huntsville, AL/Decatur, GA				
Jacksonville State University	29	2	5	
Middle Tennessee State U	10		2	
	39	**2**	**7**	
IAH=Houston-Intercontinental,TX				
Sam Houston State University	16		11	3
	16		**11**	**3**
IND=Indianapolis, IN				
Indiana State U - Main Campus	11			
	11			
JAX=Jacksonville, FL				
University of Florida	13	22	3	
	13	**22**	**3**	
JFK=New York, Kennedy Int'l, NY				
Yale University	2	2	3	
	2	**2**	**3**	
LAX=Los Angeles, CA				
Cal State College - Bakersfield	3	9	1	5
University of Redlands	101	57	24	
	104	**66**	**25**	**5**
LCH=Lake Charles, LA				
U of Southwestern Louisiana	41	1	4	
Lamar University	8	2		22
	49	**3**	**1**	**26**

248

Airport 61-80 (0500)

AIRPORT	MINORITY GROUP			
	Black	Hispanic	Asian	Native American
LIT=Little Rock, AR				
Henderson State University	13			
	13			
MCN=Macon, GA				
Clark College*	75			
GA Inst of Tech – Main Campus	13	3		
Georgia State University	64	3	2	
Morehouse College*	72			
Morris Brown College*	49			
	273	**6**	**2**	
MEM=Memphis, TN				
Arkansas State U – Main Campus	8			1
U of Mississippi – Main Campus	21		1	2
Lane College*	35			
	64		**1**	**3**
MHT=Manchester, NH				
Boston State College	19	2	2	1
Boston University	13	6	2	
U of Mass – Amherst Campus	9	3	11	2
	41	**11**	**15**	**3**
MKE=Milwaukee, WS				
Northwestern University	2		1	
U of Wisconsin – Madison	2		2	
	4		**3**	
MKL=Jackson, TN				
Mississippi Industrial College*	12			
Rust College*	24			
Memphis State University	88		9	1
	124		**9**	**1**
MLU=Monroe, LA				
Alcorn State University*	77			
	77			

Airport 61-80 (0500)

AIRPORT	MINORITY GROUP			
	Black	Hispanic	Asian	Native American
MOB=Mobile, AL/Pasagoula, MS				
U of Southern Mississippi	28	1		
	28	1		
MSN=Madison, WS				
U of Wisconsin - Milwaukee	5	5	5	
	5	5	5	
MSY=New Orleans, LA				
Louisiana State U & A&M College	12	2		3
Sthrn U A&M C - Main Cam*	183			
	195	2		3
ORF=Norfolk/Virginia Beach, VA				
Virginia State College*	168		1	
	168		1	
PVD=Providence, RI				
U of Mass - Amherst Campus	9	3	11	2
	9	3	11	2
PWA=Oklahoma City-Wiley Post, OK				
East Central Oklahoma State U		1		4
Southwest Oklahoma State U	6	1		2
	6	2		6
RDU=Raleigh/Durham, NC				
East Carolina University	12	2		
St. Paul's College*	31			
	43	2		
RIC=Richmond, VA				
Hampton Institute*	113			
Norfolk State College*	146			
St. Paul's College*	31			
U of Virginia - Main Campus	4	1		
	294	1		

Airport 61-80 (0500)

AIRPORT	MINORITY GROUP			
	Black	Hispanic	Asian	Native American
SAN=San Diego, CA				
Chapman College	14	7	4	4
U of Cal - Riverside	5	3	3	
	19	10	7	4
SAT=San Antonio, TX				
Huston-Tillotson College*	26			
U of Texas at Austin	23	71	11	2
	49	71	11	2
SAV=Savannah, GA				
Baptist College at Charleston	16			
	16			
SBA=Santa Barbara, CA				
Cal State College - Bakersfield	3	9	1	5
Cal State University - Los Angeles	50	58	153	
Cal State University - Northridge	10	24	37	15
Loyola Marymount University	13	24	11	
U of Cal - Los Angeles			1	
	76	115	203	20
SBY=Salisbury, MD				
Delaware State College*	58			
	58			
SFO=San Francisco/Oakland, CA				
Cal State University - Sacramento	30	21	50	5
University of the Pacific		3	8	1
	30	24	58	6
SHV=Shreveport, LA				
Louisiana Tech University	5			
	5			
SWI=Sherman, TX				
U of Texas at Arlington	22	13	6	1
	22	13	6	1

Airport 61-80 (0500)

AIRPORT	MINORITY GROUP			
	Black	Hispanic	Asian	Native American
TLH=Tallahassee, FL				
Albany State College*	57		1	
Valdosta State College	7			
	64		**1**	
TPA=Tampa, FL				
University of Central Florida	5	5	4	
	5	**5**	**4**	
TUL=Tulsa, OK				
Oklahoma State U - Main Campus	7	2	9	8
	7	**2**	**9**	**8**
TYR=Tyler, TX				
East Texas State University	31	5	6	1
	31	**5**	**6**	**1**

BUSINESS AND MANAGEMENT (0500)
MINORITY BACCALAUREATE DEGREES
MORE THAN 80 MILES FROM NEAREST AIRPORT

AIRPORT	MINORITY GROUP			
	Black	Hispanic	Asian	Native American
ABQ=Albuquerque, NM				
New Mexico Highlands U*		28		
		28		
AUS=Austin, TX				
Texas A&M U - Main Campus	3	13	2	8
	3	**13**	**2**	**8**
ELP=El Paso, TX				
Sul Ross State University	1	16		
	1	**16**		
IAH=Houston-Intercontinental, TX				
Texas A&M U - Main Campus	3	13	2	8
	3	**13**	**2**	**8**
MAF=Midland/Odessa, TX				
Sul Ross State University	1	16		
	1	**16**		
MSY=New Orleans, LA				
U of Southern Mississippi	28	1		
	28	**1**		
PWA=Oklahoma City-Wiley Post, OK				
Cameron University	15	1		3
	15	**1**		**3**
ROW=Roswell, NM				
Eastern NM U - Main Campus	3	21	2	5
	3	**21**	**2**	**5**
TCL=Tuscaloosa, AL				
Mississippi State University	43			
	43			

COMMUNICATIONS (0600)

COMMUNICATIONS (0600)
MINORITY BACCALAUREATE DEGREES
BY STATE AND INSTITUTION

STATE/SCHOOL	MINORITY GROUP			
	Black	Hispanic	Asian	Native American
Alabama				
Alabama A&M University*	2			
Alabama State University*	1			
Miles College*	1			
University of Alabama	17			
U at Alabama in Birmingham	1			
	22			
Arizona				
Arizona State University	3	3	1	
Northern Arizona University	3	4		
University of Arizona	1	7	2	
	7	14	3	
Arkansas				
Arkansas State U – Main Campus	9			1
Henderson State University	5			
	14			1
California				
Cal Poly State U – San Luis Obispo		1	4	1
Cal State Poly U – Pomona	1	5	1	2
Cal State University – Chico	2	2	4	
Cal State U – Dominguez Hills	5	1	1	
Cal State University – Fresno	3	3	1	
Cal State University – Fullerton	5	7	9	3
Cal State University – Hayward	7	1	1	
Cal State University – Long Beach	12	7	6	
Cal State University – Los Angeles	8	5	6	
Cal State University – Northridge	11	8	7	2
Cal State University – Sacramento	1		1	

(0600)

STATE/SCHOOL	MINORITY GROUP			
	Black	Hispanic	Asian	Native American
California (cont)				
Chapman College	1	1		
Loyola Marymount University	5	2	1	
Pacific Christian College				1
Pepperdine University	2	1	4	
San Diego State University	9	7	6	
San Francisco State University	19	11	9	1
San Jose State University	16	4	9	
Stanford University	10	7	4	
U of Cal – Berkeley		1		
U of Cal – Davis	1		1	
U of Cal – Los Angeles		4	4	
U of Cal – San Diego		3	1	
University of LaVerne	1		1	
University of San Francisco	1	1	3	
University of Southern California	17	3	4	
University of the Pacific	1			
	138	**85**	**88**	**10**
Colorado				
Metropolitan State College		1		
U of Colorado at Boulder	5	8	2	
U of Northern Colorado	5	3	2	1
U of Southern Colorado	1	1		
	11	**13**	**4**	**1**
Delaware				
University of Delaware	6			
	6			
District of Columbia				
American University	25	2		
George Washington University	5	1	1	
Howard University*	103			
University of DC*	5			
	138	**3**	**1**	

256

(0600)

STATE/SCHOOL	MINORITY GROUP			
	Black	Hispanic	Asian	Native American
Florida				
Florida Agr & Mech University*	11			
Florida Atlantic University		2		
Florida International University	6	7		
Florida State University	18	2		1
University of Central Florida	1	2		
University of Florida	20	16		
University of Miami	5	2		
University of South Florida	3	4		
University of West Florida	6	1		
	70	**36**		**1**
Georgia				
Clark College*	49			
Georgia State University	16			2
Morehouse College*	6			
Morris Brown College*	10			
University of Georgia	10	1	1	
	91	**1**	**1**	**2**
Hawaii				
University of Hawaii at Manoa*	1	1	55	
	1	**1**	**55**	
Illinois				
Bradley University	1		1	
Columbia College	42	4	4	2
Eastern Illinois University	1			
Governors State University	3			
Illinois State University	15	1		
Loyola University of Chicago	5	3		
Northern Illinois University	4			
Northwestern University	33	3	2	
Roosevelt University	3			
Southern Illinois U – Carbondale	19		1	

(0600)

STATE/SCHOOL	MINORITY GROUP			
	Black	Hispanic	Asian	Native American
Illinois (cont)				
Southern Illinois U - Edwardsville	16			
U of Illinois - Urbana Campus	7	1	1	
	149	**12**	**9**	**2**
Indiana				
Ball State University	6			
Indiana State U - Main Campus	7			
Indiana University - Bloomington	10	1	1	
Purdue University - Main Campus	8	1		
	31	**2**	**1**	
Kentucky				
Eastern Kentucky University	6			
University of Louisville	1			
Western Kentucky University	10			
	17			
Louisiana				
Grambling State University*	20			
Louisiana State U & A&M College	5		1	
Louisiana Tech University	3			
McNeese State University	1			
Northeast Louisiana University	4	1		
Sthrn U A&M College - Main Cam*	29			
Tulane U of Louisiana	1			
University of New Orleans	8	1		
U of Southwestern Louisiana	1			
Xavier University of Louisiana*	8			
	80	**2**	**1**	
Maryland				
Bowie State College*	1			
Towson State University	14			1
U of MD - College Park Campus	26	4	1	2
	41	**4**	**1**	**3**

258

(0600)

STATE/SCHOOL	MINORITY GROUP			
	Black	Hispanic	Asian	Native American
Massachussetts				
Boston University	13	2	1	
U of Mass – Amherst Campus	4			1
	17	**2**	**1**	**1**
Michigan				
Eastern Michigan University	2			
Michigan State University	34	2	2	
Oakland University	4		1	
University of Detroit	19	2		
U of Michigan – Ann Arbor	3	1	2	
Wayne State University	28	1	1	
Western Michigan University	21	1		1
	111	**7**	**6**	**1**
Minnesota				
U of Minn – Minneapolis/St. Paul	2		3	2
	2		**3**	**2**
Mississippi				
Jackson State University*	36			
Mississippi State University	10			
Mississippi University for Women	4			
U of Mississippi – Main Campus	5			
U of Southern Mississippi	9			
	64			
Missouri				
Lincoln University	3			
Park College	7			
St. Louis U – Main Campus	12		2	
U of Missouri – Columbia	11	1	1	
Washington University	1			
Webster College	2			
	36	**1**	**3**	

(0600)

STATE/SCHOOL	MINORITY GROUP			
	Black	Hispanic	Asian	Native American
Nebraska				
U of Nebraska at Omaha	3	1		
	3	**1**		
New Jersey				
Glassboro State College	12	5		3
Jersey City State College	5	1	1	
Rutgers U - New Brunswick	12	3		
Seton Hall University	9			
	38	**9**	**1**	**3**
New Mexico				
Eastern NM U - Main Campus	1	3		
New Mexico Highlands U*		3		
NM State U - Main Campus		4		
U of NM - Main Campus		3		1
	1	**13**		**1**
New York				
Adelphi University	2			
College of New Rochelle	3			
CUNY Brooklyn College	14	5	1	
CUNY Hunter College	26	15	5	2
CUNY Queen's College	26	7	8	1
Fordham University	4	5	1	
Long Island U - Brooklyn Center	3	1		
Long Island U - C W Post Center	2			
New York University	9		2	1
Pratt Institute	14	4	5	
St. John's University	7	1		
SUNY College at Buffalo	3	4		1
Syracuse University - Main Campus	14	2	2	
	127	**44**	**24**	**5**

(0600)

STATE/SCHOOL	MINORITY GROUP			
	Black	Hispanic	Asian	Native American
North Carolina				
Johnson C Smith University*	28			
Shaw University*	11			
U of NC at Chapel Hill	11	1		1
	50	**1**		**1**
North Dakota				
U of North Dakota – Main Campus		1		
		1		
Ohio				
Antioch University	4			
Bowling Green State U – Main Cam	12	2		
Central State University*	6			
Kent State U – Main Campus	18			1
Oberlin College	8		1	
Ohio State U – Main Campus	8	1		
Ohio University – Main Campus	22	1		
U of Akron – Main Campus	6			
U of Cincinnati – Main Campus	2			
University of Dayton	7	1		
University of Toledo	2			
Wilberforce University*	6			
	101	**5**	**1**	**1**
Oklahoma				
Central State University		1		
Langston University*	6			
Northeast Oklahoma State U	2	1		3
Oklahoma State U – Main Campus	4	1		2
U of Oklahoma – Norman Campus	8		1	2
	20	**3**	**1**	**7**
Oregon				
Oregon State University			1	
University of Oregon – Main Campus	2	1	8	1
	2	**1**	**9**	**1**

(0600)

STATE/SCHOOL	MINORITY GROUP			
	Black	Hispanic	Asian	Native American
Pennsylvania				
Pennsylvania State U – Main Campus	4	1		
Temple University	38	12	1	2
University of Pennsylvania	1			
	43	**13**	**1**	**2**
South Carolina				
Benedict College*	15			
U of South Carolina at Columbia	22		1	
Winthrop College	4			
	41		**1**	
Tennessee				
Lane College*	2			
Memphis State University	9		1	
Middle Tennessee State U	5	1	3	
U of Tennessee – Knoxville	13			
U of Tennessee – Martin	4			
	33	**1**	**4**	
Texas				
Angelo State University		1		
Corpus Christi State University		3		
East Texas State University	5	3	1	
Lamar University	1			2
North Texas State University	9	3	1	
Pan American University*	1	7		
Prairie View A&M University*	10			
Sam Houston State University	4		2	1
Southwest Texas State University	1			
Texas A&I University		3		
Texas A&M U – Main Campus		1		
Texas Southern University*	23			
Texas Women's University	1			
Trinity University	1	2		

262

(0600)

STATE/SCHOOL	MINORITY GROUP			
	Black	Hispanic	Asian	Native American
Texas (cont)				
U of Houston – Central Campus	7	7	1	
U of Texas at Arlington	13	2	1	1
U of Texas at Austin	15	32	1	3
U of Texas at El Paso	1	15		
	92	**79**	**7**	**7**
Utah				
Brigham Young University – Main			1	
University of Utah		1	1	
		1	**2**	
Virginia				
Hampton Institute*	39			
Norfolk State College*	30			
Virginia Commonwealth University	12			2
Virginia Union University*	2			
	83			**2**
Washington				
University of Washington	10		14	1
	10		**14**	**1**
West Virginia				
West Virginia State College	1			
	1			
Wisconsin				
U of Wisconsin – Madison	5	1		1
U of Wisconsin – Milwaukee	10			
	15	**1**		**1**
TOTALS	**1,706**	**356**	**242**	**56**

*Predominately minority institutions are those where at least 50% of the total BA Degrees awarded are to one of the minority groups being considerd.

COMMUNICATIONS (0600)
BLACK BACCALAUREATE DEGREES RANKED BY INSTITUTION

Rank	Institution	B.A.'s	Rank	Institution	B.A.'s
1	Howard U*	103	29	U of Alabama	17
2	Clark C*	49	30	San Jose State U	16
3	Columbia C	42	31	Southern Illinois U-Edwardsville	16
4	Hampton Institute*	39	32	Georgia State U	16
5	Temple U	38	33	U of Texas at Austin	15
6	Jackson State U*	36	34	Illinois State U	15
7	Michigan State U	34	35	Benedict C*	15
8	Northwestern U	33	36	Syracuse U-Main Campus	14
9	Norfolk State C*	30	37	CUNY Brooklyn C	14
10	Sthrn U A&M C-Main Campus	29	38	Towson State U	14
11	Wayne State U	28	39	Pratt Institute	14
12	Johnson C Smith U*	28	40	U of Texas at Arlington	13
13	CUNY Queen's C	26	41	Boston U	13
14	U of MD-College Park Campus	26	42	U of Tennessee-Knoxville	13
15	CUNY Hunter C	26	43	Glasssboro State C	12
16	American U	25	44	St. Louis U-Main Campus	12
17	Texas Southern U*	23	45	Bowling Green State U-Main Ca	12
18	Ohio U-Main Campus	22	46	Rutgers U-New Brunswick	12
19	U of South Carolina at Columbia	22	47	Cal State U-Long Beach	12
20	Western Michigan U	21	48	Virginia Commonwealth U	12
21	U of Florida	20	49	Shaw U*	11
22	Grambling State U*	20	50	Cal State U-Northridge	11
23	San Francisco State U	19	51	U of Missouri-Columbia	11
24	Southern Illinois U-Carbondale	19	52	Florida Agrl & Mech U*	11
25	U of Detroit	19	53	U of NC at Chapel Hill	11
26	Florida State U	18	54	Indiana U-Bloomington	10
27	Kent State U-Main Campus	18	55	Stanford U	10
28	U of Southern California	17	56	Western Kentucky U	10

264

Black B.A.'s (0600)

Rank	Institution	B.A.'s	Rank	Institution	B.A.'s
57	Morris Brown C*	10	60	Prairie View A&M U*	10
58	U of Washington	10	61	U of Georgia	10
59	Mississippi State U	10	62	U of Wisconsin-Milwaukee	10

*predominantly black institutions

Institutions not ranked have less than ten degrees conferred on blacks.

COMMUNICATIONS (0600)
HISPANIC BACCALAUREATE DEGREES RANKED BY INSTITUTION

Rank	Institution	B.A.'s	Rank	Institution	B.A.'s
1	U of Texas at Austin	32	4	CUNY Hunter C	15
2	U of Florida	16	5	Temple U	12
3	U of Texas at El Paso	15	6	San Francisco State U	11

Institutions not ranked have less than ten degrees conferred on Hispanics.

COMMUNICATIONS (0600)
ASIAN BACCALAUREATE DEGREES RANKED BY INSTITUTION

Rank	Institution	B.A.'s
1	U of Hawaii at Manoa*	55
2	U of Washington	14

*predominantly Asian institutions

Institutions not ranked have less than ten degrees conferred on Asians.

COMMUNICATIONS (0600)
MINORITY BACCALAUREATE DEGREES
WITHIN 60 MILE RADIUS OF AIRPORT

AIRPORT		MINORITY GROUP		
	Black	Hispanic	Asian	Native American
ABQ=Albuquerque, NM				
U of NM - Main Campus		3		1
		3		1
AOO=Altoona, PA				
Pennsylvania State U - Main Campus	4	1		
	4	1		
ATL=Atlanta, GA				
Clark College*	49			
Georgia State University	16			2
Morehouse College*	6			
Morris Brown College*	10			
	81			2
AUS=Austin, TX				
Southwest Texas State University	1			
U of Texas at Austin	15	32	1	3
	16	32	1	3
BAL=Baltimore, MD				
University of Delaware	6			
American University	25	2		
George Washington Univesity	5	1	1	
Howard University*	103			
University of DC*	5			
Bowie State College*	1			
Towson State University	14			1
U of MD - College Park Campus	26	4	1	2
	185	7	2	3

Airport 60 (0600)

AIRPORT	MINORITY GROUP			
	Black	Hispanic	Asian	Native American
BDL=Hartford, CT/Springfield, MA				
U of Mass – Amherst Campus	4			1
	4			1
BHM=Birmingham, AL				
Miles College*	1			
U of Alabama in Birmingham	1			
University of Alabama	17			
	19			
BKL=Cleveland–Lakefront, OH				
Kent State U – Main Campus	18			1
Oberlin College	8		1	
U of Akron – Main Campus	6			
	32		1	1
BNA=Nashville, TN				
Western Kentucky University	10			
Middle Tennessee State U	5	1	3	
	15	1	3	
BOS=Boston, MA				
Boston University	13	2	1	
	13	2	1	
BTR=Baton Rouge, LA				
Louisiana State U & A&M College	5		1	
Sthrn U A&M College – Main Cam*	29			
	34		1	
BUF=Buffalo, NY				
SUNY College at Buffalo	3	4		1
	3	4		1
CAE=Columbia, SC				
Benedict College*	15			
U of South Carolina at Columbia	22		1	
	37		1	

Airport 60 (0600)

AIRPORT	MINORITY GROUP			
	Black	Hispanic	Asian	Native American
CIC=Chico, CA				
Cal State University - Chico	2	2	4	
	2	**2**	**4**	
CLT=Charlotte, NC				
Johnson C Smith University*	28			
Winthrop College	4			
	32			
CMH=Columbus, OH				
Central State University*	6			
Ohio State U - Main Campus	8	1		
Wilberforce University*	6			
	20	**1**		
CMI=Champaign, IL				
Eastern Illinois University	1			
Illinois State University	15	1		
U of Illinois - Urbana Campus	7	1	1	
Indiana State U - Main Campus	7			
	30	**2**	**1**	
COS=Colorado Springs, CO				
U of Southern Colorado	1	1		
	1	**1**		
COU=Columbia, MO				
Lincoln University	3			
U of Missouri - Columbia	11	1	1	
	14	**1**	**1**	
CRP=Corpus Christi, TX				
Corpus Christi State University		3		
Texas A&I University		3		
		6		
CRW=Charleston, WV				
West Virginia State College	1			
	1			

268

Airport 60 (0600)

AIRPORT	MINORITY GROUP			
	Black	Hispanic	Asian	Native American
CVG=Cincinnati, OH				
Antioch University	4			
Central State University*	6			
U of Cincinnati - Main Campus	2			
University of Dayton	7	1		
Wilberforce University*	6			
	25	**1**		
DAB=Dayton Beach, FL				
University of Central Florida	1	2		
	1	**2**		
DCA=Washington-National, DC				
American University	25	2		
George Washington University	5	1	1	
Howard University*	103			
University of DC*	5			
Bowie State College*	1			
Towson State University	14			1
U of MD - College Park Campus	26	4	1	2
	179	**7**	**2**	**3**
DEN=Denver, CO				
Metropolitan State College		1		
U of Colorado at Boulder	5	8	2	
U of Northern Colorado	5	3	2	1
	10	**12**	**4**	**1**
DFW=Dallas/Fort Worth, TX				
East Texas State University	5	3	1	
North Texas State University	9	3	1	
Texas Woman's University	1			
U of Texas at Arlington	13	2	1	1
	28	**8**	**3**	**1**

Airport 60 (0600)

AIRPORT	MINORITY GROUP			
	Black	Hispanic	Asian	Native American
DTW=Detroit-Metropolitan, MI				
Eastern Michigan University	2			
Oakland University	4		1	
U of Michigan - Ann Arbor	3	1	2	
University of Detroit	19	2		
Wayne State University	28	1	1	
University of Toledo	2			
	58	**4**	**4**	
ELP=El Paso, TX				
U of Texas at El Paso	1	15		
	1	**15**		
EUG=Eugene, OR				
Oregon State University			1	
University of Oregon - Main Campus	2	1	8	1
	2	**1**	**9**	**1**
FAT=Fresno, CA				
Cal State University - Fresno	3	3	1	
	3	**3**	**1**	
FAY=Fayetteville, NC				
Shaw University*	11			
U of NC at Chapel Hill	11	1		1
	22	**1**		**1**
FLG=Flagstaff, AZ				
Northern Arizona University	3	4		
	3	**4**		
GRR=Grand Rapids, MI				
Western Michigan University	21	1		1
	21	**1**		**1**
GSO=Greensboro/High Point, NC				
U of NC at Chapel Hill	11	1		1
	11	**1**		**1**

Airport 60 (0600)

AIRPORT	MINORITY GROUP			
	Black	Hispanic	Asian	Native American
HNL=Honolulu/Oahu, HI				
University of Hawaii at Manoa*	1	1	55	
	1	**1**	**55**	
HSV=Huntsville, AL/Decatur, GA				
Alabama A&M University*	2			
	2			
IAH=Houston–Intercontinental,TX				
Prairie View A&M University*	10			
Texas Southern University*	23			
U of Houston - Central Campus	7	7	1	
	40	**7**	**1**	
IND=Indianapolis, IN				
Ball State University	6			
Indiana University - Bloomington	10	1	1	
Purdue University - Main Campus	8	1		
	24	**2**	**1**	
JAN=Jackson/Vicksburg, MS				
Jackson State University*	36			
	36			
JFK=New York, Kennedy Int'l, NY				
Jersey City State College	5	1	1	
Rutgers U-New Brunswick	12	3		
Seton Hall University	9			
Adelphi University	2			
College of New Rochelle	3			
CUNY Brooklyn College	14	5	1	
CUNY Hunter College	26	15	5	2
CUNY Queen's College	26	7	8	1
Fordham University	4	5	1	
Long Island U - Brooklyn Center	3	1		
Long Island U - C W Post Center	2			

Airport 60 (0600)

AIRPORT	MINORITY GROUP			
	Black	Hispanic	Asian	Native American
JFK (cont)				
New York University	9		2	1
Pratt Institute	14	4	5	
St. John's University	7	1		
	136	**42**	**23**	**4**
LAX=Los Angeles, CA				
Cal State Poly U - Pomona	1	5	1	2
Cal State U - Dominguez Hills	5	1	1	
Cal State University - Fullerton	5	7	9	3
Cal State University - Long Beach	12	7	6	
Cal State University - Los Angeles	8	5	6	
Cal State University - Northridge	11	8	7	2
Chapman College	1	1		
Loyola Marymount University	5	2	1	
Pacific Christian College				1
Pepperdine University	2	1	4	
U of Cal - Los Angeles		4	4	
University of Southern California	17	3	4	
University of LaVerne	1		1	
	68	**44**	**44**	**8**
LCH=Lake Charles, LA				
McNeese State University	1			
	1			
LEX=Lexington/Frankfort, KY				
Eastern Kentucky University	6			
University of Louisville	1			
	7			
MCI=Kansas City-International, MO				
Park College	7			
	7			
MDH=Carbondale, IL				
Southern Illinois U - Carbondale	19		1	
	19		**1**	

Airport 60 (0600)

AIRPORT	MINORITY GROUP			
	Black	Hispanic	Asian	Native American
MEM=Memphis, TN				
Memphis State University	9		1	
	9		1	
MFE=McAllen, TX				
Pan American University*	1	7		
	1	7		
MGM=Montgomery, GA				
Alabama State University*	1			
	1			
MIA=Miami, FL				
Florida Atlantic University		2		
Florida International University	6	7		
University of Miami	5	2		
	11	11		
MKE=Milwaukee, WS				
U of Wisconsin - Milwaukee	10			
	10			
MKL=Jackson, TN				
Lane College*	2			
U of Tennessee at Martin	4			
	6			
MLU=Monroe, LA				
Grambling State University*	20			
Louisiana Tech University	3			
Northeast Louisiana University	4	1		
	27	1		
MOB=Mobile, AL/Pasagoula, MS				
University of West Florida	6	1		
	6	1		
MSN=Madison, WS				
U of Wisconsin - Madison	5	1		1
	5	1		1

Airport 60 (0600)

AIRPORT	MINORITY GROUP			
	Black	Hispanic	Asian	Native American
MSP=Minneapolis/St. Paul, MN				
U of Minn - Minneapolis/St. Paul	2		3	2
	2		**3**	**2**
MSY=New Orleans, LA				
Tulane U of Louisiana	1			
University of New Orleans	8	1		
Xavier University of Louisiana*	8			
	17	**1**		
ORD=Chicago–O'Hare Airport, IL				
Columbia College	42	4	4	2
Governors State University	3			
Loyola University of Chicago	5	3		
Northern Illinois University	4			
Northwestern University	33	3	2	
Roosevelt University	3			
	90	**10**	**6**	**2**
ORF=Norfolk/Virginia Beach, VA				
Hampton Institute*	39			
Norfolk State College*	30			
	69			
PHL=Philadelphia, PA/Wilmington, DE				
University of Delaware	6			
Glassboro State College	12	5		3
Rutgers U - New Brunswick	12	3		
Temple University	38	12	1	2
University of Pennsylvania	1			
	69	**20**	**1**	**5**
PHX=Phoenix, AZ				
Arizona State University	3	3	1	
	3	**3**	**1**	
PIA=Peoria, IL				
Bradley University	1		1	
	1		**1**	

274

Airport 60 (0600)

AIRPORT	MINORITY GROUP			
	Black	Hispanic	Asian	Native American
PVD=Providence, RI				
Boston University	13	2	1	
	13	2	1	
PWA=Oklahoma City-Wiley Post, OK				
Central State University		1		
Langston University*	6			
Oklahoma State U - Main Campus	4	1		2
U of Oklahoma - Norman Campus	8		1	2
	18	2	1	4
RDU=Raleigh/Durham, NC				
Shaw University*	11			
U of NC at Chapel Hill	11	1		1
	22	1		1
RIC=Richmond, VA				
Virginia Commonwealth University	12			2
Virginia Union University*	2			
	14			2
SAN=San Diego, CA				
San Diego State University	9	7	6	
U of Cal - San Diego		3	1	
	9	10	7	
SAT=San Antonio, TX				
Southwest Texas State University	1			
Trinity University	1	2		
	2	2		
SBA=Santa Barbara, CA				
Pepperdine University	2	1	4	
	2	1	4	
SBP=San Luis Obispo, CA				
Cal Poly State U - San Luis Obispo		1	4	1
		1	4	1

Airport 60 (0600)

AIRPORT	MINORITY GROUP			
	Black	Hispanic	Asian	Native American
SEA=Seattle/Tacoma, WA				
University of Washington	10		14	1
	10		**14**	**1**
SFO=San Francisco/Oakland, CA				
Cal State University - Hayward	7	1	1	
San Francisco State University	19	11	9	1
San Jose State University	16	4	9	
Stanford University	10	7	4	
U of Cal - Berkeley		1		
University of San Francisco	1	1	3	
	53	**25**	**26**	**1**
SHV=Shreveport, LA				
Grambling State University*	20			
	20			
SJT=San Angelo, TX				
Angelo State University		1		
		1		
SLC=Salt Lake City, UT				
Brigham Young University - Main			1	
University of Utah		1	1	
		1	**2**	
STL=St. Louis, MO				
Southern Illinois U - Edwardsville	16			
St. Louis U - Main Campus	12		2	
Washington University	1			
Webster College	2			
	31		**2**	
SWI=Sherman, TX				
East Texas State University	5	3	1	
North Texas State University	9	3	1	
Texas Woman's University	1			
	15	**6**	**2**	

Airport 60 (0600)

AIRPORT	MINORITY GROUP			
	Black	Hispanic	Asian	Native American
SYR=Syracuse, NY				
Syracuse U-Main Campus	14	2	2	
	14	**2**	**2**	
TCL=Tuscaloosa, AL				
Miles College*	1			
U of Alabama in Birmingham	1			
University of Alabama	17			
Mississippi University for Women	4			
	23			
TLH=Tallahassee, FL				
Florida Agr & Mech University*	11			
Florida State University	18	2		1
	29	**2**		**1**
TPA=Tampa, FL				
University of South Florida	3	4		
	3	**4**		
TUL=Tulsa, OK				
Northeast Oklahoma State U	2	1		3
	2	**1**		**3**
TUS=Tucson, AZ				
University of Arizona	1	7	2	
	1	**7**	**2**	
TYS=Knoxville, TN				
U of Tennessee - Knoxville	13			
	13			

COMMUNICATIONS (0600)
MINORITY BACCALAUREATE DEGREES
WITHIN 61-80 MILE ANNULUS OF AIRPORT

AIRPORT	MINORITY GROUP			
	Black	Hispanic	Asian	Native American
ALB=Albany, NY				
U of Mass - Amherst Campus	4			1
	4			**1**
ALM=Alamogordo, NM				
NM State U - Main Campus		4		
		4		
ATL=Atlanta, GA				
University of Georgia	10	1	1	
	10	**1**	**1**	
AUS=Austin, TX				
Trinity University	1	2		
	1	**2**		
BDL=Hartford, CT/Springfield, MA				
College of New Rochelle	3			
	3			
BOS=Boston, MA				
U of Mass - Amherst Campus	4			1
	4			**1**
BTR=Baton Rouge, LA				
Tulane U of Louisiana	1			
U of Southwestern Louisiana	1			
University of New Orleans	8	1		
Xavier University of Louisiana*	8	1		
	18	**1**		
CAE=Columbia, SC				
Winthrop College	4			
	4			

Airport 61-80 (0600)

AIRPORT	MINORITY GROUP			
	Black	Hispanic	Asian	Native American
CMH=Columbus, OH				
Antioch University	4			
Ohio University - Main Campus	22	1		
University of Dayton	7	1		
	33	2		
CMI=Champaign, IL				
Purdue University - Main Campus	8	1		
	8	1		
COS=Colorado Springs, CO				
Metropolitan State College		1		
U of Colorado at Boulder	5	8	2	
	5	9	2	
CRW=Charleston, WV				
Ohio University - Main Campus	22	1		
	22	1		
DTW=Detroit-Metropolitan, MI				
Michigan State University	34	2	2	
Bowling Green State U - Main Cam	12	2		
	46	4	2	
GRR=Grand Rapids, MI				
Michigan State University	34	2	2	
	34	2	2	
GSO=Greensboro/High Point, NC				
Shaw University*	11			
	11			
HSV=Huntsville, AL/Decatur, GA				
Middle Tennessee State U	5	1	3	
	5	1	3	
IAH=Houston-Intercontinental,TX				
Sam Houston State University	4		2	1
	4		2	1

Airport 61-80 (0600)

AIRPORT	MINORITY GROUP			
	Black	Hispanic	Asian	Native American
IND=Indianapolis, IN				
Indiana State U - Main Campus	7			
	7			
JAX=Jacksonville, FL				
University of Florida	20	16		
	20	16		
LCH=Lake Charles, LA				
U of Southwestern Louisiana	1			
Lamar University	1			2
	2			2
LIT=Little Rock, AR				
Henderson State University	5			
	5			
MCN=Macon, GA				
Clark College*	49			
Georgia State University	16			2
Morehouse College*	6			
Morris Brown College*	10			
	81			2
MEM=Memphis, TN				
Arkansas State U - Main Campus	9			1
U of Mississippi - Main Campus	5			
Lane College*	2			
	16			1
MHT=Manchester, NH				
Boston University	13	2	1	
U of Mass - Amherst Campus	4			1
	17	2	1	1
MKE=Milwaukee, WS				
Northwestern University	33	3	2	
U of Wisconsin - Madison	5	1		1
	38	4	2	1

Airport 61-80 (0600)

AIRPORT	MINORITY GROUP			
	Black	Hispanic	Asian	Native American
MKL=Jackson, TN				
Memphis State University	9		1	
	9		1	
MOB=Mobile, AL/Pasagoula, MS				
U of Southern Mississippi	9			
	9			
MSN=Madison, WS				
U of Wisconsin - Milwaukee	10			
	10			
MSY=New Orleans, LA				
Louisiana State U & A&M College	5		1	
Sthrn U A&M C - Main Cam*	29			
	34		1	
PVD=Providence, RI				
U of Mass - Amherst Campus	4			1
	4			1
RIC=Richmond, VA				
Hampton Institute*	39			
Norfolk State College*	30			
	69			
SAN=San Diego, CA				
Chapman College	1	1		
	1	1		
SAT=San Antonio, TX				
U of Texas at Austin	15	32	1	3
	15	32	1	3
SBA=Santa Barbara, CA				
Cal State University - Los Angeles	8	5	6	
Cal State University - Northridge	11	8	7	2
Loyola Marymount University	5	2	1	
U of Cal - Los Angeles		4	4	
	24	19	18	2

Airport 61-80 (0600)

AIRPORT	MINORITY GROUP			
	Black	Hispanic	Asian	Native American
SFO=San Francisco/Oakland, CA				
Cal State University - Sacramento	1		1	
U of Cal - Davis	1		1	
University of the Pacific	1			
	3		2	
SHV=Shreveport, LA				
Louisiana Tech University	3			
	3			
SWI=Sherman, TX				
U of Texas at Arlington	13	2	1	1
	13	2	1	
TPA=Tampa, FL				
University of Central Florida	1	2		
	1	2		
TUL=Tulsa, OK				
Oklahoma State U - Main Campus	4	1		2
	4	1		2
TYR=Tyler, TX				
East Texas State University	5	3	1	
	5	3	1	

COMMUNICATIONS (0600)
MINORITY BACCALAUREATE DEGREES
MORE THAN 80 MILES FROM NEAREST AIRPORT

AIRPORT	MINORITY GROUP			
	Black	Hispanic	Asian	Native American
ABQ=Albuquerque, NM				
New Mexico Highlands U*		3		
		3		
AUS=Austin, TX				
Texas A&M U – Main Campus		1		
		1		
IAH=Houston–Intercontinental, TX				
Texas A&M U – Main Campus		1		
		1		
MSY=New Orleans, LA				
U of Southern Mississippi	9			
	9			
ROW=Roswell, NM				
Eastern NM U – Main Campus	1	3		
	1	3		
TCL=Tuscaloosa, AL				
Mississippi State University	10			
	10			

COMPUTER & INFORMATION SCIENCES (0700)

COMPUTER AND INFORMATION SCIENCES (0700)
MINORITY BACCALAUREATE DEGREES
BY STATE AND INSTITUTION

STATE/SCHOOL	MINORITY GROUP			
	Black	Hispanic	Asian	Native American
Alabama				
Alabama A&M University*	23			
Alabama State University*	13			
Troy State University - Main Campus	2			
Troy State University - Montgomery	1			
	39			
Arizona				
Arizona State University		3	2	
Northern Arizona University		1		
University of Arizona		3	2	
		7	**4**	
Arkansas				
Arkansas State U - Main Campus	1		1	
	1		**1**	
California				
Cal Poly State U - San Luis Obispo		1		1
Cal State Poly U - Pomona		2	1	
Cal State University - Chico	1	5		1
Cal State University - Fullerton		2	1	2
Cal State University - Northridge	2	4	5	
Cal State University - Sacramento			5	
San Diego State University	2	3	9	
U of Cal - Berkeley	3	1	27	1
U of Cal - Irvine	7		4	
U of Cal - Santa Cruz			1	
University of San Francisco	1			
University of Southern California		1	3	
	16	**19**	**58**	**5**

(0700)

STATE/SCHOOL	MINORITY GROUP			
	Black	Hispanic	Asian	Native American
Colorado				
Colorado State University	1	2		
Metropolitan State College	2	2		
U of Colorado at Boulder			1	
	3	**4**	**1**	
Connecticut				
University of Connecticut		1	1	
Yale University		1	1	
		2	**2**	
District of Columbia				
American University	8	2	1	
Howard University*	3			
University of DC*	11	1		
	22	**3**	**1**	
Florida				
Florida Agr & Mech University*	7		1	
Florida Atlantic University		2		
Florida International University	1	16	1	
University of Central Florida	2		1	
University of Florida	1	3	2	
University of Miami		4	1	
University of West Florida	3	2	1	1
	14	**27**	**7**	**1**
Georgia				
GA Inst of Tech - Main Campus		1		
Georgia State University	1			1
Morris Brown College*	1			
Spelman College*	2			
University of Georgia	1	1	1	
	5	**2**	**1**	**1**
Hawaii				
University of Hawaii at Manoa*			30	
			30	

286

(0700)

STATE/SCHOOL

	Black	Hispanic	Asian	Native American
MINORITY GROUP				
Illinois				
Bradley University	6			
DePaul University	1			
Eastern Illinois University	3		1	
Northern Illinois University	4		3	
Northeastern Illinois University	1		11	
Roosevelt University	23		3	
Southern Illinois U - Carbondale			1	
U of Illinois - Chicago Circle	1	2	5	
U of Illinois - Urbana Campus	1			
	40	**2**	**24**	
Indiana				
Indiana University - Bloomington			1	
			1	
Kentucky				
Eastern Kentucky University	5			
Kentucky State University*	3			
	8			
Louisiana				
Grambling State University*	36			
Louisiana State U & A&M College	1			
Northeast Louisiana University	2			
Sthrn U A&M College - Main Cam*	41			
U of Southwestern Louisiana	3			1
	83			**1**
Maryland				
U of MD - College Park Campus	5		1	
	5		**1**	
Michigan				
Detroit Institute of Technology	1			
Michigan State University	1		1	
Oakland University	1		1	

(0700)

STATE/SCHOOL	MINORITY GROUP			
	Black	Hispanic	Asian	Native American
Michigan (cont)				
U of Michigan - Ann Arbor	1		2	
Wayne State University	1			
	5		4	
Minnesota				
U of Minn - Minneapolis/St. Paul	1		4	
	1		4	
Mississippi				
Jackson State University*	32			
Mississippi State University	2			
Mississippi Valley State Univ*	8			
U of Southern Mississippi	3		2	
	45		2	
Missouri				
Washington University	1		1	
	1		1	
Nebraska				
U of Nebraska at Omaha	5			
	5			
New Jersey				
Kean College of New Jersey	4	2		
New Jersey Inst Technology	1		1	
Rutgers U - New Brunswick			4	
St. Peter's College		1		
	5	3	5	
New Mexico				
Eastern NM U - Main Campus	1	1		
NM State U - Main Campus		1		
U of NM - Main Campus	1	2		
	2	4		

(0700)

STATE/SCHOOL	MINORITY GROUP			
	Black	Hispanic	Asian	Native American
New York				
CUNY Bernard Baruch College	13	5	5	
CUNY Brooklyn College	17	7	2	
CUNY City College	16	8	6	1
CUNY Hunter College	5	4	2	
CUNY Queen's College	11	3	3	
New York University	2		5	
Pace University New York	2			
Polytechnic Institute New York			2	
Pratt Institute	4		1	
St. John's University	2	2	2	
SUNY at Stony Bk - Main Campus	1	1	3	
SUNY College at Buffalo	1		1	
Syracuse University - Main Campus		1		
	74	**31**	**32**	**1**
North Carolina				
Duke University	2		1	
Johnson C Smith University*	2			
	4		**1**	
Ohio				
Bowling Green State U - Main Cam	1		1	
Ohio State U - Main Campus	1			
University of Dayton	2			
Wright State U - Main Campus	1			
	5		**1**	
Oklahoma				
Central State University			2	
			2	
Oregon				
Oregon State University	1		2	
University of Oregon - Main Campus			1	
	1		**3**	

(0700)

STATE/SCHOOL	MINORITY GROUP			
	Black	Hispanic	Asian	Native American
Pennsylvania				
Drexel University	1			
Pennsylvania State U – Main Campus	2		2	
Temple University	5	1	1	
University of Pittsburgh – Main Cam	8			
	16	**1**	**3**	
South Carolina				
U of South Carolina at Columbia	6	2	1	
	6	**2**	**1**	
Tennessee				
Middle Tennessee State U			1	
U of Tennessee – Knoxville	2			
	2		**1**	
Texas				
Bishop College*	2			
Corpus Christi State University		2	1	
East Texas State University	10	3	1	
Lamar University			1	
North Texas State University	4	1		
Sam Houston State University			1	
Southwest Texas State University	2	4	1	
Texas A&I University	1	2		
Texas A&M U – Main Campus		2		
Texas Southern University*	10			
Trinity University		4	1	
U of Houston – Central Campus	1	3	7	
U of Texas at Austin		3	1	
	30	**24**	**14**	
Virginia				
Old Dominion University	2			
U of Virginia – Main Campus	1			
Virginia Commonwealth University	2			
	5			

(0700)

STATE/SCHOOL	MINORITY GROUP			
	Black	Hispanic	Asian	Native American
Washington				
University of Washington			8	
			8	
Wisconsin				
U of Wisconsin - Madison	1			
	1			
TOTALS	**444**	**131**	**213**	**9**

*Predominately minority institutions are those where at least 50% of the total BA Degrees awarded are to one of the minority groups being considered.

COMPUTER AND INFORMATION SCIENCES (0700)
BLACK BACCALAUREATE DEGREES RANKED BY INSTITUTION

Rank	Institution	B.A.'s	Rank	Institution	B.A.'s
1	Howard U*	103	29	U of Alabama	17
2	Clark C*	49	30	San Jose State U	16
3	Columbia C	42	31	Southern Illinois U-Edwardsville	16
4	Hampton Institute*	39	32	Georgia State U	16
5	Temple U	38	33	U of Texas at Austin	15
6	Jackson State U*	36	34	Illinois State U	15
7	Michigan State U	34	35	Benedict C*	15
8	Northwestern U	33	36	Syracuse U-Main Campus	14
9	Norfolk State C*	30	37	CUNY Brooklyn College	14
10	Sthrn U A&M C-Main Campus	29	38	Towson State U	14
11	Wayne State U	28	39	Pratt Institute	14
12	Johnson C Smith U*	28	40	U of Texas at Arlington	13
13	CUNY Queen's C	26	41	Boston U	13
14	U of MD-College Park Campus	26	42	U of Tennessee-Knoxville	13
15	CUNY Hunter C	26	43	Glassboro State C	12
16	American U	25	44	St. Louis U-Main Campus	12
17	Texas Southern U*	23	45	Bowling Green State U-Main Ca	12
18	Ohio U-Main Campus	22	46	Rutgers U-New Brunswick	12
19	U of South Carolina at Columbia	22	47	Cal State U-Long Beach	12
20	Western Michigan U	21	48	Virginia Commonwealth U	12
21	U of Florida	20	49	Shaw U*	11
22	Grambling State U*	20	50	Cal State U-Northridge	11
23	San Francisco State U	19	51	U of Missouri-Columbia	11
24	Southern Illinois U-Carbondale	19	52	Florida Agrl & Mech U*	11
25	U of Detroit	19	53	U of NC at Chapel Hill	11
26	Florida State U	18	54	Indiana U-Bloomington	10
27	Kent State U-Main Campus	18	55	Stanford U	10
28	U of Southern California	17	56	Western Kentucky U	10

Black B.A.'s (0700)

Rank	Institution	B.A.'s	Rank	Institution	B.A.'s
57	Morris Brown C*	10	60	Prairie View A&M U*	10
58	U of Washington	10	61	U of Georgia	10
59	Mississippi State U	10	62	U of Wisconsin-Milwaukee	10

*predominantly black institutions

Institutions not ranked have less than ten degrees conferred on blacks.

COMPUTER & INFORMATION SCIENCES (0700)
HISPANIC BACCALAUREATE DEGREES RANKED BY INSTITUTION

Rank	Institution	B.A.'s
1	Florida International U	16

Institutions not ranked have less than ten degrees conferred on Hispanics.

COMPUTER & INFORMATION SCIENCES (0700)
ASIAN BACCALAUREATE DEGREES RANKED BY INSTITUTION

Rank	Institution	B.A.'s	Rank	Institution	B.A.'s
1	U of Hawaii at Manoa*	30	3	Northeasten Illinois U	11
2	U of Cal-Berkeley	27			

*predominantly Asian institutions

Institutions not ranked have less than ten degrees conferred on Asians.

COMPUTER AND INFORMATION SCIENCES (0700)
MINORITY BACCALAUREATE DEGREES
WITHIN 60 MILE RADIUS OF AIRPORT

AIRPORT	MINORITY GROUP			
	Black	Hispanic	Asian	Native American
ABQ=Albuquerque, NM				
U of NM - Main Campus	1	2		
	1	2		
AOO=Altoona, PA				
Pennsylvania State U - Main Campus	2		2	
	2		2	
ATL=Atlanta, GA				
GA Inst of Tech - Main Campus		1		
Georgia State University	1			1
Morris Brown College*	1			
Spelman College*	2			
	4	1		1
AUS=Austin, TX				
Southwest Texas State University	2	4	1	
U of Texas at Austin		3	1	
	2	7	2	
BAL=Baltimore, MD				
American University	8	2	1	
Howard University*	3			
University of DC*	11	1		
U of MD - College Park Campus	5		1	
	27	3	2	
BDL=Hartford, CT/Springfield, MA				
Yale University		1	1	
		1	1	
BNA=Nashville, TN				
Middle Tennessee State U			1	
			1	

Airport 60 (0700)

AIRPORT	MINORITY GROUP			
	Black	Hispanic	Asian	Native American
BTR=Baton Rouge, LA				
Louisiana State U & A&M College	1			
Sthrn U A&M College - Main Cam*	41			
	42			
BUF=Buffalo, NY				
SUNY College at Buffalo	1		1	
	1		**1**	
CAE=Columbia, SC				
U of South Carolina at Columbia	6	2	1	
	6	**2**	**1**	
CIC=Chico, CA				
Cal State University - Chico	1	5		1
	1	**5**		**1**
CLT=Charlotte, NC				
Johnson C Smith University*	2			
	2			
CMH=Columbus, OH				
Ohio State U - Main Campus	1			
	1			
CMI=Champaign, IL				
Eastern Illinois University	3		1	
U of Illinois - Urbana Campus	1			
	4		**1**	
CRP=Corpus Christi, TX				
Corpus Christi State University		2	1	
Texas A&I University	1	2		
	1	**4**	**1**	
CVG=Cincinnati, OH				
University of Dayton	2			
Wright State U - Main Campus	1			
	3			

Airport 60 (0700)

AIRPORT	MINORITY GROUP			
	Black	Hispanic	Asian	Native American
DAB=Dayton Beach, FL				
University of Central Florida	2		1	
	2		1	
DCA=Washington-National, DC				
American University	8	2	1	
Howard University*	3			
University of DC*	11	1		
U of MD - College Park Campus	5		1	
	27	3	2	
DEN=Denver, CO				
Metropolitan State College	2	2		
U of Colorado at Boulder			1	
	2	2	1	
DFW=Dallas/Fort Worth, TX				
Bishop College*	2			
East Texas State University	10	3	1	
North Texas State University	4	1		
	16	4	1	
DTW=Detroit-Metropolitan, MI				
Detroit Institute of Technology	1			
Oakland University	1		1	
U of Michigan - Ann Arbor	1		2	
Wayne State University	1			
	4		3	
EUG=Eugene, OR				
Oregon State University	1		2	
University of Oregon - Main Campus			1	
	1		3	
FLG=Flagstaff, AZ				
Northern Arizona University		1		
		1		

296

Airport 60 (0700)

AIRPORT	MINORITY GROUP			
	Black	Hispanic	Asian	Native American
GLH=Greenville, MS				
Mississippi Valley State U*	8			
	8			
GSO=Greensboro/High Point, NC				
Duke University	2		1	
	2		**1**	
HNL=Honolulu/Oahu, HI				
University of Hawaii at Manoa*			30	
			30	
HSV=Huntsville, AL/Decatur, GA				
Alabama A&M University*	23			
	23			
IAH=Houston-Intercontinental,TX				
Texas Southern University*	10			
U of Houston – Central Campus	1	3	7	
	11	**3**	**7**	
IND=Indianapolis, IN				
Indiana University – Bloomington			1	
			1	
JAN=Jackson/Vicksburg, MS				
Jackson State University*	32			
	32			
JFK=New York, Kennedy Int'l, NY				
Kean College of New Jersey	4	2		
New Jersey Inst of Technology	1		1	
Rutgers U – New Brunswick			4	
St. Peter's College		1		
CUNY Bernard Baruch College	13	5	5	
CUNY Brooklyn College	17	7	2	
CUNY City College	16	8	6	1
CUNY Hunter College	5	4	2	
CUNY Queen's College	11	3	3	

Airport 60 (0700)

AIRPORT	MINORITY GROUP			
	Black	Hispanic	Asian	Native American
JFK (cont)				
New York University	2		5	
Pace University New York	2			
Polytechnic Institute New York			2	
Pratt Institute	4		1	
St. John's University	2	2	2	
SUNY at Stony Bk - Main Campus	1	1	3	
	78	**33**	**36**	**1**
LAX=Los Angeles, CA				
Cal State Poly U - Pomona		2	1	
Cal State University - Fullerton		2	1	2
Cal State University - Northridge	2	4	5	
U of Cal - Irvine	7		4	
University of Southern California		1	3	
	9	**9**	**14**	**2**
LEX=Lexington/Frankfort, KY				
Eastern Kentucky University	5			
Kentucky State University*	3			
	8			
MDH=Carbondale, IL				
Southern Illinois U - Carbondale			1	
			1	
MGM=Montgomery, GA				
Alabama State University*	13			
Troy State University - Main Campus	2			
Troy State University - Montgomery	1			
	16			
MIA=Miami, FL				
Florida Atlantic University		2		
Florida International University	1	16	1	
University of Miami		4	1	
	1	**22**	**2**	

Airport 60 (0700)

AIRPORT	MINORITY GROUP			
	Black	Hispanic	Asian	Native American
MLU=Monroe, LA				
Grambling State University*	36			
Northeast Louisiana University	2			
	38			
MOB=Mobile, AL/Pasagoula, MS				
University of West Florida	3	2	1	1
	3	**2**	**1**	**1**
MSN=Madison, WS				
U of Wisconsin - Madison	1			
	1			
MSP=Minneapolis/St. Paul, MN				
U of Minn - Minneapolis/St. Paul	1		4	
	1		**4**	
ORD=Chicago–O'Hare Airport, IL				
DePaul University	1			
Northern Illinois University	4		3	
Northeastern Illinois University	1		11	
Roosevelt University	23		3	
U of Illinois - Chicago Circle	1	2	5	
	30	**2**	**22**	
ORF=Norfolk/Virginia Beach, VA				
Old Dominion University	2			
	2			
PHL=Philadelphia, PA/Wilmington, DE				
Rutgers U - New Brunswick			4	
Drexel University	1			
Temple University	5	1	1	
	6	**1**	**5**	
PHX=Phoenix, AZ				
Arizona State University		3	2	
		3	**2**	

Airport 60 (0700)

AIRPORT	MINORITY GROUP			
	Black	Hispanic	Asian	Native American
PIA=Peoria, IL				
Bradley University	6			
	6			
PIT=Pittsburgh, PA				
U of Pittsburgh - Main Campus	8			
	8			
PWA=Oklahoma City-Wiley Post, OK				
Central State University			2	
			2	
RDU=Raleigh/Durham, NC				
Duke University	2		1	
	2		1	
RIC=Richmond, Va				
Virginia Commonwealth University	2			
	2			
SAN=San Diego, CA				
San Diego State University	2	3	9	
	2	3	9	
SAT=San Antonio, TX				
Southwest Texas State University	2	4	1	
Trinity University		4	1	
	2	8	2	
SBP=San Luis Obispo, CA				
Cal Poly State U - San Luis Obispo		1		1
		1		1
SEA=Seattle/Tacoma, WA				
University of Washington			8	
			8	
SFO=San Francisco/Oakland, CA				
U of Cal - Berkeley	3	1	27	1
University of San Francisco	1		2	
	4	1	29	1

Airport 60 (0700)

AIRPORT	MINORITY GROUP			
	Black	Hispanic	Asian	Native American
SHV=Shreveport, LA				
Grambling State University*	36			
	36			
STL=St. Louis, MO				
Washington University	1		1	
	1		**1**	
SWI=Sherman, TX				
Bishop College*	2			
East Texas State University	10	3	1	
North Texas State University	4	1		
	16	**4**	**1**	
SYR=Syracuse, NY				
Syracuse U - Main Campus		1		
		1		
TLH=Tallahassee, FL				
Florida Agr & Mech University*	7		1	
	7		**1**	
TUS=Tucson, AZ				
University of Arizona		3	2	
		3	**2**	
TYS=Knoxville, TN				
U of Tennessee - Knoxville	2			
	2			

COMPUTER AND INFORMATION SCIENCES (0700)
MINORITY BACCALAUREATE DEGREES
WITHIN 61-80 MILE ANNULUS OF AIRPORT

AIRPORT	MINORITY GROUP			
	Black	Hispanic	Asian	Native American
ALM=Alamogordo, NM				
NM State U - Main Campus		1		
		1		
ATL=Atlanta, GA				
University of Georgia	1	1	1	
	1	1	1	
AUS=Austin, TX				
Trinity University		4	1	
		4	1	
BTR=Baton Rouge, LA				
U of Southwestern Louisiana	3			1
	3			1
CMH=Columbus, OH				
University of Dayton	2			
Wright State U - Main Campus	1			
	3			
COS=Colorado Springs, CO				
Metropolitan State College	2	2		
U of Colorado at Boulder			1	
	2	2	1	
CVG=Cincinnati, OH				
Kentucky State University*	3			
	3			
DEN=Denver, CO				
Colorado State University	1	2		
	1	2		

Airport 61-80 (0700)

AIRPORT	MINORITY GROUP			
	Black	Hispanic	Asian	Native American
DTW=Detroit-Metropolitan, MI				
Michigan State University	1		1	
Bowling Green State U - Main Cam	1		1	
	2		2	
FAY=Fayetteville, NC				
Duke University	2		1	
	2		1	
GRR=Grand Rapids, MI				
Michigan State University	1		1	
	1		1	
HSV=Huntsville, AL/Decatur, GA				
Middle Tennessee State U			1	
			1	
IAH=Houston-Intercontinental,TX				
Sam Houston State University			1	
			1	
JAX=Jacksonville, FL				
University of Florida	1	3	2	
	1	3	2	
JFK=New York, Kennedy Int'l, NY				
Yale University		1	1	
		1	1	
LCH=Lake Charles, LA				
U of Southwestern Louisiana	3			1
Lamar University			1	
	3		1	1
MCN=Macon, GA				
GA Inst of Tech - Main Campus		1		
Georgia State University	1			1
Morris Brown College*	1			
Spelman College*	2			
	4	1		1

Airport 61-80 (0700)

AIRPORT	MINORITY GROUP			
	Black	Hispanic	Asian	Native American
MEM=Memphis, TN				
Arkansas State U - Main Campus	1		1	
	1		1	
MKE=Milwaukee, WS				
U of Wisconsin - Madison	1			
	1			
MOB=Mobile, AL/Pasagoula, MS				
U of Southern Mississippi	3		2	
	3		2	
MSY=New Orleans, LA				
Louisiana State U & A&M College	1			
Sthrn U A&M C - Main Cam*	41			
	42			
RIC=Richmond, VA				
U of Virginia - Main Campus	1			
	1			
SAN=San Diego, CA				
U of Cal - Irvine	7		4	
	7		4	
SAT=San Antonio, TX				
U of Texas at Austin		3	1	
		3	1	
SBA=Santa Barbara, CA				
Cal State University - Northridge	2	4	5	
	2	4	5	
SFO=San Francisco/Oakland, CA				
Cal State University - Sacramento			5	
U of Cal - Santa Cruz			1	
			6	

Airport 61-80 (0700)

AIRPORT	MINORITY GROUP			
	Black	Hispanic	Asian	Native American
TPA=Tampa, FL				
University of Central Florida	2		1	
	2		1	
TYR=Tyler, TX				
East Texas State University	10	3	1	
	10	3	1	

COMPUTER AND INFORMATION SCIENCES (0700)
MINORITY BACCALAUREATE DEGREES
MORE THAN 80 MILES FROM NEAREST AIRPORT

AIRPORT	MINORITY GROUP			
	Black	Hispanic	Asian	Native American
AUS=Austin, TX				
Texas A&M U - Main Campus		2		
		2		
IAH=Houston–Intercontinental, TX				
Texas A&M U - Main Campus		2		
		2		
MSY=New Orleans, LA				
U of Southern Mississippi	3			
	3			
ROW=Roswell, NM				
Eastern NM U - Main Campus	1	1		
	1	1		
TCL=Tuscaloosa, AL				
Mississippi State University	2			
	2			

EDUCATION (0800)

Tables	Page

EDUCATION (0800)
MINORITY BACCALAUREATE DEGREES
BY STATE AND INSTITUTION

STATE/SCHOOL	MINORITY GROUP			
	Black	Hispanic	Asian	Native American
Alabama				
Alabama A&M University*	100			
Alabama State University*	203			
Jacksonville State University	17	1		
Miles College*	17			
Oakwood College*	27			
Stillman College*	38			
Talladega College*	28			
Troy State University – Main Campus	17			
Troy State University – Montgomery	7			
Tuskegee Institute*	74			
University of Alabama	29			
U of Alabama in Birmingham	53			
University of South Alabama	21			1
	631	**1**		**1**
Arizona				
Arizona State University	11	66	2	4
Northern Arizona University	1	28	2	27
University of Arizona	14	45	7	35
	26	**139**	**11**	**66**
Arkansas				
Arkansas Baptist College*	8			
Arkansas State U – Main Campus	21	1		
Henderson State University	35			
Philander Smith College*	17			
University of Arkansas – Pine Bluff*	147			
University of Central Arkansas	16			
	244	**1**		

(0800)

STATE/SCHOOL	MINORITY GROUP			
	Black	Hispanic	Asian	Native American
California				
Cal Poly State U – San Luis Obispo	6	10	13	6
Cal State College – Bakersfield	3	3		1
Cal State College – San Bernadino	4	5	1	1
Cal State Poly U – Pomona	1	1	2	
Cal State University – Chico	3	8	3	
Cal State U – Dominguez Hills	7	1		
Cal State University – Fresno	6	21	23	1
Cal State University – Fullerton	7	17	3	2
Cal State University – Hayward	10	1	2	1
Cal State University – Long Beach	20	26	25	3
Cal State University – Los Angeles	43	71	59	2
Cal State University – Northridge	6	2	5	8
Cal State University – Sacramento	3	4	10	3
Chapman College	4	1		
San Diego State University	9	13	6	1
San Francisco State University	8	3	24	
San Jose State University	5	11	17	3
U of Cal – Berkeley	15	7	18	
U of Cal – Davis	1	1	3	
U of Cal – Los Angeles	1	3	3	
U of Cal – Santa Barbara	3	4	2	
University of LaVerne	2	7		
University of Redlands	3		2	
University of Southern California	7	13	17	
University of the Pacific	3	7	7	1
	180	**240**	**245**	**33**
Colorado				
Colorado State University	3	4		2
Metropolitan State College	11	10	2	2
U of Colorado at Boulder	1	9	5	1

(0800)

STATE/SCHOOL	MINORITY GROUP			
	Black	Hispanic	Asian	Native American
Colorado (cont)				
U of Northern Colorado	11	31	6	2
U of Southern Colorado	1	15		
	27	**69**	**13**	**7**
Connecticut				
University of Connecticut	14			1
	14			**1**
Delaware				
Delaware State College*	39			
University of Delaware	13		1	
	52		**1**	
District of Columbia				
American University	14			
George Washington University	4			
Howard University*	41			
University of DC*	117	2	3	5
	176	**2**	**3**	**5**
Florida				
Bethune Cookman College*	92			
Biscayne College*	5	42		
Edward Waters College*	24			
Florida Agr & Mech University*	123	1		
Florida Atlantic University	40	5		1
Florida International University	34	75		
Florida Memorial College*	21			
Florida State University	44	8		
University of Central Florida	11	5	1	
University of Florida	33	15		1
University of Miami	39	16	1	1
University of South Florida	56	22	1	
University of West Florida	22	5	2	
	544	**194**	**5**	**3**

310

(0800)

STATE/SCHOOL	MINORITY GROUP			
	Black	Hispanic	Asian	Native American
Georgia				
Albany State College*	65			
Clark College*	58			
Fort Valley State College*	53			
Georgia College	11			
Georgia State University	27			
Morehouse College*	8			
Morris Brown College*	51			
Paine College*	23			
Savannah State College*	39			
Spelman College*	22			
University of Georgia	16	1	1	
Valdosta State College	16			
	389	**1**	**1**	
Hawaii				
Chaminade University of Honolulu			2	
University of Hawaii at Manoa*	1	4	107	
	1	**4**	**109**	
Illinois				
Bradley University	5	1		1
Chicago State University*	170	4	1	
College of St. Francis	2	2		
DePaul University	11	3		1
Eastern Illinois University	22	1	1	
Governors State University	34	4		
Illinois State University	38	6	8	6
Loyola University of Chicago	8	2		
Northern Illinois University	47	4	1	
Northeastern Illinois University	38	23	3	
Northwestern University	7	1		
Roosevelt University	34			
Southern Illinois U - Carbondale	33	6	2	9

(0800)

STATE/SCHOOL	MINORITY GROUP			
	Black	Hispanic	Asian	Native American
Illinois (cont)				
Southern Illinois U - Edwardsville	19	1	1	
U of Illinois - Chicago Circle	37	17	3	1
U of Illinois - Urbana Campus	6	3	2	1
	511	**78**	**22**	**19**
Indiana				
Ball State University	24	1	1	2
Ind-Purdue U - Indianapolis	15	2	3	1
Indiana State U - Main Campus	21		1	1
Indiana University - Bloomington	17	4	1	
Indiana University - Northwest	7			
Purdue University - Main Campus	4	1		
	88	**8**	**6**	**4**
Kentucky				
Eastern Kentucky University	19			
Kentucky State University*	29			
University of Louisville	22		2	
Western Kentucky University	8			
	78		**2**	
Louisiana				
Dillard University*	35			
Grambling State University*	138			
Louisiana State U & A&M College	10		1	
Louisiana Tech University	19	1		
McNeese State University	21	1		
Northeast Louisiana University	21		1	
Southeastern Louisiana U	14			
Sthrn U A&M College - Main Cam*	304			
Southern U in New Orleans*	89			
Tulane U of Louisiana	1			
University of New Orleans	23	4	1	

312

(0800)

STATE/SCHOOL	MINORITY GROUP			
	Black	Hispanic	Asian	Native American
Louisiana (cont)				
U of Southwestern Louisiana	45			1
Xavier University of Louisiana*	41			
	761	**6**	**3**	**1**
Maryland				
Bowie State College*	44			
Coppin State College*	65			1
Morgan State University*	75			
Towson State University	31			
U of MD - College Park Campus	20	7	4	6
U of MD - Eastern Shore*	35			
	270	**7**	**4**	**7**
Massachussetts				
Boston State College	11	1		
Boston University	7	3	2	
Tufts University	3	1	1	
U of Mass - Amherst Campus	8	9	4	
	29	**14**	**7**	
Michigan				
Eastern Michigan University	30	7		13
Michigan State University	37	7	2	
Oakland University	4	1	1	
University of Detroit	17			
U of Michigan - Ann Arbor	33	3	1	2
Wayne State University	101	3		1
Western Michigan University	28			3
	250	**21**	**4**	**19**
Minnesota				
U of Minn - Minneapolis/St. Paul	5	3	3	
	5	**3**	**3**	
Mississippi				
Alcorn State University*	79			
Delta State University	18			

(0800)

STATE/SCHOOL	MINORITY GROUP			
	Black	Hispanic	Asian	Native American
Mississippi (cont)				
Jackson State University*	183			1
Mississippi Industrial College*	14			
Mississippi State University	45			
Mississippi University for Women	11			
Mississippi Valley State Univ*	168			
Rust College*	40			
Tougaloo College*	16			
U of Mississippi – Main Campus	16			
U of Southern Mississippi	40	2	1	
	630	**2**	**1**	**1**
Missouri				
Columbia College	3			
Harris Stowe College*	54			
Lincoln University	17			
Park College	6			1
St. Louis U – Main Campus	1			
U of Missouri – Columbia	4		2	
U of Missouri – Kansas City	11		1	
U of Missouri – St. Louis	18	1		3
Washington University	2			
Webster College		1		
	116	**2**	**3**	**4**
Montana				
Montana State University				4
				4
Nebraska				
U of Nebraska at Omaha	9	3		1
	9	**3**		**1**
New Jersey				
Glassboro State College	69	49	2	11
Jersey City State College	36	3	2	

(0800)

STATE/SCHOOL	MINORITY GROUP			
	Black	Hispanic	Asian	Native American
New Jersey (cont)				
Kean College of New Jersey	55	16	2	1
Montclair State College	11	3	1	5
Rutgers U – New Brunswick	15	4		
St. Peter's College	6	10	1	
Seton Hall University	20	1		
Trenton State College	49	4	2	3
	261	**90**	**10**	**20**
New Mexico				
Eastern NM U – Main Campus	8	35	1	7
New Mexico Highlands U*	4	65		3
NM State U – Main Campus	2	54		1
University of Albuquerque		9		1
U of NM – Main Campus	2	93		31
Western New Mexico University	1	24	1	1
	17	**280**	**2**	**44**
New York				
Adelphi University	19	12		
CUNY Bernard Baruch College	20	6	6	
CUNY Brooklyn College	123	37	7	5
CUNY City College	71	34	15	2
CUNY Hunter College	9	5	2	
CUNY Lehman College	16	19	4	
CUNY Medgar Evers College*	30	1		
CUNY Queen's College	45	10	13	2
CUNY York College	45	9	3	2
Long Island U – Brooklyn Center	8	3		
Long Island U – C W Post Center	4			
New York University	20	3	2	2
Pace University New York	7	1		1
Pratt Institute		1		
St. Francis College	2	1		

(0800)

STATE/SCHOOL	MINORITY GROUP			
	Black	Hispanic	Asian	Native American
New York (cont)				
St. John's University	5	3		
St. Joseph's College - Main Campus	1	2		
SUNY at Albany	1	2		
SUNY College at Buffalo	22	2	3	2
SUNY College at New Paltz	5	4		4
SUNY College - Old Westbury	7	3		
SUNY Empire State College	6		1	
Syracuse University - Main Campus	6			
	472	**158**	**56**	**20**
North Carolina				
Barber-Scotia College*	10			
Bennett College*	29			
East Carolina University	31			
Elizabeth City State U*	121			
Fayetteville State University*	132	1	2	
Johnson C Smith University*	50			
Livingstone College*	37			
NC Agrl & Tech State University*	134			
NC Central University*	129			1
NC State U - Raleigh	3			
Pembroke State University	16			19
St. Augustine's College*	65			
Shaw University*	51			
U of NC at Chapel Hill	14			1
U of NC at Charlotte	7			
U of NC at Greensboro	11			1
Winston-Salem State University*	85			
	925	**1**	**2**	**22**
North Dakota				
U of North Dakota - Main Campus	1			15
	1			**15**

316

(0800)

STATE/SCHOOL	MINORITY GROUP			
	Black	Hispanic	Asian	Native American
Ohio				
Antioch University	1			
Bowling Green State U – Main Cam	34	2		1
Central State University*	69			
Kent State U – Main Campus	23	1	1	3
Oberlin College	4			1
Ohio State U – Main Campus	18	1	1	1
Ohio University – Main Campus	34			
U of Akron – Main Campus	39			
U of Cincinnati – Main Campus	40	1		
University of Dayton	8			
University of Toledo	11		1	2
Wilberforce University*	18			
Wright State U – Main Campus	8		1	
	307	**5**	**4**	**8**
Oklahoma				
Cameron University	11	3		5
Central State University	26	6	2	8
East Central Oklahoma State U	6			9
Langston University*	18			
Northeast Oklahoma State U	24		2	58
Oklahoma State U – Main Campus	13	1		14
Southeast Oklahoma State U	8			14
Southwest Oklahoma State U	12			8
U of Oklahoma – Norman Campus	8	2		9
	126	**12**	**4**	**125**
Oregon				
Oregon State University	1	3	2	2
University of Oregon – Main Campus		2	8	1
	1	**5**	**10**	**3**
Pennsylvania				
Cheyney State College*	93			
Lincoln University*	21			

317

(0800)

STATE/SCHOOL	MINORITY GROUP			
	Black	Hispanic	Asian	Native American
Pennsylvania (cont)				
Pennsylvania State U – Main Campus	16	2		1
St. Joseph's University	5			1
Temple University	142	28	1	4
University of Pennsylvania	1			
U of Pittsburgh – Main Campus	23	2		1
West Chester State College	31		1	
	332	**32**	**2**	**7**
South Carolina				
Allen University*	24			
Baptist College at Charleston	14			
Benedict College*	100			
Claflin College*	57			
Morris College*	22			
South Carolina State College*	216			
U of South Carolina at Columbia	41	2		1
Voorhees College*	71			
Winthrop College	20			
	565	**2**		**1**
Tennessee				
Austin Peay State University	11		1	1
Fisk University*	21			
Knoxville College*	16			
Lane College*	35			
LeMoyne–Owen College*	32			
Memphis State University	59		1	
Middle Tennessee State U	14		2	
Tennessee State University*	105			
U of Tennessee – Knoxville	18	1	1	2
U of Tennessee – Martin	27			
	338	**1**	**5**	**3**

318

(0800)

STATE/SCHOOL	MINORITY GROUP			
	Black	Hispanic	Asian	Native American
Texas				
Angelo State University	8	18		1
Bishop College*	32			
Corpus Christi State University	1	59		1
East Texas State University	89	13	1	1
Huston-Tillotson College*	23			
Incarnate Word College	4	10		
Jarvis Christian College*	13			
Lamar University	4			28
Laredo State University*		30		
North Texas State University	56	22	4	2
Our Lady of Lake University*	1	1		
Pan American University*		327	2	
Paul Quinn College*	12			
Prairie View A&M University*	144		4	
St. Edward's University	2	24		
St. Mary's U - San Antonio	1	14		
Sam Houston State University	25		19	
Southwest Texas State University	41	123	2	7
Sul Ross State University	2	38		
Texas A&I University	9	156		
Texas A&M U - Main Campus	7	8		7
Texas College*	16			
Texas Southern University*	139	1		
Texas Women's University	29	28	2	1
Trinity University	2	11		
U of Houston - Central Campus	29	42	2	1
U of Texas at Arlington	1	1	1	
U of Texas at Austin	1	31	2	
U of Texas at El Paso	8	133	4	3
U of Texas at San Antonio	5	54		
Wiley College*	25			
	729	**1144**	**43**	**52**

(0800)

STATE/SCHOOL	MINORITY GROUP			
	Black	Hispanic	Asian	Native American
Utah				
Brigham Young University - Main			7	8
University of Utah	2	3	1	4
	2	**3**	**8**	**12**
Virginia				
Hampton Institute*	100			
Norfolk State College*	200			
Old Dominion University	17		3	1
St. Paul's College*	45			
U of Virginia - Main Campus	2			
Virginia Commonwealth University	42	2		
Virginia State College*	242			
Virginia Union University*	59			
	707	**2**	**3**	**1**
Washington				
Evergreen State College				
University of Washington	9		7	
	9		**7**	
West Virginia				
West Virginia State College	12			
	12			
Wisconsin				
U of Wisconsin - Madison	4	2		1
U of Wisconsin - Milwaukee	26	5	2	3
	30	**7**	**2**	**4**
TOTALS	**9,870**	**2,537**	**601**	**513**

*Predominately minority institutions are those where at least 50% of the total BA Degrees awarded are to one of the minority groups being considered.

EDUCATION (0800)
BLACK BACCALAUREATE DEGREES RANKED BY INSTITUTION

Rank	Institution	B.A.'s	Rank	Institution	B.A.'s
1	Sthrn U A&M C-Main Campus*	304	30	Winston-Salem State U*	85
2	Virginia State C*	242	31	Alcorn State U*	79
3	South Carolina State C*	216	32	Morgan State U*	75
4	Alabama State U*	203	33	Tuskegee Institute*	74
5	Norfolk State C*	200	34	CUNY City C	71
6	Jackson State U*	183	35	Voorhees C*	71
7	Chicago State U*	170	36	Central State U*	69
8	Mississippi Valley State U*	168	37	Glassboro State C	69
9	U of Arkansas-Pine Bluff*	147	38	Albany State C*	65
10	Prairie View A&M U*	144	39	Coppin State C*	65
11	Temple U	142	40	St. Augustine's C*	65
12	Texas Southern U*	139	41	Memphis State U	59
13	Grambling State U*	138	42	Virginia Union U*	59
14	NC Agrl & Tech State U*	134	43	Clark C*	58
15	Fayetteville State U*	132	44	Claflin C*	57
16	NC Central U*	129	45	U of South Florida	56
17	CUNY Brooklyn C	123	46	North Texas State U	56
18	Florida Agrl & Mech U*	123	47	Kean C of New Jersey	55
19	Elizabeth City State U*	121	48	Harris Stowe C*	54
20	U of DC*	117	49	Fort Valley State C*	53
21	Tennessee State U*	105	50	U of Alabama in Birmingham	53
22	Wayne State U	101	51	Shaw U*	51
23	Benedict C*	100	52	Morris Brown C*	51
24	Alabama A&M U*	100	53	Johnson C Smith U*	50
25	Hampton Institute*	100	54	Trenton State C	49
26	Cheyney State C*	93	55	Northern Illinois U	47
27	Bethune Cookman C*	92	56	CUNY Queen's C	45
28	Southern U in New Orleans*	89	57	Mississippi State U	45
29	East Texas State U	89	58	U of Southwestern Louisiana	45

Black B.A.'s (0800)

Rank	Institution	B.A.'s	Rank	Institution	B.A.'s
59	CUNY York C	45	93	Southern Illinois U-Carbondale	33
60	St. Paul's C*	45	94	U of Michigan-Ann Arbor	33
61	Florida State U	44	95	U of Florida	33
62	Bowie State C*	44	96	Bishop C*	32
63	Cal State U-Los Angeles	43	97	Le Moyne-Owen C*	32
64	Virginia Commonwealth U*	42	98	East Carolina U	31
65	Howard U*	41	99	Towson State U	31
66	U of South Carolina at Columbia	41	100	West Chester State C	31
67	Xavier U of Lousiana*	41	101	CUNY Medgar Evers C*	30
68	Southwest Texas State U	41	102	Eastern Michigan U	30
69	Rust C*	40	103	Bennett C*	29
70	U of Cincinnati-Main Campus	40	104	Kentucky State U*	29
71	Florida Atlantic U	40	105	Texas Women's U	29
72	U of Southern Mississippi	40	106	U of Alabama	29
73	Delaware State C*	39	107	U of Houston-Central Campus	29
74	Savannah State C*	39	108	Western Michigan U	28
75	U of Miami	39	109	Talladega C*	28
76	U of Akron-Main Campus	39	110	Georgia State U	27
77	Northeasten Illinois U	38	111	U of Tennessee at Martin	27
78	Illinois State U	38	112	Oakwood C*	27
79	Stillman C*	38	113	U of Wisconsin-Milwaukee	26
80	Michigan State U	37	114	Central State U	26
81	Livingstone C*	37	115	Wiley C*	25
82	U of Illinois-Chicago Circle	37	116	Sam Houston State U	25
83	Jersey City State C	36	117	Ball State U	24
84	U of MD-Eastern Shore*	35	118	Edward Waters C*	24
85	Dillard U*	35	119	Northeastern Oklahoma State	24
86	Henderson State U	35	120	Allen U*	24
87	Lane C*	35	121	U of New Orleans	23
88	Roosevelt U	34	122	Paine C*	23
89	Governors State U	34	123	U of Pittsburgh-Main Campus	23
90	Ohio U-Main Campus	34	124	Kent State U-Main Campus	23
91	Florida International U	34	125	Huston-Tillotson C*	23
92	Bowling Green State U-Main Ca	34	126	Spelman C*	22

322

Black B.A.'s (0800)

Rank	Institution	B.A.'s	Rank	Institution	B.A.'s
127	U of Louisville	22	161	Indiana U-Bloomington	17
128	Eastern Illinois U	22	162	Jacksonville State U	17
129	U of West Florida	22	163	Old Dominion U	17
130	SUNY C at Buffalo	22	164	U of Mississippi-Main Campus	16
131	Morris C*	22	165	CUNY Lehman C	16
132	Northeast Louisiana U	21	166	Valdosta State C	16
133	McNeese State U	21	167	Tougaloo C*	16
134	Indiana State U-Main Campus	21	168	U of Georgia	16
135	U of South Alabama	21	169	Knoxville C*	16
136	Florida Memorial C*	21	170	Pembroke State U	16
137	Fisk U*	21	171	Pennsylvania State U-Main Cam	16
138	Arkansas State U-Main Campus	21	172	U of Central Arkansas	16
139	Lincoln U*	21	173	Texas C*	16
140	CUNY Bernard Baruch C	20	174	U of Cal-Berkeley	15
141	U of MD-College Park Campus	20	175	Rutgers U-New Brunswick	15
142	Seton Hall U	20	176	Ind-Purdue U-Indianapolis	15
143	Cal State U-Long Beach	20	177	U of NC at Chapel Hill	14
144	New York U	20	178	American U	14
145	Winthrop C	20	179	Mississippi Industrial C*	14
146	Eastern Kentucky U	19	180	Southeastern Louisiana U	14
147	Southern Illinois U-Edwardsville	19	181	Middle Tennessee State U	14
148	Adelphi U	19	182	U of Arizona	14
149	Louisiana Tech U	19	183	Baptist C at Charleston	14
150	Wilberforce U*	18	184	Oklahoma State U-Main Campus	13
151	U of Missouri-St. Louis	18	185	Jarvis Christian C*	13
152	Ohio State U-Main Campus	18	186	U of Delaware	13
153	Delta State U	18	187	Paul Quinn C*	12
154	Langston U*	18	188	Southwestern Oklahoma State U	12
155	U of Tennessee-Knoxville	18	189	West Virginia State C	12
156	Miles C*	17	190	Georgia C	11
157	Lincoln U*	17	191	Cameron U	11
158	Troy State U-Main Campus	17	192	Florida Technological U	11
159	U of Detroit	17	193	U of Missouri-Kansas City	11
160	Philander Smith C*	17	194	Metropolitan State C	11

Black B.A.'s (0800)

Rank	Institution	B.A.'s	Rank	Institution	B.A.'s
195	U of Toledo	11	201	Mississippi U for Women	11
196	Boston State C	11	202	Arizona State U	11
197	Montclair State C	11	203	Austin Peay State U	11
198	U of Northern Colorado	11	204	Cal State U-Hayward	10
199	U of NC at Greensboro	11	205	Barber-Scotia C*	10
200	DePaul U	11	206	Louisiana State U & A&M C	10

*predominantly black institutions

Institutions not ranked have less than ten degrees conferred on blacks.

324

EDUCATION (0800)
HISPANIC BACCALAUREATE DEGREES RANKED BY INSTITUTION

Rank	Institution	B.A.'s	Rank	Institution	B.A.'s
1	Pan American U*	327	28	Western New Mexico U	24
2	Texas A&I U	156	29	St. Edward's U	24
3	U of Texas at El Paso	133	30	Northeastern Illinois U	23
4	Southwest Texas State U	123	31	U of South Florida	22
5	U of NM-Main Campus	93	32	North Texas State U	22
6	Florida International U	75	33	Cal State U-Fresno	21
7	Cal State U-Los Angeles	71	34	CUNY Lehman C	19
8	Arizona State U	66	35	Angelo State U	18
9	New Mexico Highlands U*	65	36	Cal State U-Fullerton	17
10	Corpus Christi State U	59	37	U of Illinois-Chicago Circle	17
11	NM State U-Main Campus	54	38	U of Miami	16
12	U of Texas at San Antonio	54	39	Kean C of New Jersey	16
13	Glassboro State C	49	40	U of Florida	15
14	U of Arizona	45	41	U of Southern Colorado	15
15	U of Houston-Central Campus	42	42	St. Mary's U-San Antonio	14
16	Biscayne C*	42	43	San Diego State U	13
17	Sul Ross State U	38	44	U of Southern California	13
18	CUNY Brooklyn C	37	45	East Texas State U	13
19	Eastern NM U-Main Campus	35	46	Adelphi U	12
20	CUNY City C	34	47	San Jose State U	11
21	U of Texas at Austin	31	48	Trinity U	11
22	U of Northern Colorado	31	49	CUNY Queen's C	10
23	Laredo State U*	30	50	Metropolitan State C	10
24	Texas Women's U	28	51	St. Peter's C	10
25	Northern Arizona U	28	52	Cal Poly State-San Luis Obispo	10
26	Temple U	28	53	Incarnate Word C	10
27	Cal State U-Long Beach	26			

*predominantly Hispanic institutions

Institutions not ranked have less than ten degrees conferred on Hispanics.

EDUCATION (0800)
ASIAN BACCALAUREATE DEGREES RANKED BY INSTITUTION

Rank	Institution	B.A.'s	Rank	Institution	B.A.'s
1	U of Hawaii at Manoa*	107	8	San Jose State U	17
2	Cal State U-Los Angeles	59	9	U of Southern California	17
3	Cal State U-Long Beach	25	10	CUNY City C	15
4	San Francisco State U	24	11	CUNY Queen's C	13
5	Cal State U-Fresno	23	12	Cal Poly State-San Luis Obispo	13
6	Sam Houston State U	19	13	Cal State U-Sacramento	10
7	U of Cal-Berkeley	18			

*predominantly Asian institutions

Institutions not ranked have less than ten degrees conferred on Asians.

EDUCATION (0800)
NATIVE AMERICAN BACCALAUREATE DEGREES RANKED BY INSTITUTION

Rank	Institution	B.A.'s	Rank	Institution	B.A.'s
1	Northeastern Oklahoma State	58	15	Central State U	8
2	U of Arizona	35	16	Southwest Oklahoma State U	8
3	U of NM-Main Campus	31	17	Brigham Young U-Main Campus	8
4	Lamar U	28	18	Cal State U-Northridge	8
5	Northern Arizona U	27	19	Texas A&M U-Main Campus	7
6	Pembroke State U	19	20	Eastern NM U-Main Campus	7
7	U of North Dakota-Main Campus	15	21	Southwest Texas State U	7
8	Southeast Oklahoma State U	14	22	Illinois State U	6
9	Oklahoma State U-Main Campus	14	23	U of MD-College Park Campus	6
10	Eastern Michigan U	13	24	Cal Poly State-San Luis Obispo	6
11	Glassboro State C	11	25	Montclair State C	5
12	East Central Oklahoma State	9	26	CUNY Brooklyn C	5
13	U of Oklahoma-Norman Campus	9	27	Cameron U	5
14	Southern Illinois U-Carbondale	9	28	U of DC	5

Institutions not ranked have less than five degrees conferred on Native Americans.

EDUCATION (0800)
MINORITY BACCALAUREATE DEGREES
WITHIN 60 MILE RADIUS OF AIRPORT

AIRPORT	MINORITY GROUP			
	Black	Hispanic	Asian	Native American
ABQ=Albuquerque, NM				
U of NM - Main Campus	2	93		31
University of Albuquerque		9		1
	2	**102**		**32**
ACT=Waco, TX				
Paul Quinn College*	12			
	12			
ALB=Albany, NY				
SUNY at Albany	1	2		
SUNY Empire State College	6		1	
	7	**2**	**1**	
AOO=Altoona, PA				
Pennsylvania State U - Main Campus	16	2		1
	16	**2**		**1**
ATL=Atlanta, GA				
Clark College*	58			
Georgia State University	27			
Morehouse College*	8			
Morris Brown College*	51			
Spelman College*	22			
	166			
AUS=Austin, TX				
Huston-Tillotson College*	23			
Southwest Texas State University	41	123	2	7
U of Texas at Austin	1	31	2	
	65	**154**	**4**	**7**

Airport 60 (0800)

AIRPORT	MINORITY GROUP			
	Black	Hispanic	Asian	Native American
BAL=Baltimore, MD				
University of Delaware	13		1	
American University	14			
George Washington Univesity	4			
Howard University*	41			
University of DC*	117	2	3	5
Bowie State College*	44			
Coppin State College*	65			1
Morgan State University*	75			
Towson State University	31			
U of MD - College Park Campus	20	7	4	6
Lincoln University*	21			
	445	**9**	**8**	**12**
BDL=Hartford, CT/Springfield, MA				
U of Mass - Amherst Campus	8	9	4	
	8	**9**	**4**	
BHM=Birmingham, AL				
Miles College*	17			
Stillman College*	38			
Talladega College*	28			
U of Alabama in Birmingham	53			
University of Alabama	29			
	165			
BKL=Cleveland-Lakefront, OH				
Kent State U - Main Campus	23	1	1	3
Oberlin College	4			1
U of Akron - Main Campus	39			
	66	**1**	**1**	**4**
BNA=Nashville, TN				
Western Kentucky University	8			
Austin Peay State University	11		1	1

328

Airport 60 (0800)

AIRPORT	MINORITY GROUP			
	Black	Hispanic	Asian	Native American
BNA (cont)				
Fisk University*	21			
Middle Tennessee State U	14		2	
Tennessee State University*	105			
	159		**3**	**1**
BOS=Boston, MA				
Boston State College	11	1		
Boston University	7	3	2	
Tufts University	3	1	1	
	21	**5**	**3**	
BTR=Baton Rouge, LA				
Louisiana State U & A&M College	10		1	
Sthrn U A&M College – Main Cam*	304			
Southeastern Louisiana U	14			
	328		**1**	
BUF=Buffalo, NY				
SUNY College at Buffalo	22	2	3	2
	22	**2**	**3**	**2**
CAE=Columbia, SC				
Allen University*	24			
Benedict College*	100			
Claflin College*	57			
Morris College*	22			
South Carolina State College*	216			
U of South Carolina at Columbia	41	2		1
Voorhees College*	71			
	531	**2**		**1**
CHS=Charleston, SC				
Baptist College at Charleston	14			
	14			

Airport 60 (0800)

AIRPORT	MINORITY GROUP			
	Black	Hispanic	Asian	Native American
CIC=Chico, CA				
Cal State University - Chico	3	8	3	
	3	**8**	**3**	
CLT=Charlotte, NC				
Barber-Scotia College*	10			
Johnson C Smith University*	50			
Livingstone College*	37			
U of NC at Charlotte	7			
Winthrop College	20			
	124			
CMH=Columbus, OH				
Central State University*	69			
Ohio State U - Main Campus	18	1	1	
Wilberforce University*	18			
	105	**1**	**1**	
CMI=Champaign, IL				
Eastern Illinois University	22	1	1	
Illinois State University	38	6	8	6
U of Illinois - Urbana Campus	6	3	2	1
Indiana State U - Main Campus	21		1	1
	87	**10**	**12**	**8**
COS=Colorado Springs, CO				
U of Southern Colorado	1	15		
	1	**15**		
COU=Columbia, MO				
Columbia College	3			
Lincoln University	17			
U of Missouri - Columbia	4		2	
	24		**2**	

330

Airport 60 (0800)

AIRPORT	MINORITY GROUP			
	Black	Hispanic	Asian	Native American
CRP=Corpus Christi, TX				
Corpus Christi State University	1	59		1
Texas A&I University	9	156		
	10	215		1
CRW=Charleston, WV				
West Virginia State College	12			
	12			
CVG=Cincinnati, OH				
Antioch University	1			
Central State University*	69			
U of Cincinnati - Main Campus	40	1		
University of Dayton	8			
Wilberforce University*	18			
Wright State U - Main Campus	8		1	
	144	1	1	
DAB=Dayton Beach, FL				
Bethune Cookman College*	92			
University of Central Florida	11	5	1	
	103	5	1	
DCA=Washington-National, DC				
American University	14			
George Washington University	4			
Howard University*	41			
University of DC*	117	2	3	5
Bowie State College*	44			
Coppin State College*	65			1
Morgan State University*	75			
Towson State University	31			
U of MD - College Park Campus	20	7	4	6
	411	9	7	12

Airport 60 (0800)

AIRPORT	MINORITY GROUP			
	Black	Hispanic	Asian	Native American
DEN=Denver, CO				
Metropolitan State College	11	10	2	2
U of Colorado at Boulder	1	9	5	1
U of Northern Colorado	11	31	6	2
	23	50	13	5
DFW=Dallas/Fort Worth, TX				
Bishop College*	32			
East Texas State University	89	13	1	1
North Texas State University	56	22	4	2
Texas Woman's University	29	28	2	1
U of Texas at Arlington	1	1	1	
	207	64	8	4
DTW=Detroit-Metropolitan, MI				
Eastern Michigan University	30	7		13
Oakland University	4	1	1	
U of Michigan - Ann Arbor	33	3	1	2
University of Detroit	17			
Wayne State University	101	3		1
University of Toledo	11		1	2
	196	14	3	18
ELP=El Paso, TX				
U of Texas at El Paso	8	133	4	3
	8	133	4	3
EUG=Eugene, OR				
Oregon State University	1	3	2	2
University of Oregon - Main Campus		2	8	1
	1	5	10	3
FAT=Fresno, CA				
Cal State University - Fresno	6	21	23	1
	6	21	23	1

Airport 60 (0800)

AIRPORT	MINORITY GROUP			
	Black	Hispanic	Asian	Native American
FAY=Fayetteville, NC				
Fayetteville State University*	132	1	2	
NC Central University*	129			1
NC State U - Raleigh	3			
Pembroke State University	16			19
St. Augustine's College*	65			
Shaw University*	51			
U of NC at Chapel Hill	14			1
	410	**1**	**2**	**21**
FLG=Flagstaff, AZ				
Northern Arizona University	1	28	2	27
	1	**28**	**2**	**27**
GLH=Greenville, MS				
Delta State University	18			
Mississippi Valley State U*	168			
	186			
GRR=Grand Rapids, MI				
Western Michigan University	28			3
	28			**3**
GSO=Greensboro/High Point, NC				
Bennett College*	29			
Livingstone College*	37			
NC Agrl & Tech State University*	134			
NC Central University*	129			1
U of NC at Chapel Hill	14			1
U of NC at Greensboro	11			1
Winston-Salem State University*	85			
	439			**3**
HNL=Honolulu/Oahu, HI				
Chaminade University of Honolulu			2	
University of Hawaii at Manoa*	1	4	107	
	1	**4**	**109**	

Airport 60 (0800)

AIRPORT	MINORITY GROUP			
	Black	Hispanic	Asian	Native American
HSV=Huntsville, AL/Decatur, GA				
Alabama A&M University*	100			
Oakwood College*	27			
	127			
IAH=Houston-Intercontinental,TX				
Prairie View A&M University*	144		4	
Texas Southern University*	139	1		
U of Houston - Central Campus	29	42	2	1
	312	**43**	**6**	**1**
IND=Indianapolis, IN				
Ball State University	24	1	1	2
Ind-Purdue U - Indianapolis	15	2	3	1
Indiana University - Bloomington	17	4	1	
Purdue University - Main Campus	4	1		
	60	**8**	**5**	**3**
JAN=Jackson/Vicksburg, MS				
Alcorn State University*	79			
Jackson State University*	183			1
Tougaloo College*	16			
	278			**1**
JAX=Jacksonville, FL				
Edward Waters College*	24			
	24			
JFK=New York, Kennedy Int'l, NY				
Jersey City State College	36	3	2	
Kean College of New Jersey	55	16	2	1
Montclair State College	11	3	1	5
Rutgers U-New Brunswick	15	4		
St. Peter's College	6	10	1	
Seton Hall University	20	1		
Trenton State College	49	4	2	3
Adelphi University	19	12		

334

Airport 60 (0800)

AIRPORT	MINORITY GROUP			
	Black	Hispanic	Asian	Native American
JFK (cont)				
CUNY Bernard Baruch College	20	6	6	
CUNY Brooklyn College	123	37	7	5
CUNY City College	71	34	15	2
CUNY Hunter College	9	5	2	
CUNY Lehman College	16	19	4	
CUNY Medgar Evers College*	30	1		
CUNY Queen's College	45	10	13	2
CUNY York College	45	9	3	2
Long Island U – Brooklyn Center	8	3		
Long Island U – C W Post Center	4			
New York University	20	3	2	2
Pace University New York	7	1		1
Pratt Institute		1		
St. Francis College	2	1		
St. John's University	5	3		
St. Joseph's College – Main Campus	1	2		
SUNY College – Old Westbury	7	3		
	624	**191**	**60**	**23**
LAX=Los Angeles, CA				
Cal State College – San Bernardino	4	5	1	1
Cal State Poly U – Pomona	1	1	2	
Cal State U – Dominguez Hills	7	1		
Cal State University – Fullerton	7	17	3	2
Cal State University – Long Beach	20	26	25	3
Cal State University – Los Angeles	43	71	59	2
Cal State University – Northridge	6	2	5	8
Chapman College	4	1		
U of Cal – Los Angeles	1	3	3	
University of Southern California	7	13	17	
University of LaVerne	2	7		
	102	**147**	**115**	**16**

Airport 60 (0800)

AIRPORT	MINORITY GROUP			
	Black	Hispanic	Asian	Native American
LCH=Lake Charles, LA				
McNeese State University	21	1		
	21	**1**		
LEX=Lexington/Frankfort, KY				
Eastern Kentucky University	19			
Kentucky State University*	29			
University of Louisville	22		2	
	70		**2**	
LIT=Little Rock, AR				
Arkansas Baptist College*	8			
Philander Smith College*	17			
University of Arkansas - Pine Bluff*	147			
University of Central Arkansas	16			
	188			
LRD=Laredo, TX				
Laredo State University*		30		
		30		
MCI=Kansas City-International, MO				
Park College	6			1
U of Missouri - Kansas City	11		1	
	17		**1**	**1**
MCN=Macon, GA				
Fort Valley State College*	53			
Georgia College	11			
	64			
MDH=Carbondale, IL				
Southern Illinois U - Carbondale	33	6	2	9
	33	**6**	**2**	**9**
MEM=Memphis, TN				
Mississippi Industrial College*	14			
Rust College*	40			
Le Moyne-Owen College*	32			
Memphis State University	59		1	
	145		**1**	

Airport 60 (0800)

AIRPORT	MINORITY GROUP			
	Black	Hispanic	Asian	Native American
MFE=McAllen, TX				
Pan American University*		327	2	
		327	**2**	
MGM=Montgomery, GA				
Alabama State University*	203			
Troy State University - Main Campus	17			
Troy State University - Montgomery	7			
Tuskegee Institute*	74			
	301			
MHT=Manchester, NH				
Tufts University	3	1	1	
	3	**1**	**1**	
MIA=Miami, FL				
Biscayne College*	5	42		
Florida Atlantic University	40	5		1
Florida International University	34	75		
Florida Memorial College*	21			
University of Miami	39	16	1	1
	130	**138**	**1**	**2**
MKE=Milwaukee, WS				
U of Wisconsin - Milwaukee	26	5	2	3
	26	**5**	**2**	**3**
MKL=Jackson, TN				
Lane College*	35			
U of Tennessee at Martin	27			
	62			
MLU=Monroe, LA				
Grambling State University*	138			
Louisiana Tech University	19	1		
Northeast Louisiana University	21		1	
	178	**1**	**1**	

Airport 60 (0800)

AIRPORT	MINORITY GROUP			
	Black	Hispanic	Asian	Native American
MOB=Mobile, AL/Pasagoula, MS				
University of South Alabama	21			1
University of West Florida	22	5	2	
	43	**5**	**2**	**1**
MSN=Madison, WS				
U of Wisconsin – Madison	4	2		1
	4	**2**		**1**
MSP=Minneapolis/St. Paul, MN				
U of Minn – Minneapolis/St. Paul	5	3	3	
	5	**3**	**3**	
MSY=New Orleans, LA				
Dillard University*	35			
Southeastern Louisiana U	14			
Southern U in New Orleans*	89			
Tulane U of Louisiana	1			
University of New Orleans	23	4	1	
Xavier University of Louisiana*	41			
	203	**4**	**1**	
ORD=Chicago–O'Hare Airport, IL				
Chicago State University*	170	4	1	
College of St. Francis	2	2		
DePaul University	11	3		1
Governors State University	34	4		
Loyola University of Chicago	8	2		
Northern Illinois University	47	4	1	
Northwestern University	7	1		
Northeastern Illinois University	38	23	3	
Roosevelt University	34			
U of Illinois – Chicago Circle	37	17	3	1
Indiana University – Northwest	7			
	395	**60**	**8**	**2**

338

Airport 60 (0800)

AIRPORT	MINORITY GROUP			
	Black	Hispanic	Asian	Native American
ORF=Norfolk/Virginia Beach, VA				
Elizabeth City State U*	121			
Hampton Institute*	100			
Norfolk State College*	200			
Old Dominion University	17		3	1
	438		**3**	**1**
PHL=Philadelphia, PA/Wilmington, DE				
Delaware State College*	39			
University of Delaware	13		1	
Glassboro State College	69	49	2	11
Rutgers U - New Brunswick	15	4		
Trenton State College	49	4	2	3
Cheyney State College*	93			
Lincoln University*	21			
St. Joseph's University	5			1
Temple University	142	28	1	4
University of Pennsylvania	1			
West Chester State College	31		1	
	478	**85**	**7**	**19**
PHX=Phoenix, AZ				
Arizona State University	11	66	2	4
	11	**66**	**2**	**4**
PIA=Peoria, IL				
Bradley University	5	1		1
	5	**1**		**1**
PIT=Pittsburgh, PA				
U of Pittsburgh - Main Campus	23	2		1
	23	**2**		**1**
PVD=Providence, RI				
Boston State College	11	1		
Boston University	7	3	2	
Tufts University	3	1	1	
	21	**5**	**3**	

Airport 60 (0800)

AIRPORT	MINORITY GROUP			
	Black	Hispanic	Asian	Native American
PWA=Oklahoma City-Wiley Post, OK				
Central State University	26	6	2	8
Langston University*	18			
Oklahoma State U - Main Campus	13	1		14
U of Oklahoma - Norman Campus	8	2		9
	65	**9**	**2**	**31**
RDU=Raleigh/Durham, NC				
Bennet College*	29			
Fayetteville State University*	132	1	2	
NC Agrl & Tech State University*	134			
NC Central University*	129			1
NC State U - Raleigh	3			
St. Augustine's College*	65			
Shaw University*	51			
U of NC at Chapel Hill	14			1
U of NC at Greensboro	11			1
	568	**1**	**2**	**3**
RIC=Richmond, VA				
Virginia Commonwealth University	42	2		
Virginia State College*	242			
Virginia Union University*	59			
	343	**2**		
SAN=San Diego, CA				
San Diego State University	9	13	6	1
	9	**13**	**6**	**1**
SAT=San Antonio, TX				
Incarnate Word College	4	10		
Our Lady of Lake University*	1	1		
St. Edward's University	2	24		
St. Mary's U-San Antonio	1	14		

Airport 60 (0800)

AIRPORT	MINORITY GROUP			
	Black	Hispanic	Asian	Native American
SAT (cont)				
Southwest Texas State University	41	123	2	7
Trinity University	2	11		
U of Texas at San Antonio	5	54		
	56	**237**	**2**	**7**
SAV=Savannah, GA				
Savannah State College*	39			
	39			
SBA=Santa Barbara, CA				
U of Cal – Santa Barbara	3	4	2	
	3	**4**	**2**	
SBP=San Luis Obispo, CA				
Cal Poly State U – San Luis Obispo	6	10	13	6
	6	**10**	**13**	**6**
SBY=Salisbury, MD				
U of MD – Eastern Shore*	35			
	35			
SEA=Seattle/Tacoma, WA				
University of Washington	9		7	
	9		**7**	
SFO=San Francisco/Oakland, CA				
Cal State University – Hayward	10	1	2	1
San Francisco State University	8	3	24	
San Jose State University	5	11	17	3
U of Cal – Berkeley	15	7	18	
	38	**22**	**61**	**4**
SHV=Shreveport, LA				
Grambling State University*	138			
Wiley College*	25			
	163			

Airport 60 (0800)

AIRPORT	MINORITY GROUP			
	Black	Hispanic	Asian	Native American
SJT=San Angelo, TX				
Angelo State University	8	18		1
	8	**18**		**1**
SLC=Salt Lake City, UT				
Brigham Young University - Main			7	8
University of Utah	2	3	1	4
	2	**3**	**8**	**12**
STL=St. Louis, MO				
Southern Illinois U - Edwardsville	19	1	1	
Harris Stowe College*	54			
St. Louis U - Main Campus	1			
U of Missouri - St. Louis	18	1		3
Washington University	2			
Webster College		1		
	94	**3**	**1**	**3**
SVC=Silver City, NM				
Western New Mexico University	1	24	1	1
	1	**24**	**1**	**1**
SWI=Sherman, TX				
Southeast Oklahoma State U	8			14
Bishop College*	32			
East Texas State University	89	13	1	1
North Texas State University	56	22	4	2
Texas Woman's University	29	28	2	1
	214	**63**	**7**	**18**
SYR=Syracuse, NY				
Syracuse U - Main Campus	6			
	6			
TCL=Tuscaloosa, AL				
Miles College*	17			
Stillman College*	38			

342

Airport 60 (0800)

AIRPORT		MINORITY GROUP		
	Black	Hispanic	Asian	Native American
TCL (cont)				
U of Alabama in Birmingham	53			
University of Alabama	29			
Mississippi University for Women	11			
	148			
TLH=Tallahassee, FL				
Florida Agr & Mech University*	123	1		
Florida State University	44	8		
	167	**9**		
TPA=Tampa, FL				
University of South Florida	56	22	1	
	56	**22**	**1**	
TUL=Tulsa, OK				
Northeast Oklahoma State U	24		2	58
	24		**2**	**58**
TUS=Tucson, AZ				
University of Arizona	14	45	7	35
	14	**45**	**7**	**35**
TYR=Tyler, TX				
Jarvis Christian College*	13			
Texas College*	16			
Wiley College*	25			
	54			
TYS=Knoxville, TN				
Knoxville College*	16			
U of Tennessee - Knoxville	18	1	1	2
	34	**1**	**1**	**2**

EDUCATION (0800)
MINORITY BACCALAUREATE DEGREES
WITHIN 61-80 MILE ANNULUS OF AIRPORT

AIRPORT	MINORITY GROUP			
	Black	Hispanic	Asian	Native American
ALB=Albany, NY				
U of Mass – Amherst Campus	8	9	4	
SUNY College at New Paltz	5	4		4
	13	**13**	**4**	**4**
ALM=Alamogordo, NM				
NM State U – Main Campus	2	54		1
	2	**54**		**1**
ATL=Atlanta, GA				
Jacksonville State University	17	1		
Georgia College	11			
University of Georgia	16	1	1	
	44	**2**	**1**	
AUS=Austin, TX				
Incarnate Word College	4	10		
Our Lady of Lake University*	1	1		
St. Edward's University	2	24		
St. Mary's U – San Antonio	1	14		
Trinity University	2	11		
U of Texas at San Antonio	5	54		
	15	**114**		
BAL=Baltimore, MD				
Delaware State College*	39			
Cheyney State College*	93			
	132			

344

Airport 61-80 (0800)

AIRPORT	MINORITY GROUP			
	Black	Hispanic	Asian	Native American
BDL=Hartford, CT/Springfield, MA				
SUNY at Albany	1	2		
SUNY College at New Paltz	5	4		4
	6	6		4
BHM=Birmingham, AL				
Jacksonville State University	17	1		
	17	1		
BOS=Boston, MA				
U of Mass - Amherst Campus	8	9	4	
	8	9	4	
BTM=Butte, MT				
Montana State University				4
				4
BTR=Baton Rouge, LA				
Dillard University*	35			
Southern U in New Orleans*	89			
Tulane U of Louisiana	1			
U of Southwestern Louisiana	45			1
University of New Orleans	23	4	1	
Xavier University of Louisiana*	41			
	234	4	1	1
CAE=Columbia, SC				
Paine College*	23			
Winthrop College	20			
	43			
CHS=Charleston, SC				
Savannah State College*	39			
Claflin College*	57			
South Carolina State College*	216			
	312			

Airport 61-80 (0800)

AIRPORT	MINORITY GROUP			
	Black	Hispanic	Asian	Native American
CLT=Charlotte, NC				
Wintson-Salem State University*	85			
	85			
CMH=Columbus, OH				
Antioch University	1			
Ohio University - Main Campus	34			1
University of Dayton	8			
Wright State U - Main Campus	8		1	
	51		1	1
CMI=Champaign, IL				
Purdue University - Main Campus	4	1		
	4	1		
COS=Colorado Springs, CO				
Metropolitan State College	11	10	2	2
U of Colorado at Boulder	1	9	5	1
	12	19	7	3
CRW=Charleston, WV				
Ohio University - Main Campus	34			1
	34			1
CVG=Cincinnati, OH				
Kentucky State University*	29			
	29			
DCA=Washington-National, DC				
Lincoln University*	21			
	21			
DEN=Denver, CO				
Colorado State University	3	4		2
	3	4		2
DTW=Detroit-Metropolitan, MI				
Michigan State University	37	7	2	
Bowling Green State U - Main Cam	34	2		1
	71	9	2	1

Airport 61-80 (0800)

AIRPORT	MINORITY GROUP			
	Black	Hispanic	Asian	Native American
GRR=Grand Rapids, MI				
Michigan State University	37	7	2	
	37	**7**	**2**	
GSO=Greensboro/High Point, NC				
Barber-Scotia College*	10			
NC State U - Raleigh	3			
St. Augustine's College*	65			
Shaw University*	51			
	129			
HSV=Huntsville, AL/Decatur, GA				
Jacksonville State University	17	1		
Middle Tennessee State U	14		2	
	31	**1**	**2**	
IAH=Houston-Intercontinental,TX				
Sam Houston State University	25		19	
	25		**19**	
IND=Indianapolis, IN				
Indiana State U - Main Campus	21		1	1
	21		**1**	**1**
JAX=Jacksonville, FL				
University of Florida	33	15		1
	33	**15**		**1**
JFK=New York, Kennedy Int'l, NY				
SUNY College at New Paltz	5	4		4
	5	**4**		**4**
LAX=Los Angeles, CA				
Cal State College - Bakersfield	3	3		1
University of Redlands	3		2	
	6	**3**	**2**	**1**

Airport 61-80 (0800)

AIRPORT	MINORITY GROUP			
	Black	Hispanic	Asian	Native American
LCH=Lake Charles, LA				
U of Southwestern Louisiana	45			1
Lamar University	4			28
	49			**29**
LIT=Little Rock, AR				
Henderson State University	35			
	35			
MCN=Macon, GA				
Clark College*	58			
Georgia State University	27			
Morehouse College*	8			
Morris Brown College*	51			
Spelman College*	22			
	166			
MEM=Memphis, TN				
Arkansas State U - Main Campus	21	1		
U of Mississippi - Main Campus	16			
Lane College*	35			
	72	**1**		
MGM=Montgomery, GA				
Talladega College*	28			
	28			
MHT=Manchester, NH				
Boston State College	11	1		
Boston University	7	3	2	
U of Mass - Amherst Campus	8	9	4	
	26	**13**	**6**	
MKE=Milwaukee, WS				
Northwestern University	7	1		
U of Wisconsin - Madison	4	2		1
	11	**3**		**1**

Airport 61-80 (0800)

AIRPORT	MINORITY GROUP			
	Black	Hispanic	Asian	Native American
MKL=Jackson, TN				
Mississippi Industrial College*	14			
Rust College*	40			
Memphis State University	59		1	
	113		**1**	
MLU=Monroe, LA				
Alcorn State University*	79			
	79			
MOB=Mobile, AL/Pasagoula, MS				
U of Southern Mississippi	40	2	1	
	40	**2**	**1**	
MSN=Madison, WS				
U of Wisconsin – Milwaukee	26	5	2	3
	26	**5**	**2**	**3**
MSY=New Orleans, LA				
Louisiana State U & A&M College	10		1	
Sthrn U A&M C – Main Cam*	304			
	314		**1**	
ORF=Norfolk/Virginia Beach, VA				
Virginia State College*	242			
	242			
PVD=Providence, RI				
U of Mass – Amherst Campus	8	9	4	
	8	**9**	**4**	
PWA=Oklahoma City-Wiley Post, OK				
East Central Oklahoma State U	6			9
Southwest Oklahoma State U	12			8
	18			**17**
RDU=Raleigh/Durham, NC				
East Carolina University	31			
St. Paul's College*	45			
	76			

Airport 61-80 (0800)

AIRPORT	MINORITY GROUP			
	Black	Hispanic	Asian	Native American
RIC=Richmond, VA				
Hampton Institute*	100			
Norfolk State College*	200			
St. Paul's College*	45			
U of Virginia - Main Campus	2			
	347			
SAN=San Diego, CA				
Chapman College	4	1		
	4	1		
SAT=San Antonio, TX				
Huston-Tillotson College*	23			
U of Texas at Austin	1	31	2	
	24	31	2	
SAV=Savannah, GA				
Baptist College at Charleston	14			
	14			
SBA=Santa Barbara, CA				
Cal State College - Bakersfield	3	3		1
Cal State University - Los Angeles	43	71	59	2
Cal State University - Northridge	6	2	5	8
U of Cal - Los Angeles	1	3	3	
	53	79	67	11
SBY=Salisbury, MD				
Delaware State College*	39			
	39			
SFO=San Francisco/Oakland, CA				
Cal State University - Sacramento	3	4	10	3
U of Cal - Davis	1	1	3	
University of the Pacific	3	7	7	1
	7	12	20	4

Airport 61-80 (0800)

AIRPORT	MINORITY GROUP			
	Black	Hispanic	Asian	Native American
SHV=Shreveport, LA				
Louisiana Tech University	19	1		
	19	1		
SWI=Sherman, TX				
U of Texas at Arlington	1	1	1	
	1	1	1	
TLH=Tallahassee, FL				
Albany State College*	65			
Valdosta State College	16			
	81			
TPA=Tampa, FL				
University of Central Florida	11	5	1	
	11	5	1	
TUL=Tulsa, OK				
Oklahoma State U - Main Campus	13	1		14
	13	1		14
TYR=Tyler, TX				
East Texas State University	89	13	1	1
	89	13	1	1

EDUCATION (0800)
MINORITY BACCALAUREATE DEGREES
MORE THAN 80 MILES FROM NEAREST AIRPORT

AIRPORT	MINORITY GROUP			
	Black	Hispanic	Asian	Native American
ABQ=Albuquerque, NM				
New Mexico Highlands U*	4	65		3
	4	65		3
AUS=Austin, TX				
Texas A&M U - Main Campus	7	8		7
	7	8		7
ELP=El Paso, TX				
Sul Ross State University	2	28		
	2	28		
IAH=Houston–Intercontinental, TX				
Texas A&M U - Main Campus	7	8		7
	7	8		7
MAF=Midland/Odessa, TX				
Sul Ross State University	2	28		
	2	28		
MSY=New Orleans, LA				
U of Southern Mississippi	40	2	1	
	40	2	1	
PWA=Oklahoma City–Wiley Post, OK				
Cameron University	11	3		5
	11	3		5
ROW=Roswell, NM				
Eastern NM U - Main Campus	8	35	1	7
	8	35	1	7
TCL=Tuscaloosa, AL				
Mississippi State University	45			
	45			

ENGINEERING (0900)

Tables	Page

ENGINEERING (0900)
MINORITY BACCALAUREATE DEGREES
BY STATE AND INSTITUTION

STATE/SCHOOL	MINORITY GROUP			
	Black	Hispanic	Asian	Native American
Alabama				
Alabama A&M University*	35			
Tuskegee Institute*	34		1	
University of Alabama	8			
U of Alabama in Birmingham	6		1	
University of South Alabama			2	2
	83		**4**	**2**
Arizona				
Arizona State University	3	9	16	
Northern Arizona University	2	4	4	3
University of Arizona	1	4	9	1
	6	**17**	**29**	**4**
California				
Cal Poly State U – San Luis Obispo		6	33	7
Cal State Poly U – Pomona	4	22	19	11
Cal State University – Chico		2		
Cal State University – Fresno		7	3	2
Cal State University – Fullerton		2	2	
Cal State University – Long Beach		9	17	1
Cal State University – Los Angeles	1	12	28	
Cal State University – Northridge	1	4	8	1
Cal State University – Sacramento	2	3	12	1
Loyola Marymount University	1	5	5	
San Diego State University	2	4	6	1
San Francisco State University	1	3	19	
San Jose State University	2	10	35	2
Stanford University	9	9	23	1
U of Cal – Berkeley	6	7	197	

(0900)

STATE/SCHOOL	MINORITY GROUP			
	Black	Hispanic	Asian	Native American
California (cont)				
U of Cal – Davis	4	5	37	
U of Cal – Irvine		3	8	
U of Cal – Los Angeles	2	3	88	1
U of Cal – San Diego			2	
U of Cal – Santa Barbara		8	15	
University of Redlands		1		
University of Southern California	3	12	42	4
University of the Pacific	2	1	7	
	40	**138**	**606**	**32**
Colorado				
Colorado State University		73	2	1
Metropolitan State College	8	8	2	1
U of Colorado at Boulder	3	2	10	
U of Southern Colorado	1	3	3	1
	12	**86**	**17**	**3**
Connecticut				
University of Connecticut				1
Yale University		2	5	
		2	**5**	**1**
Delaware				
University of Delaware	2		3	
	2		**3**	
District of Columbia				
George Washington University	3	4	5	
Howard University*	55		2	
University of DC*	12	3		
	70	**7**	**7**	
Florida				
Florida Agr & Mech University*	14		4	
Florida Atlantic University	1	6		
Florida International University	9	32	11	1

(0900)

STATE/SCHOOL	MINORITY GROUP			
	Black	Hispanic	Asian	Native American
Florida (cont)				
University of Central Florida	5	5	6	
University of Florida	2	41	15	
University of Miami	4	45	9	
University of South Florida	4	12	6	
University of West Florida			2	
	39	**141**	**53**	**1**
Georgia				
Fort Valley State College*	3			
GA Inst of Tech - Main Campus	36	10	13	1
Savannah State College*	12			
Spelman College*	5			
University of Georgia				2
	56	**10**	**13**	**3**
Hawaii				
University of Hawaii at Manoa*			153	
			153	
Illinois				
Bradley University	4		2	1
Illinois State University	8	2	1	2
Northern Illinois University		1	1	
Northwestern University	14	4	8	
Roosevelt University	1			
Southern Illinois U - Carbondale	7	3	3	7
U of Illinois - Chicago Circle	11	10	9	
U of Illinois - Urbana Campus	7	5	36	2
	52	**25**	**60**	**12**
Indiana				
Indiana State U - Main Campus	5		1	
Purdue University - Main Campus	22	7	20	1
	27	**7**	**21**	**1**

(0900)

STATE/SCHOOL	MINORITY GROUP			
	Black	Hispanic	Asian	Native American
Kentucky				
Eastern Kentucky University	2			
Kentucky State University*	1			
University of Louisville	3	2	2	
Western Kentucky University	3			
	9	**2**	**2**	
Louisiana				
Dillard University*				
Grambling State University*	33			
Louisiana State U & A&M College		2		
Louisiana Tech University	2	1	3	
Southeastern Louisiana U	1		1	
Sthrn U A&M College - Main Cam*	81			
Tulane U of Louisiana	10	14	2	1
University of New Orleans	2	3	2	
U of Southwestern Louisiana	4	4		1
	133	**24**	**8**	**2**
Maryland				
U of MD - College Park Campus	5	5	9	2
U of MD - Eastern Shore*	1			
	6	**5**	**9**	**2**
Massachussetts				
Boston University	1	2	3	
Harvard University	3	1	1	
Radcliffe College		1		
Tufts University	3	3	9	
U of Mass - Amherst Campus	1	3	3	
	8	**10**	**16**	
Michigan				
Detroit Institute of Technology	11		2	
Eastern Michigan University	1			
Michigan State University	8	3	4	2

(0900)

STATE/SCHOOL	MINORITY GROUP			
	Black	Hispanic	Asian	Native American
Michigan (cont)				
Oakland University	1			
University of Detroit	2	1	3	
U of Michigan - Ann Arbor	11	6	24	1
Wayne State University	14	1	8	3
Western Michigan University	4	1		
	52	**12**	**41**	**6**
Minnesota				
U of Minn - Minneapolis/St. Paul	4	3	18	2
	4	**3**	**18**	**2**
Mississippi				
Jackson State University*	25			
Mississippi State University	14			
Mississippi Valley State Univ*	12	1		
U of Mississippi - Main Campus	2		3	
	53	**1**	**3**	
Missouri				
Park College	1	1		
U of Missouri - Columbia	4	3	10	1
Washington University	7	5	10	
	12	**9**	**20**	**1**
Montana				
Montana State University			2	4
			2	**4**
New Hampshire				
Dartmouth College	5			
	5			
New Jersey				
New Jersey Inst Technology	46	31	28	
Princeton University	6	3	15	1
Rutgers U - New Brunswick	5	2	14	
Trenton State College	3	1	1	
	60	**37**	**58**	**1**

(0900)

STATE/SCHOOL	MINORITY GROUP			
	Black	Hispanic	Asian	Native American
New Mexico				
NM State U - Main Campus	2	32		3
U of NM - Main Campus	2	33	5	1
	4	**65**	**5**	**4**
New York				
Cornell U Endowed College	14	10	21	1
CUNY City College	94	45	38	4
CUNY College of Staten Island	6	3	1	
Polytechnic Institute New York	26	20	66	
Pratt Institute	25	12	5	
SUNY at Buffalo - Main Campus	4		13	
SUNY at Stony Bk - Main Campus	1	2	16	1
SUNY College at Buffalo	2	2	1	1
Syracuse University - Main Campus	1	1	3	
	173	**95**	**164**	**7**
North Carolina				
Duke University	1	2	2	
NC Agrl & Tech State University*	66			
NC State U - Raleigh	25	3		1
U of NC at Charlotte	1	2	3	
	93	**7**	**5**	**1**
North Dakota				
U of North Dakota - Main Campus	2	2	2	1
	2	**2**	**2**	**1**
Ohio				
Bowling Green State U - Main Cam			1	
Central State University*	5			
Franklin University	1			
Kent State U - Main Campus	2			
Ohio State U - Main Campus	4	2	5	
Ohio University - Main Campus	5		1	1
U of Akron - Main Campus	1	1	1	1

(0900)

STATE/SCHOOL	MINORITY GROUP			
	Black	Hispanic	Asian	Native American
Ohio (cont)				
U of Cincinnati - Main Campus	8		2	1
University of Dayton	5		2	1
University of Toledo	5	1	2	.
Wright State U - Main Campus	3			
	39	**4**	**14**	**4**
Oklahoma				
Oklahoma State U - Main Campus	12	5	12	7
Southeast Oklahoma State U	2	1	2	2
U of Oklahoma - Norman Campus	2	2	2	2
	16	**8**	**16**	**11**
Oregon				
Oregon State University		1	8	3
		1	**8**	**3**
Pennsylvania				
Cheyney State College*	16			
Drexel University	12	1	10	
Pennsylvania State U - Main Campus	1	1	6	1
Temple University	19	8	3	
University of Pennsylvania	8	1	6	
U of Pittsburgh - Main Campus	21	1		2
	77	**12**	**25**	**3**
Rhode Island				
Brown University	2		3	
	2		**3**	
South Carolina				
South Carolina State College*	17		1	
U of South Carolina at Columbia	5	2	2	
	22	**2**	**3**	
Tennessee				
Memphis State University	14	4	10	
Tennessee State University*	58			

(0900)

STATE/SCHOOL	MINORITY GROUP			
	Black	Hispanic	Asian	Native American
Tennessee (cont)				
U of Tennessee – Knoxville	11	4	2	
U of Tennessee – Martin	1			
	84	**8**	**14**	
Texas				
Lamar University	3		9	9
Prairie View A&M University*	65	4	3	
St. Mary's U – San Antonio		5	3	
Southwest Texas State University	2	3		
Texas A&I University	1	18		
Texas A&M U – Main Campus	1	38	6	6
Texas Southern University*	29			
Trinity University		1		
U of Houston – Central Campus	11	29	22	1
U of Texas at Arlington	2	3	3	
U of Texas at Austin	3	32	13	
U of Texas at El Paso	1	45	7	1
	118	**178**	**66**	**17**
Utah				
University of Utah	1	1	6	
	1	**1**	**6**	
Virginia				
Norfolk State College*	31			
Old Dominion University	2	3	1	1
U of Virginia – Main Campus	2			
	35	**3**	**1**	**1**
Washington				
University of Washington	5		45	2
	5		**45**	**2**
West Virginia				
West Virginia State College	3			
	3			

(0900)

STATE/SCHOOL		MINORITY GROUP		
	Black	Hispanic	Asian	Native American
Wisconsin				
U of Wisconsin – Madison	6	7	11	
U of Wisconsin – Milwaukee	2	1		
	8	**8**	**11**	
TOTALS	**1411**	**930**	**1536**	**131**

*Predominately minority institutions are those where at least 50% of the total BA Degrees awarded are to one of the minority groups being considered.

362

ENGINEERING (0900)
BLACK BACCALAUREATE DEGREES RANKED BY INSTITUTION

Rank	Institution	B.A.'s	Rank	Institution	B.A.'s
1	CUNY City C	94	21	South Carolina State C*	17
2	Sthrn U A&M C-Main Campus*	81	22	Cheyney State C*	16
3	NC Agrl & Tech State U*	66	23	Mississippi State U	14
4	Prairie View A&M U*	65	24	Wayne State U	14
5	Tennessee State U	58	25	Northwestern U	14
6	Howard U*	55	26	Cornel U Endowed C	14
7	New Jersey Institute Technology	46	27	Florida Agrl & Mech U*	14
8	GA Inst Tech-Main Campus	36	28	Memphis State U	14
9	Alabama A&M U*	35	29	Oklahoma State U-Main Campus	12
10	Tuskegee Institute*	34	30	Savannah State C*	12
11	Grambling State U*	33	31	Mississippi Valley Stte U*	12
12	Norfolk State C*	31	32	U of DC*	12
13	Texas Southern U*	29	33	Drexel U	12
14	Polytechnic Institute New York	26	34	Detroit Institute Technology	11
15	Pratt Institute	25	35	U of Illinois-Chicago Circle	11
16	NC State U-Raleigh	25	36	U of Tennessee-Knoxvillle	11
17	Jackson State U*	25	37	U of Michigan-Ann Arbor	11
18	Purdue U-Main Campus	22	38	U of Houston-Central Campus	11
19	U of Pittsburgh-Main Campus	21	39	Tulane U of Louisiana	10
20	Temple U	19			

*predominantly black institutions

Institutions not ranked have less than ten degrees conferred on blacks.

ENGINEERING (0900)
HISPANIC BACCALAUREATE DEGREES RANKED BY INSTITUTION

Rank	Institution	B.A.'s	Rank	Institution	B.A.'s
1	Colorado State U	73	13	Cal State Poly U-Pomona	22
2	U of Miami	45	14	Polytechnic Institute-New York	20
3	CUNY City C	45	15	Texas A&I U	18
4	U of Texas at El Paso	45	16	Tulane U of Louisiana	14
5	U of Florida	41	17	Cal State U-Los Angeles	12
6	Texas A&M U-Main Campus	38	18	U of Southern California	12
7	U of NM-Main Campus	33	19	U of South Florida	12
8	NM State U-Main Campus	32	20	Pratt Institute	12
9	Florida International U	32	21	San Jose State U	10
10	U of Texas at Austin	32	22	GA Inst of Tech-Main Campus	10
11	New Jersey Inst Technology	31	23	U of Illinois-Chicago Circle	10
12	U of Houston-Central Campus	29	24	Cornell U Endowed C	10

Institutions not ranked have less than ten degrees conferred on Hispanics.

ENGINEERING (0900)
ASIAN BACCALAUREATE DEGREES RANKED BY INSTITUTION

Rank	Institution	B.A.'s	Rank	Institution	B.A.'s
1	U of Cal-Berkeley	197	21	U fo Minn-Minneapolis/St. Paul	18
2	U of Hawaii at Manoa*	153	22	Cal State U-Long Beach	17
3	U of Cal-Los Angeles	88	23	SUNY at Stony Bk-Main Campus	16
4	Polytechnic Institute-New York	66	24	Arizona State U	16
5	U of Washington	45	25	U of Florida	15
6	U of Southern California	42	26	Princeton U	15
7	CUNY City C	38	27	U of Cal-Santa Barbara	15
8	U of Cal-Davis	37	28	Rutgers U-New Brunswick	14
9	U of Illinois-Urbana Campus	36	29	GA Inst of Tech-Main Campus	13
10	San Jose State U	35	30	SUNY at Buffalo-Main Campus	13
11	Cal Poly State-San Luis Obispo	33	31	U of Texas at Austin	13
12	New Jersey Inst Technology	28	32	Cal State U-Sacramento	12
13	Cal State U-Los Angeles	28	33	Oklahoma State U-Main Campus	12
14	U of Michigan-Ann Arbor	24	34	Florida International U	11
15	Stanford U	23	35	U of Wisconsin-Madison	11
16	U of Houston-Central Campus	22	36	Washington U	10
17	Cornell U Endowed C	21	37	Drexel U	10
18	Purdue U-Main Campus	20	38	U of Colorado at Boulder	10
19	San Francisco State U	19	39	U of Missouri-Columbia	10
20	Cal State Poly U-Pomona	19	40	Memphis State U	10

*predominantly Asian institutions

Institutions not ranked have less than ten degrees conferred on Asians.

ENGINEERING (0900)
NATIVE AMERICAN BACCALAUREATE DEGREES RANKED BY INSTITUTION

Rank	Institution	B.A.'s	Rank	Institution	B.A.'s
1	Cal State Poly U-Pomona	11	4	Southern Illinois U-Carbondale	7
2	Lamar U	9	5	Cal Poly State-San Luis Obispo	7
3	Oklahoma State U-Main Campus	7	6	Texas A&M U-Main Campus	6

Institutions not ranked have less than five degrees conferred on Native Americans.

ENGINEERING (0900)
MINORITY BACCALAUREATE DEGREES
WITHIN 60 MILE RADIUS OF AIRPORT

AIRPORT	MINORITY GROUP			
	Black	Hispanic	Asian	Native American
ABQ=Albuquerque, NM				
U of NM - Main Campus	2	33	5	1
	2	**33**	**5**	**1**
AOO=Altoona, PA				
Pennsylvania State U - Main Campus	1	1	6	1
	1	**1**	**6**	**1**
ATL=Atlanta, GA				
GA Inst of Tech-Main Campus	36	10	13	1
Spelman College*	5			
	41	**10**	**13**	**1**
AUS=Austin, TX				
Southwest Texas State University	2	3		
U of Texas at Austin	3	32	13	
	5	**35**	**13**	
BAL=Baltimore, MD				
University of Delaware	2		3	
George Washington Univesity	3	4	5	
Howard University*	55		2	
University of DC*	12	3		
U of MD - College Park Campus	5	5	9	2
	77	**12**	**19**	**2**
BDL=Hartford, CT/Springfield, MA				
Yale University		2	5	
U of Mass - Amherst Campus	1	3	3	
	1	**5**	**8**	

Airport 60 (0900)

AIRPORT	MINORITY GROUP			
	Black	Hispanic	Asian	Native American
BHM=Birmingham, AL				
U of Alabama in Birmingham	6		1	
University of Alabama	8			
	14		**1**	
BKL=Cleveland-Lakefront, OH				
Kent State U - Main Campus	2			
U of Akron - Main Campus	1	1	1	1
	3	**1**	**1**	**1**
BNA=Nashville, TN				
Western Kentucky University	3			
Middle Tennessee State U			2	
Tennessee State University*	58		.	
	61		**2**	
BOS=Boston, MA				
Boston University	1	2	3	
Harvard University	3	1	1	
Radcliffe College		1		
Tufts University	3	3	9	
Brown University	2		3	
	9	**7**	**16**	
BTR=Baton Rouge, LA				
Louisiana State U & A&M College		2		
Sthrn U A&M College - Main Cam*	81			
Southeastern Louisiana U	1		1	
	82	**2**	**1**	
BUF=Buffalo, NY				
SUNY at Buffalo - Main Campus	4		13	
SUNY College at Buffalo	2	2	1	1
	6	**2**	**14**	**1**
CAE=Columbia, SC				
South Carolina State College*	17		1	
U of South Carolina at Columbia	5	2	2	
	22	**2**	**3**	

Airport 60 (0900)

AIRPORT	MINORITY GROUP			
	Black	Hispanic	Asian	Native American
CIC=Chico, CA				
Cal State University - Chico		2		
		2		
CLT=Charlotte, NC				
U of NC at Charlotte	1	2	3	
	1	2	3	
CMH=Columbus, OH				
Central State University*	5			
Ohio State U - Main Campus	4	2	5	
	9	2	5	
CMI=Champaign, IL				
Illinois State University	8	2	1	2
U of Illinois - Urbana Campus	7	5	36	2
Indiana State U - Main Campus	5		1	
	20	7	38	4
COS=Colorado Springs, CO				
U of Southern Colorado	1	3	3	1
	1	3	3	1
COU=Columbia, MO				
U of Missouri - Columbia	4	3	10	1
	4	3	10	1
CRP=Corpus Christi, TX				
Texas A&I University	1	18		
	1	18		
CRW=Charleston, WV				
West Virginia State College	3			
	3			
CVG=Cincinnati, OH				
Central State University*	5			
Franklin University	1			
U of Cincinnati - Main Campus	8		2	1

Airport 60 (0900)

AIRPORT	MINORITY GROUP			
	Black	Hispanic	Asian	Native American
CVG (cont)				
University of Dayton	5		2	1
Wright State U – Main Campus	3			
	22		**4**	**2**
DAB=Dayton Beach, FL				
University of Central Florida	5	5	6	
	5	**5**	**6**	
DCA=Washington–National, DC				
George Washington University	3	4	5	
Howard University*	55		2	
University of DC*	12	3		
U of MD – College Park Campus	5	5	9	2
	75	**12**	**16**	**2**
DEN=Denver, CO				
Metropolitan State College	8	8	2	1
U of Colorado at Boulder	3	2	10	
	11	**10**	**12**	**1**
DFW=Dallas/Fort Worth, TX				
U of Texas at Arlington	2	3	3	
	2	**3**	**3**	
DTW=Detroit-Metropolitan, MI				
Detroit Institute of Technology	11		2	
Eastern Michigan University	1			
Oakland University	1			
U of Michigan – Ann Arbor	11	6	24	1
University of Detroit	2	1	3	
Wayne State University	14	1	8	3
University of Toledo	5	1	2	
	45	**9**	**39**	**4**
ELP=El Paso, TX				
U of Texas at El Paso	1	45	7	1
	1	**45**	**7**	**1**

Airport 60 (0900)

AIRPORT		MINORITY GROUP		
	Black	Hispanic	Asian	Native American
EUG=Eugene, OR				
Oregon State University		1	8	3
		1	8	3
FAT=Fresno, CA				
Cal State University - Fresno		7	3	2
		7	3	2
FAY=Fayetteville, NC				
NC State U - Raleigh	25	3		1
	25	3		1
FLG=Flagstaff, AZ				
Northern Arizona University	2	4	4	3
	2	4	4	3
GLH=Greenville, MS				
Mississippi Valley State U*	12	1		
	12	1		
GRR=Grand Rapids, MI				
Western Michigan University	4	1		
	4	1		
GSO=Greensboro/High Point, NC				
Duke University	1	2	2	
NC Agrl & Tech State University*	66			
	67	2	2	
HNL=Honolulu/Oahu, HI				
University of Hawaii at Manoa*			153	
			153	
HSV=Huntsville, AL/Decatur, GA				
Alabama A&M University*	35			
	35			
IAH=Houston–Intercontinental,TX				
Prairie View A&M University*	65	4	3	
Texas Southern University*	29			
U of Houston - Central Campus	11	29	22	1
	105	33	25	1

Airport 60 (0900)

AIRPORT	MINORITY GROUP			
	Black	Hispanic	Asian	Native American
IND=Indianapolis, IN				
Purdue University - Main Campus	22	7	20	1
	22	**7**	**20**	**1**
JAN=Jackson/Vicksburg, MS				
Jackson State University*	25			
	25			
JFK=New York, Kennedy Int'l, NY				
New Jersey Inst of Technology	46	31	28	
Princeton University	6	3	15	1
Rutgers U - New Brunswick	5	2	14	
Trenton State College	3	1	1	
CUNY College of Staten Island	6	3	1	
CUNY City College	94	45	38	4
Polytechnic Institute New York	26	20	66	
Pratt Institute	25	12	5	
SUNY at Stony Bk - Main Campus	1	2	16	1
	212	**119**	**184**	**6**
LAX=Los Angeles, CA				
Cal State Poly U - Pomona	4	22	19	11
Cal State University - Fullerton		2	2	
Cal State University - Long Beach		9	17	1
Cal State University - Los Angeles	1	12	28	
Cal State University - Northridge	1	4	8	1
Loyola Marymount University	1	5	5	
U of Cal - Irvine		3	8	
U of Cal - Los Angeles	2	3	88	1
University of Southern California	3	12	42	4
	12	**72**	**217**	**18**
LEX=Lexington/Frankfort, KY				
Eastern Kentucky University	2			
Kentucky State University*	1			
University of Louisville	3	2	2	
	6	**2**	**2**	

372

Airport 60 (0900)

AIRPORT	MINORITY GROUP			
	Black	Hispanic	Asian	Native American
MCI=Kansas City-International, MO				
Park College	1	1		
	1	1		
MCN=Macon, GA				
Fort Valley State College*	3			
	3			
MDH=Carbondale, IL				
Southern Illinois U - Carbondale	7	3	3	7
	7	3	3	7
MEM=Memphis, TN				
Memphis State University	14	4	10	
	14	4	10	
MGM=Montgomery, GA				
Tuskegee Institute*	34		1	
	34		1	
MHT=Manchester, NH				
Harvard University	3	1	1	
Radcliffe College		1		
Tufts University	3	3	9	
Dartmouth College	5			
	11	5	10	
MIA=Miami, FL				
Florida Atlantic University	1	6		
Florida International University	9	32	11	1
University of Miami	4	45	9	
	14	83	20	1
MKE=Milwaukee, WS				
U of Wisconsin - Milwaukee	2	1		
	2	1		
MKL=Jackson, TN				
U of Tennessee - Martin	1			
	1			

Airport 60 (0900)

AIRPORT	MINORITY GROUP			
	Black	Hispanic	Asian	Native American
MLU=Monroe, LA				
Grambling State University*	33			
Louisiana Tech University	2	1	3	
	35	**1**	**3**	
MOB=Mobile, AL/Pasagoula, MS				
University of South Alabama			2	2
University of West Florida			2	
			4	**2**
MSN=Madison, WS				
U of Wisconsin - Madison	6	7	11	
	6	**7**	**11**	
MSP=Minneapolis/St. Paul, MN				
U of Minn - Minneapolis/St. Paul	4	3	18	2
	4	**3**	**18**	**2**
MSY=New Orleans, LA				
Southeastern Louisiana U	1		1	
Tulane U of Louisiana	10	14	2	1
University of New Orleans	2	3	2	
	13	**17**	**5**	**1**
ORD=Chicago-O'Hare Airport, IL				
Northern Illinois University		1	1	
Northwestern University	14	4	8	
Roosevelt University	1			
U of Illinois - Chicago Circle	11	10	9	
	26	**15**	**18**	
ORF=Norfolk/Virginia Beach, VA				
Norfolk State College*	31			
Old Dominion University	2	3	1	1
	33	**3**	**1**	**1**
PHL=Philadelphia, PA/Wilmington, DE				
University of Delaware	2		3	
Princeton University	6	3	15	1

Airport 60 (0900)

AIRPORT	MINORITY GROUP			
	Black	Hispanic	Asian	Native American
PHL (cont)				
Rutgers U - New Brunswick	5	2	14	
Trenton State College	3	1	1	
Cheyney State College*	16			
Drexel University	12	1	10	
Temple University	19	8	3	
University of Pennsylvania	8	1	6	
	71	**16**	**52**	**1**
PHX=Phoenix, AZ				
Arizona State University	3	9	16	
	3	**9**	**16**	
PIA=Peoria, IL				
Bradley University	4		2	1
	4		**2**	**1**
PIT=Pittsburgh, PA				
U of Pittsburgh - Main Campus	21	1		2
	21	**1**		**2**
PVD=Providence, RI				
Boston University	1	2	3	
Harvard University	3	1	1	
Radcliffe College		1		
Tufts University	3	3	9	
Brown University	2		3	
	9	**7**	**16**	
PWA=Oklahoma City-Wiley Post, OK				
Oklahoma State U - Main Campus	12	5	12	7
U of Oklahoma - Norman Campus	2	2	2	2
	14	**7**	**14**	**9**
RDU=Raleigh/Durham, NC				
Duke University	1	2	2	
NC Agrl & Tech State University*	66			
NC State U - Raleigh	25	3		1
	92	**5**	**2**	**1**

Airport 60 (0900)

AIRPORT	MINORITY GROUP			
	Black	Hispanic	Asian	Native American
SAN=San Diego, CA				
San Diego State University	2	4	6	1
U of Cal – San Diego			2	
	2	4	8	1
SAT=San Antonio, TX				
St. Mary's U – San Antonio		5	3	
Southwest Texas State University	2	3		
Trinity University		1		
	2	9	3	
SAV=Savannah, GA				
Savannah State College*	12			
	12			
SBA=Santa Barbara, CA				
U of Cal – Santa Barbara		8	15	
		8	15	
SBP=San Luis Obispo, CA				
Cal Poly State U – San Luis Obispo		6	33	7
		6	33	7
SBY=Salisbury, MD				
U of MD – Eastern Shore*	1			
	1			
SEA=Seattle/Tacoma, WA				
University of Washington	5		45	2
	5		45	2
SFO=San Francisco/Oakland, CA				
San Francisco State University	1	3	19	
San Jose State University	2	10	35	2
Stanford University	9	9	23	1
U of Cal – Berkeley	6	7	197	
	18	29	274	3
SHV=Shreveport, LA				
Grambling State University*	33			
	33			

Airport 60 (0900)

AIRPORT	MINORITY GROUP			
	Black	Hispanic	Asian	Native American
SLC=Salt Lake City, UT				
University of Utah	1	1	6	
	1	1	6	
STL=St. Louis, MO				
Washington University	7	5	10	
	7	5	10	
SWI=Sherman, TX				
Southeast Oklahoma State U	2	1	2	2
	2	1	2	2
SYR=Syracuse, NY				
Cornel U Endowed College	14	10	21	1
Syracuse U-Main Campus	1	1	3	
	15	11	24	1
TCL=Tuscaloosa, AL				
U of Alabama in Birmingham	6		1	
University of Alabama	8			
	14		1	
TLH=Tallahassee, FL				
Florida Agr & Mech University*	14		4	
	14		4	
TPA=Tampa, FL				
University of South Florida	4	12	6	
	4	12	6	
TUS=Tucson, AZ				
University of Arizona	1	4	9	1
	1	4	9	1
TYS=Knoxville, TN				
U of Tennessee - Knoxville	11	4	2	
	11	4	2	

ENGINEERING (0900)
MINORITY BACCALAUREATE DEGREES
WITHIN 61-80 MILE ANNULUS OF AIRPORT

AIRPORT	MINORITY GROUP			
	Black	Hispanic	Asian	Native American
ALB=Albany, NY				
U of Mass - Amherst Campus	1	3	3	
	1	**3**	**3**	
ALM=Alamogordo, NM				
NM State U - Main Campus	2	32		3
	2	**32**		**3**
ATL=Atlanta, GA				
University of Georgia				2
				2
AUS=Austin, TX				
St. Mary's U - San Antonio		5	3	
Trinity University		1		
		6	**3**	
BAL=Baltimore, MD				
Cheyney State College*	16			
	16			
BDL=Hartford, CT/Springfield, MA				
Brown University	2		3	
	2		**3**	
BOS=Boston, MA				
U of Mass - Amherst Campus	1	3	3	
	1	**3**	**3**	
BTM=Butte, MT				
Montana State University			2	4
			2	**4**

378

Airport 61-80 (0900)

AIRPORT	MINORITY GROUP			
	Black	Hispanic	Asian	Native American
BTR=Baton Rouge, LA				
Tulane U of Louisiana	10	14	2	1
U of Southwestern Louisiana	4	4		1
University of New Orleans	2	3	2	
	16	21	4	2
CHS=Charleston, SC				
Savannah State College*	12			
South Carolina State College*	17		1	
	29		1	
CMH=Columbus, OH				
Ohio University - Main Campus	5		1	1
University of Dayton	5		2	1
Wright State U - Main Campus	3			
	13		3	2
CMI=Champaign, IL				
Purdue University - Main Campus	22	7	20	1
	22	7	20	1
COS=Colorado Springs, CO				
Metropolitan State College	8	8	2	1
U of Colorado at Boulder	3	2	10	
	11	10	12	1
CRW=Charleston, WV				
Ohio University - Main Campus	5		1	1
	5		1	1
CVG=Cincinnati, OH				
Kentucky State University*	1			
	1			
DEN=Denver, CO				
Colorado State University		73	2	1
		73	2	1

Airport 61-80 (0900)

AIRPORT	MINORITY GROUP			
	Black	Hispanic	Asian	Native American
DTW=Detroit-Metropolitan, MI				
Michigan State University	8	3	4	2
Bowling Green State U - Main Cam			1	
	8	**3**	**5**	**2**
FAY=Fayetteville, NC				
Duke University	1	2	2	
	1	**2**	**2**	
GRR=Grand Rapids, MI				
Michigan State University	8	3	4	2
	8	**3**	**4**	**2**
GSO=Greensboro/High Point, NC				
NC State U - Raleigh	25	3		1
	25	**3**		**1**
HSV=Huntsville, AL/Decatur, GA				
Middle Tennessee State U			2	
			2	
IND=Indianapolis, IN				
Indiana State U - Main Campus	5		1	
	5		**1**	
JAX=Jacksonville, FL				
University of Florida	2	41	15	
	2	**41**	**15**	
JFK=New York, Kennedy Int'l, NY				
Yale University		2	5	
		2	**5**	
LAX=Los Angeles, CA				
University of Redlands		1		
		1		
LCH=Lake Charles, LA				
U of Southwestern Louisiana	4	4		1
Lamar University	3		9	9
	7	**4**	**9**	**10**

Airport 61-80 (0900)

AIRPORT	MINORITY GROUP			
	Black	Hispanic	Asian	Native American
MCN=Macon, GA				
GA Inst of Tech - Main Campus	36	10	13	1
Spelman College*	5			
	41	**10**	**13**	**1**
MEM=Memphis, TN				
U of Mississippi - Main Campus	2		3	
	2		**3**	
MHT=Manchester, NH				
Boston University	1	2	3	
U of Mass - Amherst Campus	1	3	3	
	2	**5**	**6**	
MKE=Milwaukee, WS				
Northwestern University	14	4	8	
U of Wisconsin - Madison	6	7	11	
	20	**11**	**19**	
MKL=Jackson, TN				
Memphis State University	14	4	10	
	14	**4**	**10**	
MSN=Madison, WS				
U of Wisconsin - Milwaukee	2	1		
	2	**1**		
MSY=New Orleans, LA				
Louisiana State U & A&M College		2		
Sthrn U A&M C - Main Cam*	81			
	81	**2**		
PVD=Providence, RI				
U of Mass - Amherst Campus	1	3	3	
	1	**3**	**3**	
RIC=Richmond, VA				
Norfolk State College*	31			
U of Virginia - Main Campus	2			
	33			

Airport 61-80 (0900)

AIRPORT	MINORITY GROUP			
	Black	Hispanic	Asian	Native American
SAN=San Diego, CA				
U of Cal - Irvine		3	8	
		3	8	
SAT=San Antonio, TX				
U of Texas at Austin	3	32	13	
	3	32	13	
SBA=Santa Barbara, CA				
Cal State University - Los Angeles	1	12	28	
Cal State University - Northridge	1	4	8	1
Loyola Marymount University	1	5	5	
U of Cal - Los Angeles	2	3	88	1
	5	24	129	2
SFO=San Francisco/Oakland, CA				
Cal State University - Sacramento	2	3	12	1
U of Cal - Davis	4	5	37	
University of the Pacific	2	1	7	
	8	9	56	1
SHV=Shreveport, LA				
Louisiana Tech University	2	1	3	
	2	1	3	
SWI=Sherman, TX				
U of Texas at Arlington	2	3	3	
	2	3	3	
TPA=Tampa, FL				
University of Central Florida	5	5	6	
	5	5	6	
TUL=Tulsa, OK				
Oklahoma State U - Main Campus	12	5	12	7
	12	5	12	7

ENGINEERING (0900)
MINORITY BACCALAUREATE DEGREES
MORE THAN 80 MILES FROM NEAREST AIRPORT

AIRPORT	MINORITY GROUP			
	Black	Hispanic	Asian	Native American
AUS=Austin, TX				
Texas A&M U - Main Campus	1	38	6	6
	1	**38**	**6**	**6**
IAH=Houston–Intercontinental, TX				
Texas A&M U - Main Campus	1	38	6	6
	1	**38**	**6**	**6**
TCL=Tuscaloosa, AL				
Mississippi State University	14			
	14			

FINE & APPLIED ARTS (1000)

FINE AND APPLIED ARTS (1000)
MINORITY BACCALAUREATE DEGREES
BY STATE AND INSTITUTION

STATE/SCHOOL	MINORITY GROUP			
	Black	Hispanic	Asian	Native American
Alabama				
Jacksonville State University	1		1	
Miles College*	3			
Oakwood College*	4			
Troy State University – Main Campus	3			
University of Alabama	5			
U of Alabama in Birmingham	3			
University of South Alabama	3			
	22		**1**	
Arizona				
Arizona State University	1	5	1	
Northern Arizona University	2	4		
University of Arizona	1	3	1	
	4	**12**	**2**	
Arkansas				
Arkansas State U – Main Campus	1			
University of Arkansas – Pine Bluff*	4			
University of Central Arkansas	3			
	8			
California				
Cal State College – Bakersfield			2	
Cal State College – San Bernadino		4	1	
Cal State Poly U – Pomona	2	4		
Cal State University – Chico	1	1	2	1
Cal State U – Dominguez Hills	9	3	5	
Cal State University – Fresno	1	10	3	1
Cal State University – Fullerton	3	19	10	3
Cal State University – Hayward	9	9	3	

(1000)

STATE/SCHOOL	MINORITY GROUP			
	Black	Hispanic	Asian	Native American
California (cont)				
Cal State University - Long Beach	5	11	20	2
Cal State University - Los Angeles	18	14	18	4
Cal State University - Northridge	6	14	12	11
Cal State University - Sacramento	3	5	9	2
Chapman College		2		1
Loyola Marymount University	3	1	1	
San Diego State University	2	7	6	3
San Francisco State University	9	7	25	8
San Jose State University	4	10	31	4
Stanford University	3		2	
U of Cal - Berkeley	3	1	14	2
U of Cal - Davis	1	2	10	
U of Cal - Irvine	3	3	10	2
U of Cal - Los Angeles	16	9	43	
U of Cal - Riverside	1	1	1	1
U of Cal - San Diego		2	2	1
U of Cal - Santa Barbara	4	4	8	
U of Cal - Santa Cruz		3	2	
University of LaVerne	1			
University of Redlands		1		
University of Southern California	5	4	12	
University of the Pacific		2	4	
	112	**153**	**256**	**46**
Colorado				
Colorado State University	1	2		
Metropolitan State College	2	3		
U of Colorado at Boulder	1	2		
U of Northern Colorado	2	1		1
U of Southern Colorado		1		
	6	**9**		**1**

(1000)

STATE/SCHOOL	MINORITY GROUP			
	Black	Hispanic	Asian	Native American
Connecticut				
University of Connecticut	1			
Yale University	3	2	3	
	4	2	3	
Delaware				
University of Delaware	1			
	1			
District of Columbia				
American University	7	4		1
George Washington University	1	1	1	
Howard University*	47			
University of DC*	15			
	70	5	1	1
Florida				
Florida Agr & Mech University*	28			
Florida Atlantic University	1		1	
Florida International University		7		
Florida State University	11			
University of Central Florida	1	1		
St. Leo College		1		
University of Florida	1	5	1	
University of Miami	1	12		
University of South Florida	3	2		
University of West Florida		1	1	
	46	29	3	
Georgia				
Albany State College*	8			
Clark College*	14			
Georgia State University	3			
Morehouse College*	2			
Morris Brown College*	1			
Spelman College*	19			

(1000)

STATE/SCHOOL	MINORITY GROUP			
	Black	Hispanic	Asian	Native American
Georgia (cont)				
University of Georgia	4	1		
Valdosta State College	1			
	52	**1**		
Hawaii				
Chaminade University of Honolulu			1	
University of Hawaii at Manoa*	1	2	112	
	1	**2**	**113**	
Illinois				
Bradley University	4			
Chicago State University*	18	2		
College of St. Francis	1	1		
Columbia College	34	5	4	6
DePaul University	2			
Eastern Illinois University	2			
Governors State University	1			
Illinois State University	7		1	3
Loyola University of Chicago	4	3		
Northern Illinois University	2	1	5	
Northeastern Illinois University	5	3	1	
Northwestern University	8		1	1
Roosevelt University	9		11	
Southern Illinois U - Carbondale	5	5	4	
Southern Illinois U - Edwardsville	2		1	
U of Illinois - Chicago Circle	4	2	11	
U of Illinois - Urbana Campus	3	2	4	
	111	**24**	**43**	**10**
Indiana				
Ball State University	5			
Ind-Purdue U - Indianapolis	3			
Indiana State U - Main Campus	1			

(1000)

STATE/SCHOOL	MINORITY GROUP			
	Black	Hispanic	Asian	Native American
Indiana (cont)				
Indiana University – Bloomington	6	3	2	
Indiana University – Northwest	1	1		
Purdue University – Main Campus			2	
	16	**4**	**4**	
Kentucky				
Eastern Kentucky University	2			
Kentucky State University*	3			
Western Kentucky University	1			
	6			
Louisiana				
Dillard University*	13			
Grambling State University*	5			
Louisiana Tech University	4			
McNeese State University			1	
Northeast Louisiana University	2			
Sthrn U A&M College – Main Cam*	16			
Southern U in New Orleans*	5			
Tulane U of Louisiana	1	2	1	
University of New Orleans	2	1		
U of Southwestern Louisiana	2	2	1	2
Xavier University of Louisiana*	10			
	60	**5**	**3**	**2**
Maryland				
Bowie State College*	1			
Morgan State University*	3			
Towson State University	9		2	
U of MD – Baltimore Co Campus	6			
U of MD – College Park Campus	7	3	5	2
U of MD – Eastern Shore*	2			
	28	**3**	**7**	**2**

(1000)

STATE/SCHOOL	MINORITY GROUP			
	Black	Hispanic	Asian	Native American
Massachussetts				
Boston University	2		1	
Harvard University	2		3	
Radcliffe College	2		2	
Tufts University	6			
U of Mass – Amherst Campus		1	2	
	12	1	8	
Michigan				
Eastern Michigan University	19			1
Mercy College of Detroit	1			
Michigan State University	7	1		
Oakland University	1			
University of Detroit	1			
U of Michigan – Ann Arbor	4		1	
Wayne State University	21	5	2	
Western Michigan University	6			
	60	6	3	1
Minnesota				
U of Minn – Minneapolis/St. Paul	2	1	3	3
	2	1	3	3
Mississippi				
Delta State University			1	
Mississippi State University	2			
Mississippi University for Women	2			
Mississippi Valley State Univ*	8			
Tougaloo College*	6			
U of Southern Mississippi	3			
	21		1	
Missouri				
Columbia College	2			
Lincoln University	1			
U of Missouri – Columbia	1		1	

(1000)

STATE/SCHOOL	MINORITY GROUP			
	Black	Hispanic	Asian	Native American
Missouri (cont)				
U of Missouri - Kansas City		1		
U of Missouri - St. Louis	2			
Washington University	2		1	
Webster College	5			
	13	**1**	**2**	
Montana				
Montana State University				1
				1
New Hampshire				
Dartmouth College	4			
	4			
New Jersey				
Glassboro State College	15	5	1	3
Jersey City State College	4	8		
Kean College of New Jersey	7			
Montclair State College	3	2	2	2
Rutgers U - Camden Campus	3			
Rutgers U - New Brunswick	10	3	2	
Rutgers U - Newark Campus	12	3		
Trenton State College	9		1	
	63	**21**	**6**	**5**
New Mexico				
Eastern NM U - Main Campus	2	4		
New Mexico Highlands U*		8		
NM State U - Main Campus		1		
University of Albuquerque		2		
U of NM - Main Campus		11	2	1
Western New Mexico University	1	3		
	3	**29**	**2**	**1**
New York				
Adelphi University	16	1		
College of New Rochelle	1			

(1000)

STATE/SCHOOL	MINORITY GROUP			
	Black	Hispanic	Asian	Native American
New York (cont)				
Cornell U Endowed College	2	1	1	1
CUNY Bernard Baruch College	1			
CUNY Brooklyn College	40	13	3	1
CUNY City College	36	18	9	2
CUNY College of Staten Island	1	2		
CUNY Hunter College	21	13	5	2
CUNY Lehman College	7	7	2	
CUNY Queen's College	21	5	6	1
CUNY York College	5	1		
Fordham University	4	1		
Long Island U - Brooklyn Center	1			
Long Island U - C W Post Center	3			
New York University	16	5	3	3
Pratt Institute	16	12	5	
SUNY at Albany		2	2	
SUNY at Buffalo - Main Campus	1		1	
SUNY at Stony Bk - Main Campus	2	1		
SUNY College at Buffalo	2		1	2
SUNY College at New Paltz	5			1
SUNY College - Old Westbury	6	2		
SUNY Empire State College	3	2	1	
Syracuse University - Main Campus	7	3	3	
	217	**89**	**42**	**13**
North Carolina				
Duke University	2			
East Carolina University	4			
Johnson C Smith University*	5			
Livingstone College*	10			
NC Agrl & Tech State University*	16			
NC Central University*	35			

(1000)

STATE/SCHOOL	MINORITY GROUP			
	Black	Hispanic	Asian	Native American
North Carolina (cont)				
NC State U - Raleigh		1		
St. Augustine's College*	8			
Shaw University*	5			
U of NC at Chapel Hill	1			1
U of NC at Charlotte	2			
U of NC at Greensboro	5	1		
Winston-Salem State University*	12			
	105	**2**		**1**
North Dakota				
U of North Dakota - Main Campus				1
				1
Ohio				
Antioch University	6			
Bowling Green State U - Main Cam	6	1		
Kent State U - Main Campus	4			
Oberlin College	11	2	4	1
Ohio State U - Main Campus	6		1	
Ohio University - Main Campus	16	1		
U of Akron - Main Campus	2			
U of Cincinnati - Main Campus	8	3		
University of Dayton	2			1
University of Toledo				1
Wilberforce University*	7			
Wright State U - Main Campus	4			
	72	**7**	**5**	**3**
Oklahoma				
Cameron University		2		
Central State University	1			
East Central Oklahoma State U	1			1
Langston University*	7			

(1000)

STATE/SCHOOL	MINORITY GROUP			
	Black	Hispanic	Asian	Native American
Oklahoma (cont)				
Northeast Oklahoma State U				1
Southwest Oklahoma State U				1
U of Oklahoma - Norman Campus	6			6
	15	**2**		**9**
Oregon				
University of Oregon - Main Campus	1	4	3	1
	1	**4**	**3**	**1**
Pennsylvania				
Cheyney State College*	11			
Pennsylvania State U - Main Campus	1			
Temple University	12	5	1	
U of Pittsburgh - Main Campus	1			
	25	**5**	**1**	
Rhode Island				
Brown University	1		2	
	1		**2**	
South Carolina				
Claflin College*	3			
South Carolina State College*	4			
U of South Carolina at Columbia	4			
	11			
Tennessee				
Austin Peay State University		1		
Fisk University*	10			
Knoxville College*	3			
Lane College*	2			
LeMoyne-Owen College*	2			
Memphis State University	9		1	
Middle Tennessee State U	1			
Tennessee State University*	15			
U of Tennessee - Knoxville	2			
	44	**1**	**1**	

(1000)

STATE/SCHOOL	MINORITY GROUP			
	Black	Hispanic	Asian	Native American
Texas				
Angelo State University		4		
Corpus Christi State University		7		
East Texas State University	6	3		1
Huston-Tillotson College*	3			
Incarnate Word College		4		
Lamar University	1			4
North Texas State University	22	7	2	1
Our Lady of Lake University*	1	5		
Pan American University*		12		
Prairie View A&M University*	6			
St. Edward's University	1	1		
St. Mary's U – San Antonio	1	3		
Sam Houston State University	1		2	
Southwest Texas State University	5	12		1
Sul Ross State University		2		
Texas A&I University	1	13		
Texas College*	3			
Texas Southern University*	1			
Texas Women's University		4		
Trinity University	1	1		
U of Houston – Central Campus	5	9	2	1
U of Texas at Arlington	1	1		1
U of Texas at Austin	3	5	1	
U of Texas at El Paso	2	21	1	
U of Texas at San Antonio		5		1
Wiley College*	3			
	67	119	8	10
Utah				
Brigham Young University – Main			1	3
University of Utah	1	2	3	1
	1	2	4	4

(1000)

STATE/SCHOOL		MINORITY GROUP		
	Black	Hispanic	Asian	Native American
Virginia				
Hampton Institute*	6			
Norfolk State College*	7			
Old Dominion University	5			
U of Virginia - Main Campus	3			
Virginia Commonwealth University	22	1	1	1
Virginia State College*	17			
Virginia Union University*	1			
	61	**1**	**1**	**1**
Washington				
University of Washington	7	1	9	1
	7	**1**	**9**	**1**
West Virginia				
West Virginia State College	3			
	3			
Wisconsin				
U of Wisconsin - Madison	2		1	
U of Wisconsin - Milwaukee	5	1		1
	7	**1**	**1**	**1**
TOTALS	**1362**	**542**	**538**	**118**

* Predominately minority institutions are those where at least 50% of the total BA Degrees awarded are to one of the minority groups being considered.

FINE AND APPLIED ARTS (1000)
BLACK BACCALAUREATE DEGREES RANKED BY INSTITUTION

Rank	Institution	B.A.'s	Rank	Institution	B.A.'s
1	Howard U*	47	20	U of Cal-Los Angeles	16
2	CUNY Brooklyn C	40	21	Adelphi U	16
3	CUNY City C	36	22	Sthrn U A&M C-Main Campus*	16
4	NC Central U*	35	23	Pratt Institute	16
5	Columbia C	34	24	U of DC*	15
6	Florida Agrl & Mech U*	28	25	Glassboro State C	15
7	Virginia Commonwealth U	22	26	Tennessee State U*	15
8	North Texas State U	22	27	Clark C*	14
9	CUNY Hunter C	21	28	Dillard U*	13
10	CUNY Queen's C	21	29	Winston-Salem State U*	12
11	Wayne State U	21	30	Rutgers U-Newark Campus	12
12	Spelman C*	19	31	Temple U	12
13	Eastern Michigan U	19	32	Oberlin C	11
14	Cal State U-Los Angeles	18	33	Cheyney State C*	11
15	Chicago State U*	18	34	Florida State U	11
16	Virginia State C*	17	35	Rutgers U-New Brunswick	10
17	New York U	16	36	Xavier U of Louisiana*	10
18	NC Agrl & Tech State U*	16	37	Livingstone C*	10
19	Ohio U-Main Campus	16	38	Fisk U*	10

*predominantly black institutions

Institutions not ranked have less than ten degrees conferred on blacks.

FINE & APPLIED ARTS (1000)
HISPANIC BACCALAUREATE DEGREES RANKED BY INSTITUTION

Rank	Institution	B.A.'s	Rank	Institution	B.A.'s
1	U of Texas at El Paso	21	9	U of Miami	12
2	Cal State U-Fullerton	19	10	Pan American U*	12
3	CUNY City C	18	11	Pratt Institute	12
4	Cal State U-Northridge	14	12	Southwest Texas State U	12
5	Cal State U-Los Angeles	14	13	Cal State U-Long Beach	11
6	CUNY Hunter C	13	14	U of NM-Main Campus	11
7	CUNY Brooklyn C	13	15	Cal State U-Fresno	10
8	Texas A&I U	13	16	San Jose State U	10

*predominantly Hispanic institutions

Institutions not ranked have less than ten degrees conferred on Hispanics.

FINE & APPLIED ARTS (1000)
ASIAN BACCALAUREATE DEGREES RANKED BY INSTITUTION

Rank	Institution	B.A.'s	Rank	Institution	B.A.'s
1	U of Hawaii at Manoa*	112	8	U of Southern California	12
2	U of Cal-Los Angeles	43	9	Cal State U-Northridge	12
3	San Jose State U	31	10	Roosevelt U	11
4	San Francisco State U	25	11	U of Illinois-Chicago Circle	11
5	Cal State U-Long Beach	20	12	U of Cal-Irvine	10
6	Cal State U-Los Angeles	18	13	Cal State U-Fullerton	10
7	U of Cal-Berkeley	14	14	U of Cal-Davis	10

*predominantly Asian institutions

Institutions not ranked have less than ten degrees conferred on Asians.

FINE & APPLIED ARTS (1000)
NATIVE AMERICAN BACCALAUREATE DEGREES RANKED BY INSTITUTION

Rank	Institution	B.A.'s	Rank	Institution	B.A.'s
1	Cal State U-Northridge	11	3	Columbia C	6
2	San Francisco State U	8	4	U of Oklahoma-Norman Campus	6

Institutions not ranked have less than five degrees conferred on Native Americans.

FINE AND APPLIED ARTS (1000)
MINORITY BACCALAUREATE DEGREES
WITHIN 60 MILE RADIUS OF AIRPORT

AIRPORT	Black	Hispanic	Asian	Native American
ABQ=Albuquerque, NM				
U of NM - Main Campus		11	2	1
University of Albuquerque		2		
		13	**2**	**1**
ALB=Albany, NY				
SUNY at Albany		2	2	
SUNY Empire State College	3	2	1	
	3	**4**	**3**	
AOO=Altoona, PA				
Pennsylvania State U - Main Campus	1			
	1			
ATL=Atlanta, GA				
Clark College*	14			
Georgia State University	3			
Morehouse College*	2			
Morris Brown College*	1			
Spelman College*	19			
	39			
AUS=Austin, TX				
Huston-Tillotson College*	3			
Southwest Texas State University	5	12		1
U of Texas at Austin	3	5	1	
	11	**17**	**1**	**1**
BAL=Baltimore, MD				
University of Delaware	1			
American University	7	4		1
George Washington Univesity	1	1	1	

Airport 60 (1000)

AIRPORT		MINORITY GROUP		
	Black	Hispanic	Asian	Native American
BAL (cont)				
Howard University*	47			
University of DC*	15			
Bowie State College*	1			
Morgan State University*	3			
Towson State University	9		2	
U of MD - Baltimore Co Campus	6			
U of MD - College Park Campus	7	3	5	2
	97	**8**	**8**	**3**
BDL=Hartford, CT/Springfield, MA				
Yale University	3	2	3	
U of Mass - Amherst Campus		1	2	
	3	**3**	**5**	
BHM=Birmingham, AL				
Miles College*	3			
U of Alabama in Birmingham	3			
University of Alabama	5			
	11			
BKL=Cleveland-Lakefront, OH				
Kent State U - Main Campus	4			
Oberlin College	11	2	4	1
U of Akron - Main Campus	2			
	17	**2**	**4**	**1**
BNA=Nashville, TN				
Western Kentucky University	1			
Austin Peay State University		1		
Fisk University*	10			
Middle Tennessee State U	1			
Tennessee State University*	15			
	27	**1**		

Airport 60 (1000)

AIRPORT	MINORITY GROUP			
	Black	Hispanic	Asian	Native American
BOS=Boston, MA				
Boston University	2		1	
Harvard University	2		3	
Radcliffe College	2		2	
Tufts University	6			
Brown University	1		2	
	13		8	
BTR=Baton Rouge, LA				
Sthrn U A&M College - Main Cam*	16			
	16			
BUF=Buffalo, NY				
SUNY at Buffalo - Main Campus	1		1	
SUNY College at Buffalo	2		1	2
	3		2	2
CAE=Columbia, SC				
Claflin College*	3			
South Carolina State College*	4			
U of South Carolina at Columbia	4			
	11			
CIC=Chico, CA				
Cal State University - Chico	1	1	2	1
	1	1	2	1
CLT=Charlotte, NC				
Johnson C Smith University*	5			
Livingstone College*	10			
U of NC at Charlotte	2			
	17			
CMH=Columbus, OH				
Ohio State U - Main Campus	6		1	
Wilberforce University*	7			
	13		1	

402

Airport 60 (1000)

AIRPORT	MINORITY GROUP			
	Black	Hispanic	Asian	Native American
CMI=Champaign, IL				
Eastern Illinois University	2			
Illinois State University	7		1	3
U of Illinois - Urbana Campus	3	2	4	
Indiana State U - Main Campus	1			
	13	**2**	**5**	**3**
COS=Colorado Springs, CO				
U of Southern Colorado		1		
		1		
COU=Columbia, MO				
Columbia College	2			
Lincoln University	1			
U of Missouri - Columbia	1		1	
	4		**1**	
CRP=Corpus Christi, TX				
Corpus Christi State University		7		
Texas A&I University	1	13		
	1	**20**		
CRW=Charleston, WV				
West Virginia State College	3			
	3			
CVG=Cincinnati, OH				
Antioch University	6			
U of Cincinnati - Main Campus	8	3		
University of Dayton	2			1
Wilberforce University*	7			
Wright State U - Main Campus	4			
	27	**3**		**1**
DAB=Dayton Beach, FL				
University of Central Florida	1	1		
	1	**1**		

Airport 60 (1000)

AIRPORT	MINORITY GROUP			
	Black	Hispanic	Asian	Native American
DCA=Washington-National, DC				
American University	7	4		1
George Washington University	1	1	1	
Howard University*	47			
University of DC*	15			
Bowie State College*	1			
Morgan State University*	3			
Towson State University	9		2	
U of MD - Baltimore Co Campus	6			
U of MD - College Park Campus	7	3	5	2
	96	**8**	**8**	**3**
DEN=Denver, CO				
Metropolitan State College	2	3		
U of Colorado at Boulder	1	2		
U of Northern Colorado	2	1		1
	5	**6**		**1**
DFW=Dallas/Fort Worth, TX				
East Texas State University	6	3		1
North Texas State University	22	7	2	1
Texas Woman's University		4		
U of Texas at Arlington	1	1		
	29	**15**	**2**	**2**
DTW=Detroit-Metropolitan, MI				
Eastern Michigan University	19			1
Mercy College of Detroit	1			
Oakland University	1			
U of Michigan - Ann Arbor	4		1	
University of Detroit	1			
Wayne State University	21	5	2	
University of Toledo				1
	47	**5**	**3**	**2**

404

Airport 60 (1000)

AIRPORT	MINORITY GROUP			
	Black	Hispanic	Asian	Native American
ELP=El Paso, TX				
U of Texas at El Paso	2	21	1	
	2	21	1	
EUG=Eugene, OR				
University of Oregon – Main Campus	1	4	3	1
	1	4	3	1
FAT=Fresno, CA				
Cal State University – Fresno	1	10	3	1
	1	10	3	1
FAY=Fayetteville, NC				
NC Central University*	35			
NC State U – Raleigh		1		
St. Augustine's College*	8			
Shaw University*	5			
U of NC at Chapel Hill	1			1
	49	1		1
FLG=Flagstaff, AZ				
Northern Arizona University	2	4		
	2	4		
GLH=Greenville, MS				
Delta State University			1	
Mississippi Valley State U*	8			
	8		1	
GRR=Grand Rapids, MI				
Western Michigan University	6			
	6			
GSO=Greensboro/High Point, NC				
Duke University	2			
Livingstone College*	10			
NC Agrl & Tech State University*	16			
NC Central University*	35			

Airport 60 (1000)

AIRPORT	MINORITY GROUP			
	Black	Hispanic	Asian	Native American
GSO (cont)				
U of NC at Chapel Hill	1			1
U of NC at Greensboro	5	1		
Winston-Salem State University*	12			
	81	1		1
HNL=Honolulu/Oahu, HI				
Chaminade University of Honolulu			1	
University of Hawaii at Manoa*	1	2	112	
	1	2	113	
HSV=Huntsville, AL/Decatur, GA				
Oakwood College*	4			
	4			
IAH=Houston-Intercontinental,TX				
Prairie View A&M University*	6			
Texas Southern University*	1			
U of Houston - Central Campus	5	9	2	1
	12	9	2	1
IND=Indianapolis, IN				
Ball State University	5			
Ind-Purdue U - Indianapolis	3			
Indiana University - Bloomington	6	3	2	
Purdue University - Main Campus			2	
	14	3	4	
JAN=Jackson/Vicksburg, MS				
Tougaloo College*	6			
	6			
JFK=New York, Kennedy Int'l, NY				
Jersey City State College	4	8		
Kean College of New Jersey	7			
Montclair State College	3	2	2	2
Rutgers U - New Brunswick	10	3	2	
Rutgers U - Newark Campus	12	3		

406

Airport 60 (1000)

AIRPORT	MINORITY GROUP			
	Black	Hispanic	Asian	Native American
JFK (cont)				
Trenton State College	9		1	
Adelphi University	16	1		
College of New Rochelle	1			
CUNY Bernard Baruch College	1			
CUNY Brooklyn College	40	13	3	1
CUNY College of Staten Island	1	2		
CUNY City College	36	18	9	2
CUNY Hunter College	21	13	5	2
CUNY Lehman College	7	7	2	
CUNY Queen's College	21	5	6	1
CUNY York College	5	1		
Fordham University	4	1		
Long Island U - Brooklyn Center	1			
Long Island U - C W Post Center	3			
New York University	16	5	3	3
Pratt Institute	16	12	5	
SUNY at Stony Bk - Main Campus	2	1		
SUNY College - Old Westbury	6	2		
	242	97	38	11
LAX=Los Angeles, CA				
Cal State College - San Bernardino		4	1	
Cal State Poly U - Pomona	2	4		
Cal State U - Dominguez Hills	9	3	5	
Cal State University - Fullerton	3	19	10	3
Cal State University - Long Beach	5	11	20	2
Cal State University - Los Angeles	18	14	18	4
Cal State University - Northridge	6	14	12	11
Chapman College		2		1
Loyola Marymount University	3	1	1	
U of Cal - Irvine	3	3	10	2

Airport 60 (1000)

AIRPORT	MINORITY GROUP			
	Black	Hispanic	Asian	Native American
LAX (cont)				
U of Cal – Los Angeles	16	9	43	
U of Cal – Riverside	1	1	1	1
University of Southern California	5	4	12	
University of LaVerne	1			
	72	**89**	**133**	**24**
LCH=Lake Charles, LA				
McNeese State University			1	
			1	
LEX=Lexington/Frankfort, KY				
Eastern Kentucky University	2			
Kentucky State University*	3			
	5			
LIT=Little Rock, AR				
University of Arkansas – Pine Bluff*	4			
University of Central Arkansas	3			
	7			
MCI=Kansas City-International, MO				
U of Missouri – Kansas City		1		
		1		
MDH=Carbondale, IL				
Southern Illinois U – Carbondale	5	5	4	
	5	**5**	**4**	
MEM=Memphis, TN				
Le Moyne–Owen College*	2			
Memphis State University	9		1	
	11		**1**	
MFE=McAllen, TX				
Pan American University*		12		
		12		
MGM=Montgomery, GA				
Troy State University – Main Campus	3			
	3			

408

Airport 60 (1000)

AIRPORT	MINORITY GROUP			
	Black	Hispanic	Asian	Native American
MHT=Manchester, NH				
Harvard University	2		3	
Radcliffe College	2		2	
Tufts University	6			
Dartmouth College	4			
	14		**5**	
MIA=Miami, FL				
Florida Atlantic University	1		1	
Florida International University		7		
University of Miami	1	12		
	2	**19**	**1**	
MKE=Milwaukee, WS				
U of Wisconsin - Milwaukee	5	1		1
	5	**1**		**1**
MKL=Jackson, TN				
Lane College*	2			
	2			
MLU=Monroe, LA				
Grambling State University*	5			
Louisiana Tech University	4			
Northeast Louisiana University	2			
	11			
MOB=Mobile, AL/Pasagoula, MS				
University of South Alabama	3			
University of West Florida		1	1	
	3	**1**	**1**	
MSN=Madison, WS				
U of Wisconsin - Madison	2		1	
	2		**1**	
MSP=Minneapolis/St. Paul, MN				
U of Minn - Minneapolis/St. Paul	2	1	3	3
	2	**1**	**3**	**3**

Airport 60 (1000)

AIRPORT	MINORITY GROUP			
	Black	Hispanic	Asian	Native American
MSY=New Orleans, LA				
Dillard University*	13			
Southern U in New Orleans*	5			
Tulane U of Louisiana	1	2	1	
University of New Orleans	2	1		
Xavier University of Louisiana*	10			
	31	**3**	**1**	
ORD=Chicago–O'Hare Airport, IL				
Chicago State University*	18	2		
College of St. Francis	1	1		
Columbia College	34	5	4	6
DePaul University	2			
Governors State University	1			
Loyola University of Chicago	4	3		
Northern Illinois University	2	1	5	
Northwestern University	8		1	1
Northeastern Illinois University	5	3	1	
Roosevelt University	9		11	
U of Illinois - Chicago Circle	4	2	11	
Indiana University - Northwest	1	1		
	89	**18**	**33**	**7**
ORF=Norfolk/Virginia Beach, VA				
Hampton Institute*	6			
Norfolk State College*	7			
Old Dominion University	5			
	18			
PHL=Philadelphia, PA/Wilmington, DE				
University of Delaware	1			
Glassboro State College	15	5	1	3
Rutgers U - Camden Campus	3			
Rutgers U - New Brunswick	10	3	2	

410

Airport 60 (1000)

AIRPORT	Black	MINORITY GROUP Hispanic	Asian	Native American
PHL (cont)				
Trenton State College	9		1	
Cheyney State College*	11			
Temple University	12	5	1	
	61	**13**	**5**	**3**
PHX=Phoenix, AZ				
Arizona State University	1	5	1	
	1	**5**	**1**	
PIA=Peoria, IL				
Bradley University	4			
	4			
PIT=Pittsburgh, PA				
U of Pittsburgh – Main Campus	1			
	1			
PVD=Providence, RI				
Boston University	2		1	
Harvard University	2		3	
Radcliffe College	2		2	
Tufts University	6			
Brown University	1		2	
	13		**8**	
PWA=Oklahoma City-Wiley Post, OK				
Central State University	1			
Langston University*	7			
U of Oklahoma – Norman Campus	6			6
	14			**6**
RDU=Raleigh/Durham, NC				
Duke University	2			
NC Agrl & Tech State University*	16			
NC Central University*	35			
NC State U – Raleigh		1		

411

Airport 60 (1000)

AIRPORT	MINORITY GROUP			
	Black	Hispanic	Asian	Native American
RDU (cont)				
St. Augustine's College*	8			
Shaw University*	5			
U of NC at Chapel Hill	1			1
U of NC at Greensboro	5	1		
	72	**2**		**1**
RIC=Richmond, VA				
Virginia Commonwealth University	22	1	1	1
Virginia State College*	17			
Virginia Union University*	1			
	40	**1**	**1**	**1**
SAN=San Diego, CA				
San Diego State University	2	7	6	3
U of Cal - San Diego		2	2	1
	2	**9**	**8**	**4**
SAT=San Antonio, TX				
Incarnate Word College		4		
Our Lady of Lake University*	1	5		
St. Edward's University	1	1		
St. Mary's U - San Antonio	1	3		
Southwest Texas State University	5	12		1
Trinity University	1	1		
U of Texas at San Antonio		5		1
	9	**31**		**2**
SBA=Santa Barbara, CA				
U of Cal - Santa Barbara	4	4	8	
	4	**4**	**8**	
SBY=Salisbury, MD				
U of MD - Eastern Shore*	2			
	2			
SEA=Seattle/Tacoma, WA				
University of Washington	7	1	9	1
	7	**1**	**9**	**1**

412

Airport 60 (1000)

| AIRPORT | MINORITY GROUP | | | |
	Black	Hispanic	Asian	Native American
SFO=San Francisco/Oakland, CA				
Cal State University - Hayward	9	9	3	
San Francisco State University	9	7	25	8
San Jose State University	4	10	31	4
Stanford University	3		2	
U of Cal - Berkeley	3	1	14	2
	28	**27**	**75**	**14**
SHV=Shreveport, LA				
Grambling State University*	5			
Wiley College*	3			
	8			
SJT=San Angelo, TX				
Angelo State University		4		
		4		
SLC=Salt Lake City, UT				
Brigham Young University - Main			1	3
University of Utah	1	2	3	1
	1	**2**	**4**	**4**
STL=St. Louis, MO				
Southern Illinois U - Edwardsville	2		1	
U of Missouri - St. Louis	2			
Washington University	2		1	
Webster College	5			
	11		**2**	
SVC=Silver City, NM				
Western New Mexico University	1	3		
	1	**3**		
SWI=Sherman, TX				
East Texas State University	6	3		1
North Texas State University	22	7	2	1
Texas Woman's University		4		
	28	**14**	**2**	**2**

Airport 60 (1000)

AIRPORT	MINORITY GROUP			
	Black	Hispanic	Asian	Native American
SYR=Syracuse, NY				
Cornel U Endowed College	2	1	1	1
Syracuse U - Main Campus	7	3	3	
	9	**4**	**4**	**1**
TCL=Tuscaloosa, AL				
Miles College*	3			
U of Alabama in Birmingham	3			
University of Alabama	5			
Mississippi University for Women	2			
	13			
TLH=Tallahassee, FL				
Florida Agr & Mech University*	28			
Florida State University	11			
	39			
TPA=Tampa, FL				
St. Leo College		1		
University of South Florida	3	2		
	3	**3**		
TUL=Tulsa, OK				
Northeast Oklahoma State U				1
				1
TUS=Tucson, AZ				
University of Arizona	1	3	1	
	1	**3**	**1**	
TYR=Tyler, TX				
Texas College*	3			
Wiley College*	3			
	6			
TYS=Knoxville, TN				
Knoxville College*	3			
U of Tennessee - Knoxville	2			
	5			

FINE AND APPLIED ARTS (1000)
MINORITY BACCALAUREATE DEGREES
WITHIN 61–80 MILE ANNULUS OF AIRPORT

AIRPORT	MINORITY GROUP			
	Black	Hispanic	Asian	Native American
ALB=Albany, NY				
U of Mass - Amherst Campus		1	2	
SUNY College at New Paltz	5			1
	5	1	2	1
ALM=Alamogordo, NM				
NM State U - Main Campus		1		
		1		
ATL=Atlanta, GA				
Jacksonville State University	1		1	
University of Georgia	4	1		
	5	1	1	
AUS=Austin, TX				
Incarnate Word College		4		
Our Lady of Lake University*	1	5		
St. Edward's University	1	1		
St. Mary's U - San Antonio	1	3		
Trinity University	1	1		
U of Texas at San Antonio		5		1
	4	19		1
BAL=Baltimore, MD				
Cheyney State College*	11			
	11			
BDL=Hartford, CT/Springfield, MA				
College of New Rochelle	1			
SUNY at Albany		2	2	
SUNY College at New Paltz	5			1
Brown University	1		2	
	7	2	4	1

Airport 61-80 (1000)

AIRPORT	MINORITY GROUP			
	Black	Hispanic	Asian	Native American
BHM=Birmingham, AL				
Jacksonville State University	1		1	
	1		1	
BOS=Boston, MA				
U of Mass - Amherst Campus		1	2	
		1	2	
BTM=Butte, MT				
Montana State University				1
				1
BTR=Baton Rouge, LA				
Dillard University*	13			
Southern U in New Orleans*	5			
Tulane U of Louisiana	1	2	1	
U of Southwestern Louisiana	2	2	1	2
University of New Orleans	2	1		
Xavier University of Louisiana*	10			
	33	5	2	2
CHS=Charleston, SC				
Claflin College*	3			
South Carolina State College*	4			
	7			
CLT=Charlotte, NC				
Wintson-Salem State University*	12			
	12			
CMH=Columbus, OH				
Antioch University	6			
Ohio University - Main Campus	16	1		
University of Dayton	2			1
Wright State U - Main Campus	4			
	28	1		1

416

Airport 61-80 (1000)

AIRPORT	MINORITY GROUP			
	Black	Hispanic	Asian	Native American
CMI=Champaign, IL				
Purdue University - Main Campus			2	
			2	
COS=Colorado Springs, CO				
Metropolitan State College	2	3		
U of Colorado at Boulder	1	2		
	3	5		
CRW=Charleston, WV				
Ohio University - Main Campus	16	1		
	16	1		
CVG=Cincinnati, OH				
Kentucky State University*	3			
	3			
DEN=Denver, CO				
Colorado State University	1	2		
	1	2		
DTW=Detroit-Metropolitan, MI				
Michigan State University	7	1		
Bowling Green State U - Main Cam	6	1		
	13	2		
FAY=Fayetteville, NC				
Duke University	2			
	2			
GRR=Grand Rapids, MI				
Michigan State University	7	1		
	7	1		
GSO=Greensboro/High Point, NC				
NC State U - Raleigh		1		
St. Augustine's College*	8			
Shaw University*	5			
	13	1		

Airport 61-80 (1000)

AIRPORT	MINORITY GROUP			
	Black	Hispanic	Asian	Native American
HSV=Huntsville, AL/Decatur, GA				
Jacksonville State University	1		1	
Middle Tennessee State U	1			
	2		1	
IAH=Houston-Intercontinental,TX				
Sam Houston State University	1		2	
	1		2	
IND=Indianapolis, IN				
Indiana State U - Main Campus	1			
	1			
JAX=Jacksonville, FL				
University of Florida	1	5	1	
	1	5	1	
JFK=New York, Kennedy Int'l, NY				
Yale University	3	2	3	
SUNY College at New Paltz	5			1
	8	2	3	1
LAX=Los Angeles, CA				
Cal State College - Bakersfield			2	
University of Redlands		1		
		1	2	
LCH=Lake Charles, LA				
U of Southwestern Louisiana	2	2	1	2
Lamar University	1			4
	3	2	1	6
MCN=Macon, GA				
Clark College*	14			
Georgia State University	3			
Morehouse College*	2			
Morris Brown College*	1			
Spelman College*	19			
	39			

Airport 61-80 (1000)

AIRPORT	MINORITY GROUP			
	Black	Hispanic	Asian	Native American
MEM=Memphis, TN				
Arkansas State U – Main Campus	1			
Lane College*	2			
	3			
MHT=Manchester, NH				
Boston University	2		1	
U of Mass – Amherst Campus		1	2	
	2	**1**	**3**	
MKE=Milwaukee, WS				
Northwestern University	8		1	1
U of Wisconsin – Madison	2		1	
	10		**2**	**1**
MKL=Jackson, TN				
Memphis State University	9		1	
	9		**1**	
MOB=Mobile, AL/Pasagoula, MS				
U of Southern Mississippi	3			
	3			
MSN=Madison, WS				
U of Wisconsin – Milwaukee	5	1		1
	5	**1**		**1**
MSY=New Orleans, LA				
Sthrn U A&M C – Main Cam*	16			
	16			
ORF=Norfolk/Virginia Beach, VA				
Virginia State College*	17			
	17			
PVD=Providence, RI				
U of Mass – Amherst Campus		1	2	
		1	**2**	

Airport 61-80 (1000)

AIRPORT	MINORITY GROUP			
	Black	Hispanic	Asian	Native American
PWA=Oklahoma City-Wiley Post, OK				
East Central Oklahoma State U	1			1
Southwest Oklahoma State U				1
	1			2
RDU=Raleigh/Durham, NC				
East Carolina University	4			
	4			
RIC=Richmond, VA				
Hampton Institute*	6			
Norfolk State College*	7			
U of Virginia - Main Campus	3			
	16			
SAN=San Diego, CA				
Chapman College		2		1
U of Cal - Irvine	3	3	10	2
U of Cal - Riverside	1	1	1	1
	4	6	11	4
SAT=San Antonio, TX				
Huston-Tillotson College*	3			
U of Texas at Austin	3	5	1	
	6	5	1	
SBA=Santa Barbara, CA				
Cal State College - Bakersfield			2	
Cal State University - Los Angeles	18	14	18	4
Cal State University - Northridge	6	14	12	11
Loyola Marymount University	3	1	1	
U of Cal - Los Angeles	16	9	43	
	43	38	76	15
SFO=San Francisco/Oakland, CA				
Cal State University - Sacramento	3	5	9	2
U of Cal - Davis	1	2	10	

420

Airport 61-80 (1000)

AIRPORT	MINORITY GROUP			
	Black	Hispanic	Asian	Native American
SFO (cont)				
U of Cal - Santa Cruz		3	2	
University of the Pacific		2	4	
	4	12	25	2
SHV=Shreveport, LA				
Louisiana Tech University	4			
	4			
SWI=Sherman, TX				
U of Texas at Arlington	1	1		
	1	1		
TLH=Tallahassee, FL				
Albany State College*	8			
Valdosta State College	1			
	9			
TPA=Tampa, FL				
University of Central Florida	1	1		
	1	1		
TYR=Tyler, TX				
East Texas State University	6	3		1
	6	3		1

FINE AND APPLIED ARTS (1000)
MINORITY BACCALAUREATE DEGREES
MORE THAN 80 MILES FROM NEAREST AIRPORT

AIRPORT	MINORITY GROUP			
	Black	Hispanic	Asian	Native American
ABQ=Albuquerque, NM				
New Mexico Highlands U*		8		
		8		
ELP=El Paso, TX				
Sul Ross State University		2		
		2		
MAF=Midland/Odessa, TX				
Sul Ross State University		2		
		2		
MSY=New Orleans, LA				
U of Southern Mississippi	3			
	3			
PWA=Oklahoma City-Wiley Post, OK				
Cameron University		2		
		2		
ROW=Roswell, NM				
Eastern NM U - Main Campus	2	4		
	2	**4**		
TCL=Tuscaloosa, AL				
Mississippi State University	2			
	2			

FOREIGN LANGUAGES (1100)

FOREIGN LANGUAGES (1100)
MINORITY BACCALAUREATE DEGREES
BY STATE AND INSTITUTION

STATE/SCHOOL	MINORITY GROUP			
	Black	Hispanic	Asian	Native American
Alabama				
Alabama State University*	1			
Jacksonville State University			1	
University of Alabama	1			
U of Alabama in Birmingham		1		
	2	**1**	**1**	
Arizona				
Arizona State University		2		
Northern Arizona University		2		1
University of Arizona		8	2	
		12	**2**	**1**
Arkansas				
Henderson State University	1			
	1			
California				
Cal State College – Bakersfield		5		
Cal State College – San Bernadino	1	4		
Cal State University – Chico		5	1	
Cal State U – Dominguez Hills		10		1
Cal State University – Fresno	1	10		
Cal State University – Fullerton		14		
Cal State University – Hayward		2	1	
Cal State University – Long Beach		14	1	
Cal State University – Los Angeles	1	31		
Cal State University – Northridge	1	7	2	1
Cal State University – Sacramento		4		
Chapman College		1		
Loyola Marymount University	1	3		

(1100)

STATE/SCHOOL	MINORITY GROUP			
	Black	Hispanic	Asian	Native American
California (cont)				
San Diego State University	2	20	1	
San Francisco State University	1	9	16	
San Jose State University		11	1	1
Stanford University		2		
U of Cal – Berkeley		4	18	
U of Cal – Davis		2		1
U of Cal – Irvine		6	1	
U of Cal – Los Angeles	2	17	13	
U of Cal – Riverside		2	1	
U of Cal – San Diego		1	1	
U of Cal – Santa Barbara		15	1	1
University of LaVerne		1		
University of San Francisco		4		
University of Southern California	2	3	4	
University of the Pacific	1	1		
	13	**208**	**62**	**5**
Colorado				
Colorado State University		1		
Metropolitan State College	1			
U of Colorado at Boulder		11	2	1
U of Northern Colorado		2		
U of Southern Colorado		1		
	1	**15**	**2**	**1**
Connecticut				
University of Connecticut	2			
Yale University	1	3		
	3	**3**		
Delaware				
Delaware State College*				
University of Delaware	1	2		
	1	**2**		

(1100)

STATE/SCHOOL		MINORITY GROUP		
	Black	Hispanic	Asian	Native American
District of Columbia				
American University	1			
George Washington University		3	1	
Howard University*	5			
University of DC*	3	2	1	
	9	**5**	**2**	
Florida				
Biscayne College*		42		
Florida International University	1	22		
Florida State University	2			
University of Central Florida		3		
University of Florida		5		
University of Miami	1	4	1	
University of South Florida	1	4		
	5	**80**	**1**	
Georgia				
Fort Valley State College*	1			
Georgia State University	1			
Morehouse College*	2			
Morris Brown College*	1			
Spelman College*	3			
	8			
Hawaii				
University of Hawaii at Manoa*			67	
			67	
Illinois				
Bradley University	1			
Chicago State University*	1	4		
DePaul University	1	3		
Illinois State University	3	1		
Loyola University of Chicago	1	2		

426

(1100)

STATE/SCHOOL	MINORITY GROUP			
	Black	Hispanic	Asian	Native American
Illinois (cont)				
Northern Illinois University	2	3	1	
Northeastern Illinois University		10		
Northwestern University	3	2	1	
Roosevelt University	1	2	1	
Southern Illinois U - Carbondale	1			
U of Illinois - Chicago Circle	3	12	1	
U of Illinois - Urbana Campus		3	1	
	17	**42**	**5**	
Indiana				
Ball State University		2		
Indiana University - Bloomington	1		3	
Indiana University - Northwest		2		
Purdue University - Main Campus	2	2		
	3	**6**	**3**	
Kentucky				
Eastern Kentucky University	1			
Kentucky State University*	2			
University of Louisville	1	1		
	4	**1**		
Louisiana				
Grambling State University*	2			
Louisiana State U & A&M College	1	3		
McNeese State University	1			
Southeastern Louisiana U	1			
Southern U in New Orleans*	1			
Tulane U of Louisiana		2		
University of New Orleans	1	2		
U of Southwestern Louisiana		1		
	7	**8**		

(1100)

STATE/SCHOOL	MINORITY GROUP			
	Black	Hispanic	Asian	Native American
Maryland				
Morgan State University*	3			
Towson State University		1		
U of MD - Baltimore Co Campus	1			
U of MD - College Park Campus	1	1		
	5	2		
Massachussetts				
Boston State College	1	3		
Harvard University	1			
Radcliffe College	1			
Tufts University	2	3	2	
U of Mass - Amherst Campus	1	1		
	6	7	2	
Michigan				
Michigan State University		2		
Oakland University	1			
U of Michigan - Ann Arbor	5	2		
Wayne State University	1	3	2	
Western Michigan University		1		
	7	8	2	
Minnesota				
U of Minn - Minneapolis/St. Paul	1	1		
	1	1		
Mississippi				
U of Mississippi - Main Campus	1	1		
	1	1		
Missouri				
St. Louis U - Main Campus		2		
U of Missouri - Kansas City			1	
U of Missouri - St. Louis		2		
Washington University	2	7		
	2	11	1	

428

(1100)

STATE/SCHOOL	MINORITY GROUP			
	Black	Hispanic	Asian	Native American
New Hampshire				
Dartmouth College	5	1		1
	5	1		1
New Jersey				
Glassboro State College	4	6		2
Kean College of New Jersey		21		
Montclair State College	1	15	1	3
Princeton University	3	1		
Rutgers U - Camden Campus	3			1
Rutgers U - New Brunswick	4	10	1	
Rutgers U - Newark Campus	2	7		
St. Peter's College		9		
	17	69	2	6
New Mexico				
Eastern NM U - Main Campus		2		
New Mexico Highlands U*		2		
NM State U - Main Campus		7		
U of NM - Main Campus		7		
Western New Mexico University		2		
		20		
New York				
Adelphi University		1		
College of New Rochelle		1		
Cornell U Endowed College	1		1	
CUNY Bernard Baruch College	3	1	1	
CUNY Brooklyn College	14	4	1	1
CUNY City College	15	7	3	
CUNY Hunter College	12	8	3	
CUNY Lehman College	6	8	2	
CUNY Queen's College	10	3	3	
CUNY York College	4	1		

(1100)

STATE/SCHOOL	MINORITY GROUP			
	Black	Hispanic	Asian	Native American
New York (cont)				
Fordham University	1	15		
Long Island U – C W Post Center		1		
Mercy College		26		
New York University	3	10	2	
St. John's University			1	
SUNY at Albany	1	12	1	
SUNY at Buffalo – Main Campus	1	2	2	
SUNY at Stony Bk – Main Campus	1	3		
SUNY College at New Paltz	3	2		
Syracuse University – Main Campus	2	1		
	77	**106**	**20**	**1**
North Carolina				
Duke University	1	1		
East Carolina University	1			
NC Central University*	1			
St. Augustine's College*	2			
U of NC at Chapel Hill		1		
U of NC at Charlotte	1			
U of NC at Greensboro	1			
	7	**2**		
Ohio				
Antioch University		4		
Bowling Green State U – Main Cam	1			
Oberlin College	1		1	
Ohio State U – Main Campus	1			
U of Akron – Main Campus	2	1	1	
University of Dayton	2			
	7	**5**	**2**	
Oklahoma				
Oklahoma State U – Main Campus	1	2		
	1	**2**		

(1100)

STATE/SCHOOL	MINORITY GROUP			
	Black	Hispanic	Asian	Native American
Oregon				
University of Oregon – Main Campus	1	1		
	1	1		
Pennsylvania				
Cheyney State College*	1			
Lincoln University*	6			
Pennsylvania State U – Main Campus	1			
St. Joseph's University				1
Temple University	1	1	1	
University of Pennsylvania	1		1	
U of Pittsburgh – Main Campus	1	1		
	11	2	2	1
Rhode Island				
Brown University	2	2	1	
	2	2	1	
South Carolina				
U of South Carolina at Columbia	1			
Winthrop College	1			
	2			
Tennessee				
Fisk University*	2			
Middle Tennessee State U		1		
Tennessee State University*	2			
U of Tennessee – Knoxville		1		
U of Tennessee at Martin	1			
	5	2		
Texas				
Angelo State University		6		
Bishop College*	2			
Corpus Christi State University		5		
Incarnate Word College		1		
Lamar University				1

(1100)

STATE/SCHOOL	MINORITY GROUP			
	Black	Hispanic	Asian	Native American
Texas (cont)				
Laredo State University*		28		
North Texas State University	2			
Our Lady of Lake University*		28		
Pan American University*		8		
Prairie View A&M University*	2			
St. Mary's U – San Antonio		5		
Southwest Texas State University		14		
Sul Ross State University		3		
Texas A&I University	1	7		
Texas Women's University		1		
U of Houston – Central Campus	2	8		
U of Texas at Arlington	2	8		
U of Texas at Austin	2	21		
U of Texas at El Paso	2	9		
U of Texas at San Antonio		2		
	15	**154**		**1**
Utah				
University of Utah		2		
		2		
Virginia				
Hampton Institute*	2			
Old Dominion University		1	1	
U of Virginia – Main Campus	2			
Virginia State College*	3			
Virginia Union University*	1			
	8	**1**	**1**	
Washington				
University of Washington	2		3	1
	2		**3**	**1**

432

(1100)

STATE/SCHOOL	MINORITY GROUP			
	Black	Hispanic	Asian	Native American
Wisconsin				
U of Wisconsin - Madison			1	
U of Wisconsin - Milwaukee		4		
		4	1	
TOTALS	256	786	182	18

*Predominately minority institutions are those where at least 50% of the total BA Degrees awarded are to one of the minority groups being considered.

FOREIGN LANGUAGES (1100)
BLACK BACCALAUREATE DEGREES RANKED BY INSTITUTION

Rank	Institution	B.A.'s	Rank	Institution	B.A.'s
1	CUNY City C	15	3	CUNY Hunter C	12
2	CUNY Brooklyn C	14	4	CUNY Queen's C	10

*predominantly black institutions

Institutions not ranked have less than ten degrees conferred on blacks.

FOREIGN LANGUAGES (1100)
HISPANIC BACCALAUREATE DEGREES RANKED BY INSTITUTION

Rank	Institution	B.A.'s	Rank	Institution	B.A.'s
1	Biscayne C*	42	14	Cal State U-Fullerton	14
2	Cal State U-Los Angeles	31	15	Cal State U-Long Beach	14
3	Our Lady of the Lake U*	28	16	Southwest Texas State U	14
4	Laredo State U*	28	17	U of Illinois-Chicago Circle	12
5	Mercy C	26	18	SUNY at Albany	12
6	Florida International U	22	19	San Jose State U	11
7	Kean C of New Jersey	21	20	U of Colorado at Boulder	11
8	U of Texas at Austin	21	21	Rutgers U-New Brunswick	10
9	San Diego State U	20	22	Cal State U-Fresno	10
10	U of Cal-Los Angeles	17	23	New York U	10
11	Montclair State C	15	24	Northeastern Illinois U	10
12	U of Cal-Santa Barbara	15	25	Cal State U-Dominguez Hills	10
13	Fordham U	15			

*predominantly Hispanic institutions

Institutions not ranked have less than ten degrees conferred on Hispanics.

FOREIGN LANGUAGES (1100)
ASIAN BACCALAUREATE DEGREES RANKED BY INSTITUTION

Rank	Institution	B.A.'s	Rank	Institution	B.A.'s
1	U of Hawaii at Manoa*	67	3	San Francisco State U	16
2	U of Cal–Berkeley	18	4	U of Cal–Los Angeles	13

*predominantly Asian institutions

Institutions not ranked have less than ten degrees conferred on Asians.

FOREIGN LANGUAGES (1100)
MINORITY BACCALAUREATE DEGREES
WITHIN 60 MILE RADIUS OF AIRPORT

AIRPORT	MINORITY GROUP			
	Black	Hispanic	Asian	Native American
ABQ=Albuquerque, NM				
U of NM - Main Campus		7		
		7		
ALB=Albany, NY				
SUNY at Albany	1	12	1	
	1	12	1	
AOO=Altoona, PA				
Pennsylvania State U - Main Campus	1			
	1			
ATL=Atlanta, GA				
Morehouse College*	2			
Morris Brown College*	1			
Spelman College*	3			
	6			
AUS=Austin, TX				
Southwest Texas State University		14		
U of Texas at Austin	2	21		
	2	35		
BAL=Baltimore, MD				
University of Delaware	1	2		
American University	1			
George Washington Univesity		3	1	
Howard University*	5			
University of DC*	3	2	1	
Morgan State University*	3			
Towson State University		1		
U of MD - Baltimore Co Campus	1			

436

Airport 60 (1100)

AIRPORT	MINORITY GROUP			
	Black	Hispanic	Asian	Native American
BAL (cont)				
U of MD - College Park Campus	1	1		
Lincoln University*	6			
	21	9	2	
BDL=Hartford, CT/Springfield, MA				
Yale University	1	3		
U of Mass - Amherst Campus	1	1		
	2	4		
BHM=Birmingham, AL				
U of Alabama in Birmingham		1		
University of Alabama	1			
	1	1		
BKL=Cleveland-Lakefront, OH				
Oberlin College	1		1	
U of Akron - Main Campus	2	1	1	
	3	1	2	
BNA=Nashville, TN				
Fisk University*	2			
Middle Tennessee State U		1		
Tennessee State University*	2			
	4	1		
BOS=Boston, MA				
Boston State College	1	3		
Harvard University	1			
Radcliffe College	1			
Tufts University	2	3	2	
Brown University	2	2	1	
	7	8	3	
BTR=Baton Rouge, LA				
Louisiana State U & A&M College	1	3		
Southeastern Louisiana U	1			
	2	3		

Airport 60 (1100)

AIRPORT	MINORITY GROUP			
	Black	Hispanic	Asian	Native American
BUF=Buffalo, NY				
SUNY at Buffalo - Main Campus	1	2	2	
	1	2	2	
CAE=Columbia, SC				
U of South Carolina at Columbia	1			
	1			
CIC=Chico, CA				
Cal State University - Chico		5	1	
		5	1	
CLT=Charlotte, NC				
U of NC at Charlotte	1			
Winthrop College	1			
	2			
CMH=Columbus, OH				
Ohio State U - Main Campus	1			
	1			
CMI=Champaign, IL				
Illinois State University	3	1		
U of Illinois - Urbana Campus		3	1	
	3	4	1	
COS=Colorado Springs, CO				
U of Southern Colorado		1		
		1		
CRP=Corpus Christi, TX				
Corpus Christi State University		5		
Texas A&I University	1	7		
	1	12		
CVG=Cincinnati, OH				
Antioch University		4		
University of Dayton	2			
	2	4		

438

Airport 60 (1100)

AIRPORT	MINORITY GROUP			
	Black	Hispanic	Asian	Native American
DAB=Dayton Beach, FL				
University of Central Florida		3		
		3		
DCA=Washington–National, DC				
American University	1			
George Washington University		3	1	
Howard University*	5			
University of DC*	3	2	1	
Morgan State University*	3			
Towson State University		1		
U of MD - Baltimore Co Campus	1			
U of MD - College Park Campus	1	1		
	14	7	2	
DEN=Denver, CO				
Metropolitan State College	1			
U of Colorado at Boulder		11	2	1
U of Northern Colorado		2		
	1	13	2	1
DFW=Dallas/Fort Worth, TX				
Bishop College*	2			
North Texas State University	2			
Texas Woman's University		1		
U of Texas at Arlington	2	8		
	6	9		
DTW=Detroit-Metropolitan, MI				
Oakland University	1			
U of Michigan - Ann Arbor	5	2		
Wayne State University	1	3	2	
	7	5	2	
ELP=El Paso, TX				
U of Texas at El Paso	2	9		
	2	9		

Airport 60 (1100)

AIRPORT	MINORITY GROUP			
	Black	Hispanic	Asian	Native American
EUG=Eugene, OR				
University of Oregon - Main Campus	1	1		
	1	1		
FAT=Fresno, CA				
Cal State University - Fresno	1	10		
	1	10		
FAY=Fayetteville, NC				
NC Central University*	1			
St. Augustine's College*	2			
U of NC at Chapel Hill		1		
	3	1		
FLG=Flagstaff, AZ				
Northern Arizona University		2		1
		2		1
GRR=Grand Rapids, MI				
Western Michigan University		1		
		1		
GSO=Greensboro/High Point, NC				
Duke University	1	1		
NC Central University*	1			
U of NC at Chapel Hill		1		
U of NC at Greensboro	1			
	3	2		
HNL=Honolulu/Oahu, HI				
University of Hawaii at Manoa*			67	
			67	
IAH=Houston–Intercontinental,TX				
Prairie View A&M University*	2			
U of Houston - Central Campus	2	8		
	4	8		

440

Airport 60 (1100)

AIRPORT	Black	Hispanic	Asian	Native American
		MINORITY GROUP		
IND=Indianapolis, IN				
Ball State University		2		
Indiana University - Bloomington	1		3	
Purdue University - Main Campus	2	2		
	3	**4**	**3**	
JFK=New York, Kennedy Int'l, NY				
Kean College of New Jersey		21		
Montclair State College	1	15	1	3
Princeton University	3	1		
Rutgers U - New Brunswick	4	10	1	
Rutgers U - Newark Campus	2	7		
St. Peter's College		9		
Adelphi University		1		
College of New Rochelle		1		
CUNY Bernard Baruch College	3	1	1	
CUNY Brooklyn College	14	4	1	1
CUNY City College	15	7	3	
CUNY Hunter College	12	8	3	
CUNY Lehman College	6	8	2	
CUNY Queen's College	10	3	3	
CUNY York College	4	1		
Fordham University	1	15		
Long Island U - C W Post Center		1		
Mercy College		26		
New York University	3	10	2	
New York University	3	10	2	
St. John's University			1	
SUNY at Stony Bk - Main Campus	1	3		
	79	**152**	**18**	**4**

Airport 60 (1100)

AIRPORT		MINORITY GROUP		
	Black	Hispanic	Asian	Native American
LAX=Los Angeles, CA				
Cal State College - San Bernardino	1	4		
Cal State U - Dominguez Hills		10		1
Cal State University - Fullerton		14		
Cal State University - Long Beach		14	1	
Cal State University - Los Angeles	1	31		
Cal State University - Northridge	1	7	2	1
Chapman College		1		
Loyola Marymount University	1	3		
U of Cal - Irvine		6	1	
U of Cal - Los Angeles	2	17	13	
U of Cal - Riverside		2	1	
University of Southern California	2	3	4	
University of LaVerne		1		
	8	**113**	**22**	**2**
LCH=Lake Charles, LA				
McNeese State University	1			
	1			
LEX=Lexington/Frankfort, KY				
Eastern Kentucky University	1			
Kentucky State University*	2			
University of Louisville	1	1		
	4	**1**		
LRD=Laredo, TX				
Laredo State University*		28		
		28		
MCI=Kansas City-International, MO				
U of Missouri - Kansas City			1	
			1	
MCN=Macon, GA				
Fort Valley State College*	1			
Georgia College	1			
	2			

Airport 60 (1100)

AIRPORT	MINORITY GROUP			
	Black	Hispanic	Asian	Native American
MDH=Carbondale, IL				
Southern Illinois U - Carbondale	1			
	1			
MFE=McAllen, TX				
Pan American University*		8		
		8		
MGM=Montgomery, GA				
Alabama State University*	1			
	1			
MHT=Manchester, NH				
Harvard University	1			
Radcliffe College	1			
Tufts University	2	3	2	
Dartmouth College	5	1		1
	9	4	2	1
MIA=Miami, FL				
Biscayne College*		42		
Florida International University	1	22		
University of Miami	1	4	1	
	2	68	1	
MKL=Jackson, TN				
U of Tennessee - Martin	1			
	1			
MLU=Monroe, LA				
Grambling State University*	2			
	2			
MSN=Madison, WS				
U of Wisconsin - Madison		4	1	
		4	1	
MSP=Minneapolis/St. Paul, MN				
U of Minn - Minneapolis/St. Paul	1	1		
	1	1		

Airport 60 (1100)

AIRPORT	MINORITY GROUP			
	Black	Hispanic	Asian	Native American
MSY=New Orleans, LA				
Southeastern Louisiana U	1			
Southern U in New Orleans*	1			
Tulane U of Louisiana		2		
University of New Orleans	1	2		
	3	**4**		
ORD=Chicago–O'Hare Airport, IL				
Chicago State University*	1	4		
DePaul University	1	3		
Loyola University of Chicago	1	2		
Northern Illinois University	2	3	1	
Northwestern University	3	2	1	
Northeastern Illinois University		10		
Roosevelt University	1	2	1	
U of Illinois - Chicago Circle	3	12	1	
Indiana University - Northwest		2		
	12	**40**	**4**	
ORF=Norfolk/Virginia Beach, VA				
Hampton Institute*	2			
Old Dominion University		1	1	
	2	**1**	**1**	
PHL=Philadelphia, PA/Wilmington, DE				
University of Delaware	1	2		
Glassboro State College	4	6		2
Princeton University	3	1		
Rutgers U - Camden Campus	3			1
Rutgers U - New Brunswick	4	10	1	
Cheyney State College*	1			
St. Joseph's University				1
Lincoln University*	6			
Temple University	1	1	1	
University of Pennsylvania	1		1	
	24	**20**	**3**	**4**

444

Airport 60 (1100)

AIRPORT	MINORITY GROUP			
	Black	Hispanic	Asian	Native American
PHX=Phoenix, AZ				
Arizona State University		2		
		2		
PIA=Peoria, IL				
Bradley University	1			
	1			
PIT=Pittsburgh, PA				
U of Pittsburgh - Main Campus	1	1		
	1	1		
PVD=Providence, RI				
Boston State College	1	3		
Harvard University	1			
Radcliffe College	1			
Tufts University	2	3	2	
Brown University	2	2	1	
	7	8	3	
PWA=Oklahoma City-Wiley Post, OK				
Oklahoma State U - Main Campus	1	2		
	1	2		
RDU=Raleigh/Durham, NC				
Duke University	1	1		
NC Central University*	1			
St. Augustine's College*	2			
U of NC at Chapel Hill		1		
U of NC at Greensboro	1			
	5	2		
RIC=Richmond, VA				
Virginia State College*	3			
Virginia Union University*	1			
	4			
SAN=San Diego, CA				
San Diego State University	2	20	1	
U of Cal - San Diego		1	1	
	2	21	2	

Airport 60 (1100)

AIRPORT	MINORITY GROUP			
	Black	Hispanic	Asian	Native American
SAT=San Antonio, TX				
Incarnate Word College		1		
Our Lady of Lake University*		28		
St. Mary's U – San Antonio		5		
Southwest Texas State University		14		
U of Texas at San Antonio		2		
		50		
SBA=Santa Barbara, CA				
U of Cal – Santa Barbara		15	1	1
		15	1	1
SEA=Seattle/Tacoma, WA				
University of Washington	2		3	1
	2		3	1
SFO=San Francisco/Oakland, CA				
Cal State University – Hayward		2	1	
San Francisco State University	1	9	16	
San Jose State University		11	1	1
Stanford University		2		
U of Cal – Berkeley		4	18	
University of San Francisco		4		
	1	32	36	1
SHV=Shreveport, LA				
Grambling State University*	2			
	2			
SJT=San Angelo, TX				
Angelo State University		6		
		6		
SLC=Salt Lake City, UT				
University of Utah		2		
		2		

446

Airport 60 (1100)

AIRPORT	MINORITY GROUP			
	Black	Hispanic	Asian	Native American
STL=St. Louis, MO				
St. Louis U - Main Campus		2		
U of Missouri - St. Louis		2		
Washington University	2	7		
	2	11		
SVC=Silver City, NM				
Western New Mexico University		2		
		2		
SWI=Sherman, TX				
Bishop College*	2			
North Texas State University	2			
Texas Woman's University		1		
	4	1		
SYR=Syracuse, NY				
Cornel U Endowed College	1		1	
Syracuse U - Main Campus	2	1		
	3	1	1	
TCL=Tuscaloosa, AL				
U of Alabama in Birmingham		1		
University of Alabama	1			
	1	1		
TLH=Tallahassee, FL				
Florida State University	2			
	2			
TPA=Tampa, FL				
University of South Florida	1	4		
	1	4		
TUS=Tucson, AZ				
University of Arizona		8	2	
		8	2	
TYS=Knoxville, KY				
U of Tennessee - Knoxville		1		
		1		

FOREIGN LANGUAGES (1100)
MINORITY BACCALAUREATE DEGREES
WITHIN 61-80 MILE ANNULUS OF AIRPORT

AIRPORT	MINORITY GROUP			
	Black	Hispanic	Asian	Native American
ALB=Albany, NY				
U of Mass - Amherst Campus	1	1		
SUNY College at New Paltz	3	2		1
	4	**3**		**1**
ALM=Alamogordo, NM				
NM State U - Main Campus		7		
		7		
ATL=Atlanta, GA				
Jacksonville State University			1	
Georgia College	1			
	1		**1**	
AUS=Austin, TX				
Incarnate Word College		1		
Our Lady of Lake University*		28		
St. Mary's U - San Antonio		5		
U of Texas at San Antonio		2		
		36		
BAL=Baltimore, MD				
Cheyney State College*	1			
	1			
BDL=Hartford, CT/Springfield, MA				
College of New Rochelle		1		
Mercy College		26		
SUNY at Albany	1	12	1	
SUNY College at New Paltz	3	2		1
Brown University	2	2	1	
	6	**43**	**2**	**1**

448

Airport 61-80 (1100)

AIRPORT	MINORITY GROUP			
	Black	Hispanic	Asian	Native American
BHM=Birmingham, AL				
Jacksonville State University			1	
			1	
BOS=Boston, MA				
U of Mass - Amherst Campus	1	1		
	1	1		
BTR=Baton Rouge, LA				
Southern U in New Orleans*	1			
Tulane U of Louisiana		2		
U of Southwestern Louisiana		1		
University of New Orleans	1	2		
	2	5		
CAE=Columbia, SC				
Winthrop College	1			
	1			
CMH=Columbus, OH				
Antioch University		4		
University of Dayton	2			
	2	4		
CMI=Champaign, IL				
Purdue University - Main Campus	2	2		
	2	2		
COS=Colorado Springs, CO				
Metropolitan State College	1			
U of Colorado at Boulder		11	2	1
	1	11	2	1
CVG=Cincinnati, OH				
Kentucky State University*	2			
	2			
DCA=Washington-National, DC				
Lincoln University*	6			
	6			

Airport 61-80 (1100)

AIRPORT	MINORITY GROUP			
	Black	Hispanic	Asian	Native American
DEN=Denver, CO				
Colorado State University		1		
		1		
DTW=Detroit-Metropolitan, MI				
Michigan State University		2		
Bowling Green State U - Main Cam	1			
	1	2		
FAY=Fayetteville, NC				
Duke University	1	1		
	1	1		
GRR=Grand Rapids, MI				
Michigan State University		2		
		2		
GSO=Greensboro/High Point, NC				
St. Augustine's College*	2			
	2			
HSV=Huntsville, AL/Decatur, GA				
Jacksonville State University			1	
Middle Tennessee State U		1		
		1	1	
JAX=Jacksonville, FL				
University of Florida		5		
		5		
JFK=New York, Kennedy Int'l, NY				
Yale University	1	3		
SUNY College at New Paltz	3	2		1
	4	5		1
LAX=Los Angeles, CA				
Cal State College - Bakersfield		5		
		5		

Airport 61-80 (1100)

AIRPORT	MINORITY GROUP			
	Black	Hispanic	Asian	Native American
LCH=Lake Charles, LA				
U of Southwestern Louisiana		1		
Lamar University				1
		1		1
LIT=Little Rock, AR				
Henderson State University	1			
	1			
MCN=Macon, GA				
Morehouse College*	2			
Morris Brown College*	1			
Spelman College*	3			
	6			
MEM=Memphis, TN				
U of Mississippi - Main Campus	1	1		
	1	1		
MHT=Manchester, NH				
Boston State College	1	3		
U of Mass - Amherst Campus	1	1		
	2	4		
MKE=Milwaukee, WS				
Northwestern University	3	2	1	
U of Wisconsin - Madison		4	1	
	3	6	2	
MSY=New Orleans, LA				
Louisiana State U & A&M College	1	3		
	1	3		
ORF=Norfolk/Virginia Beach, VA				
Virginia State College*	3			
	3			
PVD=Providence, RI				
U of Mass - Amherst Campus	1	1		
	1	1		

Airport 61–80 (1100)

AIRPORT	MINORITY GROUP			
	Black	Hispanic	Asian	Native American
RDU=Raleigh/Durham, NC				
East Carolina University	1			
	1			
RIC=Richmond, VA				
Hampton Institute*	2			
U of Virginia - Main Campus	2			
	4			
SAN=San Diego, CA				
Chapman College		1		
U of Cal - Irvine		6	1	
U of Cal - Riverside		2	1	
		9	2	
SAT=San Antonio, TX				
U of Texas at Austin	2	21		
	2	21		
SBA=Santa Barbara, CA				
Cal State College - Bakersfield		5		
Cal State University - Los Angeles	1	31		
Cal State University - Northridge	1	7	2	1
Loyola Marymount University	1	3		
U of Cal - Los Angeles	2	17	13	
	5	63	15	1
SFO=San Francisco/Oakland, CA				
Cal State University - Sacramento		4		
U of Cal - Davis		2		1
University of the Pacific	1	1		
	1	7		1
SWI=Sherman, TX				
U of Texas at Arlington	2	8		
	2	8		

452

Airport 61-80 (1100)

AIRPORT	MINORITY GROUP			
	Black	Hispanic	Asian	Native American
TPA=Tampa, FL				
University of Central Florida		3		
		3		
TUL=Tulsa, OK				
Oklahoma State U - Main Campus	1	2		
	1	2		

FOREIGN LANGUAGES (1100)
MINORITY BACCALAUREATE DEGREES
MORE THAN 80 MILES FROM NEAREST AIRPORT

AIRPORT	MINORITY GROUP			
	Black	Hispanic	Asian	Native American
ABQ=Albuquerque, NM				
New Mexico Highlands U*		2		
		2		
ELP=El Paso, TX				
Sul Ross State University		3		
		3		
MAF=Midland/Odessa, TX				
Sul Ross State University		3		
		3		
ROW=Roswell, NM				
Eastern NM U - Main Campus		2		
		2		

HEALTH PROFESSIONS (1200)

HEALTH PROFESSIONS (1200)
MINORITY BACCALAUREATE DEGREES
BY STATE AND INSTITUTION

STATE/SCHOOL	MINORITY GROUP			
	Black	Hispanic	Asian	Native American
Alabama				
Alabama A&M University*	16			
Alabama State University*	2			
Jacksonville State University	3			
Troy State University - Main Campus	9			
Tuskegee Institute*	42	1		
University of Alabama	10			
U of Alabama in Birmingham	26			
University of South Alabama	11		1	
	119	**1**	**1**	
Arizona				
Arizona State University	3	6		1
Northern Arizona University		5		1
University of Arizona	4	13	5	3
	7	**24**	**5**	**5**
Arkansas				
Arkansas State U - Main Campus	2			
Henderson State University	3			
University of Central Arkansas	5		1	
	10		**1**	
California				
Cal State College - Bakersfield	1	3	6	2
Cal State College - San Bernadino	3	4	1	
Cal State University - Chico	5	4	2	
Cal State U - Dominguez Hills	15	4	9	
Cal State University - Fresno	8	16	17	
Cal State University - Fullerton	1	6		2
Cal State University - Hayward	3	1	6	

(1200)

STATE/SCHOOL	MINORITY GROUP			
	Black	Hispanic	Asian	Native American
California (cont)				
Cal State University - Long Beach	16	11	19	3
Cal State University - Los Angeles	46	37	39	2
Cal State University - Northridge	14	8	8	3
Cal State University - Sacramento	7	8	7	2
Chapman College	21	3	14	4
Pepperdine University		1		
San Diego State University	7	8	6	3
San Francisco State University	27	6	85	1
San Jose State University	9	10	30	2
U of Cal - Berkeley	1	2	3	
U of Cal - Los Angeles	4	4	11	
U of Cal - San Francisco	9	12	59	
U of Cal - Santa Barbara	1	3	2	
University of LaVerne	1		2	
University of Redlands	1	3		
University of San Francisco	3	5	8	
University of Southern California		2	5	
University of the Pacific	1	3	13	
	204	**164**	**352**	**24**
Colorado				
Colorado State University		2	2	1
Metropolitan State College		8	2	9
U of Colorado at Boulder	1	1	3	
U of Northern Colorado		5	2	
U of Southern Colorado				1
	1	**16**	**9**	**11**
Delaware				
Delaware State College*	4			
University of Delaware	2			
	6			

457

(1200)

STATE/SCHOOL	MINORITY GROUP			
	Black	Hispanic	Asian	Native American
District of Columbia				
American University	4	1	1	
George Washington University	5	2	9	1
Howard University*	98		3	
University of DC*	18			
	125	**3**	**13**	**1**
Florida				
Florida Agr & Mech University*	108		1	
Florida Atlantic University	1	1		
Florida International University	29	27	4	1
Florida State University	12	3		
University of Central Florida	2		1	
University of Florida	10	9	13	1
University of Miami	4	1		
University of South Florida	12	7	3	
University of West Florida	1			
	179	**48**	**22**	**2**
Georgia				
Albany State College*	26			
Clark College*	5			
Georgia College	3			
GA Inst of Tech - Main Campus		1		
Georgia State University	22		3	
University of Georgia	5		1	1
Valdosta State College	3			
	64	**1**	**4**	**1**
Hawaii				
University of Hawaii at Manoa*		1	68	
		1	**68**	
Illinois				
Bradley University	5		1	
Chicago State University*	21			1

458

(1200)

STATE/SCHOOL	MINORITY GROUP			
	Black	Hispanic	Asian	Native American
Illinois (cont)				
College of St. Francis	160	7	10	
DePaul University	17	7	2	1
Governors State University	5	1		
Illinois State University	8		2	
Loyola University of Chicago	9	5	3	
Northern Illinois University	7		2	
Northwestern University	3		4	
Roosevelt University	6	2		
Southern Illinois U – Edwardsville	9			
U of Illinois – Urbana Campus			3	
	250	**22**	**27**	**2**
Indiana				
Ball State University	4	1	1	
Ind–Purdue U – Indianapolis	14		2	3
Indiana State U – Main Campus	14	2	2	1
Purdue University – Main Campus	7	1	2	1
	39	**4**	**7**	**5**
Kentucky				
Eastern Kentucky University	8			
University of Louisville	3		1	
Western Kentucky University	4			
	15		**1**	
Louisiana				
Dillard University*	21			
Louisiana Tech University	3			
McNeese State University	3		2	
Northeast Louisiana University	23		1	
Southeastern Louisiana U	5			
Sthrn U A&M College – Main Cam*	8			
Southern U in New Orleans*	1			

(1200)

STATE/SCHOOL	MINORITY GROUP			
	Black	Hispanic	Asian	Native American
Louisiana (cont)				
Tulane U of Louisiana	1			
U of Southwestern Louisiana	12			3
Xavier University of Louisiana*	50	1	11	
	127	**1**	**14**	**3**
Maryland				
Coppin State College*	30			
Morgan State University*	22		1	
Towson State University	1		1	
U of MD – Baltimore Co Campus	2			
U of MD – Baltimore Prof School	60	6	19	
U of MD – College Park Campus	9			1
U of MD – Eastern Shore*	2			
	126	**6**	**21**	**1**
Massachussetts				
Boston State College	2			
Boston University	2		1	1
Tufts University	2		2	
U of Mass – Amherst Campus	4	2	1	1
	10	**2**	**4**	**2**
Michigan				
Detroit Institute of Technology			1	
Eastern Michigan University	5			1
Mercy College of Detroit	14	1		
Michigan State University	12	2	1	
Oakland University	3		1	1
University of Detroit	1			
U of Michigan – Ann Arbor	36	3	3	1
Wayne State University	25	3	2	1
Western Michigan University	2		1	
	98	**9**	**9**	**4**

460

(1200)

STATE/SCHOOL	MINORITY GROUP			
	Black	Hispanic	Asian	Native American
Minnesota				
U of Minn – Minneapolis/St. Paul	3	2		
	3	**2**		
Mississippi				
Delta State University			1	
Mississippi State University	2			
Mississippi University for Women	4			
Mississippi Valley State Univ*	7			
Rust College*	2			
U of Mississippi – Main Campus	7		1	
U of Southern Mississippi	17		3	
	39		**5**	
Missouri				
Lincoln University	3			
Park College	17			
St. Louis U – Main Campus	21	1	1	2
U of Missouri – Columbia	2	1	1	3
U of Missouri – Kansas City	1	1	1	1
Washington University	1			
	45	**3**	**3**	**6**
Montana				
Montana State University		1	1	1
		1	**1**	**1**
New Jersey				
Jersey City State College	27	4	6	
Montclair State College	6		1	
Rutgers U – Camden Campus	3			
Rutgers U – New Brunswick	7	1	6	
Rutgers U – Newark Campus	13	5	6	
Seton Hall University	9	1		
Trenton State College	7	1	1	
	72	**12**	**20**	

(1200)

STATE/SCHOOL	MINORITY GROUP			
	Black	Hispanic	Asian	Native American
New Mexico				
Eastern NM U – Main Campus		1		
NM State U – Main Campus		2		
University of Albuquerque		1		
U of NM – Main Campus	2	36	4	4
	2	**40**	**4**	**4**
New York				
Adelphi University	6	3		
CUNY Brooklyn College	41	12	3	2
CUNY City College	68	31	11	2
CUNY College of Staten Island	5	4	1	
CUNY Hunter College	78	44	17	3
CUNY Lehman College	4	31	5	
CUNY Medgar Evers College*	32			
CUNY York College	30	6	2	1
Long Island U – Brooklyn Center	83	26	12	
Long Island U – C W Post Center	20	2		
New York University	57	4	4	4
Pace University New York	2	1		
St. Francis College	18	2	6	
St. John's University	2	3	6	
SUNY at Albany		1	1	1
SUNY at Buffalo – Main Campus				1
SUNY College at New Paltz				1
Syracuse University – Main Campus	5	1		
	451	**171**	**68**	**15**
North Carolina				
Duke University	3		1	
East Carolina University	3			
NC Agrl & Tech State University*	45			
NC Central University*	26			
NC State U – Raleigh	1			

(1200)

STATE/SCHOOL	MINORITY GROUP			
	Black	Hispanic	Asian	Native American
North Carolina (cont)				
Shaw University*	4			
U of NC at Chapel Hill	23	2	2	3
U of NC at Charlotte	3	1		1
U of NC at Greensboro	9			
Winston–Salem State University*	33			
	150	**3**	**3**	**4**
North Dakota				
U of North Dakota – Main Campus				2
				2
Ohio				
Antioch University	2			
Bowling Green State U – Main Cam	4			
Kent State U – Main Campus	6	1		
Ohio State U – Main Campus	7		6	2
Ohio University – Main Campus	7			
U of Akron – Main Campus	10	1	3	
U of Cincinnati – Main Campus	27	2	2	
University of Toledo	1	1	2	
Wright State U – Main Campus	8			
	72	**5**	**13**	**2**
Oklahoma				
Central State University	5	2		2
East Central Oklahoma State U				2
Southwest Oklahoma State U	3	1	2	2
U of Oklahoma – Norman Campus		1		
	8	**4**	**2**	**6**
Oregon				
Oregon State University			5	3
			5	**3**
Pennsylvania				
Pennsylvania State U – Main Campus	9	1	2	
Temple University	12	3	13	1

(1200)

STATE/SCHOOL	MINORITY GROUP			
	Black	Hispanic	Asian	Native American
Pennsylvania (cont)				
University of Pennsylvania	7	3	2	
U of Pittsburg – Main Campus	21			3
West Chester State College	4			
	53	7	17	4
South Carolina				
South Carolina State College*	14			
U of South Carolina at Columbia	25			1
	39			1
Tennessee				
Fisk University*	17			
Memphis State University	8			
Middle Tennessee State U	1			
Tennessee State University*	23			
U of Tennessee – Knoxville	8			
	57			
Texas				
Angelo State University		2		
Corpus Christi State University		18	1	
East Texas State University	4	13		1
Incarnate Word College	8	40		
Lamar University				5
Our Lady of Lake University*	1	6		
Pan American University*		23		
Prairie View A&M University*	19		2	
Sam Houston State University	3		1	
Southwest Texas State University	4	4		
Texas A&M U – Main Campus		2		1
Texas Southern University*	34	2		
Texas Women's University	51	22	6	4
U of Houston – Central Campus	7	12	7	1
U of Texas at Arlington	3	4	1	1

(1200)

STATE/SCHOOL	MINORITY GROUP			
	Black	Hispanic	Asian	Native American
Texas (cont)				
U of Texas at Austin	8	35	11	
U of Texas at El Paso	6	28	3	1
U of Texas at San Antonio		1		
	148	212	32	14
Utah				
Brigham Young University – Main			3	3
University of Utah	4	5	3	1
	4	5	6	4
Virginia				
Hampton Institute*	56			
Norfolk State College*	9			
Old Dominion University	2		3	
U of Virginia – Main Campus	6			
Virginia Commonwealth University	20	2	3	
	93	2	6	
Washington				
University of Washington	12	5	36	3
	12	5	36	3
Wisconsin				
U of Wisconsin – Madison	4	2	2	3
U of Wisconsin – Milwaukee	8	4	3	
	12	6	5	3
TOTALS	**2640**	**780**	**784**	**133**

*Predominately minority institutions are those where at least 50% of the total BA Degrees awarded are to one of the minority groups being considered.

HEALTH PROFESSIONS (1200)
BLACK BACCALAUREATE DEGREES RANKED BY INSTITUTION

Rank	Institution	B.A.'s	Rank	Institution	B.A.'s
1	C of St. Francis	160	30	U of South Carolina at Columbia	25
2	Florida Agr & Mech U*	108	31	Northeast Louisiana U	23
3	Howard U*	98	32	U of NC at Chapel Hill	23
4	Long Island U-Brooklyn Center	83	33	Tennessee State U*	23
5	CUNY Hunter C	78	34	Morgan State U*	22
6	CUNY City C	68	35	Georgia State U	22
7	U of MD-Baltimore Prof School	60	36	Chicago State U*	21
8	New York U	57	37	Chapman C	21
9	Hampton Institue*	56	38	St. Louis U-Main Campus	21
10	Texas Women's U	51	39	U of Pittsburgh-Main Campus	21
11	Xavier U of Louisiana*	50	40	Dillard U*	21
12	Cal State U-Los Angeles	46	41	Virginia Commonwealth U	20
13	NC Agrl & Tech State U*	45	42	Long Island U-C W Post Center	20
14	Tuskegee Institute*	42	43	Prairie View A & M U*	19
15	CUNY Brooklyn C	41	44	St. Francis C	18
16	U of Michigan-Ann Arbor	36	45	U of DC*	18
17	Texas Southern U*	34	46	U of Southern Mississippi	17
18	Winston-Salem State U*	33	47	DePaul U	17
19	CUNY Medgar Evers C*	32	48	Park C	17
20	Coppin State C*	30	49	Fisk U*	17
21	CUNY York C	30	50	Alabama A & M U*	16
22	Florida International U	29	51	Cal State U-Long Beach	16
23	U of Cincinnati-Main Campus	27	52	Cal State U-Dominguez Hills	15
24	Jersey City State C	27	53	Ind-Purdue U-Indianapolis	14
25	San Francisco State U	27	54	Mercy C of Detroit	14
26	NC Central U*	26	55	Cal State U-Northridge	14
27	Albany State C*	26	56	Indiana State U-Main Campus	14
28	U of Alabama in Birmingham	26	57	South Carolina State C*	14
29	Wayne State U	25	58	Rutgers U-Newark Campus	13

466

Black B.A.'s (1200)

Rank	Institution	B.A.'s	Rank	Institution	B.A.'s
59	Florida State U	12	64	U of Washington	12
60	U of South Florida	12	65	U of South Alabama	11
61	U of Southwestern Louisiana	12	66	U of Florida	10
62	Temple U	12	67	U of Akron-Main Campus	10
63	Michigan State U	12	68	U of Alabama	10

*predominantly black institutions

Institutions not ranked have less than ten degrees conferred on blacks.

HEALTH PROFESSIONS (1200)
HISPANIC BACCALAUREATE DEGREES RANKED BY INSTITUTION

Rank	Instituion	B.A.'s	Rank	Institution	B.A.'s
1	CUNY Hunter C	44	12	Texas Women's U	22
2	Incarnate Word C	40	13	Corpus Christi State U	18
3	Cal State U-Los Angeles	37	14	Cal State U-Fresno	16
4	U of NM-Main Campus	36	15	U of Arizona	13
5	U of Texas at Austin	35	16	East Texas State U	13
6	CUNY City C	31	17	U of Cal-San Francisco	12
7	CUNY Lehman C	31	18	CUNY Brooklyn C	12
8	U of Texas at El Paso	28	19	U of Houston-Central Campus	12
9	Florida International U	27	20	Cal State U-Long Beach	11
10	Long Island U-Brooklyn Center	26	21	San Jose State U	10
11	Pan American U*	23			

*predominantly Hispanic institutions

Institutions not ranked have less than ten degrees conferred on Hispanics.

HEALTH PROFESSIONS (1200)
ASIAN BACCALAUREATE DEGREES RANKED BY INSTITUTION

Rank	Institution	B.A.'s	Rank	Institution	B.A.'s
1	San Francisco State U	85	11	Chapman C	14
2	U of Hawaii at Manoa*	68	12	U of the Pacific	13
3	U of Cal-San Francisco	59	13	U of Florida	13
4	Cal State U-Los Angeles	39	14	Temple U	13
5	U of Washington	36	15	Long Island U-Brooklyn Center	12
6	San Jose State U	30	16	Xavier U of Louisiana	11
7	Cal State U-Long Beach	19	17	U of Cal-Los Angeles	11
8	U of MD-Baltimore Prof School	19	18	CUNY City C	11
9	Cal State U-Fresno	17	19	U of Texas at Austin	11
10	CUNY Hunter C	17	20	C of St. Francis	10

*predominantly Asian institutions

Institutions not ranked have less than ten degrees conferred on Asians.

HEALTH PROFESSIONS (1200)
NATIVE AMERICAN BACCALAUREATE DEGREES RANKED BY INSTITUTION

Rank	Institution	B.A.'s
1	Metropolitan State C	9
2	Lamar U	5

Institutions not ranked have less than five degrees conferred on Native Americans.

HEALTH PROFESSIONS (1200)
MINORITY BACCALAUREATE DEGREES
WITHIN 60 MILE RADIUS OF AIRPORT

AIRPORT	MINORITY GROUP			
	Black	Hispanic	Asian	Native American
ABQ=Albuquerque, NM				
U of NM - Main Campus	2	36	4	4
University of Albuquerque		1		
	2	**37**	**4**	**4**
ALB=Albany, NY				
SUNY at Albany		1	1	1
		1	**1**	**1**
AOO=Altoona, PA				
Pennsylvania State U - Main Campus	9	1	2	
	9	**1**	**2**	
ATL=Atlanta, GA				
Clark College*	5			
GA Inst of Tech - Main Campus		1		
Georgia State University	22		3	
	27	**1**	**3**	
AUS=Austin, TX				
Southwest Texas State University	4	4		
U of Texas at Austin	8	35	11	
	12	**39**	**11**	
BAL=Baltimore, MD				
University of Delaware	2			
American University	4	1	1	
George Washington Univesity	5	2	9	1
Howard University*	98		3	
University of DC*	18			
Coppin State College*	30			
Morgan State University*	22		1	

469

Airport 60 (1200)

AIRPORT	MINORITY GROUP			
	Black	Hispanic	Asian	Native American
BAL (cont)				
Towson State University	1		1	
U of MD – Baltimore Prof School	60	6	19	
U of MD – Baltimore Co Campus	2			
U of MD – College Park Campus	9			1
	251	**9**	**34**	**2**
BDL=Hartford, CT/Springfield, MA				
U of Mass – Amherst Campus	4	2	1	1
	4	**2**	**1**	**1**
BHM=Birmingham, AL				
U of Alabama in Birmingham	26			
University of Alabama	10			
	36			
BKL=Cleveland-Lakefront, OH				
Kent State U – Main Campus	6	1		
U of Akron – Main Campus	10	1	3	
	16	**2**	**3**	
BNA=Nashville, TN				
Western Kentucky University	4			
Fisk University*	17			
Middle Tennessee State U	1			
Tennessee State University*	23			
	45			
BOS=Boston, MA				
Boston State College	2			
Boston University	2		1	1
Tufts University	2		2	
	6		**3**	**1**
BTR=Baton Rouge, LA				
Sthrn U A&M College – Main Cam*	8			
Southeastern Louisiana U	5			
	13			

Airport 60 (1200)

AIRPORT	MINORITY GROUP			
	Black	Hispanic	Asian	Native American
CAE=Columbia, SC				
South Carolina State College*	14			
U of South Carolina at Columbia	25			1
	39			1
CIC=Chico, CA				
Cal State University - Chico	5	4	2	
	5	4	2	
CLT=Charlotte, NC				
U of NC at Charlotte	3	1		1
	3	1		1
CMH=Columbus, OH				
Ohio State U - Main Campus	7		6	2
	7		6	2
CMI=Champaign, IL				
Illinois State University	8		2	
U of Illinois - Urbana Campus			3	
Indiana State U - Main Campus	14	2	2	1
	22	2	7	1
COS=Colorado Springs, CO				
U of Southern Colorado				1
				1
COU=Columbia, MO				
Lincoln University	3			
U of Missouri - Columbia	2	1	1	3
	5	1	1	3
CRP=Corpus Christi, TX				
Corpus Christi State University		18	1	
		18	1	
CVG=Cincinnati, OH				
Antioch University	2			
U of Cincinnati - Main Campus	27	2	2	
Wright State U - Main Campus	8			
	37	2	2	

Airport 60 (1200)

AIRPORT	MINORITY GROUP			
	Black	Hispanic	Asian	Native American
DAB=Dayton Beach, FL				
University of Central Florida	2		1	
	2		1	
DCA=Washington–National, DC				
American University	4	1	1	
George Washington University	5	2	9	1
Howard University*	98		3	
University of DC*	18			
Coppin State College*	30			
Morgan State University*	22		1	
Towson State University	1		1	
U of MD - Baltimore Prof School	60	6	19	
U of MD - Baltimore Co Campus	2			
U of MD - College Park Campus	9			1
	249	9	34	2
DEN=Denver, CO				
Metropolitan State College		8	2	9
U of Colorado at Boulder	1	1	3	
U of Northern Colorado		5	2	
	1	14	7	9
DFW=Dallas/Fort Worth, TX				
East Texas State University	4	13		1
Texas Woman's University	51	22	6	4
U of Texas at Arlington	3	4	1	1
	58	39	7	6
DTW=Detroit-Metropolitan, MI				
Detroit Institute of Technology			1	
Eastern Michigan University	5			1
Mercy College of Detroit	14	1		
Oakland University	3		1	1
U of Michigan - Ann Arbor	36	3	3	1

472

Airport 60 (1200)

AIRPORT	MINORITY GROUP			
	Black	Hispanic	Asian	Native American
DTW (cont)				
University of Detroit	1			
Wayne State University	25	3	2	1
University of Toledo	1	1	2	
	85	8	9	4
ELP=El Paso, TX				
U of Texas at El Paso	6	28	3	1
	6	28	3	1
EUG=Eugene, OR				
Oregon State University			5	3
			5	3
FAT=Fresno, CA				
Cal State University - Fresno	8	16	17	
	8	16	17	
FAY=Fayetteville, NC				
NC Central University*	26			
NC State U - Raleigh	1			
Shaw University*	4			
U of NC at Chapel Hill	23	2	2	3
	54	2	2	3
FLG=Flagstaff, AZ				
Northern Arizona University		5		1
		5		1
GLH=Greenville, MS				
Delta State University			1	
Mississippi Valley State U*	7			
	7		1	
GRR=Grand Rapids, MI				
Western Michigan University	2		1	
	2		1	
GSO=Greensboro/High Point, NC				
Duke University	3		1	
NC Agrl & Tech State University*	45			

Airport 60 (1200)

AIRPORT	MINORITY GROUP			
	Black	Hispanic	Asian	Native American
GSO (cont)				
NC Central University*	26			
U of NC at Chapel Hill	23	2	2	3
U of NC at Greensboro	9			
Winston-Salem State University*	33			
	139	**2**	**3**	**3**
HNL=Honolulu/Oahu, HI				
University of Hawaii at Manoa*		1	68	
		1	**68**	
HSV=Huntsville, AL/Decatur, GA				
Alabama A&M University*	16			
	16			
IAH=Houston-Intercontinental,TX				
Prairie View A&M University*	19		2	
Texas Southern University*	34	2		
U of Houston - Central Campus	7	12	7	1
	60	**14**	**9**	**1**
IND=Indianapolis, IN				
Ball State University	4	1	1	
Ind-Purdue U - Indianapolis	14		2	3
Purdue University - Main Campus	7	1	2	1
	25	**2**	**5**	**4**
JFK=New York, Kennedy Int'l, NY				
Jersey City State College	27	4	6	
Montclair State College	6		1	
Rutgers U - New Brunswick	7	1	6	
Rutgers U - Newark Campus	13	5	6	
Seton Hall University	9	1		
Trenton State College	7	1	1	
Adelphi University	6	3		
CUNY Brooklyn College	41	12	3	2
CUNY College of Staten Island	5	4	1	

474

Airport 60 (1200)

AIRPORT	MINORITY GROUP			
	Black	Hispanic	Asian	Native American
JFK (cont)				
CUNY City College	68	31	11	2
CUNY Hunter College	78	44	17	3
CUNY Lehman College	4	31	5	
CUNY Medgar Evers College*	32			
CUNY York College	30	6	2	1
Long Island U - Brooklyn Center	83	26	12	
Long Island U - C W Post Center	20	2		
New York University	57	4	4	4
Pace University New York	2	1		
St. Francis College	18	2	6	
St. John's University	2	3	6	
	515	**181**	**87**	**12**
LAX=Los Angeles, CA				
Cal State College - San Bernardino	3	4	1	
Cal State U - Dominguez Hills	15	4	9	
Cal State University - Fullerton	1	6		2
Cal State University - Long Beach	16	11	19	3
Cal State University - Los Angeles	46	37	39	2
Cal State University - Northridge	14	8	8	3
Chapman College	21	3	14	4
Pepperdine University		1		
U of Cal - Los Angeles	4	4	11	
University of Southern California		2	5	
University of LaVerne	1		2	
	121	**80**	**108**	**14**
LCH=Lake Charles, LA				
McNeese State University	3		2	
	3		**2**	
LEX=Lexington/Frankfort, KY				
Eastern Kentucky University	8			
University of Louisville	3		1	
	11		**1**	

Airport 60 (1200)

AIRPORT	MINORITY GROUP			
	Black	Hispanic	Asian	Native American
LIT=Little Rock, AR				
University of Central Arkansas	5		1	
	5		**1**	
MCI=Kansas City-International, MO				
Park College	17			
U of Missouri - Kansas City	1	1	1	1
	18	**1**	**1**	**1**
MCN=Macon, GA				
Georgia College	3			
	3			
MEM=Memphis, TN				
Rust College*	2			
Memphis State University	8			
	10			
MFE=McAllen, TX				
Pan American University*		23		
		23		
MGM=Montgomery, GA				
Alabama State University*	2			
Troy State University - Main Campus	9			
Tuskegee Institute*	42	1		
	53	**1**		
MHT=Manchester, NH				
Tufts University	2		2	
	2		**2**	
MIA=Miami, FL				
Florida Atlantic University	1	1		
Florida International University	29	27	4	1
University of Miami	4	1		
	34	**29**	**4**	**1**
MKE=Milwaukee, WS				
U of Wisconsin - Milwaukee	8	4	3	
	8	**4**	**3**	

Airport 60 (1200)

AIRPORT	MINORITY GROUP			
	Black	Hispanic	Asian	Native American
MLU=Monroe, LA				
Louisiana Tech University	3			
Northeast Louisiana University	23		1	
	26		1	
MOB=Mobile, AL/Pasagoula, MS				
University of South Alabama	11		1	
University of West Florida	1			
	12		1	
MSN=Madison, WS				
U of Wisconsin - Madison	4	2	2	3
	4	2	2	3
MSP=Minneapolis/St. Paul, MN				
U of Minn - Minneapolis/St. Paul	3	2		
	3	2		
MSY=New Orleans, LA				
Dillard University*	21			
Southeastern Louisiana U	5			
Southern U in New Orleans*	1			
Tulane U of Louisiana	1			
Xavier University of Louisiana*	50		11	
	78		11	
ORD=Chicago–O'Hare Airport, IL				
Chicago State University*	21			1
College of St. Francis	160	7	10	
DePaul University	17	7	2	1
Governors State University	5	1		
Loyola University of Chicago	9	5	3	
Northern Illinois University	7		2	
Northwestern University	3		4	
Roosevelt University	6	2		
	228	22	21	2

Airport 60 (1200)

AIRPORT	MINORITY GROUP			
	Black	Hispanic	Asian	Native American
ORF=Norfolk/Virginia Beach, VA				
Hampton Institute*	56			
Norfolk State College*	9			
Old Dominion University	2		3	
	67		**3**	
PHL=Philadelphia, PA/Wilmington, DE				
Delaware State College*	4			
University of Delaware	2			
Rutgers U - Camden Campus	3			
Rutgers U - New Brunswick	7	1	6	
Trenton State College	7	1	1	
Temple University	12	3	13	1
University of Pennsylvania	7	3	2	
West Chester State College	4			
	46	**8**	**22**	**1**
PHX=Phoenix, AZ				
Arizona State University	3	6		1
	3	**6**		**1**
PIA=Peoria, IL				
Bradley University	5		1	
	5		**1**	
PIT=Pittsburgh, PA				
U of Pittsburgh - Main Campus	21			3
	21			**3**
PVD=Providence, RI				
Boston State College	2			
Boston University	2		1	1
Tufts University	2		2	
	6		**3**	**1**
PWA=Oklahoma City-Wiley Post, OK				
Central State University	5	2		2
U of Oklahoma - Norman Campus		1		
	5	**3**		**2**

478

Airport 60 (1200)

AIRPORT	MINORITY GROUP			
	Black	Hispanic	Asian	Native American
RDU=Raleigh/Durham, NC				
Duke University	3		1	
NC Agrl & Tech State University*	45			
NC Central University*	26			
NC State U - Raleigh	1			
Shaw University*	4			
U of NC at Chapel Hill	23	2	2	3
U of NC at Greensboro	9			
	111	**2**	**3**	**3**
RIC=Richmond, VA				
Virginia Commonwealth University	20	2	3	
	20	**2**	**3**	
SAN=San Diego, CA				
San Diego State University	7	8	6	3
	7	**8**	**6**	**3**
SAT=San Antonio, TX				
Incarnate Word College	8	40		
Our Lady of Lake University*	1	6		
Southwest Texas State University	4	4		
U of Texas at San Antonio		1		
	13	**51**		
SBA=Santa Barbara, CA				
Pepperdine University		1		
U of Cal - Santa Barbara	1	3	2	
	1	**4**	**2**	
SBY=Salisbury, MD				
U of MD - Eastern Shore*	2			
	2			
SEA=Seattle/Tacoma, WA				
University of Washington	12	5	36	3
	12	**5**	**36**	**3**

Airport 60 (1200)

AIRPORT	MINORITY GROUP			
	Black	Hispanic	Asian	Native American
SFO=San Francisco/Oakland, CA				
Cal State University - Hayward	3	1	6	
San Francisco State University	27	6	85	1
San Jose State University	9	10	30	2
U of Cal - Berkeley	1	2	3	
U of Cal - San Francisco	9	12	59	
University of San Francisco	3	5	8	
	52	**36**	**191**	**3**
SJT=San Angelo, TX				
Angelo State University		2		
		2		
SLC=Salt Lake City, UT				
Brigham Young University - Main			3	3
University of Utah	4	5	3	1
	4	**5**	**6**	**4**
STL=St. Louis, MO				
Southern Illinois U - Edwardsville	9			
St. Louis U - Main Campus	21	1	1	2
Washington University	1			
	31	**1**	**1**	**2**
SWI=Sherman, TX				
East Texas State University	4	13		1
Texas Woman's University	51	22	6	4
	55	**35**	**6**	**5**
SYR=Syracuse, NY				
Syracuse U - Main Campus	5	1		
	5	**1**		
TCL=Tuscaloosa, AL				
U of Alabama in Birmingham	26			
University of Alabama	10			
Mississippi University for Women	4			
	40			

Airport 60 (1200)

AIRPORT	MINORITY GROUP			
	Black	Hispanic	Asian	Native American
TLH=Tallahassee, FL				
Florida Agr & Mech University*	108		1	
Florida State University	12	3		
	120	**3**	**1**	
TPA=Tampa, FL				
University of South Florida	12	7	3	
	12	**7**	**3**	
TUS=Tucson, AZ				
University of Arizona	4	13	5	3
	4	**13**	**5**	**3**
TYS=Knoxville, TN				
U of Tennessee - Knoxville	8			
	8			

HEALTH PROFESSIONS (1200)
MINORITY BACCALAUREATE DEGREES
WITHIN 61-80 MILE ANNULUS OF AIRPORT

AIRPORT	MINORITY GROUP			
	Black	Hispanic	Asian	Native American
ALB=Albany, NY				
U of Mass - Amherst Campus	4	2	1	1
	4	**2**	**1**	**1**
ALM=Alamogordo, NM				
NM State U - Main Campus		2		
		2		
ATL=Atlanta, GA				
Jacksonville State University	3			
Georgia College	3			
University of Georgia	5		1	1
	11		**1**	**1**
AUS=Austin, TX				
Incarnate Word College	8	40		
Our Lady of Lake University*	1	6		
U of Texas at San Antonio		1		
	9	**47**		
BAL=Baltimore, MD				
Delaware State College*	4			
	4			
BDL=Hartford, CT/Springfield, MA				
SUNY at Albany		1	1	1
		1	**1**	**1**
BHM=Birmingham, AL				
Jacksonville State University	3			
	3			
BOS=Boston, MA				
U of Mass - Amherst Campus	4	2	1	1
	4	**2**	**1**	**1**

482

Airport 61-80 (1200)

AIRPORT	MINORITY GROUP			
	Black	Hispanic	Asian	Native American
BTM=Butte, MT				
Montana State University		1	1	1
		1	1	1
BTR=Baton Rouge, LA				
Dillard University*	21			
Southern U in New Orleans*	1			
Tulane U of Louisiana	1			
U of Southwestern Louisiana	12	1		3
Xavier University of Louisiana*	50		11	
	85	1	11	3
CHS=Charleston, SC				
South Carolina State College*	14			
	14			
CLT=Charlotte, NC				
Wintson-Salem State University*	33			
	33			
CMH=Columbus, OH				
Antioch University	2			
Ohio University - Main Campus	7			
Wright State U - Main Campus	8			
	17			
CMI=Champaign, IL				
Purdue University - Main Campus	7	1	2	1
	7	1	2	1
COS=Colorado Springs, CO				
Metropolitan State College		8	2	9
U of Colorado at Boulder	1	1	3	
	1	9	5	9
CRW=Charleston, WV				
Ohio University - Main Campus	7			
	7			

Airport 61-80 (1200)

AIRPORT		MINORITY GROUP		
	Black	Hispanic	Asian	Native American
DEN=Denver, CO				
Colorado State University		2	2	1
		2	**2**	**1**
DTW=Detroit-Metropolitan, MI				
Michigan State University	12	2	1	
Bowling Green State U - Main Cam	4			
	16	**2**	**1**	
FAY=Fayetteville, NC				
Duke University	3		1	
	3		**1**	
GRR=Grand Rapids, MI				
Michigan State University	12	2	1	
	12	**2**	**1**	
GSO=Greensboro/High Point, NC				
NC State U - Raleigh	1			
Shaw University*	4			
	5			
HSV=Huntsville, AL/Decatur, GA				
Jacksonville State University	3			
Middle Tennessee State U	1			
	4			
IAH=Houston-Intercontinental,TX				
Sam Houston State University	3		1	
	3		**1**	
IND=Indianapolis, IN				
Indiana State U - Main Campus	14	2	2	1
	14	**2**	**2**	**1**
JAX=Jacksonville, FL				
University of Florida	10	9	13	1
	10	**9**	**13**	**1**

484

Airport 61-80 (1200)

AIRPORT	MINORITY GROUP			
	Black	Hispanic	Asian	Native American
LAX=Los Angeles, CA				
Cal State College – Bakersfield	1	3	6	2
University of Redlands	1	3		
	2	6	6	2
LCH=Lake Charles, LA				
U of Southwestern Louisiana	12	1		3
Lamar University				5
	12	1		8
LIT=Little Rock, AR				
Henderson State University	3			
	3			
MCN=Macon, GA				
Clark College*	5			
GA Inst of Tech – Main Campus		1		
Georgia State University	22		3	
	27	1	3	
MEM=Memphis, TN				
Arkansas State U – Main Campus	2			
U of Mississippi – Main Campus	7		1	
	9		1	
MHT=Manchester, NH				
Boston State College	2			
Boston University	2		1	1
U of Mass – Amherst Campus	4	2	1	1
	8	2	2	2
MKE=Milwaukee, WS				
Northwestern University	3		4	
U of Wisconsin – Madison	4	2	2	3
	7	2	6	3

Airport 61-80 (1200)

AIRPORT	MINORITY GROUP			
	Black	Hispanic	Asian	Native American
MKL=Jackson, TN				
Rust College*	2			
Memphis State University	8			
	10			
MOB=Mobile, AL/Pasagoula, MS				
U of Southern Mississippi	17		3	
	17		**3**	
MSN=Madison, WS				
U of Wisconsin - Milwaukee	8	4	3	
	8	**4**	**3**	
MSY=New Orleans, LA				
Sthrn U A&M C - Main Cam*	8			
	8			
PVD=Providence, RI				
U of Mass - Amherst Campus	4	2	1	1
	4	**2**	**1**	**1**
PWA=Oklahoma City-Wiley Post, OK				
East Central Oklahoma State U				2
Southwest Oklahoma State U	3	1	2	2
	3	**1**	**2**	**4**
RDU=Raleigh/Durham, NC				
East Carolina University	3			
	3			
RIC=Richmond, VA				
Hampton Institute*	56			
Norfolk State College*	9			
U of Virginia - Main Campus	6			
	71			
SAN=San Diego, CA				
Chapman College	21	3	14	4
	21	**3**	**14**	**4**

Airport 61-80 (1200)

AIRPORT	MINORITY GROUP			
	Black	Hispanic	Asian	Native American
SAT=San Antonio, TX				
U of Texas at Austin	8	35	11	
	8	**35**	**11**	
SBA=Santa Barbara, CA				
Cal State College - Bakersfield	1	3	6	2
Cal State University - Los Angeles	46	37	39	2
Cal State University - Northridge	14	8	8	3
U of Cal - Los Angeles	4	4	11	
	65	**52**	**64**	**7**
SBY=Salisbury, MD				
Delaware State College*	4			
	4			
SFO=San Francisco/Oakland, CA				
Cal State University - Sacramento	7	8	7	2
University of the Pacific	1	3	13	
	8	**11**	**20**	**2**
SHV=Shreveport, LA				
Louisiana Tech University	3			
	3			
SWI=Sherman, TX				
U of Texas at Arlington	3	4	1	1
	3	**4**	**1**	**1**
TLH=Tallahassee, FL				
Albany State College*	26			
Valdosta State College	3			
	29			
TPA=Tampa, FL				
University of Central Florida	2		1	
	2		**1**	
TYR=Tyler, TX				
East Texas State University	4	13		1
	4	**13**		**1**

HEALTH PROFESSIONS (1200)
MINORITY BACCALAUREATE DEGREES
MORE THAN 80 MILES FROM NEAREST AIRPORT

AIRPORT	MINORITY GROUP			
	Black	Hispanic	Asian	Native American
AUS=Austin, TX				
Texas A&M U - Main Campus		2		1
		2		**1**
IAH=Houston–Intercontinental, TX				
Texas A&M U - Main Campus		2		1
		2		**1**
MSY=New Orleans, LA				
U of Southern Mississippi	17		3	
	17		**3**	
ROW=Roswell, NM				
Eastern NM U - Main Campus		1		
		1		
TCL=Tuscaloosa, AL				
Mississippi State University	2			
	2			

HOME ECONOMICS (1300)

HOME ECONOMICS (1300)
MINORITY BACCALAUREATE DEGREES
BY STATE AND INSTITUTION

STATE/SCHOOL	Black	Hispanic	Asian	Native American
Alabama				
Alabama A&M University*	8			
Jacksonville State University	3			
Oakwood College*	6			
Tuskegee Institute*	31			
University of Alabama	11			
	59			
Arizona				
Arizona State University		5	1	
Northern Arizona University		1	1	
University of Arizona	2	6	2	1
	2	**12**	**4**	**1**
Arkansas				
Henderson State University	2			
Philander Smith College*	3			
University of Arkansas - Pine Bluff*	12			
University of Central Arkansas	2			
	19			
California				
Cal Poly State U - San Luis Obispo	2	4	6	5
Cal State Poly U - Pomona	1	2		3
Cal State University - Chico		1	4	1
Cal State University - Fresno	2	2	6	
Cal State University - Long Beach	6	3	19	1
Cal State University - Los Angeles	8	1	18	
Cal State University - Northridge	1	2	3	2
Cal State University - Sacramento	1	1	4	1
San Diego State University		3	2	

490

(1300)

STATE/SCHOOL	MINORITY GROUP			
	Black	Hispanic	Asian	Native American
California (cont)				
San Francisco State University	5	3	18	
San Jose State University	4	3	8	
U of Cal – Davis	1		9	
	31	**25**	**97**	**13**
Colorado				
Colorado State University	1		5	
U of Northern Colorado	2	2	1	
	3	**2**	**6**	
Delaware				
Delaware State College*	1			
University of Delaware	2			
	3			
District of Columbia				
Howard University*	29			
University of DC*	5			
	34			
Florida				
Florida Agr & Mech University*	38			
Florida International University	1	7	1	
Florida State University	22	3	3	
	61	**10**	**4**	
Georgia				
Clark College*	1			
Fort Valley State College*	2			
Georgia College	4			
Morris Brown College*	9			
Savannah State College*	8			
Spelman College*	1			
University of Georgia	12	1		1
	37	**1**		**1**

(1300)

STATE/SCHOOL	MINORITY GROUP			
	Black	Hispanic	Asian	Native American
Hawaii				
University of Hawaii at Manoa*	1	3	190	
	1	**3**	**190**	
Illinois				
Bradley University	2			
Eastern Illinois University	3			
Illinois State University	5	1		1
Northern Illinois University	14	2	2	
Southern Illinois U - Carbondale	19			
U of Illinois - Urbana Campus	4		2	1
	47	**3**	**4**	**2**
Indiana				
Ball State University	1			
Indiana State U - Main Campus	6			
Indiana University - Bloomington	6		1	
Purdue University - Main Campus	5	1	2	
	18	**1**	**3**	
Kentucky				
Eastern Kentucky University	4			
Kentucky State University*	6			
University of Louisville		1		
Western Kentucky University	2			
	12	**1**		
Louisiana				
Grambling State University*	9			
Louisiana State U & A&M College	2			
Louisiana Tech University	6			
McNeese State University	3			
Northeast Louisiana University	3			
Southeastern Louisiana U	3			
Sthrn U A&M College - Main Cam*	40			
U of Southwestern Louisiana	3			2
	69			**2**

492

(1300)

STATE/SCHOOL	MINORITY GROUP			
	Black	Hispanic	Asian	Native American
Maryland				
Morgan State University*	11			
U of MD – College Park Campus	14	2	2	4
U of MD – Eastern Shore*	3			
	28	2	2	4
Massachussetts				
U of Mass – Amherst Campus	7	1	2	
	7	1	2	
Michigan				
Eastern Michigan University	3			1
Mercy College of Detroit	9	1		
Michigan State University	32		2	
Wayne State University	15	1	1	1
Western Michigan University	3		1	
	62	2	4	2
Minnesota				
U of Minn – Minneapolis/St. Paul	1	1	2	1
	1	1	2	1
Mississippi				
Alcorn State University*	11		1	
Mississippi State University	13		1	1
U of Southern Mississippi	5			
	29		2	1
Missouri				
Columbia College	3			
Lincoln University	5			
U of Missouri – Columbia	6		1	
	14		1	
Montana				
Montana State University				1
				1

(1300)

STATE/SCHOOL	MINORITY GROUP			
	Black	Hispanic	Asian	Native American
New Jersey				
Montclair State College	6	2		2
Rutgers U - New Brunswick	8	1		
	14	**3**		**2**
New Mexico				
New Mexico Highlands U*		3		
NM State U - Main Campus		5		
U of NM - Main Campus		2		
Western New Mexico University		1		
		11		
New York				
CUNY Brooklyn College	18	5	1	1
CUNY Hunter College	8	5	2	
CUNY Lehman College	7	10	1	
CUNY Queen's College	9	2	2	
New York University	5	2	1	
Pratt Institute	18	1	2	
SUNY at Buffalo - Main Campus	14			2
SUNY College at Buffalo		1		
Syracuse University - Main Campus	4		1	
	83	**26**	**10**	**3**
North Carolina				
Bennett College*	7			
East Carolina University	10			
NC Agrl & Tech State University*	46			
NC Central University*	30			
Pembroke State University	2			4
U of NC at Greensboro	11			
	106			**4**
Ohio				
Bowling Green State U - Main Cam	17		1	
Kent State U - Main Campus	11			1
Ohio State U - Main Campus	11			

(1300)

STATE/SCHOOL	MINORITY GROUP			
	Black	Hispanic	Asian	Native American
Ohio (cont)				
Ohio University – Main Campus	5			
U of Akron – Main Campus	4			
U of Cincinnati – Main Campus	2			
University of Dayton	1		1	
	51		**2**	**1**
Oklahoma				
Cameron University	2	1		
Central State University	3			
East Central Oklahoma State U	1			
Langston University*	4			
Northeast Oklahoma State U	1			6
Oklahoma State U – Main Campus	2			2
Southwest Oklahoma State U				2
U of Oklahoma – Norman Campus		1		4
	13	**2**		**14**
Oregon				
Oregon State University			1	
			1	
Pennsylvania				
Cheyney State College*	11			
Drexel University	15	1		
Pennsylvania State U – Main Campus	5		1	2
	31	**1**	**1**	**2**
South Carolina				
South Carolina State College*	18		1	
Winthrop College	6			
	24		**1**	
Tennessee				
Memphis State University	11			
Middle Tennessee State U	3			
Tennessee State University*	21			

(1300)

STATE/SCHOOL	MINORITY GROUP			
	Black	Hispanic	Asian	Native American
Tennessee (cont)				
U of Tennessee - Knoxville	11		1	
U of Tennessee - Martin	3			
	49		**1**	
Texas				
East Texas State University	5		1	
Incarnate Word College		4		
Lamar University				7
North Texas State University	5	2		
Our Lady of Lake University*		1		
Prairie View A&M University*	31			
Sam Houston State University	4		1	1
Southwest Texas State University	4	11		
Texas A&I University		4		
Texas College*	11			
Texas Southern University*	24			
Texas Women's University	3	2	1	
Trinity University		1		
U of Houston - Central Campus	11	4	3	
U of Texas at Austin		4		
	98	**33**	**6**	**8**
Utah				
Brigham Young University - Main			2	2
University of Utah			3	1
			5	**3**
Virginia				
Hampton Institute*	6			
Norfolk State College*	28			
	34			
Washington				
University of Washington			3	1
			3	**1**

(1300)

STATE/SCHOOL	MINORITY GROUP			
	Black	Hispanic	Asian	Native American
Wisconsin				
U of Wisconsin – Madison	5			
	5			
TOTALS	1045	141	351	66

*Predominately minority institutions are those where at least 50% of the total BA Degrees awarded are to one of the minority groups being considered.

HOME ECONOMICS (1300)
BLACK BACCALAUREATE DEGREES RANKED BY INSTITUTION

Rank	Institution	B.A.'s	Rank	Institution	B.A.'s
1	NC Agrl & Tech State U*	46	20	Northern Illinois U	14
2	Sthrn U A&M C-Main Campus*	40	21	SUNY C at Buffalo	14
3	Florida Agrl & Mech U*	38	22	U of MD-College Park Campus	14
4	Michigan State U	32	23	Mississippi State U	13
5	Tuskegee Institute*	31	24	U of Georgia	12
6	Prairie View A&M U*	31	25	U of Arkansas-Pine Bluff*	12
7	NC Central U	30	26	Ohio State U-Main Campus	11
8	Howard U*	29	27	Kent State U-Main Campus	11
9	Norfolk State C*	28	28	U of NC at Greensboro	11
10	Texas Southern U*	24	29	Cheyney State C*	11
11	Florida State U*	22	30	Memphis State U	11
12	Tennessee State U*	21	31	Alcorn State U*	11
13	Southern Illinois U-Carbondale	19	32	Texas C*	11
14	Pratt Institute	18	33	Morgan State U*	11
15	CUNY Brooklyn C	18	34	U of Tennessee-Knoxville	11
16	South Carolina State C*	18	35	U of Alabama	11
17	Bowling Green State U-Main Ca	17	36	U of Houston-Central Campus	11
18	Drexel U	15	37	East Carolina U	10
19	Wayne State U	15			

*predominantly black institutions

Institutions not ranked have less than ten degrees conferred on blacks.

498

HOME ECONOMICS (1300)
HISPANIC BACCALAUREATE DEGREES RANKED BY INSTITUTION

Rank	Institution	B.A.'s
1	Southwest Texas State U	11
2	CUNY Lehman C	10

Institutions not ranked have less than ten degrees conferred on Hispanics.

HOME ECONOMICS (1300)
ASIAN BACCALAUREATE DEGREES RANKED BY INSTITUTION

Rank	Institution	B.A.'s	Rank	Institution	B.A.'s
1	U of Hawaii at Manoa*	190	3	San Francisco State U	18
2	Cal State U-Long Beach	19	4	Cal State U-Los Angeles	18

*predominantly Asian institutions

Institutions not ranked have less than ten degrees conferred on Asians.

HOME ECONOMICS (1300)
NATIVE AMERICAN BACCALAUREATE DEGREES RANKED BY INSTITUTION

Rank	Institution	B.A.'s	Rank	Institution	B.A.'s
1	Lamar U	7	3	Cal Poly State-San Luis Obispo	5
2	Northeastern Oklahoma State	6			

Institutions not ranked have less than five degrees conferred on Native Americans.

HOME ECONOMICS (1300)
MINORITY BACCALAUREATE DEGREES
WITHIN 60 MILE RADIUS OF AIRPORT

AIRPORT	MINORITY GROUP			
	Black	Hispanic	Asian	Native American
ABQ=Albuquerque, NM				
U of NM - Main Campus		2		
		2		
AOO=Altoona, PA				
Pennsylvania State U - Main Campus	5		1	2
	5		**1**	**2**
ATL=Atlanta, GA				
Clark College*	1			
Morris Brown College*	9			
Spelman College*	1			
	11			
AUS=Austin, TX				
Southwest Texas State University	4	11		
U of Texas at Austin		4		
	4	**15**		
BAL=Baltimore, MD				
University of Delaware	2			
Howard University*	29			
University of DC*	5			
Morgan State University*	11			
U of MD - College Park Campus	14	2	2	4
	61	**2**	**2**	**4**
BDL=Hartford, CT/Springfield, MA				
U of Mass - Amherst Campus	7	1	2	
	7	**1**	**2**	
BHM=Birmingham, AL				
University of Alabama	11			
	11			

Airport 60 (1300)

AIRPORT	MINORITY GROUP			
	Black	Hispanic	Asian	Native American
BKL=Cleveland-Lakefront, OH				
Kent State U - Main Campus	11			1
U of Akron - Main Campus	4			
	15			1
BNA=Nashville, TN				
Western Kentucky University	2			
Middle Tennessee State U	3			
Tennessee State University*	21			
	26			
BTR=Baton Rouge, LA				
Louisiana State U & A&M College	2			
Sthrn U A&M College - Main Cam*	40			
Southeastern Louisiana U	3			
	45			
BUF=Buffalo, NY				
SUNY College at Buffalo	14	1		2
	14	1		2
CAE=Columbia, SC				
South Carolina State College*	18		1	
	18		1	
CIC=Chico, CA				
Cal State University - Chico		1	4	1
		1	4	1
CLT=Charlotte, NC				
Winthrop College	6			
	6			
CMH=Columbus, OH				
Ohio State U - Main Campus	11			
	11			
CMI=Champaign, IL				
Eastern Illinois University	3			
Illinois State University	5	1		1

Airport 60 (1300)

AIRPORT	MINORITY GROUP			
	Black	Hispanic	Asian	Native American
CMI (cont)				
U of Illinois - Urbana Campus	4		2	1
Indiana State U - Main Campus	6			
	18	**1**	**2**	**2**
COU=Columbia, MO				
Columbia College	3			
Lincoln University	5			
U of Missouri - Columbia	6		1	
	14		**1**	
CRP=Corpus Christi, TX				
Texas A&I University		4		
		4		
CVG=Cincinnati, OH				
U of Cincinnati - Main Campus	2			
University of Dayton	1		1	
	3		**1**	
DCA=Washington-National, DC				
Howard University*	29			
University of DC*	5			
Morgan State University*	11			
U of MD - College Park Campus	14	2	2	4
	59	**2**	**2**	**4**
DEN=Denver, CO				
U of Northern Colorado	2	2	1	
	2	**2**	**1**	
DFW=Dallas/Fort Worth, TX				
East Texas State University	5		1	
North Texas State University	5	2		
Texas Woman's University	3	2	1	
	13	**4**	**2**	

Airport 60 (1300)

AIRPORT	MINORITY GROUP			
	Black	Hispanic	Asian	Native American
DTW=Detroit-Metropolitan, MI				
Eastern Michigan University	3			1
Mercy College of Detroit	9	1		
Wayne State University	15	1	1	1
	27	2	1	2
EUG=Eugene, OR				
Oregon State University			1	
			1	
FAT=Fresno, CA				
Cal State University - Fresno	2	2	6	
	2	2	6	
FAY=Fayetteville, NC				
NC Central University*	30			
Pembroke State University	2			4
	32			4
FLG=Flagstaff, AZ				
Northern Arizona University		1	1	
		1	1	
GRR=Grand Rapids, MI				
Western Michigan University	3		1	
	3		1	
GSO=Greensboro/High Point, NC				
Bennett College*	7			
NC Agrl & Tech State University*	46			
NC Central University*	30			
U of NC at Greensboro	11			
	94			
HNL=Honolulu/Oahu, HI				
University of Hawaii at Manoa*	1	3	190	
	1	3	190	

Airport 60 (1300)

AIRPORT	MINORITY GROUP			
	Black	Hispanic	Asian	Native American
HSV=Huntsville, AL/Decatur, GA				
Alabama A&M University*	8			
Oakwood College*	6			
	14			
IAH=Houston-Intercontinental,TX				
Prairie View A&M University*	31			
Texas Southern University*	24			
U of Houston - Central Campus	11	4	3	
	66	**4**	**3**	
IND=Indianapolis, IN				
Ball State University	1			
Indiana University - Bloomington	6		1	
Purdue University - Main Campus	5	1	2	
	12	**1**	**3**	
JAN=Jackson/Vicksburg, MS				
Alcorn State University*	11		1	
	11		**1**	
JFK=New York, Kennedy Int'l, NY				
Montclair State College	6	2		2
Rutgers U - New Brunswick	8	1		
CUNY Brooklyn College	18	5	1	1
CUNY Hunter College	8	5	2	
CUNY Lehman College	7	10	1	
CUNY Queen's College	9	2	2	
New York University	5	2	1	
Pratt Institute	18	1	2	
	79	**28**	**9**	**3**
LAX=Los Angeles, CA				
Cal State Poly U - Pomona	1	2		3
Cal State University - Long Beach	6	3	19	1
Cal State University - Los Angeles	8	1	18	
Cal State University - Northridge	1	2	3	2
	16	**8**	**40**	**6**

504

Airport 60 (1300)

AIRPORT	MINORITY GROUP			
	Black	Hispanic	Asian	Native American
LCH=Lake Charles, LA				
McNeese State University	3			
	13			
LEX=Lexington/Frankfort, KY				
Eastern Kentucky University	4			
Kentucky State University*	6			
University of Louisville		1		
	10	1		
LIT=Little Rock, AR				
Philander Smith College*	3			
University of Arkansas - Pine Bluff*	12			
University of Central Arkansas	2			
	17			
MCN=Macon, GA				
Fort Valley State College*	2			
Georgia College	4			
	6			
MDH=Carbondale, IL				
Southern Illinois U - Carbondale	19			
	19			
MEM=Memphis, TN				
Memphis State University	11			
	11			
MGM=Montgomery, GA				
Tuskegee Institute*	31			
	31			
MIA=Miami, FL				
Florida International University	1	7	1	
	1	7	1	
MKL=Jackson, TN				
U of Tennessee - Martin	3			
	3			

Airport 60 (1300)

AIRPORT	MINORITY GROUP			
	Black	Hispanic	Asian	Native American
MLU=Monroe, LA				
Grambling State University*	9			
Louisiana Tech University	6			
Northeast Louisiana University	3			
	18			
MSN=Madison, WS				
U of Wisconsin - Madison	5			
	5			
MSP=Minneapolis/St. Paul, MN				
U of Minn - Minneapolis/St. Paul	1	1	2	1
	1	1	2	1
MSY=New Orleans, LA				
Southeastern Louisiana U	3			
	3			
ORD=Chicago-O'Hare Airport, IL				
Northern Illinois University	14	2	2	
	14	2	2	
ORF=Norfolk/Virginia Beach, VA				
Hampton Institute*	6			
Norfolk State College*	28			
	34			
PHL=Philadelphia, PA/Wilmington, DE				
Delaware State College*	1			
University of Delaware	2			
Rutgers U - New Brunswick	8	1		
Cheyney State College*	11			
Drexel University	15	1		
	37	2		
PHX=Phoenix, AZ				
Arizona State University		5	1	
		5	1	

Airport 60 (1300)

AIRPORT		MINORITY GROUP		
	Black	Hispanic	Asian	Native American
PIA=Peoria, IL				
Bradley University	2			
	2			
PWA=Oklahoma City–Wiley Post, OK				
Central State University	3			
Langston University*	4			
Oklahoma State U – Main Campus	2			2
U of Oklahoma – Norman Campus		1		4
	9	1		6
RDU=Raleigh/Durham, NC				
Bennet College*	7			
NC Agrl & Tech State University*	46			
NC Central University*	30			
U of NC at Greensboro	11			
	94			
SAN=San Diego, CA				
San Diego State University		3	2	
		3	2	
SAT=San Antonio, TX				
Incarnate Word College		4		
Our Lady of Lake University*		1		
Southwest Texas State University	4	11		
Trinity University		1		
	4	17		
SAV=Savannah, GA				
Savannah State College*	8			
	8			
SBP=San Luis Obispo, CA				
Cal Poly State U – San Luis Obispo	2	4	6	5
	2	4	6	5

Airport 60 (1300)

AIRPORT	MINORITY GROUP			
	Black	Hispanic	Asian	Native American
SBY=Salisbury, MD				
U of MD – Eastern Shore*	3			
	3			
SEA=Seattle/Tacoma, WA				
University of Washington			3	1
			3	**1**
SFO=San Francisco/Oakland, CA				
San Francisco State University	5	3	18	
San Jose State University	4	3	8	
	9	**6**	**26**	
SHV=Shreveport, LA				
Grambling State University*	9			
	9			
SLC=Salt Lake City, UT				
Brigham Young University – Main			2	2
University of Utah			3	1
			5	**3**
SVC=Silver City, NM				
Western New Mexico University		1		
		1		
SWI=Sherman, TX				
East Texas State University	5		1	
North Texas State University	5	2		
Texas Woman's University	3	2	1	
	13	**4**	**2**	
SYR=Syracuse, NY				
Syracuse U – Main Campus	4		1	
	4		**1**	
TCL=Tuscaloosa, AL				
University of Alabama	11			
	11			

508

Airport 60 (1300)

| AIRPORT | | MINORITY GROUP | | |
	Black	Hispanic	Asian	Native American
TLH=Tallahassee, FL				
Florida Agr & Mech University*	38			
Florida State University	22	3	3	
	60	**3**	**3**	
TUL=Tulsa, OK				
Northeast Oklahoma State U	1			6
	1			**6**
TUS=Tucson, AZ				
University of Arizona	2	6	2	1
	2	**6**	**2**	**1**
TYR=Tyler, TX				
Texas College*	11			
	11			
TYS=Knoxville, TN				
U of Tennessee - Knoxville	11		1	
	11		**1**	

HOME ECONOMICS (1300)
MINORITY BACCALAUREATE DEGREES
WITHIN 61-80 MILE ANNULUS OF AIRPORT

AIRPORT	MINORITY GROUP			
	Black	Hispanic	Asian	Native American
ALB=Albany, NY				
U of Mass - Amherst Campus	7	1	2	
	7	1	2	
ALM=Alamogordo, NM				
NM State U - Main Campus		5		
		5		
ATL=Atlanta, GA				
Jacksonville State University	3			
Georgia College	4			
University of Georgia	12	1		1
	19	1		1
AUS=Austin, TX				
Incarnate Word College		4		
Our Lady of Lake University*		1		
Trinity University		1		
		6		
BAL=Baltimore, MD				
Delaware State College*	1			
Cheyney State College*	11			
	12			
BHM=Birmingham, AL				
Jacksonville State University	3			
	3			
BOS=Boston, MA				
U of Mass - Amherst Campus	7	1	2	
	7	1	2	

510

Airport 61-80 (1300)

AIRPORT	MINORITY GROUP			
	Black	Hispanic	Asian	Native American
BTM=Butte, MT				
Montana State University				1
				1
BTR=Baton Rouge, LA				
U of Southwestern Louisiana	3			2
	3			2
CAE=Columbia, SC				
Winthrop College	6			
	6			
CHS=Charleston, SC				
Savannah State College*	8			
South Carolina State College*	18		1	
	26		1	
CMH=Columbus, OH				
Ohio University - Main Campus	5			
University of Dayton	1		1	
	6		1	
CMI=Champaign, IL				
Purdue University - Main Campus	5	1	2	
	5	1	2	
CRW=Charleston, WV				
Ohio University - Main Campus	5			
	5			
CVG=Cincinnati, OH				
Kentucky State University*	6			
	6			
DEN=Denver, CO				
Colorado State University	1		5	
	1		5	

Airport 61-80 (1300)

AIRPORT	MINORITY GROUP			
	Black	Hispanic	Asian	Native American
DTW=Detroit-Metropolitan, MI				
Michigan State University	32		2	
Bowling Green State U - Main Cam	17		1	
	49		3	
GRR=Grand Rapids, MI				
Michigan State University	32		2	
	32		2	
HSV=Huntsville, AL/Decatur, GA				
Jacksonville State University	3			
Middle Tennessee State U	3			
	6			
IAH=Houston-Intercontinental,TX				
Sam Houston State University	4		1	1
	4		1	1
IND=Indianapolis, IN				
Indiana State U - Main Campus	6			
	6			
LCH=Lake Charles, LA				
U of Southwestern Louisiana	3			2
Lamar University				7
	3			9
LIT=Little Rock, AR				
Henderson State University	2			
	2			
MCN=Macon, GA				
Clark College*	1			
Morris Brown College*	9			
Spelman College*	1			
	11			
MHT=Manchester, NH				
U of Mass - Amherst Campus	7	1	2	
	7	1	2	

512

Airport 61-80 (1300)

AIRPORT	MINORITY GROUP			
	Black	Hispanic	Asian	Native American
MKE=Milwaukee, WS				
U of Wisconsin - Madison	5			
	5			
MKL=Jackson, TN				
Memphis State University	11			
	11			
MLU=Monroe, LA				
Alcorn State University*	11		1	
	11		1	
MOB=Mobile, AL/Pasagoula, MS				
U of Southern Mississippi	5			
	5			
MSY=New Orleans, LA				
Louisiana State U & A&M College	2			
Sthrn U A&M C - Main Cam*	40			
	42			
PVD=Providence, RI				
U of Mass - Amherst Campus	7	1	2	
	7	1	2	
PWA=Oklahoma City-Wiley Post, OK				
East Central Oklahoma State U	1			
Southwest Oklahoma State U				2
	1			2
RDU=Raleigh/Durham, NC				
East Carolina University	10			
	10			
RIC=Richmond, VA				
Hampton Institute*	6			
Norfolk State College*	28			
	34			

Airport 61-80 (1300)

AIRPORT	MINORITY GROUP			
	Black	Hispanic	Asian	Native American
SAT=San Antonio, TX				
U of Texas at Austin		4		
		4		
SBA=Santa Barbara, CA				
Cal State University - Los Angeles	8	1	18	
Cal State University - Northridge	1	2	3	2
	9	3	21	2
SBY=Salisbury, MD				
Delaware State College*	1			
	1			
SFO=San Francisco/Oakland, CA				
Cal State University - Sacramento	1	1	4	1
U of Cal - Davis	1		9	
	2	1	13	1
SHV=Shreveport, LA				
Louisiana Tech University	6			
	6			
TUL=Tulsa, OK				
Oklahoma State U - Main Campus	2			2
	2			2
TYR=Tyler, TX				
East Texas State University	5		1	
	5		1	

514

HOME ECONOMICS (1300)
MINORITY BACCALAUREATE DEGREES
MORE THAN 80 MILES FROM NEAREST AIRPORT

AIRPORT	MINORITY GROUP			
	Black	Hispanic	Asian	Native American
ABQ=Albuquerque, NM				
New Mexico Highlands*		3		
		3		
MSY=New Orleans, LA				
U of Southern Mississippi	5			
	5			
PWA=Oklahoma City-Wiley Post, OK				
Cameron University	2	1		
	2	1		
TCL=Tuscaloosa, AL				
Mississippi State University	13		1	1
	13		1	1

LETTERS (1500)

LETTERS (1500)
MINORITY BACCALAUREATE DEGREES
BY STATE AND INSTITUTION

STATE/SCHOOL	MINORITY GROUP			
	Black	Hispanic	Asian	Native American
Alabama				
Alabama A&M University*	5			
Alabama State University*	8			
Jacksonville State University	1	1		
Oakwood College*	8			
Stillman College*	4			
Talladega College*	10			
Tuskegee Institute*	12			
University of Alabama	8			
U of Alabama in Birmingham	4			
University of South Alabama	2			
	62	**1**		
Arizona				
Arizona State University		2		
Northern Arizona University		1		
University of Arizona	1	6	1	2
	1	**9**	**1**	**2**
Arkansas				
Henderson State University	6			
Philander Smith College*	1			
University of Arkansas – Pine Bluff*	16			
University of Central Arkansas	3			
	26			
California				
Cal Poly State U – San Luis Obispo	1	1	1	2
Cal State College – Bakersfield	1	1	1	4
Cal State College – San Bernadino		1	1	
Cal State Poly U – Pomona	1		1	

(1500)

STATE/SCHOOL	MINORITY GROUP			
	Black	Hispanic	Asian	Native American
California (cont)				
Cal State University - Chico		2		
Cal State U - Dominguez Hills	12	3	3	
Cal State University - Fresno	1			
Cal State University - Fullerton	8	12	2	1
Cal State University - Hayward	8	5	1	1
Cal State University - Long Beach	7	10	10	2
Cal State University - Los Angeles	12	12	4	
Cal State University - Northridge	6	7	6	4
Cal State University - Sacramento	15	3	4	2
Chapman College	2			
Loyola Marymount University	1	8	3	
Pepperdine University			3	
San Diego State University	3	5	2	
San Francisco State University	13	6	12	1
San Jose State University	5	8	8	2
Stanford University	4	7	8	
U of Cal - Berkeley	13	7	28	
U of Cal - Davis	3	1	3	
U of Cal - Irvine	3	3	2	
U of Cal - Los Angeles	18	5	19	4
U of Cal - Riverside		1		
U of Cal - San Diego		2	2	1
U of Cal - Santa Barbara	2	3	2	
U of Cal - Santa Cruz		4	1	
University of LaVerne	1		1	
University of Redlands	1			
University of San Francisco	2	3	2	
University of Southern California	6	5	2	1
University of the Pacific		3		
	149	**128**	**132**	**25**

518

(1500)

STATE/SCHOOL	MINORITY GROUP			
	Black	Hispanic	Asian	Native American
Colorado				
Colorado State University	1	3		
Metropolitan State College	4	5		
U of Colorado at Boulder		5		
U of Northern Colorado	1	1		
U of Southern Colorado	1	2		
	7	16		
Connecticut				
University of Connecticut			3	
Yale University	5	5	4	1
	5	5	7	1
Delaware				
Delaware State College*	1			
University of Delaware	1		1	
	2		1	
District of Columbia				
American University	1			
George Washington University	5	1	1	
Howard University*	20			
University of DC*	12			
	38	1	1	
Florida				
Bethune Cookman College*	12			
Biscayne College*	1	1		
Edward Waters College*	3			
Florida Agr & Mech University*	2			
Florida Atlantic University	3	1		
Florida International University	1	6	1	
Florida State University	3	1	1	
University of Central Florida	2	1		1
University of Florida	7	8	1	
University of Miami	5	11	1	1

(1500)

STATE/SCHOOL	MINORITY GROUP			
	Black	Hispanic	Asian	Native American
Florida (cont)				
University of South Florida	4	2		
University of West Florida	2			
	45	**31**	**4**	**2**
Georgia				
Albany State College*	8			
Clark College*	12			
Fort Valley State College*	5			
Georgia College			1	
Georgia State University	3			
Morehouse College*	7			
Morris Brown College*	1			
Paine College*	9			
Savannah State College*	4			
Spelman College*	39			
University of Georgia	3			
	91		**1**	
Hawaii				
Chaminade University of Honolulu	1	1	1	
University of Hawaii at Hilo*			7	
University of Hawaii at Manoa*			71	
	1	**1**	**79**	
Illinois				
Bradley University				
Chicago State University*	11			
Columbia College	9		1	
DePaul University	2	1		
Eastern Illinois University	6			
Governors State University	1			
Illinois State University	2	1		
Loyola University of Chicago	3			
Northern Illinois University	13			1

520

(1500)

STATE/SCHOOL	MINORITY GROUP			
	Black	Hispanic	Asian	Native American
Illinois (cont)				
Northeastern Illinois University	6	5		
Northwestern University	6	2		
Roosevelt University	5		2	
Southern Illinois U - Carbondale	11			
U of Illinois - Chicago Circle	15	9	2	
U of Illinois - Urbana Campus	2		2	
	92	**18**	**7**	**1**
Indiana				
Ind-Purdue U - Indianapolis	1			
Indiana State U - Main Campus	1			
Indiana University - Bloomington	4		1	
Indiana University - Northwest	2			
Purdue University - Main Campus	2			
	10		**1**	
Kentucky				
Eastern Kentucky University	1			
Kentucky State University*	1			
University of Louisville	2			
Western Kentucky University	3			
	7			
Louisiana				
Dillard University*	7			
Grambling State University*	16			
Louisiana State U & A&M College	3			
Louisiana Tech University	5			
McNeese State University	1			
Northeast Louisiana University	2			
Southeastern Louisiana U	2			
Sthrn U A&M College - Main Cam*	11			
Southern U in New Orleans*	3			
Tulane U of Louisiana	2			1

(1500)

STATE/SCHOOL	MINORITY GROUP			
	Black	Hispanic	Asian	Native American
Louisiana (cont)				
University of New Orleans	6			
U of Southwestern Louisiana	2		1	
Xavier University of Louisiana*	4			
	64		**1**	**1**
Maryland				
Bowie State College*	5			
Coppin State College*	2			
Morgan State University*	20			
Towson State University	4			
University of Baltimore	5			
U of MD - Baltimore Co Campus	5			
U of MD - College Park Campus	7	1	4	1
U of MD - Eastern Shore*	2			
	50	**1**	**4**	**1**
Massachussetts				
Boston State College		1	1	
Boston University	5		1	
Harvard University	6		2	
Radcliffe College	1			
Tufts University	1		1	
U of Mass - Amherst Campus		1	1	
	13	**2**	**6**	
Michigan				
Detroit Institute of Technology	2			
Eastern Michigan University	8	1	1	1
Mercy College of Detroit	3			
Michigan State University		1	1	
Oakland University			1	1
Shaw College at Detroit*	2			
University of Detroit	2	3	1	
U of Michigan - Ann Arbor	18		6	1

522

(1500)

STATE/SCHOOL	MINORITY GROUP			
	Black	Hispanic	Asian	Native American
Michigan (cont)				
Wayne State University	16	1		
Western Michigan University	2		1	1
	53	6	11	4
Minnesota				
U of Minn – Minneapolis/St. Paul	1		2	1
	1		2	1
Mississippi				
Alcorn State University*	6			
Delta State University	5			
Jackson State University*	33			
Mississippi Industrial College*	2			
Mississippi State University	1			
Mississippi Valley State Univ*	15			
Rust College*	2			
Tougaloo College*	11			
U of Mississippi – Main Campus	3			
U of Southern Mississippi	1			
	79			
Missouri				
Lincoln University	3			
Park College	1			
U of Missouri – Columbia	2			1
U of Missouri – Kansas City	10	1		1
U of Missouri – St. Louis	7		1	
Washington University			1	
Webster College	2			
	25	1	2	2
New Hampshire				
Dartmouth College	8	1		2
	8	1		2

(1500)

STATE/SCHOOL	MINORITY GROUP			
	Black	Hispanic	Asian	Native American
New Jersey				
Glassboro State College	2			
Jersey City State College	4	3		
Kean College of New Jersey	1	1		1
Montclair State College	2			5
Princeton University	6	2	1	
Rutgers U – Camden Campus	8			
Rutgers U – New Brunswick	20	3	1	
Rutgers U – Newark Campus	6	2		
St. Peter's College	1	4		
Trenton State College	3		1	
	53	**15**	**3**	**6**
New Mexico				
Eastern NM U – Main Campus	1	2		
New Mexico Highlands U*		3		
NM State U – Main Campus		3		1
U of NM – Main Campus	2	9		2
Western New Mexico University				
	3	**17**		**3**
New York				
Adelphi University	1			
College of New Rochelle		1		
Cornell U Endowed College	4		1	
CUNY Bernard Baruch College	8	3	3	
CUNY Brooklyn College	37	12	2	1
CUNY City College	40	19	10	2
CUNY College of Staten Island	4	3	1	
CUNY Hunter College	20	11	4	1
CUNY Lehman College	19	18	5	
CUNY Queen's College	20	5	6	
CUNY York College	6	2		

(1500)

STATE/SCHOOL	MINORITY GROUP			
	Black	Hispanic	Asian	Native American
New York (cont)				
Fordham University	14	7		
Long Island U – Brooklyn Center	3	1		
Long Island U – C W Post Center	1			
New York University	1		1	
Pace University New York	2	1		
St. Francis College	1	1	1	
St. John's University	2	1	1	
St. Joseph's College – Main Campus		1		
SUNY at Albany	10	4	2	2
SUNY at Buffalo – Main Campus	16		1	
SUNY at Stony Bk – Main Campus	4		2	
SUNY College at Buffalo	4		1	
SUNY College at New Paltz	6	1		
SUNY Empire State College	8	1		
Syracuse University – Main Campus	5	2		
	236	**94**	**41**	**6**
North Carolina				
Bennett College*	6			
Duke University	1	1	1	
East Carolina University	1			
Elizabeth City State U*	21			
Fayetteville State University*	8			
Johnson C Smith University*	1			
Livingstone College*	2			
NC Agrl & Tech State University*	25			
NC Central University*	14			
NC State U – Raleigh	7		1	
Pembroke State University	3			3
St. Augustine's College*	10			
Shaw University*	6			
U of NC at Chapel Hill	13	1		

(1500)

STATE/SCHOOL	MINORITY GROUP			
	Black	Hispanic	Asian	Native American
North Carolina (cont)				
U of NC at Charlotte	2			
U of NC at Greensboro	5			
Winston–Salem State University*	3			
	128	**2**	**2**	**3**
North Dakota				
U of North Dakota – Main Campus	1			1
	1			**1**
Ohio				
Bowling Green State U – Main Cam	10	2		1
Central State University*	2			
Kent State U – Main Campus	8			
Oberlin College	4		3	
Ohio State U – Main Campus	17			
Ohio University – Main Campus	22			
U of Akron – Main Campus	4			
U of Cincinnati – Main Campus	7			
University of Toledo	3		1	
Wright State U – Main Campus	1	1		
	78	**3**	**4**	**1**
Oklahoma				
Cameron University	1			1
Central State University	2	1		
Northeast Oklahoma State U	1			1
Oklahoma State U – Main Campus		1		
Southeast Oklahoma State U				1
U of Oklahoma – Norman Campus	1			2
	5	**2**		**5**
Oregon				
Oregon State University				
University of Oregon – Main Campus	1		3	1
	1		**3**	**1**

526

(1500)

STATE/SCHOOL	MINORITY GROUP			
	Black	Hispanic	Asian	Native American
Pennsylvania				
Cheyney State College*	13			
Lincoln University*	12			
Pennsylvania State U - Main Campus	4		3	
St. Joseph's University	2			2
Temple University	8	3	1	
University of Pennsylvania	7	1	2	
U of Pittsburg - Main Campus	36	1	1	2
West Chester State College	1			
	83	**5**	**7**	**4**
Rhode Island				
Brown University	7	1	3	1
	7	**1**	**3**	**1**
South Carolina				
Allen University*	3			
Baptist College at Charleston	5			
Benedict College*	6			
Claflin College*	11			
South Carolina State College*	8			
U of South Carolina at Columbia	7			
Winthrop College	1			
	41			
Tennessee				
Austin Peay State University	2			
Fisk University*	20			
Knoxville College*	8			
LeMoyne-Owen College*	5			
Memphis State University	5			
Tennessee State University*	7			
U of Tennessee - Knoxville	3			
U of Tennessee - Martin	3			
	53			

(1500)

STATE/SCHOOL	MINORITY GROUP			
	Black	Hispanic	Asian	Native American
Texas				
Angelo State University	1	5		
Bishop College*	24			
East Texas State University	2			
Incarnate Word College		1		
Jarvis Christian College*	3			
Lamar University				2
Laredo State University*		19		
North Texas State University	5	2		
Our Lady of Lake University*	2	5		
Pan American University*		14		
Prairie View A&M University*	4			
St. Edward's University	3			
St. Mary's U – San Antonio	2	8		
Sam Houston State University	3			
Southwest Texas State University	2			1
Sul Ross State University		1		
Texas A&I University		12		
Texas A&M U – Main Campus		1		1
Texas College*	5			
Texas Southern University*	8			
Texas Women's University	1		1	
Trinity University		1		
U of Houston – Central Campus	3	4	2	
U of Texas at Arlington	4	1		
U of Texas at Austin	6	18	2	
U of Texas at El Paso		7		
U of Texas at San Antonio		3		
Wiley College*	5			
	83	**102**	**5**	**4**

528

(1500)

STATE/SCHOOL	MINORITY GROUP			
	Black	Hispanic	Asian	Native American
Utah				
Brigham Young University – Main				2
University of Utah	1		2	
	1		2	2
Virginia				
Hampton Institute*	9			
Norfolk State College*	8			
Old Dominion University	2	1		1
St. Paul's College*	2			
U of Virginia – Main Campus	11	1		
Virginia Commonwealth University	2			
Virginia State College*	18			
Virginia Union University*	10			
	62	2		1
Washington				
University of Washington	5	3	3	
	5	3	3	
Wisconsin				
U of Wisconsin – Madison	2	1		1
U of Wisconsin – Milwaukee	2	1	1	
	4	2	1	1
TOTALS	**1673**	**469**	**334**	**81**

*Predominately minority institutions are those where at least 50% of the total BA Degrees awarded are to one of the minority groups being considered.

LETTERS (1500)
BLACK BACCALAUREATE DEGREES RANKED BY INSTITUTION

Rank	Institution	B.A.'s	Rank	Institution	B.A.'s
1	CUNY City C	40	28	NC Central U*	14
2	Spelman C*	39	29	Fordham U	14
3	CUNY Brooklyn C	37	30	San Francisco State U	13
4	U of Pittsburgh-Main Campus	36	31	U of Cal-Berkeley	13
5	Jackson State U*	33	32	U of NC at Chapel Hill	13
6	NC Agrl & Tech State U*	25	33	Northern Illinois U	13
7	Bishop C*	24	34	Cheyney State C*	13
8	Ohio U-Main Campus	22	35	Bethune Cookman C*	12
9	Elizabeth City State U*	21	36	Clark C*	12
10	CUNY Hunter C	20	37	U of DC*	12
11	CUNY Queen's C	20	38	Tuskegee Institute*	12
12	Howard U*	20	39	Cal State U-Los Angeles	12
13	Rutgers U-New Brunswick	20	40	Cal State U-Dominguez Hills	12
14	Morgan State U	20	41	Lincoln U*	12
15	Fisk U*	20	42	Chicago State U*	11
16	CUNY Lehman C	19	43	Southern Illinois C-Carbondale	11
17	U of Michigan-Ann Arbor	18	44	Tougaloo C*	11
18	U of Cal-Los Angeles	18	45	U of Virginia-Main Campus	11
19	Virginia State C*	18	46	Sthrn U A&M C-Main Campus*	11
20	Ohio State U-Main Campus	17	47	Claflin C*	11
21	Wayne State U	16	48	St. Augustine's C*	10
22	Grambling State U*	16	49	SUNY at Albany	10
23	SUNY at Buffalo-Main Campus	16	50	Bowling Green State U-Main Ca	10
24	U of Arkansas-Pine Bluff*	16	51	U of Missouri-Kansas City	10
25	Cal State U-Sacramento	15	52	Talladega C*	10
26	Mississippi Valley State U*	15	53	Virginia Union U*	10
27	U of Illinois-Chicago Circle	15			

*predominantly black institutions

Institutions not ranked have less than ten degrees conferred on blacks.

LETTERS (1500)
HISPANIC BACCALAUREATE DEGREES RANKED BY INSTITUTION

Rank	Institution	B.A.'s	Rank	Institution	B.A.'s
1	Laredo State U*	19	7	Cal State U-Los Angeles	12
2	CUNY City C	19	8	CUNY Brooklyn C	12
3	U of Texas at Austin	18	9	Texas A&I U	12
4	CUNY Lehman C	18	10	U of Miami	11
5	Pan American U*	14	11	CUNY Hunter C	11
6	Cal State U-Fullerton	12	12	Cal State U-Long Beach	10

*predominantly Hispanic institutions

Institutions not ranked have less than ten degrees conferred on Hispanics.

LETTERS (1500)
ASIAN BACCALAUREATE DEGREES RANKED BY INSTITUTION

Rank	Institution	B.A.'s	Rank	Institution	B.A.'s
1	U of Hawaii at Manoa*	71	4	San Francisco State U	12
2	U of Cal-Berkeley	28	5	Cal State U-Long Beach	10
3	U of Cal-Los Angeles	19	6	CUNY City C	10

*predominantly Asian institutions

Institutions not ranked have less than ten degrees conferred on Asians.

LETTERS (1500)
NATIVE AMERICAN BACCALAUREATE DEGREES RANKED BY INSTITUTION

Rank	Institution	B.A.'s
1	Montclair State C	5

Institutions not ranked have less than five degrees conferred on Native Americans

LETTERS (1500)
MINORITY BACCALAUREATE DEGREES
WITHIN 60 MILE RADIUS OF AIRPORT

AIRPORT	MINORITY GROUP			
	Black	Hispanic	Asian	Native American
ABQ=Albuquerque, NM				
U of NM - Main Campus	2	9		2
	2	**9**		**2**
ALB=Albany, NY				
SUNY at Albany	10	4	2	2
SUNY Empire State College	8	1		
	18	**5**	**2**	**2**
AOO=Altoona, PA				
Pennsylvania State U - Main Campus	4		3	
	4		**3**	
ATL=Atlanta, GA				
Clark College*	12			
Georgia State University	3			
Morehouse College*	7			
Morris Brown College*	1			
Spelman College*	39			
	62			
AUS=Austin, TX				
Southwest Texas State University	2			1
U of Texas at Austin	6	18	2	
	8	**18**	**2**	**1**
BAL=Baltimore, MD				
University of Delaware	1		1	
American University	1			
George Washington Univesity	5	1	1	
Howard University*	20			
University of DC*	12			

Airport 60 (1500)

AIRPORT		MINORITY GROUP		
	Black	Hispanic	Asian	Native American
BAL (cont)				
Bowie State College*	5			
Coppin State College*	2			
Morgan State University*	20			
Towson State University	4			
U of MD - Baltimore Co Campus	5			
U of MD - College Park Campus	7	1	4	1
University of Baltimore	5			
Lincoln University*	12			
	99	**2**	**6**	**1**
BDL=Hartford, CT/Springfield, MA				
Yale University	5	5	4	1
U of Mass - Amherst Campus		1	1	
	5	**6**	**5**	**1**
BHM=Birmingham, AL				
Stillman College*	4			
Talladega College*	10			
U of Alabama in Birmingham	4			
University of Alabama	8			
	26			
BKL=Cleveland-Lakefront, OH				
Kent State U - Main Campus	8			
Oberlin College	4		3	
U of Akron - Main Campus	4			
	16		**3**	
BNA=Nashville, TN				
Western Kentucky University	3			
Austin Peay State University	2			
Fisk University*	20			
Tennessee State University*	7			
	32			

Airport 60 (1500)

AIRPORT	MINORITY GROUP			
	Black	Hispanic	Asian	Native American
BOS=Boston, MA				
Boston State College		1	1	
Boston University	5		1	
Harvard University	6		2	
Radcliffe College	1			
Tufts University	1		1	
Brown University	7	1	3	1
	20	**2**	**8**	**1**
BTR=Baton Rouge, LA				
Louisiana State U & A&M College	3			
Sthrn U A&M College - Main Cam*	11			
Southeastern Louisiana U	2			
	16			
BUF=Buffalo, NY				
SUNY at Buffalo - Main Campus	16		1	
SUNY College at Buffalo	4		1	
	20		**2**	
CAE=Columbia, SC				
Allen University*	3			
Benedict College*	6			
Claflin College*	11			
South Carolina State College*	8			
U of South Carolina at Columbia	7			
	35			
CHS=Charleston, SC				
Baptist College at Charleston	5			
	5			
CIC=Chico, CA				
Cal State University - Chico		2		
		2		

534

Airport 60 (1500)

AIRPORT		MINORITY GROUP		
	Black	**Hispanic**	**Asian**	**Native American**
CLT=Charlotte, NC				
Johnson C Smith University*	1			
Livingstone College*	2			
U of NC at Charlotte	2			
Winthrop College	1			
	6			
CMH=Columbus, OH				
Central State University*	2			
Ohio State U - Main Campus	17			
	19			
CMI=Champaign, IL				
Eastern Illinois University	6			
Illinois State University	2	1		
U of Illinois - Urbana Campus	2		2	
Indiana State U - Main Campus	1			
	11	**1**	**2**	
COS=Colorado Springs, CO				
U of Southern Colorado	1	2		
	1	**2**		
COU=Columbia, MO				
Lincoln University	3			
U of Missouri - Columbia	2			1
	5			**1**
CRP=Corpus Christi, TX				
Texas A&I University		12		
		12		
CVG=Cincinnati, OH				
Central State University*	2			
U of Cincinnati - Main Campus	7			
Wright State U - Main Campus	1	1		
	10	**1**		

Airport 60 (1500)

AIRPORT	MINORITY GROUP			
	Black	Hispanic	Asian	Native American
DAB=Dayton Beach, FL				
Bethune Cookman College*	12			
University of Central Florida	2	1		1
	14	**1**		**1**
DCA=Washington–National, DC				
American University	1			
George Washington University	5	1	1	
Howard University*	20			
University of DC*	12			
Bowie State College*	5			
Coppin State College*	2			
Morgan State University*	20			
Towson State University	4			
U of MD - Baltimore Co Campus	5			
U of MD - College Park Campus	7	1	4	1
University of Baltimore	5			
	86	**2**	**5**	**1**
DEN=Denver, CO				
Metropolitan State College	4	5		
U of Colorado at Boulder	5			
U of Northern Colorado	1	1		
	5	**11**		
DFW=Dallas/Fort Worth, TX				
Bishop College*	24			
East Texas State University	2			
North Texas State University	5	2		
Texas Woman's University	1		1	
U of Texas at Arlington	4	1		
	36	**3**	**1**	
DTW=Detroit-Metropolitan, MI				
Detroit Institute of Technology	2			
Eastern Michigan University	8	1	1	1

Airport 60 (1500)

AIRPORT	MINORITY GROUP			
	Black	Hispanic	Asian	Native American
DTW (cont)				
Mercy College of Detroit	3			
Oakland University			1	1
Shaw College at Detroit*	2			
U of Michigan – Ann Arbor	18		6	1
University of Detroit	2	3	1	
Wayne State University	16	1		
University of Toledo	3		1	
	54	**5**	**10**	**3**
ELP=El Paso, TX				
U of Texas at El Paso		7		
		7		
EUG=Eugene, OR				
University of Oregon – Main Campus	1		3	1
	1		**3**	**1**
FAT=Fresno, CA				
Cal State University – Fresno	1			
	1			
FAY=Fayetteville, NC				
Fayetteville State University*	8			
NC Central University*	14			
NC State U – Raleigh	7		1	
Pembroke State University	3			3
St. Augustine's College*	10			
Shaw University*	6			
U of NC at Chapel Hill	13	1		
	61	**1**	**1**	**3**
FLG=Flagstaff, AZ				
Northern Arizona University		1		
		1		

Airport 60 (1500)

AIRPORT		MINORITY GROUP		
	Black	Hispanic	Asian	Native American
GLH=Greenville, MS				
Delta State University	5			
Mississippi Valley State U*	15			
	20			
GRR=Grand Rapids, MI				
Western Michigan University	2		1	1
	2		**1**	**1**
GSO=Greensboro/High Point, NC				
Bennett College*	6			
Duke University	1	1	1	
Livingstone College*	2			
NC Agrl & Tech State University*	25			
NC Central University*	14			
U of NC at Chapel Hill	13	1		
U of NC at Greensboro	5			
Winston-Salem State University*	3			
	69	**2**	**1**	
HNL=Honolulu/Oahu, HI				
Chaminade University of Honolulu	1	1	1	
University of Hawaii at Manoa*			71	
	1	**1**	**72**	
HSV=Huntsville, AL/Decatur, GA				
Alabama A&M University*	5			
Oakwood College*	8			
	13			
IAH=Houston-Intercontinental,TX				
Prairie View A&M University*	4			
Texas Southern University*	8			
U of Houston - Central Campus	3	4	2	
	15	**4**	**2**	

538

Airport 60 (1500)

AIRPORT	MINORITY GROUP			
	Black	Hispanic	Asian	Native American
IND=Indianapolis, IN				
Ind-Purdue U Indianapolis	1			
Indiana University - Bloomington	4		1	
Purdue University - Main Campus	2			
	7		1	
ITO=Hilo, HI				
University of Hawaii at Hilo*			7	
			7	
JAN=Jackson/Vicksburg, MS				
Alcorn State University*	6			
Jackson State University*	33			
Tougaloo College*	11			
	50			
JAX=Jacksonville, FL				
Edward Waters College*	3			
	3			
JFK=New York, Kennedy Int'l, NY				
Jersey City State College	4	3		
Kean College of New Jersey	1	1		1
Montclair State College	2			5
Princeton University	6	2	1	
Rutgers U - New Brunswick	20	3	1	
Rutgers U - Newark Campus	6	2		
St. Peter's College	1	4		
Trenton State College	3		1	
Adelphi University	1			
College of New Rochelle		1		
CUNY Bernard Baruch College	8	3	3	
CUNY Brooklyn College	37	12	2	1
CUNY College of Staten Island	4	3	1	
CUNY City College	40	19	10	2
CUNY Hunter College	20	11	4	1

Airport 60 (1500)

AIRPORT	MINORITY GROUP			
	Black	Hispanic	Asian	Native American
JFK (cont)				
CUNY Lehman College	19	18	5	
CUNY Queen's College	20	5	6	
CUNY York College	6	2		
Fordham University	14	7		
Long Island U - Brooklyn Center	3	1		
Long Island U - C W Post Center	1			
New York University	1		1	
Pace University New York	2	1		
St. Francis College	1	1	1	
St. John's University	2	1	1	
St. Joseph's College - Main Campus		1		
SUNY at Stony Bk - Main Campus	4		2	
	226	**101**	**39**	**10**
LAX=Los Angeles, CA				
Cal State College - San Bernardino		1	1	
Cal State Poly U - Pomona	1		1	
Cal State U - Dominguez Hills	12	3	3	
Cal State University - Fullerton	8	12	2	1
Cal State University - Long Beach	7	10	10	2
Cal State University - Los Angeles	12	12	4	
Cal State University - Northridge	6	7	6	4
Chapman College	2			
Loyola Marymount University	1	8	3	
Pepperdine University			3	
U of Cal - Irvine	3	3	2	
U of Cal - Los Angeles	18	5	19	4
U of Cal - Riverside		1		
University of Southern California	6	5	2	1
University of LaVerne	1		1	
	77	**67**	**57**	**12**

Airport 60 (1500)

AIRPORT	MINORITY GROUP			
	Black	Hispanic	Asian	Native American
LCH=Lake Charles, LA				
McNeese State University	1			
	1			
LEX=Lexington/Frankfort, KY				
Eastern Kentucky University	1			
Kentucky State University*	1			
University of Louisville	2			
	4			
LIT=Little Rock, AR				
Philander Smith College*	1			
University of Arkansas - Pine Bluff*	16			
University of Central Arkansas	3			
	20			
LRD=Laredo, TX				
Laredo State University*		19		
		19		
MCI=Kansas City-International, MO				
Park College	1			
U of Missouri - Kansas City	10	1		1
	11	1		1
MCN=Macon, GA				
Fort Valley State College*	5			
Georgia College			1	
	5		1	
MDH=Carbondale, IL				
Southern Illinois U - Carbondale	11			
	11			
MEM=Memphis, TN				
Mississippi Industrial Colege*	2			
Rust College*	2			
Le Moyne-Owen College*	5			
Memphis State University	5			
	14			

541

Airport 60 (1500)

AIRPORT		MINORITY GROUP		
	Black	Hispanic	Asian	Native American
MFE=McAllen, TX				
Pan American University*		14		
		14		
MGM=Montgomery, GA				
Alabama State University*	8			
Tuskegee Institute*	12			
	20			
MHT=Manchester, NH				
Harvard University	6		2	
Radcliffe College	1			
Tufts University	1		1	
Dartmouth College	8	1		2
	16	**1**	**3**	**2**
MIA=Miami, FL				
Biscayne College*	1	1		
Florida Atlantic University	3	1		
Florida International University	1	6	1	
University of Miami	5	11	1	1
	10	**19**	**2**	**1**
MKE=Milwaukee, WS				
U of Wisconsin - Milwaukee	2	1	1	
	2	**1**	**1**	
MKL=Jackson, TN				
U of Tennessee - Martin	3			
	3			
MLU=Monroe, LA				
Grambling State University*	16			
Louisiana Tech University	5			
Northeast Louisiana University	2			
	23			

542

Airport 60 (1500)

AIRPORT	MINORITY GROUP			
	Black	Hispanic	Asian	Native American
MOB=Mobile, AL/Pasagoula, MS				
University of South Alabama	2			
University of West Florida	2			
	4			
MSN=Madison, WS				
U of Wisconsin - Madison	2	1		1
	2	**1**		**1**
MSP=Minneapolis/St. Paul, MN				
U of Minn - Minneapolis/St. Paul	1		2	1
	1		**2**	**1**
MSY=New Orleans, LA				
Dillard University*	7			
Southeastern Louisiana U	2			
Southern U in New Orleans*	3			
Tulane U of Louisiana	2			1
University of New Orleans	6			
Xavier University of Louisiana*	4			
	24			**1**
ORD=Chicago-O'Hare Airport, IL				
Chicago State University*	11			
Columbia College	9		1	
DePaul University	2	1		
Governors State University	1			
Loyola University of Chicago	3			
Northern Illinois University	13			1
Northwestern University	6	2		
Northeastern Illinois University	6	5		
Roosevelt University	5		2	
U of Illinois - Chicago Circle	15	9	2	
Indiana University - Northwest	2			
	73	**17**	**5**	**1**

Airport 60 (1500)

AIRPORT	MINORITY GROUP			
	Black	Hispanic	Asian	Native American
ORF=Norfolk/Virginia Beach, VA				
Elizabeth City State U*	21			
Hampton Institute*	9			
Norfolk State College*	8			
Old Dominion University	2	1		1
	40	**1**		**1**
PHL=Philadelphia, PA/Wilmington, DE				
Delaware State College*	1			
University of Delaware	1		1	
Glassboro State College	2			
Princeton University	6	2	1	
Rutgers U – Camden Campus	8			
Rutgers U – New Brunswick	20	3	1	
Trenton State College	3		1	
Cheyney State College*	13			
Lincoln University*	12			
St. Joseph's University	2			2
Temple University	8	3	1	
University of Pennsylvania	7	1	2	
West Chester State College	1			
	84	**9**	**7**	**2**
PHX=Phoenix, AZ				
Arizona State University		2		
		2		
PIT=Pittsburgh, PA				
U of Pittsburgh – Main Campus	36	1	1	2
	36	**1**	**1**	**2**
PVD=Providence, RI				
Boston State College		1	1	
Boston University	5		1	
Harvard University	6		2	

544

Airport 60 (1500)

AIRPORT	MINORITY GROUP			
	Black	Hispanic	Asian	Native American
PVD (cont)				
Radcliffe College	1			
Tufts University	1		1	
Brown University	7	1	3	1
	20	**2**	**8**	**1**
PWA=Oklahoma City-Wiley Post, OK				
Central State University	2	1		
Oklahoma State U - Main Campus		1		
U of Oklahoma - Norman Campus	1			2
	3	**2**		**2**
RDU=Raleigh/Durham, NC				
Bennet College*	6			
Duke University	1	1	1	
Fayetteville State University*	8			
NC Agrl & Tech State University*	25			
NC Central University*	14			
NC State U - Raleigh	7		1	
St. Augustine's College*	10			
Shaw University*	6			
U of NC at Chapel Hill	13	1		
U of NC at Greensboro	5			
	95	**2**	**2**	
RIC=Richmond, VA				
Virginia Commonwealth University	2			
Virginia State College*	18			
Virginia Union University*	10			
	30			
SAN=San Diego, CA				
San Diego State University	3	5	2	
U of Cal - San Diego		2	2	1
	3	**7**	**4**	**1**

Airport 60 (1500)

AIRPORT		MINORITY GROUP		
	Black	Hispanic	Asian	Native American
SAT=San Antonio, TX				
Incarnate Word College		1		
Our Lady of Lake University*	2	5		
St. Edward's University	3			
St. Mary's U – San Antonio	2	8		
Southwest Texas State University	2			1
Trinity University		1		
U of Texas at San Antonio		3		
	9	**18**		**1**
SAV=Savannah, GA				
Savannah State College*	4			
	4			
SBA=Santa Barbara, CA				
Pepperdine University			3	
U of Cal – Santa Barbara	2	3	2	
	2	**3**	**5**	
SBP=San Luis Obispo, CA				
Cal Poly State U – San Luis Obispo	1	1	1	2
	1	**1**	**1**	**2**
SBY=Salisbury, MD				
U of MD – Eastern Shore*	2			
	2			
SEA=Seattle/Tacoma, WA				
University of Washington	5	3	3	
	5	**3**	**3**	
SFO=San Francisco/Oakland, CA				
Cal State University – Hayward	8	5	1	1
San Francisco State University	13	6	12	1
San Jose State University	5	8	8	2
Stanford University	4	7	8	
U of Cal – Berkeley	13	7	28	
University of San Francisco	2	3	2	
	45	**36**	**59**	**4**

546

Airport 60 (1500)

AIRPORT	MINORITY GROUP			
	Black	Hispanic	Asian	Native American
SHV=Shreveport, LA				
Grambling State University*	16			
Wiley College*	5			
	21			
SJT=San Angelo, TX				
Angelo State University	1	5		
	1	5		
SLC=Salt Lake City, UT				
Brigham Young University - Main				2
University of Utah	1		2	
	1		2	2
STL=St. Louis, MO				
U of Missouri - St. Louis	7		1	
Washington University			1	
Webster College	2			
	9		2	
SWI=Sherman, TX				
Southeast Oklahoma State U				1
Bishop College*	24			
East Texas State University	2			
North Texas State University	5	2		
Texas Woman's University	1		1	
	32	2	1	1
SYR=Syracuse, NY				
Cornel U Endowed College	4		1	
Syracuse U - Main Campus	5	2		
	9	2	1	
TCL=Tuscaloosa, AL				
Stillman College*	4			
U of Alabama in Birmingham	4			
University of Alabama	8			
	16			

Airport 60 (1500)

AIRPORT	MINORITY GROUP			
	Black	Hispanic	Asian	Native American
TLH=Tallahassee, FL				
Florida Agr & Mech University*	2			
Florida State University	3	1	1	
	5	1	1	
TPA=Tampa, FL				
University of South Florida	4	2		
	4	2		
TUL=Tulsa, OK				
Northeast Oklahoma State U	1			1
	1			1
TUS=Tucson, AZ				
University of Arizona	1	6	1	2
	1	6	1	2
TYR=Tyler, TX				
Jarvis Christian College*	3			
Texas College*	5			
Wiley College*	5			
	13			
TYS=Knoxville, TN				
Knoxville College*	8			
U of Tennessee - Knoxville	3			
	11			

LETTERS (1500)
MINORITY BACCALAUREATE DEGREES
WITHIN 61-80 MILE ANNULUS OF AIRPORT

AIRPORT	MINORITY GROUP			
	Black	Hispanic	Asian	Native American
ALB=Albany, NY				
U of Mass - Amherst Campus		1	1	
SUNY College at New Paltz	6	1		
	6	2	1	
ALM=Alamogordo, NM				
NM State U - Main Campus		3		1
		3		1
ATL=Atlanta, GA				
Jacksonville State University	1	1		
Georgia College			1	
University of Georgia	3			
	4	1	1	
AUS=Austin, TX				
Incarnate Word College		1		
Our Lady of Lake University*	2	5		
St. Edward's University	3			
St. Mary's U - San Antonio	2	8		
Trinity University		1		
U of Texas at San Antonio		3		
	7	18		
BAL=Baltimore, MD				
Delaware State College*	1			
Cheyney State College*	13			
	14			
BDL=Hartford, CT/Springfield, MA				
College of New Rochelle		1		
SUNY at Albany	10	4	2	2

Airport 61-80 (1500)

AIRPORT	MINORITY GROUP			
	Black	Hispanic	Asian	Native American
BDL (cont)				
SUNY College at New Paltz	6	1		
Brown University	7	1	3	1
	23	**7**	**5**	**3**
BHM=Birmingham, AL				
Jacksonville State University	1	1		
	1	**1**		
BOS=Boston, MA				
U of Mass - Amherst Campus		1	1	
		1	**1**	
BTR=Baton Rouge, LA				
Dillard University*	7			
Southern U in New Orleans*	3			
Tulane U of Louisiana	2			1
U of Southwestern Louisiana	2		1	
University of New Orleans	6			
Xavier University of Louisiana*	4			
	24		**1**	**1**
CAE=Columbia, SC				
Paine College*	9			
Winthrop College	1			
	10			
CHS=Charleston, SC				
Savannah State College*	4			
Claflin College*	11			
South Carolina State College*	8			
	23			
CLT=Charlotte, NC				
Wintson-Salem State University*	3			
	3			

550

Airport 61-80 (1500)

AIRPORT	MINORITY GROUP			
	Black	Hispanic	Asian	Native American
CMH=Columbus, OH				
Ohio University - Main Campus	22			
Wright State U - Main Campus	1	1		
	23	1		
CMI=Champaign, IL				
Purdue University - Main Campus	2			
	2			
COS=Colorado Springs, CO				
Metropolitan State College	4	5		
U of Colorado at Boulder		5		
	4	10		
CRW=Charleston, WV				
Ohio University - Main Campus	22			
	22			
CVG=Cincinnati, OH				
Kentucky State University*	1			
	1			
DCA=Washington-National, DC				
Lincoln University*	12			
	12			
DEN=Denver, CO				
Colorado State University	1	3		
	1	3		
DTW=Detroit-Metropolitan, MI				
Michigan State University		1	1	
Bowling Green State U - Main Cam	10	2		1
	10	3	1	1
FAY=Fayetteville, NC				
Duke University	1	1	1	
	1	1	1	

Airport 61-80 (1500)

AIRPORT	MINORITY GROUP			
	Black	Hispanic	Asian	Native American
GRR=Grand Rapids, MI				
Michigan State University		1	1	
		1	1	
GSO=Greensboro/High Point, NC				
NC State U - Raleigh	7		1	
St. Augustine's College*	10			
Shaw University*	6			
	23		1	
HSV=Huntsville, AL/Decatur, GA				
Jacksonville State University	1	1		
	1	1		
IAH=Houston-Intercontinental,TX				
Sam Houston State University	3			
	3			
IND=Indianapolis, IN				
Indiana State U - Main Campus	1			
	1			
JAX=Jacksonville, FL				
University of Florida	7	8	1	
	7	8	1	
JFK=New York, Kennedy Int'l, NY				
Yale University	5	5	4	1
SUNY College at New Paltz	6	1		
	11	6	4	1
LAX=Los Angeles, CA				
Cal State College - Bakersfield	1	1	1	4
University of Redlands	1			
	2	1	1	4
LCH=Lake Charles, LA				
U of Southwestern Louisiana	2		1	
Lamar University				2
	2		1	2

Airport 61-80 (1500)

AIRPORT		MINORITY GROUP		
	Black	Hispanic	Asian	Native American
LIT=Little Rock, AR				
Henderson State University	6			
	6			
MCN=Macon, GA				
Clark College*	12			
Georgia State University	3			
Morehouse College*	7			
Morris Brown College*	1			
Spelman College*	39			
	62			
MEM=Memphis, TN				
U of Mississippi - Main Campus	3			
	3			
MGM=Montgomery, GA				
Talladega College*	10			
	10			
MHT=Manchester, NH				
Boston State College		1	1	
Boston University	5		1	
U of Mass - Amherst Campus		1	1	
	5	**2**	**3**	
MKE=Milwaukee, WS				
Northwestern University	6	2		
U of Wisconsin - Madison	2	1		1
	8	**3**		**1**
MKL=Jackson, TN				
Mississippi Industrial College*	2			
Rust College*	2			
Memphis State University	5			
	9			

Airport 61-80 (1500)

AIRPORT	Black	Hispanic	Asian	Native American
MLU=Monroe, LA				
Alcorn State University*	6			
	6			
MOB=Mobile, AL/Pasagoula, MS				
U of Southern Mississippi	1			
	1			
MSN=Madison, WS				
U of Wisconsin - Milwaukee	2	1	1	
	2	**1**	**1**	
MSY=New Orleans, LA				
Louisiana State U & A&M College	3			
Sthrn U A&M C - Main Cam*	11			
	14			
ORF=Norfolk/Virginia Beach, VA				
Virginia State College*	18			
	18			
PVD=Providence, RI				
U of Mass - Amherst Campus		1	1	
		1	**1**	
RDU=Raleigh/Durham, NC				
East Carolina University	1			
St. Paul's College*	2			
	3			
RIC=Richmond, VA				
Hampton Institute*	9			
Norfolk State College*	8			
St. Paul's College*	2			
U of Virginia - Main Campus	11	1		
	30	**1**		

MINORITY GROUP

554

Airport 61-80 (1500)

AIRPORT	MINORITY GROUP			
	Black	Hispanic	Asian	Native American
SAN=San Diego, CA				
Chapman College	2			
U of Cal – Irvine	3	3	2	
U of Cal – Riverside		1		
	5	4	2	
SAT=San Antonio, TX				
U of Texas at Austin	6	18	2	
	6	18	2	
SAV=Savannah, GA				
Baptist College at Charleston	5			
	5			
SBA=Santa Barbara, CA				
Cal State College – Bakersfield	1	1	1	4
Cal State University – Los Angeles	12	12	4	
Cal State University – Northridge	6	7	6	4
Loyola Marymount University	1	8	3	
U of Cal – Los Angeles	18	5	19	4
	38	33	33	12
SBY=Salisbury, MD				
Delaware State College*	1			
	1			
SFO=San Francisco/Oakland, CA				
Cal State University – Sacramento	15	3	4	2
U of Cal – Davis	3	1	3	
U of Cal – Santa Cruz		4	1	
University of the Pacific		3		
	18	11	8	2
SHV=Shreveport, LA				
Louisiana Tech University	5			
	5			

Airport 61-80 (1500)

AIRPORT	MINORITY GROUP			
	Black	Hispanic	Asian	Native American
SWI=Sherman, TX				
U of Texas at Arlington	4	1		
	4	1		
TLH=Tallahassee, FL				
Albany State College*	8			
	8			
TPA=Tampa, FL				
University of Central Florida	2	1		1
	2	1		1
TUL=Tulsa, OK				
Oklahoma State U - Main Campus		1		
		1		
TYR=Tyler, TX				
East Texas State University	2			
	2			

556

LETTERS (1500)
MINORITY BACCALAUREATE DEGREES
MORE THAN 80 MILES FROM NEAREST AIRPORT

AIRPORT	MINORITY GROUP			
	Black	Hispanic	Asian	Native American
ABQ=Albuquerque, NM				
New Mexico Highlands U*		3		
		3		
AUS=Austin, TX				
Texas A&M U – Main Campus		1		1
		1		1
ELP=El Paso, TX				
Sul Ross State University		1		
		1		
IAH=Houston-Intercontinental, TX				
Texas A&M U – Main Campus		1		1
		1		1
MAF=Midland/Odessa, TX				
Sul Ross State University		1		
		1		
MSY=New Orleans, LA				
U of Southern Mississippi	1			
	1			
PWA=Oklahoma City-Wiley Post, OK				
Cameron University	1			1
	1			1
ROW=Roswell, NM				
Eastern NM U – Main Campus	1	2		
	1	2		
TCL=Tuscaloosa, AL				
Mississippi State University	1			
	1			

MATHEMATICS (1700)

MATHEMATICS (1700)
MINORITY BACCALAUREATE DEGREES
BY STATE AND INSTITUTION

STATE/SCHOOL	MINORITY GROUP			
	Black	Hispanic	Asian	Native American
Alabama				
Alabama A&M University*	3			
Jacksonville State University		1	2	
Miles College*	2			
Oakwood College*	1			
Stillman College*	3			
Talladega College*	9			
Troy State University - Main Campus	2			
Troy State University - Montgomery				
Tuskegee Institute*	10			
University of Alabama	3			
U of Alabama in Birmingham	1			
	34	**1**	**2**	
Arizona				
Arizona State University			1	
Northern Arizona University		1		
University of Arizona		1		
		2	**1**	
Arkansas				
Philander Smith College*	2			
University of Arkansas - Pine Bluff*	9			
	11			
California				
Cal Poly State U - San Luis Obispo		1	1	
Cal State College - Bakersfield	1			2
Cal State College - San Bernadino		1	1	
Cal State University - Chico			1	
Cal State University - Fresno	1	1	1	

(1700)

STATE/SCHOOL	MINORITY GROUP			
	Black	Hispanic	Asian	Native American
California (cont)				
Cal State University - Fullerton			2	
Cal State University - Hayward	2	1	2	
Cal State University - Long Beach	1	2	5	
Cal State University - Los Angeles	4	2	7	
Cal State University - Northridge			2	
Cal State University - Sacramento			2	
Loyola Marymount University		1		
Pepperdine University		1		
San Diego State University			4	
San Francisco State University		2	13	
San Jose State University	4		8	
Stanford University	1	3	4	
U of Cal - Berkeley	1		20	
U of Cal - Davis	4			
U of Cal - Irvine		2	3	
U of Cal - Los Angeles	5	2	45	1
U of Cal - Riverside	1		3	
U of Cal - San Diego		1		
U of Cal - Santa Barbara			2	
University of LaVerne			1	
University of Redlands			1	
University of San Francisco		1		
University of Southern California	2		3	
University of the Pacific	1			
	28	**21**	**131**	**3**
Colorado				
Metropolitan State College	2	2		
U of Colorado at Boulder	1		1	
	3	**2**	**1**	
Connecticut				
Yale University	1			
	1			

560

(1700)

STATE/SCHOOL		MINORITY GROUP		
	Black	Hispanic	Asian	Native American
Delaware				
Delaware State College*	1			
	1			
District of Columbia				
American University	4		1	
George Washington University	1			1
Howard University*	5			
University of DC*	5			
	15		1	1
Florida				
Bethune Cookman College*	9			
Biscayne College*		3		
Edward Waters College*	2			
Florida International University		3		
Florida Memorial College*	2			
Florida State University	1			
University of Florida	1	2	1	
University of Miami		3	1	
University of South Florida	1			
University of West Florida			1	
	16	11	3	
Georgia				
Albany State College*	5			
Clark College*	6			
Fort Valley State College*	5			
Georgia State University	2			
Morehouse College*	5			
Morris Brown College*	4			
Paine College*	3			
Savannah State College*	2			
Spelman College*	10			
Valdosta State College	1			
	43			

(1700)

STATE/SCHOOL		MINORITY GROUP		
	Black	Hispanic	Asian	Native American
Hawaii				
University of Hawaii at Hilo*			2	
University of Hawaii at Manoa*			14	
			16	
Illinois				
Chicago State University*	10			
DePaul University			1	
Illinois State University	1		1	
Loyola University of Chicago		1	1	
Northern Illinois University	1			
Northwestern University	3		1	
Southern Illinois U - Carbondale			1	
Southern Illinois U - Edwardsville				1
U of Illinois - Chicago Circle	4	1	8	
U of Illinois - Urbana Campus	1		1	1
	20	**2**	**14**	**2**
Indiana				
Ball State University	1			
Indiana State U - Main Campus	1			
Indiana University - Bloomington	2		1	1
Purdue University - Main Campus	1		1	
	5		**2**	**1**
Kentucky				
University of Louisville		1	1	
		1	**1**	
Louisiana				
Grambling State University*	1			
Sthrn U A&M College - Main Cam*	6			
Southern U in New Orleans*	1			
Tulane U of Louisiana	2			
University of New Orleans			1	

(1700)

STATE/SCHOOL	MINORITY GROUP			
	Black	Hispanic	Asian	Native American
Louisiana (cont)				
U of Southwestern Louisiana	1			
Xavier University of Louisiana*	5			
	16		1	
Maryland				
Coppin State College*	3			
Morgan State University*	12			
Towson State University	4			
U of MD - College Park Campus		2		
U of MD - Eastern Shore*	4			
	23	2		
Massachussetts				
Boston State College	1			
Boston University	5		1	
Harvard University	2			3
Radcliffe College	2			
U of Mass - Amherst Campus			1	
	10		2	3
Michigan				
Eastern Michigan University	1			
Michigan State University			1	
Shaw College at Detroit*	1			
University of Detroit	1	1	3	
U of Michigan - Ann Arbor			2	
Wayne State University	3		1	
Western Michigan University	1			
	7	1	7	
Minnesota				
U of Minn - Minneapolis/St. Paul			2	
			2	
Mississippi				
Alcorn State University*	10			
Delta State University	2			

(1700)

STATE/SCHOOL	MINORITY GROUP			
	Black	Hispanic	Asian	Native American
Mississippi (cont)				
Jackson State University*	2			
Mississippi Industrial College*	1			
Mississippi State University	1			
Mississippi Valley State Univ*	5			
Tougaloo College*	4			
U of Southern Mississippi	2			
	27			
Missouri				
Park College	4			
St. Louis U - Main Campus	1			
Washington University	4		2	
Webster College	1			
	10		2	
Montana				
Montana State University				1
				1
Nebraska				
U of Nebraska at Omaha		1		
		1		
New Hampshire				
Dartmouth College	1			
	1			
New Jersey				
Glassboro State College	1			
Jersey City State College	1	3		
Kean College of New Jersey	1	1		
Montclair State College	1		1	
Princeton University				1
Rutgers U - Camden Campus	2			
Rutgers U - New Brunswick	4	1	1	

(1700)

STATE/SCHOOL	MINORITY GROUP			
	Black	Hispanic	Asian	Native American
New Jersey (cont)				
Rutgers U - Newark Campus		2	1	
Trenton State College	1			
	11	**7**	**3**	**1**
New Mexico				
Eastern NM U - Main Campus	1		1	
NM State U - Main Campus		3		
University of Albuquerque		2		
U of NM - Main Campus		2		
Western New Mexico University		2		
	1	**9**	**1**	
New York				
Adelphi University	1			
Cornell U Endowed College		1	3	1
CUNY Bernard Baruch College	2	1		
CUNY Brooklyn College	7			3
CUNY City College	6	2	1	
CUNY College of Staten Island	3	1		
CUNY Hunter College	5	2	1	
CUNY Lehman College	4	4	1	
CUNY Queen's College	7	2	2	
CUNY York College	7	2		
Fordham University	1	1	1	
Long Island U - Brooklyn Center	2		1	
Long Island U - C W Post Center			1	
Mercy College	2	1		
New York University	3	1	6	1
Pace University New York	1			
Polytechnic Institute New York	1	1	2	
St. John's University	1			
SUNY at Albany	1			
SUNY at Buffalo - Main Campus			1	

(1700)

STATE/SCHOOL	MINORITY GROUP			
	Black	Hispanic	Asian	Native American
New York (cont)				
SUNY at Stony Bk - Main Campus	1	1	6	
SUNY College at New Paltz		1		2
	55	21	26	7
North Carolina				
Bennett College*	1			
East Carolina University	1			
Elizabeth City State U*	6			
Fayetteville State University*	15			
Johnson C Smith University*	1			
Livingstone College*	1			
NC Agrl & Tech State University*	4			
NC Central University*	8			
NC State U - Raleigh	5			
Pembroke State University	1			3
St. Augustine's College*	3			
Shaw University*	4			
U of NC at Chapel Hill	2			1
U of NC at Charlotte	6	1		
U of NC at Greensboro	3			
Winston-Salem State University*	2			
	63	1		4
Ohio				
Bowling Green State U - Main Cam			1	
Central State University*	2			
Oberlin College	1		1	
Ohio State U - Main Campus	1			
U of Cincinnati - Main Campus	2	1		
University of Toledo	1			
Wilberforce University*	1			
	8	1	2	

(1700)

STATE/SCHOOL	MINORITY GROUP			
	Black	Hispanic	Asian	Native American
Oklahoma				
Cameron University		1		
Central State University	1			
Northeast Oklahoma State U	2			
	3	**1**		
Oregon				
Oregon State University				1
University of Oregon – Main Campus			3	1
			3	**2**
Pennsylvania				
Cheyney State College*	2			
Drexel University	3			
Lincoln University*	2			
Pennsylvania State U – Main Campus	1			
St. Joseph's University				1
Temple University	1			
University of Pennsylvania		1	2	
U of Pittsburgh – Main Campus	2			1
	11	**1**	**2**	**2**
Rhode Island				
Brown University	4		1	
	4		**1**	
South Carolina				
Allen University*	2			
Benedict College*	3			
Claflin College*	15			
Morris College*	2			
South Carolina State College*	12			
U of South Carolina at Columbia	3	2	1	
Winthrop College	5			
	42	**2**	**1**	

(1700)

STATE/SCHOOL	MINORITY GROUP			
	Black	Hispanic	Asian	Native American
Tennessee				
Fisk University*	2			
Knoxville College*	2			
Lane College*	3			
LeMoyne-Owen College*	7			
Tennessee State University*	10			
U of Tennessee - Knoxville	1			
	25			
Texas				
Corpus Christi State University		1		
East Texas State University	3		2	
Huston-Tillotson College*	1			
Jarvis Christian College*	2			
Lamar University				3
Laredo State University*		11		
Pan American University*		12		
Prairie View A&M University*	7			
St. Edward's University	1	1		
St. Mary's U - San Antonio		4		
Southwest Texas State University		1		
Sul Ross State University	1	1		
Texas A&I University	1	6		
Texas A&M U - Main Campus			1	
Texas Southern University*	5			
Texas Women's University		1		
U of Houston - Central Campus	4	1	3	
U of Texas at Arlington	1	1		
U of Texas at Austin		8		
U of Texas at El Paso		7		
U of Texas at San Antonio		3		
	26	**58**	**6**	**3**

568

(1700)

<table>
<tr><td>STATE/SCHOOL</td><td colspan="4">MINORITY GROUP</td></tr>
<tr><td></td><td>Black</td><td>Hispanic</td><td>Asian</td><td>Native American</td></tr>
<tr><td>Virginia</td><td></td><td></td><td></td><td></td></tr>
<tr><td>Hampton Institute*</td><td>5</td><td></td><td></td><td></td></tr>
<tr><td>Norfolk State College*</td><td>8</td><td></td><td></td><td></td></tr>
<tr><td>Old Dominion University</td><td>1</td><td></td><td></td><td></td></tr>
<tr><td>St. Paul's College*</td><td>2</td><td></td><td></td><td></td></tr>
<tr><td>Virginia Commonwealth University</td><td>2</td><td></td><td></td><td></td></tr>
<tr><td>Virginia State College*</td><td>4</td><td></td><td></td><td></td></tr>
<tr><td>Virginia Union University*</td><td>3</td><td></td><td></td><td></td></tr>
<tr><td></td><td>25</td><td></td><td></td><td></td></tr>
<tr><td>Washington</td><td></td><td></td><td></td><td></td></tr>
<tr><td>University of Washington</td><td></td><td>1</td><td>5</td><td></td></tr>
<tr><td></td><td></td><td>1</td><td>5</td><td></td></tr>
<tr><td>West Virginia</td><td></td><td></td><td></td><td></td></tr>
<tr><td>West Virginia State College</td><td>4</td><td></td><td>1</td><td></td></tr>
<tr><td></td><td>4</td><td></td><td>1</td><td></td></tr>
<tr><td>Wisconsin</td><td></td><td></td><td></td><td></td></tr>
<tr><td>U of Wisconsin - Milwaukee</td><td>1</td><td></td><td>1</td><td></td></tr>
<tr><td></td><td>1</td><td></td><td>1</td><td></td></tr>
<tr><td>TOTALS</td><td>550</td><td>146</td><td>238</td><td>30</td></tr>
</table>

*Predominately minority institutions are those where at least 50% of the total BA Degrees awarded are to one of the minority groups being considered.

MATHEMATICS (1700)
BLACK BACCALAUREATE DEGREES RANKED BY INSTITUTION

Rank	Institution	B.A.'s	Rank	Institution	B.A.'s
1	Fayetteville State U*	15	6	Chicago State U*	10
2	Claflin C*	15	7	Tuskegee Institute*	10
3	Morgan State U*	12	8	Alcorn State U*	10
4	South Carolina State C*	12	9	Tennessee State U*	10
5	Spelman C*	10			

*predominantly black institutions

Institutions not ranked have less than ten degrees conferred on blacks.

MATHEMATICS (1700)
HISPANIC BACCALAUREATE DEGREES RANKED BY INSTITUTION

Rank	Institution	B.A.'s
1	Pan American U*	12
2	Laredo State U*	11

*predominantly Hispanic institutions

Institutions not ranked have less than ten degrees conferred on Hispanics.

MATHEMATICS (1700)
ASIAN BACCALAUREATE DEGREES RANKED BY INSTITUTION

Rank	Institution	B.A.'s	Rank	Institution	B.A.'s
1	U of Cal-Los Angeles	45	3	U of Hawaii at Manoa*	14
2	U of Cal-Berkeley	20	4	San Francisco State U	13

*predominantly Asian institutions

Institutions not ranked have less than ten degrees conferred on Asians.

MATHEMATICS (1700)
MINORITY BACCALAUREATE DEGREES
WITHIN 60 MILE RADIUS OF AIRPORT

AIRPORT	MINORITY GROUP			
	Black	Hispanic	Asian	Native American
ABQ=Albuquerque, NM				
U of NM -Main Campus		2		
University of Albuquerque		2		
		4		
ALB=Albany, NY				
SUNY at Albany	1			
	1			
AOO=Altoona, PA				
Pennsylvania State U - Main Campus	1			
	1			
ATL=Atlanta, GA				
Clark College*	6			
Georgia State University	2			
Morehouse College*	5			
Morris Brown College*	4			
Spelman College*	10			
	27			
AUS=Austin, TX				
Huston - Tillotson College*	1			
Southwest Texas State University		1		
U of Texas at Austin		8		
	1	**9**		
BAL=Baltimore, MD				
American University	4		1	
George Washington Univesity	1			1
Howard University*	5			
University of DC*	5			

Airport 60 (1700)

AIRPORT		MINORITY GROUP		
	Black	Hispanic	Asian	Native American
BAL (cont)				
Coppin State College*	3			
Morgan State University*	12			
Towson State University	4			
U of MD - College Park Campus		2		
Lincoln University*	2			
	36	**2**	**1**	**1**
BDL=Hartford, CT/Springfield, MA				
Yale University	1			
U of Mass - Amherst Campus			1	
	1		**1**	
BHM=Birmingham, AL				
Miles College*	2			
Stillman College*	3			
Talladega College*	9			
U of Alabama in Birmingham	1			
University of Alabama	3			
	18			
BKL=Cleveland-Lakefront, OH				
Oberlin College	1		1	
	1		**1**	
BNA=Nashville, TN				
Fisk University*	2			
Tennessee State University*	10			
	12			
BOS=Boston, MA				
Boston State College	1			
Boston University	5		1	
Harvard University	2			3
Radcliffe College	2			
Brown University	4		1	
	14		**2**	**3**

Airport 60 (1700)

AIRPORT		MINORITY GROUP		
	Black	Hispanic	Asian	Native American
BTR=Baton Rouge, LA				
Sthrn U A&M College - Main Cam*	6			
	6			
BUF=Buffalo, NY				
SUNY at Buffalo - Main Campus			1	
			1	
CAE=Columbia, SC				
Allen University*	2			
Benedict College*	3			
Claflin College*	15			
Morris College*	2			
South Carolina State College*	12			
U of South Carolina at Columbia	3	2	1	
	37	**2**	**1**	
CIC=Chico, CA				
Cal State University - Chico			1	
			1	
CLT=Charlotte, NC				
Johnson C Smith University*	1			
Livingstone College*	1			
U of NC at Charlotte	6	1		
Winthrop College	5			
	13	**1**		
CMH=Columbus, OH				
Central State University*	2			
Wilberforce University*	1			
	3			
CMI=Champaign, IL				
Illinois State University	1		1	
U of Illinois - Urbana Campus	1		1	1
Indiana State U - Main Campus	1			
	3		**2**	**1**

Airport 60 (1700)

AIRPORT	MINORITY GROUP			
	Black	Hispanic	Asian	Native American
CRP=Corpus Christi, TX				
Corpus Christi State University		1		
Texas A&I University	1	6		
	1	7		
CRW=Charleston, WV				
West Virginia State College	4		1	
	4		1	
CVG=Cincinnati, OH				
Central State University*	2			
U of Cincinnati - Main Campus	2	1		
Wilberforce University*	1			
	5	1		
DAB=Dayton Beach, FL				
Bethune Cookman College*	9			
	9			
DCA=Washington-National, DC				
American University	4		1	
George Washington University	1			1
Howard University*	5			
University of DC*	5			
Coppin State College*	3			
Morgan State University*	12			
Towson State University	4			
U of MD - College Park Campus		2		
	34	2	1	1
DEN=Denver, CO				
Metropolitan State College	2	2		
U of Colorado at Boulder	1		1	
	3	2	1	

574

Airport 60 (1700)

AIRPORT	MINORITY GROUP			
	Black	Hispanic	Asian	Native American
DFW=Dallas/Fort Worth, TX				
East Texas State University	3		2	
Texas Woman's University		1		
U of Texas at Arlington	1	1		
	4	**2**	**2**	
DTW=Detroit-Metropolitan, MI				
Eastern Michigan University	1			
Shaw College at Detroit*	1			
U of Michigan - Ann Arbor			2	
University of Detroit	1	1	3	
Wayne State University	3		1	
University of Toledo	1			
	7	**1**	**6**	
ELP=El Paso, TX				
U of Texas at El Paso		7		
		7		
EUG=Eugene, OR				
Oregon State University				1
University of Oregon - Main Campus			3	1
			3	**2**
FAT=Fresno, CA				
Cal State University - Fresno	1	1	1	
	1	**1**	**1**	
FAY=Fayetteville, NC				
Fayetteville State University*	15			
NC Central University*	8			
NC State U - Raleigh	5			
Pembroke State University	1			3
St. Augustine's College*	3			
Shaw University*	4			
U of NC at Chapel Hill	2			1
	38			**4**

Airport 60 (1700)

AIRPORT	Black	Hispanic	Asian	Native American
FLG=Flagstaff, AZ				
Northern Arizona University		1		
		1		
GLH=Greenville, MS				
Delta State University	2			
Mississippi Valley State U*	5			
	7			
GRR=Grand Rapids, MI				
Western Michigan University	1			
	1			
GSO=Greensboro/High Point, NC				
Bennett College*	1			
Livingstone College*	1			
NC Agrl & Tech State University*	4			
NC Central University*	8			
U of NC at Chapel Hill	2			1
U of NC at Greensboro	3			
Winston-Salem State University*	2			
	21			1
HNL=Honolulu/Oahu, HI				
University of Hawaii at Manoa*			14	
			14	
HSV=Huntsville, AL/Decatur, GA				
Alabama A&M University*	3			
Oakwood College*	1			
	4			
IAH=Houston-Intercontinental,TX				
Prairie View A&M University*	7			
Texas Southern University*	5			
U of Houston - Central Campus	4	1	3	
	16	1	3	

MINORITY GROUP

576

Airport 60 (1700)

AIRPORT	MINORITY GROUP			
	Black	Hispanic	Asian	Native American
IND=Indianapolis, IN				
Ball State University	1			
Indiana University - Bloomington	2		1	1
Purdue University - Main Campus	1		1	
	4		2	1
ITO=Hilo, HI				
University of Hawaii at Hilo*			2	
			2	
JAN=Jackson/Vicksburg, MS				
Alcorn State University*	10			
Jackson State University*	2			
Tougaloo College*	4			
	16			
JAX=Jacksonville, FL				
Edward Waters College*	2			
	2			
JFK=New York, Kennedy Int'l, NY				
Jersey City State College	1	3		
Kean College of New Jersey	1	1		
Montclair State College	1		1	
Princeton University				1
Rutgers U - New Brunswick	4	1	1	
Rutgers U - Newark Campus		2	1	
Trenton State College	1			
Adelphi University	1			
CUNY Bernard Baruch College	2	1		
CUNY Brooklyn College	7			3
CUNY College of Staten Island	3	1		
CUNY City College	6	2	1	
CUNY Hunter College	5	2	1	
CUNY Lehman College	4	4	1	

Airport 60 (1700)

AIRPORT	MINORITY GROUP			
	Black	Hispanic	Asian	Native American
JFK (cont)				
CUNY Queen's College	7	2	2	
CUNY York College	7	2		
Fordham University	1	1	1	
Long Island U – Brooklyn Center	2		1	
Long Island U – C W Post Center			1	
Mercy College	2	1		
New York University	3	1	6	1
Pace University New York	1			
Polytechnic Institute New York	1	1	2	
St. John's University	1			
SUNY at Stony Bk – Main Campus	1	1	6	
	62	26	25	5
LAX=Los Angeles, CA				
Cal State College – San Bernardino		1	1	
Cal State University – Fullerton			2	
Cal State University – Long Beach	1	2	5	
Cal State University – Los Angeles	4	2	7	
Cal State University – Northridge			2	
Loyola Marymount University		1		
Pepperdine University		1		
U of Cal – Irvine		2	3	
U of Cal – Los Angeles	5	2	45	1
U of Cal – Riverside	1		3	
University of Southern California	2		3	
University of LaVerne			1	
	13	11	72	1
LEX=Lexington/Frankfort, KY				
University of Louisville		1	1	
		1	1	

578

Airport 60 (1700)

AIRPORT	MINORITY GROUP			
	Black	Hispanic	Asian	Native American
LIT=Little Rock, AR				
Philander Smith College*	2			
University of Arkansas - Pine Bluff*	9			
	11			
LRD=Laredo, TX				
Laredo State University*		11		
		11		
MCI=Kansas City-International, MO				
Park College	4			
	4			
MCN=Macon, GA				
Fort Valley State College*	5			
	5			
MDH=Carbondale, IL				
Southern Illinois U - Carbondale			1	
			1	
MEM=Memphis, TN				
Mississippi Industrial College*	1			
Le Moyne-Owen College*	7			
	8			
MFE=McAllen, TX				
Pan American University*		12		
		12		
MGM=Montgomery, GA				
Troy State University - Main Campus	2			
Tuskegee Institute*	10			
	12			
MHT=Manchester, NH				
Harvard University	2			3
Radcliffe College	2			
Dartmouth College	1			
	5			3

Airport 60 (1700)

AIRPORT		MINORITY GROUP		
	Black	Hispanic	Asian	Native American
MIA=Miami, FL				
Biscayne College*		3		
Florida International University		3		
Florida Memorial College*	2			
University of Miami		3	1	
	2	9	1	
MKE=Milwaukee, WS				
U of Wisconsin - Milwaukee	1		1	
	1		1	
MKL=Jackson, TN				
Lane College*	3			
	3			
MLU=Monroe, LA				
Grambling State University*	1			
	1			
MOB=Mobile, AL/Pasagoula, MS				
University of West Florida			1	
			1	
MSP=Minneapolis/St. Paul, MN				
U of Minn - Minneapolis/St. Paul			2	
			2	
MSY=New Orleans, LA				
Southern U in New Orleans*	1			
Tulane U of Louisiana	2			
University of New Orleans			1	
Xavier University of Louisiana*	5			
	8		1	
ORD=Chicago–O'Hare Airport, IL				
Chicago State University*	10			
DePaul University			1	
Loyola University of Chicago		1	1	

Airport 60 (1700)

AIRPORT	MINORITY GROUP			
	Black	Hispanic	Asian	Native American
ORD (cont)				
Northern Illinois University	1			
Northwestern University	3		1	
U of Illinois - Chicago Circle	4	1	8	
	18	2	11	
ORF=Norfolk/Virginia Beach, VA				
Elizabeth City State U*	6			
Hampton Institute*	5			
Norfolk State College*	8			
Old Dominion University	1			
	20			
PHL=Philadelphia, PA/Wilmington, DE				
Delaware State College*	1			
Glassboro State College	1			
Princeton University				1
Rutgers U - Camden Campus	2			
Rutgers U - New Brunswick	4	1	1	
Trenton State College	1			
Cheyney State College*	2			
Drexel University	3			
Lincoln University*	2			
St. Joseph's University				1
Temple University	1			
University of Pennsylvania		1	2	
	17	2	3	2
PHX=Phoenix, AZ				
Arizona State University			1	
			1	
PIT=Pittsburgh, PA				
U of Pittsburgh - Main Campus	2			1
	2			1

Airport 60 (1700)

AIRPORT		MINORITY GROUP		
	Black	Hispanic	Asian	Native American
PVD=Providence, RI				
Boston State College	1			
Boston University	5		1	
Harvard University	2			3
Radcliffe College	2			
Brown University	4		1	
	14		**2**	**3**
PWA=Oklahoma City-Wiley Post, OK				
Central State University	1			
	1			
RDU=Raleigh/Durham, NC				
Bennet College*	1			
Fayetteville State University*	15			
NC Agrl & Tech State University*	4			
NC Central University*	8			
NC State U - Raleigh	5			
St. Augustine's College*	3			
Shaw University*	4			
U of NC at Chapel Hill	2			1
U of NC at Greensboro	3			
	45			**1**
RIC=Richmond, VA				
Virginia Commonwealth University	2			
Virginia State College*	4			
Virginia Union University*	3			
	9			
SAN=San Diego, CA				
San Diego State University			4	
U of Cal - San Diego		1		
		1	**4**	

Airport 60 (1700)

AIRPORT	MINORITY GROUP			
	Black	Hispanic	Asian	Native American
SAT=San Antonio, TX				
St. Edward's University	1	1		
St. Mary's U – San Antonio		4		
Southwest Texas State University		1		
U of Texas at San Antonio		3		
	1	9		
SAV=Savannah, GA				
Savannah State College*	2			
	2			
SBA=Santa Barbara, CA				
Pepperdine University		1		
U of Cal – Santa Barbara			2	
		1	2	
SBP=San Luis Obispo, CA				
Cal Poly State U – San Luis Obispo		1	1	
		1	1	
SBY=Salisbury, MD				
U of MD – Eastern Shore*	4			
	4			
SEA=Seattle/Tacoma, WA				
University of Washington		1	5	
		1	5	
SFO=San Francisco/Oakland, CA				
Cal State University – Hayward	2	1	2	
San Francisco State University		2	13	
San Jose State University	4		8	
Stanford University	1	3	4	
U of Cal – Berkeley	1		20	
University of San Francisco		1		
	8	7	47	

Airport 60 (1700)

AIRPORT	MINORITY GROUP			
	Black	Hispanic	Asian	Native American
SHV=Shreveport, LA				
Grambling State University*	1			
	1			
STL=St. Louis, MO				
Southern Illinois U - Edwardsville				1
St. Louis U - Main Campus	1			
Washington University	4		2	
Webster College	1			
	6		2	1
SVC=Silver City, NM				
Western New Mexico University		2		
		2		
SWI=Sherman, TX				
East Texas State University	3		2	
Texas Woman's University		1		
	3	1	2	
SYR=Syracuse, NY				
Cornel U Endowed College		1	3	1
		1	3	1
TCL=Tuscaloosa, AL				
Miles College*	2			
Stillman College*	3			
U of Alabama in Birmingham	1			
University of Alabama	3			
	9			
TLH=Tallahassee, FL				
Florida State University	1			
	1			
TPA=Tampa, FL				
University of South Florida	1			
	1			

584

Airport 60 (1700)

AIRPORT		MINORITY GROUP		
	Black	Hispanic	Asian	Native American
TUL=Tulsa, OK				
Northeast Oklahoma State U	2			
	2			
TUS=Tucson, AZ				
University of Arizona		1		
		1		
TYR=Tyler, TX				
Jarvis Christian College*	2			
	2			
TYS=Knoxville, TN				
Knoxville College*	2			
U of Tennessee – Knoxville	1			
	3			

MATHEMATICS (1700)
MINORITY BACCALAUREATE DEGREES
WITHIN 61-80 MILE ANNULUS OF AIRPORT

AIRPORT	MINORITY GROUP			
	Black	Hispanic	Asian	Native American
ALB=Albany, NY				
U of Mass - Amherst Campus			1	
SUNY College at New Paltz		1		2
		1	**1**	**2**
ALM=Alamogordo, NM				
NM State U - Main Campus		3		
		3		
ATL=Atlanta, GA				
Jacksonville State University		1	2	
		1	**2**	
AUS=Austin, TX				
St. Edward's University	1	1		
St. Mary's U - San Antonio		4		
U of Texas at San Antonio		3		
	1	**8**		
BAL=Baltimore, MD				
Delaware State College*	1			
Cheyney State College*	2			
	3			
BDL=Hartford, CT/Springfield, MA				
Mercy College	2	1		
SUNY at Albany	1			
SUNY College at New Paltz		1		2
Brown University	4		1	
	7	**2**	**1**	**2**
BHM=Birmingham, AL				
Jacksonville State University		1	2	
		1	**2**	

586

Airport 61-80 (1700)

AIRPORT		MINORITY GROUP		
	Black	Hispanic	Asian	Native American
BOS=Boston, MA				
U of Mass - Amherst Campus			1	
			1	
BTM=Butte, MT				
Montana State University				1
				1
BTR=Baton Rouge, LA				
Southern U in New Orleans*	1			
Tulane U of Louisiana	2			
U of Southwestern Louisiana	1			
University of New Orleans			1	
Xavier University of Louisiana*	5			
	8		1	
CAE=Columbia, SC				
Paine College*	3			
Winthrop College	5			
	8			
CHS=Charleston, SC				
Savannah State College*	2			
Claflin College*	15			
South Carolina State College*	12			
	29			
CLT=Charlotte, NC				
Wintson-Salem State University*	2			
	2			
CMH=Columbus, OH				
Ohio University - Main Campus	1			
	1			
CMI=Champaign, IL				
Purdue University - Main Campus	1		1	
	1		1	

Airport 61-80 (1700)

AIRPORT	MINORITY GROUP			
	Black	Hispanic	Asian	Native American
COS=Colorado Springs, CO				
Metropolitan State College	2	2		
U of Colorado at Boulder	1		1	
	3	2	1	
CRW=Charleston, WV				
Ohio University - Main Campus	1			
	1			
DCA=Washington-National, DC				
Lincoln University*	2			
	2			
DTW=Detroit-Metropolitan, MI				
Michigan State University			1	
Bowling Green State U - Main Cam			1	
			2	
GRR=Grand Rapids, MI				
Michigan State University			1	
			1	
GSO=Greensboro/High Point, NC				
NC State U - Raleigh	5			
St. Augustine's College*	3			
Shaw University*	4			
	12			
HSV=Huntsville, AL/Decatur, GA				
Jacksonville State University		1	2	
		1	2	
IND=Indianapolis, IN				
Indiana State U - Main Campus	1			
	1			
JAX=Jacksonville, FL				
University of Florida	1	2	1	
	1	2	1	

Airport 61-80 (1700)

AIRPORT	MINORITY GROUP			
	Black	Hispanic	Asian	Native American
JFK=New York, Kennedy Int'l, NY				
Yale University	1			
SUNY College at New Paltz		1		2
	1	1		2
LAX=Los Angeles, CA				
Cal State College - Bakersfield	1			2
University of Redlands			1	
	1		1	2
LCH=Lake Charles, LA				
U of Southwestern Louisiana	1			
Lamar University				3
	1			3
MCN=Macon, GA				
Clark College*	6			
Georgia State University	2			
Morehouse College*	5			
Morris Brown College*	4			
Spelman College*	10			
	27			
MEM=Memphis, TN				
Lane College*	3			
	3			
MGM=Montgomery, GA				
Talladega College*	9			
	9			
MHT=Manchester, NH				
Boston State College	1			
Boston University	5		1	
U of Mass - Amherst Campus			1	
	6		2	

Airport 61-80 (1700)

AIRPORT	MINORITY GROUP			
	Black	Hispanic	Asian	Native American
MKE=Milwaukee, WS				
Northwestern University	3		1	
	3		1	
MKL=Jackson, TN				
Mississippi Industrial College*	1			
	1			
MLU=Monroe, LA				
Alcorn State University*	10			
	10			
MOB=Mobile, AL/Pasagoula, MS				
U of Southern Mississippi	2			
	2			
MSN=Madison, WS				
U of Wisconsin - Milwaukee	1		1	
	1		1	
MSY=New Orleans, LA				
Sthrn U A&M C - Main Cam*	6			
	6			
ORF=Norfolk/Virginia Beach, VA				
Virginia State College*	4			
	4			
PVD=Providence, RI				
U of Mass - Amherst Campus			1	
			1	
RDU=Raleigh/Durham, NC				
East Carolina University	1			
St. Paul's College*	2			
	3			
RIC=Richmond, VA				
Hampton Institute*	5			
Norfolk State College*	8			
St. Paul's College*	2			
	15			

590

Airport 61-80 (1700)

AIRPORT	MINORITY GROUP			
	Black	Hispanic	Asian	Native American
SAN=San Diego, CA				
U of Cal - Irvine		2	3	
U of Cal - Riverside	1		3	
	1	2	6	
SAT=San Antonio, TX				
Huston-Tillotson College*	1			
U of Texas at Austin		8		
	1	8		
SBA=Santa Barbara, CA				
Cal State College - Bakersfield	1			2
Cal State University - Los Angeles	4	2	7	
Cal State University - Northridge			2	
Loyola Marymount University		1		
U of Cal - Los Angeles	5	2	45	1
	10	5	54	3
SBY=Salisbury, MD				
Delaware State College*	1			
	1			
SFO=San Francisco/Oakland, CA				
Cal State University - Sacramento			2	
U of Cal-Davis	4			
University of the Pacific	1			
	5		2	
SWI=Sherman, TX				
U of Texas at Arlington	1	1		
	1	1		
TLH=Tallahassee, FL				
Albany State College*	5			
Valdosta State College	1			
	6			
TYR=Tyler, TX				
East Texas State University	3		2	
	3		2	

MATHEMATICS (1700)
MINORITY BACCALAUREATE DEGREES
MORE THAN 80 MILES FROM NEAREST AIRPORT

AIRPORT	MINORITY GROUP			
	Black	Hispanic	Asian	Native American
AUS=Austin, TX				
Texas A&M U - Main Campus			1	
			1	
ELP=El Paso, TX				
Sul Ross State University	1	1		
	1	1		
IAH=Houston-Intercontinental, TX				
Texas A&M U - Main Campus			1	
			1	
MAF=Midland/Odessa, TX				
Sul Ross State University	1	1		
	1	1		
MSY=New Orleans, LA				
U of Southern Mississippi	2			
	2			
PWA=Oklahoma City-Wiley Post, OK				
Cameron University		1		
		1		
ROW=Roswell, NM				
Eastern NM U - Main Campus	1			1
	1			1
TCL=Tuscaloosa, AL				
Mississippi State University	1			
	1			

PHYSICAL SCIENCES (1900)

PHYSICAL SCIENCES (1900)
MINORITY BACCALAUREATE DEGREES
BY STATE AND INSTITUTION

STATE/SCHOOL	MINORITY GROUP			
	Black	Hispanic	Asian	Native American
Alabama				
Alabama A&M University*	3			
Alabama State University*	1			
Jacksonville State University			1	
Stillman College*	4			
Talladega College*	2			
Troy State University - Main Campus	2			
Tuskegee Institute*	2			
University of Alabama	2			
University of South Alabama	2		1	
	18		**2**	
Arizona				
Arizona State University	1	1	2	
University of Arizona		2	2	
	1	**3**	**4**	
Arkansas				
Arkansas State U - Main Campus	1			
Henderson State University	1			
University of Arkansas - Pine Bluff*	7			
University of Central Arkansas	3			
	12			
California				
Cal State Poly U - Pomona	1	1	1	
Cal State U - Dominguez Hills	2		2	
Cal State University - Fresno		1		1
Cal State University - Fullerton		1	4	
Cal State University - Hayward	1	3	2	1
Cal State University - Long Beach		4	3	

594

(1900)

STATE/SCHOOL	MINORITY GROUP			
	Black	Hispanic	Asian	Native American
California (cont)				
Cal State University – Los Angeles	1	3	5	
Cal State University – Northridge	1	1	1	
Cal State University – Sacramento			3	1
Chapman College	1			
Loyola Marymount University	2	1		
Pepperdine University	1			
San Diego State University	1	1	1	1
San Francisco State University	3	2	6	2
San Jose State University		3	9	
Stanford University	2	2	4	
U of Cal – Berkeley	2	2	15	1
U of Cal – Davis	1	2	1	
U of Cal – Irvine		1	12	1
U of Cal – Los Angeles	2		13	1
U of Cal – San Diego		1	3	1
U of Cal – Santa Barbara		1	2	
U of Cal – Santa Cruz		3		
University of Southern California	2	1	6	1
University of the Pacific		1		
	23	**35**	**93**	**11**
Colorado				
Colorado State University	1	1	2	
Metropolitan State College	1	1		
U of Colorado at Boulder			1	
U of Southern Colorado		2	1	
	2	**4**	**4**	
Connecticut				
Yale University		2	2	
		2	**2**	

(1900)

STATE/SCHOOL	MINORITY GROUP			
	Black	Hispanic	Asian	Native American
Delaware				
Delaware State College*	3			
University of Delaware				1
	3			**1**
District of Columbia				
George Washington University	3	1		
Howard University*	22			
University of DC*	3	1		
	28	**2**		
Florida				
Bethune Cookman College*	1	1		
Biscayne College*	1	2		
Florida Agr & Mech University*	4			
Florida Atlantic University		2	1	
Florida International University	3	11		
Florida State University	3	1	1	
University of Florida		8	3	
University of Miami	2	32	4	
University of South Florida	2	7		1
	16	**64**	**9**	**1**
Georgia				
Clark College*	2			
Fort Valley State College*	2			
GA Inst of Tech - Main Campus		3	1	
Georgia State University	1			
Morehouse College*	9			
Paine College*	1			
Savannah State College*	8			
Spelman College*	4			
University of Georgia	3			
	30	**3**	**1**	

596

(1900)

STATE/SCHOOL	MINORITY GROUP			
	Black	Hispanic	Asian	Native American
Hawaii				
Chaminade University of Honolulu			1	
University of Hawaii at Hilo*			1	
University of Hawaii at Manoa*			16	
			18	
Illinois				
Bradley University	1		1	
Chicago State University*	5			
DePaul University		2		
Illinois State University	1			
Loyola University of Chicago			1	
Northern Illinois University	1		1	
Northeastern Illinois University		1	1	
Northwestern University	4		1	1
Roosevelt University	1			
Southern Illinois U - Carbondale			2	
Southern Illinois U - Edwardsville			1	
U of Illinois - Chicago Circle	1	1	9	
U of Illinois - Urbana Campus	1		1	2
	15	4	18	3
Indiana				
Indiana State U - Main Campus	1			
Indiana University - Bloomington	2		3	
Indiana University - Northwest	1			
	4		3	
Kentucky				
University of Louisville			1	2
			1	2
Louisiana				
Dillard University*	9			
Grambling State University*	4			
McNeese State University			1	

(1900)

STATE/SCHOOL	MINORITY GROUP			
	Black	Hispanic	Asian	Native American
Louisiana (cont)				
Northeast Louisiana University	2			
Sthrn U A&M College - Main Cam*	4			
Southern U in New Orleans*	2			
Tulane U of Louisiana	2	3	1	
University of New Orleans	2	1		
U of Southwestern Louisiana	2			
Xavier University of Louisiana*	9			
	36	4	2	
Maryland				
Morgan State University*	5			
Towson State University	1		1	
U of MD - Baltimore Co Campus	1			
U of MD - College Park Campus	4	2	1	
	11	2	2	
Massachussetts				
Boston University			1	1
Harvard University	1		2	
Radcliffe College	1			
Tufts University	2	2	3	
U of Mass - Amherst Campus		2	1	
	4	4	7	1
Michigan				
Eastern Michigan University	1			
Michigan State University	1	1	2	
University of Detroit	1			
U of Michigan - Ann Arbor	1	1	1	
Wayne State University	4		1	
	8	2	4	
Minnesota				
U of Minn - Minneapolis/St. Paul			2	
			2	

598

(1900)

STATE/SCHOOL	MINORITY GROUP			
	Black	Hispanic	Asian	Native American
Mississippi				
Alcorn State University*	11			
Delta State University	1			
Jackson State University*	13			
Mississippi State University	2			
Mississippi University for Women	2		1	
Mississippi Valley State Univ*	6			
Rust College*	1			
Tougaloo College*	12			
U of Mississippi – Main Campus	5	1	2	
U of Southern Mississippi	4		1	
	57	1	4	
Missouri				
St. Louis U – Main Campus	3	2	2	
U of Missouri – St. Louis	2	1		
Washington University			2	
	5	3	4	
Montana				
Montana State University				1
				1
Nebraska				
U of Nebraska at Omaha	2	2	2	
	2	2	2	
New Hampshire				
Dartmouth College	1		2	
	1		2	
New Jersey				
Glassboro State College	2			
Kean College of New Jersey		1	1	
Montclair State College	2	2		
Princeton University	1	2	4	

(1900)

STATE/SCHOOL	MINORITY GROUP			
	Black	Hispanic	Asian	Native American
New Jersey (cont)				
Rutgers U – Camden Campus	1	1		
Rutgers U – New Brunswick	1	1	5	
Rutgers U – Newark Campus		3	3	
Trenton State College	2			
	9	**10**	**13**	
New Mexico				
New Mexico Highlands U*		3		
NM State U – Main Campus		3	1	
U of NM – Main Campus	1	3		
Western New Mexico University		1		
	1	**10**	**1**	
New York				
College of New Rochelle	1			
Cornell U Endowed College	7	3	6	
CUNY Brooklyn College	14	6	1	
CUNY City College	17	7	5	1
CUNY College of Staten Island	1			
CUNY Hunter College	6	4	1	1
CUNY Lehman College	4	2	1	
CUNY Queen's College	7	2	2	
CUNY York College	10	3	1	
Fordham University		1	1	
Long Island U – Brooklyn Center	3	2		
Long Island U – C W Post Center		3		
New York University	4		6	
Pace University New York			1	
Polytechnic Institute New York	1	1	2	
Pratt Institute	3			
St. Francis College	1			
SUNY at Albany		1	1	1
SUNY at Buffalo – Main Campus	1	1		

(1900)

STATE/SCHOOL	MINORITY GROUP			
	Black	Hispanic	Asian	Native American
New York (cont)				
SUNY at Stony Bk - Main Campus			2	
SUNY College at Buffalo				1
Syracuse University - Main Campus	1	1	1	
	81	37	31	4
North Carolina				
Bennett College*	2			
Duke University	2	2	3	
East Carolina University	1			
Elizabeth City State U*	2			
Fayetteville State University*	2			
Johnson C Smith University*	7			
Livingstone College*	6			
NC Agrl & Tech State University*	1			
NC Central University*	8			
NC State U - Raleigh	1			1
Pembroke State University				3
Shaw University*	2			
U of NC at Chapel Hill	12	1	2	
U of NC at Charlotte	2			
	48	3	5	4
North Dakota				
U of North Dakota - Main Campus			1	
			1	
Ohio				
Antioch University	1			
Bowling Green State U - Main Cam			1	
Central State University*	7			
Kent State U - Main Campus				1
Oberlin College			1	
Ohio University - Main Campus	3			

(1900)

STATE/SCHOOL	MINORITY GROUP			
	Black	Hispanic	Asian	Native American
Ohio (cont)				
U of Akron - Main Campus	1			
U of Cincinnati - Main Campus	2			
University of Toledo				1
Wilberforce University*	1			
Wright State U - Main Campus	5			
	20		**2**	**2**
Oklahoma				
Cameron University		2		
Langston University*	1			
Northeast Oklahoma State U				2
Southeast Oklahoma State U			1	
U of Oklahoma - Norman Campus			2	1
	1	**2**	**3**	**3**
Oregon				
Oregon State University				1
University of Oregon - Main Campus			3	
			3	**1**
Pennsylvania				
Cheyney State College*	8			
Lincoln University*	2			
Pennsylvania State U - Main Campus	3	2	4	2
St. Joseph's University	3			2
Temple University	1		1	
University of Pennsylvania	1		6	
U of Pittsburgh - Main Campus	7			
	25	**2**	**11**	**4**
South Carolina				
Allen University*	2			
Benedict College*	6			
Claflin College*	7			

602

(1900)

| | MINORITY GROUP | | | |
STATE/SCHOOL	Black	Hispanic	Asian	Native American
South Carolina (cont)				
South Carolina State College*	4			
U of South Carolina at Columbia	2	1		
	21	1		
Tennessee				
Austin Peay State University				
Fisk University*	10			
Knoxville College*	2			
Lane College*	1			
LeMoyne-Owen College*	1			
Memphis State University	3		1	
Middle Tennessee State U	2			1
Tennessee State University*	2			
U of Tennessee – Knoxville	1			
	22		1	1
Texas				
Bishop College*	4			
Corpus Christi State University		1		
East Texas State University		1		
Jarvis Christian College*	1			
Lamar University	1			4
North Texas State University	1			
Our Lady of Lake University*			1	
Pan American University*		5		
Prairie View A&M University*	9			
St. Mary's U – San Antonio		4		
Sam Houston State University			1	
Southwest Texas State University	1			1
Texas A&I University		5		
Texas A&M U – Main Campus		2		
Texas Southern University*	3			
Texas Women's University			1	

(1900)

STATE/SCHOOL	MINORITY GROUP			
	Black	Hispanic	Asian	Native American
Texas (cont)				
Trinity University		1		
U of Houston - Central Campus			1	
U of Texas at Arlington	3			
U of Texas at Austin	1	5	1	
U of Texas at El Paso	1	9	1	1
U of Texas at San Antonio		1	2	
	25	34	8	6
Utah				
University of Utah		1		
		1		
Virginia				
Hampton Institute*	2			
Norfolk State College*	2			
Old Dominion University	1			
Virginia Commonwealth University	3		3	
Virginia State College*	17			
Virginia Union University*	1			
	26		3	
Washington				
University of Washington	1	4	4	1
	1	4	4	1
West Virginia				
West Virginia State College			1	
			1	
Wisconsin				
U of Wisconsin - Madison			1	
			1	
TOTALS	556	240	273	44

*Predominately minority institutions are those where at least 50% of the total BA Degrees awarded are to one of the minority groups being considered.

604

PHYSICAL SCIENCES (1900)
BLACK BACCALAUREATE DEGREES RANKED BY INSTITUTION

Rank	Institution	B.A.'s	Rank	Institution	B.A.'s
1	Howard U*	22	6	Tougaloo C*	12
2	CUNY City C	17	7	U of NC at Chapel Hill	12
3	Virginia State C*	17	8	Alcorn State U*	11
4	CUNY Brooklyn C	14	9	CUNY York C	10
5	Jackson State U*	13	10	Fisk U*	10

*predominantly black institutions

Institutions not ranked have less than ten degrees conferred on blacks.

PHYSICAL SCIENCES (1900)
HISPANIC BACCALAUREATE DEGREES RANKED BY INSTITUTION

Rank	Institution	B.A.'s
1	U of Miami	32
2	Florida International U	11

Institutions not ranked have less than ten degrees conferred on Hispanics.

PHYSICAL SCIENCES (1900)
ASIAN BACCALAUREATE DEGREES RANKED BY INSTITUTION

Rank	Institution	B.A.'s	Rank	Institution	B.A.'s
1	U of Hawaii at Manoa*	16	3	U of Cal-Los Angeles	13
2	U of Cal-Berkeley	15	4	U of Cal-Irvine	12

*predominantly Asian institutions

Institutions not ranked have less than ten degrees conferred on Asians.

PHYSICAL SCIENCES (1900)
MINORITY BACCALAUREATE DEGREES
WITHIN 60 MILE RADIUS OF AIRPORT

AIRPORT	MINORITY GROUP			
	Black	Hispanic	Asian	Native American
ABQ=Albuquerque, NM				
U of NM – Main Campus	1	3		
	1	**3**		
ALB=Albany, NY				
SUNY at Albany		1	1	1
		1	**1**	**1**
AOO=Altoona, PA				
Pennsylvania State U – Main Campus	3	2	4	2
	3	**2**	**4**	**2**
ATL=Atlanta, GA				
Clark College*	2			
GA Inst of Tech – Main Campus		3	1	
Georgia State University	1			
Morehouse College*	9			
Spelman College*	4			
	16	**3**	**1**	
AUS=Austin, TX				
Southwest Texas State University	1			1
U of Texas at Austin	1	5	1	
	2	**5**	**1**	**1**
BAL=Baltimore, MD				
University of Delaware				1
George Washington Univesity	3	1		
Howard University*	22			
University of DC*	3	1		
Morgan State University*	5			
Towson State University	1		1	

Airport 60 (1900)

AIRPORT	MINORITY GROUP			
	Black	Hispanic	Asian	Native American
BAL (cont)				
U of MD - Baltimore Co Campus	1			
U of MD - College Park Campus	4	2	1	
Lincoln University*	2			
	41	**4**	**2**	**1**
BDL=Hartford, CT/Springfield, MA				
Yale University		2	2	
U of Mass - Amherst Campus		2	1	
		4	**3**	
BHM=Birmingham, AL				
Stillman College*	4			
Talladega College*	2			
University of Alabama	2			
	8			
BKL=Cleveland-Lakefront, OH				
Kent State U - Main Campus				1
Oberlin College			1	
U of Akron - Main Campus	1			
	1		**1**	**1**
BNA=Nashville, TN				
Fisk University*	10			
Middle Tennessee State U	2			1
Tennessee State University*	2			
	14			**1**
BOS=Boston, MA				
Boston University			1	1
Harvard University	1		2	
Radcliffe College	1			
Tufts University	2	2	3	
	4	**2**	**6**	**1**

Airport 60 (1900)

AIRPORT		MINORITY GROUP		
	Black	Hispanic	Asian	Native American
BTR=Baton Rouge, LA				
Sthrn U A&M College – Main Cam*	4			
	4			
BUF=Buffalo, NY				
SUNY at Buffalo – Main Campus	1	1		
SUNY College at Buffalo				1
	1	**1**		**1**
CAE=Columbia, SC				
Allen University*	2			
Benedict College*	6			
Claflin College*	7			
South Carolina State College*	4			
U of South Carolina at Columbia	2	1		
	21	**1**		
CLT=Charlotte, NC				
Johnson C Smith University*	7			
Livingstone College*	6			
U of NC at Charlotte	2			
	15			
CMH=Columbus, OH				
Central State University*	7			
Wilberforce University*	1			
	8			
CMI=Champaign, IL				
Illinois State University	1			
U of Illinois – Urbana Campus	1		1	2
Indiana State U – Main Campus	1			
	3		**1**	**2**
COS=Colorado Springs, CO				
U of Southern Colorado		2	1	
		2	**1**	

608

Airport 60 (1900)

AIRPORT	MINORITY GROUP			
	Black	Hispanic	Asian	Native American
CRP=Corpus Christi, TX				
Corpus Christi State University		1		
Texas A&I University		5		
		6		
CRW=Charleston, WV				
West Virginia State College			1	
			1	
CVG=Cincinnati, OH				
Antioch University	1			
Central State University*	7			
U of Cincinnati - Main Campus	2			
Wilberforce University*	1			
Wright State U - Main Campus	5			
	16			
DAB=Dayton Beach, FL				
Bethune Cookman College*	1	1		
	1	**1**		
DCA=Washington-National, DC				
George Washington University	3	1		
Howard University*	22			
University of DC*	3	1		
Morgan State University*	5			
Towson State University	1		1	
U of MD - Baltimore Co Campus	1			
U of MD - College Park Campus	4	2	1	
	39	**4**	**2**	
DEN=Denver, CO				
Metropolitan State College	1	1		
U of Colorado at Boulder			1	
	1	**1**	**1**	

Airport 60 (1900)

AIRPORT	MINORITY GROUP			
	Black	Hispanic	Asian	Native American
DFW=Dallas/Fort Worth, TX				
Bishop College*	4			
East Texas State University		1		
North Texas State University	1			
Texas Woman's University			1	
U of Texas at Arlington	3			
	8	1	1	
DTW=Detroit-Metropolitan, MI				
Eastern Michigan University	1			
U of Michigan - Ann Arbor	1	1	1	
University of Detroit	1			
Wayne State University	4		1	
University of Toledo				1
	7	1	2	1
ELP=El Paso, TX				
U of Texas at El Paso	1	9	1	1
	1	9	1	1
EUG=Eugene, OR				
Oregon State University				1
University of Oregon - Main Campus			3	
			3	1
FAT=Fresno, CA				
Cal State University - Fresno		1		1
		1		1
FAY=Fayetteville, NC				
Fayetteville State University*	2			
NC Central University*	8			
NC State U - Raleigh	1			1
Pembroke State University				3
Shaw University*	2			
U of NC at Chapel Hill	12	1	2	
	25	1	2	4

610

Airport 60 (1900)

AIRPORT	MINORITY GROUP			
	Black	Hispanic	Asian	Native American
GLH=Greenville, MS				
Delta State University	1			
Mississippi Valley State U*	6			
	7			
GSO=Greensboro/High Point, NC				
Bennett College*	2			
Duke University	2	2	3	
Livingstone College*	6			
NC Agrl & Tech State University*	1			
NC Central University*	8			
U of NC at Chapel Hill	12	1	2	
	31	3	5	
HNL=Honolulu/Oahu, HI				
Chaminade University of Honolulu			1	
University of Hawaii at Manoa*			16	
			17	
HSV=Huntsville, AL/Decatur, GA				
Alabama A&M University*	3			
	3			
IAH=Houston-Intercontinental,TX				
Prairie View A&M University*	9			
Texas Southern University*	3			
U of Houston - Central Campus			1	
	12		1	
IND=Indianapolis, IN				
Indiana University - Bloomington	2		3	
	2		3	
ITO=Hilo, HI				
University of Hawaii at Hilo*			1	
			1	

Airport 60 (1900)

AIRPORT	MINORITY GROUP			
	Black	Hispanic	Asian	Native American
JAN=Jackson/Vicksburg, MS				
Alcorn State University*	11			
Jackson State University*	13			
Tougaloo College*	12			
	36			
JFK=New York, Kennedy Int'l, NY				
Kean College of New Jersey		1	1	
Montclair State College	2	2		
Princeton University	1	2	4	
Rutgers U - New Brunswick	1	1	5	
Rutgers U - Newark Campus		3	3	
Trenton State College	2			
College of New Rochelle	1			
CUNY Brooklyn College	14	6	1	
CUNY College of Staten Island	1			
CUNY City College	17	7	5	1
CUNY Hunter College	6	4	1	1
CUNY Lehman College	4	2	1	
CUNY Queen's College	7	2	2	
CUNY York College	10	3	1	
Fordham University		1	1	
Long Island U - Brooklyn Center	3	2		
Long Island U - C W Post Center		3		
New York University	4		6	
Pace University New York			1	
Polytechnic Institute New York	1	1	2	
Pratt Institute	3			
St. Francis College	1			
SUNY at Stony Bk - Main Campus			2	
	78	**40**	**36**	**2**

Airport 60 (1900)

AIRPORT	MINORITY GROUP			
	Black	Hispanic	Asian	Native American
LAX=Los Angeles, CA				
Cal State Poly U - Pomona	1	1	1	
Cal State U - Dominguez Hills	2		2	
Cal State University - Fullerton		1	4	
Cal State University - Long Beach		4	3	
Cal State University - Los Angeles	1	3	5	
Cal State University - Northridge	1	1	1	
Chapman College	1			
Loyola Marymount University	2	1		
Pepperdine University	1			
U of Cal - Irvine		1	12	1
U of Cal - Los Angeles	2		13	1
University of Southern California	2	1	6	1
	13	**13**	**47**	**3**
LCH=Lake Charles, LA				
McNeese State University			1	
			1	
LEX=Lexington/Frankfort, KY				
University of Louisville		1	2	
		1	**2**	
LIT=Little Rock, AR				
University of Arkansas - Pine Bluff*	7			
University of Central Arkansas	3			
	10			
MCN=Macon, GA				
Fort Valley State College*	2			
	2			
MDH=Carbondale, IL				
Southern Illinois U - Carbondale			2	
			2	

Airport 60 (1900)

AIRPORT	MINORITY GROUP			
	Black	Hispanic	Asian	Native American
MEM=Memphis, TN				
Rust College*	1			
Le Moyne-Owen College*	1			
Memphis State University	3		1	
	5		1	
MFE=McAllen, TX				
Pan American University*		5		
		5		
MGM=Montgomery, GA				
Alabama State University*	1			
Troy State University - Main Campus	2			
Tuskegee Institute*	2			
	5			
MHT=Manchester, NH				
Harvard University	1		2	
Radcliffe College	1			
Tufts University	2	2	3	
Dartmouth College	1		2	
	5	2	7	
MIA=Miami, FL				
Biscayne College*	1	2		
Florida Atlantic University		2	1	
Florida International University	3	11		
University of Miami	2	32	4	
	6	47	5	
MKL=Jackson, TN				
Lane College*	1			
	1			
MLU=Monroe, LA				
Grambling State University*	4			
Northeast Louisiana University	2			
	6			

Airport 60 (1900)

AIRPORT	MINORITY GROUP			
	Black	Hispanic	Asian	Native American
MOB=Mobile, AL/Pasagoula, MS				
University of South Alabama	2		1	
	2		1	
MSN=Madison, WS				
U of Wisconsin – Madison			1	
			1	
MSP=Minneapolis/St. Paul, MN				
U of Minn – Minneapolis/St. Paul			2	
			2	
MSY=New Orleans, LA				
Dillard University*	9			
Southern U in New Orleans*	2			
Tulane U of Louisiana	2	3	1	
University of New Orleans	2	1		
Xavier University of Louisiana*	9			
	24	4	1	
ORD=Chicago–O'Hare Airport, IL				
Chicago State University*	5			
DePaul University		2		
Loyola University of Chicago			1	
Northern Illinois University	1		1	
Northwestern University	4		1	1
Northeastern Illinois University		1	1	
Roosevelt University	1			
U of Illinois – Chicago Circle	1	1	9	
Indiana University – Northwest	1			
	13	4	13	1
ORF=Norfolk/Virginia Beach, VA				
Elizabeth City State U*	2			
Hampton Institute*	2			
Norfolk State College*	2			
Old Dominion University	1			
	7			

Airport 60 (1900)

AIRPORT	MINORITY GROUP			
	Black	Hispanic	Asian	Native American
PHL=Philadelphia, PA/Wilmington, DE				
Delaware State College*	3			
University of Delaware				1
Glassboro State College	2			
Princeton University	1	2	4	
Rutgers U - Camden Campus	1	1		
Rutgers U - New Brunswick	1	1	5	
Trenton State College	2			
Cheyney State College*	8			
Lincoln University*	2			
St. Joseph's University	3			2
Temple University	1		1	
University of Pennsylvania	1		6	
	25	4	16	3
PHX=Phoenix, AZ				
Arizona State University	1	1	2	
	1	1	2	
PIA=Peoria, IL				
Bradley University	1		1	
	1		1	
PIT=Pittsburgh, PA				
U of Pittsburgh - Main Campus	7			
	7			
PVD=Providence, RI				
Boston University			1	1
Harvard University	1		2	
Radcliffe College	1			
Tufts University	2	2	3	
	4	2	6	1
PWA=Oklahoma City-Wiley Post, OK				
Langston University*	1			
U of Oklahoma - Norman Campus			2	1
	1		2	1

Airport 60 (1900)

AIRPORT	MINORITY GROUP			
	Black	Hispanic	Asian	Native American
RDU=Raleigh/Durham, NC				
Bennet College*	2			
Duke University	2	2	3	
Fayetteville State University*	2			
NC Agrl & Tech State University*	1			
NC Central University*	8			
NC State U – Raleigh	1			1
Shaw University*	2			
U of NC at Chapel Hill	12	1	2	
	30	3	5	1
RIC=Richmond, VA				
Virginia Commonwealth University	3		3	
Virginia State College*	17			
Virginia Union University*	1			
	21		3	
SAN=San Diego, CA				
San Diego State University	1	1	1	1
U of Cal – San Diego		1	3	1
	1	2	4	2
SAT=San Antonio, TX				
Our Lady of Lake University*			1	
St. Mary's U – San Antonio		4		
Southwest Texas State University	1			1
Trinity University		1		
U of Texas at San Antonio		1	2	
	1	6	3	1
SAV=Savannah, GA				
Savannah State College*	8			
	8			
SBA=Santa Barbara, CA				
Pepperdine University	1			
U of Cal – Santa Barbara		1	2	
	1	1	2	

Airport 60 (1900)

AIRPORT	MINORITY GROUP			
	Black	Hispanic	Asian	Native American
SEA=Seattle/Tacoma, WA				
University of Washington	1	4	4	1
	1	**4**	**4**	**1**
SFO=San Francisco/Oakland, CA				
Cal State University - Hayward	1	3	2	1
San Francisco State University	3	2	6	2
San Jose State University		3	9	
Stanford University	2	2	4	
U of Cal - Berkeley	2	2	15	1
	8	**12**	**36**	**4**
SHV=Shreveport, LA				
Grambling State University*	4			
	4			
SLC=Salt Lake City, UT				
University of Utah		1		
		1		
STL=St. Louis, MO				
Southern Illinois U - Edwardsville			1	
St. Louis U - Main Campus	3	2	2	
U of Missouri - St. Louis	2	1		
Washington University			2	
	5	**3**	**5**	
SVC=Silver City, NM				
Western New Mexico University		1		
		1		
SWI=Sherman, TX				
Southeast Oklahoma State U			1	
Bishop College*	4			
East Texas State University		1		
North Texas State University	1			
Texas Woman's University			1	
	5	**1**	**2**	

Airport 60 (1900)

AIRPORT	MINORITY GROUP			
	Black	Hispanic	Asian	Native American
SYR=Syracuse, NY				
Cornel U Endowed College	7	3	6	
Syracuse U – Main Campus	1	1	1	
	8	**4**	**7**	
TCL=Tuscaloosa, AL				
Stillman College*	4			
University of Alabama	2			
Mississippi University for Women	2		1	
	8		**1**	
TLH=Tallahassee, FL				
Florida Agr & Mech University*	4			
Florida State University	3	1	1	
	7	**1**	**1**	
TPA=Tampa, FL				
University of South Florida	2	7		1
	2	**7**		**1**
TUL=Tulsa, OK				
Northeast Oklahoma State U				2
				2
TUS=Tucson, AZ				
University of Arizona		2	2	
		2	**2**	
TYR=Tyler, TX				
Jarvis Christian College*	1			
	1			
TYS=Knoxville, TN				
Knoxville College*	2			
U of Tennessee – Knoxville	1			
	3			

PHYSICAL SCIENCES (1900)
MINORITY BACCALAUREATE DEGREES
WITHIN 61-80 MILE ANNULUS OF AIRPORT

AIRPORT	MINORITY GROUP			
	Black	Hispanic	Asian	Native American
ALB=Albany, NY				
U of Mass - Amherst Campus		2	1	
		2	1	
ALM=Alamogordo, NM				
NM State U - Main Campus		3	1	
		3	1	
ATL=Atlanta, GA				
Jacksonville State University			1	
University of Georgia	3			
	3		1	
AUS=Austin, TX				
Our Lady of Lake University*			1	
St. Mary's U - San Antonio		4		
Trinity University		1		
U of Texas at San Antonio		1	2	
		6	3	
BAL=Baltimore, MD				
Delaware State College*	3			
Cheyney State College*	8			
	11			
BDL=Hartford, CT/Springfield, MA				
College of New Rochelle	1			
SUNY at Albany		1	1	1
	1	1	1	1
BHM=Birmingham, AL				
Jacksonville State University			1	
			1	

Airport 61-80 (1900)

AIRPORT	MINORITY GROUP			
	Black	Hispanic	Asian	Native American
BOS=Boston, MA				
U of Mass - Amherst Campus		2	1	
		2	1	
BTM=Butte, MT				
Montana State University				1
				1
BTR=Baton Rouge, LA				
Dillard University*	9			
Southern U in New Orleans*	2			
Tulane U of Louisiana	2	3	1	
U of Southwestern Louisiana	2			
University of New Orleans	2	1		
Xavier University of Louisiana*	9			
	26	4	1	
CAE=Columbia, SC				
Paine College*	1			
	1			
CHS=Charleston, SC				
Savannah State College*	8			
Claflin College*	7			
South Carolina State College*	4			
	19			
CMH=Columbus, OH				
Antioch University	1			
Ohio University - Main Campus	3			
Wright State U - Main Campus	5			
	9			
COS=Colorado Springs, CO				
Metropolitan State College	1	1		
U of Colorado at Boulder			1	
	1	1	1	

Airport 61-80 (1900)

AIRPORT	MINORITY GROUP			
	Black	Hispanic	Asian	Native American
CRW=Charleston, WV				
Ohio University - Main Campus	3			
	3			
DCA=Washington-National, DC				
Lincoln University*	2			
	2			
DEN=Denver, CO				
Colorado State University	1	1	2	
	1	1	2	
DTW=Detroit-Metropolitan, MI				
Michigan State University	1	1	2	
Bowling Green State U - Main Cam			1	
	1	1	3	
FAY=Fayetteville, NC				
Duke University	2	2	3	
	2	2	3	
GRR=Grand Rapids, MI				
Michigan State University	1	1	2	
	1	1	2	
GSO=Greensboro/High Point, NC				
NC State U - Raleigh	1			1
Shaw University*	2			
	3			1
HSV=Huntsville, AL/Decatur, GA				
Jacksonville State University			1	
Middle Tennessee State U	2			1
	2		1	1
IAH=Houston-Intercontinental,TX				
Sam Houston State University			1	
			1	

622

Airport 61-80 (1900)

AIRPORT		MINORITY GROUP		
	Black	Hispanic	Asian	Native American
IND=Indianapolis, IN				
Indiana State U - Main Campus	1			
	1			
JAX=Jacksonville, FL				
University of Florida		8	3	
		8	3	
JFK=New York, Kennedy Int'l, NY				
Yale University		2	2	
		2	2	
LCH=Lake Charles, LA				
U of Southwestern Louisiana	2			
Lamar University	1			4
	3			4
LIT=Little Rock, AR				
Henderson State University	1			
	1			
MCN=Macon, GA				
Clark College*	2			
GA Inst of Tech - Main Campus		3	1	
Georgia State University	1			
Morehouse College*	9			
Spelman College*	4			
	16	3	1	
MEM=Memphis, TN				
Arkansas State U - Main Campus	1			
U of Mississippi - Main Campus	5	1	2	
Lane College*	1			
	7	1	2	
MGM=Montgomery, GA				
Talladega College*	2			
	2			

Airport 61-80 (1900)

AIRPORT		MINORITY GROUP		
	Black	Hispanic	Asian	Native American
MHT=Manchester, NH				
Boston University			1	1
U of Mass - Amherst Campus		2	1	
		2	2	1
MKE=Milwaukee, WS				
Northwestern University	4		1	1
U of Wisconsin - Madison			1	
	4		2	1
MKL=Jackson, TN				
Rust College*	1			
Memphis State University	3		1	
	4		1	
MLU=Monroe, LA				
Alcorn State University*	11			
	11			
MOB=Mobile, AL/Pasagoula, MS				
U of Southern Mississippi	4		1	
	4		1	
MSY=New Orleans, LA				
Sthrn U A&M C - Main Cam*	4			
	4			
ORF=Norfolk/Virginia Beach, VA				
Virginia State College*	17			
	17			
PVD=Providence, RI				
U of Mass - Amherst Campus		2	1	
		2	1	
RDU=Raleigh/Durham, NC				
East Carolina University	1			
	1			

624

Airport 61-80 (1900)

AIRPORT	MINORITY GROUP			
	Black	Hispanic	Asian	Native American
RIC=Richmond, VA				
Hampton Institute*	2			
Norfolk State College*	2			
	4			
SAN=San Diego, CA				
Chapman College	1			
U of Cal - Irvine		1	12	1
	1	**1**	**12**	**1**
SAT=San Antonio, TX				
U of Texas at Austin	1	5	1	
	1	**5**	**1**	
SBA=Santa Barbara, CA				
Cal State University - Los Angeles	1	3	5	
Cal State University - Northridge	1	1	1	
Loyola Marymount University	2	1		
U of Cal - Los Angeles	2		13	1
	6	**5**	**19**	**1**
SBY=Salisbury, MD				
Delaware State College*	3			
	3			
SFO=San Francisco/Oakland, CA				
Cal State University - Sacramento			3	1
U of Cal - Davis	1	2	1	
U of Cal - Santa Cruz		3		
University of the Pacific		1		
	1	**6**	**4**	**1**
SWI=Sherman, TX				
U of Texas at Arlington	3			
	3			
TYR=Tyler, TX				
East Texas State University		1		
		1		

PHYSICAL SCIENCES (1900)
MINORITY BACCALAUREATE DEGREES
MORE THAN 80 MILES FROM NEAREST AIRPORT

AIRPORT	MINORITY GROUP			
	Black	Hispanic	Asian	Native American
ABQ=Albuquerque, NM				
New Mexico Highlands U*		3		
		3		
AUS=Austin, TX				
Texas A&M U - Main Campus		2		
		2		
IAH=Houston-Intercontinental, TX				
Texas A&M U - Main Campus		2		
		2		
MSY=New Orleans, LA				
U of Southern Mississippi	4		1	
	4		1	
PWA=Oklahoma City-Wiley Post, OK				
Cameron University		2		
		2		
TCL=Tuscaloosa, AL				
Mississippi State University	2			
	2			

PSYCHOLOGY (2000)

PSYCHOLOGY (2000)
MINORITY BACCALAUREATE DEGREES
BY STATE AND INSTITUTION

STATE/SCHOOL	MINORITY GROUP			
	Black	Hispanic	Asian	Native American
Alabama				
Alabama A&M University*	5			
Alabama State University*	9			
Jacksonville State University	1			
Oakwood College*	19			
Talladega College*	15			
Troy State University - Main Campus	5			
Troy State University - Montgomery	4			
University of Alabama	4			
U of Alabama in Birmingham	3		1	
University of South Alabama	3			
	68		**1**	
Arizona				
Arizona State University	1	6	1	
Northern Arizona University	1	1		2
University of Arizona	4	9	2	2
	6	**16**	**3**	**4**
Arkansas				
Arkansas Baptist College*				
Arkansas State U - Main Campus	4			1
Henderson State University	1			
Philander Smith College*	7			
University of Arkansas - Pine Bluff*	3			
University of Central Arkansas	1			
	16			**1**
California				
Cal State College - Bakersfield	1	1		4
Cal State College - San Bernadino	2	7	1	2

628

(2000)

STATE/SCHOOL

	MINORITY GROUP			
	Black	Hispanic	Asian	Native American
California (cont)				
Cal State Poly U - Pomona	5	10	1	2
Cal State University - Chico	1	5	4	
Cal State U - Dominguez Hills	29	7	5	
Cal State University - Fresno	1	3	2	
Cal State University - Fullerton	4	12		4
Cal State University - Hayward	20	4	4	
Cal State University - Long Beach	14	18	11	3
Cal State University - Los Angeles	18	18	17	2
Cal State University - Northridge	7	12	7	1
Cal State University - Sacramento	7	6	3	3
Chapman College	9	6	1	
Loyola Marymount University	1	7	3	
Pepperdine University	7	2	4	
San Diego State University	4	13	3	3
San Francisco State University	28	18	27	3
San Jose State University	7	16	16	5
Stanford University	6	3	4	
U of Cal - Berkeley	7	5	29	
U of Cal - Davis	4	7	11	1
U of Cal - Irvine	9		1	4
U of Cal - Los Angeles	25	25	83	3
U of Cal - Riverside	2	4	3	
U of Cal - San Diego		1	4	
U of Cal - Santa Barbara	2	12	13	2
U of Cal - Santa Cruz		17	3	
University of LaVerne	3	3		
University of Redlands	1	1		
University of San Francisco	34	14	13	4
University of Southern California	19	19	27	
University of the Pacific	6	1	1	
	283	**277**	**301**	**46**

(2000)

STATE/SCHOOL	MINORITY GROUP			
	Black	Hispanic	Asian	Native American
Colorado				
Metropolitan State College	5	5		
U of Colorado at Boulder	5	2	4	
U of Northern Colorado	3	4	1	2
U of Southern Colorado		1	1	
	13	**12**	**6**	**2**
Connecticut				
University of Connecticut		6		
Yale University	10	6	2	
	10	**12**	**2**	
Delaware				
Delaware State College*	9	1		
University of Delaware	7			
	16	**1**		
District of Columbia				
American University	11	1	1	
George Washington University	7	2	1	
Howard University*	51			
University of DC*	17	7		
	86	**10**	**2**	
Florida				
Bethune Cookman College*	33			
Biscayne College*	3	22		
Florida Agr & Mech University*	26			
Florida Atlantic University	2	2		
Florida International University	3	28		
Florida State University	9	4		
University of Central Florida	5	1		
St. Leo College	4			
University of Florida	8	16	1	
University of Miami	3	18		

(2000)

STATE/SCHOOL	MINORITY GROUP			
	Black	Hispanic	Asian	Native American
Florida (cont)				
University of South Florida	5	7		2
University of West Florida	1	1		1
	102	**99**	**1**	**3**
Georgia				
Albany State College*	17			
Clark College*	13			
Fort Valley State College*	5			
Georgia College	3			
GA Inst of Tech – Main Campus		1		
Georgia State University	11			2
Morehouse College*	13			
Morris Brown College*	5			
Spelman College*	48			
University of Georgia	4	1		
Valdosta State College	6			
	125	**2**		**2**
Hawaii				
Chaminade University of Honolulu		1	3	
University of Hawaii at Hilo*			7	
University of Hawaii at Manoa*		2	157	
		3	**167**	
Illinois				
Bradley University	3			
Chicago State University*	23			
DePaul University	9	4	2	
Eastern Illinois University	4			
Governors State University	9			
Illinois State University	4			1
Loyola University of Chicago	10	3	4	
Northern Illinois University	4			
Northeastern Illinois University	6	6	1	1

(2000)

STATE/SCHOOL	MINORITY GROUP			
	Black	Hispanic	Asian	Native American
Illinois (cont)				
Northwestern University	6	2	1	
Roosevelt University	12		7	
Southern Illinois U - Carbondale	7		1	
Southern Illinois U - Edwardsville	7		2	
U of Illinois - Chicago Circle	14	5	8	1
U of Illinois - Urbana Campus	14	2	3	1
	132	**22**	**29**	**4**
Indiana				
Ball State University	7			
Ind-Purdue U - Indianapolis	8			
Indiana State U - Main Campus	4			1
Indiana University - Bloomington	10	1	1	1
Indiana University - Northwest	1			
Purdue University - Main Campus	3	1	1	1
	33	**2**	**2**	**3**
Kentucky				
University of Louisville	3			
Western Kentucky University	2			1
	5			**1**
Louisiana				
Dillard University*	11			
Grambling State University*	12			
Louisiana State U & A&M College	6			
Louisiana Tech University	1			
Northeast Louisiana University	2			
Sthrn U A&M College - Main Cam*	18			
Southern U in New Orleans*	10			
Tulane U of Louisiana	1	3	1	1
University of New Orleans	2	1		
U of Southwestern Louisiana	3			
Xavier University of Louisiana*	8			
	74	**4**	**1**	**1**

(2000)

STATE/SCHOOL	MINORITY GROUP			
	Black	Hispanic	Asian	Native American
Maryland				
Bowie State College*	13			
Morgan State University*	30			
Towson State University	13			1
University of Baltimore	1			
U of MD – Baltimore Co Campus	18			1
U of MD – College Park Campus	11	1	3	1
	86	**1**	**3**	**3**
Massachussetts				
Boston State College	6	1		
Boston University	5			
Harvard University	11	5	3	
Radcliffe College	6	1	2	
Tufts University	17	3	2	
U of Mass – Amherst Campus	4	2		
	49	**12**	**7**	
Michigan				
Detroit Institute of Technology	1			
Eastern Michigan University	4	1		
Mercy College of Detroit	13			
Michigan State University	11	2		1
Oakland University	8			1
Shaw College at Detroit*	3			
University of Detroit	3			
U of Michigan – Ann Arbor	24	5	5	1
Wayne State University	62			
Western Michigan University	4	1	1	
	133	**9**	**6**	**3**
Minnesota				
U of Minn – Minneapolis/St. Paul	3	1	3	
	3	**1**	**3**	

(2000)

STATE/SCHOOL	MINORITY GROUP			
	Black	Hispanic	Asian	Native American
Mississippi				
Jackson State University*	1			
Mississippi State University	3			
Mississippi University for Women	1			
Rust College*	2			
Tougaloo College*	11			
U of Mississippi – Main Campus	6			
U of Southern Mississippi	7			
	31			
Missouri				
Columbia College	10			
Lincoln University	4			
Park College	30	23		
St. Louis U – Main Campus	9		1	
U of Missouri – Columbia		1		1
U of Missouri – Kansas City	12			
U of Missouri – St. Louis	5		1	
Washington University	7	2		
Webster College	2			
	79	**26**	**2**	**1**
Nebraska				
U of Nebraska at Omaha	10			
	10			
New Hampshire				
Dartmouth College	11		1	
	11		**1**	
New Jersey				
Glassboro State College	9	7		1
Jersey City State College	5	6		
Kean College of New Jersey	7	4		2
Montclair State College	2	8	1	

634

(2000)

STATE/SCHOOL	MINORITY GROUP			
	Black	Hispanic	Asian	Native American
New Jersey (cont)				
Princeton University	12	2		
Rutgers U - Camden Campus	4		1	
Rutgers U - New Brunswick	20	5	2	
Rutgers U - Newark Campus	14	5	1	
St. Peter's College	1	3		
Seton Hall University	11		1	
Trenton State College	12		1	1
	97	40	7	4
New Mexico				
Eastern NM U - Main Campus	2	6		
New Mexico Highlands U*		4		
NM State U - Main Campus		5		
University of Albuquerque		5		
U of NM - Main Campus		12		4
Western New Mexico University	1	3		1
	3	35		5
New York				
Adelphi University	3	1		
College of New Rochelle	1	5		
Cornell U Endowed College	6	2	3	
CUNY Bernard Baruch College	10	4	3	
CUNY Brooklyn College	68	23	5	2
CUNY City College	47	22	11	2
CUNY College of Staten Island	16	10	4	1
CUNY Hunter College	30	17	6	2
CUNY Lehman College	23	24	6	
CUNY Medgar Evers College*	4			
CUNY Queen's College	23	6	7	1
CUNY York College	19	4	1	1
Fordham University	15	19	1	
Long Island U - Brooklyn Center	9	3		

(2000)

STATE/SCHOOL	MINORITY GROUP			
	Black	Hispanic	Asian	Native American
New York (cont)				
Mercy College	18	20	1	
New York University	5	5	1	
Pace University New York	5	3		1
St. Francis College	2	1		
St. John's University	3	1		
SUNY at Albany	5	2	1	1
SUNY at Buffalo - Main Campus	2	1		
SUNY at Stony Bk - Main Campus	6	4	1	
SUNY College at New Paltz	7	1	1	4
SUNY College - Old Westbury	9	2		
SUNY Empire State College	2		1	
Syracuse University - Main Campus	10	2		
	348	**182**	**53**	**15**
North Carolina				
Bennett College*	4			
Duke University	5	1	1	
East Carolina University	6			
Fayetteville State University*	5			
Johnson C Smith University*	16			
NC Agrl & Tech State University*	41			
NC Central University*	25			
NC State U - Raleigh	2			
Pembroke State University	3			5
St. Augustine's College*	11			
U of NC at Chapel Hill	14			
U of NC at Charlotte	7			
U of NC at Greensboro	7	2	1	
Winston-Salem State University*	25			
	171	**3**	**2**	**5**
North Dakota				
U of North Dakota - Main Campus				2
				2

636

(2000)

STATE/SCHOOL	MINORITY GROUP			
	Black	Hispanic	Asian	Native American
Ohio				
Antioch University	6			1
Bowling Green State U – Main Cam	4			
Central State University*	5			
Kent State U – Main Campus	7			
Oberlin College	3	1	1	
Ohio State U – Main Campus	2		1	1
Ohio University – Main Campus	8			
U of Akron – Main Campus	4			
U of Cincinnati – Main Campus	12	1		
University of Dayton	9	1		
University of Toledo	1		1	
Wilberforce University*	21			
Wright State U – Main Campus	1			
	83	**3**	**3**	**2**
Oklahoma				
Central State University	4			2
Northeast Oklahoma State U	3			6
Oklahoma State U – Main Campus	2			3
Southeast Oklahoma State U	3			
U of Oklahoma – Norman Campus	4		1	5
	16		**1**	**16**
Oregon				
Oregon State University			5	2
University of Oregon – Main Campus	1	1	5	
	1	**1**	**10**	**2**
Pennsylvania				
Cheyney State College*	17			
Lincoln University*	15			
Pennsylvania State U – Main Campus	8	1		
St. Joseph's University	2	1		1
Temple University	14			

(2000)

STATE/SCHOOL	MINORITY GROUP			
	Black	Hispanic	Asian	Native American
Pennsylvania (cont)				
University of Pennsylvania	11		2	1
U of Pittsburgh - Main Campus	17	1	1	1
West Chester State College	2			
	86	**3**	**3**	**3**
Rhode Island				
Brown University	5	1	1	
	5	**1**	**1**	
South Carolina				
Baptist College at Charleston	4			
South Carolina State College*	21			
U of South Carolina at Columbia	15	1		
Winthrop College	6			
	46	**1**		
Tennessee				
Austin Peay State University	3			
Fisk University*	19			
Knoxville College*	12			
Memphis State University	8			
Middle Tennessee State U	4		2	1
Tennessee State University*	30			
U of Tennessee - Knoxville	4		1	2
U of Tennessee - Martin	2		1	
	82		**4**	**3**
Texas				
Angelo State University	1	4		
Bishop College*	3			
Corpus Christi State University		15	1	
East Texas State University	4			
Incarnate Word College		5		
Lamar University				2
Laredo State University*		10		
North Texas State University	7	2		

(2000)

STATE/SCHOOL	MINORITY GROUP			
	Black	Hispanic	Asian	Native American
Texas (cont)				
Our Lady of Lake University*	4	5		
Pan American University*	1	19		
Prairie View A&M University*	2			
St. Edward's University		5		
St. Mary's U – San Antonio	1	6		
Sam Houston State University			1	
Southwest Texas State University	1	4		
Texas A&I University	1	18		
Texas A&M U – Main Campus		2	1	1
Texas Southern University*	17			
Texas Women's University	1	1		
Trinity University		5		
U of Houston – Central Campus	12	12		1
U of Texas at Arlington	2	1	1	
U of Texas at Austin	9	40	4	1
U of Texas at El Paso	2	25	1	
U of Texas at San Antonio	1	16		
	69	**195**	**9**	**5**
Utah				
Brigham Young University – Main			2	
University of Utah	5	7	1	1
	5	**7**	**3**	**1**
Virginia				
Hampton Institute*	20			
Norfolk State College*	24			
Old Dominion University	3	1	1	
U of Virginia – Main Campus	11	1	1	
Virginia Commonwealth University	17		1	
Virginia State College*	16			
Virginia Union University*	9			
	100	**2**	**3**	

(2000)

STATE/SCHOOL	MINORITY GROUP			
	Black	Hispanic	Asian	Native American
Washington				
University of Washington	9	3	14	
	9	3	14	
Wisconsin				
U of Wisconsin - Madison	2		2	
U of Wisconsin - Milwaukee	1	1		
	3	1	2	
TOTALS	2495	986	652	137

*Predominately minority institutions are those where at least 50% of the total BA Degrees awarded are to one of the minority groups being considered.

PSYCHOLOGY (2000)
BLACK BACCALAUREATE DEGREES RANKED BY INSTITUTION

Rank	Institution	B.A.'s	Rank	Institution	B.A.'s
1	CUNY Brooklyn C	68	31	Oakwood C*	19
2	Wayne State U	62	32	Fisk U*	19
3	Howard U*	51	33	U of MD-Baltimore Co Campus	18
4	Spelman C*	48	34	Cal State U-Los Angeles	18
5	CUNY City C	47	35	Sthrn U A&M C-Main Campus*	18
6	NC Agrl & Tech State U*	41	36	Mercy C	18
7	U of San Francisco	34	37	Albany State C*	17
8	Bethune Cookman C*	33	38	Tufts U	17
9	Park C	30	39	U of Pittsburgh-Main Campus	17
10	Morgan State U*	30	40	Cheyney State C*	17
11	CUNY Hunter C	30	41	Virginia Commonwealth U	17
12	Tennessee State U*	30	42	U of DC*	17
13	Cal State U-Dominguez Hills	29	43	Texas Southern U*	17
14	San Francisco State U	28	44	CUNY C of Staten Island	16
15	Florida Agrl & Mech U*	26	45	Johnson C Smith U*	16
16	Winston-Salem State U*	25	46	Virginia State C*	16
17	NC Central U*	25	47	Fordham U	15
18	U of Cal-Los Angeles	25	48	Lincoln U*	15
19	U of Michigan-Ann Arbor	24	49	Talladega C*	15
20	Norfolk State C*	24	50	U of South Carolina at Columbia	15
21	CUNY Queen's C	23	51	U of Illinois-Urbana Campus	14
22	CUNY Lehman C	23	52	U of Illinois-Chicago Circle	14
23	Chicago State U*	23	53	Rutgers U-Newark Campus	14
24	Wilberforce U*	21	54	Cal State U-Long Beach	14
25	South Carolina State C*	21	55	U of NC at Chapel Hill	14
26	Cal State U-Hayward	20	56	Temple U	14
27	Rutgers U-New Brunswick	20	57	Mercy C of Detroit	13
28	Hampton Institute*	20	58	Bowie State C*	13
29	U of Southern California	19	59	Morehouse C*	13
30	CUNY York C	19	60	Towson State U	13

Black B.A.'s (2000)

Rank	Institution	B.A.'s	Rank	Institution	B.A.'s
61	Clark C*	13	75	Michigan State U	11
62	Trenton State C	12	76	U of MD-College Park Campus	11
63	U of Missouri-Kansas City	12	77	Seton Hall U	11
64	Grambling State U*	12	78	Georgia State U	11
65	Princeton U	12	79	U of Virginia-Main Campus	11
66	Roosevelt U	12	80	St. Augustine's C*	11
67	Knoxville C*	12	81	U of Pennsylvania	11
68	U of Cincinnati-Main Campus	12	82	Loyola U of Chicago	10
69	U of Houston-Central Campus	12	83	Indiana U-Bloomington	10
70	Harvard U	11	84	Columbia C	10
71	Tougaloo C*	11	85	Yale U	10
72	Dillard U*	11	86	Syracuse U-Main Campus	10
73	Dartmouth C	11	87	Southern U in New Orleans*	10
74	American U	11	88	CUNY Bernard Baruch C	10

*predominantly black institutions

Institutions not ranked have less than ten degrees conferred on blacks.

PSYCHOLOGY (2000)
HISPANIC BACCALAUREATE DEGREES RANKED BY INSTITUTION

Rank	Institution	B.A.'s	Rank	Institution	B.A.'s
1	U of Texas at Austin	40	18	Texas A&I U	18
2	Florida International U	28	19	U of Cal–Santa Cruz	17
3	U of Cal–Los Angeles	25	20	CUNY Hunter C	17
4	U of Texas at El Paso	25	21	San Jose State U	16
5	CUNY Lehman C	24	22	U of Texas at San Antonio	16
6	CUNY Brooklyn C	23	23	U of Florda	16
7	Park C	23	24	Corpus Christi State U	15
8	CUNY City C	22	25	U of San Francisco	14
9	Biscayne C*	22	26	San Diego State U	13
10	Mercy C	20	27	Cal State U–Northridge	12
11	U of Southern California	19	28	Cal State U–Fullerton	12
12	Fordham U	19	29	U of NM–Main Campus	12
13	Pan American U*	19	30	U of Cal–Santa Barbara	12
14	Cal State U–Los Angeles	18	31	U of Houston–Central Campus	12
15	San Francisco State U	18	32	Cal State Poly U–Pomona	10
16	Cal State U–Long Beach	18	33	CUNY C of Staten Island	10
17	U of Miami	18	34	Laredo State U*	10

*predominantly Hispanic institutions

Institutions not ranked have less than ten degrees conferred on Hispanics.

PSYCHOLOGY (2000)
ASIAN BACCALAUREATE DEGREES RANKED BY INSTITUTION

Rank	Institution	B.A.'s	Rank	Institution	B.A.'s
1	U of Hawaii at Manoa*	157	8	U of Washington	14
2	U of Cal-Los Angeles	83	9	U of Cal-Santa Barbara	13
3	U of Cal-Berkeley	29	10	U of San Francisco	13
4	San Francisco State U	27	11	Cal State U-Long Beach	11
5	U of Southern California	27	12	U of Cal-Davis	11
6	Cal State U-Los Angeles	17	13	CUNY City C	11
7	San Jose State U	16			

*predominantly Asian institutions

Institutions not ranked have less than ten degrees conferred on Asians.

PSYCHOLOGY (2000)
NATIVE AMERICAN BACCALAUREATE DEGREES RANKED BY INSTITUTION

Rank	Institution	B.A.'s	Rank	Institution	B.A.'s
1	Northeastern Oklahoma State	6	3	San Jose State U	5
2	Pembroke State U	5	4	U of Oklahoma-Norman Campus	5

Institutions not ranked have less than five degrees conferred on Native Americans.

644

PSYCHOLOGY (2000)
MINORITY BACCALAUREATE DEGREES
WITHIN 60 MILE RADIUS OF AIRPORT

AIRPORT	MINORITY GROUP			
	Black	Hispanic	Asian	Native American
ABQ=Albuquerque, NM				
U of NM – Main Campus		12		4
University of Albuquerque		5		
		17		**4**
ALB=Albany, NY				
SUNY at Albany	5	2	1	1
SUNY Empire State College	2		1	
	7	**2**	**2**	**1**
AOO=Altoona, PA				
Pennsylvania State U – Main Campus	8	1		
	8	**1**		
ATL=Atlanta, GA				
Clark College*	13			
GA Inst of Tech – Main Campus		1		
Georgia State University	11			2
Morehouse College*	13			
Morris Brown College*	5			
Spelman College*	48			
	90	**1**		**2**
AUS=Austin, TX				
Southwest Texas State University	1	4		
U of Texas at Austin	9	40	4	1
	10	**44**	**4**	**1**
BAL=Baltimore, MD				
University of Delaware	7			
American University	11	1	1	
George Washington Univesity	7	2	1	
Howard University*	51			

Airport 60 (2000)

AIRPORT	Black	MINORITY GROUP Hispanic	Asian	Native American
BAL (cont)				
University of DC*	17	7		
Bowie State College*	13			
Morgan State University*	30			
Towson State University	13	1		1
U of MD - Baltimore Co Campus	18			1
U of MD - College Park Campus	11	1	3	1
University of Baltimore	1			
Lincoln University*	15			
	194	**12**	**5**	**3**
BDL=Hartford, CT/Springfield, MA				
Yale University	10	6	2	
U of Mass - Amherst Campus	4	2		
	14	**8**	**2**	
BHM=Birmingham, AL				
Talladega College*	15			
U of Alabama in Birmingham	3		1	
University of Alabama	4			
	22		**1**	
BKL=Cleveland-Lakefront, OH				
Kent State U - Main Campus	7			
Oberlin College	3	1	1	
U of Akron - Main Campus	4			
	14	**1**	**1**	
BNA=Nashville, TN				
Western Kentucky University	2			1
Austin Peay State University	3			
Fisk University*	19			
Middle Tennessee State U	4		2	1
Tennessee State University*	30			
	58		**2**	**2**

Airport 60 (2000)

AIRPORT		MINORITY GROUP		
	Black	Hispanic	Asian	Native American
BOS=Boston, MA				
Boston State College	6	1		
Boston University	5			
Harvard University	11	5	3	
Radcliffe College	6	1	2	
Tufts University	17	3	2	
Brown University	5	1	1	
	50	**11**	**8**	
BTR=Baton Rouge, LA				
Louisiana State U & A&M College	6			
Sthrn U A&M College - Main Cam*	18			
	24			
BUF=Buffalo, NY				
SUNY at Buffalo - Main Campus	2	1		
	2	**1**		
CAE=Columbia, SC				
South Carolina State College*	21			
U of South Carolina at Columbia	15	1		
	36	**1**		
CHS=Charleston, SC				
Baptist College at Charleston	4			
	4			
CIC=Chico, CA				
Cal State University - Chico	1	5	4	
	1	**5**	**4**	
CLT=Charlotte, NC				
Johnson C Smith University*	16			
U of NC at Charlotte	7			
Winthrop College	6			
	29			

Airport 60 (2000)

AIRPORT	MINORITY GROUP			
	Black	Hispanic	Asian	Native American
CMH=Columbus, OH				
Central State University*	5			
Ohio State U - Main Campus	2		1	
Wilberforce University*	21			
	28		1	
CMI=Champaign, IL				
Eastern Illinois University	4			
Illinois State University	4			1
U of Illinois - Urbana Campus	14	2	3	1
Indiana State U - Main Campus	4			1
	26	2	3	3
COS=Colorado Springs, CO				
U of Southern Colorado		1	1	
		1	1	
COU=Columbia, MO				
Columbia College	10			
Lincoln University	4			
U of Missouri - Columbia		1		1
	14	1		1
CRP=Corpus Christi, TX				
Corpus Christi State University		15	1	
Texas A&I University	1	18		
	1	33	1	
CVG=Cincinnati, OH				
Antioch University	6			1
Central State University*	5			
U of Cincinnati - Main Campus	12	1		
University of Dayton	9	1		
Wilberforce University*	21			
Wright State U - Main Campus	1			
	54	2		1

Airport 60 (2000)

AIRPORT		MINORITY GROUP		
	Black	Hispanic	Asian	Native American
DAB=Dayton Beach, FL				
Bethune Cookman College*	33			
University of Central Florida	5	1		
	38			
DCA=Washington–National, DC				
American University	11	1	1	
George Washington University	7	2	1	
Howard University*	51			
University of DC*	17	7		
Bowie State College*	13			
Morgan State University*	30			
Towson State University	13	1		1
U of MD - Baltimore Co Campus	18			1
U of MD - College Park Campus	11	1	3	1
University of Baltimore	1			
	172	12	5	3
DEN=Denver, CO				
Metropolitan State College	5	5		
U of Colorado at Boulder	5	2	4	
U of Northern Colorado	3	4	1	2
	13	11	5	2
DFW=Dallas/Fort Worth, TX				
Bishop College*	3			
East Texas State University	4			
North Texas State University	7	2		
Texas Woman's University	1	1		
U of Texas at Arlington	2	1	1	
	17	4	1	
DTW=Detroit-Metropolitan, MI				
Detroit Institute of Technology	1			
Eastern Michigan University	4	1		

Airport 60 (2000)

AIRPORT	MINORITY GROUP			
	Black	Hispanic	Asian	Native American
DTW (cont)				
Mercy College of Detroit	13			
Oakland University	8			1
Shaw College at Detroit*	3			
U of Michigan - Ann Arbor	24	5	5	1
University of Detroit	3			
Wayne State University	62			
University of Toledo	1		1	
	119	6	6	2
ELP=El Paso, TX				
U of Texas at El Paso	2	25	1	
	2	25	1	
EUG=Eugene, OR				
Oregon State University			5	2
University of Oregon - Main Campus	1	1	5	
	1	1	10	2
FAT=Fresno, CA				
Cal State University - Fresno	1	3	2	
	1	3	2	
FAY=Fayetteville, NC				
Fayetteville State University*	5			
NC Central University*	25			
NC State U - Raleigh	2			
Pembroke State University	3			5
St. Augustine's College*	11			
U of NC at Chapel Hill	14			
	60			5
FLG=Flagstaff, AZ				
Northern Arizona University	1	1		2
	1	1		2

Airport 60 (2000)

AIRPORT	MINORITY GROUP			
	Black	Hispanic	Asian	Native American
GRR=Grand Rapids, MI				
Western Michigan University	4	1	1	
	4	1	1	
GSO=Greensboro/High Point, NC				
Bennett College*	4			
Duke University	5	1	1	
NC Agrl & Tech State University*	41			
NC Central University*	25			
U of NC at Chapel Hill	14			
U of NC at Greensboro	7	2	1	
Winston-Salem State University*	25			
	121	3	2	
HNL=Honolulu/Oahu, HI				
Chaminade University of Honolulu		1	3	
University of Hawaii at Manoa*		2	157	
		3	160	
HSV=Huntsville, AL/Decatur, GA				
Alabama A&M University*	5			
Oakwood College*	19			
	24			
IAH=Houston-Intercontinental,TX				
Prairie View A&M University*	2			
Texas Southern University*	17			
U of Houston - Central Campus	12	12		1
	31	12		1
IND=Indianapolis, IN				
Ball State University	7			
Ind-Purdue U - Indianapolis	8			
Indiana University - Bloomington	10	1	1	1
Purdue University - Main Campus	3	1	1	1
	28	2	2	2

Airport 60 (2000)

AIRPORT	MINORITY GROUP			
	Black	Hispanic	Asian	Native American
ITO=Hilo, HI				
University of Hawaii at Hilo*			7	
			7	
JAN=Jackson/Vicksburg, MS				
Jackson State University*	1			
Tougaloo College*	11			
	12			
JFK=New York, Kennedy Int'l, NY				
Jersey City State College	5	6		
Kean College of New Jersey	7	4		2
Montclair State College	2	8	1	
Princeton University	12	2		
Rutgers U - New Brunswick	20	5	2	
Rutgers U - Newark Campus	14	5	1	
St. Peter's College	1	3		
Seton Hall University	11		1	
Trenton State College	12		1	1
Adelphi University	3	1		
College of New Rochelle	1	5		
CUNY Bernard Baruch College	10	4	3	
CUNY Brooklyn College	68	23	5	2
CUNY College of Staten Island	16	10	4	1
CUNY City College	47	22	11	2
CUNY Hunter College	30	17	6	2
CUNY Lehman College	23	24	6	
CUNY Medgar Evers College*	4			
CUNY Queen's College	23	6	7	1
CUNY York College	19	4	1	1
Fordham University	15	19	1	
Long Island U - Brooklyn Center	9	3		
Mercy College	18	20	1	

Airport 60 (2000)

AIRPORT	MINORITY GROUP			
	Black	Hispanic	Asian	Native American
JFK (cont)				
New York University	5	5	1	
Pace University New York	5	3		1
St. Francis College	2	1		
St. John's University	3	1		
SUNY at Stony Bk - Main Campus	6	4	1	
SUNY College - Old Westbury	9	2		
	400	**207**	**53**	**13**
LAX=Los Angeles, CA				
Cal State College - San Bernardino	2	7	1	2
Cal State Poly U - Pomona	5	10	1	2
Cal State U - Dominguez Hills	29	7	5	
Cal State University - Fullerton	4	12		4
Cal State University - Long Beach	14	18	11	3
Cal State University - Los Angeles	18	18	17	2
Cal State University - Northridge	7	12	7	1
Chapman College	9	6	1	
Loyola Marymount University	1	7	3	
Pepperdine University	7	2	4	
U of Cal - Irvine	9		1	4
U of Cal - Los Angeles	25	25	83	3
U of Cal - Riverside	2	4	3	
University of Southern California	19	19	27	
University of LaVerne	3	3		
	154	**150**	**164**	**21**
LEX=Lexington/Frankfort, KY				
University of Louisville	3			
	3			
LIT=Little Rock, AR				
Philander Smith College*	7			
University of Arkansas - Pine Bluff*	3			
University of Central Arkansas	1			
	11			

Airport 60 (2000)

AIRPORT	Black	Hispanic	Asian	Native American
		MINORITY GROUP		
LRD=Laredo, TX				
Laredo State University*		10		
		10		
MCI=Kansas City-International, MO				
Park College	30	23		
U of Missouri - Kansas City	12			
	42	**23**		
MCN=Macon, GA				
Fort Valley State College*	5			
Georgia College	3			
	8			
MDH=Carbondale, IL				
Southern Illinois U - Carbondale	7		1	
	7		**1**	
MEM=Memphis, TN				
Rust College*	2			
Memphis State University	8			
	10			
MFE=McAllen, TX				
Pan American University*	1	19		
	1	**19**		
MGM=Montgomery, GA				
Alabama State University*	9			
Troy State University - Main Campus	5			
Troy State University - Montgomery	4			
	18			
MHT=Manchester, NH				
Harvard University	11	5	3	
Radcliffe College	6	1	2	
Tufts University	17	3	2	
Dartmouth College	11		1	
	45	**9**	**8**	

654

Airport 60 (2000)

AIRPORT	MINORITY GROUP			
	Black	Hispanic	Asian	Native American
MIA=Miami, FL				
Biscayne College*	3	22		
Florida Atlantic University	2	2		
Florida International University	3	28		
University of Miami	3	18		
	11	70		
MKE=Milwaukee, WS				
U of Wisconsin - Milwaukee	1	1		
	1	1		
MKL=Jackson, TN				
U of Tennessee - Martin	2		1	
	2		1	
MLU=Monroe, LA				
Grambling State University*	12			
Louisiana Tech University	1			
Northeast Louisiana University	2			
	15			
MOB=Mobile, AL/Pasagoula, MS				
University of South Alabama	3			
University of West Florida	1	1		1
	4	1		1
MSN=Madison, WS				
U of Wisconsin - Madison	2		2	
	2		2	
MSP=Minneapolis/St. Paul, MN				
U of Minn - Minneapolis/St. Paul	3	1	3	
	3	1	3	
MSY=New Orleans, LA				
Dillard University*	11			
Southern U in New Orleans*	10			
Tulane U of Louisiana	1	3	1	1

Airport 60 (2000)

AIRPORT	MINORITY GROUP			
	Black	Hispanic	Asian	Native American
MSY (cont)				
University of New Orleans	2	1		
Xavier University of Louisiana*	8			
	32	**4**	**1**	**1**
ORD=Chicago–O'Hare Airport, IL				
Chicago State University*	23			
DePaul University	9	4	2	
Governors State University	9			
Loyola University of Chicago	10	3	4	
Northern Illinois University	4			
Northwestern University	6	2	1	
Northeastern Illinois University	6	6	1	1
Roosevelt University	12		7	
U of Illinois - Chicago Circle	14	5	8	1
Indiana University - Northwest	1			
	94	**20**	**23**	**2**
ORF=Norfolk/Virginia Beach, VA				
Hampton Institute*	20			
Norfolk State College*	24			
Old Dominion University	3	1	1	
	47	**1**	**1**	
PHL=Philadelphia, PA/Wilmington, DE				
Delaware State College*	9	1		
University of Delaware	7			
Glassboro State College	9	7		1
Princeton University	12	2		
Rutgers U - Camden Campus	4		1	
Rutgers U - New Brunswick	20	5	2	
Trenton State College	12		1	1
Cheyney State College*	17			
Lincoln University*	15			

656

Airport 60 (2000)

AIRPORT	MINORITY GROUP			
	Black	Hispanic	Asian	Native American
PHL (cont)				
St. Joseph's University	2	1		1
Temple University	14			
University of Pennsylvania	11		2	1
West Chester State College	2			
	134	16	6	4
PHX=Phoenix, AZ				
Arizona State University	1	6	1	
	1	6	1	
PIA=Peoria, IL				
Bradley University	3			
	3			
PIT=Pittsburgh, PA				
U of Pittsburgh - Main Campus	17	1	1	1
	17	1	1	1
PVD=Providence, RI				
Boston State College	6	1		
Boston University	5			
Harvard University	11	5	3	
Radcliffe College	6	1	2	
Tufts University	17	3	2	
Brown University	5	1	1	
	50	11	8	
PWA=Oklahoma City-Wiley Post, OK				
Central State University	4			2
Oklahoma State U - Main Campus	2			3
U of Oklahoma - Norman Campus	4		1	5
	10		1	10
RDU=Raleigh/Durham, NC				
Bennet College*	4			
Duke University	5	1	1	
Fayetteville State University*	5			

Airport 60 (2000)

AIRPORT	MINORITY GROUP			
	Black	Hispanic	Asian	Native American
RDU (cont)				
NC Agrl & Tech State University*	41			
NC Central University*	25			
NC State U - Raleigh	2			
St. Augustine's College*	11			
U of NC at Chapel Hill	14			
U of NC at Greensboro	7	2	1	
	114	**3**	**2**	
RIC=Richmond, VA				
Virginia Commonwealth University	17		1	
Virginia State College*	16			
Virginia Union University*	9			
	42		**1**	
SAN=San Diego, CA				
San Diego State University	4	13	3	3
U of Cal - San Diego		1	4	
	4	**14**	**7**	**3**
SAT=San Antonio, TX				
Incarnate Word College		5		
Our Lady of Lake University*	4	5		
St. Edward's University		5		
St. Mary's U - San Antonio	1	6		
Southwest Texas State University	1	4		
Trinity University		5		
U of Texas at San Antonio	1	16		
	7	**46**		
SBA=Santa Barbara, CA				
Pepperdine University	7	2	4	
U of Cal - Santa Barbara	2	12	13	2
	9	**14**	**17**	**2**

Airport 60 (2000)

AIRPORT	MINORITY GROUP			
	Black	Hispanic	Asian	Native American
SEA=Seattle/Tacoma, WA				
University of Washington	9	3	14	
	9	3	14	
SFO=San Francisco/Oakland, CA				
Cal State University - Hayward	20	4	4	
San Francisco State University	28	18	27	3
San Jose State University	7	16	16	5
Stanford University	6	3	4	
U of Cal - Berkeley	7	5	29	
University of San Francisco	34	14	13	4
	102	60	93	12
SHV=Shreveport, LA				
Grambling State University*	12			
	12			
SJT=San Angelo, TX				
Angelo State University	1	4		
	1	4		
SLC=Salt Lake City, UT				
Brigham Young University - Main			2	
University of Utah	5	7	1	1
	5	7	3	1
STL=St. Louis, MO				
Southern Illinois U - Edwardsville	7		2	
St. Louis U - Main Campus	9		1	
U of Missouri - St. Louis	5		1	
Washington University	7	2		
Webster College	2			
	30	2	4	
SVC=Silver City, NM				
Western New Mexico University	1	3		1
	1	3		1

Airport 60 (2000)

AIRPORT	MINORITY GROUP			
	Black	Hispanic	Asian	Native American
SWI=Sherman, TX				
Southeast Oklahoma State U	3			
Bishop College*	3			
East Texas State University	4			
North Texas State University	7	2		
Texas Woman's University	1	1		
	18	**3**		
SYR=Syracuse, NY				
Cornel U Endowed College	6	2	3	
Syracuse U - Main Campus	10	2		
	16	**4**	**3**	
TCL=Tuscaloosa, AL				
U of Alabama in Birmingham	3		1	
University of Alabama	4			
Mississippi University for Women	1			
	8		**1**	
TLH=Tallahassee, FL				
Florida Agr & Mech University*	26			
Florida State University	9	4		
	35	**4**		
TPA=Tampa, FL				
St. Leo College	4			
University of South Florida	5	7		2
	9	**7**		**2**
TUL=Tulsa, OK				
Northeast Oklahoma State U	3			6
	3			**6**
TUS=Tucson, AZ				
University of Arizona	4	9	2	2
	4	**9**	**2**	**2**

660

Airport 60 (2000)

<u>AIRPORT</u>

	MINORITY GROUP			
	Black	Hispanic	Asian	Native American
TYS=Knoxville, TN				
Knoxville College*	12			
U of Tennessee – Knoxville	4		1	2
	16		**1**	**2**

PSYCHOLOGY (2000)
MINORITY BACCALAUREATE DEGREES
WITHIN 61-80 MILE ANNULUS OF AIRPORT

AIRPORT	MINORITY GROUP			
	Black	Hispanic	Asian	Native American
ALB=Albany, NY				
U of Mass - Amherst Campus	4	2		
SUNY College at New Paltz	7	1	1	4
	11	**3**	**1**	**4**
ALM=Alamogordo, NM				
NM State U - Main Campus		5		
		5		
ATL=Atlanta, GA				
Jacksonville State University	1			
Georgia College	3			
University of Georgia	4	1		
	8	**1**		
AUS=Austin, TX				
Incarnate Word College		5		
Our Lady of Lake University*	4	5		
St. Edward's University		5		
St. Mary's U - San Antonio	1	6		
Trinity University		5		
U of Texas at San Antonio	1	16		
	6	**42**		
BAL=Baltimore, MD				
Delaware State College*	9	1		
Cheyney State College*	17			
	26	**1**		
BDL=Hartford, CT/Springfield, MA				
College of New Rochelle	1	5		
Mercy College	18	20	1	

Airport 61-80 (2000)

AIRPORT	MINORITY GROUP			
	Black	Hispanic	Asian	Native American
BDL (cont)				
SUNY at Albany	5	2	1	1
SUNY College at New Paltz	7	1	1	4
Brown University	5	1	1	
	36	**29**	**4**	**5**
BHM=Birmingham, AL				
Jacksonville State University	1			
	1			
BOS=Boston, MA				
U of Mass - Amherst Campus	4	2		
	4	**2**		
BTR=Baton Rouge, LA				
Dillard University*	11			
Southern U in New Orleans*	10			
Tulane U of Louisiana	1	3	1	1
U of Southwestern Louisiana	3			
University of New Orleans	2	1		
Xavier University of Louisiana*	8			
	35	**4**	**1**	**1**
CAE=Columbia, SC				
Winthrop College	6			
	6			
CHS=Charleston, SC				
South Carolina State College*	21			
	21			
CLT=Charlotte, NC				
Wintson-Salem State University*	25			
	25			
CMH=Columbus, OH				
Antioch University	6			1
Ohio University - Main Campus	8			1

Airport 61-80 (2000)

AIRPORT	MINORITY GROUP			
	Black	Hispanic	Asian	Native American
CMH (cont)				
University of Dayton	9	1		
Wright State U - Main Campus	1			
	24	1		2
CMI=Champaign, IL				
Purdue University - Main Campus	3	1	1	1
	3	1	1	1
COS=Colorado Springs, CO				
Metropolitan State College	5	5		
U of Colorado at Boulder	5	2	4	
	10	7	4	
CRW=Charleston, WV				
Ohio University - Main Campus	8			1
	8			1
DCA=Washington-National, DC				
Lincoln University*	15			
	15			
DTW=Detroit-Metropolitan, MI				
Michigan State University	11	2		1
Bowling Green State U - Main Cam	4			
	15	2		1
FAY=Fayetteville, NC				
Duke University	5	1	1	
	5	1	1	
GRR=Grand Rapids, MI				
Michigan State University	11	2		1
	11	2		1
GSO=Greensboro/High Point, NC				
NC State U - Raleigh	2			
St. Augustine's College*	11			
	13			

Airport 61-80 (2000)

AIRPORT	MINORITY GROUP			
	Black	Hispanic	Asian	Native American
HSV=Huntsville, AL/Decatur, GA				
Jacksonville State University	1			
Middle Tennessee State U	4		2	1
	5		2	1
IAH=Houston–Intercontinental,TX				
Sam Houston State University			1	
			1	
IND=Indianapolis, IN				
Indiana State U – Main Campus	4			1
	4			1
JAX=Jacksonville, FL				
University of Florida	8	16	1	
	8	16	1	
JFK=New York, Kennedy Int'l, NY				
Yale University	10	6	2	
SUNY College at New Paltz	7	1	1	4
	17	7	3	4
LAX=Los Angeles, CA				
Cal State College – Bakersfield	1	1		4
University of Redlands	1	1		
	2	2		4
LCH=Lake Charles, LA				
U of Southwestern Louisiana	3			
Lamar University				2
	3			2
LIT=Little Rock, AR				
Henderson State University	1			
	1			
MCN=Macon, GA				
Clark College*	13			
GA Inst of Tech – Main Campus		1		
Georgia State University	11			2

Airport 61-80 (2000)

AIRPORT		MINORITY GROUP		
	Black	Hispanic	Asian	Native American
MCN (cont)				
Morehouse College*	13			
Morris Brown College*	5			
Spelman College*	48			
	90	1		2
MEM=Memphis, TN				
Arkansas State U - Main Campus	4			1
U of Mississippi - Main Campus	6			
	10			1
MGM=Montgomery, GA				
Talladega College*	15			
	15			
MHT=Manchester, NH				
Boston State College	6	1		
Boston University	5			
U of Mass - Amherst Campus	4	2		
	15	3		
MKE=Milwaukee, WS				
Northwestern University	6	2	1	
U of Wisconsin - Madison	2		2	
	8	2	3	
MKL=Jackson, TN				
Rust College*	2			
Memphis State University	8			
	10			
MOB=Mobile, AL/Pasagoula, MS				
U of Southern Mississippi	7			
	7			
MSN=Madison, WS				
U of Wisconsin - Milwaukee	1	1		
	1	1		

Airport 61-80 (2000)

AIRPORT	MINORITY GROUP			
	Black	Hispanic	Asian	Native American
MSY=New Orleans, LA				
Louisiana State U & A&M College	6			
Sthrn U A&M C - Main Cam*	18			
	24			
ORF=Norfolk/Virginia Beach, VA				
Virginia State College*	16			
	16			
PVD=Providence, RI				
U of Mass - Amherst Campus	4	2		
	4	**2**		
RDU=Raleigh/Durham, NC				
East Carolina University	6			
	6			
RIC=Richmond, VA				
Hampton Institute*	20			
Norfolk State College*	24			
U of Virginia - Main Campus	11	1	1	
	55	**1**	**1**	
SAN=San Diego, CA				
Chapman College	9	6	1	
U of Cal - Irvine	9		1	4
U of Cal - Riverside	2	4	3	
	20	**10**	**5**	**4**
SAT=San Antonio, TX				
U of Texas at Austin	9	40	4	1
	9	**40**	**4**	**1**
SAV=Savannah, GA				
Baptist College at Charleston	4			
	4			
SBA=Santa Barbara, CA				
Cal State College - Bakersfield	1	1		4
Cal State University - Los Angeles	18	18	17	2

Airport 61-80 (2000)

AIRPORT	MINORITY GROUP			
	Black	Hispanic	Asian	Native American
SBA (cont)				
Cal State University - Northridge	7	12	7	1
Loyola Marymount University	1	7	3	
U of Cal - Los Angeles	25	25	83	3
	52	**63**	**110**	**10**
SBY=Salisbury, MD				
Delaware State College*	9	1		
	9	**1**		
SFO=San Francisco/Oakland, CA				
Cal State University - Sacramento	7	6	3	3
U of Cal - Davis	4	7	11	1
U of Cal - Santa Cruz		17	3	
University of the Pacific	6	1	1	
	17	**31**	**18**	**4**
SHV=Shreveport, LA				
Louisiana Tech University	1			
	1			
SWI=Sherman, TX				
U of Texas at Arlington	2	1	1	
	2	**1**	**1**	
TLH=Tallahassee, FL				
Albany State College*	17			
Valdosta State College	6			
	23			
TPA=Tampa, FL				
University of Central Florida	5	1		
	5	**1**		
TUL=Tulsa, OK				
Oklahoma State U - Main Campus	2			3
	2			**3**
TYR=Tyler, TX				
East Texas State University	4			
	4			

668

PSYCHOLOGY (2000)
MINORITY BACCALAUREATE DEGREES
MORE THAN 80 MILES FROM NEAREST AIRPORT

AIRPORT	MINORITY GROUP			
	Black	Hispanic	Asian	Native American
ABQ=Albuquerque, NM				
New Mexico Highlands U*		4		
		4		
AUS=Austin, TX				
Texas A&M U - Main Campus		2	1	1
		2	**1**	**1**
IAH=Houston-Intercontinental, TX				
Texas A&M U - Main Campus		2	1	1
		2	**1**	**1**
MSY=New Orleans, LA				
U of Southern Mississippi	7			
	7			
ROW=Roswell, NM				
Eastern NM U - Main Campus	2	6		
	2	**6**		
TCL=Tuscaloosa, AL				
Mississippi State University	3			
	3			

PUBLIC AFFAIRS & SERVICES (2100)

PUBLIC AFFAIRS AND SERVICES (2100)
MINORITY BACCALAUREATE DEGREES
BY STATE AND INSTITUTION

STATE/SCHOOL	MINORITY GROUP			
	Black	Hispanic	Asian	Native American
Alabama				
Alabama A&M University*	13			
Alabama State University*	43			
Jacksonville State University	8			
Miles College*	15			
Oakwood College*	6			
Talladega College*	11			
Troy State University - Main Campus	37		1	
Troy State University - Montgomery	19			
Tuskegee Institute*	25			
University of Alabama	14			
U of Alabama in Birmingham	23			
	214		**1**	
Arizona				
Arizona State University	8	16	1	2
Northern Arizona University	3	13		6
University of Arizona	2	11		1
	13	**40**	**1**	**9**
Arkansas				
Arkansas State U - Main Campus	7			
Henderson State University	17			
Philander Smith College*	2			
University of Arkansas - Pine Bluff*	30			
	56			
California				
Cal State College - Bakersfield	1	3		
Cal State College - San Bernadino	6	5		
Cal State Poly U - Pomona	3	11		1

(2100)

STATE/SCHOOL	MINORITY GROUP			
	Black	Hispanic	Asian	Native American
California (cont)				
Cal State University - Chico	6	11	5	3
Cal State U - Dominguez Hills	90	8	4	2
Cal State University - Fresno	8	23	8	
Cal State University - Fullerton	9	16	4	2
Cal State University - Hayward	7	6	3	
Cal State University - Long Beach	26	24	14	4
Cal State University - Los Angeles	63	54	24	4
Cal State University - Northridge	5	5	3	
Cal State University - Sacramento	34	34	28	8
Chapman College	4		1	
Pepperdine University	5		1	
San Diego State University	17	34	16	4
San Francisco State University	22	2	12	3
San Jose State University	20	36	27	5
U of Cal - Berkeley	10	10	32	1
U of Cal - Los Angeles	2	1		
U of Cal - Santa Cruz		1		
University of LaVerne	8	5	1	
University of San Francisco	49	31	22	9
University of Southern California	10	17	11	2
University of the Pacific	2	2	3	1
	407	**339**	**219**	**49**
Colorado				
Colorado State University	4	3	4	
Metropolitan State College	14	13	2	
U of Colorado at Boulder	4	2	3	
U of Northern Colorado		2		
U of Southern Colorado		1		1
	22	**21**	**9**	**1**

672

(2100)

STATE/SCHOOL	MINORITY GROUP			
	Black	Hispanic	Asian	Native American
District of Columbia				
American University	38	1	2	1
George Washington University		2		
University of DC*	56			
	94	**3**	**2**	**1**
Florida				
Biscayne College*	21	12		1
Florida Atlantic University	21	1		
Florida International University	43	51	2	1
Florida Memorial College*	2			
Florida State University	79	4	1	1
University of Central Florida	13			
St. Leo College	1			
University of Florida	7	2		
University of Miami	1			
University of South Florida	28	10		2
University of West Florida	19	2	1	
	235	**82**	**4**	**5**
Georgia				
Clark College*	14			
Fort Valley State College*	6			
Georgia College	5			
Georgia State University	27			
Morris Brown College*	4			
Savannah State College*	5			
University of Georgia	6			
	67			
Hawaii				
University of Hawaii at Manoa*			43	
			43	

(2100)

STATE/SCHOOL	MINORITY GROUP			
	Black	Hispanic	Asian	Native American
Illinois				
Bradley University	1			
Chicago State University*	30			
Eastern Illinois University	3		1	
Governors State University	48	1		
Illinois State University	27	5		2
Loyola University of Chicago	10	4		
Northeastern Illinois University	6	3		
Roosevelt University	44	5		
Southern Illinois U - Carbondale	33	3	2	1
Southern Illinois U - Edwardsville	24		1	
U of Illinois - Chicago Circle	2			
U of Illinois - Urbana Campus	1	1		1
	229	**22**	**4**	**4**
Indiana				
Ball State University	8			1
Ind-Purdue U - Indianapolis	12		1	1
Indiana State U - Main Campus	7			
Indiana University - Bloomington	21	1	2	
Indiana University - Northwest	1	1		
Purdue University - Main Campus	1			
	50	**2**	**3**	**2**
Kentucky				
Eastern Kentucky University	17			
Kentucky State University*	27			
University of Louisville	6			
Western Kentucky University	4			
	54			
Louisiana				
Dillard University*	10			
Grambling State University*	55			
Louisiana State U & A&M College		1		

674

(2100)

STATE/SCHOOL	MINORITY GROUP			
	Black	Hispanic	Asian	Native American
Louisiana (cont)				
Louisiana Tech University	4			
McNeese State University	3			
Northeast Louisiana University	10			
Southeastern Louisiana U	11			
Sthrn U A&M College - Main Cam*	35			
Southern U in New Orleans*	28			
Xavier University of Louisiana*	7			
	163	**1**		
Maryland				
Bowie State College*	12			
Coppin State College*	15			
Morgan State University*	32			
University of Baltimore	35			
U of MD - College Park Campus	7		1	
	101		**1**	
Massachussetts				
Boston State College	11	5	1	2
Boston University	2	1		
	13	**6**	**1**	**2**
Michigan				
Detroit Institute of Technology	1			
Eastern Michigan University	25	1	1	2
Mercy College of Detroit	10			
Michigan State University	27	3	1	
Oakland University	20	2	1	
University of Detroit	25		2	
Wayne State University	84	3	1	1
Western Michigan University	13	2	2	1
	205	**11**	**8**	**4**
Minnesota				
U of Minn - Minneapolis/St. Paul	7		3	
	7		**3**	

(2100)

STATE/SCHOOL		MINORITY	GROUP	
	Black	Hispanic	Asian	Native American
Mississippi				
Alcorn State University*	9			
Delta State University	13			
Jackson State University*	53			
Mississippi State University	14			
Mississippi University for Women	7			
Mississippi Valley State Univ*	28			
Rust College*	25			
U of Mississippi - Main Campus	10			
U of Southern Mississippi	27		1	
	186		**1**	
Missouri				
Columbia College	11			1
Lincoln University	10			
Park College	27	2		
St. Louis U - Main Campus	6		1	
U of Missouri - Columbia	6	1		
U of Missouri - Kansas City	5			
U of Missouri - St. Louis	20	4		2
	85	**7**	**1**	**3**
New Hampshire				
Dartmouth College			1	
			1	
New Jersey				
Glassboro State College	13	10		3
Jersey City State College	12	2		
Kean College of New Jersey	23	6		
Princeton University	3	3	1	
Rutgers U - Camden Campus	8	1		
Rutgers U - New Brunswick	2	1		
Rutgers U - Newark Campus	9			

676

(2100)

STATE/SCHOOL	MINORITY GROUP			
	Black	Hispanic	Asian	Native American
New Jersey (cont)				
Seton Hall University	1			
Trenton State College	14	1	1	
	85	24	2	3
New Mexico				
New Mexico Highlands U*		17		
NM State U - Main Campus		15		1
University of Albuquerque				1
		32		2
New York				
Adelphi University	82	14		1
College of New Rochelle		1		
CUNY Bernard Baruch College	7	3	2	
CUNY John Jay College - Crim Jus	135	65	8	10
CUNY Medgar Evers College*	4			
Long Island U - C W Post Center	10	2		
Mercy College	14	6	2	
New York University	15	5	1	
St. John's University	7	14	7	2
SUNY at Albany	4			
SUNY at Stony Bk - Main Campus	1	1		
SUNY College at Buffalo	14	3		1
SUNY Empire State College	36	7	1	2
Syracuse University - Main Campus	2	1	1	
	331	122	22	16
North Carolina				
Bennett College*	3			
Duke University	2		1	
East Carolina University	11			
Johnson C Smith University*	14			
Livingstone College*	22			
NC Agrl & Tech State University*	49			

(2100)

STATE/SCHOOL	MINORITY GROUP			
	Black	Hispanic	Asian	Native American
North Carolina (cont)				
NC Central University*	48			
NC State U - Raleigh	6	1		
St. Augustine's College*			1	
Shaw University*	13			
U of NC at Chapel Hill	13			
U of NC at Charlotte	8			
U of NC at Greensboro	4			
	193	1	2	
North Dakota				
U of North Dakota - Main Campus				5
				5
Ohio				
Antioch University	140			1
Bowling Green State U - Main Cam	15	2		
Central State University*	24			
Franklin University	2			
Kent State U - Main Campus	19		1	
Ohio State U - Main Campus	8	1		
Ohio University - Main Campus	3			
U of Akron - Main Campus	5			1
U of Cincinnati - Main Campus	29	1		
University of Dayton	8			
Wright State U - Main Campus	2			
	255	4	1	2
Oklahoma				
East Central Oklahoma State U	3			4
Langston University*	6			
Northeast Oklahoma State U				1
U of Oklahoma - Norman Campus	2			3
	11			8

(2100)

STATE/SCHOOL	MINORITY GROUP			
	Black	Hispanic	Asian	Native American
Oregon				
University of Oregon – Main Campus	6	3	6	2
	6	**3**	**6**	**2**
Pennsylvania				
Cheyney State College*	20			
Lincoln University*	6			
Pennsylvania State U – Main Campus	9	3		1
Temple University	83	18		4
U of Pittsburgh – Main Campus	40			
West Chester State College	9	1		
	167	**22**		**5**
South Carolina				
Baptist College at Charleston	9			
Benedict College*	47			
South Carolina State College*	2			
U of South Carolina at Columbia	15	1		
	73	**1**		
Tennessee				
Austin Peay State University	2			
LeMoyne–Owen College*	16			
Memphis State University	19			
Middle Tennessee State U	4			
Tennessee State University*	45			
U of Tennessee – Knoxville	7			
U of Tennessee – Martin	10		1	
	103		**1**	
Texas				
Bishop College*	5			
Corpus Christi State University		15	1	2
East Texas State University	15			
Lamar University	3		1	4
Laredo State University*		13		

(2100)

STATE/SCHOOL	MINORITY GROUP			
	Black	Hispanic	Asian	Native American
Texas (cont)				
North Texas State University	4	1		
Our Lady of Lake University*	9	37		
Pan American University*	2	61	1	
Paul Quinn College*	12			
Prairie View A&M University*	24			
St. Edward's University		8		
St. Mary's U - San Antonio		17		
Southwest Texas State University	2	25		1
Sul Ross State University		1		
Texas A&M U - Main Campus		1		
Texas Southern University*	28	2		
Texas Women's University	12	9	1	
U of Texas at Arlington	12	9	1	
U of Texas at Austin	2	11		
U of Texas at El Paso	5	66	1	1
	135	**276**	**6**	**8**
Utah				
Brigham Young University - Main			1	9
University of Utah	1		1	
	1		**2**	**9**
Virginia				
Norfolk State College*	38			
Virginia Commonwealth University	33	2		1
Virginia Union University*	6			
	77	**2**		**1**
Washington				
University of Washington	6	1	6	3
	6	**1**	**6**	**3**
West Virginia				
West Virginia State College	29		1	
	29		**1**	

(2100)

STATE/SCHOOL	MINORITY GROUP			
	Black	Hispanic	Asian	Native American
Wisconsin				
U of Wisconsin – Madison	3		2	
U of Wisconsin – Milwaukee	28	3		
	31	3	2	
TOTALS	3704	1025	353	144

*Predominately minority institutions are those where at least 50% of the total BA Degrees awarded are to one of the minority groups being considered.

PUBLIC AFFAIRS AND SERVICES (2100)
BLACK BACCALAUREATE DEGREES RANKED BY INSTITUTION

Rank	Institution	B.A.'s	Rank	Institution	B.A.'s
1	Antioch U	140	31	Morgan State U*	32
2	CUNY Joh Jay C-Crim Jus	135	32	Chicago State U*	30
3	Cal State U-Dominguez Hills	90	33	U of Arkansas-Pine Bluff*	30
4	Wayne State U	84	34	U of Cincinnati-Main Campus	29
5	Temple U	83	35	West Virginia State C	29
6	Adelphi U	82	36	Southern U in New Orleans*	28
7	Florida State U	79	37	U of South Florida	28
8	Cal State U-Los Angeles	63	38	Texas Southern U*	28
9	U of DC*	56	39	Mississippi Valley State U*	28
10	Grambling State U*	55	40	U of Wisconsin-Milwaukee	28
11	Jackson State U*	53	41	Kentucky State U*	27
12	U of San Francisco	49	42	U of Southen Mississippi	27
13	NC Agrl & Tech State U*	49	43	Georgia State U	27
14	Governors State U	48	44	Michigan State U	27
15	NC Central U*	48	45	Illinois State U	27
16	Benedict C*	47	46	Park C	27
17	Tennessee State U*	45	47	Cal State U-Long Beach	26
18	Roosevelt U	44	48	U of Detroit	25
19	Florida International U	43	49	Rust C*	25
20	Alabama State U*	43	50	Eastern Michigan U	25
21	U of Pittsburgh-Main Campus	40	51	Tuskegee Institute*	25
22	American U	38	52	Central State U	24
23	Norfolk State C*	38	53	Southern Illinois U-Edwardsville	24
24	Troy State U-Main Campus	37	54	Prairie View A&M U*	24
25	SUNY Empire State C	36	55	Kean C of New Jersey	23
26	Sthrn U A&M C-Main Campus*	35	56	U of Alabama in Birmingham	23
27	U of Baltimore	35	57	San Francisco State U	22
28	Cal State U-Sacramento	34	58	Livingstone C*	22
29	Southern Illinois U-Carbondale	33	59	Florida Atlantic U	21
30	Virginia Commonweatlh U	33	60	Biscayne C	21

682

Black B.A.'s (2100)

Rank	Institution	B.A.'s	Rank	Institution	B.A.'s
61	Indiana U-Bloomington	21	89	Glassboro State C	13
62	Oakland U	20	90	Shaw U*	13
63	Cheyney State C*	20	91	Western Michigan U	13
64	San Jose State U	20	92	Florida Technological U	13
65	U of Missouri-St. Louis	20	93	U of NC at Chapel Hill	13
66	U of West Florida	19	94	Alabama A&M U*	13
67	Kent State U-Main Campus	19	95	Bowie State C*	12
68	Troy State U-Montgomery	19	96	U of Texas at Arlington	12
69	Memphis State U	19	97	Ind-Purdue U-Indianapolis	12
70	Eastern Kentucky U	17	98	Paul Quinn C*	12
71	San Diego State U	17	99	Jersey City State C	12
72	Henderson State U	17	100	Texas Women's U	12
73	Le Moyne-Owen C*	16	101	Southeastern Louisiana U	11
74	New York U	15	102	Columbia C	11
75	Bowling Green State U-Main Ca	15	103	Boston State C	11
76	Coppin State C*	15	104	East Carolina U	11
77	East Texas State U	15	105	Talladega C*	11
78	Miles C*	15	106	Dillard U*	10
79	U of South Carolina at Columbia	15	107	Northeast Louisiana U	10
80	Mercy C	14	108	U of Cal-Berkeley	10
81	Mississippi State U	14	109	Lincoln U*	10
82	Johnson C Smith U*	14	110	Loyola U of Chicago	10
83	Trenton State C	14	111	U of Mississippi-Main Campus	10
84	Clark C*	14	112	U of Southern California	10
85	SUNY C at Buffalo	14	113	Long Island U-C W Post Center	10
86	Metropolitan State C	14	114	U of Tennessee at Martin	10
87	U of Alabama	14	115	Mercy C of Detroit	10
88	Delta State U	13			

*predominantly black institutions

Institutions not ranked have less than ten degrees conferred on blacks.

683

PUBLIC AFFAIRS & SERVICES (2100)
HISPANIC BACCALAUREATE DEGREES RANKED BY INSTITUTION

Rank	Institution	B.A.'s	Rank	Institution	B.A.'s
1	U of Texas at El Paso	66	18	Cal State U-Fullerton	16
2	CUNY John Jay C-Crim Jus	65	19	Arizona State U	16
3	Pan American U*	61	20	NM State U-Main Campus	15
4	Cal State U-Los Angeles	54	21	Corpus Christi State U	15
5	Florida International U	51	22	Adelphi U	14
6	Our Lady of the Lake U*	37	23	St. John's U	14
7	San Jose State U	36	24	Metropolitan State C	13
8	Cal State U-Sacramento	34	25	Northern Arizona U	13
9	San Diego State U	34	26	Laredo State U*	13
10	U of San Francisco	31	27	Biscayne C*	12
11	Southwest Texas State U	25	28	Cal State U-Chico	11
12	Cal State U-Long Beach	24	29	Cal State Poly U-Pomona	11
13	Cal State U-Fresno	23	30	U of Arizona	11
14	Temple U	18	31	U of Texas at Austin	11
15	U of Southern California	17	32	U of Cal-Berkeley	10
16	New Mexico Highlands U*	17	33	Glassboro State C	10
17	St. Mary's U-San Antonio	17	34	U of South Florida	10

*predominantly Hispanic institutions

Institutions not ranked have less than ten degrees conferred on Hispanics.

PUBLIC AFFAIRS & SERVICES (2100)
ASIAN BACCALAUREATE DEGREES RANKED BY INSTITUTION

Rank	Institution	B.A.'s	Rank	Institution	B.A.'s
1	U of Hawaii at Manoa*	43	6	U of San Francisco	22
2	U of Cal-Berkeley	32	7	San Deigo State U	16
3	Cal State U-Sacramento	28	8	Cal State U-Long Beach	14
4	San Jose State U	27	9	San Francisco State U	12
5	Cal State U-Los Angeles	24	10	U of Southern California	11

*predominantly Asian institutions

Institutions not ranked have less than ten degrees conferred on Asians.

PUBLIC AFFAIRS & SERVICES (2100)
NATIVE AMERICAN BACCALAUREATE DEGREES RANKED BY INSTITUTION

Rank	Institution	B.A.'s	Rank	Institution	B.A.'s
1	CUNY John Jay C-Crim Jus	10	5	Northern Arizona U	6
2	U of San Francisco	9	6	San Jose State U	5
3	Brigham Young U-Main Campus	9	7	U of North Dakota-Main Campus	5
4	Cal State U-Sacramento	8			

Institutions not ranked have less than five degrees conferred on Native Americans.

PUBLIC AFFAIRS AND SERVICES (2100)
MINORITY BACCALAUREATE DEGREES
WITHIN 60 MILE RADIUS OF AIRPORT

AIRPORT	MINORITY GROUP			
	Black	Hispanic	Asian	Native American
ABQ=Albuquerque, NM				
University of Albuquerque				1
				1
ACT=Waco, TX				
Paul Quinn College*	12			
	12			
ALB=Albany, NY				
SUNY at Albany	4			
SUNY Empire State College	36	7	1	2
	40	**7**	**1**	**2**
AOO=Altoona, PA				
Pennsylvania State U - Main Campus	9	3		1
	9	**3**		**1**
ATL=Atlanta, GA				
Clark College*	14			
Georgia State University	27			
Morris Brown College*	4			
	45			
AUS=Austin, TX				
Southwest Texas State University	2	25		1
U of Texas at Austin	2	11		
	4	**36**		**1**
BAL=Baltimore, MD				
American University	38	1	2	1
George Washington Univesity		2		
University of DC*	56			
Bowie State College*	12			
Coppin State College*	15			

Airport 60 (2100)

AIRPORT	MINORITY GROUP			
	Black	Hispanic	Asian	Native American
BAL (cont)				
Morgan State University*	32			
U of MD - College Park Campus	7		1	
University of Baltimore	35			
Lincoln University*	6			
	201	**3**	**3**	**1**
BHM=Birmingham, AL				
Miles College*	15			
Talladega College*	11			
U of Alabama in Birmingham	23			
University of Alabama	14			
	63			
BKL=Cleveland-Lakefront, OH				
Kent State U - Main Campus	19		1	
U of Akron - Main Campus	5			1
	24		**1**	**1**
BNA=Nashville, TN				
Western Kentucky University	4			
Austin Peay State University	2			
Middle Tennessee State U	4			
Tennessee State University*	45			
	55			
BOS=Boston, MA				
Boston State College	11	5	1	2
Boston University	2	1		
	13	**6**	**1**	**2**
BTR=Baton Rouge, LA				
Louisiana State U & A&M College		1		
Sthrn U A&M College - Main Cam*	35			
Southeastern Louisian U	11			
	46	**1**		

687

Airport 60 (2100)

AIRPORT	MINORITY GROUP			
	Black	Hispanic	Asian	Native American
BUF=Buffalo, NY				
SUNY College at Buffalo	14	3		1
	14	**3**		**1**
CAE=Columbia, SC				
Benedict College*	47			
South Carolina State College*	2			
U of South Carolina at Columbia	15	1		
	64	**1**		
CHS=Charleston, SC				
Baptist College at Charleston	9			
	9			
CIC=Chico, CA				
Cal State University - Chico	6	11	5	3
	6	**11**	**5**	**3**
CLT=Charlotte, NC				
Johnson C Smith University*	14			
Livingstone College*	22			
U of NC at Charlotte	8			
	44			
CMH=Columbus, OH				
Central State University*	24			
Ohio State U - Main Campus	8	1		
	32	**1**		
CMI=Champaign, IL				
Eastern Illinois University	3	•	1	
Illinois State University	27	5		2
U of Illinois - Urbana Campus	1	1		1
Indiana State U - Main Campus	7			
	38	**6**	**1**	**3**
COS=Colorado Springs, CO				
U of Southern Colorado		1		1
		1		**1**

Airport 60 (2100)

AIRPORT	MINORITY GROUP			
	Black	Hispanic	Asian	Native American
COU=Columbia, MO				
Columbia College	11			1
Lincoln University	10			
U of Missouri – Columbia	6	1		
	27	1		1
CRP=Corpus Christi, TX				
Corpus Christi State University		15	1	2
		15	1	2
CRW=Charleston, WV				
West Virginia State College	29		1	
	29		1	
CVG=Cincinnati, OH				
Antioch University	140			1
Central State University*	24			
Franklin University	2			
U of Cincinnati – Main Campus	29	1		
University of Dayton	8			
Wright State U – Main Campus	2			
	205	1		1
DAB=Dayton Beach, FL				
University of Central Florida	13			
	13			
DCA=Washington–National, DC				
American University	38	1	2	1
George Washington University		2		
University of DC*	56			
Bowie State College*	12			
Coppin State College*	15			
Morgan State University*	32			
U of MD – College Park Campus	7		1	
University of Baltimore	35			
	195	3	3	1

Airport 60 (2100)

AIRPORT	MINORITY GROUP			
	Black	Hispanic	Asian	Native American
DEN=Denver, CO				
Metropolitan State College	14	13	2	
U of Colorado at Boulder	4	2	3	
U of Northern Colorado		2		
	18	17	5	
DFW=Dallas/Fort Worth, TX				
Bishop College*	5			
East Texas State University	15			
North Texas State University	4	1		
Texas Woman's University	12	9	1	
U of Texas at Arlington	12	9	1	
	48	19	2	
DTW=Detroit-Metropolitan, MI				
Detroit Institute of Technology	1			
Eastern Michigan University	25	1	1	2
Mercy College of Detroit	10			
Oakland University	20	2	1	
University of Detroit	25		2	
Wayne State University	84	3	1	1
	165	6	5	3
ELP=El Paso, TX				
U of Texas at El Paso	5	66	1	1
	5	66	1	1
EUG=Eugene, OR				
University of Oregon - Main Campus	6	3	6	2
	6	3	6	2
FAT=Fresno, CA				
Cal State University - Fresno	8	23	8	
	8	23	8	
FAY=Fayetteville, NC				
NC Central University*	48			
NC State U - Raleigh	6	1		

690

Airport 60 (2100)

AIRPORT

	MINORITY GROUP			
	Black	Hispanic	Asian	Native American
FAY (cont)				
St. Augustine's College*			1	
Shaw University*	13			
U of NC at Chapel Hill	13			
	80	**1**	**1**	
FLG=Flagstaff, AZ				
Northern Arizona University	3	13		6
	3	**13**		**6**
GLH=Greenville, MS				
Delta State University	13			
Mississippi Valley State U*	28			
	41			
GRR=Grand Rapids, MI				
Western Michigan University	13	2	2	1
	13	**2**	**2**	**1**
GSO=Greensboro/High Point, NC				
Bennett College*	3			
Duke University	2		1	
Livingstone College*	22			
NC Agrl & Tech State University*	49			
NC Central University*	48			
U of NC at Chapel Hill	13			
U of NC at Greensboro	4			
	141		**1**	
HNL=Honolulu/Oahu, HI				
University of Hawaii at Manoa*			43	
			43	
HSV=Huntsville, AL/Decatur, GA				
Alabama A&M University*	13			
Oakwood College*	6			
	19			

Airport 60 (2100)

AIRPORT	MINORITY GROUP			
	Black	Hispanic	Asian	Native American
IAH=Houston-Intercontinental,TX				
Prairie View A&M University*	24			
Texas Southern University*	28	2		
	52	**2**		
IND=Indianapolis, IN				
Ball State University	8			1
Ind-Purdue U – Indianapolis	12		1	1
Indiana University – Bloomington	21	1	2	
Purdue University – Main Campus	1			
	42	**1**	**3**	**2**
JAN=Jackson/Vicksburg, MS				
Alcorn State University*	9			
Jackson State University*	53			
	62			
JFK=New York, Kennedy Int'l, NY				
Jersey City State College	12	2		
Kean College of New Jersey	23	6		
Princeton University	3	3	1	
Rutgers U – New Brunswick	2	1		
Rutgers U – Newark Campus	9			
Seton Hall University	1			
Trenton State College	14	1	1	
Adelphi University	82	14		1
College of New Rochelle		1		
CUNY Bernard Baruch College	7	3	2	
CUNY John Jay College – Crim Jus	135	65	8	10
CUNY Medgar Evers College*	4			
Long Island U – C W Post Center	10	2		
Mercy College	14	6	2	
New York University	15	5	1	
St. John's University	7	14	7	2
SUNY at Stony Bk – Main Campus	1	1		
	339	**124**	**22**	**13**

692

Airport 60 (2100)

AIRPORT	MINORITY GROUP			
	Black	Hispanic	Asian	Native American
LAX=Los Angeles, CA				
Cal State College - San Bernardino	6	5		
Cal State Poly U - Pomona	3	11		1
Cal State U - Dominguez Hills	90	8	4	2
Cal State University - Fullerton	9	16	4	2
Cal State University - Long Beach	26	24	14	4
Cal State University - Los Angeles	63	54	24	4
Cal State University - Northridge	5	5	3	
Chapman College	4		1	
Pepperdine University	5		1	
U of Cal - Los Angeles	2	1		
University of Southern California	10	17	11	2
University of LaVerne	8	5	1	
	231	**146**	**63**	**15**
LCH=Lake Charles, LA				
McNeese State University	3			
	3			
LEX=Lexington/Frankfort, KY				
Eastern Kentucky University	17			
Kentucky State University*	27			
University of Louisville	6			
	50			
LIT=Little Rock, AR				
Philander Smith College*	2			
University of Arkansas - Pine Bluff*	30			
	32			
LRD=Laredo, TX				
Laredo State University*		13		
		13		
MCI=Kansas City-International, MO				
Park College	27	2		
U of Missouri - Kansas City	5			
	32	**2**		

Airport 60 (2100)

AIRPORT	MINORITY GROUP			
	Black	Hispanic	Asian	Native American
MCN=Macon, GA				
Fort Valley State College*	6			
Georgia College	5			
	11			
MDH=Carbondale, IL				
Southern Illinois U - Carbondale	33	3	2	1
	33	3	2	1
MEM=Memphis, TN				
Rust College*	25			
Le Moyne-Owen College*	16			
Memphis State University	19			
	60			
MFE=McAllen, TX				
Pan American University*	2	61	1	
	2	61	1	
MGM=Montgomery, GA				
Alabama State University*	43			
Troy State University - Main Campus	37		1	
Troy State University - Montgomery	19			
Tuskegee Institute*	25			
	124		1	
MHT=Manchester, NH				
Dartmouth College			1	
			1	
MIA=Miami, FL				
Biscayne College*	21	12		1
Florida Atlantic University	21	1		
Florida International University	43	51	2	1
Florida Memorial College*	2			
University of Miami	1			
	88	64	2	2

Airport 60 (2100)

AIRPORT	MINORITY GROUP			
	Black	Hispanic	Asian	Native American
MKE=Milwaukee, WS				
U of Wisconsin – Milwaukee	28	3		
	28	3		
MKL=Jackson, TN				
U of Tennessee at Martin	10		1	
	10		1	
MLU=Monroe, LA				
Grambling State University*	55			
Louisiana Tech University	4			
Northeast Louisiana University	10			
	69			
MOB=Mobile, AL/Pasagoula, MS				
University of West Florida	19	2	1	
	19	2	1	
MSN=Madison, WS				
U of Wisconsin – Madison	3		2	
	3		2	
MSP=Minneapolis/St. Paul, MN				
U of Minn – Minneapolis/St. Paul	7		3	
	7		3	
MSY=New Orleans, LA				
Dillard University*	10			
Southeastern Louisiana U	11			
Southern U in New Orleans*	28			
Xavier University of Louisiana*	7			
	56			
ORD=Chicago–O'Hare Airport, IL				
Chicago State University*	30			
Governors State University	48	1		
Loyola University of Chicago	10	4		
Northeastern Illinois University	6	3		

Airport 60 (2100)

AIRPORT	MINORITY GROUP			
	Black	Hispanic	Asian	Native American
ORD (cont)				
Roosevelt University	44	5		
U of Illinois - Chicago Circle	2			
Indiana University - Northwest	1	1		
	141	**14**		
ORF=Norfolk/Virginia Beach, VA				
Norfolk State College*	38			
	38			
PHL=Philadelphia, PA/Wilmington, DE				
Glassboro State College	13	10		3
Princeton University	3	3	1	
Rutgers U - Camden Campus	8	1		
Rutgers U - New Brunswick	2	1		
Trenton State College	14	1	1	
Cheyney State College*	20			
Lincoln University*	6			
Temple University	83	18		4
West Chester State College	9	1		
	158	**35**	**2**	**7**
PHX=Phoenix, AZ				
Arizona State University	8	16	1	2
	8	**16**	**1**	**2**
PIA=Peoria, IL				
Bradley University	1			
	1			
PIT=Pittsburgh, PA				
U of Pittsburgh - Main Campus	40			
	40			
PVD=Providence, RI				
Boston State College	11	5	1	2
Boston University	2	1		
	13	**6**	**1**	**2**

696

Airport 60 (2100)

AIRPORT	MINORITY GROUP			
	Black	Hispanic	Asian	Native American
PWA=Oklahoma City-Wiley Post, OK				
Langston University*	6			
U of Oklahoma – Norman Campus	2			3
	8			3
RDU=Raleigh/Durham, NC				
Bennet College*	3			
Duke University	2		1	
NC Agrl & Tech State University*	49			
NC Central University*	48			
NC State U – Raleigh	6	1		
St. Augustine's College*			1	
Shaw University*	13			
U of NC at Chapel Hill	13			
U of NC at Greensboro	4			
	138	1	2	
RIC=Richmond, VA				
Virginia Commonwealth University	33	2		1
Virginia Union University*	6			
	39	2		1
SAN=San Diego, CA				
San Diego State University	17	34	16	4
	17	34	16	4
SAT=San Antonio, TX				
Our Lady of Lake University*	9	37		
St. Edward's University		8		
St. Mary's U – San Antonio		17		
Southwest Texas State University	2	25		1
	11	87		1
SAV=Savannah, GA				
Savannah State College*	5			
	5			

697

Airport 60 (2100)

AIRPORT	MINORITY GROUP			
	Black	Hispanic	Asian	Native American
SBA=Santa Barbara, CA				
Pepperdine University	5		1	
	5		1	
SEA=Seattle/Tacoma, WA				
University of Washington	6	1	6	3
	6	1	6	3
SFO=San Francisco/Oakland, CA				
Cal State University - Hayward	7	6	3	
San Francisco State University	22	2	12	3
San Jose State University	20	36	27	5
U of Cal - Berkeley	10	10	32	1
University of San Francisco	49	31	22	9
	108	85	96	18
SHV=Shreveport, LA				
Grambling State University*	55			
	55			
SLC=Salt Lake City, UT				
Brigham Young University - Main			1	9
University of Utah	1		1	
	1		2	9
STL=St. Louis, MO				
Southern Illinois U - Edwardsville	24		1	
St. Louis U - Main Campus	6		1	
U of Missouri - St. Louis	20	4		2
	50	4	2	2
SWI=Sherman, TX				
Bishop College*	5			
East Texas State University	15			
North Texas State University	4	1		
Texas Woman's University	12	9	1	
	36	10	1	

698

Airport 60 (2100)

AIRPORT	MINORITY GROUP			
	Black	Hispanic	Asian	Native American
SYR=Syracuse, NY				
Syracuse U - Main Campus	2	1	1	
	2	**1**	**1**	
TCL=Tuscaloosa, AL				
Miles College*	15			
U of Alabama in Birmingham	23			
University of Alabama	14			
Mississippi University for Women	7			
	59			
TLH=Tallahassee, FL				
Florida State University	79	4	1	1
	79	**4**	**1**	**1**
TPA=Tampa, FL				
St. Leo College	1			
University of South Florida	28	10		2
	29	**10**		**2**
TUL=Tulsa, OK				
Northeast Oklahoma State U				1
				1
TUS=Tucson, AZ				
University of Arizona	2	11		1
	2	**11**		**1**
TYS=Knoxville, TN				
U of Tennessee - Knoxville	7			
	7			

PUBLIC AFFAIRS AND SERVICES (2100)
MINORITY BACCALAUREATE DEGREES
WITHIN 61–80 MILE ANNULUS OF AIRPORT

AIRPORT	MINORITY GROUP			
	Black	Hispanic	Asian	Native American
ALM=Alamogordo, NM				
NM State U – Main Campus		15		1
		15		**1**
ATL=Atlanta, GA				
Jacksonville State University	8			
Georgia College	5			
University of Georgia	6			
	19			
AUS=Austin, TX				
Our Lady of Lake University*	9	37		
St. Edward's University		8		
St. Mary's U – San Antonio		17		
	9	**62**		
BAL=Baltimore, MD				
Cheyney State College*	20			
	20			
BDL=Hartford, CT/Springfield, MA				
College of New Rochelle		1		
Mercy College	14	6	2	
SUNY at Albany	4			
	18	**7**	**2**	
BHM=Birmingham, AL				
Jacksonville State University	8			
	8			
BTR=Baton Rouge, LA				
Dillard University*	10			
Southern U in New Orleans*	28			
Xavier University of Louisiana*	7			
	45			

699

700

Airport 61-80 (2100)

AIRPORT	MINORITY GROUP			
	Black	Hispanic	Asian	Native American
CHS=Charleston, SC				
Savannah State College*	5			
South Carolina State College*	2			
	7			
CMH=Columbus, OH				
Antioch University	140			1
Ohio University - Main Campus	3			
University of Dayton	8			
Wright State U - Main Campus	2			
	153			1
CMI=Champaign, IL				
Purdue University - Main Campus	1			
	1			
COS=Colorado Springs, CO				
Metropolitan State College	14	13	2	
U of Colorado at Boulder	4	2	3	
	18	15	5	
CRW=Charleston, WV				
Ohio University - Main Campus	3			
	3			
CVG=Cincinnati, OH				
Kentucky State University*	27			
	27			
DCA=Washington-National, DC				
Lincoln University*	6			
	6			
DEN=Denver, CO				
Colorado State University	4	3	4	
	4	3	4	
DTW=Detroit-Metropolitan, MI				
Michigan State University	27	3	1	
Bowling Green State U - Main Cam	15	2		
	42	5	1	

Airport 61-80 (2100)

AIRPORT	MINORITY GROUP			
	Black	Hispanic	Asian	Native American
FAY=Fayetteville, NC				
Duke University	2		1	
	2		1	
GRR=Grand Rapids, MI				
Michigan State University	27	3	1	
	27	3	1	
GSO=Greensboro/High Point, NC				
NC State U - Raleigh	6	1		
St. Augustine's College*			1	
Shaw University*	13			
	19	1	1	
HSV=Huntsville, AL/Decatur, GA				
Jacksonville State University	8			
Middle Tennessee State U	4			
	12			
IND=Indianapolis, IN				
Indiana State U - Main Campus	7			
	7			
JAX=Jacksonville, FL				
University of Florida	7	2		
	7	2		
LAX=Los Angeles, CA				
Cal State College - Bakersfield	1	3		
	1	3		
LCH=Lake Charles, LA				
Lamar University	3		1	4
	3		1	4
LIT=Little Rock, AR				
Henderson State University	17			
	17			

702

Airport 61-80 (2100)

AIRPORT	MINORITY GROUP			
	Black	Hispanic	Asian	Native American
MCN=Macon, GA				
Clark College*	14			
Georgia State University	27			
Morris Brown College*	4			
	45			
MEM=Memphis, TN				
Arkansas State U – Main Campus	7			
U of Mississippi – Main Campus	10			
	17			
MGM=Montgomery, GA				
Talladega College*	11			
	11			
MHT=Manchester, NH				
Boston State College	11	5	1	2
Boston University	2	1		
	13	6	1	2
MKE=Milwaukee, WS				
U of Wisconsin – Madison	3		2	
	3		2	
MKL=Jackson, TN				
Rust College*	25			
Memphis State University	19			
	44			
MLU=Monroe, LA				
Alcorn State University*	9			
	9			
MOB=Mobile, AL/Pasagoula, MS				
U of Southern Mississippi	27		1	
	27		1	
MSN=Madison, WS				
U of Wisconsin – Milwaukee	28	3		
	28	3		

Airport 61-80 (2100)

AIRPORT	MINORITY GROUP			
	Black	Hispanic	Asian	Native American
MSY=New Orleans, LA				
Louisiana State U & A&M College		1		
Sthrn U A&M C – Main Cam*	35			
	35	**1**		
PWA=Oklahoma City-Wiley Post, OK				
East Central Oklahoma State U	3			4
	3			**4**
RDU=Raleigh/Durham, NC				
East Carolina University	11			
	11			
RIC=Richmond, VA				
Norfolk State College*	38			
	38			
SAN=San Diego, CA				
Chapman College	4		1	
	4		**1**	
SAT=San Antonio, TX				
U of Texas at Austin	2	11		
	2	**11**		
SAV=Savannah, GA				
Baptist College at Charleston	9			
	9			
SBA=Santa Barbara, CA				
Cal State College – Bakersfield	1	3		
Cal State University – Los Angeles	63	54	24	4
Cal State University – Northridge	5	5	3	
U of Cal – Los Angeles	2	1		
	71	**63**	**27**	**4**
SFO=San Francisco/Oakland, CA			•	
Cal State University – Sacramento	34	34	28	8
U of Cal – Santa Cruz		1		
University of the Pacific	2	2	3	1
	36	**37**	**31**	**9**

Airport 61-80 (2100)

AIRPORT	MINORITY GROUP			
	Black	Hispanic	Asian	Native American
SHV=Shreveport, LA				
Louisiana Tech University	4			
	4			
SWI=Sherman, TX				
U of Texas at Arlington	12	9	1	
	12	**9**	**1**	
TPA=Tampa, FL				
University of Central Florida	13			
	13			
TYR=Tyler, TX				
East Texas State University	15			
	15			

PUBLIC AFFAIRS AND SERVICES (2100)
MINORITY BACCALAUREATE DEGREES
MORE THAN 80 MILES FROM NEAREST AIRPORT

AIRPORT		MINORITY GROUP		
	Black	Hispanic	Asian	Native American
ABQ=Albuquerque, NM				
New Mexico Highlands U*		17		
		17		
AUS=Austin, TX				
Texas A&M U - Main Campus		1		
		1		
ELP=El Paso, TX				
Sul Ross State University		1		
		1		
IAH=Houston-Intercontinental, TX				
Texas A&M U - Main Campus		1		
		1		
MAF=Midland/Odessa, TX				
Sul Ross State University		1		
		1		
MSY=New Orleans, LA				
U of Southern Mississippi	27			1
	27			**1**
TCL=Tuscaloosa, AL				
Mississippi State University	14			
	14			

SOCIAL SCIENCES (2200)

SOCIAL SCIENCES (2200)
MINORITY BACCALAUREATE DEGREES
BY STATE AND INSTITUTION

STATE/SCHOOL	MINORITY GROUP			
	Black	Hispanic	Asian	Native American
Alabama				
Alabama A&M University*	54			
Alabama State University*	29			
Jacksonville State University	18	1		
Miles College*	21			
Oakwood College*	9			
Stillman College*	26	1		
Talladega College*	21			
Troy State University - Main Campus	13	1		
Troy State University - Montgomery	7	2		
Tuskegee Institute*	50			
University of Alabama	9			
U of Alabama in Birmingham	13			
University of South Alabama	6	1		1
	276	**6**		**1**
Arizona				
Arizona State University	7	30	1	
Northern Arizona University	2	7		8
University of Arizona	4	23	5	3
	13	**60**	**6**	**11**
Arkansas				
Arkansas Baptist College*	37			
Arkansas State U - Main Campus	14			
Henderson State University	6			
Philander Smith College*	5			
University of Arkansas - Pine Bluff*	33			
University of Central Arkansas	5			
	100			

708

(2200)

STATE/SCHOOL

	MINORITY GROUP			
	Black	Hispanic	Asian	Native American
California				
Cal Poly State U – San Luis Obispo	2	5	4	2
Cal State College – Bakersfield	2	3		6
Cal State College – San Bernadino	22	27	1	1
Cal State Poly U – Pomona	2	8		1
Cal State University – Chico	4	13	2	1
Cal State U – Dominguez Hills	69	11	6	2
Cal State University – Fresno	14	36	13	5
Cal State University – Fullerton	9	48	8	3
Cal State University – Hayward	25	11	7	2
Cal State University – Long Beach	24	32	25	5
Cal State University – Los Angeles	51	94	15	5
Cal State University – Northridge	25	37	18	12
Cal State University – Sacramento	18	6	5	3
Chapman College	18	9	6	1
Loyola Marymount University	16	19	3	1
Pacific Christian College	11			
Pepperdine University	9	2		1
San Diego State University	15	21	12	
San Francisco State University	43	32	38	6
San Jose State University	28	36	27	5
Stanford University	25	25	20	4
U of Cal – Berkeley	66	33	108	12
U of Cal – Davis	8	6	15	5
U of Cal – Irvine	7	6	10	
U of Cal – Los Angeles	99	73	120	5
U of Cal – Riverside	22	20	2	
U of Cal – San Diego		29	9	3
U of Cal – Santa Barbara	14	31	26	2
U of Cal – Santa Cruz		10	2	
University of LaVerne	8	4	2	
University of Redlands	1	2	1	

(2200)

STATE/SCHOOL	MINORITY GROUP			
	Black	Hispanic	Asian	Native American
California (cont)				
University of San Francisco	6	7	8	1
University of Southern California	27	20	18	3
University of the Pacific	3		8	
	693	**716**	**539**	**97**
Colorado				
Colorado State University	1	2	1	
Metropolitan State College	8	12	3	
U of Colorado at Boulder	6	18	8	3
U of Northern Colorado	3	3		1
U of Southern Colorado	7	26		
	25	**61**	**12**	**4**
Connecticut				
University of Connecticut	6			
Yale University	20	10	11	1
	26	**10**	**11**	**1**
Delaware				
Delaware State College*	11			
University of Delaware	17	2	2	
	28	**2**	**2**	
District of Columbia				
American University	35	10	2	
George Washington University	7	15	5	1
Howard University*	127			
University of DC*	42	6	2	2
	211	**31**	**9**	**3**
Florida				
Bethune Cookman College*	60			
Biscayne College*	1	26		
Edward Waters College*	26			
Florida Agr & Mech University*	89			
Florida Atlantic University	6	5		

710

(2200)

STATE/SCHOOL	MINORITY GROUP			
	Black	Hispanic	Asian	Native American
Florida (cont)				
Florida International University	13	66		
Florida Memorial College*	26			
Florida State University	24	4		2
University of Central Florida	5		1	
St. Leo College	28	8		
University of Florida	25	18	1	
University of Miami	16	20	1	
University of South Florida	45	17	4	
University of West Florida	5		2	
	369	**164**	**9**	**2**
Georgia				
Albany State College*	40			
Clark College*	33			
Fort Valley State College*	34			
Georgia College	11			
Georgia State University	29			1
Morehouse College*	42			
Morris Brown College*	31			
Paine College*	16			
Savannah State College*	24			
Spelman College*	92			
University of Georgia	8	1		1
Valdosta State College	13			
	373	**1**		**2**
Hawaii				
Chaminade University of Honolulu	2	1	15	
University of Hawaii at Hilo*		3	15	
University of Hawaii at Manoa*	2	5	211	1
	4	**9**	**241**	**1**

711

(2200)

STATE/SCHOOL	MINORITY GROUP			
	Black	Hispanic	Asian	Native American
Illinois				
Bradley University	4		1	
Chicago State University*	29			
College of St. Francis	2	1		
DePaul University	15	8	2	
Eastern Illinois University	11			
Governors State University	3	4		
Illinois State University	24	1	1	1
Loyola University of Chicago	13	9	1	
Northern Illinois University	18	1	1	1
Northeastern Illinois University	23	16	2	
Northwestern University	37	2	6	
Roosevelt University	22	8	10	
Southern Illinois U – Carbondale	7	1		
Southern Illinois U – Edwardsville	7			
U of Illinois – Chicago Circle	62	35	7	
U of Illinois – Urbana Campus	17	2	7	
	294	**88**	**38**	**2**
Indiana				
Ball State University	6	1		
Ind–Purdue U – Indianapolis	3			
Indiana State U – Main Campus	17	1	1	1
Indiana University – Bloomington	18	2		1
Indiana University – Northwest	13	3		
Purdue University – Main Campus	7	2	1	
	64	**9**	**2**	**2**
Kentucky				
Eastern Kentucky University	4			
Kentucky State University*	15			
University of Louisville	12		1	1
Western Kentucky University	6	1		
	37	**1**	**1**	**1**

712

(2200)

STATE/SCHOOL	MINORITY GROUP			
	Black	Hispanic	Asian	Native American
Louisiana				
Dillard University*	14			
Grambling State University*	49			
Louisiana State U & A&M College	7	3	1	
Louisiana Tech University	8			
McNeese State University	2			
Northeast Louisiana University	2			
Southeastern Louisiana U	2			
Sthrn U A&M College – Main Cam*	45			
Southern U in New Orleans*	26			
Tulane U of Louisiana	4	8	2	1
University of New Orleans	14	2	1	
U of Southwestern Louisiana	17	2		
Xavier University of Louisiana*	22			
	212	**15**	**4**	**1**
Maryland				
Bowie State College*	13			
Coppin State College*	23			
Morgan State University*	66		1	
Towson State University	17	2	1	1
University of Baltimore	9	1		
U of MD – Baltimore Co Campus	48		1	2
U of MD – College Park Campus	44	5	11	7
U of MD – Eastern Shore*	16			
	236	**8**	**14**	**10**
Massachussetts				
Boston State College	16	3	2	
Boston University	5	5	5	1
Harvard University	53	15	12	2
Radcliffe College	25	5	4	1
Tufts University	24	6	5	2
U of Mass – Amherst Campus	6	1	5	
	129	**35**	**33**	**6**

(2200)

STATE/SCHOOL	MINORITY GROUP			
	Black	Hispanic	Asian	Native American
Michigan				
Detroit Institute of Technology	6			
Eastern Michigan University	33	1	1	
Mercy College of Detroit	6			
Michigan State University	57	4	2	5
Oakland University	19	1		
Shaw College at Detroit*	23			
University of Detroit	34	1		
U of Michigan – Ann Arbor	25	7	6	1
Wayne State University	73	3	2	1
Western Michigan University	23	5	1	
	299	**22**	**12**	**7**
Minnesota				
U of Minn – Minneapolis/St. Paul	18	9	6	1
	18	**9**	**6**	**1**
Mississippi				
Alcorn State University*	44			
Delta State University	7			
Jackson State University*	50			
Mississippi Industrial College*	6			
Mississippi State University	11			
Mississippi University for Women	2			
Mississippi Valley State Univ*	65			
Rust College*	4			
Tougaloo College*	38			
U of Mississippi – Main Campus	11			
U of Southern Mississippi	12			
	250			
Missouri				
Columbia College	2			
Lincoln University	12			
Park College	6			

(2200)

STATE/SCHOOL	MINORITY GROUP			
	Black	Hispanic	Asian	Native American
Missouri (cont)				
St. Louis U - Main Campus	22	1		
U of Missouri - Columbia	6		4	
U of Missouri - Kansas City	3	3	4	
U of Missouri - St. Louis	4	2	3	
Washington University	13		2	
Webster College	9			
	77	**6**	**13**	
Montana				
Montana State University		2		2
		2		**2**
Nebraska				
U of Nebraska at Omaha	10		1	
	10		**1**	
New Hampshire				
Dartmouth College	31	1	2	1
	31	**1**	**2**	**1**
New Jersey				
Glassboro State College	17	17		
Jersey City State College	13	12		
Kean College of New Jersey	18	8	2	
Montclair State College	6	15		
Princeton University	27	18	6	1
Rutgers U - Camden Campus	27	4		
Rutgers U - New Brunswick	110	33	14	1
Rutgers U - Newark Campus	49	10	4	
St. Peter's College	9	11		
Seton Hall University	5	2		
Trenton State College	8	2		1
	289	**132**	**26**	**3**

(2200)

STATE/SCHOOL	MINORITY GROUP			
	Black	Hispanic	Asian	Native American
New Mexico				
Eastern NM U - Main Campus	4	8		2
New Mexico Highlands U*		21		1
NM State U - Main Campus	4	23		2
University of Albuquerque		10		1
U of NM - Main Campus		25		4
Western New Mexico University		3		1
	8	90		11
New York				
Adelphi University	21	4		
College of New Rochelle	2	1		
Cornell U Endowed College	17	6	12	1
CUNY Bernard Baruch College	13	5	4	
CUNY Brooklyn College	147	56	13	4
CUNY City College	70	34	21	3
CUNY College of Staten Island	24	13	6	1
CUNY Hunter College	66	40	15	4
CUNY John Jay College - Crim Jus	31	14	2	2
CUNY Lehman College	46	45	12	1
CUNY Medgar Evers College*	9			
CUNY Queen's College	66	20	20	1
CUNY York College	43	9	3	1
Fordham University	73	53	3	
Long Island U - Brooklyn Center	15	5	2	
Long Island U - C W Post Center	5			
Mercy College	63	7	1	1
New York University	30	6	9	
Pace University New York	5	4		
St. Francis College	3	1		
St. John's University	5	4	3	
St. Joseph's College - Main Campus	4	2	2	
SUNY at Albany	25	6	1	3

716

(2200)

STATE/SCHOOL	MINORITY GROUP			
	Black	Hispanic	Asian	Native American
New York (cont)				
SUNY at Buffalo - Main Campus	19	2	2	
SUNY at Stony Bk - Main Campus	22	7	12	1
SUNY College at Buffalo	15	3		3
SUNY College at New Paltz	21	9	4	3
SUNY College - Old Westbury	18	5	1	
SUNY Empire State College	4	1	1	
Syracuse University - Main Campus	12	3	2	
	894	**365**	**151**	**29**
North Carolina				
Barber-Scotia College*	19			
Bennett College*	7			
Duke University	20	3	1	1
East Carolina University	8			1
Elizabeth City State U*	71			
Fayetteville State University*	64	4	2	1
Johnson C Smith University*	26			
Livingstone College*	19			
NC Agrl & Tech State University*	29			
NC Central University*	88	1		
NC State U - Raleigh	12		1	
Pembroke State University	19			39
St. Augustine's College*	44			
Shaw University*	43			
U of NC at Chapel Hill	22	2	1	2
U of NC at Charlotte	11	1	1	
U of NC at Greensboro	11			
Winston-Salem State University*	47			
	560	**11**	**6**	**44**
North Dakota				
U of North Dakota - Main Campus	1			
	1			

(2200)

STATE/SCHOOL	MINORITY GROUP			
	Black	Hispanic	Asian	Native American
Ohio				
Antioch University	8		2	1
Bowling Green State U – Main Cam	8	2		
Central State University*	33			
Kent State U – Main Campus	12	1		
Oberlin College	11	3	8	
Ohio State U – Main Campus	26		2	
Ohio University – Main Campus	14		1	1
U of Akron – Main Campus	4			
U of Cincinnati – Main Campus	29		1	
University of Dayton	6			
University of Toledo	9	2	1	
Wilberforce University*	11			
Wright State U – Main Campus	9			1
	180	**8**	**15**	**3**
Oklahoma				
Cameron University	11	2	1	5
Central State University	22			3
East Central Oklahoma State U		1		2
Langston University*	10			
Northeast Oklahoma State U	13			17
Oklahoma State U – Main Campus	2			3
Southeast Oklahoma State U	1			
Southwest Oklahoma State U	1			1
U of Oklahoma – Norman Campus	9	2	2	4
	69	**5**	**3**	**35**
Oregon				
Oregon State University		2	1	
University of Oregon – Main Campus	9	3	5	1
	9	**5**	**6**	**1**

718

(2200)

STATE/SCHOOL	MINORITY GROUP			
	Black	Hispanic	Asian	Native American
Pennsylvania				
Cheyney State College*	43			
Lincoln University*	48			
Pennsylvania State U – Main Campus	5	2	1	
St. Joseph's University	10			15
Temple University	41	8	6	4
University of Pennsylvania	35	10	8	1
U of Pittsburg – Main Campus	41			2
West Chester State College	5	1		
	228	**21**	**15**	**22**
Rhode Island				
Brown University	30	3	7	
	30	**3**	**7**	
South Carolina				
Allen University*	21			
Baptist College at Charleston	8			
Benedict College*	21			
Claflin College*	42			
Morris College*	26			
South Carolina State College*	48			
U of South Carolina at Columbia	34	1		
Voorhees College*	47			
Winthrop College	16	1		
	263	**2**		
Tennessee				
Austin Peay State University	20	1	1	1
Fisk University*	42			
Knoxville College*	12			
Lane College*	25			
LeMoyne-Owen College*	12			
Memphis State University	27			
Middle Tennessee State U	18		2	

(2200)

STATE/SCHOOL	MINORITY GROUP			
	Black	Hispanic	Asian	Native American
Tennessee (cont)				
Tennessee State University*	51			
U of Tennessee - Knoxville	11	1	2	
U of Tennessee - Martin	3			
	221	**2**	**5**	**1**
Texas				
Angelo State University	4	12		
Bishop College*	21			
Corpus Christi State University	1	17		
East Texas State University	19	1		2
Huston-Tillotson College*	12	1		
Incarnate Word College	2	10		
Jarvis Christian College*	8			
Lamar University	2			7
Laredo State University*		26		
North Texas State University	10	3		
Our Lady of Lake University*	3	10		
Pan American University*		76	1	1
Prairie View A&M University*	27			
St. Edward's University	2	21		
St. Mary's U - San Antonio	3	27	5	
Sam Houston State University	26	2	20	
Southwest Texas State University	5	16	1	
Sul Ross State University		8		
Texas A&I University	3	27		
Texas A&M U - Main Campus	1	5	2	1
Texas College*	10			
Texas Southern University*	35			
Texas Women's University	5			
Trinity University	3	9		
U of Houston - Central Campus	24	16	1	
U of Texas at Arlington	13	4	2	

720

(2200)

STATE/SCHOOL	MINORITY GROUP			
	Black	Hispanic	Asian	Native American
Texas (cont)				
U of Texas at Austin	20	76		4
U of Texas at El Paso	5	49		
U of Texas at San Antonio	2	38		
Wiley College*	14			
	280	**454**	**32**	**15**
Utah				
Brigham Young University – Main			3	3
University of Utah	6	9	2	4
	6	**9**	**5**	**7**
Virginia				
Hampton Institute*	53			
Norfolk State College*	64			
Old Dominion University	12	1	2	
St. Paul's College*	19			
U of Virginia-Main Campus	19		2	
Virginia State College*	77			
Virginia Union University*	21			
	282	**2**	**4**	**1**
Washington				
Evergreen State College				
University of Washington	30	9	49	5
	30	**9**	**49**	**5**
West Virginia				
West Virginia State College	11		1	
	11		**1**	

(2200)

STATE/SCHOOL		MINORITY GROUP		
	Black	Hispanic	Asian	Native American
Wisconsin				
U of Wisconsin – Madison	22	7	7	4
U of Wisconsin – Milwaukee	8	1		2
	30	**8**	**7**	**6**
TOTALS	**7166**	**2382**	**1288**	**338**

*Predominately minority institutions are those where at least 50% of the total BA Degrees awarded are to one of the minority groups being considered.

SOCIAL SCIENCES (2200)
BLACK BACCALAUREATE DEGREES RANKED BY INSTITUTION

Rank	Institution	B.A.'s	Rank	Institution	B.A'.s
1	CUNY Brooklyn C	147	31	Tuskegee Institute*	50
2	Howard U*	127	32	Grambling State U*	49
3	Rutgers U-New Brunswick	110	33	Rutgers U-Newark Campus	49
4	U of Cal-Los Angeles	99	34	South Carolina State C*	48
5	Spelman C*	92	35	U of MD-Baltimore Campus	48
6	Florida Agrl & Mech U*	89	36	Lincoln U*	48
7	NC Central U*	88	37	Winston-Salem State U*	47
8	Virginia State C*	77	38	Voorhees C*	47
9	Fordham U	73	39	CUNY Lehman C	46
10	Wayne State U	73	40	Sthrn U A&M C-Main Campus*	45
11	Elizabeth City State U*	71	41	U of South Florida	45
12	CUNY City C	70	42	St. Augustine's C*	44
13	Cal State U-Dominguez Hills	69	43	Alcorn State U*	44
14	CUNY Hunter C	66	44	U of MD-College Park Campus	44
15	Morgan State U*	66	45	Cheyney State C*	43
16	CUNY Queen's C	66	46	CUNY York C	43
17	U of Cal-Berkeley	66	47	San Francisco State U	43
18	Mississippi Valley State U*	65	48	Shaw U*	43
19	Fayetteville State U*	64	49	Claflin C*	42
20	Norfolk State C*	64	50	Morehouse C*	42
21	Mercy C	63	51	Fisk U*	42
22	U of Illinois-Chicago Circle	62	52	U of DC*	42
23	Bethune Cookman C*	60	53	U of Pittsburgh-Main Campus	41
24	Michigan State U	57	54	Temple U	41
25	Alabama A&M U*	54	55	Albany State C*	40
26	Harvard U	53	56	Tougaloo C*	38
27	Hampton Institue*	53	57	Northwestern U	37
28	Cal State U-Los Angeles	51	58	Arkansas Baptist C*	37
29	Tennessee State U*	51	59	U of Pennsylvania	35
30	Jackson State U*	50	60	American U	35

Black B.A.'s (2200)

Rank	Institution	B.A.'s	Rank	Institution	B.A.'s
61	Texas Southern U*	35	95	Cal State U-Hayward	25
62	Fort Valley State C*	34	96	Cal State U-Northridge	25
63	U of Detroit	34	97	Stanford U	25
64	U of South Carolina at Columbia	34	98	Radcliffe C	25
65	Clark C*	33	99	U of Michigan-Ann Arbor	25
66	Central State U*	33	100	U of Florida	25
67	Eastern Michigan U	33	101	SUNY at Albany	25
68	U of Arkansas-Pine Bluff*	33	102	Lane C*	25
69	CUNY John Jay C-Crim Jus	31	103	Illinois State U	24
70	Dartmouth C	31	104	Savannah State C*	24
71	Morris Brown C*	31	105	Cal State U-Long Beach	24
72	Brown U	30	106	Tufts U	24
73	New York U	30	107	CUNY C of Staten Island	24
74	U of Washington	30	108	Florida State U	24
75	Georgia State U	29	109	U of Houston-Central Campus	24
76	NC Agrl & Tech State U*	29	110	Shaw C at Detroit*	23
77	Chicago State U*	29	111	Northeastern Illinois U	23
78	U of Cincinnati-Main Campus	29	112	Western Michigan U	23
79	Alabama State U*	29	113	Coppin State C*	23
80	San Jose State U	28	114	U of NC at Chapel Hill	22
81	St. Leo C	28	115	SUNY at Stony Brook-Main Ca	22
82	Rutgers U-Camden Campus	27	116	Roosevelt U	22
83	U of Southern California	27	117	Central State U*	22
84	Memphis State U	27	118	U of Cal-Riverside	22
85	Princeton U	27	119	St. Louis U-Main Campus	22
86	Prairie View A&M U*	27	120	Xavier U of Louisiana*	22
87	Florida Memorial C	26	121	Cal State C-San Bernandino	22
88	Edward Waters C*	26	122	U of Wisconsin-Madison	22
89	Johnson C Smith U*	26	123	SUNY C at New Paltz	21
90	Southern U in New Orleans*	26	124	Allen U*	21
91	Ohio State U-Main Campus	26	125	Miles C*	21
92	Morris C*	26	126	Bishop C*	21
93	Stillman C*	26	127	Adelphi U	21
94	Sam Houston State U	26	128	Benedict C*	21

Black B.A.'s (2200)

Rank	Institution	B.A.'s	Rank	Institution	B.A.'s
129	Talladega C*	21	163	U of MD–Eastern Shore*	16
130	Virginia Union U*	21	164	U of Miami	16
131	Duke U	20	165	Winthrop C	16
132	Austin Peay State U	20	166	DePaul U	15
133	Yale U	20	167	Kentucky State U*	15
134	U of Texas at Austin	20	168	Long Island U–Brooklyn Center	15
135	Pembroke State U	19	169	San Diego State U	15
136	Barber-Scotia C*	19	170	SUNY C at Buffalo	15
137	SUNY at Buffalo-Main Campus	19	171	U of New Orleans	14
138	East Texas State U	19	172	Cal State U–Fresno	14
139	Oakland U	19	173	Dillard U*	14
140	St. Paul's C*	19	174	U of Cal-Santa Barbara	14
141	Livingstone C*	19	175	Ohio U–Main Campus	14
142	U of Virginia–Main Campus	19	176	Arkansas State U–Main Campus	14
143	Indiana U–Bloomington	18	177	Wiley C*	14
144	Chapman C	18	178	Loyola U of Chicago	13
145	Kean C of New Jersey	18	179	Jersey City State C	13
146	Northern Illinois U	18	180	Indiana U–Northwest	13
147	U of Minn-Minneapolis/St. Paul	18	181	Washington U	13
148	Cal State U–Sacramento	18	182	Valdosta State C	13
149	SUNY C–Old Westbury	18	183	Northeastern Oklahoma State	13
150	Jacksonville State U	18	184	Bowie State C*	13
151	Middle Tennessee State U	18	185	CUNY Bernard Baruch C	13
152	Towson State U	17	186	Troy State U–Main Campus	13
153	Indiana State U–Main Campus	17	187	Florida International U	13
154	U of Southwestern Louisiana	17	188	U of Alabama in Birmingham	13
155	U of Delaware	17	189	U of Texas at Arlington	13
156	Cornel U Endowed C	17	190	Syracuse U–Main Campus	12
157	U of Illinois-Urbana Campus	17	191	Kent State U–Main Campus	12
158	Glassboro State C	17	192	U of Southern Mississippi	12
159	Virginia Commonweatlh U	17	193	Le Moyne-Owen C*	12
160	Paine C*	16	194	NC State U–Raleigh	12
161	Boston State C	16	195	Huston-Tillotson C*	12
162	Loyola Marymount U	16	196	Lincoln U*	12

Black B.A.'s (2200)

Rank	Institution	B.A.'s	Rank	Institution	B.A.'s
197	Knoxville C*	12	207	Oberlin C	11
198	U of Louisville	12	208	Georgia C	11
199	Old Dominion U	12	209	U of Tennessee-Knoxville	11
200	U of NC at Greensboro	11	210	Mississippi State U	11
201	Cameron U	11	211	West Virginia State C	11
202	U of NC at Charlotte	11	212	Eastern Illinois U	11
203	Wilberforce U*	11	213	North Texas State U	10
204	Delaware State C	11	214	Texas C*	10
205	U of Mississippi-Main Campus	11	215	Langston U*	10
206	Pacific Christian C	11	216	St. Joseph's U	10

*predominantly black institutions

Institutions not ranked have less than ten degrees conferred on blacks.

726

SOCIAL SCIENCES (2200)
HISPANIC BACCALAUREATE DEGREES RANKED BY INSTITUTION

Rank	Institution	B.A.'s	Rank	Institution	B.A.'s
1	Cal State U-Los Angeles	94	31	U of NM-Main Campus	25
2	U of Texas at Austin	76	32	Stanford U	25
3	Pan American U*	76	33	NM State U-Main Campus	23
4	U of Cal-Los Angeles	73	34	U of Arizona	23
5	Florida International U	66	35	San Diego State U	21
6	CUNY Brooklyn C	56	36	New Mexico Highlands U*	21
7	Fordham U	53	37	St. Edward's U	21
8	U of Texas at El Paso	49	38	U of Southern California	20
9	Cal State U-Fullerton	48	39	U of Cal-Riverside	20
10	CUNY Lehman C	45	40	U of Miami	20
11	CUNY Hunter C	40	41	CUNY Queen's C	20
12	U of Texas at San Antonio	38	42	Loyola Marymount U	19
13	Cal State U-Northridge	37	43	U of Florida	18
14	San Jose State U	36	44	U of Colorado at Boulder	18
15	Cal State U-Fresno	36	45	Princeton U	18
16	U of Illinois-Chicago Circle	35	46	U of South Florida	17
17	CUNY City C	34	47	Corpus Christi State U	17
18	U of Cal-Berkeley	33	48	Glassboro State C	17
19	Rutgers U-New Brunswick	33	49	Southwest Texas State U	16
20	San Francisco State U	32	50	Northeastern Illinois U	16
21	Cal State U-Long Beach	32	51	U of Houston-Central Campus	16
22	U of Cal-Santa Barbara	31	52	George Washington U	15
23	Arizona State U	30	53	Montclair State C	15
24	U of Cal-San Diego	29	54	Harvard U	15
25	St. Mary's U-San Antonio	27	55	CUNY John Jay C-Crim Jus	14
26	Cal State C-San Bernardino	27	56	CUNY C of Staten Island	13
27	Texas A&I U	27	57	Cal State U-Chico	13
28	U of Southern Colorado	26	58	Metropolitan State C	12
29	Biscayne C*	26	59	Jersey City State C	12
30	Laredo State U*	26	60	Angelo State U	12

Hispanic B.A.'s (2200)

Rank	Institution	B.A.'s	Rank	Institution	B.A.'s
61	Cal State U-Hayward	11	67	Our Lady of the Lake U*	10
62	St. Peter's C	11	68	U of Albuquerque	10
63	Cal State U-Dominguez Hills	11	69	Incarnate Word C	10
64	Yale U	10	70	American U	10
65	Rutgers U-Newark Campus	10	71	U of Pennsylvania	10
66	U of Cal-Santa Cruz	10			

*predominantly Hispanic institutions

Institutions not ranked have less than ten degrees conferred on Hispanics.

SOCIAL SCIENCES (2200)
ASIAN BACCALAUREATE DEGREES RANKED BY INSTITUTION

Rank	Institution	B.A.'s	Rank	Institution	B.A.'s
1	U of Hawaii at Manoa*	211	17	Chaminade U of Honolulu	15
2	U of Cal-Los Angeles	120	18	U of Cal-Davis	15
3	U of Cal-Berkeley	108	19	U of Hawaii at Hilo*	15
4	U of Washington	49	20	Rutgers U-New Brunswick	14
5	San Francisco State U	38	21	CUNY Brooklyn C	13
6	San Jose State U	27	22	Cal State U-Fresno	13
7	U of Cal-Santa Barbara	26	23	Cornell U Endowed C	12
8	Cal State U-Long Beach	25	24	San Diego State U	12
9	CUNY City C	21	25	SUNY at Stony Bk-Main Campus	12
10	Stanford U	20	26	Harvard U	12
11	CUNY Queen's C	20	27	CUNY Lehman C	12
12	Sam Houston State U	20	28	Yale U	11
13	Cal State U-Northridge	18	29	U of MD-College Park Campus	11
14	U of Southern California	18	30	U of Cal-Irvine	10
15	Cal State U-Los Angeles	15	31	Roosevelt U	10
16	CUNY Hunter C	15			

*predominantly Asian institutions

Institutions not ranked have less than ten degrees conferred on Asians.

SOCIAL SCIENCES (2200)
NATIVE AMERICAN BACCALAUREATE DEGREES RANKED BY INSTITUTION

Rank	Institution	B.A.'s	Rank	Institution	B.A.'s
1	Pembroke State U	39	11	Cal State U-Fresno	5
2	Northeastern Oklahoma State	17	12	Cal State U-Long Beach	5
3	St. Joseph's U	15	13	Sn Jose State U	5
4	U of Cal-Berkeley	12	14	U of Cal-Los Angeles	5
5	Cal State U-Northridge	12	15	Michigan State U	5
6	Northern Arizona U	8	16	Cal State U-Los Angeles	5
7	U of MD-College Park Campus	7	17	Cameron U	5
8	Lamar U	7	18	U of Cal-Davis	5
9	San Francisco State U	6	19	U of Washington	5
10	Cal State C-Bakersfield	6			

Institutions not ranked have less than five degrees conferred on Native Americans.

SOCIAL SCIENCES (2200)
MINORITY BACCALAUREATE DEGREES
WITHIN 60 MILE RADIUS OF AIRPORT

AIRPORT	MINORITY GROUP			
	Black	Hispanic	Asian	Native American
ABQ=Albuquerque, NM				
U of NM - Main Campus		25		4
University of Albuquerque		10		1
		35		5
ALB=Albany, NY				
SUNY at Albany	25	6	1	3
SUNY Empire State College	4	1	1	
	29	7	2	3
AOO=Altoona, PA				
Pennsylvania State U - Main Campus	5	2	1	
	5	2	1	
ATL=Atlanta, GA				
Clark College*	33			
Georgia State University	29			1
Morehouse College*	42			
Morris Brown College*	31			
Spelman College*	92			
	227			1
AUS=Austin, TX				
Huston-Tillotson College*	12	1		
Southwest Texas State University	5	16	1	
U of Texas at Austin	20	76		4
	37	93	1	4
BAL=Baltimore, MD				
University of Delaware	17	2	2	
American University	35	10	2	
George Washington Univesity	7	15	5	1

Airport 60 (2200)

AIRPORT	MINORITY GROUP			
	Black	Hispanic	Asian	Native American
BAL (cont)				
Howard University*	127			
University of DC*	42	6	2	2
Bowie State College*	13			
Coppin State College*	23			
Morgan State University*	66		1	
Towson State University	17	2	1	1
U of MD - Baltimore Co Campus	48		1	2
U of MD - College Park Campus	44	5	11	7
University of Baltimore	9	1		
Lincoln University*	48			
	496	41	25	13
BDL=Hartford, CT/Springfield, MA				
Yale University	20	10	11	1
U of Mass - Amherst Campus	6	1	5	
	26	11	16	1
BHM=Birmingham, AL				
Miles College*	21			
Stillman College*	26	1		
Talladega College*	21			
U of Alabama in Birmingham	13			
University of Alabama	9			
	90	1		
BKL=Cleveland-Lakefront, OH				
Kent State U - Main Campus	12	1		
Oberlin College	11	3	8	
U of Akron - Main Campus	4			
	27	4	8	
BNA=Nashville, TN				
Western Kentucky University	6	1		
Austin Peay State University	20	1	1	1

Airport 60 (2200)

AIRPORT	MINORITY GROUP			
	Black	Hispanic	Asian	Native American
BNA (cont)				
Fisk University*	42			
Middle Tennessee State U	18		2	
Tennessee State University*	51			
	137	2	3	1
BOS=Boston, MA				
Boston State College	16	3	2	
Boston University	5	5	5	1
Harvard University	53	15	12	2
Radcliffe College	25	5	4	1
Tufts University	24	6	5	2
Brown University	30	3	7	
	153	37	35	6
BTR=Baton Rouge, LA				
Louisiana State U & A&M College	7	3	1	
Sthrn U A&M College – Main Cam*	45			
Southeastern Louisiana U	2			
	54	3	1	
BUF=Buffalo, NY				
SUNY at Buffalo – Main Campus	19	2	2	
SUNY College at Buffalo	15	3		3
	34	5	2	3
CAE=Columbia, SC				
Allen University*	21			
Benedict College*	21			
Claflin College*	42			
Morris College*	26			
South Carolina State College*	48			
U of South Carolina at Columbia	34	1		
Voorhees College*	47			
	239	1		

Airport 60 (2200)

AIRPORT	MINORITY GROUP			
	Black	Hispanic	Asian	Native American
CHS=Charleston, SC				
Baptist College at Charleston	8			
	8			
CIC=Chico, CA				
Cal State University - Chico	4	13	2	1
	4	**13**	**2**	**1**
CLT=Charlotte, NC				
Barber-Scotia College*	19			
Johnson C Smith University*	26			
Livingstone College*	19			
U of NC at Charlotte	11	1	1	
Winthrop College	16	1		
	91	**2**	**1**	
CMH=Columbus, OH				
Central State University*	33			
Ohio State U - Main Campus	26		2	
Wilberforce University*	11			
	70		**2**	
CMI=Champaign, IL				
Eastern Illinois University	11			
Illinois State University	24	1	1	1
U of Illinois - Urbana Campus	17	2	7	
Indiana State U - Main Campus	17	1	1	1
	69	**4**	**9**	**2**
COS=Colorado Springs, CO				
U of Southern Colorado	7	26		
	7	**26**		
COU=Columbia, MO				
Columbia College	2			
Lincoln University	12			
U of Missouri - Columbia	6		4	
	20		**4**	

734

Airport 60 (2200)

AIRPORT	MINORITY GROUP			
	Black	Hispanic	Asian	Native American
CRP=Corpus Christi, TX				
Corpus Christi State University	1	17		
Texas A&I University	3	27		
	4	**44**		
CRW=Charleston, WV				
West Virginia State College	11		1	
	11		**1**	
CVG=Cincinnati, OH				
Antioch University	8		2	1
Central State University*	33			
U of Cincinnati - Main Campus	29		1	
University of Dayton	6			
Wilberforce University*	11			
Wright State U - Main Campus	9			1
	96		**3**	**2**
DAB=Dayton Beach, FL				
Bethune Cookman College*	60			
University of Central Florida	5		1	
	65		**1**	
DCA=Washington–National, DC				
American University	35	10	2	
George Washington University	7	15	5	1
Howard University*	127			
University of DC*	42	6	2	2
Bowie State College*	13			
Coppin State College*	23			
Morgan State University*	66		1	
Towson State University	17	2	1	1
U of MD - Baltimore Co Campus	48		1	2
U of MD - College Park Campus	44	5	11	7
University of Baltimore	9	1		
	431	**39**	**23**	**13**

Airport 60 (2200)

AIRPORT	MINORITY GROUP			
	Black	Hispanic	Asian	Native American
DEN=Denver, CO				
Metropolitan State College	8	12	3	
U of Colorado at Boulder	6	18	8	3
U of Northern Colorado	3	3		1
	17	**33**	**11**	**4**
DFW=Dallas/Fort Worth, TX				
Bishop College*	21			
East Texas State University	19	1		2
North Texas State University	10	3		
Texas Woman's University	5			
U of Texas at Arlington	13	4	2	1
	68	**8**	**2**	**3**
DTW=Detroit-Metropolitan, MI				
Detroit Institute of Technology	6			
Eastern Michigan University	33	1	1	
Mercy College of Detroit	6			
Oakland University	19	1		
Shaw College at Detroit*	23			
U of Michigan - Ann Arbor	25	7	6	1
University of Detroit	34	1		
Wayne State University	73	3	2	1
University of Toledo	9	2	1	
	228	**15**	**10**	**2**
ELP=El Paso, TX				
U of Texas at El Paso	5	49		
	5	**4**		
EUG=Eugene, OR				
Oregon State University		2	1	
University of Oregon - Main Campus	9	3	5	1
	9	**5**	**6**	**1**

736

Airport 60 (2200)

AIRPORT	MINORITY GROUP			
	Black	Hispanic	Asian	Native American
FAT=Fresno, CA				
Cal State University - Fresno	14	36	13	5
	14	**36**	**13**	**5**
FAY=Fayetteville, NC				
Fayetteville State University*	64	4	2	1
NC Central University*	88	1		
NC State U - Raleigh	12		1	
Pembroke State University	19			39
St. Augustine's College*	44			
Shaw University*	43			
U of NC at Chapel Hill	22	2	1	2
	292	**7**	**4**	**42**
FLG=Flagstaff, AZ				
Northern Arizona University	2	7		8
	2	**7**		**8**
GLH=Greenville, MS				
Delta State University	7			
Mississippi Valley State U*	65			
	72			
GRR=Grand Rapids, MI				
Western Michigan University	23	5	1	
	23	**5**	**1**	
GSO=Greensboro/High Point, NC				
Bennett College*	7			
Duke University	20	3	1	1
Livingstone College*	19			
NC Agrl & Tech State University*	29			
NC Central University*	88	1		
U of NC at Chapel Hill	22	2	1	2
U of NC at Greensboro	11			
Winston-Salem State University*	47			
	243	**6**	**2**	**3**

Airport 60 (2200)

AIRPORT	MINORITY GROUP			
	Black	Hispanic	Asian	Native American
HNL=Honolulu/Oahu, HI				
Chaminade University of Honolulu	2	1	15	
University of Hawaii at Manoa*	2	5	211	
	4	**6**	**226**	
HSV=Huntsville, AL/Decatur, GA				
Alabama A&M University*	54			
Oakwood College*	9			
	63			
IAH=Houston–Intercontinental,TX				
Prairie View A&M University*	27			
Texas Southern University*	35			
U of Houston - Central Campus	24	16	1	
	86	**16**	**1**	
IND=Indianapolis, IN				
Ball State University	6	1		
Ind-Purdue U - Indianapolis	3			
Indiana University - Bloomington	18	2		1
Purdue University - Main Campus	7	2	1	
	34	**5**	**1**	**1**
ITO=Hilo, HI				
University of Hawaii at Hilo*		3	15	
		3	**15**	
JAN=Jackson/Vicksburg, MS				
Alcorn State University*	44			
Jackson State University*	50			
Tougaloo College*	38			
	132			
JAX=Jacksonville, FL				
Edward Waters College*	26			
	26			

Airport 60 (2200)

AIRPORT	MINORITY GROUP			
	Black	Hispanic	Asian	Native American
JFK=New York, Kennedy Int'l, NY				
Jersey City State College	13	12		
Kean College of New Jersey	18	8	2	
Montclair State College	6	15		
Princeton University	27	18	6	1
Rutgers U - New Brunswick	110	33	14	1
Rutgers U - Newark Campus	49	10	4	
St. Peter's College	9	11		
Seton Hall University	5	2		
Trenton State College	8	2		1
Adelphi University	21	4		
College of New Rochelle	2	1		
CUNY Bernard Baruch College	13	5	4	
CUNY Brooklyn College	147	56	13	4
CUNY College of Staten Island	24	13	6	1
CUNY City College	70	34	21	3
CUNY Hunter College	66	40	15	4
CUNY John Jay College - Crim Jus	31	14	2	2
CUNY Lehman College	46	45	12	1
CUNY Medgar Evers College*	9			
CUNY Queen's College	66	20	20	1
CUNY York College	43	9	3	1
Fordham University	73	53	3	
Long Island U - Brooklyn Center	15	5	2	
Long Island U - C W Post Center	5			
Mercy College	63	7	1	1
New York University	30	6	9	
Pace University New York	5	4		
St. Francis College	3	1		
St. John's University	5	4	3	

Airport 60 (2200)

AIRPORT	MINORITY GROUP			
	Black	Hispanic	Asian	Native American
JFK (cont)				
St. Joseph's College - Main Campus	4	2	2	
SUNY at Stony Bk - Main Campus	22	7	12	1
SUNY College - Old Westbury	18	5	1	
	1026	**446**	**155**	**22**
LAX=Los Angeles, CA				
Cal State College - San Bernardino	22	27	1	1
Cal State Poly U - Pomona	2	8		1
Cal State U - Dominguez Hills	69	11	6	2
Cal State University - Fullerton	9	48	8	3
Cal State University - Long Beach	24	32	25	5
Cal State University - Los Angeles	51	94	15	5
Cal State University - Northridge	25	37	18	12
Chapman College	18	9	6	1
Loyola Marymount University	16	19	3	1
Pacific Christian College	11			
Pepperdine University	9	2		1
U of Cal - Irvine	7	6	10	
U of Cal - Los Angeles	99	73	120	5
U of Cal - Riverside	22	20	2	
University of Southern California	27	20	18	3
University of LaVerne	8	4	2	
	419	**410**	**234**	**40**
LCH=Lake Charles, LA				
McNeese State University	2			
	2			
LEX=Lexington/Frankfort, KY				
Eastern Kentucky University	4			
Kentucky State University*	15			
University of Louisville	12		1	1
	31		**1**	**1**

740

Airport 60 (2200)

AIRPORT	MINORITY GROUP			
	Black	Hispanic	Asian	Native American
LIT=Little Rock, AR				
Arkansas Baptist College*	37			
Philander Smith College*	5			
University of Arkansas - Pine Bluff*	33			
University of Central Arkansas	5			
	80			
LRD=Laredo, TX				
Laredo State University*		26		
		26		
MCI=Kansas City-International, MO				
Park College	6			
U of Missouri - Kansas City	3	3	4	
	9	**3**	**4**	
MCN=Macon, GA				
Fort Valley State College*	34			
Georgia College	11			
	45			
MDH=Carbondale, IL				
Southern Illinois U - Carbondale	7	1		
	7	**1**		
MEM=Memphis, TN				
Mississippi Industrial College*	6			
Rust College*	4			
Le Moyne-Owen College*	12			
Memphis State University	27			
	49			
MFE=McAllen, TX				
Pan American University*		76	1	1
		76	**1**	**1**
MGM=Montgomery, GA				
Alabama State University*	29			
Troy State University - Main Campus	13	1		

Airport 60 (2200)

AIRPORT	MINORITY GROUP			
	Black	Hispanic	Asian	Native American
MGM (cont)				
Troy State University - Montgomery	7	2		
Tuskegee Institute*	50			
	99	**3**		
MHT=Manchester, NH				
Harvard University	53	15	12	2
Radcliffe College	25	5	4	1
Tufts University	24	6	5	2
Dartmouth College	31	1	2	1
	133	**27**	**23**	**6**
MIA=Miami, FL				
Biscayne College*	1	26		
Florida Atlantic University	6	5		
Florida International University	13	66		
Florida Memorial College*	26			
University of Miami	16	20	1	
	62	**117**	**1**	
MKE=Milwaukee, WS				
U of Wisconsin - Milwaukee	8	1	1	2
	8	**1**	**1**	**2**
MKL=Jackson, TN				
Lane College*	25			
U of Tennessee at Martin	3			
	28			
MLU=Monroe, LA				
Grambling State University*	49			
Louisiana Tech University	8			
Northeast Louisiana University	2			
	59			
MOB=Mobile, AL/Pasagoula, MS				
University of South Alabama	6	1		1
University of West Florida	5		2	
	11	**1**	**2**	**1**

Airport 60 (2200)

AIRPORT	MINORITY GROUP			
	Black	Hispanic	Asian	Native American
MSN=Madison, WS				
U of Wisconsin - Madison	22	7	7	4
	22	**7**	**7**	**4**
MSP=Minneapolis/St. Paul, MN				
U of Minn - Minneapolis/St. Paul	18	9	6	1
	18	**9**	**6**	**1**
MSY=New Orleans, LA				
Dillard University*	14			
Southeastern Louisiana U	2			
Southern U in New Orleans*	26			
Tulane U of Louisiana	4	8	2	1
University of New Orleans	14	2	1	
Xavier University of Louisiana*	22			
	82	**10**	**3**	**1**
ORD=Chicago-O'Hare Airport, IL				
Chicago State University*	29			
College of St. Francis	2	1		
DePaul University	15	8	2	
Governors State University	3	4		
Loyola University of Chicago	13	9	1	
Northern Illinois University	18	1	1	1
Northwestern University	37	2	6	
Northeastern Illinois University	23	16	2	
Roosevelt University	22	8	10	
U of Illinois - Chicago Circle	62	35	7	
Indiana University - Northwest	13	3		
	237	**87**	**29**	**1**
ORF=Norfolk/Virginia Beach, VA				
Elizabeth City State U*	71			
Hampton Institute*	53			
Norfolk State College*	64			
Old Dominion University	12	1	2	
	200	**1**	**2**	

Airport 60 (2200)

AIRPORT	MINORITY GROUP			
	Black	Hispanic	Asian	Native American
PHL=Philadelphia, PA/Wilmington, DE				
Delaware State College*	11			
University of Delaware	17	2	2	
Glassboro State College	17	17		
Princeton University	27	18	6	1
Rutgers U – Camden Campus	27	4		
Rutgers U – New Brunswick	110	33	14	1
Trenton State College	8	2		1
Cheyney State College*	43			
Lincoln University*	48			
St. Joseph's University	10			15
Temple University	41	8	6	4
University of Pennsylvania	35	10	8	1
West Chester State College	5	1		
	399	**95**	**36**	**23**
PHX=Phoenix, AZ				
Arizona State University	7	30	1	
	7	**30**	**1**	
PIA=Peoria, IL				
Bradley University	4		1	
	4		**1**	
PIT=Pittsburgh, PA				
U of Pittsburgh – Main Campus	41			2
	41			**2**
PVD=Providence, RI				
Boston State College	16	3	2	
Boston University	5	5	5	1
Harvard University	53	15	12	2
Radcliffe College	25	5	4	1
Tufts University	24	6	5	2
Brown University	30	3	7	
	153	**37**	**35**	**6**

Airport 60 (2200)

AIRPORT	MINORITY GROUP			
	Black	Hispanic	Asian	Native American
PWA=Oklahoma City-Wiley Post, OK				
Central State University	22			3
Langston University*	10			
Oklahoma State U - Main Campus	2			3
U of Oklahoma - Norman Campus	9	2	2	4
	43	**2**	**2**	**10**
RDU=Raleigh/Durham, NC				
Bennet College*	7			
Duke University	20	3	1	1
Fayetteville State University*	64	4	2	1
NC Agrl & Tech State University*	29			
NC Central University*	88	1		
NC State U - Raleigh	12		1	
St. Augustine's College*	44			
Shaw University*	43			
U of NC at Chapel Hill	22	2	1	2
U of NC at Greensboro	11			
	340	**10**	**5**	**4**
RIC=Richmond, VA				
Virginia Commonwealth University	17	1		1
Virginia State College*	77			
Virginia Union University*	21			
	115	**1**		**1**
SAN=San Diego, CA				
San Diego State University	15	21	12	
U of Cal - San Diego		29	9	3
	15	**50**	**21**	**3**
SAT=San Antonio, TX				
Incarnate Word College	2	10		
Our Lady of Lake University*	3	10		
St. Edward's University	2	21		

Airport 60 (2200)

AIRPORT	MINORITY GROUP			
	Black	Hispanic	Asian	Native American
SAT (cont)				
St. Mary's U – San Antonio	3	27	5	
Southwest Texas State University	5	16	1	
Trinity University	3	9		
U of Texas at San Antonio	2	38		
	20	131	6	
SAV=Savannah, GA				
Savannah State College*	24			
	24			
SBA=Santa Barbara, CA				
Pepperdine University	9	2		1
U of Cal – Santa Barbara	14	31	26	2
	23	33	26	3
SBP=San Luis Obispo, CA				
Cal Poly State U – San Luis Obispo	2	5	4	2
	2	5	4	2
SBY=Salisbury, MD				
U of MD – Eastern Shore*	16			
	16			
SEA=Seattle/Tacoma, WA				
University of Washington	30	9	49	5
	30	9	49	5
SFO=San Francisco/Oakland, CA				
Cal State University – Hayward	25	11	7	2
San Francisco State University	43	32	38	6
San Jose State University	28	36	27	5
Stanford University	25	25	20	4
U of Cal – Berkeley	66	33	108	12
University of San Francisco	6	7	8	1
	198	144	208	30

746

Airport 60 (2200)

AIRPORT	MINORITY GROUP			
	Black	Hispanic	Asian	Native American
SHV=Shreveport, LA				
Grambling State University*	49			
Wiley College*	14			
	63			
SJT=San Angelo, TX				
Angelo State University	4	12		
	4	12		
SLC=Salt Lake City, UT				
Brigham Young University – Main			3	3
University of Utah	6	9	2	4
	6	9	5	7
STL=St. Louis, MO				
Southern Illinois U – Edwardsville	7			
St. Louis U – Main Campus	22	1		
U of Missouri – St. Louis	4	2	3	
Washington University	13		2	
Webster College	9			
	55	3	5	
SVC=Silver City, NM				
Western New Mexico University		3		1
		3		1
SWI=Sherman, TX				
Southeast Oklahoma State U	1			
Bishop College*	21			
East Texas State University	19	1		2
North Texas State University	10	3		
Texas Woman's University	5			
	56	4		2
SYR=Syracuse, NY				
Cornel U Endowed College	17	6	12	1
Syracuse U – Main Campus	12	3	2	
	29	9	14	1

Airport 60 (2200)

AIRPORT	MINORITY GROUP			
	Black	Hispanic	Asian	Native American
TCL=Tuscaloosa, AL				
Miles College*	21			
Stillman College*	26	1		
U of Alabama in Birmingham	13			
University of Alabama	9			
Mississippi University for Women	2			
	71	**1**		
TLH=Tallahassee, FL				
Florida Agr & Mech University*	89			
Florida State University	24	4		2
	113	**4**		**2**
TPA=Tampa, FL				
St. Leo College	28	8		
University of South Florida	45	17	4	
	73	**25**	**4**	
TUL=Tulsa, OK				
Northeast Oklahoma State U	13			17
	13			**17**
TUS=Tucson, AZ				
University of Arizona	4	23	5	3
	4	**23**	**5**	**3**
TYR=Tyler, TX				
Jarvis Christian College*	8			
Texas College*	10			
Wiley College*	14			
	32			
TYS=Knoxville, TN				
Knoxville College*	12			
U of Tennessee - Knoxville	11	1	2	
	23	**1**	**2**	

SOCIAL SCIENCES (2200)
MINORITY BACCALAUREATE DEGREES
WITHIN 61-80 MILE ANNULUS OF AIRPORT

AIRPORT	MINORITY GROUP			
	Black	Hispanic	Asian	Native American
ALB=Albany, NY				
U of Mass - Amherst Campus	6	1	5	
SUNY College at New Paltz	21	9	4	3
	27	10	9	3
ALM=Alamogordo, NM				
NM State U - Main Campus	4	23		2
	4	23		2
ATL=Atlanta, GA				
Jacksonville State University	18	1		
Georgia College	11			
University of Georgia	8	1		1
	37	2		1
AUS=Austin, TX				
Incarnate Word College	2	10		
Our Lady of Lake University*	3	10		
St. Edward's University	2	21		
St. Mary's U - San Antonio	3	27	5	
Trinity University	3	9		
U of Texas at San Antonio	2	38		
	15	115	5	
BAL=Baltimore, MD				
Delaware State College*	11			
Cheyney State College*	43			
	54			
BDL=Hartford, CT/Springfield, MA				
College of New Rochelle	2	1		
Mercy College	63	7	1	1

Airport 61-80 (2200)

AIRPORT	MINORITY GROUP			
	Black	Hispanic	Asian	Native American
BDL (cont)				
SUNY at Albany	25	6	1	3
SUNY College at New Paltz	21	9	4	3
Brown University	30	3	7	
	141	**26**	**13**	**7**
BHM=Birmingham, AL				
Jacksonville State University	18	1		
	18	**1**		
BOS=Boston, MA				
U of Mass – Amherst Campus	6	1	5	
	6	**1**	**5**	
BTM=Butte, MT				
Montana State University		2		2
		2		**2**
BTR=Baton Rouge, LA				
Dillard University*	14			
Southern U in New Orleans*	26			
Tulane U of Louisiana	4	8	2	1
U of Southwestern Louisiana	17	2		
University of New Orleans	14	2	1	
Xavier University of Louisiana*	22			
	97	**12**	**3**	**1**
CAE=Columbia, SC				
Paine College*	16			
Winthrop College	16	1		
	32	**1**		
CHS=Charleston, SC				
Savannah State College*	24			
Claflin College*	42			
South Carolina State College*	48			
	114			

750

Airport 61-80 (2200)

AIRPORT	MINORITY GROUP			
	Black	Hispanic	Asian	Native American
CLT=Charlotte, NC				
Wintson-Salem State University*	47			
	47			
CMH=Columbus, OH				
Antioch University	8		2	1
Ohio University - Main Campus	14		1	1
University of Dayton	6			
Wright State U - Main Campus	9			1
	37		3	3
CMI=Champaign, IL				
Purdue University - Main Campus	7	2	1	
	7	2	1	
COS=Colorado Springs, CO				
Metropolitan State College	8	12	3	
U of Colorado at Boulder	6	18	8	3
	14	30	11	3
CRW=Charleston, WV				
Ohio University - Main Campus	14		1	1
	14		1	1
CVG=Cincinnati, OH				
Kentucky State University*	15			
	15			
DCA=Washington-National, DC				
Lincoln University*	48			
	48			
DEN=Denver, CO				
Colorado State University	1	2	1	
	1	2	1	
DTW=Detroit-Metropolitan, MI				
Michigan State University	57	4	2	5
Bowling Green State U - Main Cam	8	2		
	65	6	2	5

Airport 61-80 (2200)

AIRPORT	MINORITY GROUP			
	Black	Hispanic	Asian	Native American
FAY=Fayetteville, NC				
Duke University	20	3	1	1
	20	**3**	**1**	**1**
GRR=Grand Rapids, MI				
Michigan State University	57	4	2	5
	57	**4**	**2**	**5**
GSO=Greensboro/High Point, NC				
Barber-Scotia College*	19			
NC State U - Raleigh	12		1	
St. Augustine's College*	44			
Shaw University*	43			
	118		**1**	
HSV=Huntsville, AL/Decatur, GA				
Jacksonville State University	18	1		
Middle Tennessee State U	18		2	
	36	**1**	**2**	
IAH=Houston-Intercontinental,TX				
Sam Houston State University	26	2	20	
	26	**2**	**20**	
IND=Indianapolis, IN				
Indiana State U - Main Campus	17	1	1	1
	17	**1**	**1**	**1**
JAX=Jacksonville, FL				
University of Florida	25	18	1	
	25	**18**	**1**	
JFK=New York, Kennedy Int'l, NY				
Yale University	20	10	11	1
SUNY College at New Paltz	21	9	4	3
	41	**19**	**15**	**4**
LAX=Los Angeles, CA				
Cal State College - Bakersfield	2	3		6
University of Redlands	1	2	1	
	3	**5**	**1**	**6**

Airport 61-80 (2200)

AIRPORT	MINORITY GROUP			
	Black	Hispanic	Asian	Native American
LCH=Lake Charles, LA				
U of Southwestern Louisiana	17	2		
Lamar University	2			7
	19	2		7
LIT=Little Rock, AR				
Henderson State University	6			
	6			
MCN=Macon, GA				
Clark College*	33			
Georgia State University	29			1
Morehouse College*	42			
Morris Brown College*	31			
Spelman College*	92			
	227			1
MEM=Memphis, TN				
Arkansas State U – Main Campus	14			
U of Mississippi – Main Campus	11			
Lane College*	25			
	50			
MGM=Montgomery, GA				
Talladega College*	21			
	21			
MHT=Manchester, NH				
Boston State College	16	3	2	
Boston University	5	5	5	1
U of Mass – Amherst Campus	6	1	5	
	27	9	12	1
MKE=Milwaukee, WS				
Northwestern University	37	2	6	
U of Wisconsin – Madison	22	7	7	4
	59	9	13	4

753

Airport 61-80 (2200)

AIRPORT	MINORITY GROUP			
	Black	Hispanic	Asian	Native American
MKL=Jackson, TN				
Mississippi Industrial College*	6			
Rust College*	4			
Memphis State University	27			
	37			
MLU=Monroe, LA				
Alcorn State University*	44			
	44			
MOB=Mobile, AL/Pasagoula, MS				
U of Southern Mississippi	12			
	12			
MSN=Madison, WS				
U of Wisconsin - Milwaukee	8	1	1	2
	8	1	1	2
MSY=New Orleans, LA				
Louisiana State U & A&M College	7	3	1	
Sthrn U A&M C - Main Cam*	45			
	52	3	1	
ORF=Norfolk/Virginia Beach, VA				
Virginia State College*	77			
	77			
PVD=Providence, RI				
U of Mass - Amherst Campus	6	1	5	
	6	1	5	
PWA=Oklahoma City-Wiley Post, OK				
East Central Oklahoma State U		1		2
Southwest Oklahoma State U	1			1
	1	1		3
RDU=Raleigh/Durham, NC				
East Carolina University	8			1
St. Paul's College*	19			
	27			1

754

Airport 61-80 (2200)

AIRPORT	MINORITY GROUP			
	Black	Hispanic	Asian	Native American
RIC=Richmond, VA				
Hampton Institute*				
Norfolk State College*	53			
St. Paul's College*	64			
U of Virginia - Main Campus	19		2	
	155		2	
SAN=San Diego, CA				
Chapman College	18	9	6	1
U of Cal - Irvine	7	6	10	
U of Cal - Riverside	22	20	2	
	47	35	18	1
SAT=San Antonio, TX				
Huston-Tillotson College*	12	1		
U of Texas at Austin	20	76		4
	32	77		4
SAV=Savannah, GA				
Baptist College at Charleston	8			
	8			
SBA=Santa Barbara, CA				
Cal State College - Bakersfield	2	3		6
Cal State University - Los Angeles	51	94	15	5
Cal State University - Northridge	25	37	18	12
Loyola Marymount University	16	19	3	1
U of Cal - Los Angeles	99	73	120	5
	193	226	156	29
SBY=Salisbury, MD				
Delaware State College*	11			
	11			
SFO=San Francisco/Oakland, CA				
Cal State University - Sacramento	18	6	5	3
U of Cal - Davis	8	6	15	5

755

Airport 61-80 (2200)

AIRPORT	MINORITY GROUP			
	Black	Hispanic	Asian	Native American
SFO (cont)				
U of Cal - Santa Cruz		10	2	
University of the Pacific	3		8	
	29	22	30	8
SHV=Shreveport, LA				
Louisiana Tech University	8			
	8			
SWI=Sherman, TX				
U of Texas at Arlington	13	4	2	1
	13	4	2	1
TLH=Tallahassee, FL				
Albany State College*	40			
Valdosta State College	13			
	53			
TPA=Tampa, FL				
University of Central Florida	5		1	
	5		1	
TUL=Tulsa, OK				
Oklahoma State U - Main Campus	2			3
	2			3
TYR=Tyler, TX				
East Texas State University	19	1		2
	19	1		2

SOCIAL SCIENCES (2200)
MINORITY BACCALAUREATE DEGREES
MORE THAN 80 MILES FROM NEAREST AIRPORT

AIRPORT	MINORITY GROUP			
	Black	Hispanic	Asian	Native American
ABQ=Albuquerque, NM				
New Mexico Highlands U*		21		1
		21		1
AUS=Austin, TX				
Texas A&M U - Main Campus	1	5	2	1
	1	5	2	1
ELP=El Paso, TX				
Sul Ross State University		8		
		8		
IAH=Houston-Intercontinental, TX				
Texas A&M U - Main Campus	1	5	2	1
	1	5	2	1
MAF=Midland/Odessa, TX				
Sul Ross State University		8		
		8		
MSY=New Orleans, LA				
U of Southern Mississippi	12			
	12			
PWA=Oklahoma City-Wiley Post, OK				
Cameron University	11	2	1	5
	11	2	1	5
ROW=Roswell, NM				
Eastern NM U - Main Campus	4	8		2
	4	8		2
TCL=Tuscaloosa, AL				
Mississippi State University	11			
	11			

INTERDISCIPLINARY STUDIES (2400)

INTERDISCIPLINARY STUDIES (2400)
MINORITY BACCALAUREATE DEGREES
BY STATE AND INSTITUTION

STATE/SCHOOL	MINORITY GROUP			
	Black	Hispanic	Asian	Native American
Alabama				
Oakwood College*	27			
U of Alabama in Birmingham			1	
	27		**1**	
Arizona				
University of Arizona		2		
		2		
Arkansas				
Philander Smith College*	2			
University of Arkansas – Pine Bluff*	4			
	6			
California				
Cal Poly State U – San Luis Obispo	1	4	1	
Cal State College – Bakersfield	3	11		5
Cal State College – San Bernadino	6	14	1	1
Cal State Poly U – Pomona	3	13		
Cal State University – Chico	2	8	3	4
Cal State U – Dominguez Hills	36	12	5	1
Cal State University – Fresno	1	26	10	3
Cal State University – Fullerton		7	1	
Cal State University – Hayward	5	2	2	3
Cal State University – Long Beach	11	18	12	1
Cal State University – Los Angeles	7	18	15	
Cal State University – Northridge	11	22	16	7
Cal State University – Sacramento	7	10	7	
Chapman College	4	2		
Loyola Marymount University	6	5		
Pepperdine University	37	3	3	

(2400)

STATE/SCHOOL	MINORITY GROUP			
	Black	Hispanic	Asian	Native American
California (cont)				
San Diego State University	8	41	7	3
San Francisco State University	18	9	19	2
San Jose State University	16	18	17	2
Stanford University	1	2		
U of Cal – Berkeley	8	5	45	
U of Cal – Davis	10	9	27	3
U of Cal – Irvine	16	9	22	1
U of Cal – Los Angeles	3	4	16	1
U of Cal – Riverside	13	14	2	1
U of Cal – San Diego		9	10	1
U of Cal – San Francisco	1		1	
U of Cal – Santa Barbara	8	5	13	2
U of Cal – Santa Cruz		8	3	
University of LaVerne		58		
University of Redlands	17	8	5	
University of Southern California	1	2	2	
University of the Pacific	2	1	5	1
	262	**377**	**270**	**42**
Colorado				
Colorado State University		1	1	
Metropolitan State College		3		
U of Colorado at Boulder	2	3		
U of Northern Colorado			1	
	2	**7**	**2**	
Connecticut				
University of Connecticut	3	3		
Yale University	3	1	2	
	6	**4**	**2**	

(2400)

STATE/SCHOOL	MINORITY GROUP			
	Black	Hispanic	Asian	Native American
District of Columbia				
American University	2			
George Washington University	2			
University of DC*	1			
	5			
Florida				
Florida Atlantic University		1		
Florida International University	4	3	1	
University of Central Florida	2	1	1	
University of Florida	1	2		
University of Miami	1	1		1
University of South Florida	1	1	1	
	9	9	3	1
Georgia				
Morehouse College*	8			
Spelman College*	3		1	
University of Georgia	1			
	12		1	
Hawaii				
University of Hawaii at Hilo*		2	13	
University of Hawaii at Manoa*			30	
		2	43	
Illinois				
Bradley University	1		1	
Chicago State University*	95	2		1
Columbia College	5	1	1	
Daniel Hale Williams University*	45			
DePaul University	13	1		
Eastern Illinois University	5			
Governors State University	43			
Northern Illinois University	2			
Northeastern Illinois University	20	9	5	1

(2400)

STATE/SCHOOL	MINORITY GROUP			
	Black	Hispanic	Asian	Native American
Illinois (cont)				
Southern Illinois U – Carbondale	27	4	3	7
Southern Illinois U – Edwardsville	2			
U of Illinois – Chicago Circle	15	2	2	1
U of Illinois – Urbana Campus	3			
	276	**19**	**12**	**10**
Indiana				
Indiana University – Bloomington	1	1	1	
Purdue University – Main Campus	2		1	
	3	**1**	**2**	
Kentucky				
Kentucky State University*	1			
University of Louisville	1			
	2			
Louisiana				
Louisiana State U & A&M College	8	2	1	
Louisiana Tech University	4			
McNeese State University	4	1	1	1
Northeast Louisiana University	18			
Sthrn U A&M College – Main Cam*	11			
University of New Orleans			1	
U of Southwestern Louisiana	1			
	46	**3**	**3**	**1**
Maryland				
Towson State University	13			
U of MD – Baltimore Co Campus	8			
U of MD – College Park Campus	15		1	4
U of MD – University College	103	14	14	6
	139	**14**	**15**	**10**
Massachussetts				
Boston State College	1			
Boston University	1			

762

(2400)

STATE/SCHOOL	MINORITY GROUP			
	Black	Hispanic	Asian	Native American
Massachusetts (cont)				
Harvard University	1			
Tufts University	1			
U of Mass – Amherst Campus	5	4	1	1
	9	**4**	**1**	**1**
Michigan				
Detroit Institute of Technology	1		1	
Michigan State University	5	3	1	2
Oakland University	1			
Shaw College at Detroit*	11			
University of Detroit	2			
U of Michigan – Ann Arbor	37	7	7	2
Wayne State University	85	3	3	2
Western Michigan University	1			
	143	**13**	**12**	**6**
Minnesota				
U of Minn – Minneapolis/St. Paul	11	8	4	
	11	**8**	**4**	
Mississippi				
Mississippi State University		1		
		1		
Missouri				
Columbia College	27	2		1
U of Missouri – Columbia	2		1	
U of Missouri – St. Louis	2			1
Webster College	18			
	49	**2**	**1**	**2**
New Jersey				
Montclair State College	1	2		
Princeton University			3	
Rutgers U – New Brunswick	12	2		

(2400)

STATE/SCHOOL	MINORITY GROUP			
	Black	Hispanic	Asian	Native American
New Jersey (cont)				
Rutgers U - Newark Campus	2	1		
St. Peter's College		4		
	15	**9**	**3**	
New Mexico				
Eastern NM U - Main Campus	1			1
NM State U - Main Campus	6	5		2
University of Albuquerque		4		
U of NM - Main Campus	6	52	1	8
Western New Mexico University		1		
	13	**62**	**1**	**11**
New York				
Adelphi University	3			
College of New Rochelle	121	22	3	
Cornell U Endowed College	4	1	2	
CUNY Bernard Baruch College	9	4	3	
CUNY City College	3	2	1	
CUNY College of Staten Island	6	4	2	
CUNY Graduate School & U Center	60	27	12	2
CUNY Hunter College	5	3	1	
CUNY John Jay College - Crim Jus	5	3		
CUNY Lehman College	2	3		
CUNY Queen's College	14	4	4	
Fordham University	5	2	1	
New York University	7	4	1	
St. Francis College	150	5	26	
St. Joseph's College - Main Campus	266	5	11	
SUNY at Albany			3	1
SUNY at Buffalo - Main Campus	13		1	
SUNY at Stony Bk - Main Campus	3	3		
SUNY College at Buffalo	6	1		
SUNY College at New Paltz	1	1	1	

(2400)

STATE/SCHOOL	MINORITY GROUP			
	Black	Hispanic	Asian	Native American
New York (cont)				
SUNY College - Old Westbury	7	1		
SUNY Empire State College	4			
Syracuse University - Main Campus	3	1	1	
	697	**96**	**73**	**3**
North Carolina				
Bennett College*	18			
NC Agrl & Tech State University*	1			
NC State U - Raleigh	2			
St. Augustine's College*	1			
Shaw University*	1			
Winston-Salem State University*	5			
	28			
North Dakota				
U of North Dakota - Main Campus				1
				1
Ohio				
Antioch University	22	55		1
Bowling Green State U - Main Cam	3			
Kent State U - Main Campus	5	1		
Oberlin College	2			
Ohio State U - Main Campus	6		1	
Ohio University - Main Campus	20	1		2
U of Akron - Main Campus				1
U of Cincinnati - Main Campus	6			
University of Toledo	9	1	5	
Wilberforce University*	2			
	75	**58**	**6**	**4**
Oklahoma				
Central State University	1			
East Central Oklahoma State U				2

(2400)

| STATE/SCHOOL | MINORITY GROUP | | | |
	Black	Hispanic	Asian	Native American
Oklahoma (cont)				
Oklahoma State U – Main Campus	1			
Southeast Oklahoma State U	1			2
	3			4
Oregon				
Oregon State University	2			
University of Oregon – Main Campus			3	
	2		3	
Pennsylvania				
Cheyney State College*	6			
Drexel University	3			
Pennsylvania State U – Main Campus	7	1		
Temple University	9	3	2	
University of Pennsylvania	6	2		
U of Pittsburgh – Main Campus	16	1		1
West Chester State College	1			
	48	7	2	1
Rhode Island				
Brown University	2			
	2			
South Carolina				
Morris College*	15			
U of South Carolina at Columbia	22	2		
	37	2		
Tennessee				
Memphis State University	2		1	
U of Tennessee – Knoxville	1			
	3		1	
Texas				
Angelo State University		2		
Lamar University	1			

(2400)

STATE/SCHOOL	MINORITY GROUP			
	Black	Hispanic	Asian	Native American
Texas (cont)				
St. Edward's University	2	3		
U of Texas at Austin	3	3		
	6	8		
Utah				
Brigham Young University – Main				3
				3
Virginia				
Old Dominion University	1			
U of Virginia – Main Campus	2			
Virginia Union University*	4			
	7			
Washington				
Evergreen State College	19	7	5	17
University of Washington	3	5	11	1
	22	12	16	18
West Virginia				
West Virginia State College	18	1		
	18	1		
Wisconsin				
U of Wisconsin – Madison	3		1	
U of Wisconsin – Milwaukee	11	1		
	14	1	1	
TOTALS	1997	722	478	118

*Predominately minority institutions are those where at least 50% of the total BA
Degrees awarded are to one of the minority groups being considered.

INTERDISCIPLINARY STUDIES (2400)
BLACK BACCALAUREATE DEGREES RANKED BY INSTITUTION

Rank	Institution	B.A.'s	Rank	Institution	B.A.'s
1	St. Joseph's C-Main Campus	266	24	Bennett C*	18
2	St. Francis C	150	25	West Virginia State C	18
3	C of New Rochelle	121	26	U of Redlands	17
4	U of MD-University C	103	27	U of Cal-Irvine	16
5	Chicago State U*	95	28	San Jose State U	16
6	Wayne State U	85	29	U of Pittsburgh-Main Campus	16
7	CUNY Graduate School & U Ctr	60	30	U of MD-College Park Campus	15
8	Daniel Hale Williams U*	45	31	U of Illinois-Chicago Circle	15
9	Governors State U	43	32	Morris C*	15
10	U of Michigan-Ann Arbor	37	33	CUNY Queen's C	14
11	Pepperdine U	37	34	Towson State U	13
12	Cal State U-Dominguez Hills	36	35	U of Cal-Riverside	13
13	Columbia C	27	36	SUNY at Buffalo-Main Campus	13
14	Southern Illinois U-Carbondale	27	37	DePaul U	13
15	Oakwood C*	27	38	Rutgers U-New Brunswick	12
16	Antioch U	22	39	Cal State U-Northridge	11
17	U of South Carolina at Columbia	22	40	Cal State U-Long Beach	11
18	Northeastern Illinois U	20	41	Shaw C at Detroit*	11
19	Ohio U-Main Campus	20	42	Sthrn U A&M C-Main Campus*	11
20	Evergreen State C	19	43	U of Minn-Minneapolis/St. Paul	11
21	San Francisco State U	18	44	U of Wisconsin-Milwaukee	11
22	Webster C	18	45	U of Cal-Davis	10
23	Northeast Louisiana U	18			

*predominantly black institutions

Institutions not ranked have less than ten degrees conferred on blacks.

768

INTERDISCIPLINARY STUDIES (2400)
HISPANIC BACCALAUREATE DEGREES RANKED BY INSTITUTION

Rank	Institution	B.A.'s	Rank	Institution	B.A.'s
1	U of La Verne	58	10	Cal State U-Long Beach	18
2	Antioch U	55	11	San Jose State U	18
3	U of NM-Main Campus	52	12	U of Cal-Riverside	14
4	San Diego State U	41	13	Cal State C-San Bernardino	14
5	CUNY Graduate School & U Ctr	27	14	U of MD-University C	14
6	Cal State U-Fresno	26	15	Cal State U-Pomona	13
7	Cal State U-Northridge	22	16	Cal State U-Dominguez Hills	12
8	C of New Rochelle	22	17	Cal State C-Bakersfield	11
9	Cal State U-Los Angeles	18	18	Cal State U-Sacramento	10

Institutions not ranked have less than ten degrees conferred on Hispanics.

INTERDISCIPLINARY STUDIES (2400)
ASIAN BACCALAUREATE DEGREES RANKED BY INSTITUTION

Rank	Institution	B.A.'s	Rank	Institution	B.A.'s
1	U of Cal-Berkeley	45	11	U of MD-University C	14
2	U of Hawaii at Manoa*	30	12	U of Cal-Santa Barbara	13
3	U of Cal-Davis	27	13	U of Hawaii at Hilo*	13
4	St. Francis C	26	14	CUNY Graduate School & U Ctr	12
5	U of Cal-Irvine	22	15	Cal State U-Long Beach	12
6	San Francisco State U	19	16	St. Joseph's C-Main Campus	11
7	San Jose State U	17	17	U of Washington	11
8	Cal State U-Northridge	16	18	Cal State U-Fresno	10
9	U of Cal-Los Angeles	15	19	U of Cal-San Diego	10
10	Cal State U-Los Angeles	15			

*predominantly Asian institutions

Institutions not ranked have less than ten degrees conferred on Asians.

INTERDISCIPLINARY STUDIES (2400)
NATIVE AMERICAN BACCALAUREATE DEGREES RANKED BY INSTITUTION

Rank	Institution	B.A.'s	Rank	Institution	B.A.'s
1	Evergreen State C	17	4	Cal State U–Northridge	7
2	U of NM–Main Campus	8	5	U of MD–University C	6
3	Southern Illinois U–Carbondale	7	6	Cal State C–Bakersfield	5

Institutions not ranked have less than five degrees conferred on Native Americans.

INTERDISCIPLINARY STUDIES (2400)
MINORITY BACCALAUREATE DEGREES
WITHIN 60 MILE RADIUS OF AIRPORT

AIRPORT	MINORITY GROUP			
	Black	Hispanic	Asian	Native American
ABQ=Albuquerque, NM				
U of NM - Main Campus	6	52	1	8
University of Albuquerque		4		
	6	**56**	**1**	**8**
ALB=Albany, NY				
SUNY at Albany			3	1
SUNY Empire State College	4			
	4		**3**	**1**
AOO=Altoona, PA				
Pennsylvania State U - Main Campus	7	1		
	7	**1**		
ATL=Atlanta, GA				
Morehouse College*	8			
Spelman College*	3		1	
	11		**1**	
AUS=Austin, TX				
U of Texas at Austin	3	3		
	3	**3**		
BAL=Baltimore, MD				
American University	2			
George Washington Univesity	2			
University of DC*	1			
Towson State University	13			
U of MD - University College	103	14	14	6
U of MD - College Park Campus	15		1	4
University of Baltimore	8			
	144	**14**	**15**	**10**

Airport 60 (2400)

AIRPORT	MINORITY GROUP			
	Black	Hispanic	Asian	Native American
BDL=Hartford, CT/Springfield, MA				
Yale University	3	1	2	
U of Mass - Amherst Campus	5	4	1	1
	8	5	3	1
BHM=Birmingham, AL				
U of Alabama in Birmingham			1	
			1	
BKL=Cleveland-Lakefront, OH				
Kent State U - Main Campus	5	1		
Oberlin College	2			
U of Akron - Main Campus				1
	7	1		1
BOS=Boston, MA				
Boston State College	1			
Boston University	1			
Harvard University	1			
Tufts University	1			
Brown University	2			
	6			
BTR=Baton Rouge, LA				
Louisiana State U & A&M College	8	2	1	
Sthrn U A&M College - Main Cam*	11			
	19	2	1	
BUF=Buffalo, NY				
SUNY at Buffalo - Main Campus	13		1	
SUNY College at Buffalo	6	1		
	19	1	1	
CAE=Columbia, SC				
Morris College*	15			
U of South Carolina at Columbia	22	2		
	37	2		

Airport 60 (2400)

AIRPORT	MINORITY GROUP			
	Black	Hispanic	Asian	Native American
CIC=Chico, CA				
Cal State University - Chico	2	8	3	4
	2	8	3	4
CMH=Columbus, OH				
Ohio State U - Main Campus	6		1	
Wilberforce University*	2			
	8		1	
CMI=Champaign, IL				
Eastern Illinois University	5			
U of Illinois - Urbana Campus	3			
	8			
COU=Columbia, MO				
Columbia College	27	2		1
U of Missouri - Columbia	2		1	
	29	2	1	1
CRW=Charleston, WV				
West Virginia State College	18	1		
	18	1		
CVG=Cincinnati, OH				
Antioch University	22	55		1
U of Cincinnati - Main Campus	6			
Wilberforce University*	2			
	30	55		1
DAB=Dayton Beach, FL				
University of Central Florida	2	1	1	
	2	1	1	
DCA=Washington-National, DC				
American University	2			
George Washington University	2			
University of DC*	1			
Towson State University	13			

Airport 60 (2400)

AIRPORT	MINORITY GROUP			
	Black	Hispanic	Asian	Native American
DCA (cont)				
U of MD - University College	103	14	14	6
U of MD - College Park Campus	15		1	4
University of Baltimore	8			
	144	**14**	**15**	**10**
DEN=Denver, CO				
Metropolitan State College		3		
U of Colorado at Boulder	2	3		
U of Northern Colorado			1	
	2	**6**	**1**	
DTW=Detroit-Metropolitan, MI				
Detroit Institute of Technology	1		1	
Oakland University	1			
Shaw College at Detroit*	11			
U of Michigan - Ann Arbor	37	7	7	2
University of Detroit	2			
Wayne State University	85	3	3	2
University of Toledo	9	1	5	
	146	**11**	**16**	**4**
EUG=Eugene, OR				
Oregon State University	2			
University of Oregon - Main Campus			3	
	2		**3**	
FAT=Fresno, CA				
Cal State University - Fresno	1	26	10	3
	1	**26**	**10**	**3**
FAY=Fayetteville, NC				
NC State U - Raleigh	2			
St. Augustine's College*	1			
Shaw University*	1			
	4			

Airport 60 (2400)

AIRPORT	MINORITY GROUP			
	Black	Hispanic	Asian	Native American
GRR=Grand Rapids, MI				
Western Michigan University	1			
	1			
GSO=Greensboro/High Point, NC				
Bennett College*	18			
NC Agrl & Tech State University*	1			
Winston-Salem State University*	5			
	24			
HNL=Honolulu/Oahu, HI				
University of Hawaii at Manoa*		2	30	
		2	30	
HSV=Huntsville, AL/Decatur, GA				
Oakwood College*	27			
	27			
IND=Indianapolis, IN				
Indiana University - Bloomington	1	1	1	
Purdue University - Main Campus	2		1	
	3	1	2	
ITO=Hilo, HI				
University of Hawaii at Hilo*		2	13	
		2	13	
JFK=New York, Kennedy Int'l, NY				
Montclair State College	1	2		
Princeton University			3	
Rutgers U - New Brunswick	12	2		
Rutgers U - Newark Campus	2	1		
St. Peter's College		4		
Adelphi University	3			
College of New Rochelle	121	22	3	
CUNY Bernard Baruch College	9	4	3	
CUNY College of Staten Island	6	4	2	
CUNY City College	3	2	1	

Airport 60 (2400)

AIRPORT	MINORITY GROUP			
	Black	Hispanic	Asian	Native American
JFK (cont)				
CUNY Graduate School & U Center	60	27	12	2
CUNY Hunter College	5	3	1	
CUNY John Jay College – Crim Jus	5	3		
CUNY Lehman College	2	3		
CUNY Queen's College	14	4	4	
Fordham University	5	2	1	
New York University	7	4	1	
St. Francis College	150	5	26	
St. Joseph's College – Main Campus	266	5	11	
SUNY at Stony Bk – Main Campus	3	3		
SUNY College – Old Westbury	7	1		
	681	**101**	**68**	**2**
LAX=Los Angeles, CA				
Cal State College – San Bernardino	6	14	1	1
Cal State Poly U – Pomona	3	13		
Cal State U – Dominguez Hills	36	12	5	1
Cal State University – Fullerton		7	1	
Cal State University – Long Beach	11	18	12	1
Cal State University – Los Angeles	7	18	15	
Cal State University – Northridge	11	22	16	7
Chapman College	4	2		
Loyola Marymount University	6	5		
Pepperdine University	37	3	3	
U of Cal – Irvine	16	9	22	1
U of Cal – Los Angeles	3	4	16	1
U of Cal – Riverside	13	14	2	1
University of Southern California	1	2	2	
University of LaVerne		58		
	154	**201**	**95**	**13**

Airport 60 (2400)

AIRPORT	MINORITY GROUP			
	Black	Hispanic	Asian	Native American
LCH=Lake Charles, LA				
McNeese State University	4	1	1	1
	4	**1**	**1**	**1**
LEX=Lexington/Frankfort, KY				
Kentucky State University*	1			
University of Louisville	1			
	2			
LIT=Little Rock, AR				
Philander Smith College*	2			
University of Arkansas – Pine Bluff*	4			
	6			
MDH=Carbondale, IL				
Southern Illinois U – Carbondale	27	4	3	7
	27	**4**	**3**	**7**
MEM=Memphis, TN				
Memphis State University	2		1	
	2		**1**	
MHT=Manchester, NH				
Harvard University	1			
Tufts University	1			
	2			
MIA=Miami, FL				
Florida Atlantic University		1		
Florida International University	4	3	1	
University of Miami	1	1		1
	5	**5**	**1**	**1**
MKE=Milwaukee, WS				
U of Wisconsin – Milwaukee	11	1		
	11	**1**		

Airport 60 (2400)

AIRPORT	MINORITY GROUP			
	Black	Hispanic	Asian	Native American
MLU=Monroe, LA				
Louisiana Tech University	4			
Northeast Louisiana University	18			
	22			
MSN=Madison, WS				
U of Wisconsin - Madison	3		1	
	3		1	
MSP=Minneapolis/St. Paul, MN				
U of Minn - Minneapolis/St. Paul	11	8	4	
	11	8	4	
MSY=New Orleans, LA				
University of New Orleans			1	
			1	
ORD=Chicago-O'Hare Airport, IL				
Chicago State University*	95	2		1
Columbia College	5	1	1	
Daniel Hale Williams University*	45			
DePaul University	13	1		
Governors State University	43			
Northern Illinois University	2			
Northeastern Illinois University	20	9	5	1
U of Illinois - Chicago Circle	15	2	2	1
	238	15	8	3
ORF=Norfolk/Virginia Beach, VA				
Old Dominion University	1			
	1			
PHL=Philadelphia, PA/Wilmington, DE				
Princeton University			3	
Rutgers U - New Brunswick	12	2		
Cheyney State College*	6			
Drexel University	3			
Temple University	9	3	2	

Airport 60 (2400)

AIRPORT	MINORITY GROUP			
	Black	Hispanic	Asian	Native American
PHL (cont)				
University of Pennsylvania	6	2		
West Chester State College	1			
	37	**7**	**5**	
PIA=Peoria, IL				
Bradley University	1		1	
	1		**1**	
PIT=Pittsburgh, PA				
U of Pittsburgh - Main Campus	16	1		1
	16	**1**		**1**
PVD=Providence, RI				
Boston State College	1			
Boston University	1			
Harvard University	1			
Tufts University	1			
Brown University	2			
	6			
PWA=Oklahoma City-Wiley Post, OK				
Central State University	1			
Oklahoma State U - Main Campus	1			
	2			
RDU=Raleigh/Durham, NC				
Bennet College*	18			
NC Agrl & Tech State University*	1			
NC State U - Raleigh	2			
St. Augustine's College*	1			
Shaw University*	1			
	23			
RIC=Richmond, VA				
Virginia Union University*	4			
	4			

Airport 60 (2400)

AIRPORT	MINORITY GROUP			
	Black	Hispanic	Asian	Native American
SAN=San Diego, CA				
San Diego State University	8	41	7	3
U of Cal – San Diego		9	10	1
	8	50	17	4
SAT=San Antonio, TX				
St. Edward's University	2	3		
	2	3		
SBA=Santa Barbara, CA				
Pepperdine University	37	3	3	
U of Cal – Santa Barbara	8	5	13	2
	45	8	16	2
SBP=San Luis Obispo, CA				
Cal Poly State U – San Luis Obispo	1	4	1	
	1	4	1	
SEA=Seattle/Tacoma, WA				
Evergreen State College	19	7	5	17
University of Washington	3	5	11	1
	22	12	16	18
SFO=San Francisco/Oakland, CA				
Cal State University – Hayward	5	2	2	3
San Francisco State University	18	9	19	2
San Jose State University	16	18	17	2
Stanford University	1	2		
U of Cal – Berkeley	8	5	45	
U of Cal – San Francisco	1		1	
	49	36	84	7
SJT=San Angelo, TX				
Angelo State University		2		
		2		
SLC=Salt Lake City, UT				
Brigham Young University – Main				3
				3

Airport 60 (2400)

AIRPORT	MINORITY GROUP			
	Black	Hispanic	Asian	Native American
STL=St. Louis, MO				
Southern Illinois U - Edwardsville	2			
U of Missouri - St. Louis	2			1
Webster College	18			
	22			1
SVC=Silver City, NM				
Western New Mexico University		1		
		1		
SWI=Sherman, TX				
Southeast Oklahoma State U	1			2
	1			2
SYR=Syracuse, NY				
Cornel U Endowed College	4	1	2	
Syracuse U - Main Campus	3	1	1	
	7	2	3	
TCL=Tuscaloosa, AL				
U of Alabama in Birmingham			1	
			1	
TPA=Tampa, FL				
University of South Florida	1	1	1	1
	1	1	1	1
TUS=Tucson, AZ				
University of Arizona		2		
		2		
TYS=Knoxville, TN				
U of Tennessee - Knoxville	1			
	1			

INTERDISCIPLINARY STUDIES (2400)
MINORITY BACCALAUREATE DEGREES
WITHIN 61-80 MILE ANNULUS OF AIRPORT

AIRPORT	MINORITY GROUP			
	Black	Hispanic	Asian	Native American
ALB=Albany, NY				
U of Mass - Amherst Campus	5	4	1	1
SUNY College at New Paltz	1	1	1	
	6	5	2	1
ALM=Alamogordo, NM				
NM State U - Main Campus	6	5		2
	6	5		2
ATL=Atlanta, GA				
University of Georgia	1			
	1			
AUS=Austin, TX				
St. Edward's University	2	3		
	2	3		
BAL=Baltimore, MD				
Cheyney State College*	6			
	6			
BDL=Hartford, CT/Springfield, MA				
College of New Rochelle	121	22	3	
SUNY at Albany			3	1
SUNY College at New Paltz	1	1	1	
Brown University	2			
	124	23	7	1
BOS=Boston, MA				
U of Mass - Amherst Campus	5	4	1	1
	5	4	1	1
BTR=Baton Rouge, LA				
U of Southwestern Louisiana	1			
University of New Orleans			1	
	1		1	

782

Airport 61-80 (2400)

AIRPORT	MINORITY GROUP			
	Black	Hispanic	Asian	Native American
CLT=Charlotte, NC				
Wintson-Salem State University*	5			
	5			
CMH=Columbus, OH				
Antioch University	22	55		1
Ohio University – Main Campus	20	1		2
	42	56		3
CMI=Champaign, IL				
Purdue University – Main Campus	2		1	
	2		1	
COS=Colorado Springs, CO				
Metropolitan State College.		3		
U of Colorado at Boulder	2	3		
	2	6		
CRW=Charleston, WV				
Ohio University – Main Campus	20	1		2
	20	1		2
CVG=Cincinnati, OH				
Kentucky State University*	1			
	1			
DEN=Denver, CO				
Colorado State University		1	1	
		1	1	
DTW=Detroit-Metropolitan, MI				
Michigan State University	5	3	1	2
Bowling Green State U – Main Cam	3			
	8	3	1	2
GRR=Grand Rapids, MI				
Michigan State University	5	3	1	2
	5	3	1	2

Airport 61-80 (2400)

AIRPORT	MINORITY GROUP			
	Black	Hispanic	Asian	Native American
GSO=Greensboro/High Point, NC				
NC State U - Raleigh	2			
St. Augustine's College*	1			
Shaw University*	1			
	4			
JAX=Jacksonville, FL				
University of Florida	1	2		
	1	2		
JFK=New York, Kennedy Int'l, NY				
Yale University	3	1	2	
SUNY College at New Paltz	1	1	1	
	4	2	3	
LAX=Los Angeles, CA				
Cal State College - Bakersfield	3	11		5
University of Redlands	17	8	5	
	20	19	5	5
LCH=Lake Charles, LA				
U of Southwestern Louisiana	1			
Lamar University	1			
	2			
MCN=Macon, GA				
Morehouse College*	8			
Spelman College*	3		1	
	11		1	
MHT=Manchester, NH				
Boston State College	1			
Boston University	1			
U of Mass - Amherst Campus	5	4	1	1
	7	4	1	1
MKE=Milwaukee, WS				
U of Wisconsin - Madison	3		1	
	3		1	

Airport 61-80 (2400)

AIRPORT	MINORITY GROUP			
	Black	Hispanic	Asian	Native American
MKL=Jackson, TN				
Memphis State University	2		1	
	2		1	
MSN=Madison, WS				
U of Wisconsin - Milwaukee	11	1		
	11	1		
MSY=New Orleans, LA				
Louisiana State U & A&M College	8	2	1	
Sthrn U A&M C - Main Cam*	11			
	19	2	1	
PVD=Providence, RI				
U of Mass - Amherst Campus	5	4	1	1
	5	4	1	1
PWA=Oklahoma City-Wiley Post, OK				
East Central Oklahoma State U				2
				2
RIC=Richmond, VA				
U of Virginia - Main Campus	2			
	2			
SAN=San Diego, CA				
Chapman College	4	2		
U of Cal - Irvine	16	9	22	1
U of Cal - Riverside	13	14	2	1
	33	25	24	2
SAT=San Antonio, TX				
U of Texas at Austin	3	3		
	3	3		
SBA=Santa Barbara, CA				
Cal State College - Bakersfield	3	11		5
Cal State University - Los Angeles	7	18	15	
Cal State University - Northridge	11	22	16	7

Airport 61-80 (2400)

AIRPORT	MINORITY GROUP			
	Black	Hispanic	Asian	Native American
SBA (cont)				
Loyola Marymount University	6	5		
U of Cal - Los Angeles	3	4	16	1
	30	**60**	**47**	**13**
SFO=San Francisco/Oakland, CA				
Cal State University - Sacramento	7	10	7	
U of Cal - Davis	10	9	27	3
U of Cal - Santa Cruz		8	3	
University of the Pacific	2	1	5	1
	19	**28**	**42**	**4**
SHV=Shreveport, LA				
Louisiana Tech University	4			
	4			
TPA=Tampa, FL				
University of Central Florida	2	1	1	
	2	**1**	**1**	
TUL=Tulsa, OK				
Oklahoma State U - Main Campus	1			
	1			

INTERDISCIPLINARY STUDIES (2400)
MINORITY BACCALAUREATE DEGREES
MORE THAN 80 MILES FROM NEAREST AIRPORT

AIRPORT	MINORITY GROUP			
	Black	Hispanic	Asian	Native American
ROW=Roswell, NM				
Eastern NM U - Main Campus	1			1
	1			1
TCL=Tuscaloosa, AL				
Mississippi State University		1		
		1		

787

REFERENCES

1. Marvin W. Peterson et al. Black Students on White Campuses: The Impact of Increased Black Enrollments (Ann Arbor: Survey Research Center Institute for Social Research, The University of Michigan, 1978), p. 16.

2. National Advisory Committee on Black Higher Education and Black Colleges and Universities. A Losing Battle: The Decline in Black Participation in Graduate and Professional Education (Washington, D.C.: U.S. Department of Education, October, 1980), p. 4.

3. Alexander W. Astin et al. Minorities in American Higher Education: Recent Trends, Current Prospects, and Recommendations (San Francisco: Jossey-Bass, 1982), p. 51; A Losing Battle, pp. 35-36; James E. Blackwell. Mainstreaming Outsiders: The Production of Black Professionals (Bayside, NY: General Hall, 1981), p. 3.

4. Frank J. Atelsek and Irene L. Gomberg. Bachelor's Degrees Awarded to Minority Students 1973-74, Higher Education Panel Reports, #24, (Washington, DC: American Council on Education, January, 1977), pp. 8-10; Astin et al. Minorities in American Higher Education, pp. 52-76; Blackwell, Mainstreaming Outsiders, pp. 296-297; and National Board on Graduate Education. Minority Group Participation in Graduate Education, #5 (Washington D.C.: National Academy of Sciences, June, 1976) p. 46.

5. A Losing Battle, p. 1; Blackwell. Mainstreaming Outsiders, pp. 311-312; and Peterson et al. Black Students on White Campuses, p. 29.

6. A Losing Battle, pp. 1-3.

7. A Losing Battle, p. 17.

8. Astin et al. Minorities in American Higher Education, p. 202.

9. National Center for Educational Statistics. Earned Degrees Conferred 1972-73 and 1973-74 Summary Data #105, (Washington, D.C.: U.S. Government Printing Office, 1976).

10. "1978-79 Higher Education General Information Survey Earned Degree Tapes" (Washington, D.C.: U.S. Department of Education).

788

11. Arthur Podolsky and Carolyn R. Smith. Education Directory, Colleges and Universities 1978-79, (Washington D.C.: National Center for Educational Statistics, 1979), p. xxix.

12. Atelsek and Gomberg. Bachelor's Degrees Awarded to Minority Students 1973-74, p. 36.

13. A Classification of Institutions of Higher Education, revised edition, (Berkeley: Carnegie Foundation for the Advancement of Teaching, 1976).

14. Airports used in this study are those listed in Official Airline Guide, North American edition, (Oak Brook, Ill.: Official Airline Guides, August, 1981).

APPENDIX A

MINORITY GROUP DEFINITIONS

For the purpose of this study the four minority groups included are defined as:

1. Black. A person having origins in any of the black racial groups (except those of Hispanic origin);

2. Hispanic. A person of Mexican, Puerto Rican, Cuban, Central or South American, or other Spanish culture or origin, regardless of race;

3. Asian or Pacific Islander. A person having origins in any of the original peoples of the Far East, Southeast Asian, or the Pacific Islands. This area includes, for example, China, Japan, Korea, the Philippine Islands and Samoa;

4. American Indian or Alaskan Native (Native American). A person having origins in any of the original peoples of North America.

These minority designations follow those used in the "Higher Education General Information Survey, 1978-1979" (HEGIS). They do not denote scientific definitions or the anthropological origins of the four minority groups included. According to the HEGIS Survey:

a student may be included in the (minority) group to which he or she appears to belong, identifies with, or is regarded in the community as belonging (to). However, no person may be counted in more than one (minority) group.

The manner of collecting the (minority) information is left to the discretion of the institution (reporting) provided that the system which is established results in reasonably accurate data. One acceptable method is a properly controlled system of post-enrollment self-identification by students. If a self-identification method is utilized, a verification procedure to ascertain the completeness and accuracy of student submissions should also be employed where feasible. In order to provide reasonably accurate data, the institution may require students to complete a questionnaire and/or identify themselves by name or otherwise when providing information.

Resident Aliens who are not citizens of the United States, who are permanent residents and who hold the "green card" - Form 1-151, are included in the appropriate minority categories along with the U.S. citizens.

APPENDIX B

DISCIPLINARY DIVISIONS

The twenty-four major disciplinary divisions used in this study with the disciplines and subfields included are:

AGRICULTURE AND NATURAL RESOURCES (0100)

0101   Agriculture, general
0102   Agronomy (field crops and crop management)
0103   Soils science (management and conservation)
0104   Animal science (husbandry)
0105   Diary science (husbandry)
0106   Poultry science
0107   Fish, game, and wildlife management
0108   Horticulture (fruit and vegetable production)
0109   Ornamental horticulture (floriculture, nursery science)
0110   Agricultural and farm management
0111   Agricultural economics
0112   Agricultural business
0113   Food science and technology (including dairy mfg. & tech.)
0114   Forestry
0115   Natural resources management
0116   Agriculture and forestry technologies
0117   Range management

ARCHITECTURE AND ENVIRONMENTAL DESIGN (0200)

0201   Environmental design, general
0202   Architecture
0203   Interior design
0204   Landscape architecture
0205   Urban architecture
0206   City, community, and regional planning

AREA STUDIES (0300)

0301   Asian studies, general
0302   East Asian studies
0303   South Asian studies (Indian, etc.)
0304   Southeast Asian studies
0305   African studies
0306   Islamic studies
0307   Russian and Slavic studies
0308   Latin American studies
0309   Middle Eastern studies
0310   European studies, general
0311   Eastern European studies
0312   West European studies
0313   American studies
0314   Pacific area studies

BIOLOGICAL SCIENCES (0400)

0401   Biology, general
0402   Botany, general
0403   Bacteriology
0404   Plant pathology
0405   Plant pharmacology
0406   Plant physiology
0407   Zoology, general
0408   Pathology, human and animal
0409   Pharmacology, human and animal
0410   Physiology, human and animal
0411   Microbiology
0412   Anatomy
0413   Histology
0414   Biochemistry (including agricultural chemistry)
0415   Biophysics
0416   Molecular biology
0417   Cell biology (cytology, cell physiology)
0418   Marine biology
0419   Biometrics and biostatistics
0420   Ecology
0421   Entomology
0422   Genetics (including experimental plant and animal breeding)
0423   Radiobiology
0424   Nutrition, scientific (excluding nutrition in home economics and dietetics)
0425   Neurosciences
0426   Toxicology
0427   Embryology

BUSINESS AND MANAGEMENT (0500)

0501   Business and commerce, general
0502   Accounting
0503   Business statistics
0504   Banking and finance
0505   Investments and securities
0506   Business management and administration
0507   Operations research
0508   Hotel and restaurant management
0509   Marketing and purchasing
0510   Transportation and public utilities
0511   Real estate
0512   Insurance
0513   International business
0514   Secretarial studies
0515   Personnel management
0516   Labor and industrial relations
0517   Business economics

COMMUNICATIONS (0600)

0601   Communications, general
0602   Journalism (printed media)
0603   Radio/television
0604   Advertising
0605   Communication media (use of videotape, films, etc., oriented specifically toward radio/television)

COMPUTER AND INFORMATION SCIENCES (0700)

0701   Computer and information sciences, general
0702   Information sciences and systems
0703   Data processing
0704   Computer programming
0705   Systems anaysis

EDUCATION (0800)

0801   Education, general
0802   Elementary education, general
0803   Secondary education, general
0804   Junior high school education
0805   Higher education, general
0806   Junior and community college education
0807   Adult and continuing education
0808   Special education, general
0809   Administration of special education
0810   Education of the mentally retarded
0811   Education of the gifted
0812   Education of the deaf
0813   Education of the culturally disadvantaged
0814   Education of the visually handicapped
0815   Speech correction
0816   Education of the emotionally disturbed
0817   Remedial education
0818   Special learning disabilities
0819   Education of physically handicapped
0820   Education of the multiple handicapped
0821   Social foundations (history and philosophy of education)
0822   Educational psychology (including learning theory)
0823   Pre-elementary education (kindergarten)
0824   Educational statistics and research
0825   Educational testing, evaluation and measurement
0826   Student personnel (counseling and guidance)
0827   Educational administration
0828   Educational supervision
0829   Curriculum and instruction
0830   Reading education (methodology and theory)
0831   Art education (methodology and theory)
0832   Music education (methodology and theory)

EDUCATION (0800) (Continued)

0833   Mathematics education (methodology and theory)
0834   Science education (methodology and theory)
0835   Physical education
0836   Driver and safety education
0837   Health education (including family life education)
0838   Business, commerce, and distributive education
0839   Industrial arts, vocational, and technical education
0899-1   Agricultural education
0899-2   Education of exceptional children, not classifiable above
0899-3   Home economics education
0899-4   Nursing education (training of school nurses and of teachers of nursing)

ENGINEERING (0900)

0901   Engineering, general
0902   Aerospace, aeronautical and astronautical engineering
0903   Agricultural engineering
0904   Architectural engineering
0905   Bioengineering and biomedical engineering
0906   Chemical engineering (including petroleum refining)
0907   Petroleum engineering (excluding petroleum refining)
0908   Civil, construction, and transportation engineering
0909   Electrical, electronics, and communications engineering
0910   Mechanical engineering
0911   Geological engineering (including mining geology)
0912   Geophysical engineering
0913   Industrial and management engineering
0914   Metallurgical engineering
0915   Materials engineeirng
0916   Ceramic engineering
0917   Textile engineering
0918   Mining and mineral engineering
0919   Engineering physics
0920   Nuclear engineering
0921   Engineering mechanics
0922   Environmental and sanitary engineering
0923   Naval architecture and marine engineering
0924   Ocean engineering

FINE AND APPLIED ARTS (1000)

1001   Fine arts, general
1002   Art (painting, drawing, sculpture)
1003   Art history and appreciation
1004   Music (performing, composition, theory)
1005   Music (liberal arts program)
1006   Music history and appreciation (musicology)

FINE AND APPLIED ARTS (1000) (Continued)

1007 Dramatic arts
1010 Cinematography
1011 Photography

FOREIGN LANGUAGES (1100)

1102 French
1103 German
1104 Italian
1105 Spanish
1106 Russian
1107 Chinese
1108 Japanese
1109 Latin
1110 Greek, classical
1111 Hebrew
1112 Arabic
1113 Indian (Asiatic)
1114 Scandinavian languages
1115 Slavic languages (other than Russian)
1116 African languages (non-Semitic)

HEALTH PROFESSIONS (1200)

1201 Health professions, general
1202 Hospital and health care administration
1203 Nursing
1208 Occupational therapy
1211-2 Pharmacy
1212 Physical therapy
1213 Dental hygiene
1214 Public health
1215 Medical record librarianship
1217 Biomedical communication
1220 Speech pathology and audiology
1222 Clinical social work (medical and psychiatric and specialized rehabilitation services)
1223 Medical laboratory technologies
1224 Dental technologies
1225 Radiologic technologies

HOME ECONOMICS (1300)

1301 Home economics, general
1302 Home decoration and home equipment (including home furnishings and housing)
1303 Clothing and textiles
1304 Consumer economics and home management (including family economics and management

HOME ECONOMICS (1300) (Continued)

1305	Family relations and child development
1306	Foods and nutrition (including dietetics)
1307	Institutional management and cafeteria management

LAW (1400)

1401-2	Law, general (Prelaw)

LETTERS (1500)

1501	English, general
1502	Literature, English
1503	Comparative literature
1504	Classics
1505	Linguistics (including phonetics, semantics, and philology)
1506	Speech, debate, forensic science (rhetoric, public address)
1507	Creative writing
1508	Teaching of English as a foreign language
1509	Philosophy
1510	Religious studies (excluding theological professions)

LIBRARY SCIENCE (1600)

1601	Library science, general

MATHEMATICS (1700)

1701	Mathematics, general
1702	Statistics, mathematical and theoretical
1703	Applied mathematics

MILITARY SCIENCES (1900)

1801	Military science (Army)
1802	Naval science (Navy, Marines)
1803	Aerospace science (Air Force)
1899-1	Merchant Marine (deck officer)

PHYSICAL SCIENCES (1900)

1901	Physical sciences, general
1902	Physics, general (excluding biophysics)
1903	Molecular physics
1904	Nuclear physics
1905	Chemistry, general (excluding biochemistry)
1906	Inorganic chemistry
1907	Organic chemistry
1908	Physical chemistry
1909	Analytical chemistry
1910	Pharmaceutical chemistry

PHYSICAL SCIENCES (1900) (Continued)

1911   Astronomy
1912   Astrophysics
1913   Atmospheric sciences and meteorology
1914   Geology
1915   Geochemistry
1916   Geophysics and seismology
1917   Earth sciences, general
1918   Paleontology
1919   Oceanography
1920   Metallurgy

PSYCHOLOGY (2000)

2001   Psychology, general
2002   Experimental psychology (animal and human)
2003   Clinical psychology
2004   Psychology for counseling
2005   Social psychology
2006   Psychometrics
2007   Statistics in psychology
2008   Industrial psychology
2009   Developmental psychology
2010   Physiological psychology

PUBLIC AFFAIRS AND SERVICES (2100)

2101   Community services, general
2102   Public administration
2103   Parks and recreation management
2104   Social work, helping services (other than clinical soc. wk.)
2105   Law enforcement and corrections

SOCIAL SCIENCES (2200)

2201   Social sciences, general
2202   Anthropology
2203   Archaeology
2204   Economics
2205   History
2206   Geography
2207   Political science and government
2208   Sociology
2209   Criminology
2210   International relations
2211   Afro-American studies (black culture)
2212   American Indian cultural studies
2213   Mexican-American cultural studies
2214   Urban studies
2215   Demography

THEOLOGY (2300)

2301-2   Theological professions, general
2302   Religious music
2303   Biblical languages
2304   Religious education

INTERDISCIPLINARY STUDIES (4900)

4901   General liberal arts and sciences
4902   Biological and physical sciences
4903   Humanities and social sciences
4904   Engineering and other disciplines

The classification of these major disciplinary divisions follows the system presented in A Taxonomy of Instructional Programs in Higher Education and are used throughout the HEGIS Survey as well.

APPENDIX C

ENVIRONMENTAL SETTING

There is some value in knowing the environmental setting in which an institution is located. Not only does the environment have an impact on the character of the institution it impacts the students who attend as well. Knowledge of a student's undergraduate institution's environmental setting can be quite useful when adjustment to a new environment becomes a problem. Each of the institutions selected for this study have been classified by the nature of their location into one of the following three environmental categories:

Urban. When an institution is located in a city that has a population of 100,000 or more, it is considered to be in an urban setting.

Suburban. An institution is considered to be in a suburban environment when it is located in a city adjacent to a central city with a population of 1000,000 or more or is in the central city's urbanized area.

Rural. If an institution is located in a city with a population of less than 100,000 which is not adjacent to a central city or in its urbanized area, it is considered to be within a rural environment.

APPENDIX D

HISTORICAL GROUPINGS OF INSTITUTIONS:
CONSORTIA AND LARGE SYSTEMS

Since this study is concerned with baccalaureate degrees awarded to minority students only those institutions in the various groupings, consortia and systems considered that meet the selection criteria are included.

Ivy League. Comprised of eight institutions the Ivy League is the nation's oldest organization of institutions of higher education. All of its affiliates are privately endowed institutions:

Columbia University
Cornell University Endowed Colleges
Dartmouth College
Brown University
Harvard University/Radcliffe College
Princeton University
University of Pennsylvania
Yale University

All the member institutions are included except Columbia University which does not meet the selection criteria.

Committee on Institutional Cooperation (CIC). Established in 1958, the CIC is a consortium of eleven institutions with nine of its memberships being large State Universities with only University of Chicago and Northwestern University being privately supported. The consortium has engaged in numerious academic activities, among them is the CIC Minority fellowship program. The number of portable fellowships available annually through this program is only slightly exceeded by the National Science Foundation fellowships for Minority students which is nationwide in coverage. Member Institutions of the CIC are:

University of Chicago
University of Illinois
Indiana University
University of Iowa
Michigan State University
University of Michigan
University of Minnesota
Northwestern University
Ohio State University
Purdue University
University of Wisconsin

Of this group, only Chicago and Iowa fall short of the inclusion criteria.

California University System. The University of California is a state supported system organized on ten campuses. All of the following campuses are included except the Hastings College of Law: University of Califoria, Berkeley

> University of California, Davis
> University of California, Irvine
> University of California, Los Angeles
> University of California, Riverside
> University of California, San Diego
> University of California, San Francisco
> University of California, Santa Barbara
> University of California, Santa Cruz

California State University and College System. In addition to the California University System, public institutions in the state are also organized in a state university and college system. Nineteen institutions are members of this system:

> California Polytechnic State University – San Luis Obispo
> California State College – Bakersfield
> California State College – San Bernadino
> California State College – Sonoma
> California State College – Stanislaus
> California State Polytechnic University – Pomona
> California State University – Chico
> California State University – Dominquez Hills
> California State University – Fresno
> California State University – Fullerton
> California State University – Hayward
> California State University – Long Beach
> California State University – Los Angeles
> California State University – Northridge
> California State University – Sacramento
> Humbolt State University
> San Diego State University
> San Francisco State University
> San Jose State University

Only three of these institutions; Sonoma, Stanislaus and Humbolt did not have sufficient minority baccalaureate degrees awarded to be included.

City University of New York (CUNY). This publicly supported system has eleven institutions which award the baccalaureate degrees as well as a number of other institutions which do not offer degrees at this level. Following are the institutions in the system that grant baccalaureate degrees:

CUNY Bernard Baruch College
CUNY Brooklyn College
CUNY City College
CUNY College at Staten Island
CUNY Graduate School and University Center
CUNY Hunter College
CUNY John Jay College – Criminal Justice
CUNY Lehman College
CUNY Medgar Evers College
CUNY Queens College
CUNY York College

All of these institutions produce a sufficient number of minority baccalaureate degrees to qualify for inclusion in the study.

State University of New York (SUNY). In addition to its CUNY System New York also has the state supported State University of New York System. Although this is a large system only twenty-four of its campuses offer undergraduate degrees. They are:

SUNY at Albany
SUNY of Buffalo – Main Campus
SUNY of Binghamton
SUNY at Stoney Brook
SUNY College at Brockport
SUNY College at Buffalo
SUNY College at Cortland
SUNY College at Fredonia
SUNY College at Geneseo
SUNY College at New Paltz
SUNY College at Old Westbury
SUNY College at Oneonota
SUNY College at Oswego
SUNY College at Plattsburgh
SUNY College at Potsdam
SUNY College at Purchase
SUNY College at Utica – Rome
SUNY College Empire State
SUNY Downstate Medical Center
SUNY Health Sciences Center at Buffalo
SUNY Health Sciences Center at Stoney Brook
SUNY Upstate Medical Center
SUNY College of Environmental Science and Forestry
SUNY Maritime College

Less than 1/3 of these institutions produce enough minority baccalaureate degrees to be included in this study. Among the university campuses only Albany, Buffalo, and Stoney Brook are included with Buffalo, New Paltz, Old Westbury and Empire State among the colleges.

APPENDIX E

CARNEGIE CLASSIFICATION

All Institutions of Higher Education are not the same, they differ in size, the curricula offered and in the way in which they are organized. Nevertheless, it is possible to classify institutions by these dimensions. To accommodate the need for a framework to discuss groups of institutions in this study the Carnegie Classification of Institutions of Higher Education is used[1]. Although the Carnegie classification of institutions is divided into 19 categories, the institutions considered in the study fall into only 14 of these categories under four major groupings:

Research and Doctorate - Granting Instututions
    1.1   Reseach Universities I
    1.2   Research Universities II
    1.3   Doctorate - Granting Universities I
    1.4   Doctorate - Granting Universities II

Comprehensive Universities and Colleges
    2.1   Comprehensive Universities and Colleges I
    2.2   Comprehensive Universities and Colleges II

Liberal Arts Colleges
    3.1   Liberal Arts Colleges I
    3.2   Liberal Arts Colleges II

All Other Institutions
    5.2   Medical Schools and Medical Centers
    5.4   Schools of Engineering and Technology
    5.5   Schools of Business and Management
    5.8   Teachers Colleges
    5.9   Other Specialized Institutions
    6.0   Institutions for Non-traditional Study

The categories listed in the group "All Other Institutions" are self explicit and will not be further defined here. However, some explanation is necessary to distinquish among the four categories listed under Research and Doctorate Granting Institutions as well as what is the destinction between Comprehensive Universities and Colleges and Liberal Arts Colleges, as well as the difference in the categories within these respective groups.

It is obvious that all the institutions in the four categories under Research and Doctorate-Granting Institutions produce Ph.D.'s and are involved in research activities. They are not distinguished so much by what they do but rather by the degree to which they are involved in doctorate production and research activity. Those institutions following in the 1.1 category produce at least 50 Ph.D.'s annually and are among the top 50 universities in obtaining federal research funding. For an institution to be classified as 1.2 it is necessary that it produce 50 but no less than 25 Ph.D.'s annually and be ranked among the 100 leading universities receiving federal financial support for research as well as being among the top 60 institutions in terms of Ph.D. production between 1965-66 and 1974-75. Forty or more Ph.D.'s awarded in at least 5 fields with a minimum of 20 or receipt of 3 million federal research dollars in a year places an institution in the Doctorate-Granting University, 1.3 category. Those institutions which produce between 20 Ph.D.'s without regard to field or 10 Ph.D.'s in at least three fields or are expected to do so in the near future are classified as Doctorate-Granting Universities 1.2.

Comprehensive Universities and Colleges are those Institutions that may award master's degrees, but no doctorate degrees that have liberal arts programs as well as several other professional and occupational programs. Those institutions classified as 2.1 meet this criteria and must have enrollments in the professional or occupational programs that are at least 2,000. To be placed in Liberal Arts 2.2 category the institution must have at least one professional program with an enrollment between 1,000 and 1,500.

Liberal Arts dominates the curriculum of those institutions classified as such. For an institution to qualify for the Liberal Arts 3.1 category it must have scored 1030 or more on Astin's selectivity index [2] or be listed among the 200 baccalaureate-granting institutions in terms of the number of their graduates receiving Ph.D.'s at the 40 top doctorate-granting institutions between 1920 and 1966[3]. All other Liberal Arts institutions which do not meet the above criteria are classified as Liberal Arts 3.2.

It is obvious that it is difficult to distinguish between some institutions particularly Liberal Arts and Comprehensive Universities and Colleges. Therfore, those who conceived this taxonomy had to exercise their judgement in placing some institutions in the various categories. This practice is sound and acceptable and does not detract from the usefulness of this classification scheme because it places the 362 institutions used in this study into 14 categories or different academic studies. All of the 362 institutions selected for this study were listed in the Carnegie classification system except Franklin University which was placed in the Schools of Engineering and Technology category. More details on the Carnegie classification can be found in A Classification of Institutions of Higher Education, revised edition (Berkeley: Carnegie Foundation for the Advancement of Teaching, 1976).

APPENDIX F

CHARACTERISTICS OF INSTITUTIONS AWARDING
MINORITY BACCALAUREATE DEGREES

STATE/SCHOOL	Total BA's	Total Minority BA's	Con-trol	Size of Insti-tution	Environ-mental setting	Carnegie Classifi-cation
Alabama						
Alabama A&M University*	569	390		M	S	2.1
Alabama State University*	401	400		S	U	2.2
Jacksonville State University	944	105		M	R	2.1
Miles College*	150	142	1	S	S	3.2
Oakwood College*	196	187	1	S	R	3.2
Stillman College*	136	133	1	S	U	3.2
Talladega College*	111	109	1	S	R	3.2
Troy State University - Main Campus	1097	138		L	R	2.1
Troy State University - Montgomery	379	64		S	U	2.1
Tuskegee Institute*	494	432	1	S	R	2.1
University of Alabama	2409	175		VL	S	1.3
U of Alabama in Birmingham	1180	168		L	U	2.1
University of South Alabama	815	72		M	U	2.1
	8,881	**2,515**				
Arizona						
Arizona State University	4544	307		VL	S	1.3
Northern Arizona University	1508	158		L	R	2.1
University of Arizona	3452	355		VL	U	1.1
	9,504	**820**				
Arkansas						
Arkansas Baptist College*	50	45	1	S	R	3.2
Arkansas State U - Main Campus	865	75		M	R	2.1
Henderson State University	407	94		S	R	2.1
Philander Smith College*	78	63	1	S	U	3.2
University of Arkansas - Pine Bluff*	385	341		S	R	2.1
University of Central Arkansas	638	50		M	R	2.1
	2,423	**668**				

(Characteristics)

STATE/SCHOOL	Total BA's	Total Minority BA's	Control	Size of Institution	Environmental setting	Carnegie Classification
California						
Cal Poly State U – San Luis Obispo	2670	240		VL	R	2.1
Cal State College – Bakersfield	459	98		S	R	2.1
Cal State College – San Bernadino	595	151		M	S	2.2
Cal State Poly U – Pomona	1960	269		L	S	2.1
Cal State University – Chico	2462	167		VL	R	2.1
Cal State U – Dominguez Hills	1050	531		L	S	2.1
Cal State University – Fresno	2240	431		VL	S	2.1
Cal State University – Fullerton	2874	375		VL	S	2.1
Cal State University – Hayward	1371	292		L	S	2.1
Cal State University – Long Beach	4153	769		VL	S	2.1
Cal State University – Los Angeles	2595	1230		VL	U	2.1
Cal State University – Northridge	2022	487		VL	S	2.1
Cal State University – Sacramento	2427	429		VL	S	2.1
Chapman College	818	149	1	M	S	2.2
Loyola Marymount University	681	179	1	M	U	2.1
Pacific Christian College	253	96	1	S	S	3.2
Pepperdine University	677	150	1	M	S	2.1
San Diego State University	4128	464		VL	U	2.1
San Francisco State University	3262	914		VL	U	2.1
San Jose State University	3865	808		VL	U	2.1
Stanford University	1619	261	1	L	S	1.1
U of Cal – Berkeley	4996	1140		VL	S	1.1
U of Cal – Davis	2801	342		VL	S	1.1
U of Cal – Irvine	1575	190		L	S	1.2
U of Cal – Los Angeles	4420	913		VL	S	1.1
U of Cal – Riverside	745	128		M	S	1.3
U of Cal – San Diego	1308	115		L	S	1.1
U of Cal – San Francisco	330	82		S	U	5.2
U of Cal – Santa Barbara	2807	258		VL	S	1.3
U of Cal – Santa Cruz	1218	74		L	S	1.3
University of LaVerne	521	145	1	M	S	2.1

(Characteristics)

STATE/SCHOOL	Total BA's	Total Minority BA's	Control	Size of Institution	Environmental setting	Carnegie Classification
California (cont)						
University of Redlands	1299	232	1	L	S	2.2
University of San Francisco	1144	295	1	L	U	2.1
University of Southern California	2501	623	1		U	1.1
University of the Pacific	690	134	1	M	S	1.4
	68,536	**13,161**				
Colorado						
Colorado State University	2640	152		VL	R	1.1
Metropolitan State College	1257	198		L	U	2.1
U of Colorado at Boulder	3192	193		VL	S	1.1
U of Northern Colorado	1884	124		L	R	1.3
U of Southern Colorado	490	92		S	S	2.1
	9,463	**759**				
Connecticut						
University of Connectcut	3073	81		VL	R	1.2
Yale University	1270	154	1	L	U	1.1
	4,343	**235**				
Delaware						
Delaware State College*	256	134		S	R	2.2
University of Delaware	2577	78		VL	R	1.3
	2,833	**212**				
District of Columbia						
American University	1404	216	1	L	U	1.3
George Washington University	1376	159	1	L	U	1.2
Howard University*	1026	783	1	L	U	1.2
University of DC*	652	490		M	U	2.1
	4,458	**1,648**				
Florida						
Bethune Cookman College*	310	288	1	S	S	2.2
Biscayne College*	415	241	1	S	U	2.2
Edward Waters College*	78	76	1	S	U	3.2
Florida Agr & Mech University*	712	627		M	R	2.1

(Characteristics)

STATE/SCHOOL	Total BA's	Total Minority BA's	Con-trol	Size of Insti-tution	Environ-mental setting	Carnegie Classifi-cation
Florida (cont)						
Florida Atlantic University	1405	131		L	S	2.1
Florida International University	2124	753		VL	S	2.1
Florida Memorial College*	69	69	1	S	U	3.2
Florida State University	3636	327		VL	R	1.2
University of Central Florida	1928	97		L	U	2.1
Saint Leo College	663	100	1	M	R	3.2
University of Florida	4747	397		VL	R	1.1
University of Miami	1717	416	1	L	S	1.1
University of South Florida	3689	353		VL	S	1.4
University of West Florida	1285	103		L	R	2.1
	22,778	**3,978**				
Georgia						
Albany State College*	240	230		S	R	2.2
Clark College*	297	296	1	S	U	2.2
Fort Valley State College*	166	146		S	R	2.2
Georgia College	440	57		S	R	2.2
GA Inst of Tech – Main Campus	1467	91		L	U	1.2
Georgia State University	1853	226		L	U	1.3
Morehouse College*	214	214	1	S	U	3.2
Morris Brown College*	173	173	1	S	U	2.2
Paine College*	88	88	1	S	R	3.2
Savannah State College*	178	161		S	S	2.1
Spelman College*	274	274	1	S	U	3.2
University of Georgia	3599	122		VL	R	1.1
Valdosta State College	619	49		M	R	2.1
	9,608	**2,127**				
Hawaii						
Chaminade University of Honolulu	280	66	1	S	U	2.1
University of Hawaii at Hilo*	159	108		S	R	2.2
University of Hawaii at Manoa*	2733	2021		VL	U	1.1
	3,172	**2,195**				

(Characteristics)

STATE/SCHOOL	Total BA's	Total Minority BA's	Con- trol	Size of Insti- tution	Environ- mental setting	Carnegie Classifi- cation
Illinois						
Bradley University	845	64	1	M	U	2.1
Chicago State University*	741	575		M	U	2.1
College of St. Francis	1004	188	1	L	R	2.2
Columbia College	310	120	1	S	U	3.2
Daniel Hale Williams University*	70	70	1	S	U	3.2
DePaul University	1070	164	1	L	U	2.1
Eastern Illinois University	1878	80		L	R	2.1
Governors State University	403	166		S	S	2.1
Illinois State University	3361	222		VL	S	1.4
Loyola University of Chicago	1281	146	1	L	U	1.3
Northern Illinois University	3260	194		VL	R	1.3
Northeastern Illinois University	1253	229		L	U	2.2
Northwestern University	1735	187	1	L	S	1.1
Roosevelt University	819	406	1	M	U	2.1
Southern Illinois U - Carbondale	3756	278		VL	R	1.3
Southern Illinois U - Edwardsville	1119	121		L	R	2.1
U of Illinois - Chicago Circle	2267	444		VL	U	1.3
U of Illinois - Urbana Campus	5466	228		VL	R	1.1
	30,638	**3,882**				
Indiana						
Ball State University	2336	86		VL	R	1.3
Ind-Purdue U - Indianapolis	1204	89		L	U	2.1
Indiana State U - Main Campus	1447	111		L	R	1.4
Indiana University - Bloomington	4108	183		VL	R	1.2
Indiana University - Northwest	215	62		S	S	2.1
Purdue University - Main Campus	4604	173		VL	R	1.1
	13,914	**704**				
Kentucky						
Eastern Kentucky University	1561	81		L	R	2.1
Kentucky State University*	139	110		S	R	2.2

(Characteristics)

STATE/SCHOOL	Total BA's	Total Minority BA's	Con-trol	Size of Insti-tution	Environ-mental setting	Carnegie Classifi-cation
Kentucky (cont)						
University of Louisville	1377	97		L	U	1.3
Western Kentucky University	1224	56		L	R	2.1
	4,301	**344**				
Louisiana						
Dillard University*	194	188	1	S	U	3.2
Grambling State University*	535	526		M	R	2.1
Louisiana State U & A&M College	2820	85		VL	S	1.2
Louisiana Tech University	1242	74		L	R	2.1
McNeese State University	595	63		M	R	2.1
Northeast Louisiana University	1063	127		L	R	2.1
Southeastern Louisiana U	779	55		M	R	2.1
Sthrn U A&M College - Main Cam*	978	904		M	S	2.1
Southern U in New Orleans*	298	295		S	U	2.2
Tulane U of Louisiana	1083	99	1	L	U	1.2
University of New Orleans	1107	119		L	U	2.1
U of Southwestern Louisiana	1335	178		L	R	2.1
Xavier University of Louisiana*	300	268	1	S	U	2.2
	12,329	**2,981**				
Maryland						
Bowie State College*	214	140		S	R	2.2
Coppin State College*	163	143		S	U	2.2
Morgan State University*	489	442		S	U	2.1
Towson State University	1992	156		L	S	2.1
University of Baltimore	606	112		M	U	2.1
U of MD - Baltimore Co Campus	662	93		M	S	2.2
U of MD - Baltimore Prof School	616	85		M	U	5.2
U of MD - College Park Campus	5230	383		VL	S	1.1
U of MD - Eastern Shore*	107	88		S	R	3.2
U of MD - University College	1035	137		L	S	6.0
	11,114	**1,779**				

811

(Characteristics)

STATE/SCHOOL	Total BA's	Total Minority BA's	Control	Size of Institution	Environmental setting	Carnegie Classification
Massachussetts						
Boston State College	845	98		M	U	2.2
Boston University	2720	108	1	VL	U	1.1
Harvard University	1751	187	1	L	S	1.1
Radcliffe College	493	79	1	S	S	1.1
Tufts University	1016	121	1	L	S	1.2
U of Mass - Amherst Campus	3986	135		VL	R	1.2
	10,811	**728**				
Michigan						
Detroit Institute of Technology	196	58	1	S	U	2.2
Eastern Michigan University	2170	221		VL	S	2.1
Mercy College of Detroit	342	73	1	S	U	2.1
Michigan State University	6872	364		VL	S	1.1
Oakland University	1258	93		L	S	2.1
Shaw College at Detroit*	68	68	1	S	U	3.2
University of Detroit	640	185	1	M	U	1.4
U of Michigan - Ann Arbor	4856	363		VL	S	1.1
Wayne State University	2893	709		VL	U	1.2
Western Michigan University	3231	178		VL	U	1.4
	22,526	**2,312**				
Minnesota						
U of Minn - Minneapolis/St. Paul	5886	206		VL	U	1.1
	5,886	**206**				
Mississippi						
Alcorn State University*	289	287		S	R	2.1
Delta State University	416	73		S	R	2.1
Jackson State University*	718	654		M	U	2.1
Mississippi Industrial College*	40	40	1	S	R	3.2
Mississippi State University	1952	182		L	R	1.2
Mississippi University for Women	381	51		S	R	2.1
Mississippi Valley State Univ*	376	376		S	R	2.1
Rust College*	117	117	1	S	R	3.2

812

(Characteristics)

STATE/SCHOOL	Total BA's	Total Minority BA's	Con-trol	Size of Insti-tution	Environ-mental setting	Carnegie Classifi-cation
Mississippi (cont)						
Tougaloo College*	131	127	1	S	S	3.2
U of Mississippi - Main Campus	1446	102		L	R	1.3
U of Southern Mississippi	1749	175		L	R	1.3
	7,615	2,184				
Missouri						
Columbia College	602	101	1	M	R	2.2
Harris Stowe College*	90	54		S	U	5.8
Lincoln University	216	84		S	R	2.1
Park College	865	209	1	M	S	2.1
St. Louis U - Main Campus	1135	116	1	L	U	1.2
U of Missouri - Columbia	3475	93		VL	R	1.1
U of Missouri - Kansas City	976	72		M	U	1.3
U of Missouri - St. Louis	1259	121		L	S	2.1
Washington University	1223	100	1	L	S	1.1
Webster College	281	51		S	S	3.2
	10,122	1,001				
Montana						
Montana State University	1543	29		L	R	1.3
	1,543	29				
Nebraska						
U of Nebraska at Omaha	1109	74		L	U	2.1
	1,109	74				
New Hampshire						
Dartmouth College	986	86	1	M	R	1.3
	986	86				
New Jersey						
Glassboro State College	1725	296		L	R	2.2
Jersey City State College	978	161		M	U	2.2
Kean College of New Jersey	1445	214		L	S	2.1
Montclair State College	1843	148		L	S	2.1
New Jersey Inst Technology	705	133		M	U	5.4

(Characteristics)

STATE/SCHOOL	Total BA's	Total Minority BA's	Control	Size of Insti- tution	Environ- mental setting	Carnegie Classifi- cation
New Jersey (cont)						
Princeton University	1034	137	1	L	R	1.1
Rutgers U - Camden Campus	597	81		M	U	2.1
Rutgers U - New Brunswick	4436	420		VL	S	1.2
Rutgers U - Newark Campus	1045	248		L	U	2.1
St. Peter's College	546	112	1	M	U	2.1
Seton Hall University	1018	81	1	L	S	2.1
Trenton State College	1565	139		L	U	2.1
	16,937	**2,170**				
New Mexico						
Eastern NM U - Main Campus	543	127		M	R	2.1
New Mexico Highlands U*	226	180		S	R	2.2
NM State U - Main Campus	1300	276		L	R	1.3
University of Albuquerque	275	89	1	S	S	2.1
U of NM - Main Campus	1884	433		L	U	1.2
Western New Mexico University	143	67		S	R	2.2
	4,371	**1,172**				
New York						
Adelphi University	1471	214	1	L	S	1.4
College of New Rochelle	466	169	1	S	S	2.2
Cornell U Endowed College	1733	174	1	L	R	1.1
CUNY Bernard Baruch College	1549	671		L	U	5.5
CUNY Brooklyn College	2472	947		VL	U	2.1
CUNY City College	1812	1070		L	U	2.1
CUNY College of Staten Island	488	129		S	S	2.1
CUNY Graduate School & U Center	268	101		S	U	1.2
CUNY Hunter College	1537	573		L	U	2.1
CUNY John Jay College - Crim Jus	698	275		M	U	5.9
CUNY Lehman College	1201	423		L	U	2.1
CUNY Medgar Evers College*	126	123		S	U	2.2
CUNY Queen's College	2714	488		VL	U	2.1
CUNY York College	411	239		S	U	2.2

814

(Characteristics)

STATE/SCHOOL	Total BA's	Total Minority BA's	Control	Size of Institution	Environmental setting	Carnegie Classification
New York (cont)						
Fordham University	1587	295	1	L	U	1.3
Long Island U - Brooklyn Center	518	249	1	M	S	2.1
Long Island U - C W Post Center	1384	73	1	L	U	2.1
Mercy College	814	249	1	M	S	2.2
New York University	2185	352	1	VL	U	1.1
Pace University New York	665	155	1	M	U	2.1
Polytechnic Institute New York	376	122	1	S	U	1.3
Pratt Institute	617	169	1	M	U	2.1
St. Francis College	664	251	1	M	U	2.1
St. John's University	1933	128	1	L	U	1.3
St. Joseph's College - Main Campus	420	295	1	S	U	3.2
SUNY at Albany	2309	132		VL	S	1.3
SUNY at Buffalo - Main Campus	2677	104		VL	S	1.2
SUNY at Stony Bk - Main Campus	1809	133		L	R	1.2
SUNY College at Buffalo	1988	121		L	U	2.2
SUNY College at New Paltz	885	91		M	R	2.2
SUNY College - Old Westbury	320	101		S	S	2.2
SUNY Empire State College	862	129		M	R	6.0
Syracuse University - Main Campus	2433	147	1	VL	U	1.2
	41,392	**8,892**				
North Carolina						
Barber-Scotia College*	52	51	1	S	R	3.2
Bennett College*	85	85	1	S	U	3.2
Duke University	1530	77	1	L	S	1.1
East Carolina University	1871	96		L	R	2.1
Elizabeth City State U*	321	302		S	R	2.2
Fayetteville State University*	392	305		S	R	2.2
Johnson C Smith University*	203	200	1	S	U	2.2
Livingstone College*	141	129	1	S	R	3.2
NC Agrl & Tech State University*	662	602		M	U	2.1
NC Central University*	638	617		M	U	2.1

(Characteristics)

STATE/SCHOOL	Total BA's	Total Minority BA's	Control	Size of Institution	Environmental setting	Carnegie Classification
North Carolina (cont)						
NC State U - Raleigh	2338	102		VL	U	1.1
Pembroke State University	478	143		S	R	2.2
St. Augustine's College*	215	204	1	S	U	2.2
Shaw University*	212	193	1	S	U	3.2
U of NC at Chapel Hill	3173	187		VL	R	1.1
U of NC at Charlotte	1302	76		L	S	2.1
U of NC at Greensboro	1403	92		L	U	1.4
Winston-Salem State University*	342	309		S	U	2.2
	15,358	**3,770**				
North Dakota						
U of North Dakota - Main Campus	1373	43		L	R	1.3
	1,373	**43**				
Ohio						
Antioch University	750	264	1	M	R	2.2
Bowling Green State U - Main Cam	2704	166		VL	R	1.4
Central State University*	282	225		S	R	2.1
Franklin University	439	66	1	S	U	5.4
Kent State U - Main Campus	2820	149		VL	S	1.3
Oberlin College	667	87	1	M	R	3.1
Ohio State U - Main Campus	6355	177		VL	U	1.1
Ohio University - Main Campus	1982	209		L	R	1.3
U of Akron - Main Campus	1834	106		L	U	1.4
U of Cincinnati - Main Campus	2847	247		VL	U	1.2
University of Dayton	1250	82	1	L	U	2.1
University of Toledo	1422	89		L	U	1.3
Wilberforce University*	119	112	1	S	R	3.2
Wright State U - Main Campus	1163	58		L	S	2.1
	24,634	**2,037**				
Oklahoma						
Cameron University	470	70		S	R	2.1
Central State University	1387	135		L	R	2.1

(Characteristics)

STATE/SCHOOL	Total BA's	Total Minority BA's	Control	Size of Institution	Environmental setting	Carnegie Classification
Oklahoma (cont)						
East Central Oklahoma State U	400	39		S	R	2.1
Langston University*	84	77		S	R	2.2
Northeast Oklahoma State U	838	184		M	R	2.1
Oklahoma State U – Main Campus	3070	124		VL	R	1.2
Southeast Oklahoma State U	566	41		M	R	2.1
Southwest Oklahoma State U	660	44		M	R	2.1
U of Oklahoma – Norman Campus	2070	116		VL	S	1.2
	9,545	**830**				
Oregon						
Oregon State University	2546	76		VL	R	1.1
University of Oregon – Main Campus	2207	123		VL	U	1.2
	4,753	**199**				
Pennsylvania						
Cheyney State College*	345	303		S	R	2.2
Drexel University	997	78	1	M	U	2.1
Lincoln University*	181	172		S	R	3.2
Pennsylvania State U – Main Campus	7802	148		VL	R	1.1
St. Joseph's University	742	103	1	M	U	2.1
Temple University	3139	612		VL	U	1.2
University of Pennsylvania	2200	194	1	VL	U	1.1
U of Pittsburg – Main Campus	3139	277		VL	U	1.1
West Chester State College	1171	58		L	R	2.1
	19,716	**1,945**				
Rhode Island						
Brown University	1296	108	1	L	U	1.2
	1,296	**108**				
South Carolina						
Allen University*	66	66	1	S	U	3.2
Baptist College at Charleston	277	58	1	S	R	2.1
Benedict College*	300	296	1	S	U	2.2
Claflin College*	150	147	1	S	R	3.2

(Characteristics)

STATE/SCHOOL	Total BA's	Total Minority BA's	Con-trol	Size of Insti-tution	Environ-mental setting	Carnegie Classifi-cation
South Carolina (cont)						
Morris College*	89	89	1	S	R	3.2
South Carolina State College*	476	470		S	R	2.1
U of South Carolina at Columbia	2797	282		VL	U	1.3
Voorhees College*	525	164	1	M	R	3.2
Winthrop College	188	73		S	R	2.1
	4,868	**1,645**				
Tennessee						
Austin Peay State University	457	57		S	R	2.1
Fisk University*	219	217	1	S	U	3.2
Knoxville College*	108	104	1	S	U	3.2
Lane College*	110	109	1	S	R	3.2
LeMoyne-Owen College*	114	114	1	S	U	3.2
Memphis State University	1756	305		L	U	1.4
Middle Tennessee State U	1359	93		L	R	2.1
Tennessee State University*	519	500		M	U	2.1
U of Tennessee - Knoxville	3676	153		VL	U	1.2
U of Tennessee - Martin	638	75		M	R	2.1
	8,956	**1,727**				
Texas						
Angelo State University	575	87		M	R	2.1
Bishop College*	155	155	1	S	S	2.2
Corpus Christi State University	491	185		S	U	2.2
East Texas State University	1506	262		L	R	1.4
Huston-Tillotson College*	94	68	1	S	U	3.2
Incarnate Word College	258	104	1	S	U	3.2
Jarvis Christian College*	47	45	1	S	R	3.2
Lamar University	1100	142		L	S	2.1
Laredo State University*	183	163		S	R	3.2
North Texas State University	1923	252		L	R	1.3
Our Lady of Lake University*	237	164	1	S	U	2.2
Pan American University*	890	729		M	R	2.1

(Characteristics)

STATE/SCHOOL	Total BA's	Total Minority BA's	Con- trol	Size of Insti- tution	Environ- mental setting	Carnegie Classifi- cation
Texas (cont)						
Paul Quinn College*	53	44	1	S	R	3.2
Prairie View A&M University*	493	488		S	R	2.1
St. Edward's University	324	94	1	S	U	2.2
St. Mary's U – San Antonio	341	184	1	S	U	2.1
Sam Houston State University	1778	159		L	R	2.1
Southwest Texas State University	2437	322		VL	R	2.1
Sul Ross State University	258	81		S	R	2.1
Texas A&I University	758	357		M	R	2.1
Texas A&M U – Main Campus	4742	183		VL	R	1.1
Texas College*	99	99	1	S	R	3.2
Texas Southern University*	732	469		M	U	2.1
Texas Women's University	1099	213		L	R	1.4
Trinity University	610	85	1	M	U	2.1
U of Houston – Central Campus	2948	516		VL	U	1.3
U of Texas at Arlington	1911	161		L	S	2.1
U of Texas at Austin	6657	621		VL	U	1.1
U of Texas at El Paso	1486	667		L	U	2.1
U of Texas at San Antonio	737	226		M	U	2.1
Wiley College*	96	93	1	S	R	3.2
	35,018	**7,418**				
Utah						
Brigham Young University – Main	4115	62	1	VL	R	1.3
University of Utah	2556	103		VL	U	1.1
	6,671	**165**				
Virginia						
Hampton Institute*	458	444	1	S	U	2.1
Norfolk State College*	648	603		M	U	2.1
Old Dominion University	1600	91		L	U	2.1
St. Paul's College*	102	102	1	S	R	3.2
U of Virginia – Main Campus	2442	78		VL	R	1.2

(Characteristics)

STATE/SCHOOL	Total BA's	Total Minority BA's	Con-trol	Size of Insti-tution	Environ-mental setting	Carnegie Classifi-cation
Virginia (cont)						
Virginia Commonwealth University	1796	247		L	U	1.3
Virginia State College*	601	594		M	R	2.1
Virginia Union University*	162	162	1	S	U	3.2
	7,809	**2,321**				
Washington						
Evergreen State College	535	48		M	R	3.2
University of Washington	5247	533		VL	U	1.1
	5,782	**581**				
West Virginia						
West Virginia State College	404	104		S	R	2.1
	404	**104**				
Wisconsin						
U of Wisconsin – Madison	5098	141		VL	U	1.1
U of Wisconsin – Milwaukee	2553	155		VL	U	1.3
	7,651	**296**				
TOTALS	**495,427**	**80,051**				

*Predominately minority institutions are those where at least 50% of the total BA Degrees awarded are to one of the minority groups being considered.